Routledge Handbook of Constitutional Law

The *Routledge Handbook of Constitutional Law* is an advanced-level reference work that surveys the current state of constitutional law. Featuring new, specially commissioned papers by a range of leading scholars from around the world, it offers a comprehensive overview of the field as well as identifying promising avenues for future research. The book presents the key issues in constitutional law thematically, allowing for a truly comparative approach to the subject. It also pays particular attention to constitutional design, identifying and evaluating various solutions to the challenges involved in constitutional architecture.

The book is split into four parts for ease of reference:

- **Part I**: General issues—sets issues of constitutional law firmly in context including topics such as the making of constitutions, the impact of religion and culture on constitutions, and the relationship between international law and domestic constitutions.
- **Part II**: Structures—presents different approaches in regard to institutions or state organization, and structural concepts such as emergency powers and electoral systems.
- **Part III**: Rights—covers the key rights often enshrined in constitutions.
- **Part IV**: New challenges—explores issues of importance such as migration and refugees, sovereignty under pressure from globalization, supranational organizations and their role in creating post-conflict constitutions, and new technological challenges.

Providing up-to-date and authoritative articles covering all the key aspects of constitutional law, this reference work is essential reading for advanced students, scholars and practitioners in the field.

Mark Tushnet is William Nelson Cromwell Professor of Law, Harvard Law School and author of "Why the Constitution Matters," "The Constitution of the United States: A Contextual Analysis," and numerous other books on constitutional law and US legal history.

Thomas Fleiner is Professor Emeritus, University of Fribourg, Switzerland and was formerly director of the Institute of Federalism. President Emeritus, International Association of Constitutional Law. Professor Fleiner has served as a legal expert for Swiss and foreign governments and has been a guest professor in eight countries.

Cheryl Saunders is Laureate Professor, Melbourne Law School and President Emeritus, International Association of Constitutional Law. Professor Saunders also served as president of the International Association of Centers for Federal Studies. She is the author of *The Constitution of Australia: A Contextual Analysis* (Hart Publishing Ltd, 2011) and various books, chapters and articles on comparative constitutional law and method.

Routledge Handbook of Constitutional Law

*Edited by Mark Tushnet, Thomas Fleiner
and Cheryl Saunders*

LONDON AND NEW YORK

First published 2013
This version published 2015
by Routledge
2 Park Square, Milton Park, Abingdon, Oxon, OX14 4RN

and by Routledge
711 Third Avenue, New York, NY 10017

Routledge is an imprint of the Taylor & Francis Group, an informa business

© 2013, 2015 selection of editorial material, Mark Tushnet, Thomas Fleiner
and Cheryl Saunders; individual chapters, the contributors

The right of Mark Tushnet, Thomas Fleiner and Cheryl Saunders
to be identified as editors of this work has been asserted by them
in accordance with sections 77 and 78 of the Copyright, Designs
and Patents Act 1988.

British Library Cataloguing in Publication Data
A catalogue record for this book is available from the British Library

Library of Congress Cataloging-in-Publication Data
A catalog record for this book has been requested

ISBN: 978-0-415-78220-3 (hbk)
ISBN: 978-0-203-07257-8 (ebk)
ISBN: 978-1-138-85767-4 (pbk)

Typeset in Bembo
by RefineCatch Limited, Bungay, Suffolk

Contents

Contents

Contributors

Bipin Adhikari: Nepal Consulting Lawyers, Nepal

Zaid Al-Ali: Attorney, New York, United States, and Senior Advisor for Constitution Building, International IDEA

Denis Baranger: Professor of Public Law, University of Paris II, Panthéon-Assas, France

Lidija R Basta Fleiner: Professor, University of Fribourg, Switzerland

Juan F González-Bertomeu: J.S.D. NYU School of Law

Markus Böckenförde: Adviser to the German Federal Ministry for Economic Cooperation and Development, Germany

Pierre Bosset: Professor, Law School, University of Quebec at Montreal, Canada

Sophie Boyron: Senior Lecturer, Birmingham Law School, Birmingham, England

Brun-Otto Bryde: University of Giessen, Germany

Thomas Bull: Professor, Uppsala Faculty of Law, Uppsala, Sweden

Wen-Chen Chang: Associate Professor, College of Law, National Taiwan University

Albert HY Chen: Chan Professor of Constitutional Law, Faculty of Law, University of Hong Kong

Hong Sik Cho: Professor, Seoul National University School of Law, Korea

Margit Cohn: Senior Lecturer, Faculty of Law, Hebrew University of Jerusalem, Israel

Xenophon Contiades: Professor of Public and Social Law and Dean at the School of Social Sciences, University of Peloponnese, Greece

Hugh Corder: Professor of Public Law, University of Cape Town, South Africa

Robert J Cottrol: Professor of Law, History, and Sociology, and Harold Paul Green Research Professor of Law, George Washington University School of Law, United States

Iain Currie: Professor of Law, University of the Witwatersrand, Johannesburg, South Africa

Megan Davis: Professor of Law and Director, Indigenous Law Centre, Faculty of Law, University of New South Wales, Sydney, Australia

Solomon Dersso: Senior Researcher, Peace and Security Council Report Programme, Institute of Security Studies, Addis Ababa, Ethiopia

Catherine Dupré: Senior Lecturer, University of Exeter Law School, England

W Cole Durham, Jr: Susa Young Gates University Professor of Law, Brigham Young University Law School, United States

Carolyn Evans: Dean, University of Melbourne Law School, Australia

Thomas Fetzer: Assistant Professor, University of Mannheim Law School, Germany

Thomas Fleiner: Professor Emeritus, Faculty of Law, University of Fribourg, Switzerland

Michelle Foster: Associate Professor and Director of the International Refugee Law Research Programme in the Institute for International Law and the Humanities, Melbourne Law School, Australia

Anna Gamper: Professor, Department of Public Laws, State and Administrative Theory, University of Innsbruck, Austria

Roberto Gargarella: Professor, Universidad de Buenos Aires and Universidad Torcuato Di Tella, Argentina

Jean-François Gaudreault-DesBiens: Canada Research Chair, Faculty of Law, University of Montreal, Canada

Kirsty Gover: Senior Lecturer, University of Melbourne Law School, Australia

Dieter Grimm: Professor of Law, Humboldt University, Berlin, Germany

Menaka Guruswamy: Lawyer, Supreme Court of India

Yasuo Hasebe: Professor of Constitutional Law, University of Tokyo, Japan

Michael M Karayanni: Bruce W. Wayne Chair in International Law and Director, The Sacher Institute, Faculty of Law, Hebrew University of Jerusalem, Israel

George Katrougalos: Assistant Professor, Demokritos University, Athens, Greece

Jonathan Klaaren: Professor of Law, University of the Witwatersrand, Johannesburg, South Africa

Atsushi Kondo: Professor, Faculty of Law, Meijo University, Nagoya, Japan

Wendy Lacey: Associate Professor of Law, School of Law, University of South Australia, Adelaide, Australia

Máximo Langer: Professor of Law, University of California Los Angeles Law School, Los Angeles, United States

Patrick Macklem: Professor and William C. Graham Professor of Law, University of Toronto Faculty of Law, Canada

Janet McLean: Professor, Law School, University of Auckland, New Zealand

Miguel Poaires Maduro: Joint Chair, RSCAS & Department of Law, Professor of European Law, European University Institute, San Domencico de Fiesole, Italy

Denise Meyerson: Professor, Macquarie Law School, Sydney, Australia

Christina Murray: Professor of Constitutional and Human Rights Law, University of Cape Town, South Africa

Enyinna Nwauche: Director, Centre for African Legal Studies and Associate Professor, Faculty of Law, Rivers State University of Science and Technology, Port Harcourt, Nigeria

Colm O'Cinneide: Reader in Law, University College London, England

Paul O'Connell: Lecturer, School of Law, University of Leicester, England

Theo Öhlinger: Professor, University of Vienna, Austria

Brian Opeskin: Professor of Law and Legal Governance, Macquarie Law School, Sydney, Australia

Francesco Palermo: Associate Professor of Law, University of Verona, Italy

Ole W Pedersen: Senior Lecturer in Law, Newcastle Law School, England

Anne Peters: Professor of Public International Law, University of Basel, Switzerland

Cesare Pinelli: Professor, Faculty of Law, University of Rome 'La Sapienza', Italy

Dragoljub Popović: Judge, European Court of Human Rights

Ulrich K Preuss: Professor of Law, Hertie School of Governance, Berlin, Germany

Victor V Ramraj: Associate Professor, Law School, National University of Singapore

Kent Roach: Prichard-Wilson Chair in Law and Public Policy and Professor of Law, University of Toronto Law School, Canada

Ruth Rubio-Marín: Professor of Constitutional and Public Comparative Law, European University Institute, San Domencico de Fiesole, Italy

Daniel Sabsay: Professor and Chair in Constitutional Law, University of Buenos Aires, Argentina

Cheryl Saunders: Laureate Professor, University of Melbourne Law School, Australia

Martin Scheinin: Professor of Public International Law, European University Institute, San Domencico de Fiesole, Italy

Mahendra Pal Singh: Chair, Delhi Judicial Academy, Delhi, India

Michael Ashley Stein: Visiting Professor and Executive Director, Harvard Law School Project on Disability, Harvard Law School, United States

Manfred Stelzer: Professor of Law, University of Vienna, Austria

Arun K Thiruvengadam: Assistant Professor, Law School, National University of Singapore

Mark Tushnet: William Nelson Cromwell Professor of Law, Harvard Law School, United States

Carlos Viver Pi-Sunyer: Professor of Law, University Pompeu Fabre, Barcelona, Spain

Jeremy Webber: Professor of Law, University of Victoria, British Columbia, Canada

Jennifer Widner: Professor of Politics and International Affairs, Woodrow Wilson School, Princeton University, United States

Adrien K Wing: Bessie Dutton Murray Professor of Law, University of Iowa College of Law, United States

Jiunn-rong Yeh: Professor of Law, College of Law, National Taiwan University

Christopher S Yoo: John H. Chestnut Professor of Law, Communication, and Computer & Information Science, and Director, Center for Technology, Innovation & Competition, University of Pennsylvania Law School, United States

Table of cases

Cases of the Bundesverfassungsgericht [Federal Constitutional Court]

Introduction

Mark Tushnet

Every nation—indeed, every institution that has a more or less continuous life over a reasonably sustained period—has a constitution, understood to be a way of organizing the exercise of collective power within the nation and institution. And every nation has constitutional law, understood as a series of normative regularities in power's actual exercise. A half-century ago, a handbook on constitutional law would have taken its domain to be the constitution of a single nation. Today, the appropriate domain is the world. For this Handbook's editors, 'constitutional law' is the genus, the constitutional law of individual nations the various species. Our decision to give the book the title 'Handbook on Constitutional Law' rather than 'Handbook on Comparative Constitutional Law' was quite deliberate.

Yet, to pursue the biological metaphor, our work evolved from the field of comparative law, in which studies of constitutional law have had a contested place. The Montesquieuan standpoint—that every nation's laws grew out of that nation's specific experiences and character (and geography)—was difficult to supplement, much less displace in comparative law generally. The sense that public law remained nationally distinctive retained its hold even when increasing commercial interactions within Europe, between Europe and the Americas, and between European powers and their colonies made it possible to see how the similar functions performed by private law in different societies could support serious comparative work. During the period when scholars of comparative law devoted a great deal of attention to classifying families of legal systems (David & Brierley; Zweigert & Kötz), constitutional law seemed even more an outlying field because the core distinction in comparative law between common law and civil law systems, drawn initially because of different ways of 'doing' private law, did not seem to correspond well with the observed variations in constitutional law. A classic study demonstrated, for example, that the major variants of constitutional review—centralized or diffuse, abstract or concrete—were compatible with both civil and common law traditions (Brewer-Carias).

The integration of regional economies in Latin America and Europe produced some work comparing constitutions within those regions, but interest in constitutional law as a global phenomenon was driven primarily by successive waves of constitution-making—in the immediate aftermath of World War II, in the period of decolonization, in response to a democratization wave in South America in the 1980s, and probably most importantly with the end of the Soviet Union and its domination of central and eastern Europe and the end of the South African *apartheid* regime in the 1990s. Some of that interest was purely academic, some was associated with the practice of constitutional 'advice giving' to those drafting constitutions, especially in what came to be known as post-conflict societies. The ready availability of information on the internet has simplified researchers' tasks. Our analytic tools and our knowledge have grown substantially over the past generation.

Defining the distinctive subject matter of (worldwide) constitutional *law* remains contested. Because constitutional law implicates the organization and application of public power, its study cannot be hermetically isolated from the study of political power, and indeed there is a field, sometimes identified as 'constitutional studies,' that takes questions about organizing power to be central. Yet, there must be a distinct field of worldwide constitutional law both because of professional specialization and because lawyers are right in thinking that constitutional law, though connected to power, is distinct from it. So, for example, students of political economy have asked whether and under what conditions parliamentary systems are more stable than presidential ones (Linz; Cheibub), or what the economic effects of parliamentary systems are compared with those of presidential ones (Persson & Tabellini). Scholarship in constitutional *law* notices these studies, but they lie at the periphery of interest. Scholars of constitutional law are likely to be more interested in examining the different ways in which power is distributed between legislature and president in a presidential system, or what powers the executive has in a parliamentary one.

A natural temptation is to take the field to be the study of constitutional*ism*—that is, of a set of normative propositions about the good or wise exercise of public power. One difficulty associated with doing so is that it might constrict the field dramatically. The reason is twofold. First, the criteria for determining when a system satisfies the requirements of constitutionalism are themselves contested: How much protection must a system provide against imposing defamation liability for statements about leading political figures for it to be a constitutional system? One might be inclined to say that the extraordinarily stringent requirements for defamation liability in the United States go beyond the minimum requirements of constitutionalism, but that the lax ones in Singapore cast doubt on whether that nation is a constitutionalist one. Perhaps, but then what of liability standards in Great Britain or Australia in the 1970s? Focusing on normative constitutionalism may produce work dealing with identifying the margins while leaving too much taken for granted.

Second, and related, an enormous range of institutional forms conform to constitutionalism's requirements, once constitutionalism is given a sensible definition. Charles McIlwain's definition is widely used in the Anglo-American world: 'All constitutional government is by definition limited government,' he wrote, continuing with, 'constitutionalism has one essential quality; it is a legal limitation on government; it is the antithesis of arbitrary rule; its opposite is despotic government, the government of will instead of law' (McIlwain, 20, 21). With such an expansive definition, constitutional law would consist of little more than the enumeration of the various modes people have devised to limit government. And, perhaps equally important, constitutionalism's focus on *limiting* government makes it more difficult to discern the ways in which constitutions organize power for its effective use, whether for bad or for the good that constitutionalism seeks to advance.

Defining the field with reference to normative constitutionalism has one large advantage—not enough to overcome its disadvantages, but important nonetheless. Normative constitutionalism provides some baseline for comparisons across systems. We can ask whether one institution does 'better' than another at promoting constitutionalism's values, and under what conditions. So, for example, we can ask whether proportional representation or minority vetoes has done a better job in sustaining constitutionalism in post-conflict situations where conflict was predicated on ethnic divisions. Methodologists of comparative law generally have worried about the basis for comparison. There functionalism, here constitutionalism can provide that basis. Yet, both there and here, those baselines pose their own problems: functionalism (which has its attractions in public as well as private law) can push national distinctiveness to the background, just as constitutionalism can lead us to be overwhelmed by variation.

In developing this Handbook, the editors chose to avoid making methodological choices to as great an extent as we could. Of course, developing an outline of subjects, writing a proposed table of contents, requires that some choices be made. On the surface those choices are about subjects to be discussed, but inevitably choice carries with it some implicit methodological decisions. Even the classic form of comparative study—the juxtaposed country studies of specific subjects—makes methodological choices when the editors provide contributors with the outline of subjects and subtopics to be discussed.

We took a different course. After developing our proposed table of contents—which interestingly underwent modest transformation as the project developed—we sought out contributors but gave them no instructions about how to develop their chapters. We hoped that doing so would lead to what we might think of as an 'emergent' methodology, emerging from the relatively uncoordinated choices made by specialists. Of course, the fact that all of our contributors *are* specialists means that their choices were not entirely uncoordinated, because all shared the professional orientation of academic lawyers. We tried to offset that by *pairing* authors. We did our best to locate authors—not necessarily ones who had previously worked together—from different constitutional and legal traditions, and asked them to work out between themselves the approach they wanted to take. We hoped that this would promote methodological pluralism because scholars socialized into their specialties within different traditions would implicitly have different methodological orientations.

Our choice of contributors/collaborators was driven by an additional consideration. Scholarship in our field has been dominated by scholars from, and attention to, Anglo-European traditions. We sought out scholars from other traditions to ensure as best we could that perspectives on constitutional law from East Asia, South Asia, and elsewhere were brought to the subjects. Ideally we would have had greater representation from regions outside Europe and North America, although the Handbook's contributors do include authors from Africa, the Middle East, and Latin America. It is worth noting that we asked contributors to draft their chapters in English, not the first language for many, which we tried to offset by encouraging authors to provide references to materials in languages other than English. Even with those qualifications, we believe that we have made some progress in showing that the study of constitutional law is a worldwide endeavor whose practitioners do not inevitably start their analysis with presuppositions drawn from the Anglo-European experience. Chapter after chapter draws attention to literature on constitutional questions outside the Anglo-European mainstream, and in languages other than English.

One result of our choice of contributors emerges even from the most traditional methodology of the country study. As noted above, country studies juxtapose the ways in which different national systems treat specific topics. Their benefits are twofold. They allow readers to notice or impute common themes, but they can also have a 'defamiliarizing' effect as readers see that what they might have assumed from their own domestic experience were inevitable features of the topic's legal treatment were actually contingent ones. The larger the net of the country studies, the more likely that some defamiliarization will occur for almost all readers on one or another topic. And, because authors write from within their own traditions, we thought that bringing together authors from different traditions would enhance the value of whatever country studies our authors offered.

Our hope that questions of method would emerge from and be addressed by collaboration came with another hope—that substantive themes would emerge as authors addressed the topics we selected. That proved true at least in part. Perhaps the dominant emergent theme, coming from a large number of the Handbook's chapters, is the importance of non-domestic law in shaping domestic constitutional law. References to the role international and supra-national law plays in domestic constitutional law are pervasive. Importantly, that role is not simply as hierarchically superior law to which domestic constitutional law must conform because of the legal supremacy of international or supra-national law. Indeed, legal supremacy plays a rather small—and in some settings quite contested—role in shaping domestic constitutional law. Nor is the role often a result of direct imposition of 'outside' norms. Rather, international and supra-national law provides a model for domestic law through processes ranging from advice from outsiders such as the Venice Commission, and experts consulted in processes of constitution-making, to learning from networking and observing, with much in between. We believe that an important scholarly task suggested by many Handbook chapters is a more detailed exploration of the modes through which international and supra-national law enters domestic constitutional law.

Another emergent theme is the unsurprising one that comparative study reveals both broad similarities and large variations in how specific topics are treated in domestic constitutional law. Again, that similarities will be found is an almost inevitable feature of the comparative enterprise itself. The possibility of identifying similarities is what drives functionalist methodologies in comparative law, as those methodologies are predicated on identifying and then describing in detail how the 'same' or similar functions are carried out in different systems. Beyond that, though, the very fact of identifying specific topics *within* constitutional law will induce the identification of common themes. To take an obvious example: Placing a discussion of the constitutional treatment of abortion in a chapter on the constitutional law of privacy will connect it to issues of informational secrecy, the treatment of the home, and the like, while placing the discussion in a chapter on the constitutional law of women's rights will connect it to issues of workplace equality, affirmative action, and the like. Expository coherence almost requires that authors find something in common with the different national systems they describe.

Here, too, a theme emerges from many Handbook chapters, which many scholars might not have expected to see. Though comparative constitutional law has not taken legal 'families' as an important organizing theme, more than a few chapters note what appear to be reasonably systematic differences in the ways specific topics are dealt with depending on whether the nation is in the common law or the civil law tradition. Because the observation of the traditions' effects are emergent, our authors do not offer much in the way of explanation, and some future scholarship might productively deal with the reasons the traditions appear to be influential as such. In broad outline, the principal (although probably not sole) source of difference lies in the histories of the respective legal traditions. Different historical paths produced and then supported systematic differences in concepts and doctrines (e.g. the scope of executive power and the status of international law), constitutional theories (e.g. constituent power), and institutions (e.g. the organization of adjudication in public and private law). The various features of each 'family' have become increasingly integrated and interdependent over time, and differences have been further supported by, until recently, the lack of regular and sustained discourse between legal families and their constitutional complements. This last, at least, has now changed and is contributing to the convergence of the families, which is still far from complete. As noted earlier, some analytic work suggests that these traditions need not—as a conceptual matter—produce different approaches on specific matters. Yet, even after some convergence has occurred, institutions' location within historical traditions affects the ways in which those institutions function.

Of course, descriptive accuracy requires the acknowledgement of difference and variation, features in every comparative exercise that bedevil the field by increasing the degree of complexity necessary for accuracy—or, perhaps, raise questions about whether there *is* a field. After identifying some themes to be found in the domestic constitutional law of various nations as they deal with specific topics, chapter after chapter in this Handbook notes that fully understanding any nation's domestic law will require attention to details that vary substantially from nation to nation. The Montesquieuan specter, it seems, cannot be completely banished from the field of constitutional law.

Comparativists generally, and those of constitutional law specifically, still can take heart from T.S. Eliot's observation, well known to specialists, 'the end of all our exploring/Will be to arrive where we started/And know the place for the first time.'

References

Brewer-Carias, A-R (1989). *Judicial Review in Comparative Law* (New York: Cambridge University Press).

Cheibub, JA (2007). *Presidentialism, Parliamentarism, and Democracy* (New York, Cambridge University Press).

David, R & Brierley, J (1985). *Major Legal Systems in the World Today: An Introduction to the Comparative Study of Law* (London: Stevens).

Linz, J (1994). 'Presidential or Parliamentary Democracy: Does It Make a Difference?' in Linz, JJ & Valenzuela, A, *Presidential Democracy: Comparative Perspectives*, vol I (Baltimore, Johns Hopkins University Press).

McIlwain, C (1947). *Constitutionalism: Ancient and Modern* (Ithaca: Cornell University Press).

Persson, T & Tabellini, G (2003). *The Economic Effects of Constitutions* (Cambridge, MIT Press).

Zweigert, K & Kötz, H (1987). *An Introduction to Comparative Law* (2nd rev edn New York: Oxford University Press).

Part I
General issues

1

Constitutions

Yasuo Hasebe and Cesare Pinelli

1.1 'Constitution': families of meanings

The term 'constitution' corresponds etymologically to the Latin *constitutio*.[1] The noun derives from the verb *con-stituo*,[2] whose root *statuo* ('to set up') is a transitive form of *sto* ('to stand') (Ernout & Meillet, keyword *sto*).

Accordingly, two families of meanings are likely to stem from *constitutio*, namely the condition of an erect body, or the bodily predisposition as regards health or strength,[3] and the action of building or of constituting something.[4] These families might be considered as designating, respectively, the substance of which a certain entity is constituted, and the artificial production of a certain entity. A substantial (or organic) notion of *constitutio* might then be distinguished from a formal (or artificial) one.

But *statuo* is also at the origins of *status*. While distinguishing public law as *quod ad statum rei romanae spectat* (what pertains to the Roman polity) from private law as *quod ad singulorum utilitatem* (what pertains to the utility of individuals),[5] the Justinian code employs *status* as the condition of a certain entity, the Roman polity, that was not a state in the sense of a legal organization acting upon a certain territory. This is rather the modern sense of the notion, firstly emerging from Machiavelli's assertion that '[a]ll states, all powers, that have held and hold rule over men have been and are either republics or princedoms' (Machiavelli, 1). In turn, Hobbes's celebrated definition of the 'commonwealth or state' as 'an artificial man' is centred on 'art', namely on how the state is formed (Hobbes, 9).[6]

---

1 *Constitutio* affords the etymon for the word 'constitution' not only in English-speaking and in Latin-speaking countries, but also in others, such as Russian-speaking countries. To the contrary, the ancient Greek *politeia* and the current German *Verfassung* exhibit different etymologic roots.

2 Designating the act of building: Vergil, *Aeneid*, 12, 194.

3 See Cicero, *De Officiis*, 3, 33, 117: 'if not only the utility, but the whole happiness of life consists in a firm constitution of the body and in the experimented hope in such constitution'.

4 See Apuleius, *De Platone et Eius Dogmate*, 2: 'constitution of the polity'.

5 *Corpus Iuris* (*Institutiones*, vol. I, 1, 4; *Digestus*, vol. I, 1, 2).

6 The notion of 'art' as a technique was then widely diffused; see Maravall 58 ff.

It is still disputed whether the alternative constitutional theories that prepared, or accompanied, the rise of the modern state maintained some correspondence with the ambivalent meaning of *constitutio*. With that rise, the old meaning of *constitutio* as condition or structure of a certain body (constitution in the organic sense) might have been converted into theories of the constitution focused on the state's organization, or 'institution'.[7] Conversely, Hobbes's vision of the state as an exclusively artificial creation might be viewed as the epistemological premise of the purely procedural notion of constitution formulated by Kelsen.[8]

At any rate, it was a theoretical dichotomy between a substantial (or institutional) and a formal (or procedural) notion of constitution that dominated the European debate throughout the twentieth century. That dichotomy was then discussed in abstract terms, and therefore disconnected from the meaning of constitution as adopted from legally issued authorities and/or from the people.

However, since the Roman Republic, 'constitution' has frequently been used in the latter meaning. While noticing that 'this religious constitution does not differ much from the laws of Numa and our customs' (see Cicero, *De Legibus* 2, 10, 23), Cicero refers himself to some accepted meaning of constitution. The same occurs in the Digest, enacted in the late Roman Empire, where it is reported that the legislative acts of the Emperor are designated *constitutiones* (see *Digestus* 1, 4), or in Glanvill, who defines *legalis ista constitutio* as King Henry II's ordinance, establishing the rules for the assizes (de Glanvill 63). These authors or texts content themselves with describing the legal meaning of constitution as it is accepted in their time, without engaging in theoretical statements.

Nonetheless, references to a constitution's accepted meaning may go beyond mere descriptions. In *De Re Publica* Cicero asserts that a *constitutio*, in the sense of the foundation of a republic, cannot result from the capacity of a single man, but from that of many men acting through centuries and ages rather than within a single generation (Cicero, *De Re Publica*, vol. II, 1), adding that such constitution is provided with a great deal of equity, without which men could not preserve their freedom for long (Cicero, *De Re Publica*, vol. I, 45). While recalling the making of the Roman republic's *constitutio*, which resulted in a mixed form of government, Cicero introduces here a normative notion of constitution, whose content consists in virtues (equity and freedom) that were attached to it by various generations of Roman citizens. The author's account, although far from being neutral, relies on the historical evidence that such notion resulted from an incremental understanding from citizens of the virtues of their own constitution.

A more ambitious enterprise was attempted in the case of Article 16 of the 1789 Declaration of the Rights of Man and the Citizen, according to which '[a]ny society in which rights are not guaranteed, nor the separation of powers determined, has no constitution'. Unlike Cicero, the authors of the Declaration aimed at giving once and for all a universal normative definition of constitution, grounded on the basic elements of the emergent constitutionalism, such as the separation of powers and the guarantee of rights.

It has been noticed that 'separation of powers', far from consisting in the establishment of independent and specialised authorities, was intended by the Framers of the Declaration in the negative sense suggested by Locke and Montesquieu, namely that concentration of powers engenders despotism, a regime where the power of changing both the content and the

---

7 Hence the 'institutional theories' of Santi Romano and Maurice Hauriou.

8 Such continuity goes beyond the fact that, while Hobbes conceives the state as the subject of sovereignty, Kelsen converts it into the point of imputation to which public legal acts are imputed. On Kelsen's thesis of the identity of law and state see MacCormick, 21 ff.

procedure of rules rests upon the despot's arbitrary will (Troper, ch. XVII). However, a positive sense is given to the whole proposition from the connection of 'separation of powers' with 'guarantee of rights', set forth in the Preamble to the Declaration as 'the natural, unalienable and sacred rights of man'. While stating that societies in which rights are not guaranteed, nor the separation of powers determined, have no constitution, Article 16 reflects the fundamental precept of the natural law theory according to which unjust laws are not laws. Hence emerges a content-based notion of constitution, irrespective of whether and how citizens apprehend its basic elements, and by what processes it is made.

In spite of its universalistic ambition, this notion reflected an emphasis on the proclamation of rights and a relative lack of attention to the corresponding remedies, as criticised by Dicey with a view to indicate the superiority of the British practice: 'The Habeas Corpus Acts declare no principle and define no rights, but they are for practical purposes worth a hundred constitutional articles guaranteeing individual liberty' (Dicey, 199).

The question of whether the British practice guarantees rights better than that of continental European states has lost significance in our time. Constitutions adopted in contemporary states—with the exceptions of the United Kingdom, Israel, and New Zealand—consist in a document or a series of documents enacted through a specific procedure, providing both the distribution of power among the state's authorities and the fundamental rights of citizens. But the worldwide diffusion of written texts with these characters is far from confirming the beliefs lying at the core of the 1789 Declaration. Unlike the age of innocence of constitutionalism, the awareness is now widespread that '[c]onstitution-texts can be mere façade legitimation, mere window-dressing on actual state practice. The practice may be of one-party rule, of police torture, of corrupt and intimidated judges, of a military or militia barely if at all under civilian rule, of business practices distorted by the need for systematic bribery of officials, and so on' (MacCormick, 24; see also Sartori).

The question therefore remains open as to which criteria are needed for distinguishing façade or sham constitutions and which are not. Attention should of course be focused on whether constitutional rules and principles are sufficiently enforced, and, first and foremost, on the meanings that may be attached to the text both on formal grounds and in relation to its content. In particular, a brief account will be given of the sense of the constitution's amending procedures (see § 2), and of the evolution of the ideas and practices affecting constitutionalism (see § 3).

1.2 Flexible and rigid constitutions

James Bryce first formulated what has become a generally acknowledged distinction affecting the constitution's procedure. Bryce distinguished between 'flexible constitutions' that 'proceed from the same authorities which make the ordinary laws' and 'are promulgated or repealed in the same way as ordinary laws', and 'rigid constitutions' that 'stand above the other laws of the country which they regulate. The instrument (or instruments) in which such a constitution is embodied proceeds from a source different from that whence spring the other laws, is repealable in a different way, exerts a superior force. It is enacted, not by ordinary legislative authority, but by some higher or specially empowered person or body' (Bryce, 128 ff).

Although grounding the distinction on a formal criterion, Bryce was interested in the historical roots of those types with a view to examine their respective stability. Flexible or common law constitutions such as the Roman and the English, he argued, consist in a mass of precedents, of dicta of lawyers or statesmen, of customs and beliefs, together with a certain number of statutes, whose changes or transgressions, albeit formally easy, did not alter for centuries the main lines of the frame of government (id 141). This 'apparent paradox' was due to the balance of social and economic forces standing behind and supporting the constitution, whose 'natural affinity for an aristocratic structure of government' brought Bryce to challenge implicitly Montesquieu's famous dictum: 'The very fact that the legal right to make extensive changes has long existed, and has not been abused, disposes an assembly to be cautious and moderate in the use of that right. *Those who have always enjoyed power are least likely to abuse it*' (see id 142, emphasis added).

A rigid or 'documentary' constitution, which Bryce suggested usually arises when the mass of the people are anxious to secure their rights against the invasion of power (id 200), is affected by two opposing tendencies, namely 'the growth of the respect for the Constitution which increasing age brings', and the fact that time, 'in changing the social and material condition of a people, makes the old political arrangements as they descend from one generation to another a less adequate expression of their political needs' (id 191). Since the majority requested for constitutional amendments might then be higher than that which can be secured, it remains the expedient of 'Extensive Interpretation', which in the United States is afforded by the Judiciary: 'Human affairs being what they are, there must be a loophole for expansion or extension in some part of every scheme of government: and if the Constitution is Rigid, Flexibility must be supplied from the minds of Judges' (id 197).

However, Bryce was not sufficiently aware of the enduring debate on the constitution's relation with time, which took place among theorists and at the Constituent Assemblies since the eighteenth century's Revolutions.

It is worth mentioning Article 28 of the Declaration of the Rights of Man and the Citizen, attached to the Constitution of 1793, according to which '[a] people has always the right to review, to reform, and to alter its constitution. One generation cannot subject to its law the future generations'. Similarly, Jefferson and Payne were convinced that 'the present generation has an unlimited and illimitable right to new-model the institutions under which it lives. The only consent that legitimates any form of government is "the consent of the living"' (Holmes 202). Madison replied that, rather than enslaving future generations, precommitments enable the possibility of democracy by stipulating restraints upon one generation from preventing the future ones from experimenting with democracy (id 200 ff).

The issue of the Constitution's amendment procedure was connected with the Jefferson–Madison debate, as well as that, contextually arising in France, between Sieyès and Barnave (see Chabot).[9] While constitutions allowing the ordinary legislator to amend constitutional provisions, or flexible constitutions in Bryce's terms, corresponded to the Jeffersonian perspective, the rigid type reflected that of Madison. But, rather than Bryce's distinction between a venerable, aristocratic common law constitution and a modern, popular one, the French alternative concerned the *pouvoir constituant*'s legitimacy in binding future generations, an issue inherent in the rise of modern constitutionalism.

1.3 The emergence of constitutionalism

Broadly defined, 'constitutionalism' is the practice and method whereby limits on governmental powers are established and maintained. Constitutionalism promotes the rule of law over the rule of men. It is in this sense of the term that we discuss the idea of 'ancient

---

9 Chabot affirms that Barnave's thought foresaw that of Tocqueville.

constitutionalism' in Plato's *Statesman*, or the 'medieval constitutionalism' of Bracton (McIlwain, chs. II, IV).[10]

Defined strictly, 'constitutionalism' refers to the idea of limiting governmental powers in modern states. This idea, also called 'modern constitutionalism', presupposes the distinction between the public and private spheres, which ancient or medieval constitutionalism did not recognise (Beaud 134).[11] In the modern state, ancient or medieval constitutionalism would not work because, first, any customary limit on governmental powers is subject to change by the sovereign legislative power; and second, the Reformation brought the loss of a unified worldview that maintained moral limits on governmental powers.

Under medieval constitutionalism, it was said that 'the King shall not be subject to men, but to God and the law: since law makes the King' (Bracton 33), but no mechanism existed either to effectuate this legal constraint or to make the government accountable before the people, other than violent revolt (McIlwain 80–83). As Parliament emerged as the supreme legislature, some recognised that it had the power to do what it ought not to do. While Sir Edward Coke recommended that Parliament 'leave all causes to be measured by the golden and straight metwand of the law, and not to the incertain and crooked cord of discretion' (Coke, *Institutes of the Laws of England*, vol. 4, 40–41), he also admitted that even statutes that were unjust or contrary to fundamental common law stood as law if they were enacted by Parliament (Burgess 191–3).

To constrain political powers effectively requires a conception of the state as an independent agent of governmental powers composed of legal institutions, and a conception of rulers and officials, including princes and kings, as being entrusted to exercise governmental powers in the name of the common good (Skinner). It also requires the invention of various non-violent, normal mechanisms to circumscribe political powers within legal bounds.[12] The replacement of the medieval feudal system, where each person's social status was intimately related to his privileges and duties, by the sovereign state, which concentrated the society's political powers within the central government by dissolving intermediate bodies and creating autonomous individuals endowed with equal civil rights, was the essential prerequisite of the emergence of modern constitutionalism. Such ideas and mechanisms find grounds in social contract theories, in which a populace is conceived as a corporation consenting to be ruled under terms that protect it from the abuse of power by its rulers. When rulers violate these terms, the power with which they are entrusted may be reclaimed by the populace, and even violent resistance may be justified (see Locke, chs. 11, 19).[13]

However, Europe in the sixteenth and seventeenth centuries was not inherently conducive to the establishment of such a social order. Rather, it was deeply mired in political turmoil because of the Reformation and the division of churches it entailed. Instead of commonly revering one supreme God, people held various, conflicting and even incommensurable worldviews. Individuals were required to choose their faith in accordance with conscience.

---

10 Plato says that the strict rule of law is a 'perfectly acceptable second-best' when ideal rulers are not available: Plato 1995, p 64 para. 297e.

11 See below n 15 on Tuck.

12 Burgess points out, '[r]esistance is not the essence of constitutionalism, but its antithesis': Burgess 162.

13 Thomas Hobbes also recognises that, when their lives are threatened, people have the right to join together and rebel against the sovereign: Hobbes', ch. XXI, 152.

To understand the resolution of this turmoil under modern constitutionalism, it is helpful to conceive of each individual's reasoning as divided between private and public matters.[14] Despite the plurality of values arising in post-medieval societies, people are inclined to participate in the wider life of their society, and to share fairly in its benefits and burdens. In the private sphere, an individual leads her life in accordance with her own comprehensive conception of the good. However, in the public sphere, people don the mantle of equal citizenship and participate in rational public deliberation on the interests of the society as a whole. Individuals' reasoning in public deliberation must be independent of their private conceptions of the good to preclude the collision of irreconcilable values, which might destroy the fragile, artificial public sphere and fragment society into camps of ideological friends and foes. To safeguard the division of reasoning regarding the two spheres, modern constitutionalism entails the protection of fundamental rights, and in particular freedoms of speech and conscience, by independent courts.

Richard Tuck points out that 'the extraordinary burst of moral and political theorising in terms of natural rights which marks the seventeenth century, and which is associated particularly with the names of Grotius, Hobbes, Pufendorf and Locke, was primarily an attempt by European theorists to deal with the problem of deep cultural differences, both within their own community (following the wars of religion) and between Europe and the rest of the world (particularly the world of the various pre-agricultural peoples encountered around the globe)' (Tuck 1994).[15] Many fundamental rights perform the double function of ensuring the free pursuit of individual happiness, and promoting the long-term public interests of a society (Hasebe 2003, 240–1). This observation accords with John Rawls's vision of irreconcilable conflict as the starting point of modern liberal democracy (Rawls xvi–xvii):

> What is new about this clash [irreconcilable conflict] is that it introduces into people's conceptions of the good a transcendent element not admitting of compromise. This element forces either mortal conflict moderated only by circumstance and exhaustion, or equal liberty of conscience and freedom of thought. Except on the basis of these last, firmly founded and publicly recognized, no reasonable political conception of justice is possible. Political liberalism starts by taking to heart the absolute depth of that irreconcilable latent conflict.

Hereafter, the term 'constitutionalism' will be used in the strict sense, presupposing the distinction between the public and private spheres, unless otherwise indicated.

1.4 Constitutionalism and the rule of law

Constitutionalism is closely interrelated with the rule of law, in that both function as means to decrease the risk of the abusive use of political powers. The dominant understanding of the

---

14 The division between the private and public in question here is not that between two kinds of social interactions but one drawn by reason, which means that we should not decide on matters of the public good on reasons deriving from some conception of the good belonging to the private sphere.

15 Tuck 1993, xiv–xvii, points out that Grotius and his followers treated the universality of the principle of self-preservation as a device to undermine scepticism, which had been generated by the deep cultural conflicts resulting from the Reformation (for a view against the sixteenth- and seventeenth-century division of the Western legal history into 'medieval' and 'modern', see Berman, esp. pp. 377–80).

rule of law is that it represents the ideal state of a legal system, under which people can lead their lives with sufficient knowledge of when and how their government can exercise its coercive powers.[16] This ideal state is generally understood to require that laws be made public, general, clear and reasonably stable, not retrospective but prospective, and consistent; that laws do not demand impossible conduct; and that particular government actions be subject to review by independent courts to ensure their accordance with general laws. Even an immoral law, like one discriminating against a specific race, must conform to these requirements of the rule of law to be effective. These requirements enable laws to work effectively as laws (Raz 2009, 223–6).

This conception of the rule of law may be considered 'thin' in that it does not entail substantive political justice as a defining element of the legal system. More precisely, this thin conception does not require that a legal system enable people who embrace various world-views to conduct their lives freely and to participate fairly in the reflective deliberative process that furthers public welfare in their society.

Constitutionalism requires more than this thin idea of the rule of law. However, opinions differ on just how thick constitutionalism should or can be, in part because the demarcating line between the private and the public spheres varies from society to society.[17] It should also be noted that demands of these two ideas conflict with each other, since constitutionalism tells that, in order to achieve appropriate solutions that conform to the requirements of funda-mental rights, we should sometimes avoid the application of established statutes or precedents, which conform to the requirements of the rule of law.

1.5 Scepticism about constitutionalism

Constitutionalism may fail to achieve its purposes in many ways. A ruler may reject constitu-tionalism outright; political elites may ostensibly adopt a liberal constitutional code, but disregard it in ruling their society; or conflicts between cultural, ethnic or religious factions within a constitutional democracy may undermine its national integrity.

Moreover, some scholars argue that constitutionalism entails inherent contradictions in its project of limiting state powers with, among other mechanisms, written, rigid constitutional codes and constitutional review systems. According to Hans Kelsen's theory of 'unconstitu-tional' statutes (Kelsen 1945, 1556; Kelsen 1967, 271–6), '[t]he statement that a valid statute is "unconstitutional" is a self-contradiction; for a statute can be valid only on the basis of the constitution'. A statute cannot be unconstitutional because, if it is truly unconstitutional, it is invalid and an invalid statute is not a statute at all. In other words, although the content of a statute may be contrary to the constitution, it has been enacted by a legislature that draws *its* authority from the constitution and remains valid until annulled by the body constitutionally entitled to do so. Thus, because of the essential requirement of hierarchical validation for every legal norm, the project of constitutionalism cannot eliminate all state actions contrary to the constitution.

Other scholars maintain the more radical view that since a constitutional code is just an assemblage of texts, the meanings of which are accorded only by authoritative interpreters, constitutionalism amounts to no more than rule by these authoritative interpreters, usually the highest court in a given legal system. According to this view, the logic of constitutionalism in

16 The elements and virtues of this conception are analysed by, among others, Raz 2009, ch. 11.
17 See above n 15 on Tuck.

the broad sense entails an inherent contradiction. Michel Troper's realist theory of interpretation offers one of the most prominent developments of this line of reasoning (Troper 332–4).

Yet the notion that a text must be interpreted to be understood leads to the conclusion that it is impossible to determine the meaning of any expression. If it is necessary to interpret a text in order to understand its meaning, then any authoritative interpretation of a text, to the extent that it is expressed in language, must itself also require authoritative interpretation. We are thus plunged into a bottomless pit: no interpretation can restate a text so as to close the gap between the text and its meaning. To prevent this infinite regress, the meaning of a text must at some stage of understanding be grasped, in accordance with rules and conventions widely shared, at least among lawyers, within a society. In other words, interpretation should be an exceptional, not the standard, form of understanding of what a law means (Marmor, ch. 2). Any communication between individuals would be impossible unless the meanings of texts are graspable according to shared rules and conventions. Such a basis of communication among lawyers in a given society is a prerequisite for constitutionalism to function effectively (Hasebe 2004).[18]

Obviously this does not mean that judicial interpretation of constitutional law, when it is necessary, does not pose serious problems regarding its relation with constitutionalism and democracy. In particular, constitutional texts referring to fundamental rights give the judiciary the vast opportunity to take moral considerations into account in deciding cases with significant political implications.

1.6 Constitutionalism and democracy

Tensions between democracy and constitutionalism are likely to arise whenever statutes are not applied or invalidated by courts because of their contrast with constitutional provisions. Since democratically elected officials approve statutes, so the argument goes, the popular legitimacy with which they are provided should not be overridden by that of unelected authorities such as courts. Hence derives the 'counter-majoritarian difficulty' (Bickel 16 ff). But democracy's functioning, it is objected, is governed by the rule of majority, which from Tocqueville onwards is believed to create inescapably a monolithic power, the 'tyranny of the majority' (see Holmes 1993, 28). Once again, constitutionalism stands as a means for limiting power, referring to the legislator the very suspicion about power's arbitrary exertion from unchecked authorities that brought Montesquieu to advocate the need for the separation of powers. Furthermore, in deeply divided countries, constitutionalism aims at preventing majorities from suppressing the identities of minorities, which are founded not only on political, but also on cultural, linguistic or religious claims (see Chapters 13 and 26).

A 'difficulty', however, be it 'counter-majoritarian' or 'majoritarian', leaves open the question of how it might be surmounted. So far, attempts at composing the tension between constitutionalism and democracy are not unthinkable (see Bickel 99 ff). However, in recent literature a different approach to the issue emerges, one that appears founded on a comparison between the goods that constitutionalism and democracy are respectively believed to pursue.

---

18 This does not eliminate the possibility that the contents of a functioning constitution are different from the meanings that ordinary citizens ascribe to the text of the constitutional code. In such cases, the relevant constitution is the functioning one, not the text of the constitutional code. On this question, see Raz 1998, 173 arguing that constitutions 'are self-validating'.

Such a comparison might of course drive to opposite conclusions. Influential German constitutionalists tend to reduce democracy to the institutionalisation of the imperative of human dignity, viewed as 'the cultural anthropological premise of the constitutional State' (Häberle 18 ff). At the same time, attempts are made in the Anglo-American scholarly debate to demonstrate that representatives are better equipped in moral reasoning than courts (Waldron 2 ff), or that 'competitive party, parliamentary democracy with majority rule outperforms courts significantly without their having substantive advantages', with respect to 'the procedural virtues of equality of participation, equity in representation and influence, accountability and contestation' (Bellamy 244).

Although reacting to theories that reflect heterogeneous traditions and conceptual categories,[19] both these assumptions produce the effect of shifting the attention from the question of how the tension between constitutionalism and democracy might be, or should be, assessed, to a comparison between these on purely normative grounds. Something important is thus left aside. In the practice of constitutional democracies, the exertion of fundamental rights is inextricably connected with the democracy's functioning and vice versa, to the point that the latter is inconceivable without the former, and vice versa. This assumption corresponds to the idea that 'human rights do not compete with popular sovereignty', but 'are identical with the constitutive conditions of a self-limiting practice of publicly discursive will-formation' (Habermas 264). It is this inextricable connection that makes both the 'tyranny of the majority' and the 'counter-majoritarian difficulty' the premises for the debates. These are questions of legitimacy, namely of how power should be exerted in compliance with democratic constitutions that recognise the rights of citizens outside the realm of politics, and in the meanwhile give citizens the chance to ensure the legitimacy of such realm through the exertion of their own political rights. The two spheres are thus intrinsically connected from the perspective of citizens, although they are structurally divided, powering the institutions of government.

In spite of their being claimed 'in the name of citizens', disputes concerning the latter field consist in diverging interpretations of the power's structural divide as settled in the constitution, and of the conflicting conceptions of power that the constitution embodies. That is, the constitution itself presupposes conflicts as physiological moments of its own development, in light of its relation with time (see § 2).

'It is the very purpose of our Constitution,' wrote Justice Brennan, 'to declare certain values transcendent, beyond the reach of temporary political majorities' (Michelman 1502 n. 28). Such a notion, it should only be added, goes beyond a single constitution, being widely shared among constitutional democracies. And democracy pertains there to those 'transcendent values' as well as constitutionalism. Laws are subordinated to the constitution not just on procedural grounds, but because these, being the contingent product of a certain political majority, might infringe rights as set in constitutional principles intended to endure through diverse ages. On the other hand, the temporary limitations requested for the mandate of elected officials inhere to a positive expectation, which is related to the functioning of the accountability rule and to the renewal of the political power's legitimacy. Most importantly, both the devices presupposing these conflicting attitudes, respectively judicial review of legislation and the accountability rule, not only co-exist but are necessarily affected by a temporal dimension.

---

19 Respectively, the reaction against Schmitt's vision of the people as a natural source of the constituent power (see Häberle 35), and the 'Republican revival' vis-à-vis the longstanding tradition of judicial activism in the US (see Sunstein 1493 ff, 1539 ff, respectively).

The same occurs with the dialectical relation between constitutional interpretation and constitutional amendment procedures, to the extent that their effects consist of achieving shifting balances between stability and change. While courts are empowered to afford interpretations of the text as far as amendments on the matter are not enacted, the meaning of these might in turn be shaped from judicial decisions over time. Such process should be presumed as open-ended, since constitutions fail to designate a depositary of the final word. Conflicts opposing constitutionalism to democracy appear physiological within the framework of democratic constitutions, to the point that genuinely authoritative constitutional interpretations, or decisions, are virtually banned from their perspective.

These constitutions have abandoned the pretention of possessing time, be it of Lycurgus or the opposite claim reflecting a revolutionary epoch, that each generation should master its own future. The amending procedures may demonstrate this point, as well as the poor predictive capacity of constitutional principles. It should rather be noted that, while structuring the interplay of the authorities that are variously enabled to pursue these principles, democratic constitutions rely on time. Memories of the constitutional past are thus differentiated over time, and transformative virtues and self-correction among citizens are correspondingly enhanced, with a view to preparing the future. At the exact opposite of the 'eternal present' that permeates post-modernity, thus eliminating both the past and the future from our imagination, '[a] written constitution's normative force depends ultimately on whether it works to recall a people to itself over time: a means by which a people re-collects itself and its fundamental commitments' (Rubenfeld 177).

References

Beaud, O (2003). 'Constitution et constitutionnalisme' in Raynaud, P & Rials, S (eds) *Dictionnare de philosophie politique* (Paris, Presses Universitaires de France, 3rd edn).

Bellamy, R (2007). *Political Constitutionalism: A Republican Defence of the Constitutionality of Democracy* (Cambridge, Cambridge University Press).

Berman, H (2003). *Law and Revolution II: The Impact of the Protestant Reformations on the Western Legal Tradition* (Cambridge, Harvard University Press).

Bickel, A (1986). *The Least Dangerous Branch* (New Haven, Yale University Press, 2nd edn).

Bryce, J (1901) 'Flexible and Rigid Constitutions' in *Studies in History and Jurisprudence*, vol. I (Oxford, Clarendon Press).

Burgess, G (1996). *Absolute Monarchy and the Stuart Constitution* (New Haven, Yale University Press).

Chabot, J (1995). 'Barnave et le pouvoir constituant' in Martucci, R (ed) *Constitution et Révolution aux Etats-Unis d'Amérique et en Europe (1776–1815)* (Macerata, Laboratorio di Storia Costituzionale).

de Bracton, H (1968). *On the Laws and Customs of England*, Thorne, S (trans) vol. 2 (Cambridge, Harvard University Press).

de Glanvill, R (1932). *De Legibus et Consuetudinibus Angliae*, Woodbine, GE (ed) (New Haven, Yale University Press).

Dicey, A (1959). *Introduction to the Study of the Law of the Constitution* (London, Macmillan, 10th edn).

Ernout, A & Meillet, A (1951). *Dictionnaire étymologyque de la langue latine* (Paris, Librairie C. Klinksieck).

Häberle, P (1982). *Verfassungslehre als Kulturwissenschaft* (Berlin, Duncker & Humblot).

Habermas, J (1996). *Between Facts and Norms: Contributions to a Discourse Theory of Law and Democracy* (Cambridge, MIT Press).

Hasebe, Y (2003). 'Constitutional Borrowing and Political Theory', *International Journal of Constitutional Law* 1:224.

—— (2004). 'The Rule of Law and Its Predicament', *Ratio Juris* 17:489.

Hobbes, T (1996). *Leviathan*, Tuck, R (ed) (Cambridge University Press).

—— (1988). 'Precommitment and the Paradox of Democracy' in Elster, J & Slagstad, R (eds) *Constitutionalism and Democracy* (Cambridge, Cambridge University Press).

Holmes, S (1993). 'Tocqueville and Democracy' in Copp, D, Hampton, J & Roemer, JR (eds) *The Idea of Democracy* (Cambridge, Cambridge University Press).

Kelsen, H (1945). *General Theory of Law and State*, Wedberg, A (trans) (Cambridge, Harvard University Press).

—— (1967). *Pure Theory of Law*, Knight, M (trans) (Berkeley, University of California Press).

Locke, J (1988). *Two Treatises of Government*, Laslett, P (ed) (Cambridge, Cambridge University Press).

MacCormick, N (1999). *Questioning Sovereignty* (Oxford, Oxford University Press).

Machiavelli, N (1988). *The Prince*, Skinner, Q & Price, R (eds) (Cambridge, Cambridge University Press).

Maravall, JA (1972). *Estado moderno y mentalidad social: Siglos XV a XVII* (Madrid, Revista de Occidente).

Marmor, A (2005). *Interpretation and Legal Theory* (Oxford, Hart Publishing, 2nd edn).

McIlwain, CH (1947). *Constitutionalism: Ancient and Modern* (Ithaca, Cornell University Press).

Michelman, F (1988). 'Law's Republic' *Yale Law Journal* 97:1493.

Plato (1995). *Statesman*, Annas, J & Waterfield, R (eds) (Cambridge, Cambridge University Press).

Rawls, J (1996). *Political Liberalism* (New York, Columbia University Press).

Raz, J (1998). 'On the Authority and Interpretation of Constitutions: Some Preliminaries' in Alexander, L (ed) *Constitutionalism: Philosophical Foundations* (Cambridge, Cambridge University Press).

—— (2009). *The Authority of Law: Essays on Law and Morality* (Oxford, Oxford University Press, 2nd edn).

Rubenfeld, J (2001). *Freedom and Time: A Theory of Constitutional Self-Government* (New Haven, Yale University Press).

Sartori, G (1962). 'Constitutionalism: A Preliminary Discussion' *American Political Science Review* 56:853.

Skinner, Q (2002). 'The State of Princes to the Person of the State' in *Vision of Politics*, vol. II (Cambridge, Cambridge University Press).

Sunstein, C (1988). 'Beyond the Republican Revival' *Yale Law Journal* 97:1539.

Troper, M (1994). *Pour une théorie juridique de l'État* (Paris, Presses Universitaires de France).

Tuck, R (1993). *Philosophy and Government 1572–1651* (Cambridge, Cambridge University Press).

—— (1994). 'Rights and Pluralism' in Tully, J (ed) *Philosophy in an Age of Pluralism: The Philosophy of Charles Taylor in Question* (Cambridge, Cambridge University Press).

Waldron, J (2009). 'Judges as Moral Reasoners' *International Journal of Constitutional Law* 7:2.

Additional reading

Alexander, L (ed) (1998). *Constitutionalism: Philosophical Foundations* (Cambridge, Cambridge University Press).

Dobner, P & Loughlin, M (eds) (2010). *The Twilight of Constitutionalism?* (Oxford, Oxford University Press).

Elster, J & Slagstad, R (eds) (1988). *Constitutionalism and Democracy* (Cambridge, Cambridge University Press).

Loughlin, M & Walker, N (eds) (2007). *The Paradox of Constitutionalism: Constituent Power and Constitutional Form* (Oxford, Oxford University Press).

Maravall, JM & Przeworsky, A (eds) (2003). *Democracy and the Rule of Law* (Cambridge, Cambridge University Press).

McIlwain, CH (1947). *Constitutionalism: Ancient and Modern* (Ithaca, Cornell University Press).

Constitutions embedded in different legal systems

Thomas Fleiner and Cheryl Saunders

2.1 Introduction

This chapter examines how and why constitutional arrangements vary depending on the legal systems in which they are embedded. We confine our attention almost entirely to the civil law and common law legal families, with which we are most familiar. Both have their origins in Western legal thought and practice from which they have spread in varying degrees to much of the rest of the world (Mitchell & Powell, 26). Despite the considerable similarities between these families of law, however, we show that there are relatively consistent and significant differences in the constitutional concepts, doctrines, norms, and institutions found in common law and civil law states (Damaska).

We begin with three disclaimers:

1 We do not overlook the significance of other legal systems and the potential for the constitutional arrangements associated with them to be equally, if not more, distinctive. Socialist legal theory affects both the concept of a constitution and its operation in practice (Sidel). Theories of sovereignty and legitimacy in Islamic legal systems might have implications for the status of a constitution, the institutions of government, and the constitutional relationship between religion and the state (El Fadl). Variations in constitutional phenomena should also be expected in states where forms of chthonic law or other religious legal traditions have a significant influence (Glenn). In the world of the twenty-first century, however, these are never the sole sources of law but typically co-exist, formally or informally, with other bodies of law, the form and operation of which may be modified accordingly.

2 We acknowledge that neither of these two legal families is homogenous, either generally or from a constitutional perspective. Within the common law legal world, the divergence of the traditions of the United Kingdom and the United States manifests itself in various ways in other common law states. Within the civil law legal family there are major differences between the French and German spheres of constitutional influence and, within each, between individual states. To complicate generalisation further, many states have mixed legal systems and others combine a civilian legal system with common law constitutional features or vice versa. The adoption of elements of the US Constitution by many

Latin American countries, otherwise in the civil law tradition, is a case in point (Kleinheisterkamp, 261). Such variations do not disprove the relevance of the legal setting for comparative constitutional law but they should be taken into account in detailed comparative work.

3   We note that no constitutional tradition is static and that this is a time of comparatively rapid change, marked by the interpenetration of domestic and international law and considerable cross-systemic borrowing, creating a perception of constitutional convergence. In due course, these trends may negate the usefulness of legal systems as a tool for comparative constitutional analysis. That time has not yet arrived, however, and for the moment seems unlikely to do so.

The chapter begins by identifying how the constitutional arrangements of civil law and common law states diverged historically, as a key to understanding the differences between them now. The ensuing part examines five areas of difference: the concept of a constitution; the separation of powers; the process of constitutional review; the form of the state; and the relationship between domestic and international law. A final part explores the phenomenon of convergence more fully, by way of conclusion.

2.2 History

All European states, England included, were exposed to similar influences on the development of their early legal and constitutional arrangements, including the principles of Roman law through the *Corpus Juris Civilis* and the methods and doctrines of the Christian Church (Loughlin, 17–49). All experienced periods of royal absolutism. Many used Charters, of which Magna Carta was only one example, to restrain the exercise of arbitrary power in mediaeval times (van Caenegem, 80).

The causes of legal, including constitutional, divergence between what subsequently became two distinctive legal families inevitably are complex. On any view, however, one is the Norman conquest of England, the aftermath of which laid many of the foundations of the common law legal system including the prominent function played by judges in 'finding' the law, the institution of the jury, the emphasis on procedure and remedies, and the adversarial character of the legal process (Glenn 224–72). Another is the Reformation, which consolidated the authority of the Monarch in Parliament in England at a time when representative assemblies were in decline elsewhere, and provided encouragement to dissent through its emphasis on individual responsibility. Conversely, Catholicism reinforced both the inquisitorial procedure and its pursuit of truth in the continental states in which it remained dominant. The higher the position of officials in the feudal hierarchy, the closer they were to God, and thus to truth and justice (Damaska 36).

Most decisive of all were the different routes to constitutionalism, in the sense of limited government, taken in England and on the continent. In England, the revolutions of the seventeenth century represented a victory for Parliament rather than a notionally sovereign people, left the functions of the common law courts intact, retained the monarchy with significantly limited power, and drew on earlier seeds of constitutionalism, including Magna Carta and habeas corpus, to develop a self-understanding of the constitution as organic, evolutionary, and protective of liberty. In France a century later, by contrast, the Revolution and the Napoleonic era that followed swept away the existing social, legal, and political structures including the Crown and placed obligations on the new state to replace the feudal society and to develop equality and social justice. The sovereign now was the nation that, as the constituent power, empowered and limited the institutions of the new state through a constitution. The legislature represented the general will of free and equal citizens and was the sole law-making authority (Declaration of the Rights of Man and the Citizen 1789, Article 6). The courts, losers in the revolutionary struggle, were reduced to the application of legislation. And public authorities were no longer subject to private law courts, founding a relatively sharp distinction between public and private law.

Through Napoleonic conquest and imitation, these institutions and concepts ultimately spread in various forms to the rest of continental Europe and provided the base for subsequent developments wherever the civil law applied. The monopoly of the legislature over law-making, for example, coupled with the distinction between public and private law, paved the way for the Kelsenian view of the law as a hierarchy of abstract norms. The removal from the ordinary courts of authority over the lawfulness of public action led, in due course, to the development of the innovative principles of administrative law of the French *Conseil d'Etat*, an institution also much copied elsewhere. The view of the constitution as the sole source of authority for public institutions, together with the exclusion of ordinary courts from public law, also explains the creation of specialist constitutional courts in civil law states, empowered by the constitution. A civil law court could not assume authority for constitutional review without express constitutional authorisation, as in the United States or Australia.

In the United States, a revolution created a new order based on a written constitution that claimed the authority of a sovereign people. But this was a political revolution that did not seek to create a new social order. And, comparatively speaking, there was significant continuity between the old and the new, not least in relation to the function of courts and the interstitial role of the common law. Similarly, legal, institutional, and often constitutional continuity have been features of the post-independence constitutional arrangements of most other common law states, reflecting the influence of the British constitutional tradition, despite reliance on written constitutions with the status of fundamental law.

2.3 Concept of a constitution

The different historical paths of common law and civil law constitutionalism have left a residual distinction in the concept of a constitution itself.

In a civil law system, a constitution is conceived as a 'big bang': an originally revolutionary act, undertaken by a homogenous and indivisible sovereign people, constructed either as an *ethnos* (Germany) or *demos* of *citoyens* (France), acting as the constituent power. The constitution legitimates the institutions of government and is the sole source of law and justice. In a common law system, by contrast, a constitution may be a product of revolution but, equally, it may not. In admittedly rare cases, there may be no formal written constitution at all. While the authority for a common law constitution is now invariably ascribed to a sovereign people, earlier constitutions attributable to such alternative forms of sovereign authority as an imperial power are not denied constitutional status for that reason.[1] The delineation of a *demos* is less of a concern[2] and sovereignty is regarded as more readily

---

1 The Australian Constitution, enacted by the British Parliament before full independence, is a case in point (Saunders 44).
2 Thus from a common law perspective, the prospect of a Constitution for Europe may have encountered political difficulties related to its potential impact on national sovereignty but did not raise theoretical concerns arising from the character of the *demos* or the question whether Europe could be equated with a state.

divisible.[3] A common law constitution may well be regarded as the source of the legitimacy of institutions and the primary source of law but this does not necessarily preclude recognition of the creative function of courts in determining the law, acting on assumptions about the role of the judiciary that preceded the written constitution.

While the passage of time has rendered this distinction between civil law and common law constitutions more subtle, its effects continue to manifest themselves both in constitutional discourse and in the ways in which constitutions are made and changed. In civil law states, constitutions are expected to be made by a process that equates to an act of a sovereign people. Avoidance of a constituent assembly or other comparable process creates theoretical difficulties, as evidenced by the discussions of elite round-tables in Hungary and elsewhere in the constitutional revisions that followed the fall of the Berlin Wall. Conversely, use of a sovereign process suggests that the product has constitutional status; hence the refusal of the German authorities to convene a Constituent Assembly before unification, in the immediate aftermath of World War II, in the face of American pressure (Preuss 2006). By contrast, in common law states, popular involvement is also important, but for practical rather than for theoretical reasons.

More significantly still, civil law states distinguish more sharply than do common law states between the original exercise of constituent power and the authorities empowered by the constitution, whether as institutions of the state or for the purposes of constitution alteration. This distinction has doctrinal consequences. First, it causes many civil law constitutions to distinguish between the procedures used for a total and a partial constitutional revision (for example, Constitution of Switzerland, Articles 193, 194). Second, it prompts theoretical inquiry about whether the authority of the constituent power is tamed by the constitution, as opposed to remaining latent, with recognised capacity to replace the constitution with a new one if appropriately roused. In this latter case, any attempt to place certain provisions of the constitution beyond alteration could be circumvented by abrogating the constitution and creating a new one; alteration of continuing provisions within the framework of the original constitution would give rise to an unconstitutional constitutional amendment. By a parallel process of reasoning, even where a constitution has no explicit eternity clause, some amendments may be deemed unconstitutional because they are deemed to be reserved for the original constituent power.

Common law constitutions may also provide different mechanisms for alteration of different parts of the constitution. Failure to comply with the prescribed requirements may also lead to an unconstitutional constitutional amendment. In this case the problem is one of process rather than substance, however, and likely to be analysed in terms of constitutional interpretation rather than by reference to constituent power. Nevertheless, in this as in other respects, there is evidence of cross-fertilisation of ideas. The emergence of the basic structure doctrine in India, prompted by German influence, is a familiar example (Noorani).

2.4 Separation of powers

Both the common law and civil law constitutional traditions subscribe broadly to a tripartite separation of powers (Declaration of the Rights of Man and the Citizen 1789, Article 17; Federalist Papers no. 48). For reasons that are attributable partly to history and partly to

---

3 Thus the potential for a Canadian Province to derogate from the Charter of Rights and Freedoms (section 33), even for a limited period, would be inconsistent with the concept of a Constitution in a civil law state.

institutional choice, however, there are differences between them affecting both concept and practice. To generalise, in a civil law system there is a somewhat greater institutional separation, less of a functional separation, and less emphasis on the role of checks and balances.

At the heart of these differences is the concept of a constitution as it emerged from the various revolutionary struggles by the end of the eighteenth century. Civil law constitutional theory tends to conceptualise the sovereign people itself as a constitutional organ and thus an element in the separation of powers (Heun 88). In principle, sovereignty is absolute and indivisible. At root, therefore, power is not divided, even though it is exercised through state institutions with distinct functions. To complicate separation further, the legislature expresses the general will and thus is the 'mouthpiece' of the sovereign (Baranger 220). The scope of power to be exercised by the legislature, and by extension that of the executive and the judiciary, is determined against this backdrop of principle, subject to anything to the contrary in the constitution. The exercise of legislative power may also be conditioned by other principles, derived from the very conception of law-making or from the rule of law (Heun 37–42). The judiciary has the most tenuous link with the sovereign with the consequence that in some states, including France, it is described as an 'authority' rather than as a 'power' (Constitution of France 1958, Title VIII; Zoller 238). The inability of ordinary courts to deal with questions of public law is often understood as an element in the separation of powers.

By contrast, the less institutionalised notion of the people in common law constitutionalism allows for a functional as well as an institutional separation of powers, popular sovereignty notwithstanding. Each branch exercises the power assigned to it, effectively in its own right. Checks and balances have greater prominence, reflecting different expectations of the state. The respective boundaries of legislative, executive, and judicial power are broadly attributable to the outcomes of the seventeenth-century constitutional struggles in England, although there has been considerable subsequent redefinition at the margins through written constitutions and evolutionary change. The judicial branch is weak in terms of electoral legitimacy but, in theory at least, it is co-equal with the others, in an interdependent system of checks and balances.

How this works out in practice depends on institutional design. The nature and degree of separation of powers varies between presidential and parliamentary systems, both of which exist in both legal systems. Even so, there are variations worth noting. Civil law states commonly adopt either a parliamentary form of government or a modified version along the lines of the fifth French Republic, sometimes described as semi-presidential, in which executive power is shared between a directly elected President and a government responsible to the legislature (Elgie). A civil law legislature is more likely to be elected through some form of proportional representation, whereas in common law systems majoritarian electoral systems are typically in use, creating a different institutional dynamic. Ministers in a civil law parliamentary system are unlikely to be required to hold seats as Members of Parliament and may be constitutionally precluded from doing so, whereas common law systems typically insist that ministers remain members of the parliament throughout their term of office.

There are some differences too in the extent to which an executive can exercise, or be authorised to exercise, law-making power, in the concept of legislative power itself and in the theory that underpins these arrangements. Parliamentary supremacy in a common law parliamentary system denies legislative power to the executive but accepts delegation by parliament to the executive, typically without limit as a matter of law. By contrast, a civil law system may draw a more deliberate distinction between 'law' and 'regulation' that constrains both the scope and manner of the delegation of power by the Parliament to the executive (for example, German Basic Law, Article 80). In a novel variation, the Constitution of the Fifth French

Republic and others influenced by it use a distinction between law and regulation to confine the role of the legislature to the prescription of general rules, leaving the executive with the authority to make laws on matters of relative detail, in its own right (Constitution of France 1958, Articles 34, 37; Baranger 229).

It follows from what has already been said that different conceptions of the separation of powers are also manifested in the function and constitution of courts. Common law courts deal with public as well as private law. Common law judges enjoy substantial independence, which is viewed as an attribute of the separation of powers. Judicial independence is formally protected through guarantees of tenure, remuneration, and insulation from the other branches that separation of powers provides. Less formally, it is buttressed by constitutional culture and the expectations of the legal profession from which judges are drawn.

Judges of ordinary civil law courts, on the other hand, are career judges. Their independence is valued but is protected differently, through the career structure and institutions calibrated by reference to it (Bell). Separation of powers precludes these courts from dealing with questions of public law. Public law adjudication takes place instead through specialist adjudicatory bodies. Examples include the Conseil d'Etat and Conseil Constitutionnel in France, the Federal Administrative Court and the Federal Constitutional Court in Germany. The procedures for appointment to these bodies and the tenure of members are designed to satisfy civil law sensitivities about the relationship between institutions that draw their authority from the sovereign people and those that do not. These matters are taken up in the next section, in the context of constitutional review.

One final point of difference concerns remedies. Common law judges have at their disposal a range of coercive remedies, backed by a power to deal with contempt of court. By contrast, in the civil law tradition, administrative and constitutional courts had no power to impose their decision on the administration or to find a civil servant in contempt of court. Thus, the remedy of an injunction did not traditionally exist in civil law systems and courts had no remedy to prevent the commission of an illegal act. An administrative court might quash an illegal decision of the administration. Illustrating the effects of convergence, a civil law court might also now declare an act or an omission to be unlawful. But, at least in the European context, a civil law court typically lacks power to enforce execution through a contempt order. The distinction has important consequences for the protection of human rights.

In one example of the collective, practical implications of these differences between court systems, the 1974 decision of the Supreme Court in *United States v Nixon*[4] that a District Court had power to order an *in camera* examination of tapes recording private conversations in the White House would be inconceivable in the civil law. This would not be a matter for an ordinary court. And a court would lack authority to compel compliance with such an order in any event.

2.5 Process of constitutional review

Constitutional review, understood as the power of a court to determine the constitutionality even of legislation appeared first in the United States as a concomitant of a written constitution with the status of fundamental law. Justifying the practice in 1803, Marshall CJ reasoned that '[i]f ... the Courts are to regard the Constitution, and the Constitution is superior to any ordinary act of the Legislature, the Constitution, and not such ordinary act, must govern the

---

4 418 US 683 (1974).

case to which they both apply'.[5] Constitutional review in this sense broke with the British tradition of parliamentary sovereignty, which had long since repudiated any earlier claim by common law courts to declare an Act of Parliament to be void.[6] Nevertheless, review of the constitutionality of legislation subsequently became a feature of the constitutional arrangements of all other common law states that adopted written constitutions with superior legal status. Typically in such a common law state, any court can apply the constitution, together with other sources of law, although sometimes constitutional jurisdiction is confined to higher courts. In older common law constitutions in particular, the authority for constitutional review may be assumed, rather than explicitly authorised.

Constitutional review is now also available under the constitutions of most, although not all, civil law states. Differences in both history and the way in which review is conceived and justified, however, mean that it operates in somewhat different ways. Common law systems typically accept that courts have an inherent power to secure a 'government by law and not by men', whatever the source of the law. Their power in this regard is linked to their function of determining cases and controversies. In the civil law tradition, by contrast, courts must be specifically empowered to decide cases by reference to the constitution. Power to resolve other questions of a constitutional nature also may be delegated by the constitution to them.

Civil law states resisted constitutional review until well into the twentieth century. The model that ultimately proved widely influential was first given effect in the Austrian Constitution of 1920, drafted by Hans Kelsen. The Kelsenian solution concentrated constitutional review in a single Constitutional Court, specially constituted for the purpose with an eye to its legitimacy and specifically empowered to control the conformity of lower norms, including those that derived from legislation, with the highest domestic norm, which derived from the Constitution according to the theory of the hierarchy of norms (Steltzer 23–7). Following World War II, this model was adopted and adapted to provide a mechanism for review by reference to the new, supreme constitutional instruments in Germany and Italy. It now prevails in most continental European states including, for example, Bulgaria, Hungary, Portugal, Slovenia, and Spain, and is also influential elsewhere including, for example, Indonesia, South Korea, Mongolia, and Chile. It has influenced the design of the European Court of Justice.

The French approach originally was distinctive, although still clearly the product of ideas characteristic of the civil law tradition. Although the institution of the Conseil Constitutionnel was introduced by the French Constitution of 1958, its authority could be invoked only prior to formal enactment to avoid conflict with the general will and by only a small range of institutional parties deemed to represent the nation (Zoller 221). The distinctiveness of the French position within Europe gradually eroded. In 1971 the Constitution was interpreted to incorporate and give effect to the rights in the 1789 Declaration and the preamble to the Constitution of 1946.[7] In 1974 it was amended to extend the right to refer laws to the Conseil Constitutionnel, in effect, to opposition parties (Constitution of France 1958, Article 61). Nevertheless, the distinction has by no means entirely disappeared, despite provision for a priority preliminary ruling on the constitutionality of promulgated law by an alteration of the Constitution that took effect in 2010 (Constitution of France 1958, Article 61(1); Pfersmann).

5 *Marbury v Madison*, 5 US 137, 178 (1803).
6 *Bonham v College of Physicians (Dr Bonham's Case)* (1610) 8 Co Rep 114.
7 Conseil Constitutionnel [Constitutional Council of France], Decision 71-44 DC (16 July 1971).

There are variations among states in the model of concentrated constitutional review, complicating generalisation. Nevertheless, common features include a Constitutional Court that is not part of the regular judiciary; a selection process designed to reinforce the legitimacy of the Court, typically through a process of election for a lengthy but fixed term by designated organs of the state; an explicit constitutional conferral of jurisdiction on the Court; a conception of review that divorces norm control from the concrete case; and, often, a range of additional functions that require the Court to deal with disputes between governmental bodies at the instance of an authorised party. Matters may reach such a Court in a range of ways that also vary between states. Procedures currently in use include abstract review of a challenged statute at the instance of a designated and restricted range of public actors; concrete review at the instance of a judge of another court who considers that a statute germane to an issue before the court is unconstitutional; and complaints by an individual about infringement of that person's constitutional rights.

Operational differences that stem from these alternative broad models of constitutional review include the following. Courts in a common law constitutional setting typically apply the Constitution as one of a number of sources of law available to them, to resolve a legal dispute before them. Matters typically are presented in factual context, requiring a plaintiff with an interest in the outcome. Constitutional cases share the features of any other form of litigation: proceedings are adversarial; a formal doctrine of precedent applies, with the usual caveats about the discretion of an apex court to depart from former decisions; the ordinary range of judicial remedies is available to the court. By contrast, a Constitutional Court in a civil law setting typically deals only with the constitutional question, presenting consequential problems for the relationship between the Constitutional Court and other courts, which are resolved differently in different states. This form of constitutional review places little, if any, weight on the factual context in which the constitutional question arises. By definition, neither abstract review nor political questions are a bar to the exercise of jurisdiction. There is no formal doctrine of precedent although the values of decisional consistency may produce a similar effect.

Differences in judicial reasoning in constitutional cases in the two systems may be attributed to differences both in the conception of the judicial role and in substantive principles. In identifying these, allowance must be made for cultural factors that often found distinctive approaches to judicial reasoning between states in the same legal tradition. Paradigmatically, nevertheless, common law judicial reasoning builds on the facts of the instant case while that of civil law judges is more inclined to begin with principle. The distinction is less pronounced in constitutional litigation but helps to account for some differences in the way in which reasons are framed. Constitutional interpretation is a potentially controversial exercise in any system but the search for 'objective interpretation' in civil law jurisdictions through a range of broadly accepted techniques, only one of which relies on history,[8] gives the debate a somewhat different cast in these states in contrast, at least, to the focus on originalism in the United States. Legal realism, an economic approach to law, and comparative reasoning have less influence in the civil law tradition, where the judge is not accepted as a law maker. Differences in constitutional principle that also affect reasoning include a greater willingness in civil law states to employ the principle of proportionality; different understandings of the rule of law; and different conceptions of the role of the state, with implications for the scope and application of constitutional rights (Grimm 2005).

8 Others include textual, grammatical, systemic, and teleological techniques (Heun 181).

2.6 Form of the state

The first modern federation, which emerged in the United States, was conceived in the common law legal tradition. Sixty years later, Switzerland became the first federation in a civil law setting. In the early twenty-first century there are approximately 25 federations in the world, distributed between the two legal systems, sometimes also in conditions of significant legal pluralism. For comparative purposes, federations are often treated as a genus, to be further analysed by reference to such considerations as the manner in which each federation was formed. This part shows that legal culture also may affect the design and operation of federal constitutions.

The most obvious difference stems from the recognition of legislation as the only source of law in civil law states (Fleiner & Basta Fleiner 541). In a common law legal system, by contrast, private law, criminal law, and legal procedure are sourced in the common law in the sense of judge-made law, subject to the possibility of statutory overlay. It follows that, in a civil law federation, these areas of law must be distributed through an allocation of legislative power whereas, in a common law federation, they may be distributed implicitly through the way in which judicial power is organised. The significance of the civil, criminal, and procedural codes in the civil law tradition, coupled with the significance attached to the generality of law, suggests that legislative authority in these matters is more likely to be allocated to the federation.

A second point of distinction that generally, though not invariably, coincides with the legal tradition in which the federation is formed concerns the manner of the allocation of powers. The classical common law federation is dualist, with parallel sets of institutions in each sphere. In accordance with this model, each order of government administers its own legislation and may provide for its own adjudication as well. By contrast, a civil law federation typically also divides legislation and administration, often conferring substantial legislative power on the federation, leaving the administration of federal law to the federated units, in their own constitutional right.

This significant difference in federal design can also be attributed to the influence of the hierarchy of norms in civil law legal systems, militating against competitive, parallel normative orders. In these circumstances, civil law federations necessarily are more collaborative than those in the common law tradition; the principle of 'federal loyalty' that applies in the former, as opposed to the more combative implied limitations claimed to preclude the use of federal legislative power to impair the capacity of the federated units to function in the United States and Australia are telling, in this respect. The execution of federal law by the federated units in civil law federations also necessitates additional procedures to prescribe the extent of federal control and enforcement, which are lacking in established federations in the common law tradition (Heun 63).

A third difference lies in the structure of the judiciary. The common law federal model lends itself to dual or parallel court systems in which each order of government has a court system that applies its own law irrespective of the public/private divide. By contrast, for reasons canvassed earlier, in a civil law federation, distinct institutions are used for adjudication in private and public law. Further, the same specialist court hierarchy is likely to deal with all cases in that category, without distinguishing between federal and state jurisdiction. In the case of administrative courts, this arrangement also corresponds neatly to the separation of law-making from the administration of the law.

There may be other differences as well, which should be borne in mind in federal comparisons. Different conceptions of the scope of executive power may play out differently in analysing such problems as the scope of a federal spending power or the legal status of inter-governmental agreements. Implied power is less usual in a civil law than in a common law federation, for reasons attributable to the concept of a constitution. Even the familiar federal conundrum of how to explain divided sovereignty sparks differences of discourse in the two systems, pitting common law pragmatism on the one hand against the writings of Althusius or the Kelsenian theory of the third sphere on the other (Steltzer 150).

2.7 Status of international law

The relationship between domestic and international law is yet another area in which there is some difference between constitutions embedded respectively in common law and civil law legal systems.

As a generalisation, civil law countries are more likely to be monist, recognising the direct effect in domestic law of both customary international law and treaties to which the state is a party as long as the treaty is construed as self-executing. There are variations between such states in regard to the status accorded international law but it is often hierarchically superior at least to statute (for example, Constitution of France 1958, Article 55). Common law countries, by contrast, are more likely to be dualist, requiring treaties to be incorporated into domestic law by legislation even where, as is usually the case, they accept the direct effect of customary international law. An incorporating statute has the same status as other legislation and breach attracts the same array of domestic judicial remedies. The distinction is not neatly drawn along jurisdictional lines, however, as the important examples of Germany and the United States show. While Germany has a civilian legal system, under the Basic Law treaties must be ratified by a law, in a form of 'mitigated dualism' (Article 59(2); Schermers & Waelbroeck 155). Conversely, Article VI of the Constitution of the United States declares treaties to be supreme law, although in practice they are not directly applied if determined to be non-self-executing, as is typically the case.

At least from a common law perspective, one rationale for the difference lies in the separation of powers. In most common law legal systems, with the United States a telling exception, the power to sign and ratify treaties falls within the assumed scope of executive power, making dualism necessary to avoid breach of the principle that the executive cannot make or change law. The constitutions of most civil law states, by contrast, involve the legislature in some way in the treaty ratification process, minimising objections to the effects of monism on separation of powers grounds (Fleiner & Basta Fleiner 324).

Another rationale points to differences in attitudes to the international legal system. Once again, generalisation is fraught, yet there is somewhat greater willingness on the part of states in the civil law legal family to acknowledge universal values expressed through international law as part and parcel of a single legal system comprising both domestic and international law. Thus understood, the willingness of some civil law states to accept the jurisdiction of ordinary courts to review the compatibility of legislation with international law while rejecting constitutional review, at least by ordinary courts, is less remarkable (Zoller 222–23).

2.8 Conclusion

Our argument in this chapter is that the legal system in which a constitution is embedded offers a guide to its form and operation and to the theories that underpin it. We reiterate our earlier caveats, however. There are differences between the constitutional arrangements of states within each legal family and numerous states in which, in one way or another, legal families and the constitutional arrangements associated with them are mixed. And there is evidence that differences attributable to the legal systemic context are diminishing, in consequence of a degree of constitutional convergence, which is a feature of our times.

One of the principal catalysts for convergence is the influence of international law on domestic constitutional systems, understood to include the intense impact of supra-national arrangements within Europe on the constitutions of participating states.[9] Another is the extent of horizontal borrowing of constitutional arrangements between states, both at the point at which a constitution is made and during its operation in practice, through processes that range from the eclectic provision of 'expert' advice in the course of constitution-making processes to the impact of real and virtual networks of jurists and scholars. Between them, these forces are eroding the relevance of legal systemic differences, most obviously in relation to rights but with implications for institutions and other constitutional principles as well. Thus, to take only a few examples, the principle of proportionality is now used for purposes of analysis and evaluation by judges in many common law as well as civil law states; a more homogenised conception of judicial independence, drawing on common law procedures, has affected traditional modes of public law adjudication in some civil law states; and semi-presidentialism is in vogue in many newly democratising states, whatever their legal tradition. Even the distinction between monism and dualism, long discredited in international law scholarship in any event, requires qualification in the context of comparative constitutional law as courts in even the most dualist of common law states draw indirectly on international law to resolve domestic constitutional problems.

Nevertheless, for the moment at least, the degree of correlation between legal systems and constitutional arrangements makes the former a useful tool for constitutional comparison. In many cases, moreover, superficial convergence masks underlying differences in the ways in which constitutional institutions and principles are understood, explained, and discussed. In our view, the relevance of the distinction is unlikely ever to disappear entirely. And this is no bad thing. The different ways of thinking about constitutions that derive from different legal traditions enrich the constitutional commons of the world of the twenty-first century.

References

Baranger, D (2006). 'Executive Power in France' in Craig, P & Tomkins, A (eds), *The Executive and Public Law* (Oxford, Oxford University Press).

Bell, J (2010). *Judiciaries within Europe: A Comparative Review* (Cambridge, Cambridge University Press).

Damaska, MR (1986). *The Faces of Justice and State Authority* (New Haven, Yale University Press).

El Fadl, KA (2004). *Islam and the Challenge of Democracy* (Princeton, Princeton University Press).

Elgie, R (2011). *Semi-Presidentialism: Sub-Types and Democratic Performance* (Oxford, Oxford University Press).

Fleiner, T & Basta Fleiner, L (2009). *Constitutional Democracy in a Multicultural and Globalised World* (Berlin, Springer-Verlag).

Glenn, HP (2007). *Legal Traditions of the World* (Oxford, Oxford University Press, 3rd edn).

Grimm, D (2005). 'The Protective Function of the State' in Georg, N (ed) *European and US Constitutionalism* (Cambridge, Cambridge University Press).

Heun, W (2011). *The Constitution of Germany: A Contextual Analysis* (Oxford, Hart Publishing).

Kleinheisterkamp, J in Reimann, M & Zimmerman, R (2006). *The Oxford Handbook of Comparative Law* (Oxford, Oxford University Press).

---

9 We include here both the European Union and relevant features of membership of the Council of Europe, including the European Convention on Human Rights and the European Commission for Democracy through Law (Venice Commission).

Loughlin, M (2010). *Foundations of Public Law* (Oxford, Oxford University Press).

Mitchell, SM & Powell, EJ (2011). *Domestic Law Goes Global* (Cambridge, Cambridge University Press).

Noorani, AG (2001). 'Beyond the "Basic Structure" Doctrine' *Frontline* 18(9) (28 April).

Pfersmann, O (2010). 'Concrete Review as Indirect Constitutional Complaint in French Constitutional Law: A Comparative Perspective' *European Constitutional Law Review* 6:223.

Preuss, UK (2006). 'Post-Conflict Constitutionalism: Reflections on Regime Change through External Constitutionalization' *New York Law School Law Review* 51:467.

Saunders, C (2011). *The Constitution of Australia: A Contextual Analysis* (Oxford, Hart Publishing).

Schermers, HG & Waelbroeck, DF (1995). *Judicial Protection in the European Union* (The Hague, Kluwer Law International, 5th edn).

Sidel, M (2009). *The Constitution of Vietnam: A Contextual Analysis* (Oxford, Hart Publishing).

Steltzer, M (2011). *The Constitution of Austria: A Contextual Analysis* (Oxford, Hart Publishing).

Van Caenegem, RC (1995). *An Historical Introduction to Western Constitutional Law* (Cambridge, Cambridge University Press).

Zoller, E (2008). *Introduction to Public Law: A Comparative Study* (Leiden, Martinus Nijhoff).

International relations and international law

Anne Peters and Ulrich K Preuss

Recent developments of international relations and international law in times of globalization have had a profound impact on the form and substance of domestic constitutional law, and on the concept and theory of the constitution itself (Tushnet, 142–64; Peters 2007; Auby, 236–40).

3.1 Constitutional references to international relations and international law

Constitutions have traditionally defined the powers of state organs in foreign affairs, especially with regard to the conclusion of international treaties. Modern constitutions additionally often provide for the binding force of international law within the domestic sphere, sometimes recognize the primacy of international law over domestic law, refer to international organizations, especially to the United Nations, or regulate the state's accession to international organizations. In the constitutions of EU member states, provision is made for the transfer of sovereign powers to the EU or the pooling of sovereignty within the EU (Grewe). Clauses regarding the International Criminal Court (ICC), concerning its jurisdiction or surrender of persons to the Court, have been introduced. Frequently, special constitutional clauses enshrine international human rights, give them priority over domestic law, or guarantee access to international control mechanisms.

The proliferation of such constitutional references to international law reflects major changes in international relations since the 1980s. First and foremost, the liberalization of world markets in the last three decades led to intensified economic and cultural cross-border activities, with state borders no longer constituting serious barriers to such transactions. The thrust towards a unified global economic space required new legal, including constitutional, norms to satisfy the functional imperatives of globalized markets.

Second, the collapse of authoritarian regimes predominantly, but not exclusively, in Southern Europe in the 1970s and in East and Central Europe after 1989, necessitated the elaboration of entirely new constitutions. Geared to Western models of constitutionalism, they were ready (or were urged) to pledge fidelity to international law.[1] Third, the international community, or at least its most powerful members, have been supervising regime changes and have induced, accompanied, steered, or even installed new state constitutions, such as the constitutions of Cambodia (1993), Bosnia and Herzegovina (1995), South Africa (1996), East Timor (2002), Afghanistan (2004), Iraq (2006), Kosovo (2008), and South Sudan (2011).[2] Fourth, the creation and power gain of international organizations such as the EU and the ICC have necessitated constitutional adaptations to permit the states' integration into and cooperation with those regimes.

3.2 Constitutional convergence through internationalization

These factors have led to a 'permeation' of national constitutions by international law (Wendel), towards a 'vertical' convergence of international law and domestic constitutional law, and thereby also to a 'horizontal' convergence of constitutions *inter se*.

3.2.1 Vertical

National constitutional principles (such as human rights and self-determination/democracy, or the rule of law and good governance) have previously been 'upgraded' to international standards, both as principles governing the functioning of the international institutions themselves, and as a point of reference from which to evaluate a national constitution (Franck). These norms thus guide constitution-making, constitutional reform, and judge-made *Verfassungswandel*. A pertinent example is the international prescription of free and regular elections. The most intense and far-reaching pressure or stimulation of domestic constitutional reform has been exercised by the Council of Europe, the EU, and NATO. Empirical studies have demonstrated that the 'international socialization' of states of Eastern and Central Europe took place due to these organizations' accession conditionalities (Schimmelfennig).

The Treaty of Maastricht of 1992, which founded the EU and which substantially reformed the European Community, triggered constitutional revisions in most of the then 12 member states. The United Kingdom's current constitutional evolution has, to a significant extent, been induced by European integration and by the Human Rights Act of 1998, which implements the European Convention on Human Rights (ECHR).

3.2.2 Horizontal

Simultaneously, a 'horizontal' approximation of state constitutions is taking place. In particular, new state constitutions designed under international guidance are 'chipped off the same block', based on the modern canon of fundamental rights, rule of law, democracy, and separation of powers (Thürer, 25). Examples of principles that have travelled transnationally and spread through the case-law are notably human rights, the idea of legitimate expectations, and the constitutional principle of proportionality (Stone Sweet & Mathews).

The overall approximation is promoted by the (constitutional) judiciary. Increasingly, both international and foreign constitutional law is used as an argument in the national constitutional discourse (Jackson). These processes have been called 'constitutional

---

1 Greece art 28 (1975); Portugal art 8 (1976); Spain art 96 (1978); Bulgaria art 5(4)(1991); Poland art 9 (1997); Romania art 11 (1991/2003).
2 See Al-Ali, with case studies on Afghanistan, Iraq, and Bosnia.

cross-fertilization' (Slaughter, 1116–19) and a 'migration of constitutional ideas' (Choudhry). They entail a considerable expansion of judicial authority at the expense of law-making democratic bodies that may end up in a juristocracy (Hirschl).

Although both types of convergence have happened mostly in Europe, non-European proponents of 'subaltern cosmopolitan legality' also advocate a change of perspective on globalized law that 'shifts from the North to the South, with the South expressing not a geographical location but all forms of subordination (economic exploitation; gender, racial, and ethnic oppression...)' (de Sousa Santos & Rodríguez-Garavito, 14). Cosmopolitan legalists claim that 'whoever lives in misery in a world of wealth needs cosmopolitan solidarity' (ibid), and hence call for an involvement in transnational constitutional discourses that aim at furthering global justice.

3.3 The dark side of internationalization

The phenomenon that 'international law is now in the process of creating and defining the "democratic State"' is not a purely positive one (Chimni, 8). Critics, especially in post-colonial countries, suspect a 'shrinking space for domestic politics in developing countries'.[3] The internationalization of property rights, concomitant processes of the privatization of state-owned property and the intervention-prone internationalization of the human rights discourse are considered as negative examples. From that perspective, the sovereign state should remain a hurdle against the creation of a 'unified global economic space' and against the economic power of international organizations that are suspected to limit 'the possibilities of third-world states to pursue independent self-reliant development' (Chimni, 7).

Indeed, globalization and global governance belie the national constitutions' claims of uniqueness, totality, and supremacy, and also undermine the operation of constitutional principles. Global problems compel states to cooperate within international organizations, and through bilateral and multilateral treaties. Previously typical governmental functions, such as guaranteeing human security, freedom and equality, are in part transferred to 'higher' levels. Moreover, non-state actors (acting in a transboundary fashion) are increasingly entrusted with the exercise of traditional state functions, even with core tasks such as military and police activity. All this has led to governance exercised beyond the states' constitutional confines. This means that state constitutions can no longer regulate the totality of governance in a comprehensive way. Thereby, the original claim of state constitutions to form a complete basic order is defeated. National constitutions are, so to speak, hollowed out; traditional constitutional principles become dysfunctional or empty. This affects the rule of law, the principle of social security and the organization of territory, and notably the constitutional principle of democracy.

The impairment of democracy within states through globalization and through the concomitant zoning-up of governance functions is basically three-fold.[4] First, the reduced capacity of nation states to tackle and solve political problems by themselves reduces the self-determination of citizens within their national polity, hence the democratic output. Second, in the age of global interdependencies, state activities have become further reaching and more extraterritorial. This means that political decisions (ranging from the utilization of nuclear power over tax reductions to raising environmental standards) produce externalities by

---

3 Cf. Kelly.
4 Seminally, Kaiser.

affecting people across state borders. The democratic difficulty here lies in the fact that the affected individuals have not elected the decision-makers and can in no way control them.

Third, complexities of globalization increase the influence of unelected experts ('technocracy'). All this means that it is no longer possible for democratic states to be fully democratic in a non-democratic international system. In consequence, if the basic principles of constitutionalism, including democracy, are to be preserved, compensatory constitutionalisation on the international plane must happen (Peters 2006).

3.4 Normative hierarchies between international law and constitutional law

3.4.1 Supremacy of (some) international law over constitutional law

The position of international adjudicatory bodies is that (all) international law supersedes all national law, including constitutional law.[5] However, only very few state constitutions, such as the Constitution of Belgium (1994)[6] and the Constitution of the Netherlands (1983),[7] accept that claim.

Other countries treat only international human rights treaties as supreme, notably the ECHR, which is itself a kind of 'constitutional instrument'.[8] Along this line, the constitutions of several post-transition countries (Romania,[9] Slovakia,[10] and the Czech Republic[11]) explicitly grant international treaties on human rights precedence over domestic 'law', plausibly including domestic constitutional law.

Some countries, obviously more concerned about their sovereignty, are more cautious. Argentina has chosen a complex middle course between the legal and the constitutional rank of international human rights instruments: according to a 1994 constitutional amendment,

---

5 Case of the 'Montijo': Agreement between the United States and Colombia of 17 August 1874, award of 26 July 1875, in Bassett Moore, J, *History and Digest of International Arbitrations to which the United States has been a Party* (Washington, Government Printing Office, 1898) vol 2, 1421, 1440; PCIJ, *Treatment of Polish Nationals and other Persons of Polish Origin or Speech in the Danzig Territory*, Series A/B, no 44 (1932), 24; ECJ, case 11/70, *Internationale Handelsgesellschaft v Einfuhr- und Vorratsstelle für Getreide- und Futtermittel*, [1970] ECR 1125, para. 3; ECHR, *Open Door v Ireland*, Series A no 246-A, para. 69; ECHR, no. 27996/06 and 34836/06, *Sejdić and Finci v Bosnia Hercegovina* (2009).

6 There is no explicit constitutional provision to this effect. See Cour de cassation (première chambre), *Etat Belge v Fromagerie Franco-Suisse Le Ski*, 27 May 1971, RTDE 7: 494–501 (1971), English translation in Common Market Law Review 9: 229, 230 (1972); Belgian Cour de cassation, 9 Nov 2004, para. 14.1.

7 The Constitution of the Netherlands of 17 February 1983 prescribes in art 91(3): 'Any provisions of a treaty that conflict with the Constitution or which lead to conflicts with it may be approved by the Houses of the States General only if at least two-thirds of the votes cast are in favour.' Art 94 explicitly grants precedence to international treaties only over statutes, but prevailing scholarship and some practice supports the view that Art 94 applies also to the Constitution itself. In any case, if parliament determines that a treaty conflicts with the constitution and, under art 91(3) approves a treaty by a 2/3 majority, courts are able to let that treaty prevail over the constitution. But this is different if parliament does not determine such a conflict and hence does not approve a treaty by a 2/3 majority, since that would implicitly mean that the court could review a decision of parliament against the constitution, which is not allowed under art 120 of the Constitution. We thank André Nollkaemper for this clarification.

8 ECHR, *Loizidou v Turkey* (preliminary objections), Series A 310 (1995), para 75.

9 Art 20 of the Constitution of 8 December 1991.

10 Art 11 of the Constitution of 1 September 1992.

11 Art 10 of the Constitution of 16 December 1992.

international treaties take precedence over ordinary law without having constitutional rank. However, a list of two international human rights declarations[12] and eight international covenants on human rights are declared part of the constitution. All other human rights treaties have constitutional rank only if approved by congress with a two-thirds majority of the members of each chamber.[13] Likewise, an amendment of 2004 to Brazil's Constitution of 1988 establishes that international human rights treaties and conventions require the approval in each house of national congress, in two rounds, by three-fifths of votes of the respective members, and will have the rank of constitutional amendments.[14]

In the Constitution of Colombia of 1991, two inconsistent principles apply: the supremacy of the constitution[15] and the priority of 'international treaties and agreements ratified by the Congress that recognize human rights and that prohibit their limitation in states of emergency'. Consequently, fundamental rights of the constitution have to 'be interpreted in accordance with international treaties on human rights ratified by Colombia'.[16] Pursuant to the jurisprudence of the Colombian Constitutional Court, universal and regional human rights treaties form part of the 'constitutional block' of the country's legal order and hence have constitutional rank (Ramelli). The same applies to the 1917 Constitution of Mexico after the Federal Congress enacted the amendment of 10 June 2011, which implicitly assigns constitutional rank to human rights treaties to which Mexico is a party.[17]

Peremptory norms of international law are in some states accepted as superseding the constitution. The Swiss Constitution makes this explicit.[18] Finally, some state constitutions grant (some) international instruments a status equal to the state constitution.[19]

3.4.2 Supremacy of (some) constitutional law over international law

Most states do *not* grant international law unconditional priority (Peters 2009). Traditional case law often rejects international law's claim to supremacy over domestic constitutional

---

12 Including the American Declaration of the Rights and Duties of Man of April 1948, and the Universal Declaration of Human Rights of 10 December 1948.

13 Art 75(22) of the Constitution of 1853, amended 1994; see Pagliari, 195 et seq.; León. We thank Eduardo Pintore for his advice.

14 Art 5(3) added by constitutional amendment no 45 of 8 December 2004; cf. Maliska.

15 Art 4(1).

16 Art 93(1) and (2).

17 Art 1, see 'Decreto por el que se modifica la denominación del Capítulo I del Título Primero y reforma diversos artículos de la Constitución Política de los Estados Unidos Mexicanos, Diario Oficial de la Federación, Tomo DCXCIII, No. 8, Primera Sección, 10 June de 2011, pp. 2–5. We thank Alfredo Narváez Medécigo for his advice.

18 Art 139(2) and 194(2) Swiss Constitution (*Bundesverfassung*).

19 This appears to be the case for Austria and Italy. Revision of art 50 of the Austrian Constitution, with a new clause 4, amendment through Änderungsgesetz Bundes-Verfassungsgesetz (in force since 1 January 2008), art 1, no 13 (Bundesgesetzblatt für die Republik Österreich, Teil I, of 4 January 2008, no 2, 7; www.ris.bka.gv.at). See the explanatory comment in no 314 der Beilagen XXIIII.GP – Regierungsvorlage – Vorblatt und Erläuterungen, on Z 10, Z 11, and Z 13 (art 50), para 4. See art 117 of the Italian Constitution as amended on 18 October 2001: '(1) Legislative power belongs to the state and the regions in accordance with the constitution and *within the limits set by European Union law and international obligations*.' (Emphasis added.)

law.[20] Granting only international treaties had the rank of federal laws was standard for constitutions created in the spirit of the principle of national sovereignty before the wave of international human rights covenants was stimulated by the UN Declaration of 1948. For example, the Indian Constitution of 1950 assigns the rank of ordinary law to international treaties, agreements or conventions transformed into domestic law by Parliament.[21] The same applies, albeit indirectly, to the 1947 Constitution of Japan, which defines the constitution as the supreme law of the nation without any exception with respect to international law.[22] Even under the relatively new Constitution of South Africa of 1996, which is deeply committed to the protection of human rights, international treaties including human rights treaties approved by the National Assembly and the National Council of Provinces have no higher rank than that of ordinary laws.[23] However, when interpreting the Constitutional Bill of Rights, courts must consider international law;[24] thus, international human rights treaties assume a quasi-constitutional rank.

With regard to young, mostly post-transition state constitutions, 'a clear tendency towards "de jure recognition" of the primacy of international law by new constitutions … but not [a placement of international law] above the constitution itself' has been noted (Vereshtin, 29, 37). Examples of state constitutions that claim the superiority of state constitutional law over international law (or parts of it) are the Constitutions of Russia,[25] Belarus,[26] Georgia,[27] and South Africa.[28] Some state constitutions grant international law priority over ordinary statutes, but not over the domestic constitution itself (see e.g. the Greek Constitution,[29] the Constitution of Estonia,[30] the Constitution of Poland[31] and the Constitution of Paraguay[32]). The Lithuanian Constitutional Court ruled that Lithuania's Constitution of 1992 is superior to international treaties.[33] Finally, EU member states' courts have tended to refuse the

20 See for the USA art 6 of the Constitution and on the supremacy of the US American Constitution over international law, *Reid v Covert*, 354 US 1, 16–17 (1957). For France, arts 54 and 55 of the Constitution and *Conseil d'État*, 30 October 1998, *Sarran*, RFDA 1081–90 (1998); *Cour de Cassation*, *Pauline Fraisse*, decision no 450 of 2 June 2000; *Conseil d'État, Société Arcelor Atlantique et Lorraine*, 8 February 2007 (no. 287110). For Austria: Austrian Constitutional Court (*Verfassungsgerichtshof*), 14 October 1987, *Miltner*, part 4g, VfSlg. 11500/1987. For Germany: BVerfGE 111, 307 (2004) – *Görgülü*, para 35; engl. at www.bverfg.de.

21 Art 253.

22 Art 98(1).

23 Art 231(2) and (4).

24 Art 39(1); see infra sec 3.5.

25 Art 79 of the Russian Constitution of 12 December 1993. Supreme Court of the Russian Federation (plenum), decision no 5 of 10 October 2003 on the application by ordinary courts of the universally recognized principles and norms of international law and the international treaties of the Russian Federation, holding that international law has priority over the laws of the Russian Federation, but not over the Russian Constitution, except maybe for the generally recognized principles of international law, 'deviation from which is impermissible', HRLJ 25: 108–111 (2004), paras 1 and 8.

26 Constitution of Belarus of 1 March 1994, art 128 (2).

27 Constitution of Georgia of 24 August 1995, art 6 (2).

28 Constitution of South Africa of 8 May 1996, art 232 on customary international law.

29 Art 28 of the Greek Constitution of 11 June 1975.

30 Art 123 of the Estonian Constitution of 28 June 1992.

31 Art 91 of the Polish Constitution of 2 April 1997.

32 Art 141, 137(1) of the Constitution of 20 June 1992.

33 Constitutional Court of Lithuania, case no 17/02-24/02-06/03-22/04 on the limitation of the rights of ownership in areas of particular value and in forest land, 14 March 2006, para 9.4. Engl. at <http://www.lrkt.lt/Documents1_e.html>.

application of EU law when this would infringe the 'constitutional identity' of the member state.[34] The domestic constitutional actors' assertion of the supremacy of the state constitution as a whole, or of core constitutional principles, over international law is normally accompanied by those domestic actors' procedural claim to have the final word on this question.[35] Technically, this 'final word' is normally clothed in a scrutiny of the relevant domestic acts or statutes that transfer powers to the EU, against the yardstick of the states' constitution.[36] In particular, the German Constitutional Court has also directly subjected EU Acts to constitutional scrutiny, based on the argument that these Acts ultimately depend on a previous transfer of powers to the EU by a treaty that is in turn dependent on legislative consent, which means that EU Acts manifestly transgressing this consent must be considered unconstitutional, especially if they affect the 'constitution's identity' ('ultra-vires control').[37]

3.5 The 'direct effect' and 'indirect effect' of international law

Another constitutional issue is the 'direct effect' ('direct applicability' or 'self-executingness') of international law (notably of the provisions of international treaties).[38] Domestic courts in various legal orders rely on quite similar criteria to grant or reject such an effect, namely on the intentions of the contracting parties and of the domestic bodies participating in the ratification process, and on the content, objective, and wording of the relevant treaty provision. A state's attitude towards direct effect has eminent constitutional implications because it concerns the distribution of powers among courts, the executive, and parliaments, and also affects the constitutional principles of legality and democracy.

Besides, or as an alternative to, a 'direct effect' of international law, its 'indirect effect' is acknowledged in state practice. Clashes between domestic constitutional law and international law are reduced to a minimum through consistent interpretation of state constitutions. For example, the Portuguese Constitution,[39] the Spanish Constitution,[40] the Romanian Constitution,[41] and the South African Constitution[42] explicitly require that the state constitution must be interpreted in conformity with international human rights law. Notably, the South African Constitutional Court has become famous for its universalist approach to

---

34 Spanish Constitutional Court, declaration DTC 1/2004 of 13 December 2004, *French Conseil constitutionnel*, décision no 2006-540 DC of 27 July 2006, para. 19; German Constitutional Court, BVerfG, 2 BvE 2/08 of 30 June 2009, para. 340 (*Treaty of Lisbon*).

35 The Spanish Constitutional Court, in judgment 64/91 of 22 March 1991, *Asepesco*, implies that the national authorities are bound by the Spanish Constitution when implementing EU law. See also Danish High Court, 6 April 1998, para 9.6. [1998] Ugeskrift for Retsvaesen, H 800; Irish Supreme Court, judgment of 19 December 1989, *Society for the Protection of Unborn Children Ireland v Grogan*, [1990] ILRM 350, 361 (separate opinion Walsh, J.).

36 See, e.g. German BVerfGE 89, 155 (1992) – *Maastricht*; BVerfG of 30 June 2009 – *Lisbon*.

37 BVerfG, 2BvR 2661/06, 6 July 2010, paras 55-56 – *Honeywell*.

38 We understand by direct effect the legal mechanism that a domestic body (especially a court) may apply an international rule directly, and that this application can render a contrary rule of domestic law illegal.

39 Art 16 (2) of the Portuguese Constitution of 2 April 1976.

40 Art 10 (2) of the Spanish Constitution of 29 December 1978.

41 Art 20 (1) of the Romanian Constitution of 8 December 1991.

42 Art 233 of the Constitution of South Africa of 8 May 1996.

constitutional rights, in a series of judgments relating mostly to criminal processes.[43] The Supreme Court of Canada also relies quite heavily on constitutional comparison and on international law in constitutional cases,[44] but explicitly rejected any binding force of international law over the Canadian Constitution.[45]

The German Constitutional Court has held that the constitutional principle of 'friendliness towards international law' requires that the Convention's text and the case law of the Strasbourg Court must, on the level of constitutional law, serve as interpretative guidelines for the determination of the content and scope of fundamental rights and principles of the Basic Law, but only within the limits of constitutional principles.[46]

The UK's Human Rights Act (1998) requires domestic courts to interpret domestic legislation (which includes provisions with constitutional substance) in conformity with the ECHR and to take into account the case-law of the European Court of Human Rights.[47] In a landmark decision, the House of Lords declared illegal the indefinite detention of foreigners suspected of terrorism without charge or trial. The Law Lords drew on decisions of the European Court of Human Rights, on the UN Human Rights Covenant, on various other international instruments, and on opinions of the Supreme Courts of Canada and the United States, and other US courts.[48]

The United States Supreme Court has moved in the direction of interpreting the US Constitution consistently with international law. In 2003, the Court began to cite foreign and international case law and has admitted it to be materially relevant for the Court's majority's analysis.[49] In 2005, the Supreme Court departed from precedent and declared the death penalty for juvenile offenders a 'cruel and unusual punishment' in terms of the Eighth Amendment to the US Constitution, referring to the 'opinion of the world community' as supportive, but not decisive, in its conclusions.[50] This trend has been sharply criticized by individual justices.

The practice of consistent interpretation implies that constitutional law does not, in a technical sense, 'supersede' international law, because a hierarchically inferior norm could not have an impact on the reading of a 'higher' norm. The courts' practice rather suggests that both types of norms cannot be clearly 'ranked'. This strategy is laudable. It should be

---

43 See Constitution of South Africa of 8 May 1996: art 233 (Application of international law): 'When interpreting any legislation, every court must prefer any reasonable interpretation of the legislation that is *consistent with international law* over any alternative interpretation that is inconsistent with international law.' Article 39 on Interpretation of Bill of Rights: '(1) When interpreting the Bill of Rights, a court, tribunal or forum (a) must promote the values that underlie an open and democratic society based on human dignity, equality and freedom; (b) *must consider international law*; and (c) *may consider foreign law.*' (Emphasis added.) See du Plessis, 309–40 with further references.

44 E.g. Supreme Court of Canada, *Baker v Canada*, [1999] 2 S.C.R. 817; *USA v Burns* [2001] 1 S.C.R. 283, paras 79–92; *R v Hape*, [2007] SCC 26, paras 55–56; Supreme Court of Canada, *Suresh v Canada (Minister of Citizenship and Immigration)*, 11 January 2002, ILM 41: 945 (2002), para 59.

45 *Suresh*, para 60.

46 BVerfG, 18 December 2008, 1 BvR 2604/06, para 24; BVerfG, 4 May 2011, 2 BvR 2365/09, paras 86–94.

47 Human Rights Act of 1998, s 3(1), see also s 2 (1).

48 House of Lords, *Anti-Terrorism Crime and Security Act* (2001), 16 December 2004, [2004] UKHL 56.

49 In *Atkins v Virginia*, 536 US 304 (2002) on the death penalty for mentally ill offenders, the Court cited an *amicus curiae* brief of the EU in a footnote. The breakthrough was *Lawrence v Texas*, 123 S. Ct. 2472, 2483 (2003) on homosexual conduct ('sodomy'), citing case-law of the ECHR in order to bolster departure from precedent. See also *Grutter v Bollinger*, 539 US 309, 342 (2003), concurring opinion Justice Ginsburg, with reference to the International Convention on the Elimination of All Forms of Racism.

50 *Roper v Simmons*, 543 US 551 (2005).

complemented by the – inverse – consistent interpretation of international law in the light of domestic constitutional law.[51] In the EU, the principles of loyal cooperation and respect of national identity of the member states (Art 4 (2) and (3) EU) already form a possible legal basis for a European principle in that sense.

3.6 Pluralism as promise and peril

The examples of national constitutions and case-law have demonstrated that there is indeed a worldwide constitutional practice highly responsive to international law but jealous of safeguarding at least domestic core constitutional principles against international intrusion. In parallel, a growing body of international legal scholarship has begun to call into question the unconditional supremacy of international law over domestic constitutional law, notably in the event of a conflict with constitutional core values (Cottier & Wüger, 263–64; Nollkaemper; von Bogdandy & Schill).

3.6.1 A pluralism of perspectives

The new label given to these judicial practices and scholarly proposals is the label of pluralism. Pluralism here refers first of all to perspectives and denies the existence of an absolute external observer standpoint. The consequence is that there is no absolute vantage point from which to decide where the rule for deciding a conflict sits and what its content is. The plurality of perspectives is accompanied by a plurality of legal orders, a plurality of legal actors claiming ultimate authority, and a plurality of rules of conflict. In this intellectual framework, there is no legal rule to decide which norm should prevail, in other words there is no supremacy. There is also no legal meta-rule to resolve the competing claims to authority raised by the international and the domestic constitutional actors. Different legal actors, for example courts, necessarily belong to one of the various orders, therefore necessarily speak from their own perspective, and can only apply a rule of priority residing in their own legal system. In the absence of an overarching, institutionalized power that could decide a conflict, the different actors' perspectives are – in legal terms – equally valid and consistent: there is no conflict of validity. But unlike (academic) observers who may simply diagnose plurality and leave it there, the participants in the legal process must resolve upcoming conflicts and must decide which of the contrary rules to apply. Under the premise of pluralism, such conflicts in norm application cannot be decided by legal argument, but are ultimately resolved politically.

3.6.2 Mechanisms of coordination

The task ahead is therefore to identify and to develop further the procedural mechanisms of reciprocal restraint, respect, and cooperation needed for the adjustment of competing claims of authority, in order to realize what has been called a 'pluralisme ordonné' (Delmas-Marty). Besides, substantive common principles underlying both international law and national (constitutional) law might be fleshed out.[52]

Some of these mechanisms are already in place. As mentioned, domestic (constitutional) courts take into consideration international law in good faith and interpret the domestic

---

51 See, e.g., ECJ, joint cases 46/87 and 227/88, *Hoechst v Commission*, ECR 1989, 2859, paras 33–4.
52 Mattias Kumm has suggested the following principles: legality, subsidiarity, due process, good governance, democracy, and human rights. Kumm, 258–326, 273–310.

constitution in the light of international law (see above). This practice should be regularized.

Second, courts should be asked to give reasons for any non-application of international law, and these should be accepted as valid only if the application of international law risks violating the core principles of the domestic constitution ('constitutional identity').

Third, the *Solange* and *Bosphorus* strategy should be generalized. Courts should employ a legal presumption that a legal act performed by a body rooted in 'another' legal system is in conformity with their 'own' standards, coupled with the reciprocal recognition of such acts, 'as long as' some minimum requirements are not undercut.[53] In this scheme, domestic courts refuse to revisit (judicial or quasi-judicial) decisions taken by an international body on the basis of the rebuttable presumption that the international regime offers a functionally equivalent legal protection to that in domestic constitutional law.

Fourth, the international bodies should grant a margin of appreciation to national decision-makers with a strong democratic legitimation,[54] and should themselves interpret international law in the light of domestic constitutional law.

3.6.3 Balancing in the concrete case instead of a formal hierarchy

Fifth, and most importantly, conflicts between international law and constitutional law should be resolved by balancing in the concrete case, not on the basis of a normative hierarchy. Less attention should be paid to the formal sources of law, and more to the substance of the rules in question. The ranking of the norms at stake should be assessed in a more subtle manner, according to their substantial weight and significance. Such a non-formalist, substance-oriented perspective implies that, on the one hand, certain less significant provisions in state constitutions would have to give way to important international norms. Inversely, fundamental rights guarantees should prevail over less important norms (independent of their locus and type of codification). This approach is in fact already implicitly present in the emerging national constitutional practice of treating international human rights treaties differently from ordinary international law, either by granting them precedence over state constitutions, or by using them, more than any other category of international law, as guidelines for the interpretation of state constitutions. Admittedly, this new approach does not offer strict guidance, because it is debatable which norms are 'important' in terms of substance, and because it does not resolve clashes between a 'domestic' human right on the one side and an 'international' human right on the other. However, the fundamental idea is that what counts is the substance, not the formal category, of conflicting norms. Such a flexible approach appears to correspond better with the current state of global legal integration than does the idea of a strict hierarchy, particularly in human rights matters. From this perspective, international law and constitutional law find themselves in a fluent state of interaction and reciprocal influence, based on discourse and mutual adaptation, but not in a hierarchical relationship.

3.6.4 Risks and opportunities

It would be naïve to expect that identical norms will be interpreted and applied identically by all actors. Any interpretation of a constitutional norm by a national constitutional court or by

---

53 Cf. BVerfGE 37, 271 (1974) – *Solange I*; ECHR, *Bosphorus v Ireland*, appl. no 45036/98, 30 June 2005.
54 ECHR, *Hatton v UK*, appl. no 36022/97, 8 July 2003, para 97.

an international tribunal is likely to be influenced to some extent by the acting body's institutional bias. Moreover, the practical impact of the meaning given to a norm in a judgment or decision will depend on the institution's legal and political authority. It is therefore misleading to celebrate the openness of the question 'who decides who decides' and the lack of ultimate authority. While it is true that such openness in theory constitutes an additional mechanism for limiting power, it seems more likely that legal openness tends to result in the political dominance of the more powerful actors, which are normally the domestic ones. Therefore, pluralism in the sense just described bears the real risk of reinforcing the perception that international law is only soft law or even no law at all.

On the other hand, constitutional resistance might constitute an 'emergency brake' and thereby one condition for the opening-up of states' constitutions towards the international sphere. In the long run, reasonable resistance by national actors – if it is exercised under respect of the principles for ordering pluralism, notably in good faith and with due regard for the overarching ideal of international cooperation – might build up the political pressure necessary to promote the progressive evolution of international law in the direction of a system more considerate of human rights and democracy.

References

Al-Ali, Z (2011). 'Constitutional Drafting and External Influence' in Ginsburg, T & Dixon, R (eds), *Comparative Constitutional Law* (Cheltenham, Elgar), 77–95.

Auby, J-B (2010). *La globalisation, le droit et l'Etat* (2nd edn, Paris, LGDJ).

Chimni, BS (2006). 'Third World Approaches to International Law: A Manifesto', International Community Law Review 8: 3–27.

Choudhry, S (ed) (2006). *The Migration of Constitutional Ideas* (Cambridge, Cambridge University Press).

Cottier, T & Wüger, D (1999). 'Auswirkungen der Globalisierung auf das Verfassungsrecht: Eine Diskussionsgrundlage' in Beat Sitter-Liver (ed), *Herausgeforderte Verfassung: Die Schweiz im globalen Konzert* (Freiburg, Universitätsverlag), 241–281.

de Sousa Santos, B & Rodríguez-Garavito, CA (2005). 'Law, Politics, and the Subaltern in Counter-hegemonic Globalization' in de Sousa Santos, B & Rodríguez-Garavito, CA (eds), *Law and Globalization from Below: Towards a Cosmopolitan Legality* (Cambridge, Cambridge University Press), 1–26.

Delmas-Marty, M (2006). *Le pluralisme ordonné* (Paris, Seuil).

du Plessis, L (2007). 'International Law and the Evolution of (domestic) Human-rights Law in the Post-1994 South Africa', in Nijman, J & Nollkaemper, A (eds), *New Perspectives on the Divide between National and International Law* (Oxford, Oxford University Press).

Franck, TM (1992). 'The Emerging Right to Democratic Governance', American Journal of International Law 86: 46–91.

Grewe, C (2009). 'Constitutions nationales et droit de l'Union Européenne', Répertoire Communautaire: 1–29.

Hirschl, R (2004). *Towards Juristocracy: The Origins and Consequences of the New Constitutionalism* (Cambridge, MA, Harvard University Press).

Jackson, VC (2005). 'Constitutional Comparisons: Convergence, Resistance, Engagement', Harvard Law Review 119: 109–128.

Kaiser, K (1971). 'Transnational Relations as a Threat to the Democratic Process', International Organization 25: 706–720.

Kelly, JP (2008). 'International Law and the Shrinking Space for Domestic Politics in Developing Countries' in Andrews, PE & Bazilli, S (eds), *Law and Rights: Global Perspectives on Constitutionalism and Governance* (Lake Mary, FL, Vandeplas Publishing), 259–272.

Kumm, M (2009). 'The Cosmopolitan Turn in Constitutionalism: On the Relationship Between Constitutionalism in and Beyond the State' in Dunoff, JL & Trachtman, JP (eds), *Ruling the World? International Law, Global Governance, Constitutionalism* (Cambridge, Cambridge University Press), 258–326.

León, AQ (2005). 'Relaciones entre el derecho internacional y el derecho interno: Nuevas perspectivas doctrinales y jurisprudenciales en el Âmbito americano', Ius et Praxis 11: 243–267.

Maliska, MA (2011). 'Verfassung und normative Kooperation: Zum übergesetzlichen Status Internationaler Menschenrechtsverträge in Brasilien', Verfassung und Recht in Übersee 44: 316–325.

Nollkaemper, A (2010). 'Rethinking the Supremacy of International Law', Zeitschrift für öffentliches Recht/Journal of Public Law 65: 65–85.

Pagliari, AS (2007). Curso de Derecho Internacional Publico (Cordoba, Advocatus).

Peters, A (2006). 'Compensatory Constitutionalism: The Function and Potential of Fundamental International Norms and Structures', Leiden Journal of International Law 19: 579–610.

—— (2007). 'The Globalization of State Constitutions', Chapter 10 in Nijman, J & Nollkaemper, A (eds), New Perspectives on the Divide between National and International Law (Oxford, Oxford University Press), 251–308.

—— (2009). 'Supremacy Lost: International Law Meets Domestic Constitutional Law', Vienna Online Journal on International Constitutional Law 3: 170–198.

Ramelli, A (2004). 'Sistema de Fuentes de Derecho Internacional Público y 'Bloque de Constitucionalidad' en Colombia', Cuestiones Constitucionales, Revista Mexicana de Derecho Constitucional 11: 157–175.

Schimmelfennig, F (2005). 'Strategic Calculation and International Socialisation: Membership Initiatives, Party Constellations, and Sustained Compliance in Central and Eastern Europe', International Organization 59: 827–860.

Slaughter, AM (2000). 'Judicial Globalization', Virginia Journal of International Law 40: 1103–1119.

Stone Sweet, A & Mathews, J (2008). 'Proportionality Balancing and Global Constitutionalism', Columbia Journal of Transnational Law 47: 72–164.

Thürer, D (2005). 'Kosmopolitische Verfassungsentwicklungen' in Thürer, D, Kosmopolitisches Staatsrecht (Zurich, Schulthess) vol 1, 3–39.

Tushnet, M (2003). The New Constitutional Order (Princeton, Princeton University Press).

Vereshtin, VS (1996). 'New Constitutions and the Old Problem of the Relationship Between International Law and National Law', European Journal of International Law 7: 29–41.

von Bogdandy, A & Schill, S (2011). 'Overcoming Absolute Primacy: Respect for National Identity under the Lisbon Treaty', Common Market Law Review 48: 1417–1453.

Wendel, M (2011). Permeabilität im europäischen Verfassungsrecht (Tübingen, Mohr Siebeck).

Additional reading

Albi, A (2005). EU Enlargement and the Constitutions of Central and Eastern Europe (Cambridge, Cambridge University Press).

Belaid, S (1998). 'Droit international et droit constitutionnel: Les développements récents' in Achour, RB & Laghmani, S (eds), Droit international et droits internes: Développements récents (Paris, Editions A Pedone), 47–79.

Bryde, B-O (2003). 'Konstitutionalisierung des Völkerrechts und Internationalisierung des Verfassungsrechts', Der Staat 42: 61–75.

Franck, TM & Thiruvengadam, AK (2003). 'International Law and Constitution-Making', Chinese Journal of International Law 2: 467–518.

Jyränki, A (ed) (1999). National Constitutions in the Era of Integration (The Hague, Kluwer).

Klabbers, J, Peters, A & Ulfstein, G (2009). The Constitutionalization of International Law (Oxford, Oxford University Press).

Levade, A & Betrand M (2006). 'L'internationalisation du droit constitutionnel, acteurs, domaines, techniques', Revue Européenne de Droit Public 18: 161–216.

Nollkaemper, A (2011). National Courts and the International Rule of Law (Oxford, Oxford University Press).

Sanzhuam, G (2009). 'Implementation of Human Rights Treaties by Chinese Courts: Problems and Prospects', Chinese Journal of International Law 8: 161–179.

Xue, H & Jin, Q (2009). 'International Treaties in the Chinese Domestic Legal System', Chinese Journal of International Law 8: 299–322.

4

Constitutions and legitimacy over time

Catherine Dupré and Jiunn-rong Yeh

4.1 Introduction

While the spatial dimensions of constitutionalism are well-known, the study of its relationships with time is only beginning to emerge as a distinct area of investigation. Constitutions construct time in ways that raise many questions yet to be explored: issues of the constitutional culture and time (Häberle), the construction of time by constitutions (Kirste), their duration and endurance over time (Elkins, Ginsburg & Melton), and the question of the definition of power and time by constitutions (Cuocolo). Of these questions, a key issue is the democratic legitimacy of constitutions: as each society constructs its own time and temporality (Nowotny), so do constitutions. Following its authors' respective areas of expertise, this chapter focuses on European and Asian types of constitutionalism. The points made here may not have the same significance for other types of constitutionalism, but perhaps they will provide food for thought and encourage further exploration of time issues and constitutional legitimacy elsewhere in the world.

The first section argues that time has been a built-in component of constitutional legitimacy since the development of modern constitutionalism in the eighteenth century. The middle section discusses how rights and (Asian) values have played a central role in sustaining constitutional legitimacy over time. The final section considers how different constitutional temporalities affect legitimacy.

4.2 Time: built-in component of constitutional legitimacy

Time and constitutions are so tightly interwoven that it is sometimes hard to disentangle them. Arguably, the adoption of codified constitutions in Europe signalled the emergence of specific constitutional (i.e. man-made) time in contrast with the God-given eternity of the Ancien Régime. The 1791 French Constitution offers a clear example of this shift in temporality.[1] Constructing time through constitutions was arguably an essential component of democratic legitimacy from the start.

---

1 The approach to time in the very first codified constitution, namely that of the US adopted in 1776, differs from the European approach, see Tushnet; Rubenfeld.

4.2.1 Inventing constitutionalism: constructing human time

The French revolutionary project of constitution-making was driven by the effort to claim the exercise and control of political power, by moving its origin away from God and placing it squarely within the people and the newly invented citizens (Gauchet). This move away from divine origin of power arguably went together with a shift from divine temporality to a human temporality. As opposed to the apparent eternity of the sovereign power mirroring that of God ('the King is dead, long live the King'), by becoming constitutional, time became finite.

Therefore, a key question of early constitutionalism became to set a timescale for political power through appropriate constitutional design, a long process of trials and errors that spanned almost two centuries. Setting the duration of each power was essential as no branch could any longer be conceived as eternal; the rules for their renewal were enshrined in the constitution as a form of democratic control through the *pouvoir constituant*. Arguably as essential was the fact that each branch of power acquired a different temporality, which strengthened the separation of power by making simultaneous renewal of all branches of power almost impossible. The dyschrony resulting from these deliberately different temporalities has created a complex pattern, with each institution operating on a different time zone (Kirste, 66–68). This is an essential feature of legitimacy as it is meant to ensure a better quality of mutual checks on power. Moreover, the interplay of these disjointed temporalities arguably creates a space of constitutional freedom that is not dominated by the temporality of a single institution (with a single constitutional and political agenda) (Kirste, 67). Being the time of no one in particular, these spaces become the time of all; issues arising therein are arguably addressed with the interests of all in mind, a crucial factor in ensuring democratic legitimacy.

Finally, constitutions are designed to outlast the singular temporalities of each branch. While not being set by the constitution-makers, the time of the overall constitution is itself conceived as being finite and the ultimate legitimacy of democratic constitutions may derive from the fact that constitutions contain the rules for their partial revision and amendment, as well as for their complete replacement. In the absence of a set date or term for the renewal of the constitution, the emphasis is put on enshrining procedural, and sometimes substantive, rules for total revision. These rules vary, but their aim is to ensure that the timing of the renewal is right and that the adoption of the new constitution will unfold on, and represent a temporality of, the people and not of the political party in power.

4.2.2 Self-aware location in time: construction of a memory and response to the past

The temporality created by (European) constitutions is not neutral and proceeds from the drafters' self-awareness of their particular location on the time line. The adoption of the constitution itself is what makes the difference between the time before (e.g. the Ancien Régime, or a dictatorial regime) and the time after, as constructed by the new constitution. The timing of this moment is either decided by the rules of the constitution (where a complete revision has occurred) or, more often than not, by historical factors so momentous that they cannot be claimed by a single party or person (e.g. defeat or victory in war, end of dictatorship, total financial and economic collapse).[2] Constitution-drafters may be aware of their

---

2 See below on constitutional moment.

particular position in time and include in the constitutional text, mainly but not exclusively in the preamble (Frosini, 91), explicit indications of their image of the past. As a result, constitutional rhetoric is not impartial: it generally emphasizes the negative quality of the past from which the constitution endeavours to break away and its positive elements (the slightly glorified traditions and heritage with which the *pouvoir constituant* wants to be identified) are meant to provide solid foundations (Orgad). This construction of the past is inevitably selective and aimed to position the constitution in relation to a particular historical event or period in a way that will give it the strongest legitimacy possible. However, as both constitutional and cultural times are tightly interwoven, constitution-drafters cannot construct the past in a way that is completely out of line with what people perceive it to be and detached from its wider historical and cultural realities (Häberle, 648). Failing to acknowledge this and attempting to construct a past that is too overtly and bluntly selective (e.g. negating crucial periods or years of the country's history) might alienate both the people in the name of whom the constitution is formally adopted and other states that have some history in common and may not recognize their shared past in the constitutional reconstruction of it.

Finally, in preserving the past, codified constitutions perform a deliberate memory function that anchors them in history and legitimizes their overall agenda as a response to the immediate past. The 1789 Declaration of the Rights of Man and the Citizen included at the start of the first French Constitution of 1791 is paradigmatic in this respect:[3] '[the] National Assembly, considering ignorance, forgetfulness or contempt of the rights of man to be the only causes of public misfortunes and the corruption of Governments, have resolved to set forth, in a solemn Declaration, the natural, inalienable and sacred rights of man, to the end that this Declaration, constantly present to all members of the body politic, may remind them unceasingly of their rights and their duties'. These opening lines, or similar ones in other constitutional preambles, arguably shape the constitution's legitimacy over time by giving it the explicit purpose to avoid repetition of 'ignorance, forgetfulness or contempt of rights'. By responding to the past in this way, the constitution aims to guarantee a certain quality of the present and projects it into the future.

4.2.3 Making space for the future: aspirations, protection of mankind and 'future generations'

The last factor considered here is the explicit space made within and by constitutions for the possibility of a future. The importance of this built-in constitutional future for legitimacy can be understood by contrasting it with the seemingly eternal present under the God-given temporality of (absolute) monarchies or the single deterministic future under constitutions of (communist) dictatorships. In the constitutional text, the future is presented as being open while being identified through a range of aspirations (i.e. broad and inclusive constitutional objectives such as peace, justice or equality), the understanding and interpretation of which can and will vary over time. Their never-ending quest ensures that there is always a constitutional future in the sense that the quality of these objectives can always reach higher levels and constitutions therefore never lose their purpose. Moreover, essential to democratic legitimacy is a constitution's ability to allow for the unexpected and make space for discontinuities and unpredictability (Ost, 27, 30; Lefort). This approach to the future is the opposite of a deterministic construction of it that closes down the possibilities of

---

3 See generally Keiser; Christodoulidis & Veitch. On transitional constitutionalism, see below.

developments and changes in the name of a higher agenda (e.g. ideology). This openness to change makes it possible to respond effectively to crises and guarantees the continuity of constitutions.

While the future is not defined by constitutions, the concern that humanity should have a future has begun to appear in constitutional texts. This has been expressed in at least two ways: the protection of genetic identity of human beings enshrined as a distinct human right, and, more generally, references to the protection of future generations.[4] This novel face of the future as designed by constitutions has emerged as a response to environmental and bioethics concerns in the 1990s, with the summit of Rio in 1992 (Brown Weiss) and the adoption by the Council of Europe of the Oviedo Convention in 1997 based on the 'conviction of the need to respect the human being both as an individual and as a member of the human species and recognising the importance of ensuring the dignity of the human being'.[5] (See Chapter 31.) The exact constitutional shape that these new concerns will take is not completely clear because of their novelty and the fact that they do not easily fit with the more familiar and better established categories of constitutional law and theory. What seems to appear clearly, at least in the European context, is that a constitution that did not provide for some protection and at least acknowledgment of mankind's future would miss out on a key dimension, and its legitimacy might be questioned accordingly.

4.3 Sustaining constitutional legitimacy over time: protecting rights and core values

Effective and ongoing control over government and law-making procedures, and regular and smooth renewal of the judiciary and parliament, are all essential factors that sustain constitutional legitimacy over time. This section focuses on the key role played by the protection of human rights in the European context and the construction and promotion of constitutional values in the Asian context.

4.3.1 A rejected past and a dynamics of interpretation

In Europe, the devastating impact of the Nazi regime and World War II followed by a number of lasting and harsh dictatorships have led to a constitutional emphasis on human rights protection as a key component of constitutional legitimacy. This in turn has led to a 'never again' type of constitutionalism, of which the German Basic Law adopted in 1949 is the paradigmatic example (Mahlmann) and which has unfolded in three directions since then.

(1) European constitutionalism guarantees a core of absolute and unconditional rights, enshrined in the European Convention on Human Rights (ECHR) adopted in 1950 and ratification of which has become a pre-condition for EU membership. Member States cannot derogate from these rights (art. 15 ECHR). Moreover, articles 3 and 4 tolerate no exceptions and, while art. 2.2 necessarily provides for some strictly defined exceptions

---

4 Häberle, 630, highlighted the need to protect future generations against financial debts contracted by the past or current generations, a topical concern at the time of writing.

5 Convention for the Protection of Human Rights and Dignity of the Human Being with regard to the Application of Biology and Medicine, adopted at Oviedo, 4 April 1997, preamble.

(self-defence, lawful arrest or prevention of escape of a person lawfully detained, and for the purpose of quelling a riot or an insurrection), the death penalty has been abolished in all EU Member States. The EU Charter (in force since December 2009 as part of the Lisbon Treaty) confirmed and developed this approach and commits the EU and its Member States to the protection of the same rights, to which the Charter added the 'right to physical and mental integrity' (art. 3) and the prohibition of human trafficking (art. 5). Implementation of these rights is worked in European constitutionalism through two types of mechanisms: the possibility of an alleged victim to sue a Member State before the European Court of Human Rights for a breach of ECHR rights and the possibility of imposing sanctions (including the suspension of voting rights for the culprit states) on states that would breach human rights in 'a serious and persistent way' (art. 7 of the 2009 Lisbon Treaty).

(2) This imbrication of normative layers of human rights guarantees and remedies is the second feature of sustained constitutional legitimacy in Europe. Since 2009, the EU Charter has made respect of human rights a requirement for 'the institutions, bodies, offices and agencies of the EU with due regard to the principle of subsidiarity and to the Member States only when they are implementing Union law' (under art. 51 EU Charter). By filling the gap created in previous treaties (Alston), the EU Charter renders official and visible the complex human rights body developed so far largely by the European Court of Justice and establishes a clear normative link between the ECHR, the EU systems of human rights protection and the 'constitutional traditions common to the member states' (art. 6.3 Lisbon Treaty) (Peers & Ward).

(3) The third feature is the dynamic interpretation of these rights. The European Court of Human Rights (ECtHR) has constructed the ECHR as a 'living instrument, which [. . .] must be interpreted in the light of present-day conditions'.[6] In other words the decisive factor is not the intention of the drafters, but the aim of the ECHR understood as striving to establish an always higher degree of human rights protection (Letsas, ch 3). This logic has explicitly shaped the interpretation of the prohibition of torture, inhuman and degrading treatment or punishment under art. 3, in the sense that while the ECtHR requires a 'minimum threshold of severity' of the treatment inflicted for art. 3 to be engaged, it has made it very clear that 'certain acts which were classified in the past as "inhuman and degrading treatment" as opposed to "torture" could be classified differently in future'. The effect of this dynamic approach was particularly clear in the *Gäfgen v Germany* ruling where the Court held that a police officer's threat of torturing the kidnapper of a young child in order to ascertain where the child had been hidden amounted to a breach of art. 3.[7] Second, interpretation of human rights in Europe has been driven by a sort of judicial dialogue (Glendon; Lenearts; Wildhaber), in which (constitutional) courts have engaged and which has encouraged the European Court of Justice to protect human rights,[8] sped up the development of domestic case law during democratic transitions (Dupré 2003), and interwoven the various layers of human rights protection to create very tight (if not perfect) judicial protection of rights.

---

6 ECtHR *Tyrer v UK*, 25 April 1978 at para 31.
7 ECtHR *Gäfgen v Germany*, Appl. no 22978/05, 30 June 2008, Grand Chamber.
8 German Federal Constitutional Court 'solange I' ruling, *Internationale Handelsgesellschaft GmbH v Einfuhr-und Vorratstelle für Getreide und Futtermittel*, [1974] 2 *Common Market Law Reports* 540 and 'solange II' ruling *Wünsche Handelsgesellschaft* [1987] 3 *Common Market Law Reports* 225.

The emphasis on a high level of human rights protection rests on the belief that human rights are essential in preventing the return of a darker past that still haunts most European constitutions (Joerges & Singh Ghaleigh). However, this effort to sustain constitutional legitimacy through human rights is vulnerable to at least three sorts of attack. Some states resent the increasingly tight supranational control imposed on them and claim that this impinges on their national sovereignty presented as the main (if not the only) factor of constitutional legitimacy (Dzehtsiarou & Green). Second, what makes this human rights dynamics strong may well weaken it as well: it is effective as long as most (if not all) states work towards an enhanced level of human rights protection. However, were some states to choose not to do so, there is no built-in mechanism in the judicial dialogue described above and, in particular, in the use of foreign and comparative law by courts to prevent them from doing so. Therefore, if things were to go wrong within the EU, art. 7 Lisbon Treaty would only represent a weak barrier against human rights abuse (Pernice). Ultimately, this way of sustaining constitutional legitimacy relies on judicial reasoning being of high quality. In the context of ever-growing supranational courts (the ECtHR has 47 judges) and a method of interpretation by reference to comparative and foreign law that is still in the infant stages (Dupré 2009), this is its Achilles heel.

4.3.2 Asian Values: construction and dynamics

Human rights became a key component of constitutional legitimacy in response to the rejected past in Europe. By enshrining human rights as an absolute and unconditioned core value, (European) constitutionalism represents determination of 'never again' against the 'rejected past'. This level of universality and eternity, however, has not been so sure in Asian context and temporality.

Some Asian political leaders have argued for Asian values against the universal claim of democratic values, human rights and constitutionalism. They hold the view that Asia has different historical roots, social values and ongoing progress of development, and for that reason, Asians are entitled to develop their own constitutional agenda and system.[9]

Although usually characterized as a discourse of geographical difference, Asian values bear strong implications for time and constitutionalism. First, the past is important for Asian Values, not for the guarantee of universal human rights but for the shaping of Asian uniqueness in the path and speed of developing constitutionalism. Proponents of Asian Values did not totally reject democratic values and human rights; instead they argued for a stage-by-stage temporal agenda in their recognition and implementation. They considered the state-led economic developmental model, placing development ahead of democracy and human rights, as the basic engine for the remarkable economic growth in East Asia (Yeh 2008, 35). Second, having a strong state with limited human rights was necessary for economic development. Asia will follow the West in the recognition of universal values once economic development has been achieved. In this discourse, (Western) constitutionalism was reconstructed in a different temporal order: rights come after duties; social welfare and political liberty come after economic growth. Incremental realization becomes the essence of the Asian path to constitutionalism.

The real experience of Asian constitutionalism, however, has not squarely fit in the reconstructed sequential order in the discourse of Asian values. First and foremost, there has never

---

9 For a more detailed discussion of the Asian Values debate, see e.g. Engle.

been any ideological struggle for the prioritization between civil/political rights and social/economic rights (Yeh & Chang, 832–33, 837–38). In contrast with what was emphasized in Asian values, courts in Asia have affirmed constitutional rights in response to social and political progress. In Japan, South Korea and Taiwan—three vibrant constitutional jurisdictions—for example, political rights, social security and labour rights were recognized almost simultaneously, and courts have shown no preferred agenda on the realization of rights and freedoms other than responding to social and political demands (Yeh & Chang, 832–33).

In addition, the claim that Asians weigh duty or collective interests more than individual rights is not always true. As rapid industrialization and economic growth greatly challenged the traditional family structure, Asian courts have been trying to reconcile these rapidly shifting social relationships and norms with the emerging concept of individual rights (Yeh & Chang, 833). The judicial handling of gender equality issues presented a liberal attitude towards growing women's movements. These decisions never emphasized a citizen's duty, but rather found it to be the state's duty to protect citizens' fundamental rights—a duty well recognized in international human rights law.

Asian values discourse underestimates the differences among Asian countries, and fails to appreciate the roles of both human agency and institutions in the transformative process of cultural discourse (Davis, 110). Rather than being deep-rooted cultural heritage or consensus of the society, Asian Values discourse has been criticized for compelling the acceptance of a single and state-defined ideology (Robison, 311).

In the light of a dynamic Asia, both universalism and particularism should understand their position in a humble way. Between the two claims exists a giant middle, a negotiated zone of constitutional rights and principles in relative terms. This is a dialectic space for further dialogue and construction. Exactly because of this dialectic nature, constitutional temporality is required for better deliberation in the recognition and implementation of rights and principles.

4.4 Multiple constitutional temporalities and specific issues of legitimacy

At the institutional and operational levels, constitutionalism bears even stronger temporal connotations. In comparison to rights, constitutional institutions and the exercise of powers are more subject to change against the backdrop of social and political transformation. Two issues of temporal significance are examined here. They are the theory of constitutional moment and transitional justice. A third issue also linking constitutions and time is emergency constitutionalism (see Chapter 7).

4.4.1 The constitutional moment

In the conventional story, sovereignty, people and constitution-making are three elements mutually constituted at a single moment. At that moment, multitudes of different ethnicities, religions, origins and cultures transform into a unified 'People' (Rosenfeld 1993, 500). The People express the general will and legitimize the sovereignty of the state and the constitution (*see* generally Rousseau).

Moreover, constitution-making is depicted as a founding moment. Following a revolution, the newly written constitution can dynamically institutionalize the resulting power allocation by directly establishing a new order. Yet, at this moment, long-existing values may still be entrenched in the constitution and formulated as the guiding framework for future generations. For some scholars like Bruce Ackerman, during the constitutional moment the general public is to be deeply engaged in deliberation with public virtues, and the People in the aggregate take a relatively impartial view in forming the constitutional order (*see* generally Ackerman 1993). The constitutional moment gives the constitution a normative priority over later actions. The decisions made in the constitutional moment can thus legitimately constrain the choice made by the people of today.

Although traditional constitutionalism presumes a once-and-for-all and stable framework, social changes and dynamics have generated variants of constitutionalism, mainly transitional constitutionalism and emergency constitutionalism that involve temporal aspects and raise special issues of legitimacy.

4.4.2 Transitional constitutionalism

Traditional constitutionalism focuses on the moment at which a constitution is made and expects the constitution made at this very moment to be entrenched into the future. In this sense, constitutionalism defines fundamental rules of government established on the basis of enduring values. In a time of transition, the constitution also responds to the past and the future. However, the time-sensitivity differs in many ways.[10]

The most salient issue of transitional constitutionalism is transitional justice. In many cases, serious oppression created social cleavage or exaggerated social distrust. As the European experience shows, the old constitution usually constructs the collective memory. How the constitution deals with past wrongs, deconstructs the past and facilitates future integration has troubled many new democracies.[11] To address transitional justice, one must strike a balance between the past and the future. Substantive justice with reference to prior wrongs has to be achieved, while stability and the predictability of the legal order have to be embraced. Compromise has to be made against the flux of social transformation. The ways past wrong-doings are redressed are not always consistent with purely normative standards but mixed with practical concerns. Many societies have undertaken transitional justice issues with punishments offset by pardons, and investigations undertaken by truth and reconciliation commissions.

During democratic transitions, the functions of the constitution shift from constraining government powers and inspiring the future to steering reform agendas and social integration (Yeh & Chang 2009, 162–65). Further, transitional democracies usually emerge from a period of illegitimate government and fragmented constitutional identity, unlike the conventional story where the legitimacy of a regime, identity and the constitution were mutually constructed at the founding moment and sustained continually. When the legitimacy of the previous regime disappeared and the new regime was not yet consolidated, how to make or amend the constitution to consolidate legitimacy and identity stays at the top of the political agenda.[12]

---

10 On the features and diverse perspectives of transitional constitutionalism, see e.g. Yeh & Chang 2009, 148–61.

11 See generally Hesse & Post (discussing experiences of various countries in their redressing past human rights abuses); Teitel 2000 (discussing a great deal of institutional difficulties in dealing with transitional justice).

12 See Arato (arguing various models of constitutional-making facilitate to various extents the construction of a new political community); Rosenfeld 1998 (arguing that negotiated changes by which groups of various identities are embraced facilitate successful construction of a new collective political identity).

Various processes of rebuilding constitutional legitimacy present another temporal dimension of transitional constitutionalism. Some transitional democracies made new constitutions after democratic transitions had taken place.[13] Facing the legitimacy crisis during transition, these countries preferred a brand-new constitution to represent a break with the past regime and to construct needed legitimacy for the new one. Many democracies, on the other hand, chose to deal with the legitimacy deficit in a slower and more gradual way. Patterns and processes vary. Some preferred to revise the constitution incrementally, some chose to enact an interim constitution, and still others made political statements consented to by all political parties (Yeh & Chang 2009, 150–53). Despite a conventional understanding that a constitution must be created at one moment and last forever, these temporary and incremental constitutional arrangements proved to be quite helpful when final, settled constitutional solutions had not yet emerged or been agreed upon. In this sense, constitutionalism performs functions beyond restraining government power and extends to facilitating, integrating and empowering democratic values with varying degrees of time-sensitivity.

The incremental scenario of constitutional change also generates the time-sensitive issue of the reform agenda (Teitel 1997, 2057–58). When Polish constitutional reform put property rights, freedom of contract and the effective rule of law at the top of the reform list, aiming at building a workable free market, different priorities such as separation of powers and fair elections were emphasized in South Korea and Taiwan. Decision-makers in transitional democracies took cautions in prioritizing reform agenda, showing a time-sensitive constitutional agenda.

In transitional constitutionalism, courts are also expected to be more time-sensitive (Yeh & Chang 2009, 162–65). For instance, faced with an unconstitutional statute enacted in the previous regime, many constitutional courts of transitional democracies were troubled by a similar dilemma—whether to declare it unconstitutional and annul it right away or leave it to political process for resolution. A possible third way is a prospective ruling, finding the statute unconstitutional while imposing a deadline for political compliance. By doing so, the already declared unconstitutional legislation remained effective for a certain period of time in order to allow an extended space of political resolution. But, how much time is required? In Taiwan, one of the most significant decisions rendered by the Constitutional Court was the Interpretation No. 261, in that the Court ordered old members of the parliament to leave office in one-and-a-half years when a new national election should be held. Some reacted to this length of time as being too long, while others criticized it as too short. Long or short, courts must balance the time-sensitivity against profound transitionality and their judicial wisdom is put to serious test.

4.5 Conclusion

Legitimacy has been the central issue since the creation of modern constitutionalism. There have been many scholarly attempts to establish and sustain constitutional legitimacy, but little attention has been paid to the temporal dimension. Scholars thereby ignore the interwoven relation between time and constitutionalism.

---

13 Romania, the Czech Republic, the Baltic States, Mongolia and the Philippines were some of the examples. See e.g. Linz & Stepan, 293–434 (discussing constitution-making politics in Bulgaria, Romania, the former USSR states and the Baltic states).

As we have shown, time has been one essential part of constitutional legitimacy. Establishing and sustaining legitimacy involves temporality, but other temporal dimensions of constitutionalism also challenge the traditional understanding of constitutional legitimacy.

The creation of constitutionalism establishes the very basis of legitimacy. As a response to the past and an aspiration to the future, the establishment of legitimacy has to be worked through a time line. Constitutional legitimacy needs to be sustained over time as well. The question is, how? European constitutionalists entrench rights protection based on past experience and interpret the constitution dynamically. When Europeans hold the view that human rights are universal, they encounter a challenge from proponents of Asian Values. The debate over Asian Values does not subject constitutional legitimacy to cultural or geographical difference, but rather discloses a dynamic Asia in which cultural differences, historical legacies and the mobility of civil society all participate in the construction of rights and its content, categories and phases of protection, which call for more time and space for deliberation.

Revealing the temporal dimension of constitutionalism empowers us to see the complexity and possibility of constitutional legitimacy. Constructing and sustaining constitutional legitimacy are not efforts of a single time, in any fixed and absolute way. The construction and deconstruction of legitimacy are always occurring as constitutionalism persists. The source, speed and pattern are always in flux, and we need to devote some attention to the relation between the constitution and time.

Catherine Dupré was the primary author of Sections 4.1–4.3.1, Jiunn-rong Yeh was the primary author of Sections 4.3.2 through to 4.5.

References

Ackerman, B (1993). *We The People, Volume 1: Foundations.* Cambridge: Harvard University Press.

Alston, P (ed) (1999). *The EU and Human Rights.* Oxford: Oxford University Press.

Arato, A (1994). Dilemmas Arising from the Power to Create Constitutions in Eastern Europe, in Rosenfeld M (ed), *Constitutionalism, Identity, Difference, And Legitimacy: Theoretical Perspective*, 413–22.

Brown Weiss, E (1990). Our Rights and Obligations to Future Generations for the Environment, *American Journal of International Law*, 84, 198–207.

Christodoulidis, E & Veitch, S (eds), (2011). *Lethe's Law. Justice, Law and Ethics in Reconciliation.* Oxford: Oxford University Press.

Cuocolo, L (2009). *Tempo e Potere nel diritto costituzionale.* Milano: Giuffré.

Davis, M (1998). Constitutionalism and Political Culture: The debate over Human Rights and Asian Values, *Harvard Human Rights Journal*, 11, 109–147.

Dupré, C (2003). *Importing the Law in Post-Communist Transitions, The Hungarian Constitutional Court and the Right to Human Dignity.* Oxford: Hart Publishing.

— (2009). 'Globalisation and Judicial Reasoning: Building Blocks for a Method of Intepretation' in Halpin, A & Roeben, V (eds) *Theorising the Global Legal Order*, 190–206. Oxford: Hart Publishing.

Dzehtsiarou, K & Green, A (2011). Legitimacy and the Future of the European Court of Human Rights: Critical Perspectives from Academia and Practitioners, *German Law Journal*, 12, 1707–15.

Elkins, Z, Ginsburg, T & Melton, J (2009). *The Endurance of National Constitutions.* Cambridge: Cambridge University Press.

Frosini JO (2011). Changing Notions of Democracy: A Comparative Analysis of Constitutional Preambles, in Filibi, I, Cornago, N & Frosini, JO (eds) *Democracy with(out) nation? Old and New Foundations for Political Communities in a Changing World*, 83–109. Bilbao: University of the Basque Country Press.

Gauchet, M (1989). *La révolution des droits de l'homme.* Paris: Gallimard.

Glendon, MA (1991). *Rights Talk: The Impoverishment of Political Discourse.* New York and Toronto: Free Press.

Häberle, P (1992). Zeit und Verfassungskultur, in P Häberle (ed) *Rechtsvergleichung im Kraftfeld des Verfassungsstaates*, 627–72. Berlin: Duncker und Humblot.

Hesse, C & Post, R (eds) (1999). *Human Rights in Political Transitions: Gettysburg To Bosnia*. New York: Zone Books.

Joerges, C & Singh Ghaleigh, N (eds) (2003). *The Darker Legacies of Law in Europe*. Oxford: Hart Publishing.

Keiser, T (2005). 'Europeanization as a Challenge to Legal History' 6, *German Law Journal* 473–81.

Kirste, S (2008). Die Zeit der Verfassung, Jahrbuch des öffentlichen Rechts der Gegenwart, 56, 35–74.

Lefort, C (1986). *Essai sur le politique*, Paris: Payot.

Letsas, G (2009). *A Theory of Interpretation of the European Convention on Human Rights*. Oxford: Oxford University Press.

Lenearts, K (2003). Interlocking Legal Orders in EU and Comparative Law, *International and Human Rights Law Quarterly*, 52, 873.

Linz, J & Stepan, A (1996). *Problems of Democratic Transition And Consolidation: Southern Europe, South America, And Post-Communist Europe*. Baltimore, MD: The Johns Hopkins University Press.

Mahlmann, M (2010). The Basic Law at 60 – Human Dignity and the Culture of Republicanism, *German Law Journal*, 11, 9–31.

Nowotny, H (1996). *Time. The Modern and Post-modern Experience*, Cambridge: Polity Press.

Orgad, L (2010). The Preamble in Constitutional Interpretation, *International Journal of Constitutional Law*, 8, 714–38.

Ost, F (1999). *Le Temps du Droit*. Paris: Odile Jacob.

Peers, S & Ward, A (eds) (2004). *The EU Charter of Fundamental Rights: Context and Possibilities*. Oxford: Hart Publishing.

Pernice, I (2008). 'The Treaty of Lisbon and Fundamental Rights', in Griller, S & Ziller, J (eds), *The Lisbon Treaty, EU Constitutionalism without a Constitutional Treaty?* 235. New York: Springer.

Rousseau, JJ (1762). *The Social Contract Or Principles of Political Right* (Cole GDH trans).

Robison, R (1996). The politics of 'Asian Values', *Pacific Review*, 9 (3), 309–27.

Rosenfeld, M (1993). Modern Constitutionalism as Interplay between Identity and Diversity: An Introduction, *Cardozo Law Review*, 14, 497–531.

—— (1998). Constitution-Making, Identity Building, and Peaceful Transition to Democracy: Theoretical Reflections Inspired by the Spanish Example, *Cardozo Law Review*, 19, 1891–1920.

Rubenfeld, J (2001). *Freedom and Time: A Theory of Constitutional Self-Government*. New Haven: Yale University Press.

Teitel, R (1997). Transitional Jurisprudence: The Role of Law in Political Transformation, *Yale Law Journal*, 2009–82.

—— (2000). *Transitional Justice*. New York: Oxford University Press.

Tushnet, M (2009). *The Constitution of the United States of America. A Contextual Analysis*. Oxford: Hart Publishing.

Wildhaber, L (2005). The Role of Comparative Law in the Case-Law of the European Court of Human Rights, in Broehmer, J *et al.* (eds), *Internationale Gemeinschaft und Menschenrechte, Festschrift f Georg Ress*, 1101–07. München: Carl Heymanns Verlag.

Yeh, J-R (2008). Democracy-driven Transformation to Regulatory State: The Case of Taiwan, *National Taiwan University Law Review*, 3(2), 31–59.

—— & Chang, WC (2009). The Changing Landscape of Modern Constitutionalism: Transitional Perspective, *National Taiwan University Law Review*, 4(1), 145–83.

—— & Chang, WC (2011). The Emergence of East Asian Constitutionalism: Features in Comparison, *American Journal of Comparative Law*, 59, 805–40.

Additional reading

Barshack, L (2009). 'Time and the Constitution' *International Journal of Constitutional Law*, 7, 553–76.

Häberle, P (1992). Zeit und Verfassungskultur, in Häberle, P (ed) *Rechtsvergleichung im Kraftfeld des Verfassungsstaates*, 627–72. Berlin: Duncker und Humblot.

Hutchings, K (2008). Time and World Politics, Thinking the Present. Manchester: Manchester University Press.

Kirste, SJ (2008). 'Die Zeit der Verfassung', Jahrbuch des öffentlichen Rechts der Gegenwart, 56, 35–74.

Kirste, S (2002). The Temporality of Law and the Plurality of Social Times – the Problem of Synchronising Different Time Concepts through Law, in Troper, M and Verza, A (eds), *Legal Philosophy: General Aspects, Concepts, Rights and Doctrines*, 82, 23–45. *Archiv der Rechts-und Sozialphilosophie* (Beiheft).

Ost, F & Van Hoecke, M (eds) (1998). *Time and Law. Is it the Nature of Law to Last?* Bruxelles: Bruylant.

Yeh, J-R (2003). Constitutional Reform and Democratization in Taiwan: 1945–2000, in Chow, P (ed), *Taiwan's Modernization In Global Perspective*, 47–77.

5

Constitution-writing processes

Jennifer Widner and Xenophon Contiades

During the past three decades, new constitutions have appeared in many parts of the world, often in the aftermath of civil wars, but also in response to demands for more democratic political systems or for resolution of institutional crises. Constitutional theory intersects political practice when these new constitutions are made. Notions of constituent power and amending power have evolved and the range of procedural choices has expanded. An important question is whether the approaches chosen to prepare and ratify new constitutions shape content and other outcomes such as levels of trust or the degree to which constitutional principles take root in public consciousness. In particular, are some kinds of drafting processes more likely than others to produce terms that limit executive abuse of power and promote inclusive governments and societies? In theory, rules that allow broad participation, encourage attention to long-term general interests, limit opportunities for grandstanding, and provide for careful drafting are more likely than others to produce these kinds of results.

Although the complex interactions among rules, leadership aptitudes, and underlying conditions make it impossible to determine an optimal strategy, it is possible to point to some of the advantages and disadvantages of the main procedural choices. Constitutional change occurs in many ways, both formal and informal (Contiades & Fotiadou). Focusing on constitution-making, this Chapter deals almost exclusively with formal methods of constitution-making and revision.

5.1 Defining the constitution-making power

Constitution-making encompasses a variety of constitutional design processes rooted in exercise of either the constituent or the amending power. The constituent power (*pouvoir constituant*), conceptualized as the source of the constitution exercised at an original founding moment, has its roots in the eighteenth and nineteenth centuries (Sieyès). A pre-constitutional political authority crafts a new order, then dissolves itself or self-destructs (Carré de Malberg). Understood as an unlimited sovereign power underlying the enactment of constitutions, this idea is the basis for belief in the constitution's supremacy over ordinary law. Exactly what is required in terms of process and how participation should be organized is likely to vary between states, however, depending on the issues at stake and the interests of the protagonists.

Modern constitution-making, taking place mostly in the context of democratic transitions, is no longer conceived as the exercise of limitless power. Norms of international law, principles of constitutionalism, and understandings of the notion of the constitution have evolved since the first era of constitution-making. Today, the prevailing view is that the very nature of the constituent power creates procedural standards or principles that govern constitution-making (Häberle). Sincere deliberation cannot occur without respect for these limits. In the early understandings of the constituent power, that power was simply a brute fact of political life. The constituent power was unrestrained, creating a constitutional order and then disappearing (Carré de Malberg). Today, the prevailing view is that there are implicit substantive limits built into the concept of constituent power, which derive from the fact that the constituent power's exercise is supposed to give the constitution it enacts normative force: Without substantive limits on the constituent power, the ensuing constitution cannot be normatively binding (Häberle). Questions raised by the older theory remain: Who identifies those who possess the constituent power, an issue of special concern when the very boundaries of the territory to be regulated by the constitution are contested, as in cases of purported secession; to what degree the constituent power is absorbed by the constituted powers and so can be exercised through discrete amendments rather than total constitutional revision; and, related, do the people retain an unlimited power to rearrange their constitution? Modern conditions may have reversed the traditional conceptualization of a limitless constituent power and a constrained amending power: Now the constituent power is subject to the substantive limitations alluded to above, while the amending power is said to authorize constitutional changes of any scope whatsoever in the name of the sovereign people.

Constitutions may also change through exercise of the amending power (part of the *pouvoir constitué*). The amending power is subject to constraints set forth in an existing constitution, which usually specifies procedures for making changes and often imposes substantive limits. The basic principles that limit the amending power are constitutional continuity, constitutional coherence, and the need for broad consensus, all of which must be balanced against each other. Over the past several decades, a substantial jurisprudence has developed around the world about the possibility of unconstitutional amendments, adopted through formally correct procedures but inconsistent with substantive limits on the amending power (Gözler).

Constitutional replacement, which lies closer to the exercise of constituent power rather than the amending power on the continuum of constitution-making, involves the possibility of renegotiating fundamental issues even if the act of replacement occurs within already formed constitutional cultures. Similarly, extensive revision may take place through the amending power, but because of the scope of the changes envisioned, theoretically such a revision requires respect for the same principles that shape the creation of new constitutions. The boundaries between replacement and large-scale revision within an otherwise persisting constitution are obscure, in part because political actors might try to present a replacement as a revision to signal continuity and preserve legitimacy. Allowing the reconsideration of principles and values through constitutional amendment might even go so far as to blur the distinction between the constituent and the amending power, for the constituent power might be allowed to resurface as a prerequisite for the democratic legitimation of the constitution (Colón-Ríos). Constitutional courts have struggled with the issues arising from this way of thinking about revision and replacement. The Colombian constitutional court, for example, held that allowing a president to seek a third term was a total revision requiring the convening of a constituent assembly to exercise the constituent power (Congressional Research Service).

Whether nations choose large-scale revision, complete replacement, or incremental change through formal and informal methods of constitutional alteration depends on factors such as the complexity and stringency of amending formulas, the capacity of the political system to foster consensus or compromise on constitutional issues, and the power of the judiciary to trigger constitutional moments.

The delimitation of the constitution-making power through the adoption of amending formulas designed to set out the rules for future constitution writing has generated combinations of procedural and material limits interwoven in different blends. Continuity is usually pursued through material limits such as the non-amendability of fundamental constitutional principles, the form of government, or specific rights and principles, while qualified majority rules, time constraints, and veto powers are techniques designed to block temporary majorities from changing the constitution at will, aiming also to ensure wider legitimation. The amending formula's success depends on various parameters that shape, in different legal orders, the role and status of the actors involved, and account for the specific features of the means used to induce constitutional change. Tradition and polity, state structure, ethnic, linguistic and religious composition, party system and patterns of democracy, polarization and consent, the system of judicial review, and constitutional ethos can all have major effects.

Earlier, constitutions sometimes gained legitimacy through forms of cultural mystification and, on some views, may continue to do so as well. Today, though, the authority of a constitution depends in large measure on how it can be made to matter through the successful regulation of politics (Tushnet). Through this prism, drafters must be more aware of the link between adaptability and durability, and of the need for conscious choices about the effect of substantive terms on democratic deliberation or constitutionalism (the appropriation of the principles into the everyday actions of citizens and their political representatives).

5.2 Outcomes & procedures

The success of constitutions relies largely on their compatibility with the legal and socio-political environment they aim to address, providing the polity's rule of recognition.

5.2.1 Outcomes

Recent research on state capacity and conflict has stressed the importance of inclusive institutions that also limit executive abuse of power (World Development Report; Besley & Persson; Acemoglu & Robinson). Research links these institutions not only to reduced levels of violence but also to higher levels of public goods provision, innovation, and investment.

Historically, constitutions have often developed as contracts or compacts designed to limit the sovereign's ability to expropriate or coerce others. Concern about executive abuse of power and misuse of security forces is a common theme in most constitutional conversations today. The legal and intellectual resources these new constitutions provide for policing the executive vary enormously and implicate many parts of the document. Legislative review of the budget, legislative oversight or ratification of appointees, the majorities required for overriding executive vetoes: these exemplify measures that are part of executive restraint. The scope of bills of rights clearly matters as well, along with rights enforcement provisions and limitations on suspension of bills of rights. Term limits are an easy-to-measure restriction, although political parties often find ways to coordinate candidates to circumvent them. Independent auditors general, courts, human rights boards, and anti-corruption commissions also target executive abuse of power. (See Chapter 6 in this volume.)

Inclusiveness also rests on a variety of provisions, but what to include in assessing this outcome is at least as difficult as evaluating executive restraint. Equality clauses that explicitly extend rights regardless of gender or cultural background may help generate inclusive institutions and policies, provided people are able to bring cases to independent courts to animate these provisions. The phrasing of language about the role of religion in the state also matters. Where state law must be consistent with the law of a religious group, inclusiveness is lower than in constitutions that may acknowledge religion but do not contain provisions to enforce religious law—or than in constitutions that require separation of religion and the state. In many contemporary constitutions, guarantees that women and minority groups will have seats in the legislature or be included on party lists also contribute to inclusiveness, as do voting rights for refugees and other citizens living abroad.

Other outcomes often appear as measures of success, too. Although rarely discussed, drafting quality—clarity, concision, coherence—matters greatly and is often directly related to the organization of a constitution-writing process. A constitution that has many terms designed to prevent executive abuse of power may fail in that objective if the language is ambiguous.

Further, constitution-drafting procedures may shape political behavior in ways that have little to do with the actual substantive terms accepted. The models they set may influence whether citizens channel conflict into non-violent forums, enter sustained dialogue, and adopt constitutional principles as part of the vocabulary of popular politics. Some constitutions remain pieces of paper that command little attention from political elites or ordinary citizens, while others have become focal points for political debate and the source of norms that shape everyday behavior. In theory, procedural choices affect reception of core principles as well as the actual terms selected.

By contrast, a constitution's durability—how long it remains in force—may not always deserve the attention it has received in lists of desirable results. It may be helpful and appropriate to build in some flexibility and encourage substantial revision in post-conflict settings where initial terms tend to over-represent the views of armed parties to peace agreements at the expense of the broader population. The prospect of revision may encourage a longer-term view and may make it possible to craft a satisfactory document in stages. The exploration of alternative routes that constitution-making may follow in post-conflict contexts, setting different priorities from the traditional model, has led to new conceptualizations of what constitution writing may involve based on comparative data (Jackson).

5.2.2 Links to procedural choice

Decision-making procedures can shape all of these outcomes. In theory, procedures are linked to outcomes like inclusiveness or executive restraint by a number of different causal pathways. Most of these linkages emphasize the effects of rules on delegate willingness to put aside short-term personal or partisan advantage and to consider the long-term welfare of the broader political community.

1) Where the body that deliberates and takes the key decisions is itself inclusive, it is arguably more likely that the final document will preserve minority rights more strongly, at least if the decision rules that govern deliberations require super-majorities. Constitution-building programs that exclude key players or social segments generally result in short-lived documents and rarely reduce violence, at least in theory.

2) The size of the assembly may affect ability to persuade or deliberate, ability to compromise, and drafting quality. Large groups are rarely able to function effectively as deliberative forums. Insufficient time for individual contributions, delays in translation, and other

problems make these forums less effective than smaller ones. Creation of technical committees to deliberate and draft can help counter these problems. Vesting the responsibility for the draft in a smaller body that takes general instruction from the larger group is another alternative. How well these measures compensate depends on details of structure and membership.

3) Publicity rules, or transparency, influence compromise and polarization. An example of this kind of claim is Jon Elster's proposition that highly public processes, in which negotiators deliberate in front of the media or audiences, promote grandstanding and are less friendly to compromise (Elster 2000). Many constitution-writing processes have committee deliberations closed to the media for this reason, allowing coverage of the occasional plenary session only, although the media have often reported extensively on the outcome of committee deliberations.

4) Veil rules increase each delegate's uncertainty about his future position or the future position of his constituents. They introduce prospectivity and generality into decision-making, increasing the likelihood that drafters will weigh a broad range of interests. Rules in this category block clear conflicts of interest, where a delegate's decisions affect his or her immediate economic or political status. Recusal requirements, delay between the ratification of a new constitution and first election, and bans on delegates running for election are all examples.

5) If delegates know that there is a downstream check on what they do, in the form of a court hearing, referendum, or vote by another assembly, they may take the assumed preferences of those who man the later checkpoint as a guide to how far they can push for terms they want (Elster 1995, 1998, 2000).

6) If citizens are engaged in the process through public consultation and civic education, they are more likely to have some passing familiarity with the principles introduced, which may then allow them to monitor the behavior of officials and object when a government agency transgresses. Where leaders are aware that citizens are better able to monitor boundary lines, they may refrain from actions that break the rules, anticipating that they will meet resistance. However, the form of involvement is likely to matter too. A broad, cursory canvas prior to constitutional deliberations may produce little extra knowledge, though it may focus public attention on the news the assembly puts out. Civic group engagement in public hearings may produce higher levels of knowledge, but mainly among elites whose connection to other citizens will vary, depending on the country. As part of its transition to majority rule, South Africa created a distinctive process that empowered a new constitutional court to hear challenges brought by citizens and civic groups who believed that the terms in the draft constitution matched a set of 34 principles set forth in an initial political agreement. This form of participation helped disseminate knowledge, as did the activities of the political parties and civic groups (Murray).

5.2.3 The risky business of generalization

Understandably, practitioners and many scholars want to know the 'optimal' or best way to design a constitution-writing process in a given context. However, the rules interact strongly with elements of context, including the distribution of preferences and styles among those who participate in the drafting process. Bold generalizations are difficult for this reason, and there will always remain much room for political savvy and local knowledge.

Constitution-writing processes are complex bundles of rules governing deliberation and interaction among many people and groups. They usually include multiple forums (for setting ground rules, articulating principles, developing preliminary drafts, deliberation, ratification). At each stage, decision rules, conflict of interest provisions, deadlines, deadlock procedures, committee structures, and transparency/publicity will shape the incentives delegates have to take the long view and to eschew short-term personal advantage in favor of broader considerations. Because of the many rules in effect simultaneously, the simple causal paths sketched earlier may blur.

Personal aptitudes of the people who lead constitution writing separately affect outcomes and tend to interact with procedure. Some leaders have the magnetism and interactive skill to convince others to look forward and consider the long term, while others cannot or choose not to. Some are innate deal-makers, while others are not. Some are more comfortable in small-group settings, while others rise to the challenge of herding crowds. A well-designed process may make outcomes less vulnerable to individual talents, but there can be little doubt that what leaders say and do exercises an independent effect.

Underlying conditions also shape the options available. Elections are expensive and difficult to run, and where there is a limited tradition, some other method of delegate selection may make more sense. In parts of Africa, the national conference, with representatives from a wide variety of corporate groups, gained some popularity in the 1990s as an alternative to elected constituent assemblies. However, the same conditions that shaped these decisions also influence the ability to manage these large assemblies effectively. National conferences impose stringent demands on management skills, speed of translation, and other support. Where management is weak or support slow, suspicions rise. Although there are some instances of success, this choice can aggravate conflict rather than foster compromise and a long view.

For all these reasons, it is difficult to draw reliable causal inferences about the effects of procedures, writ large, on constitution-writing outcomes. The best we can do is to evaluate the pros and cons of specific measures, as these are likely to play out in given circumstances.

5.3 Forums and procedures

When people talk about constitution-writing procedures, they usually focus on the main deliberative body, referred to here as a 'constitutional reform model.' Six main alternatives are in use today: commission or committee and the legislature; commission or committee and an elected Constituent Assembly; a National Conference and commission with a transitional legislature; roundtables, including many processes linked to peace settlements; executive-directed processes; and hybrid approaches, including those in which non-national actors are engaged. (See Chapter 36 in this volume.)

The character of the main deliberative body is only one part of the larger procedural landscape, however. Within each constitutional reform model, countries vary with respect to ground rules and rules of representation, and the structure of deliberative forums at each stage: decision rules, time limits, 'veil rules,' and steps for overcoming deadlock, opportunity for public involvement, and use of referenda and other devices as part of the ratification process.

5.3.1 Setting ground rules and frameworks

Where an existing constitution is not a source of guidance about how constitutional reform should unfold, the first task is to win agreement on a way to move forward. Usually these bargains re-legalize opposition, set forth a framework for subsequent negotiation, specify the rules that will govern elections for constituent assemblies or some other method for delegate selection, and identify the laws that will govern in the interim. Sometimes, as in South Africa, these agreements identify essential features or principles that the delegates who craft the final draft must respect.

The usual venue for these conversations is a roundtable that includes key actors, whether these are political parties, social leaders, or the heads of warring factions. Much has been written about roundtables in East European drafting processes, but roundtables were also important in South Africa, Benin, Spain, and, informally, in many or most other settings (Widner). In most post-conflict constitution building programs, roundtables have negotiated at least the interim framework, and some have played a central role in drafting. It may be critical to build consensus on many of the most difficult issues to avoid later disruption by potential spoilers, who might feel left out, as well as to lessen the risk that the electoral process will polarize factions on central issues.

In the wave of constitution writing in the 1990s, the Polish roundtable occurred earlier than other East European examples and offered a model. It developed a relationship between the Communist establishment and the opposition. The idea was not to replace the existing system, but rather to open participation to Solidarity. It took several months to organize, as each side grew to understand what was involved. Eventually it convened with government and Solidarity representatives, as well as Catholic Church observers, although it really only met twice. Between the opening and closing meetings, committees and sub-committees dealt with the real issues. When disputes arose, the sub-committees sent the problems to the committees, and the committees sent the problems they could not resolve for mediation at high levels, usually informally. The sides cut deals about which group would hold each of several key positions and how the reform process would unfold. The roundtable performed three tasks in Poland. It addressed what would happen to Solidarity by re-legalizing the union as an opposition party. It prepared an election in which Solidarity could contest seats and win representation. Finally, it offered some guarantees to the Communists. Afterwards the parliament pursued the actual job of writing a new constitution (Widner).

Depending on public willingness to accept past constitutions, interim provisions may either resurrect an older document for a defined period or provide new essential language and leave the rest for delineation in the official constitution-writing process. Latvia resurrected its pre-war 1923 constitution, just as Poland revived its earlier constitution, with amendments. After the coup in 1991, the Republic of Georgia also felt it was not possible to retain the old Soviet constitution. Georgians lived for three years under a combination of the restored 1921 constitution and interim laws put in place by a national consultative conference. At the other end of the spectrum, in South Africa the pre-existing constitution was not accepted by all sides, and an interim document was put in place, a step that was feasible in part because the interim constitution would only last for two years. Even in South Africa, there were significant elements of continuity, in contrast to the even more radical break with continuity in Nepal.

Because bills of rights are essential for free and fair elections, they are important parts of interim laws and constitutions. In Eastern Europe, countries essentially adopted a bill of rights by ratifying the European Convention on Human Rights. (See Chapter 36.)

Ideally, the roundtable should also specify that there will be an opportunity for the parties to step back and discuss the kind of society they want to build before deliberations on the final draft begin. This step helps distance the subsequent process from fighting or polarized political conflict.

Where the appropriate authority for developing a new constitutional text does not appear in the existing constitution or where there is no accepted constitution, the roundtable typically also determines the procedure for developing an initial text and for deliberating, revising, and adopting a final draft.

5.3.2 Developing an initial text

The initial text may appear before any sort of consultative and deliberative process begins, after a national consultative process but before deliberation, or as a product of the main deliberative body.

Who prepares the initial text is important, in part because its content tends to shape the final document. Later deliberation might produce a more inclusive text that restrains executive power, but it takes more time, effort, and political capital to win changes in provisions than it does to start with content that represents broad interests. For this reason many countries form special commissions or committees that are broadly representative or made up of widely respected citizens to prepare a first draft.

Without a commission, political parties will tend to push their drafts, leading to a focus on short-term partisan advantage. Alternatively, if a large assembly or national conference assumes responsibility, incoherence is a likely result. For example, in Brazil, an array of committees prepared the initial constitutional draft and the consequence was a mélange of inconsistent pieces (Widner). By contrast, a commission, if representative, can carry out an investigation and prepare a detailed report for submission to the main deliberative body, which can then debate and modify the text.

In countries with a tradition of free and fair elections, the legislature often appoints a commission to prepare a draft, choosing people who attract the respect of all parties and social groups. The commission may be composed entirely of legislators or it may draw on people outside the legislature. In many developing countries, the pool of lawyers, politicians, and elder statesmen may be limited, making it sensible to include legislators on the drafting commission. Experts could be placed on the commission, but they would still have to consult with the politicians to know how much power to vest in different parts of the government. The best alternative approach is probably to create a commission within the parliament but with enhanced autonomy.

Practice is often at odds with this approach, either because the legislature lacks legitimacy or because tradition gives the executive the power to appoint a commission. In Latin America, the president often issues an emergency decree to establish the rules for election of the assembly and sometimes provides a draft text. In parts of Africa, proposals for constitutional reform have often been presented to regular legislatures in the form of a bill drafted by the executive branch (Widner).

In countries without a record of free and fair elections, the legislature lacks the legitimacy that voting may confer. In these cases, alternative methods of appointment merit attention. In Benin's 1990 move to multi-party democracy, a transitional legislature appointed the drafting commission, itself indirectly elected from the ranks of a large national conference. The transitional legislature named technical experts to the commission along with some of its own members, and the conference designated some other representatives. In other cases, the executive has appointed a commission but has taken care to make the body representative.

Initial texts produced by the main deliberative body itself are rarely successful because the process of deliberation in a large group becomes laborious and representatives tend to push language that their constituents favor, leading to incoherence within the overall constitution. Even here there are exceptions. In South Africa's transition to majority rule, a roundtable set forth many principles and the legislature, sitting as a constituent assembly, wrote the initial text. The legislature created technical committees to say what should go into specific provisions, and these texts then went to a special committee for harmonization and professional drafting before a vote.

However the development of the initial text takes place, the more inclusive and forward-thinking the drafters, the more likely the final results will satisfy widely accepted standards. Requiring an extensive consultative process can help broaden the horizons of representatives and reduce partisanship, as well as boost levels of popular trust. Some sort of consultation usually attends this stage of constitution writing—usually through hearings or solicitation of written comments from civic groups and citizens. Public participation can raise hopes, however, and the people who develop the initial text must be prepared to explain why some recommendations appeared in the draft while others did not.

The use of experts has expanded in this phase of constitution writing. Expert involvement sometimes comes from a perceived need for technocratic legitimation, but it can have other roots as well. For example, in the aftermath of conflict or where distrust runs deep and information is scarce, experts may appear more neutral than political representatives and may be able to bring a broad range of options into the discussion. In long-standing democracies, the pattern varies. Where there is a tradition of popular mobilization on behalf of constitutional change, suspicion of experts is greater than in countries where political elites take the lead. For example, in Ireland and Switzerland, where constitutional revision had its roots in citizen action, experts work mainly behind the scenes, whereas in Germany and Finland, where revisions are political elite-driven, a distinct feature of constitution-making is openness toward expert participation.

5.3.3 Deliberating

A final draft constitution usually results from debate and amendment in some sort of deliberative body. Elected constituent assemblies, legislatures, and some types of national conferences, are today the main forums in most parts of the world. Together, the constituent assembly model and the legislature model were employed in about 60 percent of the new constitutions that came to a conclusion between 1995 and 2003, the period when many new constitutions emerged. In this same era, national conferences and roundtables sometimes played a larger role in settings where experience with parliamentary government and the management of competitive elections was scant, or where civil war limited the capacity either to hold elections or undermined the legislature's legitimacy. Executive-directed processes accounted for only a small minority of contemporary reform cases. Hybrid approaches have since gained traction, as countries pick and choose procedural elements.

Elected assemblies—constituent assemblies or legislatures sitting as constituent assemblies—have strengths and weaknesses. They promote buy-in and in theory they confer a popular mandate. Depending on the electoral rules and whether electoral competition is free and fair, such an assembly may be broadly representative or quite narrow. The degree to which elections capture popular preferences varies enormously. For example, if conflict caused groups of people to flee and elections do not allow refugee voting, the final draft constitution is unlikely to represent the interests of the citizenry writ large. If districting or the electoral system leads to over-representation of some regions or types of people over others, the composition of the body that prepares the final draft may privilege some points of view over others. The more proportional the system, the more representative the forum, provided the people who stand for election have a strong ties to communities. If political parties are elite clubs whose members have only a weak rapport with voters, the results may have political buy-in but little popular support.

Special problems may arise in bicameral systems, although the problem is mainly one of time and not substance. It is usually best to avoid launching a process in all chambers simultaneously, because each then creates its own draft, and the results must then be reconciled. (In 1978, Spain's constitutional deliberations took place in two chambers. One house had to revisit its deliberations after the other made changes in the draft.)

Out of tradition, or out of lack of capacity to organize an election with little notice, some countries have convened unelected—but nonetheless representative—national conferences on the model of the French *états généraux*. Generally, these serve as devices for building consensus or identifying important principles prior to the creation of a transitional legislature and the development of a draft constitution, or prior to legislature-based constitutional reform. The transitional legislature may be indirectly elected from the ranks of the conference. In a few instances, conferences have also produced initial texts and final drafts themselves.

Conferences are usually large, ranging from several hundred people to over 2,000 delegates. Usually the potential spoilers, the main parties, sit down to agree on a set of rules first. They may set limits on the numbers of seats allocated to different types of delegates—for example, for farmers, traditional authorities, and political parties. They may set eligibility rules as well. The associations that organize these groups—unions, for example—then have responsibility for selecting the people who will represent them.

Where used as deliberative bodies to produce a final draft constitution, national conferences have their own distinct set of maladies. The risk of dominance by the incumbent is high unless the roundtable that establishes eligibility rules and numbers of delegates is carefully balanced. Phantom political parties tend to proliferate prior to registration of delegates, empowering small groups or disguised representatives of the incumbent political party. Perhaps more seriously, it is difficult to finance the kind of sustained deliberation necessary for constitution writing by a large group of people, and most conferences are relatively short, partly for this reason. Sheer size means that most delegates will have little time to speak and may feel they have not really been consulted. Slow translation or publication of proceedings may breed distrust. The tone set by the chair often influences the ability of delegates to work together. As a result, even though the forum may look more representative of the society than others, the outcomes often disappoint.

The rules that shape representation are only one of several procedural elements that define the results of deliberation. Among the many others that matter, the most visible are usually the decision rules that determine whether proposed language stands or falls. In theory, a constitution that takes into account the interests of the larger community is more likely to emanate from assemblies with super-majority rules than from assemblies that require only simple majorities. Super-majority requirements may force compromise, depending on the degree to which one group or another predominates. If the threshold is up for discussion and not fixed in stone, then it is worth considering the kind of margin that would generate give and take in the particular circumstances and whether this rule should apply to all matters or just the most sensitive. Requiring full consensus tends to over-endow small minorities with power and may prolong the discussion for so long that the process loses legitimacy. Consensus or large super-majority rules also place high demands on the skills of the assembly leadership to build support.

Limiting the numbers of points at which votes are taken can also prove useful in defusing conflict and bringing people together. According to close observers, much of the real action in the South African process was almost informal. In the constituent assembly proceedings, although committees drafted text to go to the plenary sessions, real negotiations between party representatives often happened one-on-one or in small groups, outside any formal setting. The chairs of the committees knew not to push hard issues to a vote and referred matters that were too difficult. (Murray, interview with author and '"A Constitutional Beginning": Making South Africa's Final Constitution'.)

Publicity and transparency during deliberation and revision have distinct pros and cons. The conversation can provide a focal point and help transfer knowledge of basic principles to the public at large, but it can trigger grandstanding that interferes with compromise and persuasion. If delegates think citizens are watching their speeches and actions in constitutional negotiations and may form opinions of them on that basis, they may try to pitch toward their likely electoral bases. Grandstanding may also heighten tensions and kindle or re-kindle conflict, reducing inclusiveness.

Where the public has low trust in politicians or representatives, high transparency may be necessary. To avoid polarization, it may be better to allow coverage of regular 'reporting out' sessions and keep other deliberations quiet.

5.3.4 Incorporating veil rules and sunset clauses

To enhance inclusiveness and encourage adoption of terms that constrain executive abuse of power, encouraging delegates to take the long view is critical. Ideally, each delegate would stand behind a 'veil of ignorance' about his or her future position in society, forcing consideration of the interests of the poorest or most insecure. Several kinds of rules can help simulate this veil in a limited sense.

1) Creating a multi-stage process may help separate immediate interests from the final deliberations. To empower those who would prevail in peace-time where militarized factions are present, allowing faction leaders to help draft some procedures and possibly some guiding principles in a roundtable forum, then creating a process for ensuring a final draft, developed by civilians, which respects these agreements, may hold promise. This arrangement aided successful constitution writing in South Africa, but few other countries have experimented with this strategy.
2) Taking immediate political fortune off the table helps limit individual calculations of short-term partisan advantage. Allowing the constituent assembly to become a sitting legislature, and thereby postponing new elections for several years, is one useful device. Where that is not possible, countries have sometimes banned delegates from running for election to public office within a specified period after ratification of a new constitution, However, where people with the skills to serve their countries well in these sorts of capacities are limited, this rule may be counter-productive.
3) A unity government that endures for several years beyond the adoption of a new constitution may also lift some of the pressure to consider short-term advantage.

Sunset clauses may help accomplish some of the same goals as veil rules, though they act differently. Sunset clauses can be used to offer potential spoilers some time to adjust and create enough ambiguity about the future that delegates are able to think about the next generation instead of immediate individual circumstances.

5.3.5 Adoption and ratification

Adoption and ratification rules can produce downstream constraints that shape constitutional content. There are two main methods, with a few rare variants. Where an elected constituent assembly produces the final draft, a vote of the assembly is often all that is required to adopt and ratify. The main alternative is a national referendum—usually an up or down vote on the whole document. A super-majority is usually required for ratification by an assembly, although there are regional variations in the kinds of margins favored. Many referenda require simple majorities of the voters who turn out. A referendum could induce greater inclusiveness if minorities are distributed across voting districts in such a way that they could block acceptance—and if delegates take this possibility seriously in their deliberations.

Variations in ratification rules may exercise more influence over substantive terms. South Africa added a certification process that empowered a new constitutional court to hold hearings and evaluate a draft's compliance with 34 principles set out by an initial roundtable. The hearings provided an opportunity for a unique form of popular participation, while the prospect of review by a thoughtful court may have moved delegates to think carefully before proposing terms that diminished inclusiveness or ran counter to the spirit of initial agreements. The United States provides another variant with probable effect on some centrally important outcomes. The amendment procedures set out in the US Constitution assign a role to state legislatures in approving amendments. This process potentially motivates restrictions on executive abuse of power, because state legislatures are likely to pay particular attention to any amendment that might allow the federal government to encroach on their powers. Only if the party in office at the national level also controlled many state legislatures—and continued to do so for the duration of the ratification process—or if there was wide agreement on the need to lift restrictions would this kind of downstream constraint ease.

Amending formulas are designed to balance the need for stability with the need for change and their ratios reflect the way in which drafters envisage the future function of the polity. Yet, quite often, amending procedures lead to unintended consequences under the influence of external factors, and formulas may be eroded or by-passed. The US Constitution is so difficult to amend that constitutional evolution usually takes place through jurisprudence. In Denmark, formal amendments happen rarely, because the requirement that constitutional revisions be approved through popular vote and by at least 40 percent of the voting population has led to constitutional inertia, while in Belgium and the Netherlands the hurdles set by amending formulas have led politicians to find ways to bypass the limitations in order to effect desired changes.

5.4 Conclusion

This depiction of the procedural complexity of most constitution-writing projects only scratches the surface. The constitutional toolkit has expanded since the first era of constitution-making and the boundaries between the constituent and the amending power have become more fluid. It is clear that the design of a process matters for a range of important outcomes, but because of the interactions between rules and context, bold generalizations are risky. Careful consideration of local circumstances is essential. The point of the description offered here is to show the very different effects many common rules have, depending on the underlying distribution of preferences, the political context, and leader aptitudes.

It is also worth noting that most successful constitution-building ventures also entail a healthy dose of practical politicking on the side. Mediators have intervened in many episodes. Heads of State, including monarchs, have sometimes played this role, as have high-level party officials, who are often kept out of daily involvement for just this purpose. Study tours that help delegates on different sides of an issue build friendships and a basis for compromise can help remedy procedures that might otherwise polarize. Technical workshops that distract committee members from differences and focus them on learning play a similar role. These stratagems, and others, help overcome some of the inevitable downsides associated with any specific procedural choice and keep participants focused on the future and the outcomes that matter.

References

Acemoglu, D & Robinson, J (2012). Why Nations Fail. New York: Crown Publishers.

Besley, T & Persson, S (2011). Pillars of Prosperity: The Political Economics of Development Clusters. Princeton University Press.

Carré de Malberg, R (1922). Contribution à la théorie générale de l'État, Sirey.

Colón-Ríos, J (2010). 'The Legitimacy of the Juridical: Constituent Power, Democracy, and the Limits of Constitutional Reform', Osgoode Hall Law Journal, pp 200 ff.

Congressional Research Service Colombia: Issues for Congress (2010).

Contiades, X & Fotiadou, A (2012). 'Models of Constitutional Change', in Contiades, X (ed), Engineering Constitutional Change in Europe, Canada and the USA, Routledge, pp 417 ff.

Elster, J (2000). 'Arguing and Bargaining in Two Constituent Assemblies', *University of Pennsylvania Journal of Constitutional Law*, 2 (March): 345 ff.

—— (1995). 'Forces and Mechanisms in the Constitution-Making Process', *Duke Law Journal*, 45: 364 ff.

—— (1998). Offe, C & Preuss, U, *Institutional Design in Post-Communist Societies* (Cambridge).

Gözler, K (2008). Judicial Review of Constitutional Amendments (Bursa, Elkin Press).

Häberle, P (1987). Die verfassunggebende Gewalt des Volkes im Verfassungsstaat, AöR, pp 85 ff.

Jackson, VC (2008). 'What's in a Name? Reflections on Timing, Naming and Constitution-making', 49 Wm & Mary L Rev, pp 1249 ff.

Murray, C (2000–2001). '"A Constitutional Beginning": Making South Africa's Final Constitution', University of Arkansas at Little Rock Law Review, 23, 809 ff.

Sieyès, EJ (1963). What is the Third Estate?, trans by Blondel, M (Pall Mall Press).

Tushnet, M (2010). Why the Constitution Matters, Yale University Press.

Widner, J (2008). 'Constitution Writing & Conflict Resolution' Data Project, http://www.princeton.edu/~pcwcr/ Accessed on 15 June 2012. Parts of this project also appear in Widner, J, 'Constitution Writing in Post-Conflict Settings: An Overview', Wm and Mary L Rev, 49, 4 (March): 1513 ff.

World Bank (2011). World Development Report 2011: Conflict, Security, and Development, Washington, DC: The World Bank.

Part II
Structures

6

Systems of government

Denis Baranger and Christina Murray

The word 'government' has long been used to describe the way collective decisions are taken and implemented in a particular community by specially designated people.[1] Be they a single individual, a small group, or the entire community, the decision-makers are called 'rulers', while the members of the community are 'the governed'. People are governed in the sense that their conduct is directed (or influenced) by rules, institutions, and sanctions. The considerable power of the state is exercised through this process in modern democracies.

We are 'governed' by many people and institutions, at different levels. 'Systems of government' are the different arrangements according to which these institutions interact and co-operate in making and enforcing law. They are influenced by such things as how democratic a system is; political parties; the electoral system; the distribution of wealth; the degree of decentralisation of power in the state; and more. Constitutional law has a rather narrow approach to government, taking for granted that what matters is the decision-making process by state institutions, especially legislatures, executives, and courts. Since at least the late eighteenth century, the state has governed in ways unknown in past political forms. In particular, it legislates abundantly, and it relies on a specialized bureaucracy.

This chapter provides an introductory description of the main systems of government in democratic countries that seek to promote the rule of law.[2]

6.1 Preliminary questions

6.1.1 Law, government, and politics

There is much more to government than law but law permeates the modern state. In modern societies, government is readily equated with the process of law-making (with many different

---

1 Sometimes terminological confusion arises because scholars of the British system, and more generally parliamentary systems, often use the word 'government' to refer only to the executive government. We use the term to encompass all 'branches' of government comprehensively.

2 This chapter does not discuss non-democratic systems in which power is concentrated in the hands of a few.

kinds of laws, including statutes, regulations, and international treaties), and a developed administrative structure that implements laws and makes sure that 'private' entities act in accordance with them. As the application of laws is not always straightforward—laws may conflict, be ambiguous, or be wrongly applied—institutions, usually the courts, are needed to oversee their application.

The emphasis on law-making, implementation, and enforcement has led lawyers to tend to equate the state with law-making and implementation. The perceived benefit is that issues of power and politics can be set aside, if not altogether banished, from the business of describing the state in legal terms. On this view, 'government' is the business of political scientists, dealing with 'positive' facts, while 'positive law' is the proper study of lawyers.

The success of this scientific agenda is staggering, and so are its shortcomings. Politics is pervasive. It is about collective decision-making and how it takes place: preferences and demands of individuals and groups; the pressure they put on decision-makers; appointment and dismissal of officials at different levels; policy-making and the bargaining it entails; and a great deal more. Constitutions provide the framework within which this political activity is organized through expressing values, setting out decision-making procedures, and creating the institutions that give shape to political action and that seek to constrain its inherent propensity to conflict.

Constitutions do not always 'work', of course. While France's record of recovering from World War II in the 1945–1958 era was impressive in economic and social terms, its 1946 constitution (the 'Fourth Republic') is generally seen as having significantly impeded its development, generating political instability and preventing the finding of a peaceful solution in the decolonisation conflicts, notably in Algeria. France, it was perceived at the time, was no longer 'governed'. In the summer of 2011, the US showed a remarkable example of constitutional inadequacy with a Democratic President and a Republican majority in one of the Houses of Congress nearly unable to reach a deal on the issue of debt, the public deficit, and reining in public spending.

Moreover, constitutional arrangements that 'work' in one context may fail or operate very differently in another. The parliamentary system, which has endured in the United Kingdom, survived only a few years after independence in most of the UK's former African colonies. The reasons for this failure are complex and diverse but in part it can be attributed to the very different political context of those young African states. In other cases, small variations in the political environment or rules mean that systems that are formally similar, with similar institutions and rules, work quite differently. Again, parliamentary systems provide examples: compare the relationship of the executive to Parliament in the UK—where vigorous Question Time sessions require the Prime Minister to defend government policy and enhance accountability and open government—with that in South Africa where Question Time is organised to benefit the majority party and members of the executive answer questions reluctantly. Consider also the way in which Germany has managed to govern with stable coalitions for decades while Belgium has repeatedly struggled to form governments.

These examples show how constitutional processes and institutions influence politics and vice versa. Ignoring the relationship between them can lead to misunderstandings of both law and politics.

6.1.2 'Governance' in a changing world

The word 'governance' has recently been revived to capture an understanding of government that is broader than formal rules, and to cover 'a variety of recent changes in governmental practice arising from globalizing social, economic and technological developments' (Loughlin).

To a large extent, modern governance is a universal phenomenon and states with different systems (be they parliamentary, presidential, or whatever else) are faced with similar problems (environment, economic policy-making, multiculturalism, 'law and order' concerns), under similar constraints (scarcity of state resources, rising demands for a better protection of individual rights), and have found solutions of a broadly similar nature, often through processes of cross-fertilisation. Moreover, 'governance' is now often of a transnational nature: regional courts may have authority over a number of states (such as the European Court of Justice and the East African Court of Justice); and institutions such as the UN World Trade Organization, the Basel Banking Committee mechanism, North American Free Trade Agreement (NAFTA), the Southern African Development Community (SADC), and, at a more integrated level, the European Union are examples of transnational governance. A country's international and regional economic, security, and other obligations constrain its constitutional choices and its law-making and implementation just as international human rights obligations do—a point dramatically illustrated by the replacement of Italy and Greece's governments under extreme pressure from the EU by 'governments of experts' in the 2011 financial crisis.

6.2 The classic framework

1. A poorly charted territory called 'comparative government' lies at the crossroads of political science and law. It consists in an attempt to understand scientifically the way in which countries are governed through constitutions and institutionalised politics. The vocabulary of comparative government has a reassuring quality: we talk of 'systems', 'structures', 'régimes'. This lends a veneer of rationality to our approach but it can be quickly displaced by disenchantment. As a result, the very word 'system', which appears in the title of this chapter, has aroused increasing scepticism from the ranks of political scientists, some of whom have tried to replace it with 'situations', 'fields', or even 'games' to describe patterns of action in which actors and even rules are constantly changing.

The theory of comparative government has struggled to reduce the immense variety of existing systems of government to a small number of identifiable categories but it has proved extremely difficult to categorise particular régimes. Even more disconcertingly, it produces mere categories, rather than fully fledged explanations of the way in which each régime actually works. Nonetheless, although the explanatory power of the intellectual categories is limited, they have proved rather robust and have not been superseded. Despite its shortcomings, the standard categorisation of comparative government has the advantage of being standard: people speak more or less the same language.

One concluding caveat about the categories of governmental systems concerns their scope. They fit Western liberal democracies fairly well. But, first, the standard categorisation described here simply does not apply to many important non-Western political régimes, China being the main example. Secondly, the widespread use of Western constitutional categories or principles in non-Western political cultures does not mean that these government systems can always be understood in Western terms. The parliamentary system of, say, India, generates a kind of party politics and institutional configurations remarkably similar to a Western 'Westminster-style' régime. On the other hand, although Thailand has a parliamentary government and the Republic of the Philippines an American-style presidential system, the culture, politics, and values in these countries differ vastly from those of their Western constitutional role models, and the functioning of their systems has to be described quite differently.

2. The standard categorisation distinguishes between two main forms of government: parliamentary and presidential. We follow suit, while acknowledging that other, less easily identifiable forms, such as the Swiss system or the institutions of the European Union, need to be identified.

The categorization 'parliamentary/presidential' is structured around the concept of separation of powers: it aims to describe the ways in which separation of powers is positively transcribed into a set of working institutions. Separation of powers should not be misunderstood as a single, straightforward, constitutional blueprint. It is first and foremost a principle of political morality, expressed as a core requirement to secure political liberty. As such, its only demand is that all the powers of the state should not be devolved to a single institution. All Western democracies achieve this. The particular way in which different countries arrange the institutions of the state to distribute competences is what differentiates the several 'systems' of government. There is only a limited number of models available and they are mostly the products of history and, in particular, of struggles to contain power. The mother of all government systems, the British parliamentary government, has arisen from practice—and an impressive amount of background political thinking (from Locke to, say, Walter Bagehot)—rather than from deliberate, voluntary constitution-making. The 'prototype' presidential system, the US system, was developed in a more formal process of constitution-making but it too was very much a product of its political and historical context as was, most famously, the French system in which executive power is shared between a directly elected head of state and a Prime Minister who emerges from Parliament.

Separation of powers is most closely associated with the US where it dominates descriptions of the political arrangements and particularly the sharing of power between Congress, the President, and the Courts derived from the 1787 Constitution. While generally accepted, this nomenclature has obvious flaws: 'powers' in the sense of functions (legislative, executive, judicial) are not entirely separated in the several institutions of government. Executives routinely make laws (often called regulations), fulfil quasi-judicial functions in tribunals, and may have the power to veto laws; legislatures may appoint members of courts or the executive; courts, and particularly courts with the power to review laws for constitutionality, may make law.

The inadequacy of the description 'separation of powers' is even more evident in parliamentary régimes that follow, more or less closely, the British (Westminster) model. There, members of the executive are often members of Parliament and, until 2005, the House of Lords was at the same time a part of the legislature and the highest court in the land. Nonetheless, even in parliamentary systems, in practice functions are separated to some extent. For example, the bureaucracy is separate from the legislature, and courts are not subject to executive or parliamentary control.

6.2.1 Parliamentary government

1. 'Parliamentary government' is the most widespread form of democratic government. This quantitative success may be due to the fact that the label 'parliamentary' hardly denotes a uniform structure of government. At best, it identifies a basic criterion that many systems satisfy. The criterion can be stated thus: a collective executive is accountable to an elected legislative chamber. This accountability is expressed through expressions of 'confidence' by

the chamber. Should this confidence be withdrawn (by what is usually called a 'vote of no confidence'), a (written or unwritten) constitutional rule prescribes that the executive (i.e. Prime Minister and major cabinet ministers) must resign. Nothing else is needed to join the club of parliamentary governments, not even some other common features such as a separate head of state (sometimes a monarch) and head of government, or the executive's power to dissolve Parliament. This apparently straightforward criterion expresses a more subtle underlying constitutional reality. Parliamentary systems are normally found in contexts where the best solution to legitimising executives has proved to be a functional link between the executive and the elected chamber(s) of Parliament. Votes of no confidence have always been rare.

In practice in a parliamentary system, after each parliamentary election the largest party in the legislature, or largest coalition of parties, forms a government (the executive). Usually, the leader of this group becomes head of the executive (and is usually called Prime Minister) and chooses a cabinet with which to govern collectively. Thus, the executive generally commands the support of Parliament and 'confidence' is mostly a positive political relationship. It means that a parliamentary majority expresses its approval of the cabinet's political intentions (the 'programme' of art 49 of the French Constitution of 1958, or the 'mandate' of British democratic theory) and is willing to support its legislative implementation. Co-operation between Parliament and the executive maintains the executive in office. Conversely, rejecting the smallest piece of legislation that has been declared to be a confidence issue (a single item in an Appropriation Act, an unimportant measure that has nothing to do with the hot political issues of the day) can convey the message that the cabinet has been defeated and that its political existence is in jeopardy.

The requirement in parliamentary systems that the executive must retain the confidence of Parliament does not mean that Parliament is politically dominant in the state. Rather, in most cases, the executive is in charge of 'developing and implementing national policy' (section 85(2)(b) South African Constitution of 1996) or 'determining the nation's policies' (art 20, French Constitution of 1958). Despite many claims to the contrary (including those expressed in some constitutions), the function of the deliberative Houses of Parliament is not to devise policies or make ultimate political decisions but rather (to borrow from a medieval phrase still to be found in every British Act of Parliament) to 'advise and consent' on policies and statutes devised by better equipped executives. Executives make decisions that are scrutinised and ultimately approved in legally authoritative form by democratic, deliberative chambers of Parliament. The executive can act in this way only because it enjoys the 'confidence' of Parliament. In many cases, this has involved the decline of the power of heads of state. Being left outside the magic circle of legitimacy, the monarch or the elected President is unable to wield effective power or engage in political action. He/she retains formal powers of appointment and dismissal, and perhaps some leeway on the appointment and dismissal of the Prime Minister or the decision to dissolve Parliament. But generally in modern 'monistic' parliamentary government, the head of state is deprived of an active part in political decision-making. As the 1975 dismissal of the Whitlam government by the Australian Governor-General demonstrates, political decision-making by an unelected head of state in a parliamentary system is deeply problematic.

2. In 'continental' Europe, the British constitutional model has long attracted praise for its conduciveness to political stability. Starting with the Belgian Constitution of 1831, written constitutions have tried to reproduce the British model's main features. This increasingly took the form of an attempt to formulate the unwritten 'conventions' of the British Constitution into entrenched constitutional clauses and the development of new

constitutional rules to respond to differing circumstances. This process was brought to another level by the German and Austrian Constitutions of 1919–1920 and the process known as the 'rationalization' of parliamentary government. Specific rules and detailed procedures purported to bring more clarity and greater constraining power to the core elements of the parliamentary model. At least three aspects were dealt with.

(a) *The executive's internal functioning.* The natural tendency to 'monism' was supported by formal rules limiting the power of the head of state and/or extending the Prime Minister or Chancellor's prerogatives. Both goals could be achieved by requiring all (or some) of the acts of the head of state to be countersigned by ministers. As ministers were accountable for these measures in Parliament, they would insist that they approve of their political content.

(b) *Ministers' appointment and dismissal.* While in the UK the monarch still formally appoints and dismisses ministers, modern parliamentary constitutions have insisted on what has been called an 'elective function' of parliaments. This can consist of a preliminary vote of confidence at the moment ministers are appointed (France 1946) or a direct election of the Prime Minister by Parliament (Germany 1949; South Africa 1996). At least one attempt to take this a step further by having the Prime Minister directly elected by the electorate (Israel 1996–2001) ended in failure because it broke the link between the executive and the legislature that underpins the parliamentary system. The cabinet's dismissal can also be organised so as to ensure political stability. This is emphatically the function of article 67 of the German Basic Law ('constructive vote of no confidence'), which forces a majority in the lower House to appoint a successor if it wants to topple the Chancellor and his/her cabinet.

(c) *Dissolution* has also been 'rationalised'. In parliamentary regimes based on the Westminster model, a (written or unwritten) rule stipulates the maximum term of Parliament and gives the head of state the power to dissolve Parliament. In all but the most exceptional circumstances, the head of state is required to act 'on the advice of' the Prime Minister and the decision to dissolve Parliament thus lies with the government. In these systems, the power to determine when Parliament should be dissolved is a powerful political tool allowing the governing party to determine the election date strategically. Rationalisation has constrained the dissolution power in a number of newer parliamentary systems. For example, its use, while remaining discretionary, has been conditioned upon certain circumstances (a formal vote of no confidence with a supermajority: France, 1946; the Bundestag's failure to appoint a Chancellor: Germany, 1949). Or, it may be restrained by time (not permissible until three years after an election: South Africa, 1996).

3. There are many other variations on the traditional Westminster-style parliamentary regime. In the UK and other Commonwealth countries with parliamentary systems, ministers are usually appointed from Parliament, or, if they are drawn from outside Parliament, an arrangement is made to secure them parliamentary seats as soon as possible. But, in a number of European parliamentary systems, for instance, ministers need not be members of Parliament (e.g. Denmark, Germany, Finland, Italy) or may not be (e.g. Luxembourg, Norway, the Netherlands) (Andeweg & Nijzink, 160). In South Africa, the National Assembly elects the President, who is both head of state and head of the executive, from amongst its members but he or she must leave Parliament once elected. None of these variations affects the basic feature of parliamentary systems: the accountability of a collective executive to the legislature.

The most profound variation on the traditional parliamentary model is found in the French system, which has been followed in Francophone African countries and forms the basis of many of the new systems in Eastern Europe. While often ranked among 'presidential' forms of government (and variously referred to as hybrid, premier-presidential, or semi-presidential), these systems are often specific instances of parliamentary government in which the head of state is elected by universal suffrage and granted important constitutional prerogatives. At the same time, the cabinet is accountable to Parliament and the criterion of parliamentary government is therefore satisfied. In France, where the President is elected by universal suffrage, there can be two different configurations. If the parliamentary majority is the same as that which has elected the President, it becomes 'the President's majority'. It is elected on his/her own political agenda and supports the cabinets that the President has appointed and can freely dismiss. This is why France's system is sometimes called 'semi-parliamentary' or 'semi-presidential'. Yet there can be a second political configuration in which the President and the parliamentary majority do not belong to the same political side. In these (rarer) phases of 'cohabitation', the President's formal constitutional powers are intact, but his/her political authority is diminished. The French system then functions as a classic 'monistic' parliamentary government, in which the Prime Minister sets the political agenda and is accountable only to the majority in Parliament.

The tendency to call these régimes 'presidential' stems from the fact that the actual seat of power appears to be the head of state. He or she appoints and dismisses ministers according to his/her own political will and does not have to bow to the will of Parliament. This can lead to a form of political authoritarianism (Russia) or to a régime that works very differently from the Westminster model (France's Fifth Republic, Finland, Austria). Yet calling these régimes presidential creates a misleading analogy with the American model. Rather, they are parliamentary regimes that co-exist with a strong, and sometimes overbearing, President elected by universal suffrage.

6.2.2 The American 'presidential' model

6.2.2.1 The US Constitution

The American system is the classic presidential system. In the United States, the label 'presidential' should not be construed as implying that the constitution puts the President, the constitution's executive authority, to the forefront at the expense of Congress (the legislative branch). When Woodrow Wilson, then a professor of political science, wrote an authoritative account of the régime in 1885, he called it 'congressional government' in order to emphasize (and deplore) Congressional prominence. This prominence has later waned, but the US model of government still relies on a balanced relationship between both branches.

The core features of the presidential model, US style, can be expressed in the language of separation of powers. The constitution creates three 'powers' or three branches of government: the legislative function is devolved to Congress; the executive power to the President (and that institution alone); and the judicial power is 'vested' in the Supreme Court, and in 'inferior Courts' (s 1, art III). This vesting of powers, which takes place in the first three Articles of the Constitution and dominates understanding of it, is not absolute. Functions overlap. In part, this is because it is impossible to define functions absolutely—the interpretation of law necessarily involves some law-making; executing legislative programmes necessarily involves some law-making and adjudication of interests. In part, however, functions are shared to prevent any branch of government from monopolising power: it is, famously, a system of 'checks and balances'. For example, the grant of legislative power to Congress is mitigated by the presidential power to veto laws, and the executive power of the

President is tempered by the involvement of the Senate in certain appointments to the executive and in approving international agreements. Moreover, even though the requirements of justice are such that courts are expected to enjoy greater independence than the two other branches of government, there are some limits on the 'separation' of the judicial branch. Most notably, judges are chosen by the other two branches.

The three branches of government are deprived of the means of institutional pressure that characterise parliamentary government. The separately elected President and Congress have independent legitimacy. Accordingly, the President cannot dissolve either House of Congress and, in turn, neither the House of Representatives nor the Senate can force the President to resign by way of a vote of no confidence. The President can be removed from office only through a deliberately complex process of 'impeachment' by Congress in which it is established that he or she has (or has not) been 'guilty' of 'Treason, Bribery, or other high Crimes and Misdemeanors'. Certain aspects of this procedure replicate some features of criminal justice and, unlike the Queen of England, who enjoys full constitutional immunity, the US President is both subject to criminal liability and can be removed from office through the impeachment procedure. As far as the President is concerned, impeachment is better approached as a very specific instance of political accountability. The President cannot be removed merely because a majority (or even a super-majority) in Congress disapprove of his or her policies. Political disagreements between Congress and the President must be resolved by negotiation or, at worst, at the next scheduled election. Unlike votes of no confidence in a parliamentary government, impeachment does not sanction poor (but legal) political choices ('maladministration'). Rather, it aims at protecting the constitution and the system of government against egregious behaviour that is likely to imperil the whole constitutional edifice and is perceived as a 'breach of trust'.

6.2.2.2 Presidentialism outside the US

In the past, about 30 countries around the world have followed the United States and adopted 'presidential democracy', many of them in Latin America. However, many deviate from the US model in significant ways. In many South American and African countries, the powers of the President are substantially greater than those of the US President and checks and balances weaker. For example, many Presidents have substantial law-making powers. When such power is granted by a law passed by the legislature, the legislative check on executive power remains in place, at least formally, as the legislature can revoke the grant of power (see Chapter 10). However, presidential constitutions may grant the President the power to make laws (often referred to as decrees) and sometimes these powers are broad. Emergency powers also often give Presidents the power to suspend rights. Sometimes legislative oversight of this is required (Namibia art 26), but not universally (see Chapter 7). Similarly, few presidential systems follow the US example and require legislative approval for cabinet appointments. Often too, the judiciary is weakened because the President controls the appointment of judges. And, some Presidents have the power to dissolve the legislature either under circumscribed conditions or more generally.

These and other variations in the design of presidential systems may affect the way in which the doctrine of separation of powers operates. The terms 'hyper-presidentialism' and 'imperial presidency' have been coined to describe cases in which few democratic checks operate, and many scholars argue that these are not examples of a classic presidential system at all. These examples, together with the poor record of presidential regimes in South America, have provoked a lively debate about whether presidential or parliamentary systems are better.

6.2.3 Systems that are neither parliamentary nor presidential

The standard analysis has to make some room for long-standing exceptions to the parliamentary/presidential divide. An obvious example is Switzerland. In Switzerland, the seven-member Federal Council, the federal executive, is elected by the Federal Assembly, a joint assembly of the two houses of the Federal Parliament. Annually, the Assembly must also elect a Federal President from the members of the Council, to serve for one year only. Like executives in parliamentary systems, the Council operates as a collective (it is subject to the principle of collegiality: art 177). But, although the Assembly has 'supervisory control' over the Federal Council (art 169), the Council is not subject to the confidence of the Assembly—there is no procedure for the dismissal of the government by a vote of no confidence. Thus the Swiss system has been described as 'non-parliamentary' (because the executive is not dependent on legislative confidence) and 'non-presidential' (because there is no head of state directly elected by the people) (Linder & Steffan, 298).[3]

The Swiss system also provides an excellent example of how poorly formal descriptions of systems of government explain the processes of government. For more than 40 years, the Federal Council has been composed of a coalition of four political parties, holding seats in the ratio of 2:2:2:1, which reflects their representation in the elected legislature. Thus, a hallmark of the Swiss system is its consensual nature. As Linder and Steffan comment, 'political decisions are not found by majority decisions but through negotiations and compromise among the important political forces' (Linder & Steffan, 291–92).

6.3 Government systems in flux: pathologies, cures, and 'fit'

6.3.1 Pathologies

Parliamentary government and presidential government are faced with major challenges. Most of these challenges are common to all systems of government: instability; insufficient accountability; and 'crisis in governance' because, in the words of Davina Cooper, 'welfare provisions can no longer be sustained, political authority and legitimacy are in decline, [and] the state as we know it is in jeopardy' (Cooper). Yet experience has shown that each main model is prone to specific pathologies.

Parliamentary government is often perceived as being beset by political instability and powerlessness: Belgium has not had a cabinet enjoying a majority in Parliament from June 2010 to December 2011; during the Fourth Republic (1946–1958), France had 26 ministries and more than a year of interim administrations. There have been 61 administrations in Italy since 1945. Other parliamentary systems seem to have escaped this fate: since 1949, Germany has succeeded in achieving the aim of having one administration per legislative term.

The presidential system, on the other hand, is associated with problems of immobilisation. In the United States, there are ever-growing signs that political polarisation and failure to reform the Constitution have brought about a state of recurring tension between President and Congress resulting in 'endless backbiting, mutual recrimination, partisan deadlock … the House will harass the executive and the President will engage in unilateral action whenever he can get away with it' (Ackerman).

---

3 Linder & Steffan, 298 citing Riklin, A & Ochsner, A, 'Parliament', Handbuch Politisches System der Schweiz, eds Klöti U, Knoepfel P, Kriesi H, Linder W & Papadopoulos Y (Zurich: NZZ, 2004) p 210–11.

The case has also been made that presidentialism has sometimes been detrimental to the countries to which it has been exported. In Latin America, presidentialism has coincided with a record level of regime instability, and a propensity to give way to military dictatorships. Juan Linz has been the outspoken proponent of the view that this is due to some inherent features of presidentialism as a form of government. In the 'Linzian' account, presidentialism is based on 'mutual independence' between the executive and the legislature. This generates irresolvable conflicts between a President elected by the electorate and who is also the head of government on one side, and on the other side an elected assembly that cannot either be dissolved by the President or force him or her to resign. Interdepartmental conflicts are more likely than co-operation (Linz).

Other scholars are less prone to hold the institutional framework of presidential government responsible for the failure of South American presidential régimes. As Cheibub demonstrates, there is no evidence that presidential systems are less able to deal with deadlock than parliamentary ones. Instead, he argues, 'the reason for the instability of presidential democracies (...) lies in the fact that presidential institutions tend to exist in countries that also more likely to suffer from dictatorships led by the military' (Cheibub, 3). In this context, he concludes, democratic failure is due to the 'military–presidential nexus', namely that 'democracies following military dictatorships are more likely to become a dictatorship and that presidential democracies are more likely to follow military dictatorships' (Cheibub, 141).

6.3.2 Cures?

Many of the political reforms that try to address the pathologies are not specific to the particular model of government. For instance, as a solution to issues of 'good governance', accountability and a crisis in 'state delivery', significant state competences have been devolved to independent agencies that are not subject to the authority of parliaments or executives and are not directly accountable to them ('quangos' in the UK, 'autorités administratives indépendantes' in France). In systems with newer constitutions, the inability of classic systems to control abuses of power has led to a proliferation of constitutionally entrenched 'independent institutions', which are sometimes characterised as additional branches of government: Central Banks; Electoral Commissions; Human Rights Commissions; Auditor Generals/Cours de Audit. (The 2009 Kenyan Constitution establishes 12 such independent institutions.) (See Chapter 10.)

Inside each type of government, critiques often focus on the shortcomings of the classic separation of powers model. Experts are often prone to think that the grass is greener on the other side of the separation of powers fence. In Europe, initial fascination with the Westminster model was replaced with attempts to repatriate some features of the US presidential system. In France, this used to mean increasing the President's domination and moving away from parliamentarism. Yet the 2008 overhaul of the Constitution took the reverse approach: it aimed at creating a greater balance between the executive on one side, courts and parliament on the other.

On the other side of the fence, in the face of what was perceived as a failure of presidential government outside US borders, notably in South America, a plea has been entered in favour of 'constrained parliamentarism', a system that would resort to the core mechanisms of parliamentary government while constraining law-making through a greater involvement of the people and increased judicial review of higher 'substantive political principles' (Ackerman, 663 ff).

6.3.3 Fitness issues: adjusting governmental systems to political realities

There is much debate about what system of government is 'better'. The question of what system of government to adopt is perhaps the most difficult question for constitutional designers in a new state (like South Sudan) or in the many countries emerging from authoritarian rule or contemplating substantial constitutional change (such as Eastern European countries after 1989; South Africa in 1994; Pakistan in 2010; Tunisia in 2011; and Kenya between 2001 and 2010).

In this context, abstract discussions about the vices and virtues of government systems can be misleading. A better understanding of just how constitutional engineering can help fix political problems may depend on a closer look at national contexts and their interaction with the details of the design of each system. This is a lesson lawyers might draw from the active debate triggered in the field of political science by the work of Juan Linz. Linz argues that his analysis of presidential systems demonstrates their particular unsuitability for societies deeply divided by ethnic or other differences.

Current discussion of what system is best in ethnically divided societies is framed by a famous debate between Arend Lijphart and Donald Horowitz. Lijphart's position is that 'majority rule in plural societies spells majority dictatorship and civil strife' (Lijphart 1985, 19)—in other words, neither a 'pure' parliamentary or presidential model is appropriate—and that in such circumstances the answer is 'consociational democracy', a system in which as many people as possible are involved in decision-making. For Lijphart, 'the consensus model tries to share, disperse and limit power in a variety of ways' (Lijphart 2008). A consociational system has many components—autonomy for different groups (for instance through federal arrangements), power sharing, and the careful distribution of civil service positions, among other things. In the context of systems of government, Lijphart prescribes 'executive power sharing in broad multi-party coalitions' and 'executive–legislative balance of power'. Here, what is important is that all significant political groupings should have a say in decision-making. The system in Switzerland and Kenya's 'grand coalition' government established in 2008 after ethnically based violence tore the country apart are examples of the type of arrangements Lijphart favours. The Kenyan system saw a President and Prime Minister from opposing sides share power with a cabinet composed of an equal number of ministers from each side. A similar system in South Africa under the 1993 'Interim' Constitution provided for the appointment of Executive Deputy Presidents from any party with more than 20 percent of the seats in Parliament and required the President to consult them on most executive decisions.

Horowitz thinks consociational systems of government proposed by Lijphart will not work when they are most needed, in part because they rely on greater idealism from the leaders of ethnic groups than is likely to exist. He proposes an alternative, dubbed 'centripetal' because, in his words, 'its principal tool is not a regime of ethnic guarantees but the provision of incentives, usually elective incentives, that accord an advantage to ethnically based parties that are willing to appeal … to voters other than their own' (Horowitz 2008; see also Horowitz 2002). The goal is to develop institutions that will encourage accommodation amongst groups before elections rather than to secure the representation of groups. Carefully designed electoral systems may contribute to achieving this goal. For Horowitz, the choice of system of government is less important as a tool in managing ethnic division but not irrelevant. In particular, he disagrees with both Lijphart and Linz in his preference for a—specially designed—presidential system. The model he points to is Nigeria where the President must secure at least 25 percent of the vote in at least two-thirds of all the states (Nigeria art 134), a requirement that is intended to require candidates to build multi-ethnic alliances and to lead to 'pan-ethnic' presidents.

6.4 Conclusion

A nation's system of government is the backbone of its constitutional system—if the system of government is ineffective, free and fair elections are unlikely, rights will not be implemented or protected by courts, and national resources will not be distributed to the people. Yet we lack systematic knowledge of these systems' consequences. In particular, relatively small changes in design (the scheduling of legislative and presidential elections, for example), in the political context (such as the number and stability of political parties) or in the broader social and economic context (the economic dependency of constituents on public representatives or the importance of consensus in a society perhaps) may have unpredictable consequences for the way in which a system actually operates. Moreover, the 'choice' of system, in those newer cases where it has been a deliberate choice, is frequently driven by history and the short-term interests of those making the choice and their understanding of the options available. Nonetheless, as we pay more attention to systems of government, their relationship to constitutionalism and the rule of law, and their design and implementation, we may come to understand better their strengths and weaknesses. The theory of governmental systems does not provide ready-made constitutional blueprints or panaceas. But it is a necessary appendage to the science of constitutions and (at times) a helpful guide for constitution drafters.

References

Ackerman, B (2000). 'The New Separation of Powers,' *Harvard Law Review* 113, no. 3 (1 January): 646.

Andeweg, RB & Nijzink, L (1995). 'Beyond the Two-Body Image: Relations between Ministers and MPs', in Herbert Doring (ed), *Parliaments and Majority Rule in Western Europe*, 152.

Cheibub, JA (2006). *Presidentialism, Parliamentarism, and Democracy* (Cambridge University Press).

Cooper, D (1998). Governing out of Order: Space, Law and the Politics of Belonging (Rivers Oram, London and New York University Press, New York, USA).

Horowitz, DL (2002). 'Constitutional design: proposals versus processes', in Reynolds, A (ed), The Architecture of Democracy: Constitutional Design, Conflict Management, and Democracy (Oxford: Oxford University Press).

—— (2008). Conciliatory Institutions and Constitutional Processes in Post-conflict States, 49 *Wm & Mary L Rev* 1213.

Linder, L & Steffan, S (2006). 'Switzerland' in *Legislative, Executive and Judicial Governance in Federal Countries*, Saunders, C & Le Roy, K (eds) (McGill-Queens University Press) p 298.

Lijphart, A (1985). *Power-Sharing in South Africa* (Univ California Press, Berkeley).

—— (2008). *Thinking About Democracy: Power Sharing and Majority Rule in Theory and Practice*, New edn (Routledge).

Linz, JJ (1990). 'The Perils of Presidentialism', *Journal of Democracy* 1, no. 1: 51–69.

Loughlin, M (2009). 'In Defence of Staatslehre', *Der Staat* (Berlin: Duncker und Humblot) 48 (1), 1–28.

Emergency powers

Victor V Ramraj and Menaka Guruswamy

7.1 Emergency powers and constitutionalism

Emergency powers pose a serious challenge to one key objective of modern constitutionalism—limiting state power. How, if at all, can a legal order respond to an emergency within a constitutional framework? Is it consistent with the general aims of constitutionalism for a constitution to authorize the suspension of constitutional guarantees, in whole or in part, in times of emergency? There are also important questions about the definition of 'emergency', for the meaning ascribed to this idea and the power to decide when an emergency exists are themselves contentious. The definition chosen affects the ability of a legal order to respond to the emergency in a manner consistent with its fundamental normative commitments. Basic questions about the nature of constitutional government are never that far from seemingly innocuous questions about emergency powers.

Modern constitutionalism may have formalized and institutionalized the principles limiting the power of the sovereign within a professional bureaucratic state. Yet, unwritten political and social norms still play an important role in constraining government, even in times of emergency, in ways that are not always apparent on an exclusively positivist or normative account of law. While we might be tempted to think of the conundrum of emergency powers as posing a challenge only to the integrity of modern, liberal–democratic constitutional government, the challenge of remaining true to the virtues of good government in the face of crisis has ancient roots. For example, in Ottoman times, the law of the Shari'a imposed standards of governance 'that, when violated, could result in [the sovereign's] dismissal or even assassination' and that for 'political power to acquire any legitimacy, it had to meet these standards, and conduct itself in a morally and legally responsible way' (see Hallaq). And Confucian principles have been said to include a 'right of revolution … against tyrannical rulers even in extreme situations' (Chen 2004, 12)—a principle that resonates with John Locke's belief that the right to revolt against a tyrannical ruler provided the ultimate constraint on the abuse of extraordinary powers such as the prerogative—'the Power of doing Publick good without a Rule'.[1]

It is also important from a legal–historical perspective to recognize the impact of colonialism on the development of emergency powers. This can be seen, for example, in the controversy over Jamaica Governor John Eyre's brutal response to the Morant Bay rebellion in 1865, which sparked a larger debate over the limits of martial law (Kostal). Western legal thinking has also been shaped by the experience of emergency powers in Weimar Germany, apartheid South Africa, and Northern Ireland, the latter two again connected to colonialism. And many contemporary discussions of emergency powers remain inextricably linked to the 11 September 2001 attacks on the United States.

The chapter begins with a brief survey of the history of emergency powers and some of the defining events that have shaped contemporary approaches to emergency powers. It provides an analytic roadmap for approaching emergency powers before outlining the formal or structural elements of constitutional emergency powers and the substantive limits imposed on their exercise. The chapter then considers the interplay between domestic and international legal principles governing the exercise of emergency powers. It concludes by reflecting on the relationship between emergency powers and modern constitutionalism, and on the methodological challenges of comparative constitutional law.

7.2 Approaching emergency powers

In our contemporary, post-colonial world order, a layer of formal legality extends seamlessly around the globe, but the depth of the social penetration of formal constitutional law differs dramatically. In some countries it has been said that an unwritten cultural constitution (Eoseewong; Ginsburg) has more influence than the formal written constitution and better explains the constraints imposed on and experienced by government. This may be true in societies where formal law has not penetrated deeply into the popular understanding of government, or where—as in many fragile, post-conflict situations—the formal institutions of government are simply too weak. It is important to bear in mind the societal context in thinking about formal legal approaches to emergency powers precisely because these powers are often invoked, when they are formally invoked, in vastly different social and political contexts, and in societies with distinct understandings of the importance of formal law (Mattei).

That said, within the formal framework of modern constitutional government, two approaches to emergency powers have emerged whose provenance can be traced, at least in part, to differences between common law and civil law traditions. The first approach is based on the civil law tradition, which in turn can be traced to the institution of a 'constitutional dictatorship' in Roman law.[2] On this approach, emergency powers are expressly incorporated into and governed by the formal provisions of the constitution. Under the Roman model as it emerged over time, the consuls, in times of 'grievous war or serious civil unrest', could, with the approval of the Senate, appoint a dictator with almost absolute power, restrained in the duration of the appointment and the specificity of purpose—the ultimate purpose being the restoration of the constitutional order. The dictator was also dependent on the Senate for finances and had no civil jurisdiction.

---

1 *Two Treatises of Government*, Laslett, P (ed) (Cambridge: CUP, 1988), 378; on the right to revolt in such circumstances, see 380.
2 This and the subsequent paragraph rely on Rossiter.

The modern successor of the Roman model was the French state of siege (*état de siege*), which began as a military institution but was gradually transformed into a legal institution for responding to crises within a constitutional framework. On this model, as it evolved and migrated around the civil-law influenced world, the circumstances that trigger the powers, the procedure by which they are invoked, the body that is empowered to make decisions, the limits on those powers, and the procedure for returning to ordinary constitutional government are all governed by principles set out *ex ante* in the constitution itself. A clear distinction is envisioned between ordinary constitutional government and the extraordinary exercise of emergency powers under the constitution, a distinction echoed in Article 48 of the Weimar constitution, which provided a legal path for Adolf Hitler's rise to power.

The common law approach is in some respects more complex, and in other respects less defined, admitting of multiple variations. Common law jurisdictions have, over time and to different extents, adopted many of the characteristics of Roman law-influenced emergency power provisions in their constitutions. But the common law approach to emergency powers was historically characterized by the absence of a formal constitutional distinction between 'ordinary' and 'extraordinary' modes of governance, and by the pre-eminent role of the ordinary courts in policing the limits of the state's response to extraordinary circumstances, and, in contrast with the Roman and French models, by the tendency, as one critic observes, 'to work out arrangements in each case on a trial and error basis, regardless of the delay and inefficiency this may cause' (Townshend, 198).

Within this broad framework, a further question arises as to whether, to the extent that emergency powers are to be regulated *ex ante* by written law (rather than *ex post*, through judicial review), the formal regulation should take statutory or constitutional form. In some respects, this question results from local circumstances, with few general features. For example, the US Constitution says very little about emergency situations, doing no more than limiting the suspension of *habeas corpus* to 'cases of rebellion or invasion, the public safety may require it' (Art. I). In the US context, constitutional law scholars are divided on whether a formal emergency powers provision should be introduced (putting aside the effective impossibility of amending the US Constitution) or whether statutory powers are sufficient.[3] Even this seemingly insular debate resonates elsewhere. For example, it has been suggested that China's emergency law, which limits the conditions in which emergency powers may be invoked, has the potential to create a significant constraint on government power, even in a state with a strong and largely unconstrained executive (deLisle).

7.3 Formal considerations

In approaching emergency powers, most modern constitutions will provide, implicitly or explicitly, answers to the following formal questions: Who decides when emergency powers may be invoked? Under what conditions may they be exercised? What powers accrue when a state of emergency is declared? What checks exist on the exercise of those powers? How does an emergency end?

7.3.1 Who decides

In many constitutions, modelled perhaps distantly on the Roman model, the power to declare a state of emergency is expressly vested in the executive branch, subject to ratification by the

---

3 See e.g. Ferejohn & Pasquino; Ackerman.

legislature, and with the French Constitution serving as an archetype, South Africa's Constitution offers an alternative model, providing that a state of emergency 'may be declared only in terms of an Act of Parliament' (s. 37(1)). In other constitutional contexts, the answer to this fundamental question is more ambiguous, depending in part on the nature and source of the threat. Indeed, much of the controversy around martial law in the common law tradition concerns the answer to the ultimate question of control of military power in response to domestic unrest (Townshend). In the UK today (with its unwritten constitution), Parliament provides the statutory basis for the government to respond to emergencies, whether through counter-terrorism or civil emergencies legislation.

The aftermath of the 9/11 attacks in the United States saw a concentration of power in the executive branch, with Congress, at least initially, granting the President broad statutory powers to respond, and the President assuming broad powers, which he viewed as rooted in the Constitution. But common interest in strong presidential powers came under strain as the differing interpretations of the source of those powers came under the scrutiny of the Supreme Court in its first post-9/11 case, *Hamdi v Rumsfeld*,[4] and, over time, as differences between the White House and Congress appeared, the divided structure of US government became more pronounced. In France, which also has a presidential system of government, the Constitution vests the power to declare a state of emergency in the President, 'after formally consulting the Prime Minister, the Presidents of the Houses of Parliament and the Constitutional Council' (Art. 16), and specifies that the National Assembly will continue to sit as of right and will not be dissolved during the state of emergency. The advice given is non-binding, in as much as the President is not required to follow it, but the President's powers are time limited.

7.3.2 Triggering conditions and definitions of emergencies

A second formal question concerns the triggering conditions—the conditions under which an emergency may be declared. At one extreme is Schmitt's view that the most a constitution can do is to specify who decides; it cannot specify in advance the circumstances in which emergency powers may be invoked (Schmitt, 6–7). But most modern constitutions seek to do precisely that, to set out those circumstances in advance. Consider Article 187 of the Interim Constitution of South Sudan, setting out the following circumstances in which the President may declare a state of emergency (subject to ratification by the legislature): 'upon the occurrence of an imminent danger, whether it is war, invasion, blockade, natural disaster or epidemics, as may threaten the country, or any part thereof or the safety or economy of the same'. China's Constitution allows the Standing Committee of the National People's Congress to enact emergency legislation, which, in addition to legislation 'focused on the authority to use force, to displace ordinary law, and to limit citizens' rights' under the Law on Martial Law (deLisle, 358), now includes an Emergency Response Law in 2007, covering 'natural disasters, accidents, and epidemics' (Chen in Ramraj & Thiuvengadam, 82).

Other constitutions have less to say in this respect. As noted earlier, the US Constitution, which does not contain an emergency powers clause, allows Congress to suspend *habeas corpus* when, in 'cases of rebellion or invasion, the public safety may require it'. Singapore's Constitution allows Parliament to enact emergency legislation in relation to threats of organized violence or against the President or government, acts that 'promote feelings of ill-will and hostility between different races or other classes of the population likely to cause violence'

---

4 542 US 507 (2004). See also *Rasul v Bush*, 542 US 466 (2004), *Hamdan v Rumsfeld*, 548 US 557 (2006), *Boumediene v Bush*, 128 SCt 2229 (2008).

or that attempt to change the law 'otherwise than by lawful means', and acts 'prejudicial to the security of Singapore' (s. 149). In India, the Constitution specifically provides for situations that qualify as 'emergencies'. War, external aggression, and armed rebellion can all trigger the proclamation of an emergency (Art. 352). Less conventionally, an emergency may be declared when the President is satisfied that the government of an individual state within the country cannot be 'carried on in accordance with the provisions of the Constitution' (Art. 356).[5] In some jurisdictions, constitutionally entrenched emergency powers provisions have been invoked in response to economic crises (Negretto & Aguilar Rivera) and drug-related violence.[6]

In some jurisdictions, the triggering conditions for the invocation of emergency powers are set out not in the constitution, but in ordinary legislation, and sometimes in very precise terms. Canada's Emergencies Act creates a statutory framework to govern not only war and international emergencies, but also 'public welfare emergencies' (defined to encompass 'fire, flood, drought, storm, earthquake or other natural phenomenon, disease in human beings, animals or plants, or accident or pollution ... that results or may result in a danger to life or property, social disruption or a breakdown in the flow of essential goods, services or resources, so serious as to be a national emergency') and 'public order emergencies', such as serious threats to the security of Canada. In the context of the UK's unwritten constitution, the Civil Contingencies Act 2004 similarly establishes a framework for the roles and responsibility of local authorities in an emergency, while allowing, in Part II, for special legislative measures in the most serious emergencies. Among the circumstances covered by Part II of the Act are threats of 'serious damage to human welfare' (which is defined in the Act) or to the environment, or war or terrorism that threatens serious damage to the UK (s. 19).

7.3.3 Powers that accrue

Some constitutions specify the powers that accrue to the executive or other bodies and the limits on those powers. The general, substantive legal principles (non-derogation, proportionality) limiting emergency powers are considered in detail later in this chapter. But a constitutional framework of emergency powers might (1) transfer powers ordinarily exercised by one branch of government to another; (2) authorize the use of powers or measures not ordinarily permitted within the constitutional framework; or (3) permit the executive or other body to derogate from fundamental constitutional rights or freedoms, in whole or in part. For example, the Constitution of Trinidad and Tobago expressly provides 'exceptionally' for the detention of persons (s. 7(2)) and a specific review procedure (s. 11) during a proclaimed public emergency. On the other hand, some constitutions place strikingly few limitations on the powers that accrue. The French Constitution, for example, provides only that the President may take 'such measures as are required in the circumstances' (Article 16).

---

5 Even so, pursuant to an amendment to the Constitution, the right to life guaranteed by it cannot be suspended in any emergency. Therefore, *habeas corpus* cannot be suspended in India when an emergency is proclaimed: see below on the principle of non-derogation.

6 Ranald C. Archibald, 'Trinidad and Tobago Declares Emergency Over Drug Crimes', *The New York Times* (24 August 2011). Emergency powers in Trinidad and Tobago are governed by Part III of The Constitution of the Republic of Trinidad and Tobago, Act 4 of 1976 (as amended).

7.3.4 Separation of powers: legislative and judicial checks

Emergencies alter the balance of separation of powers, since usually the executive engages in actions that infringe on the domain of the legislature. Executive actions usually impact well-established constitutional rights. The respective roles of the various branches of government in relation to emergency powers are therefore the subject of considerable academic controversy. For example, Mark Tushnet argues that 'the substantive law of emergency specifies what the executive can do to whom when there are rationally indisputable major threats to the continued stable operation of a democratic nation's political and social order' and he considers the checks on emergency powers to be primarily political rather than legal (Tushnet, 1452). Also rejecting the centrality of legal checks, Oren Gross argues that extra-legal measures taken by public officials to address extraordinary threats should be checked through democratic or political mechanisms rather than by bending or diluting legal principles, such as the prohibition on torture, to accommodate them (Gross 2003). In contrast, Bruce Ackerman and William Scheuerman argue that the main checks on emergency powers are found in formal political and legislative processes (Ackerman; Scheuerman), while David Dyzenhaus and David Cole insist that the responsibility for holding emergency power to account resides in the courts, through judicial review (Dyzenhaus; Cole). These tensions are reflected in the diversity of approaches taken by different constitutions to the separation of powers in an emergency.

When the power to declare a state of emergency is vested in the executive branch, some constitutions include formal legislative checks on the declaration and on the exercise of emergency powers. For example, the constitution itself may provide that the declaration of a state of emergency by the executive is subject to legislative ratification within a specified period. Elsewhere, the judiciary is formally assigned or, in constitutional practice, assumes a primary role in reviewing the invocation of emergency powers, whether by the executive or the legislature. The South African Constitution categorically provides that the Court will decide the validity of the declaration of the state of emergency, extension of emergency and validity of any legislation enacted or other action taken in consequence of a declaration of emergency.[7] Conversely, the Malaysian Constitution does not permit any court to entertain or determine any application, question, or proceeding on any ground regarding the validity of the proclamation or continuation of emergency or any law under it.[8] Likewise, the Constitution of Bangladesh allows for all fundamental rights (Bill of Rights) to be suspended during an emergency, and also permits the executive to suspend the right to move the courts in such times, as does Pakistan, albeit in somewhat different terms.[9] Given the weaknesses in both constitutions, in tandem with the ability of the military regimes of both to stage coups and take over political power, emergencies have been frequently proclaimed in Bangladesh and Pakistan (Jalal; Siddiqa; Rizvi).

Courts that are formally prohibited by the text of a constitution from reviewing emergency powers might yet draw on first principles and generalities about the rule of law to find constitutional justifications for doing so. But even when judicial review of the invocation or exercise of emergency powers is not formally prohibited by the constitution, courts can be more or less deferential to the executive. It is therefore important to distinguish the threshold question of

---

7 Section 37 (3), Constitution of South Africa.
8 Article 150 (8)(a), Constitution of Malaysia.
9 Article 141 B and C of the Constitution of Bangladesh. Pakistan allows for fundamental rights to be suspended, and allows the Executive to prohibit any challenges relating to the emergency in a court of law: Article 233, Constitution of Pakistan.

whether the courts have the formal power to review (and whether this matters), from the question of whether they will or ought to defer to the executive on questions of national security. When courts do review the exercise of emergency powers, further questions arise as to the substantive principles they should adopt (a question we consider in the next section).

7.3.5 Extension, lapse, and termination

While indefinite states of emergency are not uncommon (Israel, Malaysia and, until recently, Egypt[10] have been described as countries under a perpetual state of emergency), some constitutions provide that a state of emergency will lapse after a specified period if it is not renewed or extended by the legislature. For example, East Timor's Constitution provides that the suspension of fundamental rights, freedoms, or guarantees in a state of siege or state of emergency 'shall not last for more than thirty days, without prejudice of possible justified renewal, when strictly necessary, for equal periods of time' (s. 25). In South Africa, a declaration of a state of emergency, which is limited in the first instance to 21 days, lapses thereafter unless extended by the National Assembly for a period of no more than three months at a time (s. 37(2)(b)). A first extension may be obtained with the support of a simple majority, but subsequent extensions require the support of at least 60 percent of the members of the Assembly. In a distant echo of the Roman model, the Constitution of the Democratic Republic of East Timor provides expressly that the authorities 'shall restore constitutional normality as soon as possible' (s. 25). Some constitutions do not provide for a lapse, nor do they specify how a state of emergency ends. For instance, as of 2011, Malaysia remains technically under a state of emergency proclaimed in 1969. That state of emergency was not rescinded even after the immediate conditions that triggered the emergency (ethnic unrest in the wake of general elections) had long since passed.

7.4 Substantive principles: non-derogation and proportionality

Two substantive legal principles limit the extent to which emergency powers can suspend constitutional rights: non-derogation and proportionality. These constitutional principles reflect, and in many instances can be traced in part to, the major international human rights instruments, including the International Covenant on Civil and Political Rights (ICCPR) and the European Convention on Human Rights (ECHR).

7.4.1 The principle of non-derogation

The principle of non-derogation holds that there is a core of fundamental rights that may not be infringed or limited, even in an emergency.[11] Although it is often conceded in many

---

10 As we were revising this chapter for publication, the status of Egypt's emergency laws remained ambiguous. The military-led post-Mubarak government has yet to formally rescind those powers, promising only to 'limit the use of extrajudicial arrests and detentions to cases of … "thuggery"' ('Egypt Military Council Party Curbs State of Emergency Law', *The New York Times*, 24 January 2012).

11 ICCPR, art. 4; ECHR, art. 15(2). The non-derogable rights in the ICCPR include the right to life (Art 6), right to freedom from torture, cruel and degrading treatment (Art 7), freedom from slavery (Art 8), the right against punishment for breach of contract (Art 11), the unenforceability of retroactive legislation (Art 16), freedom of thought, conscience and religion (Art 18), and right not to be subject to death penalty (Art 6).

constitutions, as it is in international human rights instruments, that the state may derogate from its obligations in an emergency, it is also acknowledged that certain essential protections and rights cannot be derogated from (i.e. those protections/obligations are non-derogable). For instance, the right against torture is generally regarded as a principle of *jus cogens*, a peremptory norm not subject to derogation (Allain).

The principle of non-derogation can be found in the text of many modern constitutions. For example, East Timor's Constitution limits the extent to which a state of siege can limit fundamental rights: 'In no case shall a declaration of a state of siege affect the right to life, physical integrity, citizenship, non-retroactivity of the criminal law, defence in a criminal case and freedom of conscience and religion, the right not to be subjected to torture, slavery or servitude, the right not to be subjected to cruel, inhuman or degrading treatment or punishment, and the guarantee of non-discrimination.'[12] Similar limitations can be found in Sudan (prohibiting derogation from the rights to life, prohibitions against slavery and torture, right of non-discrimination on the basis of race, sex, religion, and the right to fair trial),[13] South Africa (prohibiting derogation from, among others, the rights to equality, human dignity, life, prohibitions against torture and slavery),[14] and Russia (prohibiting limits on, among others, the rights to life, dignity, privacy, appeals, against self-incrimination, access to courts and counsel, and prohibitions on torture).[15] The Interim Constitution of Nepal, which is in force until a final constitution is passed by the Constituent Assembly, provides that the rights to equality, environment, health, social justice (among others) and the rights against torture, exploitation, and exile cannot be suspended in an emergency.[16] In some contexts, the principle of non-derogation has a longer history, and has attracted considerable judicial scrutiny. For example, according to the Supreme Court of India, the constitutional prohibition on derogation from the rights against self-incrimination, double-jeopardy, retroactive criminal legislation and the rights to life and liberty[17] was added to the Constitution to protect people from 'executive and legislative despotism'.[18]

In jurisdictions with newer constitutions, where the principle of non-derogation has not been tested judicially, the international jurisprudence may be helpful and, in some cases, is explicitly invoked by the constitutional text. For example, Colombia prohibits derogation from or suspension of any human rights or fundamental freedoms or international humanitarian laws in times of emergency.[19] But even apart from these explicit textual links, the work of international law jurists might yet shed some light on the principle of non-derogation in domestic constitutional law. The United Nations Human Rights Committee's General Comment No. 29 (24 July 2001) elaborates on the derogation provision Article 4 of the ICCPR, setting out principles limiting derogation under domestic law: that derogations are

---

12 Section 25(5).

13 Article 188, Constitution of Sudan.

14 Section 37, Constitution of South Africa.

15 Article 56, Constitution of Russia.

16 Article 143 (7), Interim Constitution of Nepal.

17 Articles 20 and 21 cannot be derogated from: see Constitution of India, Article 359. This, the Supreme Court of India declared, has been added into the Constitution by subsequent amendments to protect people from 'executive and legislative despotism' (*State of Maharashtra v Bhairao Punjabrao Gawande*, (2008) 3 SCC 613, para. 23.

18 *State of Maharashtra v Bhairao Punjabrao Gawande*, (2008) 3 SCC 613, at para. 23.

19 Article 214, Constitution of Colombia. The Constitution also explicitly states that international treaties that prohibit limitations on their provisions in times of emergency that have been ratified by Colombia have priority: Article 93.

time bound (i.e. they must be terminated as soon as the situation ceases to be a threat to the life of the nation) (Gross 1998, 455); that the state remains bound by the principle of legality and the rule of law[20]; and that the derogation can be in force only for the duration of the proclaimed emergency.[21] Whether the international jurisprudence is ultimately embraced by domestic constitutional law will likely be a function of a range of factors, including the degree of interplay between the domestic and international legal orders—a point that we will return to in the final section.

7.4.2 The principle of proportionality

The principle of proportionality is a second critical principle that regulates the conduct of states in times of emergency. This principle has been formulated in different ways in the domestic and international case law, but it is expressed in Article 4 of the ICCPR as providing that measures that derogate from fundamental rights are permissible in a 'time of public emergency which threatens the life of the nation' but only 'to the extent strictly required by the exigencies of the situation'.

For example, in Canada, the general proportionality test developed by the Supreme Court of Canada is its jurisprudence on the *Canadian Charter of Rights and Freedoms*, known as the *Oakes* test,[22] has been used to determine whether, in the event of a *prima facie* violation of a *Charter* right, that violation can be justified in a free and democratic society. A finding of proportionality requires '(a) means rationally connected to the objective; (b) minimal impairment of rights; and (c) proportionality between the effects of the infringement and the importance of the objective'.[23] In a case with parallels to emergency powers in other jurisdictions, the Supreme Court of Canada, applying this test, found that a procedure that permits the deportation of a foreign citizen or permanent resident on national security grounds without providing the person access to some or all of the information that formed the basis for the deportation, was disproportionate since there were other ways 'to protect sensitive information while treating individuals fairly' (para 70).

Similarly, in *A and Others v Secretary of State for the Home Department*,[24] the House of Lords was asked to decide, under the Human Rights Act 1998, whether the indefinite detention of foreign terrorist suspects under Part IV of the Anti-Terrorism, Crime and Security Act 2001, in respect of which the United Kingdom purported to derogate from the European Convention on Human Rights, was permissible. The answer to that question turned on whether the UK's derogation was justified under Article 15 of the Convention on the ground that the post-9/11 terrorist threat in the UK amounted to a 'public emergency threatening the life of the nation' for which derogating measures were permissible under Article 15 of the Convention 'to the extent strictly required by the exigencies of the situation'. With only Lord Hoffmann holding (in dissent) that there was no threat to the life of the nation, the majority of the House of Lords deferred to the government's view of the threat. However, the majority found that the indefinite detention of non-nationals was discriminatory: since the legislation either detained indefinitely or allowed 'non-UK suspected terrorists to leave the country with

---

20 General Comment No. 29 States of Emergency (Article 4) CCPR/C/21/Rev.1/Add.11 at para 16.
21 *Ibid*, para 4.
22 [1986] 1 SCR 103.
23 *Charkaoui v Canada (Citizenship and Immigration)* [2007] 1 SCR 350.
24 [2005] 1 AC 68.

impunity' while 'leaving British terrorists at large' (at para. 43), it was a disproportionate derogation from the right to liberty that was 'not strictly required by the exigencies of the situation'.[25] The Belmarsh case eventually made its way to Strasbourg. And while earlier jurisprudence of the European Court of Human Rights was largely deferential to state authorities in cases involving national security (see, for example, the lines of cases on Northern Ireland, beginning with *Ireland v United Kingdom*),[26] the Strasbourg Court showed little sign of deference in this case, affirming that 'the derogating measures were disproportionate in that they discriminated unjustifiably between nationals and non-nationals'.[27]

7.5 Constitutional emergency powers and international law

The preceding sections demonstrate the interplay between international legal principles and domestic constitutional norms governing the exercise of emergency powers in the formal structure of emergency powers and in the broad principles seeking to limit them. This interplay takes place in three spheres: constitution-making, constitutional principle, and in the global counter-terrorism regime.

The interplay is evident in constitution-making, where formal structures and broad principles relating to emergency powers have been adapted from a range of international instruments such as the ICCPR and the ECHR, and from other constitutions that have drawn inspiration from these sources. The international principles, in turn, themselves drew support from the structure and principles of domestic constitutionalism, reaching as far back (at least in the Western tradition) as the Roman Republic. The development of substantive legal principles demonstrates a similar tendency, with a vertical interplay between domestic and international orders and a horizontal borrowing of principles and approaches. The principle of proportionality is a good example of a principle that moves between the international and domestic legal orders, and across domestic constitutional boundaries.

Finally, the interplay between international and domestic constitutional principles governing emergency powers can be seen in the aftermath of the 9/11 attacks on the United States and the interplay between an 'international state of emergency' (Jayasuriya), international human rights law, and the domestic constitutional order. In response to the 9/11 attacks, the Security Council of the United Nations adopted Resolution 1373,[28] and subsequent resolutions that mandated counter-terrorism legislation and enhanced the UN sanctions regime (initiated by Resolution 1267[29]) by compelling member states to restrict the movement and freeze the assets of suspected terrorists (see Roach 2011, 21–76). These developments at the international level acknowledged the need for states to complement international cooperation by taking measures to prevent and suppress terrorism financing, leading to the development of a sophisticated counter-terrorism financing regime co-administered by global governance bodies such as the Financial Action Task Force, which influence domestic governments and financial institutions by developing 'soft law' standards and principles, and publicly monitoring compliance with them.

25 This decision marked a departure from its deferential approach in the World War II case, *Liversidge v Anderson*, [1942] AC 206 (HL).
26 [1978] ECHR 1.
27 *A and others v United Kingdom*, Application No. 3455/05 (19 February 2009), para 190.
28 SC Res 1373, UN Doc S/RES/1373 (28 September 2001)
29 SC Res 1267, UN Doc S/RES/1267 (15 October 2009).

At the same time, the interplay between this global counter-terrorism regime and domestic and regional legal orders is evident from the attempt by domestic constitutional courts and regional bodies to remedy the procedural defects of the UN sanctions regime. For example, the decision of the European Court of Justice in *Kadi and Al-Barakaat v Council of the European Union*,[30] which found the direct implementation of the UN sanctions blacklist in the European Union to be contrary to fundamental human rights in the absence of procedural safeguards for individuals named on the list, along with similar domestic constitutional decisions in Canada and the United Kingdom, collectively exposed flaws in the UN sanction regime. The Security Council sought to remedy these flaws by reforming its de-listing procedures.[31] This example demonstrates the complex interplay among different legal orders in the development and refinement of an international 'emergency powers' regime, an interplay that raises important questions about the nature of the legal order beyond the state in the context of a supranational emergency.

7.6 Conclusion

This chapter opened with the claim that emergency powers raise fundamental issues about law and constitutionalism. We can now discern several reasons why this is so. For one, the invocation of emergency powers throws into question the normative principles governing state conduct as well as the usual relationship among the branches of government; as power is concentrated into one branch of government, typically the executive, the role of the other branches in checking that power comes under stress. More fundamentally, the invocation of emergency powers throws into question the role of law itself in limiting state power. The concentration of power in a particular branch or agency of the government is an important test—perhaps even the ultimate 'litmus' test—of the depth of a society's commitment to the goal of moderating state power through law; but it also invites a closer examination of the informal, social, and political mechanisms that might complement or compete with formal constitutional mechanisms in limiting power in times of emergency. And finally, emergency powers give rise to fundamental questions of constitutional design by exposing the sheer diversity of mechanisms, principles, and practices that constitutions and constitutional actors employ in confronting these issues.

This diversity leads to a final point concerning comparative constitutional methodology. We have chosen in this chapter to draw on a wide range of examples, from liberal democracies with a stable legal system and a developed legal infrastructure to post-conflict states struggling to establish stable, effective institutions to deliver basic public goods, sometimes in the face of residual political violence. From the experience of emergency powers in such diverse settings, common themes might be identified at a high level of generality, but prescription becomes more tenuous. Yet here, in the extreme circumstances that trigger the exercise of emergency powers, we might find the aspiration of constitutional government in its basic aspirational form—as it seeks to subordinate sheer political power to a core set of limiting principles, formal or informal, but appropriate to the particular social, political, and historical context, that can be effectively enforced.

30 (3 September 2008), C-402/05 P & 415/15 P.
31 SC Res 1904, UN Doc S/RES/1904 (17 December 2009).

References

Ackerman, B (2004). 'The Emergency Constitution', 113 *Yale Law Journal* 1029–91.

Allain, J (2005). 'Derogation from the European Convention of Human Rights in the light of the "Other Obligations under International Law"', 11 *European Human Rights Law Review* 480.

Chen, A (2010). 'Emergency Powers, Constitutionalism and Legal Transplants: The East Asia Experience,' in Ramraj, VV & Thiruvengadam, A (eds), *Emergency Powers in Asia* (Cambridge: CUP), 56–88.

Chen, AHY (2004). *An Introduction to the Legal System of the People's Republic of China*, 3rd edn (Hong Kong: LexisNexis).

Cole, D (2004). 'The Priority of Morality: The Emergency Constitution's Blind Spot', 113 *Yale Law Journal* 1753.

deLisle, J (2010). 'States of Exception in an Exceptional State: Emergency Powers Law in China' in Ramraj, VV & Thiruvengadam, A (eds), *Emergency Powers in Asia* (Cambridge: CUP), 342–90.

Dyzenhaus, D (2006). *The Constitution of Law: Legality in a Time of Emergency* (Cambridge: CUP).

Eoseewong, N (2003). 'The Thai Cultural Constitution' (Baker C, trans), *Kyoto Review of Southeast Asia* 3 (March).

Ferejohn, J & Pasquino, P (2004). 'The Law of the Exception: A Typology of Emergency Powers', 2 *International Journal of Constitutional Law* 210.

Ginsburg, T (2009). 'Constitutional Afterlife: The Continuing Impact of Thailand's Postpolitical Constitution', 7 *International Journal of Constitutional Law* 83.

Gross, O (1998). 'Once More Unto the Breach: The Systemic Failure of Applying the European Convention on Human Rights to Entrenched Emergencies', 23 *Yale Journal of International Law* 437.

—— (2003). 'Chaos and Rules: Should Responses to Violent Crises Always be Constitutional?' 112 *Yale Law Journal* 1011.

Hallaq, W (2009). *An Introduction to Islamic Law* (Cambridge: CUP).

Jalal, A (1995). *Democracy and Authoritarianism in South Asia* (Cambridge University Press).

Jayasuriya, K (2008). 'The Struggle over Legality in the Midnight Hour: Governing the International State of Emergency' in Ramraj, VV (ed), *Emergencies and the Limits of Legality* (Cambridge: Cambridge University Press), 360–84.

Kostal, RW (2005). *A Jurisprudence of Power: Victorian Empire and the Rule of Law* (Oxford: Oxford University Press).

Mattei, U (1997). 'Three Patterns of Law: Taxonomy and Change in the World's Legal Systems', 45 *American Journal of Comparative Law* 5.

Negretto, GL & Aguilar Rivera, JA (2000). 'Liberalism and Emergency Powers in Latin America: Reflections on Carl Schmitt and the Theory of Constitutional Dictatorship', 21 *Cardozo Law Rev* 1797.

Rizvi, H-A (2000). *Military, State and Society in Pakistan* (Macmillan Press).

Roach, K (2011). *The 9/11 Effect: Comparative Counter-Terrorism* (New York: CUP).

Rossiter, CL (2002). *Constitutional Dictatorship: Crisis Government in Modern Democracies* (New Brunswick: Transaction Publishers).

Scheuerman, W (2006). 'Emergency Powers and the Rule of Law After 9/11', 14 *Journal of Political Philosophy* 61.

Schmitt, C (1922). Political Theology (trans. George Schwab, revised 1934) (University of Chicago Press).

Siddiqa, A (2007). *Military Inc., Inside Pakistan's Military Economy* (UK: Pluto Press).

Townshend, C (1982). 'Martial Law: Legal and Administrative Problems of Civil Emergency in Britain and the Empire, 1800–1940', 25(1) *The Historical Journal* 167–95.

Tushnet, M (2006–2007). 'The Political Constitution of Emergency Powers: Some Lessons from Hamdan', 91 *Minn L Rev* 1451.

Additional reading

Fitzpatrick, J (1994). *Human Rights in Crisis: The International System for Protecting Rights During States of Emergency* (Philadelphia: University of Pennsylvania Press).

Gross, O & Ní Aoláin, F (2006). *Law in Times of Crisis: Emergency Powers in Theory and Practice* (Cambridge: Cambridge University Press).

Ramraj, VV (ed) (2008). *Emergencies and the Limits of Legality* (Cambridge: Cambridge University Press).

8

The judiciary and constitutional review

Albert HY Chen and Miguel Poiares Maduro*

How can we ensure that a written constitution's promises will be translated into reality? There is a world of difference between a paper constitution that is merely nominal or semantic (Loewenstein, 147–53), and a normative constitution that constrains and regulates the exercise of political power and secures the enjoyment of human rights. The challenge is one of institutional design: What kind of political and legal structures should be put in place to ensure that a constitution's provisions will be put into practice? Constitutional rules might be embedded in political practice by the symbolic power of constitutional rules in shaping political discourse or by institutional competition and countervailing powers, both of which prevent breaches of constitutional provisions. Sometimes, though, the constitution may require effective sanctions for such breaches.

Modern constitutional law has developed various means of 'controls of constitutionality' to supervise and guarantee the effective implementation of constitutional rules. Cappelletti (1971) draws a distinction between political control[1] and judicial control. Judicial control of constitutionality, also known as constitutional judicial review, is the review by a court of the constitutionality of legislation enacted by parliament. This has become a dominant feature of modern constitutionalism, although it has not always been a necessary feature of constitutionalism. In some constitutional cultures, political constitutionalism is still dominant.[2]

In contemporary constitutionalism, two well-known models of constitutional judicial review exist: the American model of 'decentralised' review by ordinary courts, and the continental European model of 'centralised' review by a specialised constitutional court. There also exist mixed or hybrid systems that contain features of both these models. Systems of constitutional judicial review also differ in terms of the extent to which the system provides for a stronger or weaker form of judicial review.

---

* The authors' names here are in alphabetical order.
1 Political control is exercised by political or non-judicial organs.
2 For recent defences of political constitutionalism, see, e.g. Tushnet; Bellamy. Tushnet calls his version 'populist constitutionalism'.

The US model of constitutional judicial review is usually traced back to *Marbury v Madison*,[3] although there is a close relationship between the American system and British colonial constitutional law. Chief Justice Marshall pointed out in the *Marbury* case that the power of the legislature is limited by the constitution established by the people; any law made by the legislature that is repugnant to the constitution is void; and it is the power and responsibility of the court to determine the applicable legal norm where there is a conflict between a statute and the constitution. In the US system, every court has the power to determine whether a statutory provision is unconstitutional and therefore void. Standing at the apex of the hierarchy of courts, the US Supreme Court is the final court of appeal in deciding whether any statutory provision is inconsistent with the constitution.

Britain does not have a written constitution, and there is therefore no practice of constitutional judicial review.[4] Colonies in the British Empire had written constitutions enacted by the Crown or Parliament in Britain. Colonial courts had the power, under the colonial constitution, to review whether any provision in an enactment of the colonial legislature was *ultra vires* and therefore void. This tradition was inherited by Commonwealth countries such as Canada and Australia. The written constitutions of both Canada and Australia provide for a federal system characterised by a constitutionally entrenched division of power between the federal government and the provincial or state governments. Constitutional judicial review in these jurisdictions was mainly concerned with the enforcement of this federal division of power, until Canada in 1982 enacted, by way of constitutional amendment, the Canadian Charter of Rights and Freedoms, which inaugurated in Canada the era of constitutional judicial review in the human rights domain. Constitutional judicial review by ordinary courts is also practised to varying extents in newly independent countries that were formerly parts of the British Empire, such as India, Pakistan, Bangladesh, Sri Lanka, and some other common law countries in Asia and Africa, such as Malaysia and Kenya.

The European model of constitutional judicial review by a specialised constitutional court can be traced back to the Austrian Constitution of 1920, which, under the influence of Hans Kelsen's jurisprudence, established a constitutional court (Cappelletti 1971, 46–47, 71–72). According to Kelsen's theory of the hierarchy of legal norms, the constitution stands at the foundational level; the validity of all legal norms is ultimately derived from it. Kelsen proposed the creation of a constitutional court that (unlike the ordinary courts) has jurisdiction to determine whether any legal norm is consistent with the constitution. In his view, the constitutional court is the complement to the legislature; it performs a political and legislative function—that of negative legislation, or nullification of an unconstitutional norm. In Kelsen's theory, such constitutional judicial review was limited to dealing with inconsistencies between constitutional norms—particularly norms governing the division of power between various state organs—and other lower-level legal norms; it was not concerned with the protection of human rights.[5]

---

3 1 Cranch 137 (1803).
4 However, under the law of the European Communities (now the European Union), British courts (if necessary, on the basis of interpretations of EU law provided by the European Court of Justice) may review and invalidate UK law that is inconsistent with applicable EU law. Moreover, under the European Convention on Human Rights, the European Court of Human Rights may review the compatibility of UK law with the Convention. After the enactment by the British Parliament of the Human Rights Act 1998, the highest courts in the UK may also review the compatibility of UK law with the Convention (as incorporated into the Act), though they may not invalidate such incompatible law.
5 See generally Kelsen 1942; Kelsen 1961.

Constitutional review was also established in Czechoslovakia in 1920, in Liechtenstein in 1921, and in Spain in 1931.[6] In Ireland, the 1937 Constitution expressly provided for judicial review of legislation.[7] The Austrian constitutional court epitomised the 'archetypal form' (Cappelletti 1971, 69) of the kind of constitutional judicial review that is (a) centralised, (b) abstract (i.e. review of a law's constitutionality not in the context of the facts and circumstances of any concrete case litigated before a court) rather than concrete review (as in the American system or the systems in former British colonies, under which the court reviews the constitutionality of a law only where the application of that law is relevant to a case litigated before the court), and (c) review *principaliter* (i.e. review in a legal action where the principal or only issue is the constitutionality of a law) rather than review *incidenter* (as in the US system or the systems in former British colonies, where the review is only incidental to the making of a judicial decision as to which party wins the case) (Cappelletti 1971, 69). In the Austrian system that existed in 1920–1929, the constitutional court conducted only abstract review of laws in actions initiated by other governmental organs for the purpose of such review. The system was modified by the constitutional amendment of 1929, under which the supreme court and central administrative court acquired the right to refer the question of a law's constitutionality to the constitutional court when such a question arose in cases being tried by them (Cappelletti 1971, 72–74). An element of concrete review or review *incidenter* was thereby introduced into the Austrian system.

Before the Second World War, ordinary courts in Germany and France made some attempts to practise the American system of constitutional review but did not succeed (Favoreu, 43; Jackson & Tushnet, 527–28). However, the influence of the US system of constitutional review was considerable in Latin America. Brewer-Carías pointed out that there is no necessary connection between a legal system based on the common law and the US system of decentralized constitutional review[8]; nor is there a necessary connection between a civil law-based legal system and the Austrian model of centralised review. Some civil law countries in Latin America—including Mexico, Argentina, and Brazil—have adopted the American system of constitutional review (Brewer-Carías, 128). At the same time, a hybrid system of constitutional judicial review, in which 'the ordinary courts may have power to refuse to apply an unconstitutional law, but only a single court has the power to declare a law invalid' (Jackson & Tushnet, 466), evolved in the course of the nineteenth century in some Latin American countries, including Venezuela and Columbia (Brewer-Carías, 128, 130). By the early twenty-first century, the Supreme Court in 10 Latin American countries has the power to declare a law unconstitutional and to annul it; five of these 10 countries have a special constitutional chamber in the Supreme Court.[9] In six other Latin American countries, the power of constitutional review is exercised by a specialised

---

6 Ferreres Comella 2009, 3.

7 Koopmans 2003, 42.

8 Brewer-Carías (1989, 186–87) provides the following examples of common law countries with a centralised form of constitutional review by a single court: Papua New Guinea, Uganda (under its 1966 Constitution), and Ghana (under its Constitutions of 1960, 1969, and 1979). He draws three conclusions from his comparative study (at 188): 'first, the concentrated system of judicial review can only exist when it is established *expressis verbis* in a Constitution, ... second, the concentrated system of judicial review is compatible with any legal system, whether common law or Roman law legal systems; third, the concentrated system of judicial review does not imply the attribution of the functions of constitutional justice to a special Constitutional Court, Tribunal or Council ... It may also exist when constitutional justice functions are attributed to the existing Supreme Court of the country ...'

9 Jackson & Tushnet, 493; Ferreres Comella, 5.

constitutional court.[10] For example, since the 1970s, constitutional courts or 'constitutional guarantee tribunals' have been established in Chile, Ecuador, and Peru.[11] In Argentina and Brazil, a lower court's decision may be brought before the Supreme Court for review by an 'extraordinary recourse of unconstitutionality' (Brewer-Carías, 129).

After the Second World War, major developments in constitutional judicial review occurred in Europe. These developments may be understood in the context of the post-War international movement to enhance the protection of human rights, including the adoption by the United Nations of the Universal Declaration of Human Rights in 1948, and the signature of the European Convention on Human Rights and Fundamental Freedoms in 1950. Both the 1949 Basic Law of West Germany and the new 1947 Constitution of Italy provide for the establishment of constitutional courts, which started to operate in these countries in 1951 and 1956 respectively. In France, the 1958 Constitution of the Fifth Republic provides for a constitutional council. Constitutional courts were established in Spain and Portugal in 1978 and 1982, respectively, after their transition to democracy. Poland also established a constitutional court in 1985. Another wave of founding of constitutional courts followed the collapse of Communism in the former Soviet Union and eastern Europe. Since the early 1990s, constitutional courts have been established in most of the new democracies in Russia, and eastern and central Europe. By the early twenty-first century, constitutional courts exist in 18 of the 27 member states of the European Union, while American-style constitutional judicial review exists in Denmark, Sweden, Finland,[12] and Switzerland. Ireland, Portugal, Greece, Cyprus, and Estonia have hybrid systems of constitutional review (Ferreres Comella, 154). The Netherlands and the United Kingdom are exceptional in the sense that they do not have a formal mechanism of constitutional review. Under the Human Rights Act 1998, UK courts may declare the incompatibility of statutory provisions with the European Convention on Human Rights, though they have no power to invalidate such provisions. Dutch courts may review whether legislation is inconsistent with the European Convention on Human Rights, and to strike down statutory provisions that are inconsistent (Koopmans, 44). EU law has also given to all courts in EU member states the power to set aside national legal provisions contrary to EU rules. This is akin to constitutional review and has served, in fact, to promote a system of decentralised constitutional review in EU member states.

From its European and American roots, constitutional judicial review has spread to all parts of the world, and is now clearly a global phenomenon. The institution of constitutional review by ordinary courts is widespread among common law jurisdictions, and has also been introduced in post-War Japan. At the same time, constitutional courts have been established all over the world. Examples of countries outside the European and American continents that have established constitutional courts include Turkey, Egypt, South Africa,[13]

---

10 They are Peru, Guatemala, Chile, Ecuador, Bolivia, and Colombia: see Ferreres Comella, 5; Jackson & Tushnet, 493.

11 Brewer-Carías, 190; Ferreres Comella, 5.

12 Finland has a tradition of *ex ante* review of the constitutionality of bills by the Parliament's Constitutional Law Committee. This committee consists only of Members of Parliament, but in its decision-making process it consults academic experts whose opinions are given considerable weight. In addition to this kind of constitutional review, the Finnish Constitution of 1999 also introduced a system of *ex post* review by courts in cases where 'the application of an Act of Parliament would be in manifest conflict with the Constitution'. See Lavapuro *et al.*

13 The South African Constitution of 1996 not only establishes a constitutional court but expressly provides that when interpreting the constitutional bill of rights, a court 'must consider international law' and 'may consider foreign law': see Article 39 of the Constitution.

Ethiopia,[14] Senegal,[15] Taiwan (Republic of China), Mongolia, South Korea, Cambodia,[16] Thailand, and Indonesia. It is no coincidence that some of these courts were established in the 1980s (in South Korea), 1990s (in Mongolia, South Africa, and Thailand), or the first decade of the twenty-first century (in Indonesia) at the time of the transition of their countries from authoritarianism to liberal constitutional democracy, which was also the case in European countries that have undergone such a transition. In the early twenty-first century, a well-developed system of constitutional review is now generally accepted as an essential or desirable feature of a liberal constitutional democracy.

Why did many European states and new democracies in other parts of the world choose to establish specialised constitutional courts instead of adopting US-style constitutional review by ordinary courts? In the case of the civil law jurisdictions in Continental Europe, factors that have favoured the option of having a constitutional court include the following[17]: (a) the traditional conception of separation of powers according to which the judiciary (of the ordinary courts) should not engage in the 'political' function of invalidating Acts of Parliament; (b) the absence of a doctrine of *stare decisis* (binding precedents) in civil law countries, which means that even if one court rules that a statute is unconstitutional, the ruling does not bind other courts; (c) judicial structure and procedure (such as the plurality of courts specializing in different kinds of litigation); and (d) the legal culture and training of judges of ordinary courts being such that, some fear, these courts may not be appropriate for performing the task of constitutional review. In the case of countries undergoing a transition from authoritarianism to democracy, existing judges 'would be unlikely to have either the training or the independence from prior regimes to function with legitimacy as constitutional adjudicators'; hence the more viable option is to establish a constitutional court staffed by 'a small number of respected and untainted jurists' (Jackson & Tushnet, 468).

Constitutional courts are often given additional functions other than the review of the constitutionality of laws, such as supervising elections and referenda, determining the legality of political parties, or enforcing criminal law against senior officials (Ferreres Comella, 6). The German case provides a well-known example of the operation of a constitutional court. The Federal Constitutional Court (Bundesverfassungsgericht, or BVerG), originally of West Germany, and subsequently of the united Germany (after 1990),[18] consists of 16 judges divided into two chambers or senates. Half of the judges are elected by the Bundestag (Federal Parliament), and the other half by the Bundesrat (Council of Constituent States).[19] The types of cases over which the court has jurisdiction include, among others, (a) abstract review (upon

---

14 In Ethiopia, the Council of Constitutional Inquiry (CCI) established by the 1994 Constitution is a quasi-constitutional court. This constitution vests the power of constitutional review and interpretation in the second chamber of Ethiopia's Parliament, known as the House of the Federation, which in exercising this power acts on the (non-binding) advice of the CCI, which consists of the president and vice-president of the Supreme Court, six legal experts and three members of the House of the Federation. See Takele Soboka Bulto.

15 Senegal has a French-style constitutional council. See below on the French Conseil Constitutionnel.

16 Cambodia has a French-style constitutional council that also has some functions in *ex post* concrete review: see Menzel, 55–57.

17 Cappelletti 1971, 54–66; Jackson & Tushnet 467–68.

18 See generally Kommers.

19 See the Basic Law, Art. 94, which also provides that the court 'shall consist of federal judges and other members'. At least six of the 16 judges of the court must have served as federal judges. In practice, law professors constitute the largest group of appointees to the court, which is also the case in the Italian and Spanish Constitutional Courts. See generally Stone Sweet, 48.

the request of certain governmental actors, such as the federal government, a state government, or one-third of the members of the Bundestag); (b) concrete review, where other courts may, in the course of hearing cases, refer to the Constitutional Court a question regarding whether a statutory provision is unconstitutional; and (c) constitutional complaints (Verfassungsbeschwerde) by persons who allege that their basic rights have been violated by governmental actions, including administrative actions and judicial decisions. In practice, most of the cases dealt with by the Court arose from constitutional complaints, and most such complaints were against decisions of other courts (Jackson & Tushnet, 529–30). Kommers suggests that the institution of constitutional complaints has contributed to the high standing of the Constitutional Court in the eyes of members of the public, and to the 'rising constitutional consciousness among Germans generally' (Kommers, 28).

The model of the German Constitutional Court has much in common with that of other European states, such as the Italian and Spanish Constitutional Courts (Favoreu, 52–54). In France, constitutional judicial review has traditionally been much more limited. Since the French Revolution, the conception of legislation (as expressing the 'general will') and the supremacy of Parliament was such that courts did not have any power to strike down laws enacted by Parliament. The 1958 Constitution of the Fifth Republic established for the first time a constitutional council (Conseil Constitutionnel), with the role mainly of protecting the boundaries between the Parliament and the executive. The council was given the power to review the constitutionality of bills adopted by Parliament before the bills came into effect as laws. This kind of review may be characterised as 'preventive' (preventing an unconstitutional law from coming into force) or *'a priori'* review (before the formal promulgation of a law) (Ferreres Comella, 7). The role of the constitutional council expanded significantly since the council's landmark decision in 1971 in the case of *Liberté d'Association*, which *de facto* 'incorporated' into the Constitution the French Declaration of the Rights of Man and of the Citizen (of the year 1789), the Preamble to the 1946 Constitution, or 'the fundamental principles recognized by the laws of the Republic'. Since 1971, therefore, the constitutional council has used its power not only to maintain the boundary between the powers of legislative and executive organs but also to protect human rights. A constitutional reform in 1974 further expanded the council's role by empowering 60 members of either chamber of Parliament to activate the council's review jurisdiction. Almost every controversial bill is now referred to the council for review (Morton, 90–92). The council's power of review was confined to abstract preventive review until a constitutional amendment of 2008 introduced concrete review into the French system, by establishing a system of judicial referral subject to a filtering process involving the two highest courts.

There is, therefore, an increased degree of convergence in Europe with regard to the forms of constitutional judicial review and the roles attributed to constitutional courts. Some have identified a similar, albeit slower and more limited, trend towards convergence between the European and American models of constitutional review (Cappelletti 1971; Favoreu 1990). As stated above, one factor contributing to this trend is the empowerment by EU law of lower courts to review the validity of national laws in light of EU rules.

In addition to the distinction between US-style and European-style review, another distinction is that between what can be called a strong form of constitutional judicial review and a weak form. This distinction is based on the relative powers of, and relationship between, the court and the Parliament. Strong constitutional judicial review may be said to exist where the court's determination on constitutionality is final and conclusive, and is binding on all persons and organs until and unless the court overrules itself in another case, or a constitutional amendment is enacted that alters the constitutional rule on which the court's original decision was based. Strong constitutional judicial review exists in both the USA and Germany, although they practise decentralised and centralised review respectively.

Weak constitutional judicial review exists where the court's determination that a particular law is unconstitutional and invalid can be superseded or overridden by a subsequent legislative act (not a constitutional amendment) that re-affirms this law by a special majority or even just a simple majority. The most well-known example of this form is Canada under its 1982 Constitution, which provides for an 'override' mechanism[20]: Parliament may (by a simple majority) validate a statute even if it is inconsistent with certain provisions of the Canadian Charter of Rights and Freedoms as interpreted by the court. Such validation automatically expires after five years unless it is extended. This 'override' mechanism is not, however, applicable to certain Charter rights considered essential to the democratic process.

The system introduced in the UK by the Human Rights Act (HRA) 1998 may be regarded as a form of constitutional judicial review that is even weaker than the Canadian review. A British court may only declare provisions in an Act of Parliament to be inconsistent with the HRA (and the European Convention on Human Rights) but has no power to invalidate the provisions. It will then be up to Parliament to decide whether, and if so how, the former Act is to be amended. 'Preventive' or '*a priori*' review, and 'consultative' review (Cappelletti 1971, 2),[21] may also be regarded as weak forms of constitutional judicial review. In practice, however, in some of these regimes of formal weak review, the political culture has developed a deference towards judicial judgments that empowers the judiciary more than in some regimes with formal strong review.

The strongest form of constitutional judicial review may be said to exist where the court has—or has successfully claimed—the power to determine, in the final analysis, whether a constitutional amendment itself is constitutional and valid. For example, in the German Basic Law, the 'eternity clause' (Article 79(3)) prohibits constitutional amendments of certain core principles of the Basic Law. The constitutional court is the ultimate authority for determining whether a constitutional amendment is valid.[22] In India, the Supreme Court has, in the famous *Kesavananda Bharati* case (in 1973) and subsequent cases, enunciated a doctrine that the 'basic structure' of the constitution may not be validly amended (Krishnaswamy 2009; Ramachandran 2000). The constitutional court in Taiwan adopted a similar approach in 2000.[23]

Constitutional judicial review in most of its forms involves the court's invalidation of provisions in legislative Acts on the ground that the provisions are unconstitutional. Insofar as the court consists of unelected judges whereas Parliament consists of the elected representatives of the people, the institution of constitutional judicial review may appear undemocratic or counter-majoritarian. Its legitimacy has thus been questioned from time to time (Bickel 1986). A long-standing debate has taken place on what is the proper role of courts in constitutional review. The usual focus of this debate is on the methods of interpretation to be adopted by courts (Garcìa Belaunde, 3421 ff.), but the discussion is linked to broader normative preferences regarding the role of courts in shaping political and social life, and the proper balance of power between the judiciary and the political process in a democratic political community.

20 Canada Constitution Act 1982, s. 33. See Dorsen, 152.
21 Consultative review refers to the advisory or reference jurisdiction of the supreme court—upon request by the government—to deliver an advisory opinion, which is not binding, on a constitutional question. Such a system exists in Canada and India.
22 In Portugal, which has a similar clause, a long discussion has taken place on the extent to which the clause itself could be amended. See Miranda.
23 The Council of Grand Justices' Interpretation No. 499 (March 2000): see www.judicial.gov.tw/constitutionalcourt. See also Yeh, 59.

The peculiar nature of constitutional interpretation poses a major problem of method. Courts employ a variety of methods of interpretation: text, legislative history, context, purpose or telos are among those most used in judicial decisions.[24] It is through this arsenal of professional techniques that judges construct the legal arguments by which they justify their judicial decisions. This recourse to the 'language' of a particular community of judicial discourse[25] is a usual step taken by courts in the objectivisation of the process of interpretation by reference to the particular community where it takes place (Fiss, 739–63). However, such language can be used to construct rather different legal arguments. The nature of the law and its changing context of application is such that there is often a normative gap between the text and the social reality in which courts are called upon to intervene.

We can identify at least three different ways of dealing with the role of courts in addressing such normative gaps. Often presented as theories of constitutional interpretation or constitutional justice, they express, above all, different institutional preferences regarding the role to be played by courts and other institutional alternatives[26] in enforcing the constitution. First, one can simply assume that the normative gap inherent in the process of interpretation ought to be filled by courts. This is legitimated by the institutional authority of courts. Interpretation renders law objective by reason of the meaning attributed to particular norms by courts; it is the courts' interpretative authority that renders law objective and not vice versa. To a certain extent, this is the never-quite-articulated theory of interpretation and constitutional justice that has largely dominated the practice of constitutional review in Europe. Any normative gap of constitutional interpretation is construed as a delegation to courts. Constitutional review is the process through which courts exercise their exclusive authority of interpretation. This is an approach that emphasises the power of courts at the expense of the political process in giving meaning to constitutional text.

This constitutional practice is theorised in rather different ways by some versions of legal positivism,[27] legal realism,[28] and critical legal studies.[29] They all recognise, at either a normative or empirical level, that courts do have the authority to fill the normative gaps of the constitution. What varies between them is that for some, such authority derives from the construction of the legal system as complete and fully insulated from outside arguments, in which case the existence of such normative gaps is itself denied, while for others, such authority is a given of the institutional position that courts have acquired in a particular legal system. This is not to imply that under such theories, there are no constraints imposed on courts, but what they have in common is the conception of those constraints as external to the process of legal interpretation.[30] They all empower courts at the expense of the political process.

---

24 Coherently with the historical classification by Savigny (1840). For a modern (and more articulate) treatment, see Bobbitt.

25 It is a language that also varies depending on the constitutional culture that dominates a particular political community: see Kahn.

26 On comparative institutional analysis, see Komesar 1994.

27 See Kelsen 1930–31; Raz, 180 ff. and the reflections of Garlicki & Zakrzewski, 31 and Waluchow.

28 See e.g. Holmes; Ross, 108 ff.; Llewellyn; and the historical reviews in Peces-Barba Martìnez; and Tamanaha.

29 See e.g. Kennedy 1973, and the broad considerations in Kennedy 1997.

30 For an example, see Troper 1978, 287–302 (and particularly at 293–95) and Troper 1990, 31–48, departing from a notion of interpretation as an act of will and not knowledge, in a way very similar to Fish.

Such approaches to constitutional review are challenged because they keep outside of judicial reasoning other relevant constitutional dimensions and arguments in determining the appropriate levels and forms of judicial review. That there are other relevant dimensions of constitutional interpretation, in particular those concerning its relationship with the political process, is made obvious by the fact that all courts end up developing mechanisms of self-restraint.[31] They do not come in the form of theories of judicial deference but, instead, appear in the form of procedural filters,[32] narrowly tailored decisions or limitations of the effects of judicial decisions.[33] Sometimes, the resistance to the internalisation and articulation of the other dimensions of constitutional interpretation in judicial reasoning leads to apparently inconsistent judicial outcomes. This is a simple product of the fact that variations in the degree of judicial scrutiny remain unarticulated in the case law.

A second approach to constitutional review argues that the normative gaps identified in constitutional interpretation ought to be filled by the political process. The most usual version of this is to be found in some of those arguing for a formal interpretation of the law. Unlike the versions of legal formalism associated with legal positivism that believe that existing constitutional rules provide courts with all the answers, this kind of formalism recognises that rules do not provide all the answers and that, precisely because this is so, courts must develop methods of interpretation narrowing their own discretion and protecting that of the political process. We can define this approach as formal constructivism. These theories adopt formal methods of interpretation even to artificially govern areas that could be considered as involving substantive judicial discretion in light of the legal text. The argument is that formalism is what best constrains courts. These theories require, in practice, an objective meaning of the norm that is static in time. If the text itself is not clear, then such meaning is to be found in the historical context of its enactment,[34] the intent of the legislator,[35] a holistic interpretation of the language employed (Amar), a rule-bound combination of plain meaning and agency deference (Vermeule), a direct and popular decoding,[36] or any other purportedly objective and formal meaning (external to the interpreter's preferences). This appears to be the currently dominant conception of constitutional review in the United States.[37]

These theories also limit the scope of arguments to be employed by courts. They close the constitution by appealing to formal arguments; thus they are in tension with the universalist claims usually associated with constitutionalism. Constitutional norms derive their superior authority from their purporting to reflect universal principles intended to bound us under a kind of prospective veil of ignorance (Rubenfeld, 188). Agreement on such general principles is meant to be an agreement on the universal potential of such principles abstracting from their concrete historical meaning. This openness of constitutional law should not be artificially closed. This discussion highlights the fundamental challenge to formal constructivist theories: in light of the openness of constitutional law, why should the political process always be presumed to be superior to the judicial process in giving meaning to substantive areas of discretion in constitutional law?

---

31 See Komesar 2001.
32 Bickel 1961, 75. See also Bickel 1986, 111 ff.
33 Sunstein.
34 I.e. in the 'original meaning' of the norm: see Scalia 1989; Barnett. For a recent review on the subject, see Balkin.
35 See historically Crosskey; Berger; and Bork.
36 See Tushnet 1999, Kramer 2004.
37 Despite, of course, the great difference between the authors just considered.

This question is equally valid for another theory aimed at limiting the judicial role so as to empower the political process: judicial minimalism as argued by Cass Sunstein (1999). Courts should show deference to the political process by narrowing the scope and depth of their judicial decisions. They should decide only issues specific to the cases actually before them, without laying down broad rules for future application. As Chief Justice Roberts of the US Supreme Court put it, 'If it is not necessary to decide more to dispose of a case, in my view it is necessary not to decide more.'[38] Judicial minimalism may also be a simple product of the constraints of deliberation. Particularly in courts without dissents, it is usual for judges to agree on minimalist decisions, keeping disagreement on questions of principle while agreeing on how to resolve the particular case.

These approaches prefer the meaning of the constitution to be determined by the political process and not courts. Their popularity in the United States is understandable in view of the democratic concerns raised by constitutional review historically, since it was introduced by the Supreme Court in the absence of any express constitutional provision to such effect (contrary to what came to be the case in most modern constitutions). But such a general presumption in favour of the political process in interpreting constitutions is itself a product of a systemic understanding of the constitution and the legal order[39]—one that must be justified.

The third approach to constitutional review entrusts courts with a specific constitutional mission, involving a particular normative goal that ought to guide them in interpreting and applying the constitution. Both the legitimacy and the role of courts in constitutional review are determined by a particular function entrusted to them by the constitution. Adopting this approach, some defend judicial review by explaining that it enables the values in natural law to be realised in a largely positivist legal system (Cappelletti 1971). Others identify constitutional justice with a set of constitutional values (in particular, human rights or human dignity) inherent in the constitutional document interpreted as a living one.[40] Others focus on a more procedural conception of the constitutional role of courts to secure the proper functioning of the democratic process by correcting representative malfunctions.[41] Challenges to these theories would highlight, instead, how courts themselves can be victims of institutional malfunctions (Komesar 1994 and 2001).

Constitutional courts themselves rarely engage in such debates or even in justifications of the different levels of judicial scrutiny that are often employed under the same constitutional rules. The most famous exception is in a footnote of a US Supreme Court opinion highlighting that certain discrete and insular minorities deserve additional protection by constitutional justice.[42] Even outside their written judicial opinions, it remains uncommon for constitutional judges to articulate any theory of constitutional interpretation or judicial review.[43]

The scholarly debate on constitutional justice does highlight a reality where courts and the political process (as well as other institutional alternatives) compete in giving meaning to

---

38 Chief Justice John G Roberts, Jr, Georgetown Law Center Commencement Address, 21 May 2006.
39 Paradoxically, departing from such systemic understanding is in contradiction with a formalist conception of interpretation.
40 Dworkin 1977, 131 ff; Dworkin 1985, 32 ff, 69–70; Strauss.
41 See, e.g. Ely.
42 See, e.g. the famous footnote 4 of Justice Stone's opinion in *United States v Carolene Products Co* (1938) 304 US 144.
43 For recent, well-known exceptions, see Scalia 1997; Posner 1990 and 2003; and also Zagrebelsky; Barak; Lorenzetti.

constitutions. The debate is mostly about the relative merits of these institutions in the pursuit of constitutional goals.[44] But that, after all, is both what explains the emergence of constitutional judicial review and the debates surrounding it.

References

Amar, AR (2005). *America's Constitution: A Biography* (New York, Random House).

Balkin, JM (2011). *Living Originalism* (Cambridge, Harvard University Press).

Barak, A (2006). *The Judge in a Democracy* (Princeton, Princeton University Press).

Barnett, RE (2004). *Restoring the Lost Constitution: The Presumption of Liberty* (Princeton, Princeton University Press).

Bellamy, R (2007). *Political Constitutionalism* (New York, Cambridge University Press).

Berger, R (1977). *Government by Judiciary: The Transformation of the Fourteenth Amendment* (Cambridge, Harvard University Press).

Bickel, AM (1961). 'The Supreme Court 1960 Term-Foreword: The Passive Virtues', *Harvard Law Review* 75: 40–79.

—— (1986). *The Least Dangerous Branch* (New Haven, Yale University Press, 2nd edn).

Bobbitt, P (1982). *Constitutional Fate: Theory of the Constitution* (New York, Oxford University Press).

Bork, RH (1990). *The Tempting of America: The Political Seduction of the Law* (New York, Free Press).

Brewer-Carías, AR (1989). *Judicial Review in Comparative Law* (Cambridge: CUP).

Bulto, TS (2011). 'Judicial Referral of Constitutional Disputes in Ethiopia: From Practice to Theory', *African Journal of International and Comparative Law* 19(1): 99–123.

Cappelletti, M (1971). *Judicial Review in the Contemporary World* (Indianapolis, Bobbs-Merrill).

Crosskey, WW (1953). *Politics and the Constitution in the History of the United States* (Chicago, University of Chicago Press, 2 vols).

Dorsen, N et al (2010). *Comparative Constitutionalism: Cases and Materials* (St Paul, West, 2nd edn).

Dworkin, R (1977). *Taking Rights Seriously* (Cambridge, Harvard University Press).

—— (1985). *A Matter of Principle* (Cambridge, Harvard University Press).

Ely, JH (1980). *Democracy and Distrust: a Theory of Judicial Review* (Cambridge, Harvard University Press).

Favoreu, L (1990). 'Constitutional Review in Europe', in Henkin, L & Rosenthal, AJ (eds), *Constitutionalism and Rights: The Influence of the United States Constitution Abroad* (New York: Columbia University Press), 38–62.

Ferreres Comella, V (2009). *Constitutional Courts and Democratic Values: A European Perspective* (New Haven, Yale University Press).

Fish, S (1989). *Doing What Comes Naturally – Change, Rhetoric, and the Practice of Theory in Literary and Legal Studies* (Durham and London, Duke University Press).

Fiss, O (1982). 'Objectivity and Interpretation', *Stanford Law Review* 34: 739–63.

Garcìa Belaunde, D (2003). 'La interpretaciòn constitucional como problema', in Ferrer-MacGregor, E (ed), *Derecho procesal constitucional* (México, Porrùa), 3419 ff.

Garlicki, L & Zakrzewski, W (1985). 'La protection juridictionnelle de la Constitution dans le monde contemporain', in *Annuaire International de Justice Constitutionelle*, 17 ff.

Holmes, OW Jr (1897). 'The Path of the Law' *Harvard Law Review* 10: 457–78.

Jackson, VC & Tushnet, M (2006). *Comparative Constitutional Law* (New York, Foundation Press).

Kahn, P (1999). *The Cultural Study of Law: Reconstructing Legal Scholarship* (Chicago: University of Chicago Press).

Kelsen, H (1931). 'Wer soll der Hüter der Verfassung sein?', *Die Justiz* 6: 576–628 (1930–1931), reprinted in Klecatsky, H et al (eds), *Die Wiener rechtstheoretische Schule. Schriften von Hans Kelsen, Adolf Merkl, Alfred Verdross* (Vienna, Europa-Verlag), vol. II, 1873–1922.

—— (1942). 'Judicial Review of Legislation: A Comparative Study of the Austrian and the American Constitution', *Journal of Politics* 4: 183–200.

—— (1961). *General Theory of Law and the State* (New York, Russell).

---

44 Komesar 1994 and 2001; Shapiro 1964 and 1981.

Kennedy, D (1973). 'Legal Formality', *Journal of Legal Studies* 2: 351–98.
—— (1997). *A Critique of Adjudication (Fin de Siècle)* (Cambridge, Harvard University Press).
Komesar, N (1994). *Imperfect Alternatives: Choosing Institutions in Law, Economics, and Public Policy* (Chicago, University of Chicago Press).
—— (2001). *Law's Limits: The Role of Courts, the Rule of Law and the Supply and Demand of Rights* (New York, Cambridge University Press).
Kommers, DP (1997). *The Constitutional Jurisprudence of the Federal Republic of Germany* (Durham: Duke University Press, 2nd edn).
Koopmans, T (2003). *Courts and Political Institutions: A Comparative View* (Cambridge: CUP).
Kramer, L (2004). *The People Themselves: Popular Constitutionalism and Judicial Review* (New York, Oxford University Press).
Krishnaswamy, S (2009). *Democracy and Constitutionalism in India: A Study of the Basic Structure Doctrine* (New Delhi, Oxford University Press).
Lavapuro, J, Ojanen, T and Scheinin, M (2011). 'Rights-based Constitutionalism in Finland and the Development of Pluralist Constitutional Review', *International Journal of Constitutional Law* 9: 505–31.
Llewellyn, KN (1962). *Jurisprudence. Realism in Theory and Practice* (Chicago, University of Chicago Press).
Loewenstein, K (1957). *Political Power and the Government Process* (Chicago, University of Chicago Press).
Lorenzetti, RL (2006). *Teoria De La Decision Judicial: Fundamentos De Derecho* (Buenos Aires, Rubinzal-Culzoni Editores).
Menzel, J (2008). 'Cambodia: From Civil War to a Constitution to Constitutionalism?' in Hill, C and Menzel, J (eds), *Constitutionalism in Southeast Asia* (Singapore, Konrad-Adenauer-Stiftung), Vol. 2, 37–67.
Miranda, J (2007). *Manual de Direito Constitucional, Tomo II* (Lisboa, Almedina, 6th edn).
Morton, FL (1988). 'Judicial Review in France: A Comparative Analysis', *American Journal of Comparative Law* 36: 89.
Peces-Barba Martìnez, G (1984). 'La creación judicial del Derecho desde la teoría del ordenamiento jurídico', *Rivista Trimestrale di Diritto Pubblico* 4: 1010–33.
Posner, R (1990). *The Problems of Jurisprudence* (Cambridge, Harvard University Press).
—— (2003). *Law, Pragmatism and Democracy* (Cambridge, Harvard University Press).
Ramachandran, R (2000). 'The Supreme Court and the Basic Structure Doctrine', in Kirpal, BN et al (eds), *Supreme But Not Infallible: Essays in Honour of the Supreme Court of India* (New Delhi, Oxford University Press), 107–33.
Raz, J (1979). *The Authority of Law: Essays on Law and Morality* (Oxford, Clarendon Press).
Ross, A (1959). *On Law and Justice* (Berkeley, University of California Press).
Rubenfeld, J (2001). *Freedom and Time – A Theory of Constitutional Self-Government* (New Haven and London, Yale University Press).
Savigny, FC (1840). *System des heutigen römischen Rechts, I* (Berlin).
Scalia, A (1989). 'Originalism: The Lesser Evil', *University of Cincinnati Law Review* 57: 849–65.
—— (1997). *A Matter of Interpretation: Federal Courts and the Law* (Princeton, Princeton University Press).
Shapiro, M (1964). *Law and Politics in the Supreme Court: New Approaches to Political Jurisprudence* (New York, Free Press of Glencoe).
—— (1981). *Courts: A Comparative and Political Analysis* (Chicago, University of Chicago Press).
Strauss, DA (2010). *The Living Constitution* (New York, Oxford University Press).
Sunstein, C (1999). *One Case at a Time: Judicial Minimalism on the Supreme Court* (Cambridge, Harvard University Press).
Stone Sweet, A (2000). *Governing with Judges: Constitutional Politics in Europe* (Oxford, Oxford University Press).
Tamanaha, B (2009). 'Understanding Legal Realism', *Texas Law Review* 87: 731–86.
Troper, M (1978). 'La motivation des décisions constitutionnelles', in Perelman, C & Foriers, P (eds), *La motivation des décisions de justice* (Bruxelles, Établissements Émile Bruylant), 287–302.
—— (1990). 'Justice constitutionelle et démocratie', *Revue francaise de Droit constitutionnel*, 1: 31–48.
Tushnet, M (1999). *Taking the Constitution Away from Courts* (Princeton, Princeton University Press).

Vermeule, A (2006). *Judging under Uncertainty – An Institutional Theory of Legal Interpretation* (Cambridge, Harvard University Press).

Waluchow, WJ (2007). *A Common Law Theory of Judicial Review: The Living Tree* (Cambridge: CUP).

Yeh, JR (2002). 'Constitutional Reform and Democratization in Taiwan, 1945–2000', in Chow, PCY (ed), *Taiwan's Modernization in Global Perspective* (Westport, Praeger), 47–77.

Zagrebelsky, G (2005). *Principî e voti. La Corte costituzionale e la politica* (Torino, Einaudi).

Additional reading

Bachof, O (1959). *Grundgesetz und Richtermacht* (Tübingen, Mohr Grundgesetz und Richtermacht).

Beatty, DM (2004). *The Ultimate Rule of Law* (Oxford: OUP).

Böckenförde, EW (1974). 'Grundrechtstheorie und Grundrechtsinterpretation', *Neue Juristische Wochenschrift*, 27: 1536–38.

Breyer, S (2005). *Active Liberty: Interpreting Our Democratic Constitution* (New York, Knopf).

Fallon, RH Jr (2008). 'The Core of an Uneasy Case for Judicial Review', *Harvard Law Review* 121: 1693–1736.

Fernandez Segado, F (2003). 'Reflexiones en torno a la interpretaciòn de la Constituciòn', in Ferrer-MacGregor, E (ed), *Derecho procesal constitucional* (México, Porrùa), 3343 ff.

Ginsburg, T (2003). *Judicial Review in New Democracies: Constitutional Cases in Asian Courts* (Cambridge: CUP).

Pech, L (2004). 'Rule of Law in France', in Peerenboom, R (ed), *Asian Discourses of Rule of Law* (London, Routledge), 79–112.

Stephenson, MC (2003). '"When the Devil Turns ...": The Political Foundations of Independent Judicial Review', *Journal of Legal Studies* 32: 59–89.

9

Justiciability

Mark Tushnet and Juan F González-Bertomeu

9.1 Introduction

A constitutional claim is justiciable when the appropriate court or courts will decide it on the merits. The term is more useful in its negative sense: cases or issues are nonjusticiable when courts will refrain from deciding them on the merits, asserting for various reasons that the cases or issues are not suitable for judicial resolution. The question of justiciability is bound up with the scope of constitutional review generally, and so with the sources and constitutional delimitations upon constitutional review.

Constitutional review can be acknowledged in the constitution's text, as in nearly every modern constitution, or can be implied from the constitution's structure, as in the United States. The language creating constitutional review can be more or less detailed, more or less ambiguous. What the constitution says about the scope of constitutional review will have implications for a system's approach to justiciability: a broad definition of constitutional review will fit well with a narrow or non-existent definition of nonjusticiability; conversely, a narrow definition of constitutional review will fit well with a broad definition of nonjusticiability. Further, the constitution's substance might have similar implications. The more detailed a constitution is in dealing with a particular subject, the less room there might be for constitutional review, and the greater the inclination to describe constitutional challenges to legislation dealing with that subject as nonjusticiable. Yet, a detailed constitutional provision limits the law-makers' discretion, and courts might be willing to find disputes over 'abuse of discretion' justiciable because they believe that the details provide them with clear guidance for resolving the controversy.

Consider here Article 10 of the Constitution of Costa Rica, which provides, '[a] special-ized Chamber of the Supreme Court of Justice shall declare, by the absolute majority vote of its members, the unconstitutionality of provisions of any nature and acts subject to Public Law.' Similarly, Article 93 of the German Basic Law lists a large number of bases for consti-tutional review, and uses the terms 'the formal or substantive compatibility of federal law or Land law with this Basic Law', and 'alleging that one of his basic rights … has been infringed.' These terms suggest rather strongly that Costa Rica's and Germany's constitutional traditions will be unreceptive to claims of nonjusticiability, and so it has proven, with the German

Constitutional Court ruling on the merits on such questions as whether the deployment of German armed forces in support of UN operations in Iraq required consent by the legislature.[1] The more parsimonious language of the US Constitution, which gives the national courts jurisdiction over 'cases and controversies' involving 'this Constitution,' has been used to generate a robust doctrine of justiciability, with the courts regularly rejecting constitutional challenges to US military involvement abroad.

The idea of nonjusticiability has its roots in the notion of prerogative power, which is a power unconstrained by law. Courts used to dismiss challenges to exercises of prerogative power, and came to attach the label 'nonjusticiable' to such dismissals. One way to interpret this notion of unconstrained power is that courts could just as easily have said that the challenges failed on the merits, because the actions were not contrary to law, there being no law to apply.

In the most general sense, constitutionalism is the idea that all public power must be constrained by law. For constitutionalists, there is always law to apply when someone challenges an exercise of public power as unconstitutional. Many constitutional systems thus reject the very idea of nonjusticiable constitutional challenges.

Some systems, though, retain that idea, classifying some constitutional challenges—sometimes involving national security and foreign affairs—as nonjusticiable. For example, in some constitutional systems such as Japan, statutes implementing validly ratified treaties can rarely be challenged on constitutional grounds (Ejima).

9.2 Justiciability and substantive law

These systems divide subject matters into two classes, the justiciable and the nonjusticiable. Two loose uses of the term 'justiciability' should be noted:

(1) Sometimes a constitutional challenge should fail because the constitution does not place the claimed limit on public power. So, for example, a court might call a challenge to a legislative decision to set tax rates at a low rather than a high rate as nonjusticiable, or a challenge to a ministerial decision not to submit legislation on a specific subject as nonjusticiable. The reason for these decisions is that there is no law to apply, and so the dismissals should be described as on the merits. But, importantly, whether a dismissal is proper will depend on the constitution's content. A constitution might place a government under a duty to introduce legislation promised in its election manifesto, for example, in which case the second claim described above would be justiciable.

(2) A related form of dismissal on the merits sometimes described in terms of justiciability occurs when the courts apply an extremely deferential standard of review in evaluating constitutional challenges to government action. If the constitution gives the government broad, though not completely unlimited, discretion on some subject—such as the substantive content of laws for social provision of material goods—constitutional challenges will rarely succeed insofar as the government acts within that scope of discretion, to the point where some might conclude mistakenly that the subjects are nonjusticiable. The correct conclusion is that the government's broad discretion is rarely abused. Yet, questions often arise regarding whether the constitution actually gives the government this scope of discretion and what the scope precisely consists of.

---

1 Bundesverfassungsgericht [German Constitutional Court], 2 BvE 1/03, 7 May 2008 reported in (2008) 121 BVerfGE 135 (AWACS II case).

Three cases posing closely related substantive questions illustrate the point. In the 1967 Asahi case,[2] the Supreme Court of Japan heard the claim of a tuberculosis patient who was seeking restoration of a monthly allowance he had been receiving from the administration and which had been interrupted after the patient's brother started sending him money in excess of the allowance's amount. The patient argued that the allowance amount, determined by the administration 11 years before litigation started, was insufficient to maintain the constitutional right to 'healthy, cultural, and minimum standard of living' (Art. 25). The Court held that this constitutional standard did not create any direct right but generated a duty on the state, and that the right only materialized through the provisions of the statute setting up the basis for the determination of allowances. It said that the concept of 'healthy, cultural and minimum standard of living' (reproduced in the statute) was both vague and relative, and could only be determined after taking into consideration systemic elements such as the development of the economy and the national culture. This is why the authority to do so was 'first vested in the discretionary power of the Minister of Health and Welfare, and [...] his decision [did] not directly produce an issue of illegality.' While the Court did not deny that it had power to review the Minister's decision, it created a very lenient standard. Only if the administration established extremely low standards or ignored the real standard of living would the state incur responsibility, something that, after a very brief analysis, the Court found did not happen in the case. Outside that extreme possibility, the issue was political (not legal), in the sense that 'such decision might produce an issue of propriety which might lead to a political debate about governmental responsibility.'

In the United States, *Dandridge v Williams*[3] held that a state program establishing a 'standard of need' for the protection of dependent children, and imposing a maximum monthly allowance per family without regard to family size or need, did not violate the Equal Protection Clause of the Fourteenth Amendment. It claimed that in the area of economics and social welfare, the state only had to demonstrate that the classification in the program has some 'reasonable basis,' and that it was not enough for the plaintiff to show that the classification was not 'made with mathematical nicety or [that] in practice it result[ed] in some inequality.' Writing for the Court, Justice Stewart said that the Equal Protection Clause does not give federal courts any power to dictate 'their views of what constitutes wise economic or social policy' to the states.

While the level of review chosen by both Courts in *Asahi* and *Dandridge* was similarly lenient, only the Japanese Constitution recognizes a social right, making the type of intervention 'in the area of economics and social welfare' that the US Court deemed as purely political a more directly constitutional one in the case of Japan. Unlike both *Asahi* and *Dandridge*, the German Constitutional Court devised a more stringent test in the recent Hartz IV case.[4] The Court was called upon to review a new social program enacted by parliament merging different forms of social assistance 'in the shape of a uniform, means-tested basic provision for employable persons and the persons living with them in a joint household'. It decided to strike down provisions of the program concerning the standard benefit for adults and children for failing to comply with the constitutional requirement to protect human dignity following from Article 1.1 of the Basic Law (*Grundgesetz*), in connection with Article 20.1, establishing

---

2 *Asahi v Japan* (1967) 21 MINSHŪ 5, 1043 (Supreme Court of Japan, 24 May 1967). See also Itoh & Beer.

3 397 US 471 (1970).

4 Bundesverfassungsgericht [German Constitutional Court], 1 BvL 1/09, 1 BvL 3/09, 1 BvL 4/09, 9 February 2010 reported in (2010) 125 BVerfGE 175 (Hartz IV case).

that the country is a democratic and social state. The Court said that these principles could not be ignored, although, similarly to *Asahi*, it was incumbent upon the legislature to both give it concrete shape and update it. The Court argued that the exact quantification of the subsistence minimum did not follow from the Basic Law, and that substantive review could only extend to ascertaining whether the benefits were manifestly insufficient.

Unlike *Asahi*, though, the Court said its mission was to review the procedural grounds on which the assessment of the benefits was made, to determine 'whether they do justice to the objective of the fundamental right.' For this, the Court devised a four-pronged method, by which it would determine whether the legislature had: (a) 'taken up and described the objective of ensuring an existence that is in line with human dignity'; (b) 'chosen a fundamentally suitable method of calculation for assessing the subsistence minimum'; (c) 'completely and correctly ascertained the necessary facts'; and (d) kept 'within the boundaries of what is justifiable within the chosen method and its structural principles in all stages of calculation, and with plausible figures.'

It is on these procedural grounds that portions of the statute were found in contradiction with the principle of human dignity, since, without providing any justification, parliament had employed a valid statistical method to ascertain some of the benefits but had abandoned it to establish others. The Court claimed, in particular, that the determination of the social allowance for children under the age of 14 was not based 'on any justifiable method', and added that parliament 'had not ascertained the specific need of a child in any way.'

These cases illustrate the connection between justiciability as a shorthand reference for a lenient standard of review and the extent to which a constitutional court is willing (or unwilling) to engage in interpretation to fill out constitutional provisions that are not defined in precise textual terms, and therefore between the idea of justiciability and judicial willingness to interpret the constitution 'creatively'.

9.3 Related concepts

An additional consideration is sometimes classed with justiciability. In some constitutional systems there are no or few limits on the subject matters that courts will review on the merits, but the courts will sometimes insist that the litigant presenting the claim be the 'right' litigant or the 'best' litigant available, or that the claim not be presented too early or too late. In the United States these doctrines are labeled 'standing,' 'ripeness,' and 'mootness,' and have been applied with varying rigor in different historical eras. Other systems such as India's grant broad 'public interest standing,' allowing non-governmental organizations to present constitutional claims, usually on the implicit theory that the beneficiaries of the asserted constitutional rights lack sufficient resources on their own to pursue constitutional litigation. Related, some constitutional systems authorize broad *jus tertii* standing, allowing a litigant who is adversely affected by some policy but does not suffer the kind of harm associated with a constitutional violation to challenge the policy on the ground that the policy is unconstitutional as applied to some other party not before the court. Systems of constitutional review that adhere strictly to the idea that every subordinate norm must be consistent with hierarchically superior norms tend to insist that the norms themselves be assessed to determine their consistency with the constitution, without concern about the factual circumstances in which the subordinate norms are applied. Such systems tend to minimize the scope of ripeness concerns, and treat standing as, at most, an instrumental doctrine aimed at providing the constitutional court with the best possible range of legal arguments. Constitutional systems that give their courts an advisory jurisdiction or allow constitutional review prior to a statute's effective date have no or extremely weak ideas of ripeness, but they may invoke concepts similar to mootness when they require that constitutional challenges be brought *only* before a statute takes effect. As in France before constitutional revisions in 2008, such a requirement can flow from express jurisdictional limitations on the constitutional court's power, yet such limitations are not conceptually strongly distinguishable from justiciability limitations inferred in other constitutional systems from the general structure of constitutional review.

9.4 Justiciability in the proper sense

In careful use, the term 'justiciability' should probably be reserved for cases in which the constitution does supply a legal rule constraining the exercise of government power, and yet the courts nonetheless refrain from disposing of claims that an exercise of such power violates the legal constraint on power.

Courts that find challenges nonjusticiable in this sense typically offer one of two types of argument for their position. In general terms the ideas are, first, that sometimes judicially manageable rules concretely implementing general constitutional norms are unavailable (or that the rules that the courts could implement impose too heavy a price on other constitutionally relevant values), and second, that sometimes legislatures and executive ministries require discretionary power to deal with important policy matters.

The first argument may be illustrated by the AWACS II case, where the German Constitutional Court said that legislative consent was needed for military deployments since 'the individual legal and factual circumstances indicate[d] that there [was] a concrete expectation that German soldiers [would] be involved in armed conflicts.'[5] This is hardly a standard that courts can reliably invoke, for military conditions change rapidly, sometimes making armed conflict more likely, sometimes less. Yet, another way to approach the decision is that nonjusticiability in this case would have meant authorizing the federal government to engage in military conflict in the absence of the legislative involvement that the Constitutional Court believed was required by the Basic Law.

As to the second argument, broad discretion is not necessarily incompatible with justiciability, as long as the courts use appropriately generous standards in reviewing constitutional challenges to policies of this sort. Consider again the claim that treaties and statutes implementing them should be immune from judicial oversight. Courts could address constitutional challenges to treaties by distinguishing between justiciable challenges to procedure and nonjusticiable ones to substance, or could use a generous standard of review that would invalidate treaties on substantive grounds only if they seriously compromise a core of truly fundamental rights.

A third area where the government often requires a broad scope of discretion, immune from relatively immediate judicial oversight, is that meant to address internal crises or emergencies. Cases in this area abound where courts defer to the government, because they think the government needs special powers to deal with crises and there are no manageable standards to decide, or fear its retaliation against them if they dared restrict those powers. Sometimes, though, courts will intervene even on substantive grounds. An example is the Colombian Constitutional Court's refusal to defer to the government's rationale for declaring

---

5 Bundesverfassungsgericht [German Constitutional Court], 2 BvE 1/03, 7 May 2008 reported in (2008) 121 BVerfGE 135 (AWACS II case).

a state of emergency in the country (*estado de conmoción interior*). In a 1995 case,[6] the Court had to review an executive order meant to strengthen the criminal justice system to deal with what the government argued was a rise in crime and violence in the country. The order gave the executive a blanket authorization to create new crimes, increase penalties, and reform the jail system. The Court struck down the executive order, finding the government's rationale inadequate. It recognized that violence was a 'rooted pathology' in the political system. Yet, it argued that 'the government itself had not produced evidence supporting the facts it allege[d] as the basis of the [measure]: the government's figures [did] not show the alleged increase in crime.' The Court added that 'the government itself admit[ted] that the facts alleged [were] permanent', so the declaration of emergency, meant to target exceptional short-term situations, was not the proper means for addressing the crisis. While the Colombian Constitution itself regulates these emergencies and subjects them to a judicial review process, courts are often more deferential to the government when dealing with the handling of crises.

A more detailed discussion of the previous arguments follows.

9.4.1 Risks of judicial enforcement of constitutional constraints

Judicial enforcement of the constraints the constitution places on government power might be thought to pose significant risks, of a sort that the constitution itself treats as relevant. These risks take three forms.

(a) The courts may lack knowledge relevant to proper disposition of the constitutional challenge, and cannot acquire that knowledge reliably in the context of an individual lawsuit. Many challenges to actions taken in foreign affairs might pose this risk. Proper disposition of the constitutional challenge might require that the courts understand the implications for foreign policy of the rule they find in the constitution, and—really in the extreme—judicially enforced constitutional rules might imperil the nation's survival, a constitutionally relevant matter. As mentioned, this is not incompatible with allowing judicial oversight of actions taken in foreign affairs to determine whether they (seriously) compromise fundamental rights.

(b) Related but somewhat different is the idea associated with Lon Fuller that some legal problems, including some constitutional problems, are 'polycentric.' As Fuller put it, such problems are like a spider-web, where an action at one point—a decision to impose constitutional constraints on the government with respect to the challenged policy—have effects on other policies, and it is simply impossible to anticipate what those effects will be. Still, this does not necessarily point toward nonjusticiability. Claiming that courts should not be able to disrupt the government's balance among policies at the macro level, or generate negative externalities on other policies, does not mean that courts should have no role to play in seemingly 'polycentric' issues. The intervention of courts may be important in determining whether a constitutional violation (through action or omission) has taken place. Once this determination has been made, the government can have a role in designing the proper remedy to redress the violation, and courts should take into account plausible (or perhaps 'substantial') government claims about the macro implications of the decision. The relevance and extent of courts' intervention may be thought to rest on the

---

6 Corte Constitucional de Colombia [Constitutional Court of Columbia], Sentencia C-466/95 (18 October 1995).

importance of the constitutional violation itself and not—or not only—on its 'polycentric' character. Finally, since it is part of the definition of 'polycentric' problems that they may generate effects that are hard to anticipate, the position against judicial intervention risks seeing *any* problem as a polycentric one—after all, the solution to any problem can have unintended consequences.

(c) Alexander Bickel identified a third risk. Often those who advocate nonjusticiability for some matters point to the risk that the target of the ruling will disregard it, with attendant damage to the courts' standing and role in the constitutional system. Constitutionalists respond properly that courts should not assume that other actors in the government system will disregard justified judicial rulings. Bickel pointed to a different risk, the risk that other actors will *comply* with judicial rulings when they should not. This risk has two components. More obvious is the possibility that people will comply with substantively erroneous judicial decisions. Here Bickel relied on an important insight: that, too often, discussions of constitutional adjudication assume that judicial decisions interpreting the constitution are necessarily correct. Put that assumption aside, as careful analysts should, and there is a risk of compliance with mistaken rulings. In addition, compliance even with correct decisions can be thought to weaken the sense among legislatures and executives that they too have responsibility for interpreting the constitution as they consider what policies to pursue. This argument against justiciability is obviously connected to general concerns about 'juridification' and 'judicialization.'

Yet again, even though it is true that courts can err in their interpretations of the constitution, namely, in their decisions of whether there is a constitutional violation, the relevant question is what the greater risk is. As Fallon has argued, it may be better to allow the possibility of judicial error that judicial review entails if the goal is to minimize rights violations (Fallon). The bigger risk, Fallon argues, may be the under-enforcement of rights, not their over-enforcement. This is so because rarely do courts violate rights when they wrongly strike down constitutionally valid dispositions (at least when these dispositions are not implemented especially to solve a rights violation). Against this it might be said that over-enforcement of rights limits the government's ability to pursue desirable social policies that, were the constitution interpreted 'correctly,' are constitutionally permissible. As Tushnet has argued, Fallon's position rests on the proposition that less government is generally to be preferred over more government, a proposition to which only some constitutional systems are committed (Tushnet). But as González-Bertomeu has argued, Fallon's argument might apply where the constitution imposes duties on the legislature (a situation Fallon does not consider). In such cases, the courts might review and invalidate as inadequate statutes purporting to fulfill a constitutional requirement. Whether and how often judicial errors will violate rights or obstruct the implementation of constitutionally permissible policies that do not themselves violate rights is ultimately an empirical one. In some situations judicial intervention, while in some sense mistaken, would not be introducing an *original* violation *because* some rights violation or constitutional omission existed before the court's action. Perhaps taking all possible types of court intervention into account and comparing such interventions with refusals to intervene, on nonjusticiability grounds for example, may suggest that the overall level of rights violations can still be lower when courts do intervene (González-Bertomeu).

On the other hand, whether compliance with courts weakens politicians' responsibility for interpreting the constitution ultimately presents an empirical question. It is certainly conceivable that politicians within a political system operating with judicial review will have few incentives to think hard about the constitution, since courts would see to it that violations get solved. But it is at least equally conceivable that without judicial review they would have the same incentives (or even fewer incentives) to pay attention to the constitution. The fact that courts would not be there as a final check to politicians on the constitutionality of their actions may simply mean that politicians will not devote much attention to the constitution in the first place. As noted below, much here will depend on the extent to which a culture of constitutionalism is embedded in the politicians' constituents.

9.4.2 Political constitutionalism

The second type of argument for nonjusticiability rests on the idea of 'political constitutionalism,' as distinguished from 'legal constitutionalism.' Legal constitutionalism, the predominant view among constitutionalists, is that all constitutional provisions must be enforceable by the courts: *Ubi jus ibi remedium* (where there is [constitutional] law, there is a [judicial] remedy). This idea has its greatest purchase when constitutions specify the existence and scope of constitutional review, and it is probably no accident that the United States, which applies doctrines of justiciability to limit constitutional review with some regularity, has a constitution from which the power of constitutional review must be inferred.

In contrast to legal constitutionalists, political constitutionalists argue that legislatures and executives can do as good a job as courts in enforcing constitutional limits on their own power, at least with respect to some problems and under some circumstances. The core idea of political constitutionalism is that legislatures and executives often have *political* incentives to respect constitutional limits on their own power. Even if they care only about election and re-election, in the end they might have to worry that their constituents will punish them politically for adopting policies that violate the constitution as the constituents understand it. Opposition parties can use constitutional arguments to mobilize their supporters and weaken the majority, and even a majority coalition's leaders might have to be concerned about defections premised on constitutional disagreements.

Whether this system of incentives is sufficient to minimize constitutional violations (and in particular rights violations) is contingent on many matters of social, cultural, historical, and institutional detail. It may or may not be the case in particular political systems and at particular periods of time. However, a decision whether or not to implement judicial review usually has effects over the future (these decisions are often made at constitutional conventions, and conventions are purposely not frequent). Then it may be natural that the contingent character of the question about political incentives to respect the constitution affects that institutional decision. Moreover, the incentives described may obviously not be enough to protect marginalized voices or rights and interests that are not particularly popular. Further, the limited resources of the legislative agenda may make it hard at times to repeal policies that even a non-negligible portion of the population considers in violation to the constitution. Political constitutionalism might not be a comprehensive alternative to legal constitutionalism, but it might provide an account of why discrete issues might be nonjusticiable—where political incentives exist to keep legislative or executive action within constitutional bounds. For example, the US Supreme Court faced the question of whether a process for removing judges from office conformed to the constitutional requirement that judges receive a 'trial' in the Senate when Senate rules allowed testimony to be taken by a committee, which then reported to the Senate as a whole. The Court held that this was a nonjusticiable 'political question.' Justice David Souter observed, accurately, that this holding would immunize from constitutional review a decision to remove a federal judge by tossing a coin in the Senate. Against that argument, one might respond that within the US political tradition neither major political party has incentives to act arbitrarily in defining what constitutes a 'trial' by the Senate.[7] But, an answer to this is that the claim is contingent upon the political system, the period of time, and the issue involved. For instance, even within the US, situations of electoral malapportionment (apart from those stipulated in the Constitution itself) managed to survive for long periods without political parties being interested in or immediately successful in their attempts to change them.

Of the ideas of nonjusticiability described above, only the idea that some exercises of public power are entirely unconstrained by law is in tension with ideas of constitutionalism. Yet, no democratic constitutionalist really believes that law constrains absolutely everything the government does. Something must be left to democratic decision-making; the complete judicialization of policy-making in the name of constitutionalism is unacceptable where central values are not at stake. The tension is resolved by restricting the domain over which the constitution applies; matters outside that domain can be called nonjusticiable. This does not necessarily mean that this domain will be able to be defined substantively, according to a set of subject matters. A view restricting the reach of judicial review can still accept that the constitution potentially cuts across every rule in the legal system, arguing instead that what defines this restricted domain is not the area or subject matter of the rule but the type of issue involved or the intensity of judges' scrutiny. Highly deferential review is consistent with the idea of legal constitutionalism. More interestingly, political constitutionalism, confined to appropriate domains, can also be an acceptable form of constitutionalism. Relevant matters to consider here are the politically rooted incentives that legislatures and executives have to conform their actions to the constitution. This raises important empirical questions, which will receive different answers in different constitutional systems. Although abstractly there may be an acceptable concept of nonjusticiability, both its precise scope and its instantiation will be different in different political systems.

References

Bickel, AM (1986). *The Least Dangerous Branch* (New Haven, Yale University Press).

Ejima, A (2007). 'Reconsiderations on Judicial Review: A Pragmatic Approach?' (Manuscript presented at the VIIth World Congress of the International Association of Constitutional Law, Athens).

Fallon, RH Jr (2008). 'The Core of an Uneasy Case for Judicial Review', *Harvard Law Review* 121:1693.

González-Bertomeu, JF (2011). 'Against the Core of the Case: Structuring the Evaluation of Judicial Review', *Legal Theory* 17:81.

Itoh, H & Beer, LW (eds) (1978). *The Constitutional Case Law of Japan* (Seattle, University of Washington Press).

Tushnet, M (2010). 'How Different are Waldron's and Fallon's Core Cases For and Against Judicial Review?' *Oxford Journal of Legal Studies* 30:49.

Additional reading

Amoroso, D (2010). 'A Fresh Look at the Issue of Non-Justiciability of Defence and Foreign Affairs', *Leiden Journal of International Law* 23:933.

Angell, A, Schjolden, L & Sieder, R (eds) (2009). *The Judicialization of Politics in Latin America* (Basingstoke, Palgrave Macmillan).

Barton, T (1983). 'Justiciability: A Theory of Judicial Problem Solving', *Boston College Law Review* 24:505.

---

7 *Nixon v United States*, 506 US 224 (1993).

Claeys, ER (1994). 'The Article III, Section 2 Games: A Game-Theoretic Account of Standing and Other Justiciability Doctrines', *Southern California Law Review* 67:1321.

Couso, J, Huneeus, A & Sieder, R (eds) (2010). *Cultures of Legality: Judicialization and Political Activism in Latin America* (Cambridge, Cambridge University Press).

Ferreres-Comella, V (2009). *Constitutional Courts and Democratic Values: A European Perspective* (New Haven, Yale University Press).

Franck, TM (1992). *Political Questions/Judicial Answers: Does the Rule of Law Apply to Foreign Affairs?* (Princeton, Princeton University Press).

Gloppen, S, Wilson, BM, Gargarella, R, Skaar, E & Kinander, M (eds) (2010). *Courts and Power in Latin America and Africa* (New York, Palgrave Macmillan).

Graber, MA (2004). 'Resolving Political Questions into Judicial Questions: Tocqueville's Thesis Revisited', *Constitutional Commentary* 21:485.

Gunther, G (1964). 'The Subtle Vices of the 'Passive Virtues': A Comment on Principle and Expediency in Judicial Review', *Columbia Law Review* 64:1.

Hirschl, R (2007). *Towards Juristocracy: The Origins and Consequences of the New Constitutionalism* (Cambridge, Harvard University Press).

Shapiro, M & Stone Sweet, A (2002). *On Law, Politics, and Judicialization* (Oxford, Oxford University Press).

Siegel, JR (2007). 'A Theory of Justiciability', *Texas Law Review* 86:73.

Stearns, ML (1995). 'Standing Back from the Forest: Justiciability and Social Choice', *California Law Review* 83:1309.

Tribe, L (2000). *American Constitutional Law* (New York, Foundation Press, 3rd edn).

Administrative bureaucracy

Janet McLean with Mark Tushnet

10.1 Introduction

A tradition of constitutionalism extending back to at least Montesquieu describes three government functions—legislation, execution of the laws, and adjudication—and allocates them to three branches. The development of the modern administrative state introduced the administrative bureaucracy, described by US constitutionalists as a 'fourth branch', into the overall scheme of government. Constitutional systems firmly established in the late nineteenth century accommodated the new 'branch' without altering their basic constitutional texts. They conceptualized the administrative bureaucracies as recipients of delegations of rule-making ('quasi-legislative') power from the legislature, as engaged in the enforcement of existing law as arms of the executive, and as determining particular cases ('quasi-judicially') in the course of implementing delegated power. These systems did not amend their constitutions to include the fourth branch. Many adopted organic laws, such as civil service systems giving the staffs of administrative bureaucracies guarantees against political manipulation and statutes regulating the procedures adopted by many agencies, one model of which is the US Administrative Procedure Act (1946), with such scope, importance, and effective entrench-ment against substantial amendment that they could fairly be described as quasi-constitutional. As other nations drafted constitutions in the twentieth century, the model of accommodating administrative bureaucracies with the classical tripartite division exercised sufficient gravitational force that few dealt specifically and in detail with administrative bureaucracies (Ginsburg, 123–24).[1] One exception, increasingly important in recent years, has been the identification in constitutional texts of transparency and anticorruption institutions, described in Section 10.3 below.

Constitutional texts, on the whole, tend not to reflect the true extent of administrative power. Whether they have written or federal constitutions, states with Westminster-based constitutions, such as the United Kingdom, Canada, Australia, and New Zealand, tend not even to name the Prime Minister or Cabinet as the primary executive actors. The Monarch

---

1 Part IX of the Constitution of Singapore on 'The Public Service' provides an unusually detailed constitutionalized civil service system.

or Governor-General remains the legal repository of executive power even if in practice, by convention, power is usually exercised by elected responsible ministers. How *general* executive authority (as opposed to specific executive power) devolves upon the bureaucracy is also a matter that most constitutions leave opaque. In Westminster constitutions these issues have been left to scant and often contradictory common law authorities, which variously describe bureaucrats as the delegates, agents, or even alter egos of the political actors. These ambiguities can affect legal and political understandings of the power properly exercised by different actors. For example, an 'alter ego' conception might lead to assertions that especially important powers should be exercised by ministers themselves, as the legislature's alter ego, while an 'agency' conception might support delegation to career bureaucrats. Neither do the constitutional texts and doctrines of these jurisdictions reflect the true extent to which the executive enjoys law-making and judicial-type powers as well as executive powers of implementation. Administrative bureaucracies are firmly located within the executive branch, and the much praised strict separation of powers has always been more mythological than real in the British system.

Even systems firmly committed to the separation of powers tend to place administrative bureaucracies within the executive branch as a matter of form. Judicial efforts to define the limits on what law-making power can be delegated have, on the whole, not been successful and decisions about how much can be delegated have tended to be left in the hands of the legislators. The notion that the bureaucracies exercise delegated powers is often fictional, as when the purported delegations are stated in such broad terms—'in the public interest' is a common formulation in the United States—that the administrative bureaucracy, or 'agency' in the term used in the US, has law-making authority almost as extensive as the legislature's. The courts, whether of general jurisdiction or specialized in dealing with administrative law, do use the organic statutes regulating judicial review of administrative action to determine whether the agency has acted within the scope of the delegation, and sometimes these reviews to determine whether action is *ultra vires*—beyond authority—can be quite vigorous.

Modern administrative bureaucracies typically lay claim to some degree of expertise unavailable, at least to the same degree, to high political officials in either the legislative or the executive branch. The staffs of these bureaucracies may be experts in regulation of workplace safety and health, for example, or on matters of environmental pollution. The bureaucracies must be given some degree of independence from political control so that the overall policy-making process can take advantage of their expertise. Yet, the bureaucracies must also be subject to some political control to sustain the legitimacy of the policies they generate. In the most general terms, the constitutional law of administrative bureaucracies aims at achieving a suitable balance between independence and accountability—a balance that may be struck differently in various nations because of their overall cultures (Halberstam). Some national cultures may be suspicious of, others enthusiastic about, claims to expertise; the term 'politician' may be a pejorative in some national cultures, a neutral or even honourable term in others. And, of course, the claims to expertise may be warranted or unwarranted. As in much constitutional law, national peculiarities shape the precise form that more general features take.

Conceiving of administrative bureaucracies as located within the executive branch, one might nonetheless identify an internal 'separation of powers' within that branch, with some agencies held more at arm's length than others. Often the degree of independence will depend on the degree to which claims of expertise are widely accepted; and less often, but still importantly, on the degree to which independence is given especially high value. The Treasury and central banks tend to be more insulated, for example, than agencies administering the public benefits associated with the modern social welfare state.

10.2 The relationship between the bureaucracy and the political branches

The competing characterizations of administrative bureaucracies as delegees, agents, or alter egos may fit differently into parliamentary and presidential systems. The division between the legislature and the executive government is typically thin in parliamentary systems, where the executive government's power rests on its control over a parliamentary majority. In parliamentary systems, administrative bureaucracies are readily understood as components of the executive ministries, themselves understood as creatures of an executive government dependent upon the legislature. The 'agency' and 'alter ego' conceptions flow easily from this situation. In separating the legislature from the chief executive, presidential systems force consideration of the questions, 'For whom are the administrative bureaucracies the agents, and from whom do they receive their delegated power?'

Presidential systems are characterized by the separate election of the chief executive and the legislature. This presents the possibility of conflict between the executive and the legislature over a range of matters, including the substance of the policy made by the administrative bureaucracy.[2] When this conflict occurs, space opens up for the permanent, nominally non-political heads and staffs of administrative bureaucracies either to take sides with one or the other branch, or sometimes to pursue their own agendas, at least if they do not go too far beyond what either the legislature or the chief executive can tolerate. It has been claimed that political rivalry between the House, Senate, and Presidency in the US, for example, has created an excessively politicized style of bureaucratic government (Ackerman, 641). Put another way, the administrative heads and staffs of administrative bureaucracies can treat either the legislature or the president as the principal for whom they are agents.

These and related conflicts have been examined intensively in the United States, where political scientists have identified 'iron triangles' of policy-making (Rourke, 119). The vertices of the triangle are the heads of the administrative bureaucracies, the interest groups most affected by each bureaucracy's policies, and the congressional committees with jurisdiction over each bureaucracy. According to the 'iron triangle' account, policy is made as these three groups interact. Notably, the chief executive or the nominally responsible departmental head (the equivalent of the minister in parliamentary systems) are absent from the 'iron triangle' account. Examples of the iron triangles in operation include the adoption of environmental policies by the Environmental Protection Agency (EPA) or regulations adopted by the Food and Drug Administration (FDA) for the distribution of medications used to prevent conception that are at odds with the president's policy goals (or, in a weaker version, the imposition of significant political costs on the president for overriding policies proposed by the EPA or FDA). These are helpful examples because in the US the heads of the EPA and the FDA are appointed by the president and—on the predominant understanding of the US Constitution—can be fired by the president simply because the president wants the EPA or the FDA to implement different policies.

The precise contours of the 'iron triangle' may not be present in other presidential systems, sometimes because the relevant interest groups are weaker, sometimes because the agencies are more under the chief executive's control. Yet, the 'iron triangle' analysis directs attention

---

2 Whether this possibility is realized depends on the array of party power, being more substantial when different coalitions control the two branches than when a single coalition controls both. Even in the latter case, though, the possibility of conflict exists.

to the ways in which political and administrative structures can affect the policy-making out of administrative bureaucracies.

In parliamentary systems, the executive branch is drawn from the party or parties who enjoy the confidence of the majority of the legislature. As such, the executive government does not have a separate democratic mandate from that of the legislature. Usually the political parties themselves select individual cabinet ministers to form the executive government, though practices vary according to party and parliamentary rules, and in some systems (e.g. Scotland) the legislature also has a role in deciding who shall remain in ministerial office. Expectations may be changing: the overnight removal of the Prime Minister of Australia by the parliamentary party in 2010 caused considerable public disquiet and is unlikely to be repeated without more public deliberation. In most parliamentary systems, and all Westminster-style ones, political control and accountability of the bureaucracy is primarily through ministers who are Members of Parliament. They are collectively and individually responsible to parliament for both policy and operational matters. Parliamentary questions and debates, and select committees and inquiries, are all vehicles for holding the bureaucracy to account through ministers. The ultimate sanction is the resignation of the minister or loss of confidence in the government collectively. Those sanctions may be more symbolic than real, although resignations of individual ministers for misconduct or errors within the bureaucracy for which they are nominally responsible do sometimes occur.

In addition to the executive powers that inhere in the executive authority itself, the executive exercises powers delegated by the legislature. The most significant of these are delegated law-making powers, and (to a lesser extent) delegated decision-making powers (including sometimes judicial and quasi-judicial powers often exercised by tribunals or boards).[3] Delegated law-making typically occurs when an administrative body adopts a rule that applies to a large class of regulated entities. Quasi-judicial powers are exercised, among other situations, when administrators, typically on the lowest level with some degree of higher-level review, determine that applicants are eligible or ineligible for social welfare benefits.

Delegated law-making powers (exercised in practice by the executive and the bureaucracy) have been increasingly brought within parliamentary oversight, with the aid of committees, established for the purpose, that scrutinise the delegated instruments by reference to set criteria, which may include the question of whether the delegation has been exercised in an unexpected way. Where delegated instruments are subject to disallowance by one or both Houses of the legislature, such committees also may play a role in determining whether a vote on disallowance should proceed. The exercise of powers to make specific determinations (akin to adjudication) rarely attracts parliamentary oversight, except in the most politically controversial instances such as state asset sales and immigration decisions relating to alleged terrorists, which may become the subject of committee inquiry. Failing that, supervision may be available by way of the ombudsman's office or judicial review. Given that in some systems (such as the UK) a complaint to the ombudsman's office must be brought through a Member of Parliament, that oversight is considered to be taken on behalf of Parliament. The advent of contracting out of both service and policy functions to the private sector has reduced the relevance and effectiveness of some of these mechanisms of parliamentary control, and has also reduced ministerial control.

If *political* mechanisms of control and accountability are central in Westminster-style constitutions, the bureaucracy itself is politically neutral, merit based, and survives political

---

3 These powers are sometimes conceptualized as executive in nature rather than as delegated to the executive from the legislature.

changes in government. Constitutionally it is required to give 'free and frank advice' and 'speak truth to power'. Since the 1980s there has been pressure in the UK and elsewhere to make bureaucracy more responsive, outcome- and change-oriented, and citizen focused. Worldwide, the influence of neoliberalism has generated pressures to outsource both policy advice and service delivery to the private sector. This has inevitably led to strain on traditional understandings of both political control and accountability.

In practice, different parts of the bureaucracy enjoy different degrees of independence from the political branches. Civil service systems and specialised training courses for the staff of administrative bureaucracies are designed to promote independence. Increasingly, agencies have been given more formal independence from ministers—especially in relation to operational matters. This has been a deliberate attempt to lessen both political control and political accountability. Despite this, ministers have often continued to be publicly called to account and to be the locus of blame.

Constitutions differ on the question of how much independence and autonomy the bureaucracy enjoys from politicians. In some constitutions (Italy) there are large numbers of patronage appointments. In Westminster systems, patronage appointments are relatively rare. Patronage appointments involve direct connections between politicians and agency staff. Less direct connections exist as well. In many constitutional systems (such as France), executive authorities cannot act except on the basis of power granted by written enactment. Agency power is thereby sustained only through delegation of authority from the political branches and so from politicians.

On the other hand, significant executive and hence bureaucratic powers also originate in the executive itself. These so-called 'prerogative' powers include the power to make treaties, to make war and peace, and to organise its own advisors. Sometimes the notion of 'prerogative' is extended to executive decisions to make specific expenditures or to enter into particular contracts, though sometimes these decisions are treated as ordinary administrative ones subject to the usual methods of administrative review in the courts. While prerogative powers have been increasingly subject to judicial—and sometimes parliamentary—definition, they nevertheless remain large and significant. The scope of the power to conduct war in particular has become highly contested in recent decades, with courts weighing in on such questions as whether and to what extent a chief executive can commit a nation's military forces to conflicts abroad and whether the chief executive's power to determine 'battlefield' strategy extends to the long-term disposition of those taken as prisoners (AWACS II case; *Hamdi v Rumsfeld*). While often conceptualized as involving only the chief executive's power, these conflicts also implicate the armed forces, understood as bureaucracies, with military officers serving as the 'experts' who have some role in determining policy.[4]

Given that the prerogative power to organise and structure the bureaucracy itself may be exercised in ways that potentially affect the political neutrality of the bureaucracy and hence upset constitutional norms, the issue arises about how much of this power should reside in the executive acting alone (Sossin, 74) or whether it should be subject to broader constitutional oversight and control. This has been especially important in recent decades, given that the adoption of the techniques of the 'new public management' (Harlow & Rawlings 2009) has resulted in radical restructuring and increasing politicisation of the civil service. Under the new public management, for example, politicians set strategic targets that chief executives of government agencies are to meet. Agency heads have become publicly answerable for

---

4 For a discussion of whether the military and the police should be treated as elements of the executive branch or as administrative bureaucracies, see Chapter 6 of this volume.

achieving them. They are no longer anonymous and have a direct relationship with the public. Problems can arise about whether the Minister or the agency official should be held publicly to account in the event of an agency's bad performance. Perhaps the problem is that the politically-determined strategic targets are incomplete, misguided, or do not take a complete account of the real risks to the agency. Perhaps performance measures set by politicians (such as the requirement to meet standard surgery waiting times) consume disproportionate administrative effort, distort administrative behaviour, or lead to manipulation of procedures without improving real outcomes. It is difficult to know what went wrong and, more particularly, who should be held to account in such circumstances. Individual employment performance of agency heads is measured against such targets. This alignment of personal performance targets and strategic performance targets may inhibit free and frank advice from officials to politicians, and may create incentives for everyone to claim that the system is working when it is not improving real outcomes.

In addition to the effects of prerogative power and the new public management, the executive's power has effectively grown with the increasing relevance of international treaty law to domestic law. This is a general phenomenon affecting both monist and dualist systems. Executive governments are increasingly engaged in implementing law made by international institutions. Not only does this have the effect of increasing executive power but it also redirects bureaucratic effort into executing laws made by international law-makers rather than by local legislatures. This phenomenon is not restricted to Westminster systems and is particularly apparent in the EU member states. It has been politically significant given the UN Security Council Resolutions relating to terrorism and the fact that many of the 'new' post-cold war constitutions give explicit priority to international treaty law over domestic law, including constitutional and human rights law. As a result of the increasing importance and relevance of the international sphere, there have been efforts to increase legislative and public scrutiny of treaty-making processes. Given the secrecy surrounding international treaty-making, and the fact that treaties themselves tend to delegate rule-making and decision-making to international institutions, these efforts have had only limited success.

10.3 Internal modes of organization and control of the bureaucracy

The most important internal mechanism of control over bureaucracy has traditionally been budgetary. Different constitutional systems accord different powers to different parts of the political apparatus over taxing, borrowing, and spending. In Westminster-style systems, the executive government, which commands a majority of the legislature, effectively controls these areas and uses the budget as a mechanism through which to set and monitor government priorities. The same is true in most presidential systems, although agency heads there have the possibility of appealing 'over the head' of the chief executive to the legislature for protection and augmentation of their budgets.

Whoever is in political control of the budgetary processes, some central authority, almost always located within the executive branch, operates as a central controlling department *within* the bureaucracy.[5] Since the 1980s many countries have legislated for balanced budgets, or (like the UK) have adopted a fiscal 'golden rule' with the same objective. At the same time,

---

5 The Treasury or some similar title is often attached to these central bodies, especially in parliamentary systems.

more transparent mechanisms of financial reporting have been favoured. These measures have further increased the power of Treasury departments within the bureaucracy.[6]

Some parts of the bureaucracy have as their primary focus the maintenance of the integrity of other parts of the bureaucracy. Ackerman describes such agencies as part of the 'integrity branch of government'. One traditional mechanism of control that potentially comes into this category is the Audit Office. In many constitutions this office has grown in scope and changed in style from an institution narrowly concerned with financial probity to one increasingly involved in measuring efficiency, cost-effectiveness, and policy outcomes. In Westminster-style systems, the independence of the office within the bureaucracy is maintained by its special reporting relationship to Parliament and its direct relationship to special Parliamentary select committees. Audit offices can be supplemented by, or be transformed into, more general anticorruption agencies, with a remit to identify and initiate corruption prosecutions of officials, including both administrators and parliamentarians.

The Office of the Ombudsman, a Scandinavian invention that been widely adopted across a range of constitutional systems, including the EU, is also of this kind. The Office investigates individual cases of maladministration and has a role in making broad policy recommendations to the bureaucracy more generally. Ombudsman offices often have a special relationship with the legislature and exercise their oversight of the executive and bureaucracy on its behalf. Bureaucratic agencies that administer and enforce freedom of information (FOI) legislation also belong to the 'integrity branch' of the administration. Like the ombudsmen, they have a dual role in assisting and obtaining redress for individual citizens and in enhancing political mechanisms of accountability.

The 'integrity branch' emerged as a separate constitutional concern in the late twentieth century. Achieving the proper balance of independence and accountability for this branch is especially difficult. Agencies in the 'integrity branch' seek to provide information directly to the people, rather than having their decisions mediated through the political branches, precisely because these agencies' concerns lie in ensuring that the political branches perform honestly and fairly. Subjecting them even to the kinds of political control exercised over environmental and similar agencies therefore seems misguided. Yet, too much independence may lead to overly aggressive and seemingly partisan enforcement actions, which may in turn lead to attacks on the agency's independence through control of its budget and hyperpoliticisation of the mechanisms for choosing the agency heads. Maladministration and corruption are sometimes in the eye of the beholder—or, more formally, practices that some identify as corrupt or reflecting gross incompetence may be reasonable adaptations to the circumstances politicians and bureaucrats face. Integrity-branch agencies that have strong views about what is corrupt or incompetent may interfere with the smooth functioning of government. This may be exacerbated by the fact that the agencies' mission lies in identifying corruption and maladministration, and they might sometimes think that they must find some targets merely to justify their existence. These tensions have produced constitutional conflicts in several nations. The 'Scorpions', a special *South African* investigative unit targeting government corruption, were disbanded by legislation in 2008, after they investigated the head of the nation's police service. The South African Constitutional Court held the legislation unconstitutional because it replaced the Scorpions with a unit that was 'vulnerable to political influence' (*Glenister v President*).

---

6 The office of the presidency in Singapore was transformed by constitutional amendment from a largely ceremonial office to an office with important control over expenditures from the nation's reserves, though the president's powers have gradually been eroded by subsequent amendments (Tan, 90–110).

10.4 External mechanisms of control

Where delegated law-making power is concerned, most parliamentary systems have instituted systems of parliamentary scrutiny and disallowance of legislation made by the executive. The underlying structural logic is that the executive government is the creature of the parliamentary majority, which therefore has the authority to displace decisions made by the executive ministries. The structural logic in presidential systems is different because, in them, legislation requires the concurrence of both the legislature and the separately elected executive. That logic leads to the approach taken in the United States. There, delegated legislation—known as administrative regulations or rules—has the force of law unless the rules are repealed by the legislature, an action that requires the president's signature (or, in theory but never in practice, a two-thirds vote in each house of Congress to override a presidential veto).[7]

In many jurisdictions the courts are seen as the primary source of accountability and control of the bureaucracy. This is not just through the adjudication of constitutional rights but also through the less glamorous means of administrative law review, often referred to as 'judicial review' and distinguished from 'constitutional review'. Rights to administrative justice occasionally are constitutionalised: the South African Constitution is a notable example (section 33). The scope of bureaucratic activity subject to administrative review differs depending on the jurisdiction, as do the rules about who has standing to bring such a proceeding and the manner in which the proceeding is conducted. In Germany, for example, both political and administrative areas of the bureaucracy are subject to law through a system of administrative courts distinct from the general civil law courts. In France, a distinction is made between an *acte de gouvernement* outside the scope of review, and a reviewable *acte administratif*, subject to review by the Conseil d'État, which has been conceptualised from its beginning as located within the executive branch. In practice, *actes de gouvernement* unreviewable in the administrative courts are rare. The category used to include the president's prerogative of pardon (which is now treated as a reviewable judicial act). It still includes diplomatic relations. Common law systems of judicial review have steadily increased the kinds of decisions that can be reviewed (including, for example, exercises of prerogative power such as the power of pardon but not yet diplomatic relations) but tend to apply different standards of scrutiny depending on the political nature of the decision and whether human rights are at stake. The increasing use of private legal persons to deliver public services has presented a new challenge to determining the proper scope of review in both civil and common law systems: Should their actions be subjected to the scrutiny given to actions by government officials, or should they be regulated only by the general law of torts/delicts and contracts/obligations? Many common law jurisdictions have adopted public function-type tests as a way of defining the legal scope of public law controls. These resemble, superficially at least, French administrative law ideas.

The basis of administrative review tends to be both substantive and procedural. Typical grounds include procedural impropriety, illegality, absence of proportionality, and the misuse of power. Whatever the system, in the practice of judicial scrutiny, there is a delicate balance to be achieved between protecting individuals and maintaining the effectiveness of the administration. Questions of who is authorized to challenge administrative action are often answered with reference to this balance. One can coherently argue that every citizen has an

---

7 The Congressional Review Act authorizes Congress to take up bills aimed at repudiating agency rules through a 'fast-track' procedure that bypasses most of the elaborate stages of legislative consideration and proceeds directly to a vote. The procedure has been used only once since its enactment in 1996.

interest in ensuring that the government proceeds according to law, and that every citizen therefore ought to be allowed to challenge administrative action on the ground that it departs from legality. Yet, authorizing review so widely would likely impede the administrative bureaucracies' ordinary operation, contributing to what in the United States has been called the 'ossification' of the regulatory process.

Constitutional rights challenges also affect administrative bureaucracies by limiting their powers to make decisions, legislation, and rules. In many cases these challenges will go further into politically sensitive areas, and provide broader remedies than traditional administrative law review in special administrative tribunals.

10.5 Citizen participation and redress

Modern bureaucracies have been seeking more direct citizen engagement in policy and rule-making. In so doing they also seek to make themselves more directly responsive and account-able to the citizenry and often to enhance their own legitimacy. The US administrative agencies have led the way in this regard through the Administrative Procedure Act's rule-making processes, which permit interested and affected groups to participate in the rule-making process, through the submission of comments and suggestions that the agency must fully consider, at the risk of having the resulting rule overturned by the courts. Other systems have been less transparent or have opted for more ad hoc processes of inclusion, particularly where planning and environmental rule-making have been concerned—areas where the range of affected groups can vary widely depending on the nature of the action under consid-eration. Legislated consultation requirements have become more common in Western democracies and have sometimes been the subject of judicial enforcement and constitutional-ised in order to ensure consultation with particular (often indigenous) groups. The South African Constitutional Court has pioneered the idea of 'engagement' with citizens before some constitutionally sensitive quasi-judicial administrative actions take place (*Occupiers of 51 Olivia Road v City of Johannesburg*). Freedom of information (FOI) regimes potentially support these processes of direct citizen engagement and help to make them meaningful.[8]

Mechanisms for citizen engagement generally, and FOI regimes in particular, may encounter resistance from within the bureaucracy because of the complex accountability regimes operating in relation to individual bureaucrats who find themselves subject to multiple and often overlapping accountability regimes (Mulgan). They are accountable to their bureau-cratic superiors in the administrative hierarchy (upwards accountability), to ombudsman offices or information commissioners for the proper operation of FOI legislation (sideways accountability) and to the individual citizen (downwards accountability). These complexities may be exacerbated in presidential systems, where bureaucrats may have to respond to both the executive branch and to the legislature separately. Parliamentary systems may generate their own sources of resistance, especially to citizen accountability, because bureaucrats can see themselves as solely responsible to their hierarchical superiors in a unified 'government'.

In most jurisdictions, opportunities for direct citizen redress through the courts is limited in practice by the cost of access, so less formal avenues of redress have proved important. General avenues of redress include the ombudsman's role (which delivers practical redress as well as, at times, monetary remedies) and Human Rights Commissions, which have also served a grievance resolution role in some jurisdictions. In many common law jurisdictions

---

8 See Chapter 17 of this volume.

(notably Australia, see Cane 2009), specialist tribunals and administrative appeals tribunals serve a crucial role in providing an avenue for citizens' complaints. In this area, too, the privatisation and contracting-out of functions formerly performed by central bureaucracies has led to issues about the scope and continued availability of such avenues for redress. In some cases, private self-regulatory bodies have emulated the public ombudsman model (e.g. the Banking Ombudsman).

10.6 Conclusion

Administrative bureaucracy has a crucial role in any constitutional system. On it depends the operationalization of constitutional values and respect for citizens. It is surprising then that constitutions of all kinds tend not to give these issues much explicit prominence. While it is true that in the twentieth century a great deal of effort was put into devising mechanisms by which to control bureaucracy and its uses of delegated authority, crucial questions such as the proper degree of bureaucratic independence historically have tended to be under-constitutionalised. The emergence of the so-called 'integrity branch' of government, which serves as an internal mechanism for holding bureaucracies to account, may give impetus to constitutional thinking about such issues. Should rights to FOI be constitutionalized and what constitutional protections should attach to officers involved in enforcing such rights? Another constitutional challenge to administrative bureaucracies over recent years has been the impact of neoliberal policies, which have led to privatisation and contracting-out, and have resulted in perceived loss of public law control and accountability. These changes too may conceivably prompt consideration about how much the public–private distinction should or could be treated as a constitutional division.

References

Ackerman, B (2000). 'The New Separation of Powers', 113 Harv L Rev 633.

Cane, P (2009). *Administrative Tribunals and Adjudication* (Oxford: Hart).

Ginsburg, T (2010). 'Written constitutions and the administrative state: on the constitutional character of administrative law', in Rose-Ackerman, S & Lindseth, PL, *Comparative Administrative Law* (Cheltenham & Northampton: Edward Elgar).

Halberstam, D (2010). 'The promise of comparative administrative law: a constitutional perspective on independent agencies', in Rose-Ackerman, S & Lindseth, PL, *Comparative Administrative Law* (Cheltenham & Northampton: Edward Elgar).

Harlow, C & Rawlings, R (2009). *Law and Administration* (3rd edn, Cambridge: Cambridge University Press).

Mulgan, RG (2003). Holding Power to Account: Accountability in Modern Democracies (Houndsmills and New York: Palgrave Macmillan).

Rourke, F (1991). 'American Bureaucracy in a Changing Political Setting', Journal of Public Administration: Research and Theory 1(2): 111–29.

Sossin, L (2005). 'The Ambivalence of Executive Power in Canada', in Tomkins, A & Craig, P (eds), *The Executive and Public Law* (Oxford: Oxford University Press).

Tan, K (2011). Constitutional Law in Singapore (Amsterdam: Wolters Kluwer).

Additional reading

Rose-Ackerman, S & Lindseth, PL (2010). *Comparative Administrative Law* (Cheltenham & Northampton: Edward Elgar).

11

Elections and electoral systems in constitutional regimes

*Mahendra Pal Singh**

11.1 Introduction

Except in case of direct democracy where all eligible citizens participate in decision-making, some kind of electoral system is inevitable for making a democracy work. Direct democracy at the national level has long become part of history, though a handful of nations still have reasonably robust systems of direct democracy with respect to some matters, such as constitutional amendment. Direct democracy's replacement, representative democracy, requires some mechanism for making representation operational. Election of some kind is universally considered the legitimate mechanism for such representation. Article 25 of the International Covenant on Civil and Political Rights explains the connection:

> Every citizen shall have the right and the opportunity, without any of the distinctions mentioned in article 2 and without unreasonable restrictions:
>
> (a) To take part in the conduct of public affairs, directly or through freely chosen representatives;
> (b) To vote and to be elected at genuine periodic elections which shall be by universal and equal suffrage and shall be held by secret ballot, guaranteeing the free expression of the will of the electors.

Not all written constitutions, however, incorporate provisions for elections and electoral systems within them. According to one survey,

> [O]nly 19 percent of constitutions specify, in any detail, the electoral system for the lower house of the legislature. Instead most constitutions either explicitly leave to

* Chairman, Delhi Judicial Academy, New Delhi. Former Vice-Chancellor, National University of Juridical Sciences, Kolkata and Professor of Law, University of Delhi. I am grateful to Arpita, Rajat and Siddharth for their help in the preparation of this paper. But for their help it could have never been written. I also thank Ms Jasmine Joseph for her initial suggestions and assurance of support in the preparation of this paper.

ordinary law the design of electoral systems for the legislature (approximately 30 percent of constitutional texts since 1789 [year of making the US Constitution]) and the drawing of districts (approximately 10 percent since 1789), or do not mention election law issues of either kind at all (approximately 30 percent and 60 percent, respectively, since 1789). Also, 47 percent of constitutions in our study do not even mention political parties, which are surely central to constitutional governance in both democracies *and* many autocracies.

(Elkins, Ginsburg & Melton, 51–52)

The Constitution of India is exceptional in this regard, making detailed provision on most election matters, save political parties. Following a general introduction to the topic, the constitutional treatment of the electoral system in India is offered as a case study in the kinds of issues that arise in the field. It should be noted as well that the design of electoral systems is closely connected to other aspects of constitution-making (see Chapter 5).

11.2 Prevalent electoral systems

Elections form a subset of democracy that focuses more on mechanics than substance. Major discussions on election law have dealt with the relation between rules and electoral outcomes, and with the proper implementation of electoral rules. With the development of comparative studies on democracies and laws of different countries, the form of the electoral system is no longer taken for granted.

11.2.1 Systems of voting: proportional representation and plurality

Most electoral systems use plurality and list proportional representation (PR) systems (Lijphart). These forms of electoral systems are generic in nature. For example, a list proportional system and a single transferable vote system are both forms of PR. One cannot claim that PR is 'better' than plurality voting. Rather, one must specify one form of PR system out of many (Lijphart, 5–6). Further, plurality and PR systems are not necessarily at loggerheads; there can be a harmonious co-existence between the two systems, as in fact has been achieved in some countries.

The best electoral system most precisely and straightforwardly reflects the voters' opinions. But, voter choices change according to the electoral system through which they elect their representatives. Preferences and electoral systems are not mutually exclusive features. Also, every kind of electoral system has its own form of biases. Choosing from amongst these sets of electoral systems, therefore, means that one set of biases is preferred over the others. The major forms of electoral systems are:

1. First past the post (FPTP) system. Here the candidate receiving the largest number of votes wins the election, even if that candidate does not obtain an absolute majority of the votes cast. This system has been taken to be typical in English-speaking countries. Horowitz mentions that, conventionally, the FPTP system is viable when few parties (preferably two) exist. According to a 'law' propounded by French political scientist Maurice Duverger, FPTP systems tend to *generate* only two or three parties, because, with too many parties, candidates can win seats from individual districts yet be unable to co-ordinate on national policy. Under FPTP a party receiving as little as 40 to 48 percent of the votes can gain the majority and form the government. With 'seat bonuses'—produced when a party wins by small margins in many constituencies but loses some constituencies

by large margins—the party winning the largest number of seats obtains some extra seats, thereby bring stability and durability to the government (Horowitz). Political cultures that believe in consistency and stability would prefer to have an FPTP form of electoral system.

The main focus of this electoral system is effective governance and not representation of the entire spectrum of minority opinions. A significant feature is that single-member constituencies depend upon the size of the electorate, being more 'natural' when the electorate is extremely large (Norris). The United States of America, Canada, India, the United Kingdom, Malaysia, and many Anglophone Caribbean nations follow this form of electoral system. Again, a nuanced form of FPTP is practised in India, Canada, and Malaysia where the systems accommodate more than two parties, so as to deal with pluralism of ideology and principles more effectively than two or three parties can (Horowitz, 121).

2. In proportional representation (PR) systems, the number of seats won by a political party is proportionate to the number of votes received. Proponents of PR argue that it gives a fair chance to small political parties. Its main objective is to represent all opinions regardless of the position or status in the political spectrum (Horowitz, 122). Carl Friedrich observed in 1967 that opposition to PR was 'to some extent influenced by the fact that the Communist parties throughout Europe have been firmly supporting it' (Friedrich, 305). With those parties weakening, scholars have become increasingly inclined towards PR because it ensures that a party, merely by being the largest party, does not win bonus seats. Notably, Switzerland adopted PR in 1918 by popular vote, over significant opposition from the political class, well before fears of Communism affected the choice of electoral systems.

3. A third significant form of electoral system is the Alternative Voting System (AVS), widely used in Australia. AVS requires the victor to obtain an absolute majority. Voters express first, second, and third preferences. If no candidate obtains an absolute majority of first-preference votes, the system requires the candidate with the fewest of the first-preference votes to be eliminated and his second-preference votes redistributed as if they were first-preference votes. This process continues until one of the candidates receives 50 percent of the votes. Therefore, victory is attained by candidates who have some support even outside their core group of first-preference voters. Another form of AVS is known as Coomb's rule, whereby the candidate with the largest number of last preferences is eliminated and the votes are redistributed until 50 percent is achieved. The purpose of AVS and Coomb's rule is to count the second and subsequent preferences of the voters rather than discarding them altogether as in FPTP and PR systems of elections (Horowitz, 123).

4. In a system used elsewhere as well, German voters cast dual forms of votes. The first one is the candidate ballot system known as *Erststimme*. The second level of election is that of the party-list ballot, known as *Zweitstimme*. The candidate ballots are summed at the district level and the candidate with the highest number of votes at the district level becomes the district's Member of Parliament—a plurality. PR enters at the second level, when the share of parliamentary seats obtained by each party is made proportional to the percentage of votes secured by the parties in the party-list ballot. Where the number of votes received by a party through party-list ballot outnumbers the number of seats allocated to the district winners, the extra seats are allocated to the party members highest on the party list (Stratmann & Baur).

According to Lijphart, electoral reform in democracies tends to convert from plurality to PR systems as compared to the reverse (Lijphart, 8). The reason probably is the greater distribution of power in a PR system as compared to the plurality system, which tends to concentrate powers only in the winning party.

While the discussions for devising the best and most effective system of representation continue, Friedrich's observation is worth noting:

> At any rate, electoral systems must be seen and studied in relation to the whole constitutional order, as well as to the social and other conditions of the country concerned. Popular government requires the working out of a system adapted to the peculiar needs of the country' (Friedrich, 305).

11.3 Elections and electoral system in India

India's extensive treatment of the electoral system in its Constitution offers an opportunity to examine some general issues about the constitutional status of electoral systems, such as the importance of the right to vote in specific political cultures, the relation between independent electoral commissions and legislatures, and the role of courts in policing the operation of the electoral system.

11.3.1 Constitutional provisions: contents, adoption, and rationale

The Constitution of India is one of those few constitutions with detailed provisions on elections. It also provides for an independent institution—the Election Commission—for the conduct and supervision of elections. Notably, the introduction of universal adult suffrage in the Constitution was a bold step taken without any difference of opinion or commotion. As Rajni Kothari puts it, 'What amounted to a historic decision was taken quietly and without furor' (Kothari, 1970). Initially, the provision for adult franchise was made part of the fundamental rights provisions of the Constitution, until the whole subject of elections was shifted to Part XV of the Constitution (Rao, 459 ff).

In a society like India, which discriminated between its people on the basis of caste and creed, severely injuring their moral and social selves, it was hoped that rendering them all equal politically would, in due course, heal the deep wounds of social discrimination. These underlying cultural features affect how politics operates in India, and therefore influence the ways in which the electoral system works in practice.

Experiences with a sense of pluralism, says Kothari, have given Indians a certain degree of ambivalence and apathy towards political power structures, for the fundamental idea remains the recognition of both good as well as evil in every exercise of power and authority. These psychological experiences also led to the development of a rigid thought pattern within the individual, its most vigorous societal manifestation being the rigid caste structure that developed in India in the latter half of the last millennium. The fact that the child in Indian households receives an immense amount of care and devotion also ensures that the child is hardly ever required formally to be self-dependent. It is customary for an older sibling, or a parent, or a senior to take care of the younger ones. This results in the development of a culture of superior–subordinate relationships, which slowly become entrenched. Given the fact that there exists ambivalence towards authority, such relationships are usually not disrupted as people are comfortable being in a subordinate relationship with those who love and care for them.

Given these cultural contexts, democracy in India takes a wholly different form from what it does elsewhere. People in India today are still largely apolitical, content with the stable routine of their household or community lives. And yet, voter turnouts in India, especially in the rural areas, are immense. This seems a paradox but the political activity usually witnessed is not for national or meta-level political ideologies; people rather vote for their immediate representatives, especially those at the grass-roots level. It is in this context that one has to appreciate things like party structures and politics, right to vote, and the related issues of fair and free elections.

11.3.2 The right to vote

The 'right to vote' is an integral aspect of any modern democracy. Is voting merely the act of expressing the will of an individual about the choice of his or her ruler or is it something more? The concept of universal adult suffrage flows from the concept of equality before law. On an individual basis, the right to vote recognises the right of an individual to participate in a decision-making process and gives control (even by means of a single vote) to the individual, to design one's life and society according to one's own idea of what is just and fair. It recognises the individual's expressive interest in equal political standing that inheres to each citizen, taken one by one. From a group point of view, the right to vote also protects, as a matter of positive law, the interests that groups of citizens have in systems of election and representation that distribute political power 'fairly' or appropriately as between these various groups (Pildes). The fair and appropriate distribution of power, or 'equity', arises from the fact that it is a basic—indeed fundamental—requirement of democracy. A government 'by the people' must ultimately include all the people in a symmetric way, and this is also essential to enable the Government to become 'of the people and for the people' (Dreze & Sen).

The 'right to vote' in India has never been directly under the Supreme Court's scrutiny. The only cases where it is discussed are those where other issues or rights were in direct conflict with the free and fair functioning of democracy. The 'right to vote', though fundamental to a democratic system of governance, *anomalously enough*, is not considered a fundamental or common law right (*Jyoti Basu v Debi Ghosal* [1982] 1 SCC 691). The basic argument advanced in almost all the cases is that outside of statute, there is no right to elect, no right to be elected, and no right to dispute an election. What otherwise might be considered fundamental and constitutional rights are statutory creations and, therefore, subject to statutory limitation. Jurisdiction over elections is a special jurisdiction, and a special jurisdiction has always to be exercised in accordance with the statute creating it. Concepts familiar to common law and equity must remain strangers to election law unless statutorily embodied. Though this position subsists until now, the issue of the constitutional position of the right to vote has been referred by the Supreme Court to the Chief Justice to be placed before a larger bench of the Court (*PUCL v Union of India* [2009] 3 SCC 200).

In *Union of India v Association for Democratic Reforms* ([2002] 5 SCC 294), the Supreme Court upheld the directions of the Delhi High Court to the Election Commission that, to enable the voter to make the right choice of candidate for whom to cast his or her vote, the Commission must secure information from every candidate for election to Parliament or State Legislature regarding pendency of any criminal cases against them, their financial assets as well as those of their spouse and dependants, their competence and suitability as candidates, and the political party fielding them. The Court justified these directions as necessary elements of free and fair election falling within the competence of the Commission, though not covered by any existing legislation.

As democracy (*Kesavananda Bharati v State of Kerala* [AIR 1973 SC 1461]) and holding periodic free and fair elections by the Election Commission (*Gujarat Assembly Election Matter,*

In re [2002] 8 SCC 237) are parts of the basic structure of the Constitution, the core elements of the right to contest elections and the right to vote cannot be denied even by an amendment of the Constitution. Let us note, however, that although both democratic institutions and democratic practices are important in achieving democracy in the fuller sense, the presence of the former does not guarantee the latter (Dreze & Sen). Therefore, a robust right to vote has great significance in any democratic system, more so in the case of India.

11.3.3 The election process

The election process in India, which is contained in the Representation of the People Act 1951, has been summarised by the Supreme Court, in the animated words of Krishna Iyer, J:

> The scheme is this. The President of India (under Section 14 of the Representation of the People Act) ignites the general elections across the nation by calling upon the People, divided into several constituencies and registered in the electoral rolls, to choose their representatives to the Lok Sabha. The constitutionally appointed authority, the Election Commission, takes over the whole conduct and supervision of the mammoth enterprise involving a plethora of details and variety of activities, and starts off with the notification of the timetable for the several stages of the election (Section 30). The assembly line operations then begin. An administrative machinery and technology to execute these enormous and diverse jobs is fabricated by the Act, creating officers, powers and duties, delegation of functions and location of polling stations. The precise exercise following upon the calendar for the poll, commencing from presentation of nomination papers, polling drill and telling of votes, culminating in the declaration and report of results are covered by specific prescriptions in the Act and the rules. The secrecy of the ballot, the authenticity of the voting paper and its later identifiability with reference to particular polling stations, has been thoughtfully provided for. Myriad other matters necessary for smooth elections have been taken care of by several provisions of the Act (*Mohinder Singh Gill v The Chief Election Commissioner*, AIR 1978 SC 851).

Speaking of conducting the election in the Indian democratic setup, earlier Fazal-i-Ali, J in *NP Ponnuswami v Returning Officer, Namakkal Constituency* (AIR 1952 SC 64) held:

> Broadly speaking, before an election machinery can be brought into operation there are three requisites which require to be attended to, namely: (1) there should be a set of laws and rules making provisions with respect to all matters relating to, or in connection with, elections, and it should be decided as to how these laws and rules are to be made; (2) there should be an executive charged with the duty of securing the due conduct of election; and (3) there should be a judicial tribunal to deal with disputes arising out of or in connection with elections. Articles 327 and 328 deal with the first of these requisites, article 324 with the second and article 329 with the third requisite. The other two articles in Part XV viz., articles 325 and 326, deal with two matters of principle to which the Constitution framers have attached much importance. They are: (1) prohibition against discrimination in the preparation of, or eligibility for inclusion in, the electoral rolls, on grounds of religion, race, caste, sex or any of them; and (2) adult suffrage. Part XV of the Constitution is really a code in itself providing the entire ground work for enacting appropriate laws and setting up suitable machinery for the conduct of elections.

Under Article 324, the responsibility for conducting elections has been given entirely to the Election Commission of India, an autonomous constitutional body, comprising necessarily a Chief Election Commissioner and, optionally, other Election Commissioners, Joint Election Commissioners, and others. Thus, while the power to make laws with respect to electoral processes remains in the hands of the Parliament, as a matter of its privilege to determine its own constitution, the implementation of such laws and regulation of the electoral process is entirely in the hands of the Election Commission. The powers of the Election Commission, in this context, are comprehensive, and have been held by the Supreme Court of India to be plenary in their character and sweeping (see *Indira Nehru Gandhi v Raj Narain,* AIR 1975 SC 2299), free from any interference, and imbued with discretionary powers (*Mohinder Singh Gill v Chief Election Commissioner,* AIR 1978 SC 851). Dr Ambedkar, speaking on the floor of the Constituent Assembly, during the discussions on Article 324 said:

> But the House affirmed without any kind of dissent that in the interest of purity and freedom of elections to the legislative bodies, it was of the utmost importance that they should be freed from any kind of interference from the executive of the day. In pursuance of the decision of the House, the Drafting Committee removed this question from the category of Fundamental Rights and put it in a separate part containing Articles 289, 290 and so on. Therefore, so far as the fundamental question is concerned that the election machinery should be outside the control of the executive, there has been no dispute. What Article 289 does is to carry out that part of the decision of the Constituent Assembly. It transfers the superintendence, direction and control of the preparation of the electoral rolls and of all elections to Parliament and the Legislatures of States to a body outside the executive to be called the Election Commission.

The inter-relationship between the plenary powers of the Election Commission, as provided under Article 324, the power of the legislatures to make laws with respect to elections, as provided for under Articles 327 (read with Entry 72 of the Union List in the Seventh Schedule) and 328 (read with Entry 37 of the State List in the Seventh Schedule), and the power of the courts to judicially review the electoral process, has been a hotly contested point.

11.3.4 The Election Commission and the legislatures

Many nations have created independent Electoral Commissions to supervise elections (see Chapter 10). Indian jurisprudence illustrates some of the issues that arise in connection with these Commissions. The most important decision of the Indian Supreme Court in explaining the powers of the Commission and those of the legislatures within the constitutional scheme is that of *Indira Nehru Gandhi v Raj Narain* (AIR 1975 SC 2299). In that case, the then Prime Minister Indira Gandhi's election to Parliament was challenged on the basis of electoral malpractices. A Single Judge Bench of the High Court of Allahabad, acting as the election court under Section 80-A of the Representation of the People Act 1951, upheld the challenge and struck down the election of Indira Gandhi. An appeal was taken by Indira Gandhi to the Supreme Court. However, pending the appeal, the Constitution was amended by inserting Article 329-A. Clause (4) of this Article placed the election of a person to the Parliament, who holds the office of the Prime Minister, beyond the pale of judicial scrutiny, retrospectively. Attendant amendments were made to the Representation of the People Act 1951. In effect, the Constitution was amended to nullify the effect of the decision by the Allahabad High Court. The Supreme Court, sitting in appeal over the decision, struck down Article

329-A as violative of the Basic Structure of the Indian Constitution. Writing one of the opinions, Mathew, J, held along the following line:

(i) One of the essential characteristics of legislation is that it made laws generally applicable. In the instant case, Parliament had sought to amend the Constitution and the statutes, not for any general purpose, but to achieve specific ends, and such an act could not be understood as law making by the Parliament. To that effect, such an act, even if it were done with the intention to regulate its own composition by the Parliament, could not be considered as law making under Articles 327 and 328.

(ii) One of the arguments raised for Indira Gandhi was that what had been affected was in the exercise of the Parliament's constituent power, not merely its legislative power. Mathew, J, held that an exercise of constituent power should bear the same standard and vision as goes into the making of a constitution. In the instant matter, the act was merely to achieve specific political benefits, and thus could not be accorded the status of constituent power.

(iii) Referring to the practice, as it obtained in the United States, where the legislatures had the power to make laws and adjudicate upon disputes, relating to election to them, and also to the privileges of the British legislature before 1770, it was argued that the legislatures in India also had the same sweeping powers. Mathew, J, held that the provision to have the elections regulated by an autonomous body, and to render the election disputes judicially reviewable, has been adopted into the Constitution with the sole purpose to ensure fairness. He further held that the power vested in the legislature, could only be legislative power. It could not be, as had been done in the instant case by overruling the decision of the High Court, a judicial power.

The Court thus explained the limited nature of legislative power, and its recognition within Articles 327 and 328. The position established in *Indira Gandhi* has since been relied upon and approved of by successive benches of the Supreme Court. It is now settled that the powers of the Election Commission are plenary insofar as regulation of elections is concerned, and to the extent they do not encroach upon the law-making powers of the legislatures.

11.3.5 Judicial review of electoral process

Initially, the Constitution, under Article 324 (1), had empowered the Election Commission to constitute election tribunals for deciding electoral disputes. These election tribunals were *ad hoc* in nature, usually headed by a District Judge, and constituted specifically for the purposes of deciding a certain set of disputes. However, questions soon arose with respect to the jurisdiction of the *ad hoc* tribunals and their supervision by the Supreme Court and the High Courts (*Hari Vishnu Kamath v Ahmed Ishaque*, AIR 1955 SC 233). Therefore, on the recommendations of the Commission itself, Article 324 (1) was amended in 1966, divesting the Commission of the power to constitute election tribunals and vesting it in the High Courts. Since then, all disputes relating to any election have been disposed of by the High Courts acting as election courts (Section 80A of the Representation of the People Act, 1951 read with Article 329 of the Constitution of India).

Judicial review of electoral process was initially limited in view of the mandate of Article 329 of the Constitution. The issue came up before a Constitution Bench of the Supreme Court in *N P Ponnuswami*. Explaining the philosophy of Article 329, Fazal-i-Ali, J, held that the idea behind Article 329 was to ensure that elections—central to the democratic structure of the country—should not be held up by frivolous litigative enterprise, which may often be aimed merely at thwarting the chances of a deserving candidate. The judgment did refer to certain special situations in which the High Courts and the Supreme Court would be competent to judicially review the electoral process; however, it did not delve into the details of such a situation.

The issue was discussed in much greater detail in *Mohinder Singh Gill*. Krishna Iyer, J, speaking for a Constitution Bench, held that the bar of Article 329 operated only so as to safeguard smooth functioning of electoral processes. However, held the Supreme Court, if a challenge were to be brought before the Courts which would, in effect, facilitate the electoral process by enabling the court to weed out problems at their inception, then the bar of Article 329 would not operate against them.

By its decision in *L Chandra Kumar v Union of India and Others* (AIR 1997 SC 1125), the Supreme Court held judicial review to be part of the basic structure of the Indian Constitution. The superior courts in India have thus been empowered to judicially review decisions of any tribunals, including the Election Commission. However, such a review is balanced with the philosophy of Article 329.

11.4 Political parties and processes

Political parties are a *sine qua non* of democracies. Emphasising their necessity, the Supreme Court in *Kanhiya Lal Omar v RK Trivedi* [(1985) 4 SCC 628] observed that the importance of political parties is implicit in the nature of democratic government. Also, the existence of political parties is crucial and inevitable for bringing revolution through constitutional procedure with every change in government. Plurality is an inevitable part of democracy and existence of multiple political parties ensures it. 'Systemized differences' and 'unresolved conflicts', according to the Court, are the essence of the Indian political system, which establishes the convictions of the majority.

Until the enactment of the Constitution (Fifty-second Amendment) Act 1985, the Indian Constitution did not have any reference to political parties. The Amendment acknowledged the existence of political parties and gave them due recognition. Until then, the recognition of political parties and allotment of party symbols to them was regulated by the Election Symbols (Reservation and Allotment) Order 1968. The definition of political party was provided in paragraph 2(1)(h) of the Symbols Order 1968. The Symbols Order was issued by the Commission in exercise of its power under Article 324 of the Constitution, read with Rules 5 and 10 of the Conduct of Election Rules. According to Paragraph 2(h), a political party is an association or a body of individual citizens of India registered with the Commission as a political party under paragraph 3, and includes a political party deemed to be registered with the Commission under the proviso to sub-paragraph 2 of that paragraph.

A political party does not get the right to exist in perpetuity merely because it has once been registered by the Election Commission under the Symbols Order of 1968. After General Elections, the party is required to fulfill the conditions laid down in Paragraphs 6(2) and 7 of the Order in order to continue as a recognised national or state political party. Paragraph 6(2) requires a recognised political party either to remain politically active for a continuous period of five years or to return one member to the House of People for every 25 members existing in the House or any fraction elected from that state or return at least one member to the Legislative Assembly for every 30 members existing or any similar fraction. The alternative method is to fulfill the condition laid down in Paragraph 7(1). A national party under

Paragraph 7(1) is required to be recognised in more than four states. In *Janata Dal Samajwadi v Election Commission of India* (AIR 1996 SC 577), the Supreme Court declared that General Elections did not mean elections in all the states. In India, elections are generally held in groups of states at a time. Hence a party should be recognised in more than four states in order to be recognised as a national political party. Otherwise, the Election Commission may derecognise the concerned party.

11.4.1 Law against political defection

Besides this, Articles 102 and 191 of the Indian Constitution indirectly provide for certain mandates for membership in a political party at the central and the state level respectively. The tenth Schedule of the Constitution was inserted with the objective of fixing the problem of political defections, which had become a national concern aggravated by the coalition government system. Political defection in India is seen as a nuisance that undermines the basic principles of democracy (Jain 2003, 1693). The new clause added in Article 102 provided that a person ceases to be a member of either House of the Parliament if he is disqualified under the Tenth Schedule of the Constitution. The Tenth Schedule of the Constitution itself, among various significant provisions, declares that if an individual votes or abstains from voting in the House contrary to the directions of the political party, and the same has either not been done with the prior permission of the party or has not been condoned within 15 days, then the concerned person stands disqualified from the political party (ibid). A person's political identity in India cannot be divorced from the political party that he represents. When a member intends to quit the party on whose ticket he was elected, then he, according to the Constitution, has to resign and re-contest election. The underlying principle behind this provision is prevention of individual party members from deriving undue and immediate political gains in the guise of belonging to a political party (Jain, 1694).

11.5 Conclusion

Many details of Indian law—laid down in the Representation of the People Act, Rules made under it, various Orders issued by the Election Commission, and their interpretation by the courts in a large number of matters such as election symbols, use of religious symbols for electoral purposes, setting up of candidates for different political parties, merger and amalgamation of political parties, offences related to election matters which make election law a specialised branch of study could not be incorporated in this paper because of space constraints. Yet, the volume and specialised character of constitutional provision for elections in India reminds us of the importance of the subject in the constitutional structure and operation of modern democracies.

As we noted in the beginning, it is not necessary from a comparative perspective that a constitution must expressly provide for the elections and electoral machinery, but as the Indian experience has proved so far, such an arrangement in the constitution is of great support, especially in those societies that do not have a history of having worked with democratic institutions. As a society, India may or may not be included in that category, but the functioning of its constitution on expected democratic lines in the midst of all adverse calculations based on objective factors unfavourable for democracy leads us to conclude that effective provisions in the text of the constitution establishing an electoral system are conducive to its operation and healthy growth. If India has been able to sustain a democratic system and hold itself together in spite of its unfavourable history and circumstances, as well as its immense diversities and inequalities, it is first and foremost due to its constitutional guarantee of universal adult suffrage and the provisions for constitutional machinery for the realisation of that guarantee. In that light we could assume that the future constitutional democracies, especially those with no history of having worked with democratic institutions, could seek guidance from such constitutional arrangements.

References

Dreze, J & Sen, A (2002). Practice of Democracy in India (Oxford University Press).

Elkins, Z, Ginsburg, T & Melton, J (2009). The Endurance of National Constitutions (Cambridge University Press).

Friedrich, CJ (1967). Constitutional Government and Democracy (Oxford & IBH Publishing Co. New Delhi, 4th edn).

Horowitz, DL (2003). Electoral Systems: A Primer for Decision Makers, *Journal of Democracy* 14; 4 (Oct 2003), pp. 115–27.

Jain, MP (2003). Indian Constitutional Law (5th edn; Wadhwa and Company, Nagpur).

Kothari, R (1970). Politics in India (New Delhi: Orient Longman Private Ltd); reprinted 2009, published by Orient Blackswan.

Lijphart, A & Grofman, B (eds) (1984). Choosing an electoral system: Issues and alternatives (Praeger Special Studies, New York).

Norris, P (1997). Choosing Electoral System: Proportional, Majoritarian or Mixed System, Harvard University, International Political Science Review, Vol. 28(3) July, p. 297–312.

Pildes, RH (2007). What Kind of Right is 'The Right to Vote?', Virginia Law Review in Brief, Vol. 93, pp. 43–50, 23 April; NYU Law School, Public Law Research Paper No. 07-08. Available at SSRN: http://ssrn.com/abstract=987912.

Rao, BS (ed) (1968). The Framing of India's Constitution. A Study (IIPA, New Delhi).

Stratmann, T & Baur, M (2002). Working paper on Plurality Rule, Proportional Representation, and The German Bundestag: A joint initiative of Ludwig-Maximilians-Universität and Ifo Institute for Economic Research, CES Ifo Working Paper no. 650(2), January 2002.

Additional reading

Austin, G (1996). The Indian Constitution: Cornerstone of a Nation (Oxford University Press).

Balagopal, K (2011). Ear to the Ground (Navayana).

Baxi, U (1987). Law Democracy and Human Rights, Lokayukta Bulletin, 5: 4/5.

—— (2007). Parliamentary Committee on Personnel, Public Grievances, Law and Justice – Study on Electoral Reforms, 18 February.

Dhawan, R (1998). A Constitution for a Civilization: India's Constitutions and Discontents, PILSARC.

Kadambi, R (2009). 'Right to Vote as a Fundamental Right: "Mistaking the Woods for Trees"' [2009] INJlConLaw 11; 3 Indian Journal of Constitutional Law 181.

Kothari, R (1996). Elections without party system [Journal], Bombay: [s.n.], April 16–17: Vol. 31, p. 1004.

Mehta, PB (2003). The Burden of Democracy (New Delhi: Penguin Books).

Nandy, A (1989). The Intimate Enemy (New Delhi: Oxford University Press).

12

Federalism and autonomy

Lidija R Basta Fleiner and Jean-François Gaudreault-DesBiens

12.1 Introduction

Federal systems characteristically seek to establish constitutional structures reconciling self-rule and shared rule (Elazar, 5). Given the avowed objective of such systems to protect and promote self-rule, federalism inevitably relates to autonomy and its beneficiaries. Yet, there are limits to an approach linking federalism and autonomy:

(1) *Context* – The various institutional designs of federal systems address problems faced by particular political communities stemming from distinct political and legal traditions.
(2) *Descriptive v normative* – Federalism scholarship is either descriptive (analytical) or normative. This chapter will mainly privilege the former.
(3) *Variations* – Whereas federations are the main constitutional expression of federalism, a number of other federal designs cannot, strictly speaking, be assimilated to federations.
(4) *Evolutionary dynamics* – Distinctions can be drawn between *aggregative federalism* (coming-together federalism), such as the United States, Switzerland and Australia—and *disaggregative* or *devolutionary federalism* (holding-together federalism)—such as India, Belgium and Spain. Federations created through the mediation of the international community (Iraq, the Union of Serbia and Montenegro) result from a phenomenon of 'putting-together' federalism (Stepan, 23). Looking beyond the formal foundational constitutional moment of a federation may even reveal, as in Canada, more complex patterns mixing aggregative and disaggregative dynamics.

Some common trends are discernible despite these variations. One is the centrality of the constitution and consequently the critical importance of constitutional justice, with the increasingly important role of judicial review in developing federalism, and its impact on shared rule, self-rule or other forms of autonomy. Nonetheless, Swiss federalism functions effectively without having any system of constitutional judicial review of federal laws; an exception that highlights the importance of developing a truly federal culture in the daily working of the federation, in which judicial review of federal laws is seen as an instrument of unification at the federal level.

A second trend concerns the political uses of federalism, which has become an important nation-building tool in divided or post-conflict societies, particularly those where ethnicity played a significant role in triggering divisions and fuelling conflict. Yet, federalism is not a 'magic tool' for fragmented societies, as constitutional and political factors in each case tend to change its function. Appropriate distinctions therefore must be made between *monistic federalism*, inhospitable to claims for political recognition of ethnic, religious and linguistic group identities (United States, Australia), and *pluralist federalism*, embracing constitutive principles and institutions more prone to accommodate sub-state ethnic, religious or linguistic identities (Canada, Switzerland and Belgium).

The interplay between federalism and autonomy will be examined by mapping various approaches to federalism, its underlying values and the potential tensions that might erupt between the latter (see Section 12.2). Various types of federal and quasi-federal arrangements will then be described (see Section 12.3). The chapter will next focus on shared rule and constitutional limits to autonomy (see Section 12.4), closing with a look at self-rule and constitutional guarantees of autonomy (see Section 12.5). Throughout, the focus is on federations at the national level.

12.2 The values underlying federalism and the dynamic interplay of self-rule and shared rule

The self-rule/shared-rule distinction should not evoke polar opposites, but instead be understood as describing a continuum. Federations are often shaped through sinuous dynamics of aggregation (centralization) and disaggregation (decentralization). Moreover, political autonomy within a broader polity can be fostered in many ways, the creation of a federation being only one possibility. An illustration is the federalizing regionalism that has recently characterized the constitutional evolution of Italy and Spain, or the Scottish devolution within the United Kingdom.

This self-rule/shared-rule distinction serves additionally as a springboard for normative judgments about the successes and failures of particular federations, pointing to the values typically claimed by federalism. Examining the most important values sheds light on the central role of autonomy when reflecting upon federalism. Because these values sometimes clash with one another, the federal nature of a polity cannot alone explain all positive or negative outcomes; they are inevitably influenced by other variables such as the party system, the depth of identity pluralism within society, the urban–rural ratio, the level of economic disparities, or the degree of concentration of economic power. Contingency characterizes the relation that federalism entertains with the values it allegedly fosters.

12.2.1 Federalism and diversity

A federal structure is particularly appropriate for addressing a polity's *social, ethnic* and *cultural diversity,* even though these vectors of diversity can also be grasped by other political means, such as administrative decentralization. Consequently, federalism is not an end in itself, but rather a political response to the *fact* of diversity.

The nature of internal diversity and, most importantly, its political salience obviously influences the structure of a given state. The presence of political minorities, whose primary locus of identification is a sub-state entity rather than the global polity, and for whom belonging to the latter is conditional upon the respect by the polity of their primary identification, risks making a significant difference in the ultimate configuration of that state, as opposed to the mere presence of social minorities, who are in a legitimate position to advance an equality claim but whose form of belonging to the broader polity is not conditional (Lajoie, 34, 45).

All forms of federalism cannot accommodate such a deep level of diversity, but pluralist federalism seeks to do it. To sustain the viability of nation-building in multicultural and, *a fortiori*, multinational societies, such a polity embraces principles and establishes institutions designed to acknowledge the particular configuration of its *demos* and to accommodate sub-state ethnic, religious or linguistic identities (Requejo).

Among multinational or multicultural federations, differences abound as to how diversity is constitutionally recognized. One example is the manner in which Canada and Belgium deal with minority language education. Canada envisages the right to be educated in one's language as a personal right, exercisable if a sufficient number of speakers justify the funding of public schools in the official minority language (French or English); Belgium privileges the territoriality principle in linguistic policy. Another illustration is Indian federalism's embrace of diversity, while most Euro–American models of federalism seem rather inclined to tame it, even when they give it a say, for example through the enshrinement of minority rights—a structure that somehow presupposes a majoritarian cultural background.

Federalism, diversity and self-government are intertwined to a significant extent. Federalism allows federated units a regulatory space precisely as regards their particular circumstances. From that perspective, the idea of a perfectly symmetrical federalism (in law, conventions and practices) is arguably an illusion. Yet, federalism also rejects the artificial amplification of differences so common in identity politics, which brings up its potential role as a peace-making tool.

12.2.2 Federalism and peace

Enlightenment thinkers had already debated the normative potential of international federalism to promote peace in Europe (Kant). Their concern is still valid today, as federalism is often associated with *peace*, in spite of not always being conducive to it. The internal conflicts plaguing some federations have sometimes led to civil wars, such as those that erupted in the United States in the nineteenth century or in Yugoslavia more than a century later. Undoubtedly, a federation undermined by the lack of any foundational consensus can lead to social unrest if it does not otherwise find means to foster the loyalty of all segments of society. This does not mean, however, that federalism, under certain conditions, cannot help bridge longstanding antagonisms. These conditions are context-related and must first and foremost guarantee that belonging to the federation remains non-negotiable on a day-to-day basis across community lines. All three ex-communist federations dissolved precisely because no federal democratic consensus was at hand.

12.2.3 Federalism and democracy

Federalism's relation to *democracy* is ambiguous. On a positive note, the presence of federated units arguably closer to citizens than a remote central government might provide them with an enhanced opportunity to be involved in the self-government of their community. There might be some truth to that, but one can imagine a similar outcome in other forms of decentralized regimes. Still, federalism might promote such opportunities more regularly than unitary regimes.

On the other hand, federalism is accused of undermining democracy when it frustrates majority rule as a result of the division of the 'national' polity into constitutionally protected smaller segments. On certain issues falling under the sub-state units' jurisdiction, local majorities may end up defeating national ones. Nonetheless, a federal polity is not an abstract polity. It is a polity that, for diverse reasons, has been politically designed and legally constituted as federal, which by definition implies some degree of political fragmentation. Reducing democracy to majority rule therefore enshrines a normative bias against federalism. Moreover, it ignores that federalism is about political group accommodation, implying that majority alone does not express the will of the sovereign, and that the very identity of the sovereign, or of its modes of expression, is plural and highly debatable.

A more complex definition of democracy is needed in order to better grasp the relation between this concept and federalism. Human rights and the principle of the rule of law may provide further layers of complexity by supplementing the traditional majoritarian narrative of democracy. One can legitimately wonder what to make of notions of equal citizenship and human rights in a federal context, where the actual exercise of self-rule by federated units in their spheres of competence may lead to disparities in the treatment of citizens. The bare reality is that federalism, like multiculturalism or multinationalism, puts into question and aims at redefining absolute political equality as political liberty (Basta Fleiner 2011, 226). How to understand, then, differential treatments imposed upon the citizens of a federation depending on the federated unit in which they reside? If the differential treatment at stake affects the enjoyment and/or exercise of human rights, the problem becomes even more complicated given that federated units have a constitutional right to see their normative autonomy respected, provided they remain within their competences. Quebec's laws restrict the use of languages other than French in commercial advertising and force immigrants to send their children to French schools, to perpetuate the French fact in a country and on a continent where English rules. In Switzerland, the territoriality policy envisages collective language rights, allowing, for example, for the prohibition of private German schools in the French-speaking district of the bilingual canton of Bern. The solution echoes in this case the priority of inter-communal peace over individual freedoms. More importantly, it testifies to a different nature of the relation between democracy and federalism. The availability of the referendum and initiative transformed an abstract principle of people's sovereignty into participatory democracy. This original Swiss contribution to the modern democracies of the nineteenth century has a two-fold function: (1) promoting democratic integration, by maintaining and promoting communal and cantonal loyalty in light of linguistic and religious diversities; (2) making direct democracy a systemic element of checks and balances. By 'federalizing' participatory democracy federalism also plays the key competitive role in the Swiss political arena.

The tension between the asymmetries brought about by federalism on the one hand, and human rights on the other, paradoxically provides an argument in favour of federalism, tying it to the constitutionalist democratic ideal of the separation of state powers. This argument, which was first articulated in the United States, values federalism because it has the potential to increase the individual freedom of citizens by establishing structures that spread rather than concentrate power. If one level of government abuses its powers, the citizens may seek protection, or at least some form of counter-intervention, in the other level of government. A similar idea may be formulated horizontally: If a federated unit commits abuses while exercising its autonomous powers, its citizens—after having voiced their discontent to no avail—may move to other units in search of greener pastures. Here again, an element of contingency must be included. This 'checks-and-balances' argument presupposes that each level of government is meaningfully autonomous and therefore not subordinated to the other, that both levels of government respect the rule of law, and that the judiciary is independent from these governments. No constitutionally established division of powers ever prevented abuses in non-democratic 'federations'.

12.2.4 Federalism and innovation

It is often said that federalism's constitutional recognition of several self-governing federated units, and the diversity of policies they elaborate, may transform them into laboratories for innovation. This presupposes that they enjoy a meaningful legal and financial autonomy, without which it is difficult, if not outright impossible, to go off beaten paths.

12.3 Different types of federal and quasi-federal arrangements

12.3.1 Federalism between integration and accommodation

Whether federalism actively seeks to integrate sources of cultural diversity within a broader polity, thus downplaying them, or is instead open to accommodating and promoting them, remains anchored in the logic that underpins the type of federalism in question.

Monistic federalism is intrinsically suspicious of ethnic, religious and linguistic identities, tending to be hostile to their political and legal recognition, as the United States' 'melting pot' doctrine shows. Alternatively, a monistic federalism based upon a cultural nation-concept may privilege the identity of the federation's cultural majority, understood as its 'constitutive' ethno-nation (e.g. the contested German national concept of Blutgemeinschaft' [community of blood] or 'Schicksalsgemeinschaft' [community of fate]).

In contrast, pluralist federalism recognizes as the ultimate locus of political sovereignty a 'composed' nation formed by distinct and politically salient linguistic, ethnic and religious communities (Choudhry, 171). Its sub-types—multicultural/multinational and ethnic federalism—differ in terms of the scope and focus of the strategies privileged for accommodating diversity, the constitutional status of self-determination rights, and the role territory plays in identity politics. Switzerland, India, and Canada can arguably be characterized as multicultural or multinational federations, whereas Ethiopia and ex-communist federations enshrine under one form or another an ethnic-federalism model.

The choice between integration and accommodation of diversity directly leads to key constitutive differences between the two types of federalism. Whereas the United States paradigmatically represents a democratic federation and federal polity in which federalism serves as an anti-majoritarian check of governmental powers, Switzerland's federalised participatory democracy (initiative and referendum) is an answer to the dilemma about the reconciliation of divergent majority and minority interests. Such a regime protects multiple loyalties by giving collective rights to historical sub-state communities. Being a constitutive element of the sovereign people's will, these rights therefore limit governmental powers (Basta Fleiner 1996, 60–65).

Given such constitutive particularities, pluralist/multinational federations tend to entail the following complementary institutional arrangements: significant constitutionally guaranteed autonomy for federated units, and consociational decision-making rules at the federal level. The more multinational they are, the greater the probability that pluralist federations embrace the concept of divided sovereignty or sovereign powers (McGarry, O'Leary & Simeon, 64), although of course there are exceptions to this generalization. Federalism in multinational federations actually replaces sovereignty with a 'diffusion of sovereign power', which is best reflected by the fact that internal sovereignty is divided, with sovereign powers vested in both the federation and federated units.

12.3.2 Federal governance without federations

12.3.2.1 Federations without a formal federal structure

There can be no federation properly understood if the federal constitutional design is not built upon a federal polity. Consequently, communist multinational federations reflected a type of 'façade federalism' (Friedrich 1968). On the other hand, while not formally consti-tuted as a federation, South Africa is characterized by a system of federal governance. As the majority of the country's black population associated federalism with apartheid politics, it was deemed politically inappropriate to designate the new regime as a federation. The system was given strong unitary features, while federal elements—such as a separated list of competences, shared rule and a supremacy clause—were left to the interpretation of the courts. This led to a much-criticized 'judicialization of federal claims' (Basta Fleiner 2008, 80). Yet, regardless of South Africa's 'unofficial status as a federal country', its constitution establishes a federal framework because of the way 'power has been dispersed between three spheres of govern-ment (national, provincial and local) and for its explicit articulation of a principle of coopera-tive government' (Steytler, 312–13). A federal-governance dynamic without a federal constitution, strictly speaking, epitomizes the distinction between 'federal governments' and 'federal constitutions' (Wheare, 15–20).

12.3.2.2 Regionalism and crypto-federalism

Constitutionally, Italy is a 'state of regions' and Spain a 'state of autonomous communities'. In Spain, the 1978 Constitution laid down an open-ended model of a federalizing territorial organization with 'differential status' for 'historical nationalities' (Aja; Moreno, 291). Italy first introduced a *de facto* federal system by means of ordinary legislation. The constitutionali-zation of federal principles followed in the form of three constitutional laws, passed between 1999 and 2001. The new system 'considerably limits the legislative and administrative powers of the national level, abolishes State control over regional legislation and puts the presumption for general regional legislative competence in the constitution' (Palermo, 113). Spain and Italy are neither decentralized unitary states nor federations, but both have embraced, albeit differently, solutions reminiscent of federalism. Notably, both states have allowed regionalism to permanently inform their development, and have recognized the legitimacy of asymmet-rical statuses for their regions (Italy) or autonomous communities (Spain). In both cases, their institutional features reveal a federal *telos* of accommodating cultural diversities on a territo-rial basis, and specific procedures enabling regions to co-determine their status with central authorities. This last feature has effectively made Italian and Spanish regions *de facto* partners with central authorities when deciding on matters concerning them, but not other types of matters. It distinguishes their status from that of Northern Ireland and Scotland in the United Kingdom, where, due to the resilience of Parliament's absolute sovereignty, the current system of asymmetric devolution does not envisage the participation of devolved units *as such* in the central government, even on matters that concern them alone. An important aspect of the devolution settlement is the Sewel Convention, which ensures that Westminster will normally legislate on devolved matters only with the express agreement of the Scottish Parliament, after proper consideration and scrutiny of the proposal in question. In a similar vein, even though their status is arguably closer to that of federated units, Italian and Spanish regions are no more constituent units of the central state than are Northern Ireland or Scotland, as they do not participate in the constitution-making power.

12.3.2.3 Legal system underpinnings of federalism: common law v. civil law

Whether a modern federation belongs to the common-law or the civil-law tradition is critical in order to properly understand the underlying principles of that federation, as well as the institutional factors affecting its functioning dynamics. The main difference lies in fundamentally different perspectives on the nature and role of the state and, accordingly, its relation to law. In civil law countries, the resilience of Bodin's absolutist theory of sovereignty, which posits that the sovereign is the ultimate source of law, renders difficult conceiving the *de jure* and *de facto* division of sovereignty that characterizes federalism (Beaud, 58–65; Fleiner & Basta Fleiner, 311–12).

Conversely, common law jurisdictions, tending to adhere to the idea that the sovereign is bound by the fundamental law rather than being its ultimate source, are less reluctant to accept such a division of sovereignty. The acceptance of the principle of divided sovereignty in common law systems has even affected the internal working of the state, by influencing the institutional design and role that courts play. The fact that courts are viewed as law-making bodies empowered to review governmental action *ex post facto* in concrete disputes made possible an arguably broader judicial review of laws and executive acts on federalism grounds in common law federations than in civil law federations. Predictably, courts have often significantly influenced the shape of federalism in the former, the US Supreme Court being a pioneer in this respect, with its key role in the development of US federal principles, notably the allocation of powers (*McCulloch v Maryland*, 1819). On the contrary, notwithstanding the existence of a constitutional complaint procedure, judicial review on federalism groups occupies a narrower scope in civil law federations (Austria or Germany, among others), where special constitutional courts are responsible for reviewing the constitutionality and legality of legal acts, *ex ante* and abstractly.

Last, the division between constitutional law and politics is not exactly the same in common law and civil law federations. For the purpose of laying down the rules governing federalism, the latter tend to privilege formal, often detailed, legal frameworks over less specific frameworks more tolerant of political arrangements or expedients, as is the case in several common law federations (Poirier 2001, 8).

12.4 Shared rule and constitutional limits to autonomy

The key constitutional mechanisms for shared rule provided by federal constitution are: (1) representation of constitutional units in federal bodies, most importantly the second chamber; (2) distributions of powers among government levels, including which powers are to be exclusive and which are to be explicitly or implicitly concurrent; (3) allocation of residual powers; (4) institutions or mechanisms to resolve conflicts between orders of government, especially those over the distribution of powers; (5) the supremacy of federal laws enacted within the national government's sphere of constitutional authority; (6) an independent judiciary umpiring or policing the division of powers between orders of government. The aim of all these mechanisms is to guarantee the the representation of the federation's diversity within federal institutions, this in view of achieving a proper balance between unity and diversity.

Like decentralized unitary states, federations have to arbitrate centripetal and centrifugal forces. Competing claims over primarily federal legislative powers characterize all federations, the only difference lying in the type and level of conflicts. Some federations are more successful than others in managing them. The Swiss directorial system better mediates such conflicts when compared with the US presidential system or the German parliamentary regime. The key conflict-management rules and principles in the constitutional politics of all federations are generally found in their division of powers. Nonetheless, concurrent powers tend to enhance the potential for conflicts. The German 'framework legislation' on the *uniformity* of living conditions has long been targeted as one of the main constitutional avenues for federal intrusions into affairs of the Länder (interlocked systems, Politikverflechtung). A constitutional revision in 1994 reduced the veto rights of the Bundesrat, which had covered over 60 percent of federal legislation. Since 1994, the federation can pre-empt Länder only if the general interest of equivalent living conditions demands so, or in order to secure the legal and economic secutiry of the country (Gunlicks). Some constitutions expressly provide mechanisms for resolving conflicts. The Indian Constitution provides, 'If any provision of a law made by the Legislature of a State is repugnant to [...] any provision of an existing law with respect to one of the matters enumerated in the Concurrent List [...] the law made by Parliament [...] shall prevail' (Art. 254.1).

The Russian Constitution allows the President of the Federation to use dispute-settlement procedures to settle conflicts between the recognized federated units of the Russian Federation. Other federal constitutions leave this question to the judiciary (United States, Canada).

In a nutshell, concurrent powers have served more to limit autonomy by making federation stronger than to sustain autonomy through shared rule. A judicially developed common law is generally more flexible when establishing shared rule, and more adaptable to changing trends in majority/minority contestations, especially when concurrency is understood to deal with the level of government rather than division of powers. Australia is the only federation with legislative inter-delegation within uniform legislation. (...) In Canada, only administrative inter-delegation and legislation 'by reference' (i.e. legislation relying on concepts defined in laws validly enacted by another level of government) are allowed.

Given varieties in legal status and closeness to politics, intergovernmental relations are also critical for the effective application of conflict-management rules or principles in a federation.

12.4.1 Federal supremacy clause

Courts are pivotal in arbitrating centripetal and centrifugal pressures; even more so when a federal constitution is devoid of fomal conflict-management institutions, but contains constitutional principles guiding courts in solving, according to legal criteria, political conflicts over the interpretation of the constitutional allocation of powers between the federal government and federated units. The most widespread principle is expressed in *federal supremacy clauses*, whose origins can be traced back to the world's first modern federation, the United States.

12.4.2 Subsidiarity as a principle

Important conflict-management rules and principles are not always constitutionally enshrined but developed instead by constitutional courts. Whereas the Swiss Constitution provides that 'the Confederation shall only undertake tasks that the Cantons are unable to perform or which require uniform regulation by the Confederation', in Germany, the *principle of subsidiarity* has been developed in the rulings of the Federal Constitutional Court. The sometimes weak conception of subsidiarity promoted by courts of law is supplemented by the somewhat more robust understanding it receives in the political realm, which often emphasizes the federated units' autonomy.

12.4.3 Loyalty principle

The *principle of loyalty* may limit the autonomy either of the federated units or of the federal order. The weaker level is *federal comity,* formulated by *full faith and credit clauses* (Art. IV.1 of the US Constitution: 'Full faith and credit shall be given in each state to the public acts, records, and judicial proceedings of every other state'). A stronger conception of loyalty, known as *loyalty proper* (Bundestreue) or *conviviality,* has been embraced by younger federations (Germany, Belgium, post-1999 Switzerland, and South Africa, in which federal loyalty is most comprehensively enshrined). Although strictly speaking not federations, Italy and Spain, with their highly federalized structure and political dynamics, have also elevated federal loyalty to a constitutional principle. Notably, this principle always operates reciprocally, and can have vertical and horizontal dimensions. Federal loyalty proper as a constitutional principle was in fact invented under the first Constitution of the German Empire but the 1949 Fundamental Law contains no such provision. In Germany and Austria, the principle of federal loyalty became inherently linked to federalism by these countries' constitutional courts. In both cases, federal loyalty was applied when ruling on the distribution of constitutional powers and deciding how such powers are actually to be exercised by their legal holders (Gamper 2010, 163–65). Even when a federation's constitutional tradition does not formally refer to the notion of loyalty, its logic can be detected in legal developments, especially in times of crisis. When ruling on the legality of a potential unilateral declaration of independence by the province of Quebec, the Supreme Court of Canada built on implicit constitutional principles (federalism, democracy, constitutionalism and the rule of law) and imposed a reciprocal duty to negotiate, should a clear majority in favour of independence be expressed, this in view of ensuring an orderly process protective of the rights and interests of all those affected by a secession (*Reference re Secession of Quebec*, 1998).

12.4.4 Equality principle

12.4.4.1 Intergovernmental equality

The dichotomy between and the practice of *asymmetrical* and *symmetrical federalism* reveal the difficulty of implementing the notion of intergovernmental equality. Asymmetrical federalism presupposes the existence of variations in the legislative and administrative powers conferred on federated units or in the fiscal arrangements they have with their central government. Exceptionally, the possibility that asymmetries be created can also be explicitly recognized in a Bill of Rights and in a constitution's amending procedure through opting-out rights, or, implicitly, through the incremental evolution of federal constitutions (Gaudreault-DesBiens, 238–47).

Asymmetrical federalism gives more autonomy to some federated units than others, creating formal inequalities among such units. Such formal inequalities are sometimes constitutionally enshrined so as to enhance the substantive equality of particular federated units, for example when they overlap with a minority within the federation.

The Russian and Belgian federations provide interesting illustrations of asymmetrical arrangements. Russia currently represents the most asymmetrical federation, with 83 'subjects of federation', divided into five categories, according to the level of constitutionally guaranteed autonomy and participation in decision-making at federal level that is granted to them. The *situs* of federal asymmetries in Russia is territorial. The situation is different in Belgium, where a mixed form of asymmetry has been constitutionally recognized since 1993, notably through the recognition of jurisdictional differences between the three territorial regions and the three non-territorial communities.

Another important distinction is between *de jure* and *de facto* asymmetrical federalism. Conventions or political practices may lead to the creation of asymmetries with no legal formal basis, but which may reinforce the political legitimacy of the federation among all of its federated units. Particularly important as regards multinational federations is the issue as to whether asymmetrical federalism has stabilizing or destabilizing effects, the latter being the case with India.

Nonetheless, the conceptual relevance and usefulness of the symmetry/asymmetry dichotomy remains limited; a certain level of asymmetry is arguably an intrinsic consequence of any federal arrangement. Its centrality is obvious in states where the constitutional dynamics can be associated with pluralist federalism. It is the case in Spain or in Italy, as well as in the United Kingdom, where asymmetrical arrangements, whether constitutionally enshrined as in Spain or Italy, or provided for by Acts of Parliament as in the UK, give tangible meaning to regionalism. Beyond states enshrining one form or another of pluralist federalism, political asymmetry is unavoidable among the federated units of most federations, due to demographic, economic or cultural differences. Once such disparities, particularly economic ones, detrimentally affect one territorially concentrated ethnic community, serious tensions and instability can arise (in Switzerland, the internal secession of the northern French-speaking part of Jura from the canton of Bern).

Asymmetry can be further enhanced with 'soft-law' or purely political mechanisms of intergovernmental relations. In Canada, thanks to political agreements between the federal government and the province of Quebec, this province now plays a much more important role than other provinces in the management of immigration, and is significantly more active than its counterparts on the international scene.

Last, a particular design of symmetrical division of powers may nevertheless *facilitate* the creation of asymmetries. Although all Canadian provinces enjoy the same jurisdiction over 'property and civil rights' (a head of power that encompasses most private law subjects), only the province of Quebec has used it to select civil law rather than common law as its *jus commune*. The normative space created by symmetrical divisions of powers may therefore help sustain or even deepen the distinctiveness of some federated units (Gaudreault-DesBiens 2012, 232).

12.4.4.2 Interpersonal equality

Interpersonal equality in federal structures primarily addresses equality in minimal living standards for all citizens of a country, notwithstanding socio-economic disparities among federated units, including welfare services. Typically, fiscal equalization systems, based upon the redistributive-justice principle, seek to implement this type of equality.

12.4.4.3 Equal rights v. equality in rights

Except for the US Senate, where all states are equally represented regardless of population, the American federalist model affirms an absolute equality of civil and political rights. It is therefore hostile to collective rights and presents itself as the antithesis of pluralist federalism. In contrast, the Indian discourse of human rights heavily emphasizes the importance of negotiating the values of citizenship through the affirmation of differential rights in a plural and unequal society. Constitutional and statutory provisions for affirmative action in favour of disadvantaged groups became 'an arena of contestation between two constitutional principles of equality and difference, [...] calling for judicial intervention' (Suresh, 134). The Swiss model of pluralist federalism is based on collective rights as part of the citizenship principle. The territoriality principle in language rights policy allows the overruling of individual rights for the sake of protecting traditional linguistic patterns in the country. The equality of federated communities, as opposed to the equality of individuals, thus becomes the focus of the constitutional order. The Canadian situation lies somewhere in-between, recognizing two official linguistic communities and their individual members' rights to have access to public schooling wherever they are, provided that they are in sufficient number. In this model, language rights are to be understood primarily as individual, but as such may only be exercised if a broader societal culture is protected (Kymlicka, 76–77) (see Chapter 30).

12.5 Self-rule and constitutional guarantees of autonomy

Typically, the notion of autonomy is central to theorizing about both the understanding and practical functioning of federalism. We shall look, first, at some structural and normative features that, in federations, serve as safeguards for protecting the autonomy of constitutionally recognized levels of governments, and, second, at various archetypal logics underlying the organization of autonomy.

12.5.1 Structures and principles

A defining characteristic of a federation is a constitutionally entrenched division of powers, which is supreme and thus non-modifiable at the will of a single party. Within a federation, the constitutionally recognized levels of government must enjoy constitutional protection from changes imposed upon them, unless these changes are validly made according to the relevant amending procedure. In many federations, the assent of governments affected by such crucially important changes, or of a substantial majority of them, is mandatory. In Canada, the division of powers can only be amended with the assent of the federal Parliament and of seven provinces (out of 10) representing at least 50 percent of the population of all the provinces. Moreover, provinces disagreeing with an amendment modifying their legislative powers in the manner set forth above may 'opt out' of this amendment by expressing their dissent. In Switzerland, constitutional revision must be accepted by the majority of both people and cantons.

A division of powers materializes the idea that each level of government, being a legal order distinct and autonomous from the others, is immune to actions that would alter its constitutional status and prerogatives within the federation. Once created, the central government cannot be considered as a mere 'creature' of the federated units. Conversely, once created or recognized by the constitution, the federated units' existence and autonomous powers are equally guaranteed. In several federations, various interpretive theories have stemmed from such constitutional enshrinement of competences, for example the theory of sovereign powers. Essentially, they all boil down to a non-subordination principle, subject to the paramount application of federal laws in case of conflict. The division of powers therefore guarantees a relative normative and political autonomy of a federation's constitutionally recognized levels of government.

Within the parameters set forth by the federal constitution, the central government and the federated units enjoy some level of organizational and institutional autonomy: as a matter of principle, they are free to adopt or modify their internal constitution and to organize the functioning of government, encompassing the structure and interplay of legislative, executive and judicial powers. Many federal constitutions ensure that all levels of government enjoy revenue-raising powers, be they exclusive or concurrent, thereby protecting to some extent their financial and fiscal autonomy. Some even regulate financial transfers from one level, often the central government, to another, most likely the federated units, in order to stabilize and equalize the revenues of the recipient governments, thus further contributing to their financial autonomy.

Supplementing the division of powers are conflict rules or principles, broadly understood, whose aim is to ensure that there cannot be any jurisdictional vacuum or legal incoherence arising out of the division of powers. Among those rules is the allocation of residuary powers to a particular level of government. These powers are most often attributed to federated units, especially when the division of powers does not enumerate the competences of such units. The United States, Switzerland, Germany and Malaysia, among others, embraced the former solution, while in fewer federations (Canada, India, Belgium) the central government possesses residuary powers. The principle of subsidiarity—explicitly recognized or not—also contributes to regulating power transfers between levels of government, with a view to avoiding arbitrary power grabs. Moreover, federal constitutional frameworks deal with the inter-delegation of legislative powers, with some allowing it (Australia) and some prohibiting it (Canada). Another way of increasing the efficiency and predictability of division of powers is the use of the primacy principle. Most often, it is federal laws that prevail in cases of conflict, irrespective of the 'cooperative' or 'competitive' nature of federalism in question.

This distinction is not watertight, though, since some level of cooperation is arguably inevitable in any federation. Even when the federal constitution seemingly enshrines a type of federalism that is closer to the competitive model, political actors often circumvent such constitutional hurdles by resorting to intergovernmental agreements, the legal status of which varies depending on the federation. In many federations, this has led to a burgeoning practice of 'peri-constitutionalism'. Still, the distinction between 'cooperative' or 'competitive' federalism remains relevant, displaying different patterns as to the space that constitutionally recognized levels of government actually enjoy when exercising their autonomy. A competitive federalism assumes that vertical and horizontal competition between governments better serves citizens by avoiding the creation of normative or economic monopolies; a cooperative federalism model establishes to institutions that seek to reduce inter-jurisdictional conflicts to a minimum. The former tends to maximize the autonomy of both levels of government while the latter has the effect of reducing it in view of achieving its conflict-reduction objective, sometimes at the risk of inducing a centralization dynamic, as was the case in Germany. Put differently, the former is more conducive to self-reliance—a value also to be fostered by federalism—while the latter builds instead on the value of solidarity. The emergence of neo-liberal state conceptions since the 1980s, economic globalization, as well as the recurring inefficiencies caused by the often interlocking nature of cooperative federalism, resulted in the expansion of the competitive federalism model in the past two decades. This dynamic comes with a price tag, however. In India, the rise of competitive federalism has increased economic disparities across the federation (Basta Fleiner 2008, 81–83).

The distinction between these two visions of federalism also reflects the various ways in which the federation's internal division of sovereignty is shared and managed, for autonomy in a federation is always relative. Emphasis is purposely placed on *internal* sovereignty. Regarding external sovereignty, only the federation as a whole, represented by the central government, is fully sovereign. Consequently, federated units are not international legal subjects in the sense used in international law. Nevertheless, they are not entirely absent from the international scene, even though the legal framework governing their activities varies extensively depending on the federation involved. Belgium goes as far as constitutionally recognizing a limited and constrained *jus tractatus* to its federated units while others, like the United States, explicitly grant this power to the central government. Canada does not solve this question by formal constitutional means, and distinguishes between the international action of provinces as public actors and as private actors, allowing some leeway to provinces (essentially Quebec) when interacting with foreign governments and some international institutions.

Because the judiciary plays a crucial role in interpreting the division of powers in most federations, courts' independence from the central government's control needs to be built into their institutional design. This ensures that they will be impartial when they adjudicate disputes between a federation's governments. This is especially true if the polity's federal culture is weak.

The judiciary is not the only state institution arbitrating the interests of the central government and the federated units. In a number of federations, the federal parliament is also vested with such a responsibility, its second chamber's (or upper house's) primary function often being to defend, through different mechanisms, the interests of the federated units, or at least to voice their concerns. The archetypal example is Germany's *Bundesrat* (Federal Council). However, this second chamber's role is not universally shared, or carried out effectively: the American and Canadian senates provide eloquent counter-examples. Typical for old federations, the senate type of the federal house builds on the liberal model of equal representation. Federal units as constituencies are represented by an equal number of members in the chamber, directly elected in federal units as constituencies. Conversely, the council type of federal house is constituted by proportional representation of the governments of federal units. In Austria, the parliament of each Land elects its delegates to the Bundesrat. The representatives of each Land in the Federal Council reflect the proportion of the political parties as represented in the respective Land parliament. In Germany, the Bundesrat members are delegated by the respective state government, according to the votes a state has in the second chamber. Votes are allocated based on a principle that favours smaller states and aims at preventing domination by the most populous states.

The two different types of federal houses reflect different conceptions of federalism. The senate type of second chamber is asked to evaluate legislation under the criteria of common interests, taking into account the different interests of the different constituencies. In Germany and Austria, the states have to implement federal statutes. The states' governments can evaluate to what extent federal legislation is in fact appropriate and to what extent they can guarantee implementation. In the nineteenth century, the second chamber was established in Switzerland with a focus on legislation rather than administration. The Council of States accordingly replicated the US Senate type, constituted as part of the legislature to represent the interest of the cantons.

Typically, the role of one house in legislation is limited, with the fully bicameral decision-making in Switzerland and the United States representing exception.

12.5.2 *Organization of autonomy within federal structures*

Two main models of organizing autonomy of the federated units exist. The autonomy of federated units can first be anchored in a territory. Several modern federations, such as Canada, Mexico, Germany and Nigeria, have adopted this model. Under a territorial regime, all people residing in the territory of a federated unit are deemed its members, irrespective of their other identities. This territorial paradigm assumes a relative homogeneity of the population of that federated unit, or, alternatively, downplays its heterogeneity. But the socio-demographic make-up of some federations does not easily lend itself to the application of that paradigm. In Russia, there are federal republics that have a minority as the 'constitutive nation' although ethnic Russians are a majority of the population. Some historically significant and politically salient groups, sharing a language, a religion or an ethnicity, may not be territorially concentrated. One way to accommodate constitutionally their claims for recognition is to structure their status of autonomy on the basis of the personality principle. The model generally implies setting up autonomous institutions controlled by these groups, which are given jurisdiction over some core issues such as family law, personal status or education. An important feature of this model, when materialized in a democratic context, lies in the individual's self-identification with a particular community and the formal registration of that identification by the state. Moreover, the model often provides constitutional guarantees respecting representation of the recognized communities within federal institutions. Such 'personal' or 'corporate' federalism is best exemplified by the 'millet system' that was in force in the Ottoman Empire and that has strongly influenced Lebanon.

In practice, several federations have integrated the two models. Although primarily a territorial federation, Canada has incorporated elements of personal federalism through the recognition of particular rights to members of official language minorities (English or French) wherever they reside. Belgium systemically combines personal and territorial federalism, through both the territorial jurisdiction of the three communities (Flemish-speaking, French-speaking and German-speaking) and three regions (Flanders, Wallonia and Brussels-Capital), and the personal jurisdiction of the French-speaking and Flemish-speaking communities in the Brussels area (Deschouwer, 53).

12.6 Conclusion

If this cartography of the dynamic relation between federalism and autonomy has shown anything, it is not only that federalism cannot be conceptualized without reference to autonomy. The tangible implementation of autonomy within federations goes beyond constitutional norms and institutional design: it requires the presence of a federal culture that must be sustained and promoted by both institutional actors and civil society. Law, in this respect, is clearly an element of a society's culture.

References

Aja, E (2003). *El estado autonomico. Federalism y hechos diferenciales*, 2ᵃ edicion (Madrid: Allianza Editorial).

Basta Fleiner, LR (2008). 'Nation-Building and Diversity', in Watts, R & Chattopadhyay, R (eds), *Unity in Diversity*, Volume 1 (New Delhi: Forum of Federations and Viva Books), 77–88.

—— (2011). 'Nation Building: Favouring Multiculturalism through Federalism?' in LIX Annals FLB–Belgrade Law Review 3: 224–240.

—— & Fleiner, T (eds) (1996). Federalism and Multiethnic States: the Case of Switzerland (Fribourg, Institut du Fédéralisme).

Beaud, O (2007). *Théorie de la fédération* (Paris: Presses Universitaires de France).

Choudhry, S (ed) (2008). Constitutional Design for Divided Societies. Integration or Accommodation? (Oxford: Oxford University Press).

Deschouwer, K (2005). 'Kingdom of Belgium', in Kincaid, J & Tarr, GA (eds), Constitutional Origins, Structure and Change in Federal Countries (Montreal & Kingston: McGill-Queen's University Press), 48–75.

Elazar, D (1987). *Exploring Federalism* (Tuscaloosa & London: University of Alabama Press).

Gamper, A (2010). 'On Loyalty and the (Federal Constitution)', in www.cil-journal.com, Vol 4, No 2, 157–70.

Gaudreault-DesBiens, JF (2012). 'Religious Identities: Testing the Limits of Canadian Federalism?' in Appleby, G, Aroney, N & John, T (eds), The Future of Australian Federalism: Comparative and Interdisciplinary Perspectives (Cambridge: CUP), 228–49.

Gunlicks, AB (2005). German Federalism and Recent Reform Efforts in 6 *German Law Journal*. No. 10, http://www.germanlawjournal.com/pdfs/Vol06No10/PDF_Vol_06_No_10_1283-1296_SI_Articles_Gunlicks.pdf

Kymlicka, W (1995). *Multicultural Citizenship* (Oxford: Oxford University Press).

Lajoie, A (2002). *Quand les minorités font la loi* (Paris: Presses Universitaires de France).

McGarry, J, O'Leary, B & Simeon, R (2008). Integration or accommodation? The enduring debate in conflict regulation, in Choudhry, S (ed), *Constitutional Design for Divided Societies: Integration or Accommodation?* (Oxford: Oxford University Press), 41–88.

Moreno, L & Colino, C (eds) (2008). A Global Dialogue on Federalism, Volume 7: *Diversity and Unity in Federal Countries* (Montreal & Kingston: McGill-Queen's University Press).

Palermo, F (2004). 'Asymmetric, "quasi-federal" regionalism and the protection of minorities. The case of Italy', in Tarr, A, Williams, RF & Marko, J (eds), *Federalism, Subnational Constitutions and Minority Rights* (United States: Praeger Publishers), 107–32.

Poirier, J (2001). The Functions of Intergovernmental Agreements: Post-Devolution Concordats in a Comparative Perspective (London: The Constitution Unit, School of Public Policy UCL), http://www.ucl.ac.uk/spp/publications/unit-publications/75.pdf

Reference re Secession of Quebec [1998] 2 S.C.R. 217.

Requejo, F (2003). *Federalisme plurinacional I estat de les autonomies. Aspectes teòrics i aplicats* (Barcelona: Proa).

Stepan, A (1999). 'Federalism and democracy, Beyond the US Model', in *Journal of Democracy*, 10.4, 19–34, http://www.catedras.fsoc.uba.ar/deluca/Stepan.htm

Steytler, N (2005). 'The Republic of South Africa', in Kincaid, J & Tarr, GA (eds), Constitutional origins, structure and change in federal countries: Global dialogue on federalism, Vol 1 (Montreal & Kingston: McGill-Queen's University Press), 311–46.

Suresh, K (2004). 'Citizenship and Differential Rights of Minority Protection in India, Constitutional Principles and Judicial Intervention', in 2 *Indian Journal of Federal Studies* 134.

Wheare, KC (1963). *Federal Government*, 4th edn (Oxford: Oxford University Press).

Additional reading

Fabbrini, S (2007). *Compound Democracies* (Oxford: Oxford University Press).

Fleiner, T (2011). 'Constitutional Underpinnings of Federalism: Common Law vs. Civil Law', in Courchene TJ, Allan, JR, Lauprecht, C & Verrelli, N (eds), *The Federal Idea: Essays in Honour of Ronald L. Watts* (Montreal & Kingston: McGill University Press).

—— & Basta Fleiner, LR (2009). *Constitutional democracy in a Multicultural and Globalised World* (Berlin Heidelberg: Springer Verlag).

Friedrich, CJ (1968). Trends of Federalism in Theory and Practice (New York: Praeger).

Funk, A (2010). Asymetrical Federalism: A Stabilizing or Destabilizing Factor in Multinational Federations http://www.ie-ei.eu/bibliotheque/memoires2010/Funk.pdf

Gamper, A (2005). 'A Global Theory of Federalism'. The Nature and Challenges of a Federal State in 6 *German Law Journal*. No. 10 http://www.germanlawjournal.com/pdfs/Vol06No10/PDF_Vol_06_No_10_1297-1318_SI_Articles_Gamper.pdf

Gaudreault-DesBiens, JF (2010). 'The State Management of Legal and Cultural Diversity in Canada', in Foblets, MC, Gaudreault-DesBiens, JF & Dundes Renteln, A (eds), *Cultural Diversity and Law. State Responses from Around the World* (Brussels: Bruylant), 195–234.

Govinda Rao, M & Singh, N (2004). *Asymmetric Federalism in India*, http://papers.ssrn.com/sol3/papers.cfm?abstract_id=537782

Kincaid, J (2005). 'Comparative Observations', in Kincaid, J & Tarr, GA (eds), Constitutional Origins, Structures and Changes in Federal Countries, Global Dialogue, Vol. 1 (Montreal & Kingston: McGill University Press), 409–48.

Poirier, J & Saunders, C (forthcoming). *Intergovernmental Relations in Federal Countries* (Montreal & Kingston: McGill–Queen's University Press).

Saunders, C (2011). *The Constitution of Australia. A Contextual Analysis* (Oxford: Hart Publishing).

Watts, RL (2009). *Comparing Federal Systems*, 3rd edition (Montreal & Kingston: McGill Queen's University Press).

Minority rights

Solomon Dersso and Francesco Palermo

13.1 Introduction: recognition and evolution of minority rights

Ours is the time of multiculturalism. While largely homogenous societies are becoming ethnically diverse, with rising identity consciousness of groups, the diversity of multi-ethnic societies is becoming more pronounced. Amid this resurgence of ethnic consciousness and the spread of democratic changes during the post-Cold War period, claims for recognition and inclusion are increasing across the globe. In its dramatic manifestations, this has taken the form of violent ethnic conflicts, ranging from those involving the inclusion of diverse racial groups as in South Africa to longstanding religious tensions in Northern Ireland; genocidal fighting between Hutus and Tutsis in Rwanda and Burundi; civil wars in the Balkans, Sudan and the Ivory Coast; and separatist movements throughout the world.[1] As a result of these developments, States are increasingly resorting to constitutional and legislative tools to find appropriate means to accommodate ethno-cultural diversity within a democratic framework.

For centuries, the challenge of constitutionalism has been—and still is—the struggle for equality. Increasingly, however, the challenge is also about accommodating diversity. Or, as Dworkin (1977) put it, equality can be seen as treating all persons as if they were equal or as treating them equally, taking into account their real differences. Full and effective equality can be pursued only if different situations are treated differently. While for the most part of the twentieth century nation-state models of constitutionalism (which, in spite of their differences, all showed an assimilationist bias) have been dominant,[2] there is now an increasing shift towards constitutionalism that respects and accommodates minorities. This is due to both the recognition of the discriminatory effect of the nation-state model of constitutionalism on members of minorities, and to the post-Cold War resurgence in the claims of marginalised groups for equal recognition in many parts of the world.

The recognition and accommodation of minorities raises questions of critical constitutional importance. Does a right to be different—as a community—exist, and if so, what is its

---

1 For a detailed analysis of ethnic-based conflicts, see Gurr; Horowitz 1985.
2 Tully (68) notes that one of the characteristic features of the constitutional state following the French and American revolutions has been that it 'possesses an individual identity as a "nation"'.

content? Who is entitled to different treatment under the law? What are the instruments or mechanisms for granting effective protection to minorities? To what extent can these instruments be employed and what are their limits? The challenges of social and legal pluralism and the limitations to the majority rule, as exemplified by the regulation of minority rights, are essential elements of contemporary constitutional law. Against the background of these questions, this chapter identifies and explains the mechanisms for the protection of minorities that are being used in the constitutional design and practice of States. Given that the provision of constitutional mechanisms for protection of minority rights is not without its dangers, the issues one needs to take into account to avoid the pitfalls of such mechanisms, including the provision of effective guarantees for promoting and maintaining a common national identity, are also discussed.

13.1.1 The issue of definition

There is no universal legal definition of a minority, nor would a definition be possible or desirable, since the factors that might make a group a minority are potentially endless. According to Toniatti,

> Minorities as such do not exist. Rather, there exist large and small, numerous and otherwise, social groups. In abstract, all groups, each endowed with its own identity, equally represent the natural and cultural diversity of the human species. A social group may be seen as transformed into a minority when, on the basis of a shared and single feature of reference, it establishes relations with another group which, by virtue of a largely (but not solely) quantitative criterion comes to constitute the majority (Toniatti, 200).

What matters, in legal terms, is the legal recognition of a minority position and its subsequent legal treatment. Such recognition ultimately depends, among others, on a political choice. Thus it is not surprising that States take different approaches to minority issues and define minorities differently, nor that the same features can be seen as constituting a minority in some contexts and not in others, depending on circumstances such as the historical background or the overall approach of the legal system to the issue of 'difference'. For instance, in the United Kingdom and in Canada, Sikhs have been allowed to ride motorbikes without wearing a protective helmet over their traditional headgear, whereas in France they are not allowed to do so.

Law in the abstract does not have an answer to what constitutes a minority. It only deals with how a minority is identified, what instruments are used for its differential treatment, how these instruments are (or should be) used and how the rights of identified minority groups are balanced with the rights of the 'majority'. However, political choices about the recognition of the minority status and the following legal consequences are not unconstrained. Rather, they are increasingly determined by the overall constitutional developments, by international commitments[3] and by the circulation of legal models and solutions through legislation, case law[4] and academic debate.

---

3 Article 3(1) of the Council of Europe's Framework Convention for the Protection of National Minorities affirms that 'Every person belonging to a national minority shall have the right freely to choose to be treated or not to be treated as such and no disadvantage shall result from this choice (…).'
4 One may think of the recent evolution concerning the recognition of rights to homosexuals: in a growing number of countries the discrimination following from a formally equal treatment starts to be acknowledged and the right to marry and to form a family is being granted.

While there is no doubt that the potential categories of bearers of minority rights are beyond enumeration, in fact these rights and the connected instruments have been developed for specific categories of minorities: national, ethnic, religious and linguistic.[5] These have been historically, and still are, the groups characterised by 'strong' differential factors, those that have often caused violence, repression, mass deportations and threats to the integrity of States. Some of the instruments developed for the protection of these minorities represent the matrix also for new types of minorities that the legal systems may recognise: one may think, for example, of the quotas reserved for women in political and economic life, or of the attribution of cultural rights to migrant groups (see Medda-Windischer). While important aspects of minority protection such as equality in difference are being extended to the 'new' categories of minorities, the structural mechanisms identified in this chapter have largely been developed to afford protection to ethno-cultural minorities (i.e. minorities present at the founding of the State concerned).

13.1.2 Legal-historical development

Because of the relation between equality and minority status, the position of minorities became a constitutional issue with the establishment of modern States and constitutionalism. Before that, not only was it acceptable that conquered groups were often assimilated or at times exterminated, but the existence of different legal categories of peoples was considered natural. Both in the ancient civilizations and in the middle ages, people did not enjoy the same rights and differentiation was the rule. Only modern constitutionalism, born together with the concept of the State, presupposes equality of people in principle and is thus permanently confronted with the challenge of making equality and difference compatible.

The approach to and the legal instruments for the treatment of minorities have gone through different phases (Ruiz Vieytez). In recent times, the exclusively individual rights-based approach developed by international documents such as the Universal Declaration of Human Rights (1948) and the European Convention for the Protection of Human Rights and Fundamental Freedoms (1950), and by most constitutions after World War II as a reaction to the collectivistic hysteria of Fascism and Nazism, was profoundly challenged by the end of colonialism and, above all, by the post-1989 revolutions (Hadden; Fottrell & Bowring).

---

5 There is no consolidated terminology at international level on the different types of minorities. In most cases, minorities are considered to be 'a group numerically inferior to the rest of the population of a State whose members—being nationals of the State—possess ethnic, religious or linguistic characteristics differing from the rest of the population and who, if only implicitly, maintain a sense of solidarity, directed towards preserving their culture, traditions, religion or language' (Capotorti). 'National' minorities (usually an umbrella term) often coincides with this definition. In some cases it is opposed to the term 'ethnic' minorities, which means, depending on the context, either traditional minorities not having their own 'kin-State', such as the Roma (this is, for instance, the legal definition of ethnic minorities in Poland) or persons with immigration background (as in the case of most Anglo-Saxon countries). Indigenous peoples, sometimes referred to as 'first nations', are, according to a UN working definition, 'those which, having a historical continuity with pre-invasion and pre-colonial societies that developed on their territories, consider themselves distinct from other sectors of the societies now prevailing on those territories, or parts of them' (UN Doc. E/CN.4/Sub.2/1986/7 and Add. 1–4). Even apparently less contested terms such as linguistic minorities are sometimes problematic, as people can have multiple linguistic affiliations. See Advisory Committee on the Framework Convention for the Protection of National Minorities, Commentary on Language Rights of Persons Belonging to National Minorities, 24 May 2012, ACFC/44 Doc (2012) 001.

At the international level, the UN adopted the Declaration on the Rights of Persons Belonging to National or Ethnic, Religious and Linguistic Minorities (1992); the Organization for Security and Co-operation in Europe (OSCE) drafted the Copenhagen Document (1990) and created the High Commissioner on National Minorities (1993), a diplomatic instrument aimed at preventing conflicts around national minorities; the Council of Europe elaborated important multilateral treaties aimed at protecting linguistic diversity (European Charter for Regional or Minority Languages, 1992) and persons belonging to national minorities (Framework Convention for the Protection of National Minorities, 1995; so far, the only existing multilateral treaty on this issue) (Pentassuglia); and many countries signed bilateral treaties on the treatment of national minorities (Bloed & van Dijk). Most of these mechanisms are assisted by monitoring bodies. Thus,

> Issues concerning national minorities (...) [became] matters of legitimate international concern and consequently do not constitute exclusively an internal affair of the respective State.[6]

Consequently, nearly all constitutions drafted after 1989 contain detailed regulation of minority issues, largely inspired by the international standards.

13.2 Constitutional mechanisms for the protection of minorities

In a comparative constitutional perspective, the legal treatment of minorities takes different shapes. Depending on the ideological approach towards equality, it ranges from non-recognition or assimilation (often justified by the purely formal dimension of equality: the 'colour-blind' constitution)[7] to recognition and protection (with exceptional character and generally simple rules), to diversity as the rule requiring a whole set of complex rules (see below).[8] We identify three of the main sets of such mechanisms: constitutional guarantees for self-government of minorities; constitutional arrangements for effective representation and participation of minorities in public life; and constitutional provisions relating to language, culture and religion. These mechanisms might be thought in some instances to be in tension with constitutional guarantees of non-discrimination. (See Chapters 22 to 26.)

13.2.1 Self-government

Structures of self-government and/or territorial autonomy provide the strongest institutional framework for the protection of minorities. Self-government can be institutionalised within States in various ways (Benedikter; Lapidoth; Suksi). One important mechanism, increasingly used, is federalism (Watts, 117–20). What makes federalism attractive is its capacity to provide a flexible framework for balancing the demands of unity and diversity by allowing members of minorities to participate at the centre in relation to common matters through shared rule, while leaving autonomous space for minorities through self-rule for local matters. The principle of federalism, according to the Supreme Court of Canada,

---

6 Report of the CSCE Meeting of Experts on National Minorities, Geneva 1991, part II, para. 3.
7 *Shaw v Reno*, 509 US 630 (1993).
8 See *inter alia* Toniatti; Marko, J. *Autonomie und Integration* (Vienna, Böhlau, 1995), 531.

recognises the diversity of the component parts of confederation or a federation and the autonomy of the provincial governments to develop their societies within their respective sphere of jurisdiction.[9]

It is, however, important to note that whether federalism serves to accommodate the interests of minorities depends on the resolution of two questions (see Kymlicka). The first is whether, and the extent to which, the boundaries of federal units are defined to allow minorities to exercise some degree of self-government within those units. The other is the degree of autonomy that the division of powers leaves to the federal units to accommodate self-rule for the minorities concerned.

Accordingly, not any kind of federalism offers guarantees of self-government for minorities. A distinction is therefore made between territorial or administrative federalism and multinational federalism (Kymlicka, 273–77). The former is institutionalised merely on the basis of historic internal boundaries and administrative considerations, as in the US, Germany, Brazil, Mexico and Australia. But as Kymlicka observes, '[f]or a federal system to qualify as genuinely multinational, decisions about boundaries and powers must consciously reflect the needs and aspirations of minority groups' (id 276). Examples of such federal systems include Canada, India, Belgium and Spain. More recent examples include the 1994 Constitution of Ethiopia, which is unique in its formulation of ethnic federalism with a guarantee to every ethnic group of the right to form its self-governing structure.

There is no hard-and-fast rule about the degree of authority to be constitutionally vested in federal units; it is a matter to be determined according to the specific circumstances of each society and the nature of the issues affecting the minorities concerned. It is generally accepted that federal units are assigned the powers necessary for the community or communities constituting the self-governing units to exercise effective self-government over local matters and issues of particular concern to minorities. Where federalism is used in such a form, it invariably results in the emergence of minorities at the level of such federal units, a situation that is otherwise known as 'minorities within minorities'. Adequate guarantees must be put in place to safeguard the rights of such minorities. Such guarantees range from judicially enforceable bills of rights including cultural and religious rights, to allocation of seats for such minorities in proportion to their population size to a power-sharing arrangement.

When used as a mechanism to protect territorial minorities, federalism can be asymmetrical. Often, asymmetrical forms of federalism or autonomy are used to provide minority inhabited territories with special status compared to the rest of the country, precisely to provide compact minority groups with more advanced instruments of self-government. This is the case, *inter alia*, of Spain's historical autonomous communities (such as Catalonia and the Basque Country), of South Tyrol in Italy, of Scotland in the UK, and many other areas.

In the context of the discussion on self-government, it is worth noting that some countries provide for a right to self-determination: in South Africa and Ethiopia in their respective constitutions; in Canada through case law, most notably in the Supreme Court's *Reference re the Secession of Quebec*.[10] The right to self-determination in Ethiopia and Canada may include secession, whereas Section 235 of the South African Constitution is ambiguous about secession.

The institutionalisation of self-government through federalism or territorial autonomy to address minority claims is not without limits. It can be a more effective instrument in

9 *Reference re the Secession of Quebec* (1998) 2 SCR 217 para 58.
10 Supreme Court of Canada [1998] 2 SCR 217.

countries where minorities are territorially concentrated. Where minorities are dispersed it may be of very limited use, although not necessarily irrelevant. Besides, the circumstances of some societies and their minorities may not require the institutionalisation of self-government structures. Similarly, past misuse and abuse of arrangements akin to federalism such as the Bantustan system under apartheid mean that South Africa's political leaders are skittish about federalism in its strong form as a mechanism for accommodation of ethno-cultural diversity. The same goes for the communist idea of ethnic federalism, which paved the way to the dissolution of federal communist countries along ethnic lines; for this reason, in Eastern Europe federalism is often associated with a threat to territorial integrity of States.

Under such circumstances, participation rights and the manner of their institutionalisation become avenues for increased minority representation and participation. Finally, even when federalism is an option, states must still make provision for minority representation and participation in decision-making bodies.

13.2.2 Representation and participation

Besides elaborating the rights under Article 27 of the International Covenant on Civil and Political Rights (ICCPR),[11] the 1992 UN Declaration on the Rights of Persons Belonging to Ethnic, Religious and Linguistic Minorities enunciates additional rights that aim to ensure substantive equality for minorities. The most important is the right 'to participate effectively in cultural, religious, social, economic and public life'.[12] Effective participation is further elaborated in Article 2(3), which provides for

> the right to participate effectively in decisions on the national and, where appropriate, regional level concerning the minority to which they belong or the regions in which they live, in a manner not incompatible with national legislation.

It follows that, beyond and above individual participation, effective participation of minorities requires States to adopt various arrangements, such as power-sharing political processes or electoral schemes, which facilitate the representation and participation of minorities.[13]

The most important level for minority representation is the legislative process (Wheatley, 514–18): minorities can enjoy equal status only if they participate effectively in the formulation of the rules on the basis of which rights and obligations are established. One important mechanism for achieving minority representation in the legislative process is the electoral system. As Steiner points out, 'the electoral structure selected for choosing a legislature … will significantly influence the degree of representation and power of many minority groups in society' (Steiner, 107). For effective representation of minorities, preference should be given to an electoral system that can, in the particular circumstances of the country concerned, secure both a high level of representation of members of minorities and their effective participation, without institutionalising group differences.

The forms that an electoral system may take can be broadly divided into plurality or majority systems, and proportional representation (PR) and/or mixed systems (see generally Reynolds, Reilly & Ellis; Lijphart 1994). PR is the preferred electoral system for the just

---

11 See the Declaration on the Rights of Minorities Articles 2(1) and 4(2).
12 Declaration on the Rights of Minorities Article 2.
13 See Lund Recommendations on the Effective Participation of National Minorities in Public Life principle 1.1; De Varennes; Eide.

representation of minorities and their effective participation.[14] The essence of this electoral system is that votes cast are translated into a proportional number of seats for each party, and it is thus credited with fairness and inclusivity. According to Lewis,

> in a plural society, proportional representation with a few large several-member constituencies is better than electoral systems with many single-member constituencies not only because it gives more satisfaction to the minorities, but also because it reduces the geographical conflict, and the racial or other differences which go with geography.[15]

Many agree that PR better ensures fair representation of minorities in multi-ethnic societies (Reynolds 1995, 2006; Töpperwien, 47; Ghai 2005), although some versions of PR such as those that take the form of representation by quota tend to entrench divisions and exacerbate problems of national unity. Where PR is implemented in a way that allows self-identification (see Lijphart, 281), it makes the opportunity to participate in the political processes of the State available to all minorities who seek representation and participation, and thereby minimises the pattern of ethnic rivalry for control or a share of State power that the winner-takes-all system tends to produce.[16] While it facilitates the representation of minorities, PR has the advantage of not forcing people to identify with particular groups.

Effective minority representation may in particular situations call for additional arrangements (Young, 187–88), such as reserved seats or quotas (Ghai 2005).[17] The constitutional approach that India adopted vis-à-vis the 'untouchables' or the scheduled castes illustrates the need for, and the practical application of, measures to redress exclusions suffered by highly disadvantaged communities. Articles 332 and 334 of the Constitution of India guarantee reserved representation for the Scheduled Castes and Tribes. Similarly, to provide for the representation of those ethnic groups whose population size is smaller than the size of an electoral district, the 1994 Constitution of Ethiopia envisages special representation of 'minority nationalities and peoples' by reserving 20 seats.[18] The Burundian Constitution provides quotas for the representation of the minority Batwa community in the National Assembly and the Senate,[19] and similar mechanisms are provided by a large number of constitutions, from Slovenia to Kosovo, from Lebanon to Pakistan, from Jordan to Fiji.

The representation of minorities does not necessarily guarantee their effective participation.[20] Once represented in the law-making structures of a State, they need to be given opportunities to contribute to the legislative process. It is important in this regard that minorities are also allowed representation in the various committees, hearings and processes of legislative bodies.

---

14 There are, however, scholars who reject PR on the ground that instead of dampening divisions it leads to their institutional entrenchment. Thus Horowitz, for example, proposes as an alternative to PR the 'Alternative Vote' electoral system. Horowitz 1991, 188–203; Horowitz 2003. On the drawbacks of this system, see Lijphart 1991.

15 Lewis, 72. This has been affirmed also by the European Court of Human Rights, *Lindsay and others v United Kingdom*, ruling of 8-3-1979, ref 8364/78.

16 See *Cultural Liberty in Today's Diverse World*, Human Development Report (2004), 54 [Human Development Report (2004)].

17 This is done in many countries, such as Venezuela, Romania, India, Jordan, Niger, Slovenia, Colombia, Croatia and Burundi. See, for example, Human Development Report (2004), 54.

18 See Article 54(3) of the Constitution & Article 2(5) & 15(3) of the Electoral Law.

19 Articles 164, and 180, respectively.

20 For a detailed discussion on the distinction between representation and effective participation see Verstichel.

In some countries, the representation of minorities is translated into effective participation by prescribing a deliberative and participatory democratic process. This is done by providing adequate mechanisms and opportunities to facilitate direct public participation of minorities in decision-making processes, as envisaged in Articles 2(2) and (3) of the 1992 UN Declaration on Minority Rights. These may include special procedures and arrangements through which minorities can bring relevant facts to decision makers, articulate and defend their views, propose alternative courses of action, and generally get the opportunity to be heard or become co-decision makers.

The 1996 Constitution of South Africa provides for such guarantees. First, specific provisions require the inclusion of representatives of minorities in the legislative processes.[21] Second, strong rights of public participation are elaborated under Sections 19, 59(1), 59(2), 72(1) and 118(1).[22] According to the Constitutional Court of South Africa, these provisions express a constitutional commitment that all members of society, particularly minorities, 'should feel that they have been given a real opportunity to have their say, that they are taken seriously as citizens, that their views matter and will receive due consideration'.[23] In the constitutional design of some countries, minorities are guaranteed veto power with respect to identified subjects considered to be of particular concern to them. The consent of minority representatives is a pre-requisite for the legislature to enact law on these subjects.[24]

Minority representation and participation should not be limited to the law-making process alone (Wheatley, 515). They should cover the whole range of the conduct of public affairs. According to General Comment 25 of the UN Human Rights Committee (HRC):

> Conduct of public affairs ... is a broad concept which relates to the exercise of political power, in particular the exercise of legislative, executive and administrative powers ... covering *all aspects of public administration*, and the formulation and *implementation of policy* at international, national, regional and local levels.[25]

It is therefore important that minorities are represented in executive, administrative and judicial institutions as well. Ghai rightly points out that there are many good reasons for this: 'A great deal of State policy and regulation are made by public servants, and it is appropriate that officials of minorities should be able to participate in those processes' (Ghai 2003, 12). The quota system, whereby a percentage of positions available in institutions of public administration are reserved for minorities, is one possible mechanism for effecting such representation. The quota system can be particularly valuable in sharply divided societies, and for fast-tracking the inclusion of highly marginalised groups. Article 16(4) of the Constitution of India stipulates that the State may make 'provision for reservation in matters of promotion to any class or classes of posts in the services under the State in favour of the Scheduled Castes

---

21 For example, Section 57(2)(*b*) of the Constitution requires that the rules and orders of the National Assembly provide for 'the participation in the proceedings of the Assembly and its committees of minority parties represented in the national assembly, in a manner consistent with democracy'.

22 The right to public participation is given its most robust articulation by the Constitutional Court of South Africa in *Doctors for Life International v Speaker of the National Assembly* 2006 (6) SA 416 (CC), 2006 (12) BCLR 1399 (CC).

23 Id, para 235.

24 For example, Article 64 of the Slovenian constitution (absolute veto) and the 'alarm bell procedure' of Article 54 of the Belgian constitution (suspensive veto).

25 UN Human Rights Committee General Comment 25 (57) UN Doc. CCPR/C/21/Rev.1/Add.7 (1996) para 5.

and the Scheduled Tribes which, in the opinion of the State, are not adequately represented in the services under the State'.

Apart from quotas, greater minority participation can also be effected through a constitutional provision that requires institutions of government to be representative of the diversity of the society and by implementing policies that incrementally guarantee the representation of minorities in the structures of State institutions. An example of such constitutional provision is found in the 1996 Constitution of South Africa. Section 195(1)(*i*) stipulates:

> Public administration must be governed by the democratic values and principles enshrined in the constitution, including the following principles: ... (i) Public administration must be *broadly representative of the South African people*, with employment and personnel management practices based on ability, objectivity, fairness, and *the need to redress the imbalances of the past to achieve broad representation* (authors' emphasis).

While in some countries the provision of quotas in the public sector is determined in a rigidly arithmetical way, in others the constitution merely provides for an 'equitable' or 'appropriate' representation (as in Macedonia, Croatia and Montenegro) (Palermo 2010).

13.2.3 Language and cultural policies, and guarantees for cultural, religious and linguistic rights

Language policies determine the level of inclusion and protection of minorities having their own languages. With respect to language, the most important issues to be addressed include official recognition, the use of minority languages in communication with public authorities and the use of minority languages in education.

As to the official recognition of languages, there is no uniform or standard approach in the constitutional practice of States. Some countries accord official status to almost all languages. The 1996 Constitution of South Africa designates 11 languages as official languages of the country (Section 6). Additionally, it provides for the development of the indigenous Khoi, Nama and San languages along with the official languages. Similarly, in Canada the dominant English and the minority French are the official languages.

Other countries accord national official status to one or some languages, while allowing the official recognition of other languages at sub-national level. Examples include India, Ethiopia and Spain. India's Constitution regards Hindi and English as official languages, but under Article 345 allows State legislatures to adopt other languages widely spoken in the State as official. So far, 22 such languages are recognised. Additionally, Article 347 stipulates that a minority language spoken in a State of the Union may be recognised as an official language where 'a substantial proportion of the population of [that State] desire for that language to be recognised'. In Ethiopia, while Amharic serves as the working language of the Federal Government, States are guaranteed to designate their own official language (other than Amharic, four other languages serve as official languages in the different States).[26] Similarly, Spain recognises Spanish as the official language of the country, but its constitution allows other languages to be declared official by its autonomous communities.[27]

An important factor for determining the use of minority languages in communication between public institutions and citizens is usually the diversity of languages in a country. The

---

26 Art 5, the Constitution of the Federal Democratic Republic of Ethiopia.
27 Art 3, Spanish Constitution.

smaller the number of languages, the greater the possibility for using minority languages for communication between public institutions and minorities: in Canada, citizens are allowed to use either one of the two languages, the dominant English and the relatively minority French. Similarly, in Belgium and Switzerland, where the number of language groups is small, all languages are used for official purposes at federal level. The difference is that while in Canada federal government services are made available in either English or French anywhere in the country as long as numbers warrant, in Belgium the two main regions of Wallonia and Flanders are generally unilingual and so are most Swiss Cantons.

Usually, in societies with high linguistic diversity, States are expected to provide public services and communication in minority languages in places where speakers of those languages are found in significant numbers.[28] The public services in question are of a very important nature, and the resources required to provide the public services can be made available without unduly compromising the distribution of resources in other areas of public demand as well (De Varennes, 177–78).

The case of South Africa is an example. Section 6(1) of the 1996 South African Constitution recognises 11 official languages of the Republic.[29] Of these, nine are indigenous languages that were subject to discrimination during apartheid. Section 6(2) places the State under a constitutional duty 'to take practical and positive measures to elevate the status and advance the use of these (indigenous) languages' having regard to their 'historically diminished use and status'. When read with Section 6(4) of the Constitution, which requires that all languages be treated equitably, this demands that the State provide special support to the indigenous official languages (see Henrard, 119). Although the effect of the designation of 11 languages as official is to make them languages to be used for government purposes, namely legislation and administration, '[i]t will too often be practically and financially impossible to provide every type of service' (Currie, 65 ff) in all the languages. Accordingly, when national and provincial governments select any of the official languages for administration purposes, Section 6(3) envisages that consideration should be given to factors like 'usage, practicality, expense, regional circumstances, and the needs and preferences of the population as a whole or in respective provinces'.[30]

The use of minority languages in the conduct of public affairs covers, and is also particularly important in, education,[31] which is key for the reproduction and maintenance of both cultures and languages of groups. As Addis has argued, they are also instrumental in nurturing genuine dialogue across difference and developing a strong sense of pluralistic solidarity in multi-ethnic societies (Addis). Issues of particular importance with respect to the use of minority languages in education include the provision of public education in minority languages and the establishment of private educational institutions.

The Canadian Charter of Rights and Freedoms provides under Article 23 for the right of Canada's official language minorities, defined to include French and English language groups within particular regions, to receive primary and secondary education in either official language. Elucidating on the importance of this, Chief Justice Dickson opined that

---

28 In this regard, reference can be made to Article 70(2) of the Swiss Constitution, which requires the Cantons to 'respect the traditional territorial distribution of languages and take account of indigenous linguistic minorities' in determining their official languages.

29 The official languages are 'Sepedi, Sesotho, Setswana, siSwati, Tshivenda, Xitsonga, Afrikaans, English, isiNdebele, isiXhosa and isiZulu'.

30 It also provides that '[m]unicipalities must take into consideration the language usage and preferences of their residents'.

31 See Oslo Recommendations of the OSCE HCNM Regarding the Linguistic Rights of National Minorities.

Minority-language education guarantee has two purposes: first, education in one's language provides an important way to preserve and promote the minority group's language and culture ... there is also a strong remedial component designed to protect the French and English minorities from assimilation and to give recognition and encouragement to the two official language groups in Canada.[32]

Under the 1996 Constitution of South Africa, Section 29(2) guarantees the right of everyone to 'receive education in the official language or languages of their choice in public educational institutions where that education is reasonably practicable'.[33] Although this is not a membership right, it nevertheless creates for members of the groups represented by the 11 official languages the right to education in their language if they so wish.

With respect to establishment of educational institutions, the Indian Constitution stipulates under Article 30(1) that '[a]ll minorities, whether based on religion or language, shall have the right to establish and administer educational institutions of their choice'. The Constitution also gives allowance to the State to provide aid without discrimination including for minority schools. In providing for such rights, Section 29 of the Constitution of South Africa guarantees religious and cultural communities the right to establish and maintain, at their own expense, educational institutions on the basis of *their religion, culture* and *language*, subject to non-discrimination on the basis of *race*.[34]

With respect to rights of cultural, religious and linguistic minorities, it is possible to distinguish between constitutions that guarantee these rights as rights of individual members of these groups and others that regard them as group rights. Examples in the first category include the constitutions of India, South Africa and the 2010 Constitution of Kenya. Section 31 of the Constitution of South Africa envisages the rights of 'members of cultural, religious and linguistic communities' (a) to enjoy their culture, practice their religion and use their language, and (b) to form, join and maintain cultural, religious and linguistic associations. As Justice O'Regan of the Constitutional Court of South Africa put it,

[t]hese rights are important in protecting members of cultural, religious and linguistic communities who feel threatened by the dominance or hegemony of larger or more powerful groups. They are an express affirmation of those members of cultural or other groups as human beings of equal worth in our society whose community practices and associations must be treated with respect.[35]

An example of a constitution in the second category (that regards cultural, religious and linguistic rights as group rights) is the 1995 Constitution of the Federal Democratic Republic

---

32 *Mahé v Alberta,* [1990] 1 SCR 342 [*Mahé*] (CanLII) at 362–63.

33 Practicability depends on, among other things, the number of students requesting teaching in the particular language and the availability of institutions providing education in the language.

34 Justice Kriegler in this regard noted that this is the first qualification to the right of religious, cultural and linguistic minorities to establish and maintain educational institutions for the preservation of their religion, culture or language: 'A common culture, language or religion having racism as an essential element has no constitutional claim to the establishment of separate educational institutions. The Constitution protects diversity, not racial discrimination.' *Ex Parte Gauteng Provincial Legislature: In re Dispute Concerning the Constitutionality of the Gauteng School Education Bill of 1995* 1996 (3) SA 165 (CC), 1996 (4) BCLR 537 (CC) para 40.

35 *MEC for Education, KwaZulu-Natal & Others v Pillay* 2008 (1) SA 474 (CC) para. 151.

of Ethiopia. Article 39(2) states: '[e]very Nation, Nationality and People in Ethiopia has the right to speak, to write and to develop its own language; and to express, to develop and to promote its culture'.

One manifestation of the rights of cultural, religious and linguistic minorities is recognition of religious and customary laws as in the constitutions of South Africa, India and Ethiopia. Section 211(3) of the South African Constitution stipulates that 'the courts must apply customary law when the law is applicable, subject to the constitution and any other legislation that deals with customary law'. Moreover, in Section 39(2) and (3) of the Constitution courts are called upon to develop customary law, along with common law, in accordance with 'the spirit, purport and objects of the Bill of Rights'. This constitutional recognition elevates the status of customary law to be an integral part of the legal system of South Africa with its own independent standing.[36] Accordingly, the courts (and legislature) are under a constitutional obligation to respect and accommodate customary law in the South African legal system.

The precedent for such forms of accommodation of diversity goes back to the Ottoman *Millet* system, in which each minority community was entitled to self-govern its religious and cultural affairs. Legacies of this system are still to be found in a number of countries, both in the Middle East (examples include Israel and Lebanon) and elsewhere (India). The most typical manifestation of this attitude is the establishment of religious courts, which decide on religious and family matters for the members of the involved communities only.

Another dimension of cultural, religious and linguistic rights relate to exemption rights. These rights relieve members of religious or cultural minorities from complying with otherwise legitimate rules in order to enable them to observe their cultural or religious commitments (Levy, 25–29). This forms part of what Kymlicka calls 'polyethnic rights', which 'are intended to help ethnic groups and religious minorities express their cultural particularity and pride without it hampering their success in the economic and political institutions of the dominant society' (Kymlicka, 31). Underlying exemption rights is the recognition that ostensibly neutral laws that require citizens to comply with standard norms of behaviour as a condition for public opportunities impose an undue or disproportionate burden on those whose culture requires them to behave in ways that do not conform to such norms. The equal treatment of these minorities therefore entails, within the bounds of limitations that are reasonable and rational in democratic societies, that they be exempted from the requirements of such general norms.

An example from South Africa is *KwaZulu-Natal MEC on Education v Pillay*. A young woman claimed that her school's refusal to relax its dress code to allow her to wear a nose stud as a manifestation of her Hindu–Tamil culture was a violation of her rights to culture and equality. The majority of the Court held that the school's action 'constitute[d] a significant infringement of her religious and cultural identity'.[37] The Court reasoned that the school could have accommodated her cultural practice without any major violation of the rules of the school. 'The admirable purposes that uniforms serve do not seem to be undermined by granting religious and cultural exemptions. There is no reason to believe, nor has the School presented any evidence to show, that a learner who is granted an exemption from

---

36 See *Alexkor Ltd & Another v Richtersveld Community & Others* 2004 (5) SA 460 (CC) para. 51 (stating that '[w]hile in the past indigenous law was seen through the common law lens, it must now be seen as an integral part of our law' and that 'the Constitution acknowledges the originality and distinctiveness of indigenous law as an independent source of norms within the legal system').

37 Pillay case, para 85.

the provisions of the Code will be any less disciplined or that she will negatively affect the discipline of others.'[38]

13.3 Scope and limits of constitutional design for the protection of minorities

One objection that is often raised to minority rights is their frequently assumed problematic relationship to individual human rights. Critics of minority rights worry that minority rights undermine individual human rights (Glazer). This is partly attributable to the possible tension that may arise between minority rights as group rights and the individual rights of members of minorities. Partly, it is based on the fear that accepting minority rights suggests prioritising the group over the individual.

Conflicts can indeed arise between minority and individual human rights. This nevertheless does not necessarily suggest that the former are invalid. As Åkermark argues, the rejection of such rights

> on the basis of risks to individual rights ignores the fact that conflicts of rights are common also as regards individual rights, thus leading to a debate about priorities. In other words, the existence of conflicts calls for a balancing of the underlying interests. If one accepts the recognition of collective rights this does not imply automatically that those rights should always be given priority' (Spiliopoulou Åkermark, 44–45).

The recognition of minority rights does not imply the communitarian logic that group rights take precedence over individual rights.[39] It is also clear that conflicts that may arise in particular circumstances between minority and individual rights are not, and should not necessarily be seen as being, significantly different from conflicts between different individual rights.[40] Accordingly, the resolution of a conflict that may arise should be determined on a case-by-case basis rather than by applying prior principles.[41]

Minority rights are subject to limitations by certain fundamental rights. Scheinin identifies what he calls 'a tentative list of human rights that must enjoy absolute protection in

---

38 Id para 101. Case law on exemption rights is increasing throughout the world. See *inter alia* the cases of the Sikh *kirpan* in a Canadian school (*Multani v Commission scolaire Margherite-Bourgeoys*, [2006] 1 SCR 256) and of the Hindu burial in the UK (Court of Appeal, Civil Division, *Ghai v Newcastle City Council* [2009] EWHC 978 (Admin)).

39 The fear that minority rights may lead to the precedence of the community over the individual is a result of the association of minority rights with communitarianism and individual rights with liberalism. As Casalas observes, it is this association that often leads to the unfortunate depiction of group rights as being incompatible with individual rights. Casalas, Chapter I. Casalas effectively demonstrates in Chapter II of this work that group rights need not be seen as conflicting with individual rights in that way.

40 Taylor maintains that the difficulties faced as a result of the tension or conflict that may arise between the two categories of rights 'are not in principle greater than those encountered by any liberal society that has to combine, for example, liberty and equality, or prosperity and justice'. Taylor, 59–60. Similarly, Triggs maintains that 'individual rights are frequently balanced both with other individual rights and with the interests of a democratic society (the latter a collective interest)'. Triggs, 144.

41 This is also reflected in the jurisprudence of the UN HRC. See *Sandra Lovelace v Canada* (Communication No. 24/1977) UN Doc. Supp. No. 40 (A/36/40) 166 (1981) (HRC); *Ivan Kitok v Sweden* (Communication No. 197/1985) UN Doc. Supp. No. 40 (A/43/40) 221 (1988) (HRC).

relation to the regulatory authority of a minority community' (Scheinin, 233–34). These include the right to life (in all its dimensions); the prohibition against torture and inhuman, degrading or cruel treatment; the prohibition against all slavery-like practices; the prohibition against deprivation of liberty, save for cases where legislation explicitly prescribes powers of detention and they are subject to appropriate safeguards, including court review; and the prohibition against grave forms of discrimination.[42] This is also borne out in some constitutional cases. One such example is *Christian Education South Africa v Minister of Education*.[43] A unanimous court held that the administration of corporal punishment to children as part of the parents' practice of their Christian belief is subject to the prohibition against torture and inhuman, degrading or cruel treatment.[44]

In this context, an issue that often arises in constitutional cases is the question of whether minority rights undermine equality and non-discrimintion. The defendant in *Christian Education South Africa* contended that affirming the existence of a special exemption in favour of religious practices of certain children only, would be to violate the equality provisions contained in section 9 of the Bill of Rights of the Constitution. The argument here is that exempting followers of a particular religion from observing a general rule of law is discriminatory against others.

The court held in this regard that

> 'It is true that to single out a member of a religious community for disadvantageous treatment would, on the face of it, constitute unfair discrimination against that community. The contrary, however, does not hold. To grant respect to sincerely held religious views of a community and make an exception from a general law to accommodate them, would not be unfair to anyone else who did not hold those views.'[45]

Minority rights, like other human rights, are also subject to various other limitations and regulated by principles of constitutional democracy. As the jurisprudence of the HRC shows, the exercise of some of these rights is subject to considerations of the interests of other members of society or public policy, where the latter has a reasonable and objective justification.[46] Moreover, the exercise of minority rights is also subject to the regulation of certain important principles of democracy and constitutionalism. One such principle is that of stability (Norman). This principle recognises that the institutionalisation of mechanisms for the accommodation of diversity can have adverse effects on stability or national cohesion of a society even as protection of minority rights can contribute to stability. For this reason, it is generally regarded that, in giving expression to minority rights, a balance should be struck between stability and unity on the one hand, and multicultural accommodation and diversity

---

42 As Scheinin points out, inasmuch as they relate to the very core of the group's identity and hence are based on objective and reasonable grounds in specific situations, distinctions based on group membership or other grounds cannot be presumed to constitute discrimination and hence can be justified as the necessary consequence of the rights of the group to practise its culture or religion. Scheinin, 234.

43 See *Christian Education South Africa v Minister of Education* 2000 (4) SA 757 (CC), 2000 (10) BCLR 1051 (CC).

44 The same principle has been affirmed by the European Commission of Human Rights in *Campbell and Cosans v United Kingdom* (1980) 3 EHRR 531 at 556.

45 *Christian Education South Africa*, para 42.

46 See, for example, *Lovelace* para 16.

on the other. Justice Sachs of the Constitutional Court of South Africa wrote in *Christian Education* that any open and democratic society based on human dignity, equality and freedom, in which conscientious and religious freedom has to be regarded with appropriate seriousness, can cohere only if all its participants accept that certain basic norms and standards are binding.[47]

Related to the above is the principle of common national identity. The recognition and institutionalisation of membership-based rights and institutions should not obstruct the achievement of a common national identity (see Kymlicka, chapter 9; Patten). Rather, the legitimate aim to establish and to preserve national identity should go hand in hand with the protection of the rights of minorities. In other words, mechanisms should be provided to meet, to the extent possible, both the interests of particularity and the need for nurturing and maintaining a common national identity. As Donald Horowitz (1991) suggested, adopting policies and institutions that promote unity and shared sense of identity among the diverse constituent groups is necessary. One such mechanism is a just resource-sharing scheme. The experience of post-apartheid South Africa shows that a judicially enforceable bill of rights pursued in a way that is respectful of the diversity and identity of members of society can be beneficial. Where multicultural federalism is involved, one additional approach could be the inclusion of a constitutional requirement that the laws and acts of the units of the federation shall be pursued in a way that does not undermine national laws and policies.

Finally, minority rights are also informed by the principle of constitutionalism and rule of law. This entails that the enforcement or exercise of minority rights has to comply with the processes laid down under the constitution and such other relevant laws that are made following due procedure, including the participation of minorities.[48] An important aspect of this is the principle of proportionality. This entails that regard should be given to the nature of the impact of minority rights on others. As Brownlie puts it, 'the modalities of the different treatment (group-specific minority rights) must not be disproportionate in effect or involve unfairness to other ... groups' (Brownlie, 10).

13.4 Conclusion

Minority rights are always a work in progress and require constant adaptation. Nevertheless, some general trends do emerge from the comparative analysis. First, the extraordinary development of international standards over the past two decades in this field as well as the related increased awareness of minority issues by the States has led to a quick and qualitatively remarkable growth of minority rights in constitutions and legislation. Second, since the balance between equality and diversity can never be achieved once and for all, the main challenge remains effective implementation of minority rights, through judicial practice and continuous review of the legislative and administrative tools. Finally, the importance of these legal instruments to accommodate diversity is bound to increase: they are key not only to maintaining peace within and among the States, but also to meeting the quests for recognition of diversity and substantive equality, which are on the rise.

While the above offers the range of possible institutional and policy options for constitutional protection of minorities, the particular form that such constitutional design takes varies from country to country. This is attributable to a number of factors including the nature and

---

47 See *Christian Education South,* para 35.
48 Kymlicka; Patten.

saliency of ethno-cultural diversity in the history and politics of the society. The use or rejection of a particular constitutional mechanism of minority protection depends on both the policy choice of the political forces dominant at the time of the making or substantive revision of a constitution and the past experience of the society with respect to minority rights or group rights. The misuse and abuse of group identity and rights in both South Africa and Rwanda explains the aversion of these countries to group-based political rights. As France's rejection of minority rights also illustrates, the reception of minority-specific constitutional arrangements also depends on the nature of the political commitment and tradition of the society concerned.

References

Addis, A (1997). 'On Human Diversity and the Limits of Toleration', in Shapiro, I & Kymlicka, W (eds), *Ethnicity and group rights - NOMOS XXXIX* (New York, NYU Press), 112.

Benedikter, T (2007). *The World's Working Regional Autonomies: An Introduction and Comparative Analysis* (London, New York, Delhi, Anthem).

Bloed, A & van Dijk, P (eds) (1999). *Protection of Minority Rights Through Bilateral Treaties. The Case of Central and Eastern Europe* (The Hague, Kluwer).

Brownlie, I (1992). 'The Rights of Peoples in Modern International Law', in Crawford, J (ed), *The Rights of Peoples* (Oxford, Oxford University Press).

Capotorti, F (1979). *Study on the Rights of Persons Belonging to Ethnic, Religious and Linguistic Minorities* (New York - UN Doc. E/CN.4/Sub.2/384/Rev.1, UN Sales Nr. E.78.XIV.1).

Casalas, NT (2006). *Group Rights as Human Rights: A Liberal Approach to Multiculturalism* (Dordrecht, Springer).

Currie, I (2007). 'Official Languages and Language Rights', in Woolman, S et al. *Constitutional Law of South Africa* (Cape Town, Juta & Co. Ltd), 2nd edn, Chapter 65.

De Varennes, F (1996). *Language, Minorities & Human Rights* (The Hague, Nijhoff).

—— (1998). *Towards Effective Political Participation and Representation of Minorities* (E/CN.4/Sub.2/AC.5/1998/WP.5).

Dworkin, R (1977). *Taking Rights Seriously* (Cambridge, Harvard University Press).

Eide, A (2000). *Commentary to the Declaration on the Rights of Persons Belonging to National or Ethnic, Religious or Linguistic Minorities* (Working Paper, Working Group on Minorities (6th Session) E/CN.4/Sub.2/AC.5/2000/WP.1 - Commentary to the Declaration).

Fottrell, D & Bowring, B (eds) (1999), *Minority and Group Rights in the New Millennium* (The Hague, Kluwer).

Ghai, Y (2003). *Public Participation and Minorities* MRG Report.

—— (2005). 'Public Participation, Autonomy and Minorities', in Skurbaty, ZA (ed), *Beyond a One Dimensional State: An Emerging Right to Autonomy?* (Leiden/Boston, Nijhoff), 23.

Glazer, N (1995). 'Individual Rights against Group Rights', in Kymlicka, W (ed), *The Rights of Minority Cultures* (Oxford University Press), 123.

Gurr, TR (1993). *Minorities at Risk: A Global View of Ethnopolitical Conflicts.*

Hadden, T (2000). 'The Pendulum Theory of Individual, Communal and Minority Rights', 3 *Critical Review of International Social and Political Philosophy* 82: 77.

Henrard, K (2002). *Minority Protection in Post-Apartheid South Africa: Human Rights, Minority Rights and Self-determination* (Westport, Praeger).

Horowitz, DL (1985). *Ethnic groups in conflict.* (University of California Press Ltd).

—— (1991). *A Democratic South Africa? Constitutional Engineering in a Divided Society* (University of California Press).

—— (2003). 'Electoral Systems: A Primer for Decision Makers', 14 *J of Democracy.*

Kymlicka, W (2005). 'Federalism, Nationalism and Multiculturalism', in Karmis, D & Norman, W (eds), *Theories of Federalism: A Reader* (London, Palgrave Macmillan).

Lapidoth, R (1997). *Autonomy. Flexible Solutions to Ethnic Conflicts* (Washington, US Institute of Peace).

Levy, JT (1997). 'Classifying Group Rights', in Shapiro, I & Kymlicka, W (eds), *Ethnicity and group rights — NOMOS XXXIX* (New York, NYU Press).

Lewis, WA (1965). *Politics in West Africa* (London: George Allen & Unwin Ltd).

Lijphart, A (1991). 'The Alternative Vote: A Realistic Alternative for South Africa?', 18 *Politikon* 9.

—— (1994). *Electoral Systems and Party Systems: A Study of Twenty-Seven Democracies, 1945–1990* (Oxford, Oxford University Press).

—— (1995). 'Self-Determination Versus Pre-determination of Ethnic Minorities in Power-sharing Systems', in Kymlicka, W (ed), *The Rights of Minority Cultures* (Oxford University Press, 275.

Marko, J (1995). *Autonomie und Integration* (Vienna, Böhlau).

Medda-Windischer, R (2009). *Old and new minorities: reconciling diversity and cohesion. A human rights model for minority integration* (Baden Baden, Nomos).

Norman, W (2001). 'Justice and Stability in Multinational Societies', in Gagnon, AG & Tully, J (eds), *Multicultural Democracies* (Cambridge, Cambridge University Press), 90.

Palermo, F (2010). 'At the Heart of Participation and of its Dilemmas. Minorities in Executive Structures', in Weller, M (ed), *Political Participation of Minorities* (Oxford, Oxford University Press), 434–52.

Patten, A (2001). 'Liberal Citizenship in Multicultural Societies', in Gagnon, AG & Tully, J (eds), *Multicultural Democracies* (Cambridge, Cambridge University Press), 279.

Pentassuglia, G (2002). *Minorities in International Law* (Strasbourg, Council of Europe).

Reynolds, A, Reilly, B & Ellis, A with Chebub, JA et al. (2005). *Electoral System Design: The New International IDEA Handbook.*

Reynolds, A (1995). 'The Case for Proportionality', 6 (4) *J of Democracy*, 117.

—— (2006). *Report: Electoral System and the Protection and Participation of Minorities* (London, Minority Rights Group), 11.

Ruiz Vieytez, E (1999). *The History of Legal Protection of Minorities in Europe (XVIIth–XXth Centuries)* (Derby, Derby University Press).

Scheinin, M (2004). 'How to Resolve Conflicts Between Individual and Collective Rights', in Scheinin, M & Toivanen, R (eds), *Rethinking Non-Discrimination and Minority Rights* (Åbo, Institute for Human Rights).

Spiliopoulou Åkermark, A (1996). *Justification of Minority Protection in International Law* (The Hague, Nijhoff).

Steiner, HJ (1998). 'Political Participation as a Human Right' in *Harvard Human Rights Yearbook*, 77.

Suksi, M (ed) (1998). *Autonomy: Applications and Implications* (The Hague, Kluwer).

Taylor, C (1994). 'The Politics of Recognition', in Gutmann, A (ed), *Multiculturalism: Examining the Politics of Recognition* (Princeton University Press).

Toniatti, R (1995). 'Minorities and Protected Minorities: Constitutional Models Compared', in Bonazzi, T & Dunne, M (eds), *Citizenship and rights in multicultural societies* (Keele, Keele University Press).

Töpperwien, N (2004). 'Participation in the Decision-Making Process as a Means of Group Accommodation', in Tarr, GA, Williams, RF & Marko, J (eds), *Federalism, Subnational Constitutions and Minority Rights* (Westport, Praeger), 41–52.

Triggs, G (1992). 'The Rights of "Peoples" and Individual Rights: Conflict or Harmony?' in Crawford, J (ed), *The Rights of Peoples* (Oxford, Oxford University Press), 141.

Tully, J (1995). *Strange Multiplicity: Constitutionalism in an Age of Diversity.*

Verstichel, A (2009). *Participation, Representation and Identity. The Right of Persons Belonging to Minorities to Effective Participation in Public Affairs. Content, Justification and Limits* (Antwerp, Intersentia).

Watts, RL (1998). 'Federalism, Federal Political Systems, and Federations', 1 *Ann Rev Pol Sci*, 117–37.

Wheatley, S (2003). 'Deliberative Democracy and Minorities', 14 (3) *Eur J Int'l L*, 507.

Young, IM (1990). *Justice and the Politics of Difference* (Princeton, New Jersey).

Horizontal effect/state action

Colm O'Cinneide and Manfred Stelzer

14.1 Introduction

The legal doctrines of 'horizontal effect' and 'state action' are both concerned with the issue of whether constitutional rights may play a part in regulating relationships between private actors. Constitutional rights are described as having 'horizontal effect' when they can be applied by courts in moulding the private law norms that govern 'horizontal' relationships among private individuals, corporate bodies, and other non-state legal entities. In contrast, in certain legal systems, rights have limited or no horizontal effect and only regulate the 'vertical' relationship between the individual and the state. In such a situation, individuals will be protected only against violations of their constitutional rights that are attributable to 'state action'; that is, the activities of government actors or other bodies closely connected to the state.

However, where their horizontal effect is limited or non-existent, constitutional rights may nevertheless still exert some influence over how private law regulates horizontal relationships between non-state actors. National legislatures and governments may be subject to certain 'positive obligations' to take steps to ensure the effective enjoyment of fundamental rights, which can derive either from domestic constitutional law or from international human rights treaties. Giving effect to these positive obligations may require restrictions to be imposed on the freedom of other private actors. Alternatively, courts may choose to interpret and apply private law norms in a manner that reflects constitutional values, even if the provisions of the constitution only apply to state actors. Constitutional rights may thus exert considerable influence over the development of private law through a variety of different routes, even when they lack horizontal effect and only apply to 'state action'.

To understand the complex legal issues involved in this area, it is helpful to consider an example of the type of case where it may make a considerable difference as to whether constitutional rights are given horizontal effect or not. Take a situation where a landlord prohibits a tenant from installing a satellite dish on the roof of the rented building in order to receive television and/or radio programmes.[1] Whether the landlord has a right to impose such a

---

1 This example is taken from the case law of the German Federal Constitutional Court, cf. BVerfG, *Neue Juristische Wochenschrift 1993*, p. 1252.

restriction is traditionally determined by applying the relevant principles of contract and/or property law. Furthermore, in most common law or civil law jurisdictions, the landlord's property rights will normally prevail over the limited private law rights of the tenant. However, denial of access to television and radio programmes might place serious limits on the private as well as the social life of the tenant. It might also restrict the tenant's political rights, by limiting access to public information. As a result, unfairness might ensue if the legal relationship between tenants and landlords is governed solely by property law and the principle of freedom of contract. Furthermore, while private law often operates on the presumption that parties to a contract have equal bargaining power, the reality is often very different: a considerable imbalance of power may exist between the landlord and tenant in this type of scenario, which may deprive the tenant of any real opportunity to negotiate an agreement that protects his or her rights.

In such a politically and ideologically highly controversial situation, a legal system might react in one of four ways. First of all, the system could rely entirely on private law, 'leave things as they are', and trust the free market to settle the matter. Second, common law or civil law doctrine might be gradually adjusted by the courts to address some of the moral concerns raised by this type of case. For example, exceptions to the existing rules could be introduced that might dilute the principle of freedom of contract to the tenant's benefit. Third, the legislator might intervene and pass a law further regulating the private relationships in question, which might grant the tenant additional legal rights. Fourth, if neither the courts nor the legislature have adjusted private law, national law might make it possible for the tenant to invoke constitutional rights, such as political rights or a right to freedom of information (where it applies); that is, it might give horizontal effect to these rights. This would usually have the effect of triggering the application of a new 'balancing test' between the rights of the tenant and the interests of the landlord, the results of which might override the pre-existing 'orthodox' private law rules that usually apply in this type of situation.

On first sight, this fourth option might seem rather surprising. Historically, the enactment of bills of rights post-dated the establishment of a working system of common or civil law, while entrenched constitutions were designed to restrict the power of government rather than interfere with private law adjudication. As a result, constitutional rights came to be understood as primarily concerned with protecting the individual against the coercive power of the state and as lacking horizontal application in the private sphere. This view of the 'proper' role of constitutional rights still persists in many quarters: as discussed below, it shapes the doctrine of state action as applied in US constitutional law.

However, the relationship between constitutional rights and private law can be understood in a much broader manner. For example, an influential strand of thought within French constitutional doctrine (Troper, 119) treats the 1789 French Declaration of the Rights of Man as having given expression to the Enlightenment concept that every human being enjoys certain inherent rights. Specifically, they enjoy them solely by virtue of their status as free and equal beings, which should be respected both by governments and by other private individuals. If constitutionally entrenched rights are understood in this sense, then it follows as a necessary consequence that they should govern 'horizontal' legal relations between private actors as well as the 'vertical' relationship between the individual and the state.

These two positions—one emphasising the historical aim of constitutional rights to constrain government, the other focussing on entrenching the status of the free and equal human being against threats emanating from both the state and private actors—are starting points that play a key role in shaping the different approaches that exist in different jurisdictions to the question of 'horizontal effect'. The US Supreme Court still adheres to the more historical approach—constitutional rights guarantees may only be invoked in situations where 'state action' forms the subject matter of the dispute. The German Federal Constitutional Court (*Bundesverfassungsgericht*), on the other hand, emphasises the basic values that have been enshrined in the German Constitution, attributing to them a 'radiating effect' on the whole legal system. However, on close analysis, these two approaches are not based on a sharp opposition: instead they originate from different starting points but then begin to converge, with both making provision to varying degrees along a common spectrum for constitutional rights to exercise some influence over private law.

14.2 State action and vertical effect

The US Supreme Court has interpreted the constitutional rights set out in the US Bill of Rights as applicable only in situations where 'state action' is at issue; that is, where individual rights are affected by the activities of government actors. As a result, US constitutional rights lack horizontal effect: some element of government encroachment upon individual freedom is required before rights can take effect. Only the prohibition on slavery set out in the Thirteenth Amendment applies to both state and private actors.

This doctrinal position was initially adopted by the Supreme Court in its 1883 decision in the *Civil Rights Cases*, where it held that the Equal Protection Clause of the Fourteenth Amendment prohibited only discrimination by federal and state authorities, not by private businesses.[2] In a powerful dissent, Justice Harlan argued that this reading of the Fourteenth Amendment was unduly restrictive. However, the approach of the majority in the *Civil Rights Cases* has been consistently reaffirmed by subsequent Court decisions, which have concluded that the rights set out in the US Bill of Rights were only intended to impose constraints on the activities of government actors, not private individuals.[3]

This doctrinal position reflects a 'vertical' understanding of constitutional rights that sees their function as largely confined to protecting the individual against abuse of government power. In contrast, the Bill of Rights is seen as having little or no application in the private law sphere. Constitutional rights are viewed as being too vague and imprecise to be applied in the context of horizontal relationships between private individuals and corporate bodies. This means that private actors are subject to no legal obligation to respect constitutional rights, and the Bill of Rights has little or no role in private law litigation. Abuses of private power are left to be dealt with through legislation, such as the Civil Rights Act 1964.

However, this apparently straightforward position is complicated by the difficulties courts face in defining the scope of 'state action'. Laws enacted by the state play a major part in shaping horizontal relationships, while federal and state courts enforce and apply private law within the scope of their respective jurisdictions. Private actors may often act on behalf of the state, or perform functions usually carried out by public authorities. As a result, a complex case-law has emerged in the US as to when 'state action' is involved in a legal dispute.

Shelley v Kraemer[4] held that judicial enforcement of contractual provisions under specific circumstances constituted a form of state action. It concluded that courts could not grant

---

2 *Civil Rights Cases*, 109 US 3 (1883).

3 Some commentators have strongly argued that the US federal courts should abandon their adherence to the 'state action' doctrine and give horizontal effect to constitutional rights, on the basis that this represents a better understanding of the relevant constitutional provisions: see, e.g., Gardbaum 2003.

4 334 US 1 (1948).

relief in a private law action that would infringe constitutional rights. As a result, the discriminatory provisions of a restrictive covenant that prevented property owners selling their house to African-Americans could not be enforced once a house was effectively sold, even though the *Civil Rights Cases* had established that the Equal Protection Clause was not applicable to private parties—the active intervention by a court that would be required to prevent the transfer of property in question from going ahead qualified as a form of state action and therefore was subject to the constitutional prohibition on race discrimination.

The Supreme Court thus attempted in *Shelley* to circumvent the restrictions imposed on the horizontal effect of constitutional rights in US constitutional law by treating judicial enforcement of private law under the specific circumstances of the case as a form of state action. If followed to its logical limits, this approach would appear capable of being extended so as to require all American private law to conform to constitutional requirements, as all forms of legal regulation ultimately depend upon judicial enforcement to acquire force of law. However, in subsequent decisions, the US courts have declined to take account of constitutional rights in situations where they are acting as 'neutral arbiters' in private law disputes. For example, in *Evans v Abney*[5] the Supreme Court declined to alter the standard legal rules governing the validity of wills even when the bequest in question discriminated against African-Americans.

The US Supreme Court has nevertheless been willing to treat the development of the common law by the courts as a form of state action that must conform to constitutional requirements. In the famous case of *New York Times v Sullivan*,[6] the Supreme Court required that state courts modify the common law of defamation to protect the First Amendment right of freedom of expression. It concluded that only the dissemination of malicious falsehoods about a public official would give rise to liability in defamation.

The US courts have also recognised a number of situations where the actions of private individuals or corporate bodies can be treated as constituting a form of state action. For example, the performance by a private body of a function usually carried out by the state may qualify as state action,[7] as can private activity carried out as part of a joint enterprise with government.[8] Similarly, if the leadership of a private organisation is 'pervasively entwined' with that of a government authority, then its activities may constitute a form of state action.[9] However, the existence of a close relationship between a private body and state-supported institutions may not be enough in itself to establish that state action is in play.[10]

US courts have thus shown some flexibility in giving effect to constitutional rights in the context of horizontal relationships, while limiting their effect by and large to situations where government action encroaches upon the individual. However, confining the application of constitutional rights to the 'vertical' relationship between the individual and the state in this way inevitably gives rise to complex questions as to when 'state action' is in play. The case-law of the US courts in this area has attracted widespread criticism for its alleged inconsistency and incoherence (see Chemerinsky; Tushnet).

In general, the 'vertical' approach adopted by the US courts can be difficult to apply, as courts often struggle to define the limits of what constitutes 'state action'. This can be

---

5 396 US 435 (1970).
6 376 US 1 (1948).
7 *Marsh v Alabama*, 326 US 501 (1946).
8 *Burton v Wilmington Parking Authority*, 365 US 715 (1961).
9 *Brentwood Academy v Tennessee Secondary School Athletic Association*, 535 US 971 (2002).
10 *National Collegiate Athletic Association v Smith*, 525 US 459 (1999).

illustrated by reference to UK case-law as well as that of the US courts. Section 6 of the UK Human Rights Act 1998 provides that only bodies performing 'public functions' are obliged to respect the rights set out in the European Convention on Human Rights, but the English courts have faced great difficulty in defining clearly when private organisations receiving public funds can be classified as performing a 'public function'.[11] This problem of how to define the limits of state action may explain in part why courts across the world are increasingly willing to give some form of 'horizontal effect' to constitutional rights.

14.3 Horizontal effect

The doctrine of the horizontal (or third-party) effect of constitutional rights has been primarily developed in post-war Germany. Although the German Bill of Rights, Articles 1 to 19 of the Basic Law, does not explicitly provide for a third-party effect (cf. Heun, 191 ff), some of its provisions were nevertheless favourable to the development of this doctrine. Article 1, paragraph 3 of the Basic Law states that the 'basic rights shall be binding as directly valid laws' not only on the legislative and the executive branch of government but also on the judiciary. As legal conflicts between private parties may ultimately be solved by an authoritative judgement of a civil law court, the fact that civil law courts are bound by constitutional rights arguably opened the way for constitutional rights to be applied indirectly in private disputes. It is also of importance that the Federal Constitutional Court has the power to scrutinise decisions of ordinary courts; that is, civil and penal law courts. Without such a power, the horizontal-effect doctrine might not have been developed, as it then would have fallen to the civil law courts to apply constitutional law, which they arguably would have been very reluctant to do. In Austria, for instance, where the Constitutional Court has no jurisdiction over civil law courts, the third-party doctrine, although accepted in principle, still plays only a marginal part in private law adjudication (see Stelzer, 191).

Those structural features aside, the origins of the horizontal-effect doctrine lie in how the Basic Law was designed in reaction against a barbaric Nazi regime that defied all moral standards of civilised nations (Heun, 191). Hence, the bill of rights was not only placed to the forefront of the new constitution but also has been subsequently interpreted as constituting a moral code rooted in Enlightenment principles, and in particular the philosophy of Immanuel Kant, which is intended to guide the development of the entire legal system (and, consequently, German society) rather than merely designating realms of individual freedom to be safeguarded against governmental encroachment.[12]

It therefore does not come as a surprise that the leading case in which the Federal Constitutional Court expressed the idea of a horizontal effect for the very first time had a strong link to Germany's Nazi past. In 1958, the Court heard the case of Erich Lüth,[13] head of the press office of the Hamburg state government, who called for a boycott of post-war films directed by Veit Harlan, one of the leading directors under the Third Reich who was responsible for films featuring strong anti-Semitic and pro-Nazi propaganda. On the application of the distribution company alleging disturbance of their business, German civil law courts granted injunctive relief, which effectively prohibited Mr Lüth from repeating his

---

11 See, e.g., *YL v Birmingham CC* [2008] 1 AC 95 (UK House of Lords).
12 Preuß 2005, 28, explicitly speaks of a constitution as a 'normative blueprint for the whole society'.
13 Bundesverfassungsgericht [German Constitutional Court], 15 January 1958 reported in (1958) 7 BVerfG 198; this case is reported extensively by Preuß 2005, 25 ff.

boycott calls. However, Mr Lüth filed a complaint with the Constitutional Court invoking Article 5 of the Basic Law, which guarantees the right to free speech. Eventually, the Federal Constitutional Court overturned the decisions of the civil law courts, on the basis that those courts had failed sufficiently to respect Mr Lüth's constitutional rights.

In the view of the Court, the German Basic Law establishes an 'objective order of values', or, in a more contemporary phrasing, lays down general 'objective' principles (Heun, 199) penetrating the whole German legal system. As objective principles, they affect all spheres of public and private law, exercising a 'radiating effect': all actions of the legislator, the administration, and the judiciary have to be measured against their requirements. Furthermore, the Federal Constitutional Court as custodian of the Basic Law claims responsibility for ensuring that this order of values is enforced and respected.

With regard to private law, this theoretical approach requires the rules of private law to conform to this constitutional system of values and to be interpreted and applied in its spirit (cf. Heun, 198). It therefore can be said that fundamental rights guarantees have a 'horizontal effect' as they do not only take effect in the vertical dimension but also radiate horizontally. From a more procedural point of view, rights guarantees can also be described as having 'third-party effect', as the defendant in a civil lawsuit can be viewed as the third party to the legal relation between the plaintiff and the public authority (the law court).

German legal doctrine insists that this horizontal effect is 'indirect' rather than 'direct'. This distinction between direct and indirect horizontal effect again primarily reflects procedural considerations relating to the particular status of private actors.[14] Giving fundamental rights direct horizontal effect would make it possible for a private party to sue another private party (in an ordinary court or in the Constitutional Court) merely on the ground of an alleged violation of a constitutional right. The German legal system does not provide for such action, or consider it necessary or appropriate for such an action to exist. However, constitutional rights may indirectly be brought into play in private litigation. For example, a private party may sue another private party by arguing that a clause of a contract previously agreed upon was void because it offended 'public morals' (see German Civil Law Code, art 138 para 1), on the basis that it was not compatible with the objective value order established by the constitution, thus 'indirectly' invoking a fundamental rights guarantee. In general, it might be said that private law provisions that refer to 'public morals', 'common standards', 'the public good' or other vague terms that provide for significant interpretative latitude serve as important links between private law doctrine and constitutional considerations, and provide a vehicle for constitutional rights to be given 'indirect horizontal effect'.

Consequently, under the supervision of the Constitutional Court, civil law courts are obliged to interpret open-ended private law provisions in light of the provisions of the Basic Law. However, although this obligation seems to be clear and straightforward, it is much less clear in practice how courts should give effect to it. In private law litigation, both parties may often be in a position to invoke constitutional rights, especially given that freedom of contract principles in German law are underpinned by constitutional recognition of the right to property. As a result, virtually every conflict under private law is potentially capable of being reconstructed as a clash of fundamental rights positions. Such a clash may be resolved by courts balancing the rights in question through a proportionality analysis. However, this may be a highly indeterminate and uncertain process. German lawyers have at times criticised the

---

14 It may therefore be questioned if this distinction really matters in terms of substantive standards; cf. Kumm & Comella, 251.

horizontal-effect doctrine on the basis that it enables the Constitutional Court to displace highly sophisticated arguments based on hundreds of years of civil law doctrine on the basis of rather blunt balancing decisions that do not necessarily improve the overall rationality of the legal system (Roellecke, 1649). Indeed, although the German Federal Constitutional Court emphasises that it will only intervene if civil law courts have either entirely failed to consider the relevant constitutional right or seriously failed to give it due weight in its legal assessment, the Court has nevertheless reshaped private law to a comparatively large extent.[15]

Despite these concerns, the horizontal-effect doctrine has proved attractive to many other courts in a variety of common law and civil law systems.[16] How it is applied tends to vary from state to state, reflecting local constitutional factors. In some jurisdictions, constitutional rights tend to be given horizontal effect in a 'weak' or 'limited' manner, whereby courts place considerable emphasis on the importance of maintaining the stability and internal logic of existing private law rules when they balance rights in the context of private litigation. In other jurisdictions, courts appear to be readier to give 'strong' effect to rights by being comparatively more willing to adjust existing private law to conform to constitutional norms. The horizontal-effect doctrine has, in broad outline, proved to be a popular transplant, especially in states that have incorporated new or expanded charters of fundamental rights into their legal systems over the last few decades. The examples of Canada and South Africa are especially interesting.

The case law of the Canadian Supreme Court on horizontal effect is shaped by the framework provided by the 1982 reform of the Canadian Constitution. While Section 52 stipulates that the Constitution including the Charter of Rights and Freedoms is the supreme law of the land, Section 32 provides that the Charter is binding on Parliament and the government, and does not make reference to private parties. Given this ambiguity, the Supreme Court has distinguished between private law cases that involve a statute (an act of Parliament and/or government) and those based on common law only. Statutes relating to private law must be interpreted so as to fully comply with the Constitution, which confers a degree of 'indirect horizontal effect' on Charter rights. However, this requirement is not applied to the common law, which is treated as lying outside of the scope of the Charter.[17]

However, the Supreme Court of Canada also determined that the common law has to be applied, developed, and—if necessary—modified in accordance with the principles of the Charter (cf Saunders, 198). This ensures that Charter rights enjoy a degree of indirect horizontal effect in a manner broadly analogous to the approach applied in Germany, with both common law and statute law capable of being interpreted and applied with reference to the values sets out in the Charter of Fundamental Rights and Freedoms (Kumm & Comella, 259 ff). The difference between the two jurisdictions is that the influence exerted by the

15 Cf. Kumm & Cormella 2005, p. 255. It is interesting how the Federal Constitutional Court dealt with the case referred to above (section 1). Basically, a tenant can be prevented from installing a satellite dish by the landlord if access to a cable network was granted (BVerfG, *Neue Juristische Wochenschrift 1993*, 1252). But in case the tenant was a foreigner and the cable network did not offer programmes in his language, his right to free information prevailed (Bundesverfassungsgericht [German Constitutional Court], 1 BvR 2116/94 (eA), 7 February 1995 reported in (1995) 92 BVerfGE 126).

16 With respect to some Central European countries, cf. Kühn.

17 *RWDSU v Dolphin Delivery Ltd* [1986] 2 SCR 573 (Supreme Court of Canada).

Charter on Canadian common law derives from the willingness of the Supreme Court to interpret private law norms in a manner that reflects Charter values, rather than from the limited binding effect of the Charter itself. In contrast, the 'radiating effect' of the German Basic Law is based on its status as fundamental law. The Canadian approach could thus be seen as 'weaker' than its German counterpart, although in practice there appears to be relatively little difference of substance.

Both the German and Canadian approaches to attributing horizontal effect to constitutional rights attracted considerable interest during the drafting process of the 1993 Interim Constitution of South Africa.[18] They appeared to provide a way of ensuring that constitutional values could permeate private law in a manner that would help to address the devastating social and economic legacy of apartheid. Section 7 of the Interim Constitution consequently provided that constitutional rights 'would apply to all law in force', while 'juristic persons shall be entitled to the rights contained in this Chapters where, and to the extent that, the nature of the rights permits'. However, these provisions left a degree of ambiguity about the extent to which private law would have to conform to the values of the new constitutional order. In *Du Plessis v De Klerk*,[19] the majority of the South African Constitutional Court interpreted these provisions as providing for a relatively weak form of indirect horizontal effect, whereby constitutional rights did not have binding authority in the private sphere but courts should give 'due regard to the spirit, purport and objective' of the constitutional bill of rights in developing and applying the common law.[20]

This generated concern that the horizontal effect of constitutional rights could prove to be very dilute. As a result, Section 6 of the 1996 Constitution explicitly made provision for strong horizontal effect to be given to constitutional rights, which could take 'indirect' or even 'direct' form. It stipulated that a provision of the Bill of Rights is not only binding on the legislature, the executive, the judiciary, and all other organs of the state, but also on a 'natural or juristic person if, and to the extent that, it is applicable, taking into account the nature of the right and the nature of any duty imposed by the right'. The Constitution further encourages courts to apply and, if necessary, to develop the common law in order to give effect to a constitutional right if legislation does not give it adequate effect. Common law rules that limit the enjoyment of rights must also be shown to be reasonable and justifiable in an open and democratic society in line with the requirements set out in Section 36, paragraph 1 of the Constitution. These constitutional provisions have been largely interpreted in a manner that is similar to the approach adopted by the German courts, and they have played a significant part in transforming South African private law: libel law, family law, the law of inheritance, and the law of privacy have all been adjusted to conform to the requirements of the 1996 Constitution.[21]

In other countries—such as Ireland, Spain, Brazil, and India—certain specific constitutional rights can also, in particular circumstances, be given 'direct' horizontal effect; that is, they can be applied directly in the context of horizontal relationships to regulate the conduct

---

18 *Du Plessis v De Klerk* [1996] 3 SA 850 (Constitutional Court of South Africa).
19 [1996] 3 SA 850 (Constitutional Court of South Africa).
20 In contrast, Kriegler J in his dissent (at 914–15) argued that constitutional rights constituted fundamental legal norms that should be treated as superior to all other legal norms, and therefore that they should pervade and govern the application of all legal rules, whether in public or private law.
21 See, e.g., *Khumalo v Holomisa* [2002] 5 SA 401 (Constitutional Court of South Africa).

of private individuals and corporate bodies.[22] For example, the Irish Supreme Court in *Meskell v CIE* held that an employer had directly violated the constitutional right of freedom of association by terminating existing contracts of employment and replacing them with new contracts that required employees to join a union. The Court awarded damages for breach of constitutional rights, thus establishing the existence of a 'constititutional tort'.[23] Similarly, the Indian Supreme Court in *Vishaka v State of Rajasthan*[24] set out guidelines on sexual harassment in the workplace that both private and public employers were required to respect, in order to give effect to a number of fundamental constitutional rights, including the Article 14 right to equality and the Article 15 right to non-discrimination.

The willingness of courts in these jurisdictions to give direct horizontal effect to rights appears to be based in part on the expectation common to many post-colonial states that courts should play a leading role in transforming society. It also reflects the fact that serious violations of individual rights in many of these states have often been attributable to abuses of private power linked to the persistence of serious socio-economic inequalities (see Singh). However, in many of these jurisdictions, concern nevertheless exists that giving direct horizontal effect to rights risks making private law highly indeterminate. As a result, constraints are often imposed on the extent to which constitutional rights can be given direct effect. In Ireland, rights are only applied directly when existing private law cannot be interpreted in a manner that conforms to constitutional requirements, or when it manifestly fails to protect individual rights (see O'Cinneide). In India, only certain constitutional rights are treated as applicable to private actors; other rights only apply where 'state action' is at issue, which again has proved to be difficult to define.[25]

It is therefore open to question whether direct horizontal effect to rights necessarily represents a 'stronger' approach than the indirect route developed in the German, Canadian, and South African jurisprudence. The two approaches differ when it comes to the specific mode by which rights take effect in the context of horizontal relationships, but both try to balance the risk of indeterminacy with a common commitment to ensuring that private law in the final analysis recognises that rights constitute 'objective values', which all legal norms must respect.

Finally, constitutional rights can also exercise a considerable impact on the evolution of private law through the development of the concept of 'affirmative duties' or 'positive obligations', whereby the state is required not only to refrain from interfering with constitutional rights but also to take positive steps to ensure their effective enjoyment. In states where this doctrinal approach applies, all branches of government acting within their fields of responsibility are obliged to ensure individual rights are not eroded by the behaviour of third parties. When it comes to private law, the results of this doctrine often produce similar effects to those achieved through the application of the doctrine of horizontal effect. This is of especial relevance to all member states of the European Convention for the Protection of Human

---

22 See also the 1999 Swiss Constitution, which in Article 35 has entrenched the idea that fundamental rights affect the whole legal system and has stipulated that all 'authorities shall ensure that fundamental rights, where appropriate, apply to relationships among private persons' (art 35 para 3).

23 Meskell v CIE [1973] IR 121 (Supreme Court of Ireland).

24 (1997) 6 SCC 241 (Supreme Court of India). See also Apparel Export Promotion Council v Chopra, AIR (1999) SC 625 (Supreme Court of India).

25 Contrast the approach adopted by the Indian Supreme Court in MC Mehta v Union of India (1987) 1 SCC 395 with that adopted in Zee Telefilms Ltd v Union of India (2005) 4 SCC 649.

Rights and Fundamental Freedoms, as the European Court of Human Rights has interpreted the Convention as imposing a wide-ranging set of 'positive obligations' on states.[26] Again, the doctrine of positive obligations has its roots in the concept of rights as objective norms: the state is expected to take steps to ensure that rights as 'objective values' are respected in the context of both horizontal and vertical relationships.

14.4 Conclusion

In most jurisdictions, constitutional rights were originally introduced solely to govern the relation between the individual and the government ('vertical effect'). Today they are for the most part applicable in litigation between private parties as well. Some courts, in particular the US Supreme Court, still adhere to the position that constitutional rights may only be invoked where there is a specific element involved that can be classified as a form of governmental encroachment or 'state action'. However, many constitutional courts have tended over the few decades to adopt the alternative approach that constitutional rights also entrench 'objective values' or 'objective principles' that penetrate the whole legal system and serve as a benchmark for assessing all actions of legislation, administration, and adjudication. In accepting such a 'radiating effect', courts confer 'indirect' horizontal effect on fundamental rights, or even at times a form of 'direct' horizontal effect.

The powers and responsibilities of highest courts and their position within a given constitutional system tend to influence their approach to addressing the issue of whether and how fundamental rights should have an effect on private law litigation. In many jurisdictions, various national courts have effectively 'constitutionalised' private law through their development and application of doctrines of state action, horizontal effect, and positive obligations. Although some argue that this may be detrimental to the coherence of private law doctrine, it can help to transform private law and ensure that it better reflects modern concepts of justice and individual rights.

Nevertheless, there are dangers associated with the constitutionalising of private law through the operation of horizontal effect and similar doctrines. Doing so can result in private law disputes being settled by rather blunt judicial reasoning involving the balancing of rights in a fairly indeterminate manner. It is therefore the responsibility of the courts to apply these doctrines with some prudence. However, it appears as if constitutional values now play a significant role in shaping the interaction of private actors to a greater or lesser degree in virtually every state, even in jurisdictions such as the US, which still adhere to a predominantly 'vertical' approach that conceptualises rights as designed to protect the individual against state interference rather than as objective values that should infuse the entire legal order. As a result, the doctrines of state action and horizontal effect should not be regarded as opposing concepts, but rather as different points along a spectrum demarcating the extent to which constitutional rights are applicable in the context of private relationships (Gardbaum 2011).

---

26 Cf, e.g. with regard to Article 8 of the ECHR: Von Hannover v Germany (European Court of Human Rights, Chamber, Application No. 59320/00, 24 June 2004); Garlicki. Interestingly, the European Court of Justice has adopted both the doctrines of third-party/horizontal effect and positive obligation in its case-law in respect of the four fundamental freedoms enjoyed by citizens of the European Union: see Chalmers, Davies & Monti 2010, 757 ff (concerning the free movement of goods), 797 ff (concerning the free movement of services).

References

Chalmers, D, Davies, G & Monti, G (2010). *European Union Law* (Cambridge, Cambridge University Press, 2nd edn).

Chemerinsky, E (1985). 'Rethinking State Action', *North Western University Law Review* 80:503.

Gardbaum, S (2003). 'The "Horizontal Effect" of Constitutional Rights', *Michigan Law Review* 102:388.

—— (2011). 'The Structure and Scope of Constitutional Rights', in Ginsburg, T & Dixon, R (eds), *Comparative Constitutional Law* (Cheltenham, Edward Elgar Publishing).

Garlicki, L (2005). 'Relations between Private Actors and the European Convention on Human Rights', in Sajó, A & Uitz, R (eds), *The Constitution in Private Relations: Expanding Constitutionalism* (Utrecht, Eleven International Publishing).

Heun, W (2010). *The Constitution of Germany* (Oxford, Hart Publishing).

Kühn, Z (2005). 'Making Constitutionalism Horizontal: Three Different Central European Strategies', in Sajó, A & Uitz, R (eds), *The Constitution in Private Relations: Expanding Constitutionalism* (Utrecht, Eleven International Publishing).

Kumm, M & Ferreres Comella, V (2005). 'What Is So Special about Constitutional Rights in Private Litigation? A Comparative Analysis of the Function of State Action Requirements and Indirect Horizontal Effect', in Sajó, A & Uitz, R (eds), *The Constitution in Private Relations: Expanding Constitutionalism* (Utrecht, Eleven International Publishing).

O'Cinneide, C (2007). 'Grasping the Nettle: Irish Constitutional Law and Direct Horizontal Effect', in Fedtke, J & Oliver, D (eds), *Human Rights and the Private Sphere* (London, Cavendish).

Preuß, U (2005). 'The German *Drittwirkung* Doctrine and Its Socio-Political Background', in Sajó, A & Uitz, R (eds), *The Constitution in Private Relations: Expanding Constitutionalism* (Utrecht, Eleven International Publishing).

Roellecke, G (1992). 'Das Mietrecht des BVerfG', *Neue Juristische Wochenschrift*, 1649.

Saunders, C (2005). 'Constitutional Rights and the Common Law', in Sajó, A & Uitz, R (eds), *The Constitution in Private Relations: Expanding Constitutionalism* (Utrecht, Eleven International Publishing).

Singh, M (2007). 'India: Protection of Human Rights against State and Non-State Action', in Oliver, D & Fedtke, J (eds), *Human Rights and the Private Sphere* (Abingdon, Routledge-Cavendish).

Stelzer, M (2011). *The Constitution of the Republic of Austria* (Oxford, Hart Publishing).

Troper, M (2005). 'Who Needs a Third Party Effect Doctrine? — The Case of France', in Sajó, A & Uitz, R (eds), *The Constitution in Private Relations: Expanding Constitutionalism* (Utrecht, Eleven International Publishing).

Tushnet, M (1983). '*Shelley v Kraemer* and Theories of Equality', *New York Law School Law Review* 33:383.

Additional reading

Cheadle, H (2005). 'Third Party Effect in the South African Constitution', in Sajó, A & Uitz, R (eds), *The Constitution in Private Relations: Expanding Constitutionalism* (Utrecht, Eleven International Publishing).

Oliver, D & Fedtke, J (eds) (2007). *Human Rights and the Private Sphere* (Abingdon, Routledge-Cavendish).

Rüfner, W (1992). 'Grundrechtsadressaten', in Isensee, J & Kirchhof, P (eds), *Handbuch des Staatsrechts der Bundesrepublik Deutschland* (Heidelberg, CF Müller Juristischer Verlag).

Tushnet, M (2003). 'The Issue of State Action/Horizontal Effect in Comparative Constitutional Law', *International Journal of Constitutional Law* 1:79.

Part III
Rights

1. Integrity

'Human dignity' as a constitutional doctrine

Margit Cohn and Dieter Grimm

15.1 Introduction

The dignity of the human person is recognized across states and in transnational arrangements. It is expressed on several levels: as an overarching political principle underlying the constitutional framework, as a central key for the interpretation and application of other rights and values, and as a fully-fledged enforceable right. Unlike the classical libertarian civic rights, which draw their force from liberty, dignity also comprises the material preconditions of liberty and equality and becomes a source for social and economic rights. Yet, the concept is far from clear, and appears in a variety of forms. As a concept, it is also distinguished from other well-recognized human rights, it is sometimes absent, and is sometimes presented as drawing on a more state-centered rationale.

While dignity is a rather new phenomenon in a constitutional context, it is an old notion in philosophy, theology, and law. Roman times feature in many analyses, with Cicero often marking the beginning. Further roots in Judaism and Christianity are based on the *imago dei* concept, which links the value of the human being with God and divinity. The creature the most similar to God ranks higher than other creatures. The gradual move towards the positing of man at the center, from the Renaissance to Kant, led to the modern concept of dignity as an inherent value of every human being; thus concept stands at the center of this chapter. As a modern concept, it is usually linked with Enlightenment and Kantian philosophy (see e.g., McCrudden; Whitman; England).

In law, dignity was, from its Roman beginnings, mainly directed to the social role and esteem due to persons on the basis of their status, office, or rank in a hierarchically structured society. This understanding ended only with the great revolutions of the late eighteenth century, aimed at granting all members of society the rights and dignities previously offered only to high-ranking individuals. 'Dignity' was thus a mechanism for upward equalization and was simultaneously couched in the notions of liberty and equality. The absence of a collective memory of a feudal society in the United States serves to explain the absence of a distinct doctrine of dignity across the Atlantic (Whitman).

Yet, dignity played no role in early modern constitutionalism, and is absent in the foundational documents of constitutionalism. Likewise, one would seek it in vain in the many constitutions that were enacted in the nineteenth century. It first appears in a few constitutions after World War I (Germany, Ireland, Brazil), in reaction to the social problems that were the heritage of the nineteenth century.[1] Here, dignity meant the possibility for everyone to lead a dignified life, the preconditions of which had to be secured by the state. Dignity as an inherent quality of every human being was later linked with the lessons drawn from Nazism and Fascism, and entered into almost every constitution of a society that had freed itself from dictatorship in the course of the second half of the twentieth century.

Many have noted the vagueness of the concept. Laments that no definition has been adopted in constitutions or elsewhere may be answered that such is the nature of constitutional texts. Some attempts at definition do exist, such as Gewirth's emphasis on the 'Kantian injunction to treat every human being as an end'[2] rather than a mere object of the state, which is vague in itself. Distinctions among different conceptions of dignity abound. Most notably, the distinction between dignity as an intrinsic element of the human person and dignity as the source of both state duties and the setting of constraints on the human person is expressed in Brownsword's distinction between 'dignity as empowerment' and 'dignity as constraint', further developed in the literature (Brownsword, 20–28; see also Fyfe; Rao 2011).

Gewirth's distinction between 'empirical' and 'inherent' concepts of dignity offers another dimension to the distinction between a social grant of respect and one that is intrinsic to all human beings (Gewirth 1992, 11–13). This understanding clearly prevails over the idea that dignity is a merit-based quality that can be earned by leading a good life and forfeited by leading a bad life. Finally, the distinction between dignity as absolute and inalienable and dignity as balanceable and subject to limitations roughly corresponds to the continental/common law divide, an issue discussed further below.

15.2 The formal recognition of human dignity

A survey of current formal recognition of human dignity reflects a dominant pattern, with some constitutional documents offering only partial, context-based protection and a few that do not formally recognize the right. Human dignity was recognized in 1945 in the Preambles to the Charter of the United Nations and the Constitution of UNESCO. In addition to their Preambles, the Universal Declaration of Human Rights (1948) and the International Covenant on Civil and Political Rights recognize the dignity of man in the context of some specific rights, and many additional UN documents contain the term. Dignity is also central to international humanitarian law; common article 3 of the Geneva Conventions (1949) prohibits 'outrages upon personal dignity, in particular humiliating and degrading treatment'.

Dignity is now a central element of European Union (EU) law. In addition to the Preamble of the EU Charter of Fundamental Rights, in which dignity is the first of 'the indivisible, universal values' on which the Union is founded, the Charter's first chapter is entitled 'Dignity'. Article 1, which, like the German Basic Law discussed below, recognizes the

---

1 Art 151 of the Weimar Constitution of 1919 reads, 'The economic order must correspond to the principles of justice with the aim to guarantee everybody an existence in human dignity ... 'Art 115 of the Brazilian Constitution of 1934 is nearly identical with the Weimar Constitution. Ireland refers to 'dignity and freedom of the individual' in the Preamble of the Constitution of 1937.
2 Gewirth 1983, 849 (preceded by the author's attention to the absence of a definition and the usual application on the basis of 'I know it when I see it even if I cannot tell you what it is').

inviolability of human dignity, is followed by provisions that recognize and protect the right to life and the right to the integrity of the person, and prohibit torture and inhuman or degrading treatment as well as slavery and forced labor. The Treaty of the European Union, following the entry into force of the Treaty of Lisbon, likewise recognizes 'respect for human dignity' as the first of a list of basic values. Additional protection can be found in these treaties, in the context of other protected rights. Other conventions pertaining to specific areas, such as bioethics, also place dignity as a central element.[3]

Limited recognition is found in the International Covenant on Economic, Social and Cultural Rights (1966), in which dignity is protected only in the context of education. Further, dignity appears only in Protocol 13 of the European Convention on Human Rights, concerned with the death penalty, recognized there as 'inherent' to all human beings. Similar patterns can be found in national constitutions, but absence of direct protection is also found.

Several national constitutions dedicate a specific section or article to the recognition of human dignity and its protection. In the vanguard is Germany; others include Belgium, Sweden, Portugal, Spain, Brazil, Switzerland, the Czech Republic, Israel, South Africa, and Hungary, as well as Iran and Iraq. In some of these constitutions, the requirement to protect dignity is also an element of other specific protected rights, such as the protection of personal freedom, bodily integrity, working conditions, and private initiative (with variations); in a few of these constitutions, human dignity is also recognized in the preamble. More limited recognition of human dignity is found in other constitutions, such as the Italian, Greek, Argentinian, Turkish, and the provisional Egyptian constitutions, in which human dignity is mentioned only in the context of one or few specific defined rights, such as the ones mentioned above. Other constitutions address dignity only in their preamble, as is the case with the Irish Constitution. No formal recognition of human dignity can be found in the constitutions of the United States, Canada, and France. As we shall see below, the mode of adoption and the extent of application of human dignity do not derive solely from the constitutional text.

'Human dignity' is not defined in any of these constitutions. Some constitutions—for example the constitutions of Germany, the Czech Republic, and Puerto Rico—recognize human dignity as absolute, referring to it as 'inviolable' or 'inalienable'.

In addition, the duty to protect human dignity can be found in a variety of statutes across the systems, concerned *inter alia* with prisoners' rights, bioethics, and the grant of social rights.

15.3 The scope of human dignity

Clapham mentions four types of behavior against which the right to dignity protects persons or to which the right to dignity entitles persons. (1) It prohibits inhuman treatment, humiliation, and degradation. (2) It guarantees individual self-fulfillment, autonomy, or self-realization. (3) It protects group-identity and culture as essential for personal development. (4) It guarantees everybody the satisfaction of their essential needs (Clapham, 545 ff; see also McCrudden, 686 ff).

These aspects are neither exhaustive nor mutually exclusive, nor do they rest on sharp boundaries. What is in the foreground may vary over time and from place to place. Introduced in Germany in reaction to the atrocities of the Nazi regime, the scope of the right to dignity was originally derived from the first aspect. Later on, autonomy and recognition as well as fulfillment of basic needs (including participation in cultural goods) became more salient. In

---

3 E.g., Convention on Human Rights and Biomedicine, CETS No. 164 (1997).

a country like South Africa, whose past was determined by racism, the aspect of the intrinsic value of each person and the equality that flows from it is prominent. After a dictatorship, as in the post-Communist regimes, autonomy and self-realization may play a prominent role. Where large parts of the population live under conditions of extreme poverty, the right to obtain certain benefits may have particularly high importance.

But even within these aspects there is room for different emphases. In particular, dignity and the aspects covered by it can be interpreted in a more individualistic or a more communitarian way. Again, this is not a matter of either/or, but a matter of degree. Dignity is always concerned with the human being, the individual and his or her recognition as a value in itself, regardless of age, gender, class, capacities, merit, and the like. But the individual can be imagined more as an isolated being or more embedded in and dependent on society. Here, the differences between the European and the American approach become visible (Whitman; Brugger). Accordingly the scope of the right will vary.

The scope will also vary depending on the understanding of dignity as an absolute or a relative right. 'Absolute' means that the right can neither be restrained nor weighed against other rights. If this is so, it seems inevitable that protection can only be invoked against the most severe encroachments. All minor encroachments may be classified as protected by other rights such as the right to physical integrity or to privacy. If dignity is but a relative right, the scope can be drawn more widely, since limitation or balancing is allowed. Furthermore, the range of the bill of rights may play a role. If important rights, such as equality in Israel, are not contained in the catalog of rights, dignity may serve as a substitute, an aspect discussed below.

15.4 The relationship between dignity and (other) rights

The relationship between dignity and rights depends largely on the answer to the question of whether dignity is only a principle or also a right and whether, as a right, it is absolute or relative.

'Principle' here is understood not, in the sense of Robert Alexy, as a difference between principles and rules, but in the sense of a binding norm for government, which, however, does not correspond with an individual entitlement. In this case, dignity will be a guideline for any governmental agent, but will serve as the basis of direct obligations only in exceptional cases. Compared with rights, it takes effect by way of interpretation. Every fundamental right can be said to have a dignity core. If rights collide, dignity is not on the side of one right only. The closer a state action that limits a fundamental right comes to the dignity core, the more weight this right will have in the balancing process.

Whether dignity, in itself, is regarded as a right can depend on its status in the constitutional framework as an absolute or relative principle. If the guarantee is absolute, a hierarchical order between dignity and other rights is established, with dignity at the top of the hierarchy. In such a case, no limitation is justifiable and no balancing takes place. As an absolute right, when found to be affected (a question of its scope), it will always trump other rights and interests. As a relative right, dignity may still enjoy a privileged position, as in the South African Constitution with its triad of dignity, equality, and freedom: under such a structure, dignity is likely to prevail in many cases, but not in all.

A special problem exists in the context of the relationship between dignity and the right to life. One could argue that life is the precondition of the enjoyment of all other rights, dignity included. Hence, life should enjoy a preferred position. Killing a person would also be an attack on his or her dignity. However, in most jurisdictions the right to life is subject to limitations. The legal order recognizes instances in which the state can lawfully take life. In these cases, taking someone's life would not at the same time mean a violation of dignity. This is more the case when life is guaranteed in a relative way, while dignity enjoys absolute protection. Under these conditions, killing a person does not automatically violate dignity. But there may be ways or circumstances under which killing constitutes a violation of dignity.

15.5 Human dignity in the courts: models of constitutional adjudication

From formal absence and limited judicial application, to full formal recognition supplemented by judicial dedication to the eradication of breaches of human dignity, the following models are explicated by examples from several systems.

15.5.1 Absence of explicit constitutional protection: 'human dignity' as rhetoric/discursive/linguistic element

The US Constitution contains no reference to human dignity. There is, however, a growing body of literature that addresses the question of whether dignity has in fact entered the legal sphere and is used by courts as a legal doctrine. Some continue to argue that human dignity, as a constitutional doctrine, is as foreign to the US system as it is to its sociological and historical ethos (Whitman). Yet several studies insist that the Supreme Court has used the concept since the mid-twentieth century, expanding its reliance by the turn of the century (e.g. Paust; Goodman; Rao 2008; Rao 2011). These empirical studies support a variety of normative arguments regarding the value of the adoption of the concept—for some, amounting to a 'tradition' (McCrudden, 684)—but it seems these studies grant insufficient attention to the distinction between the linguistic rhetorical uses of the phrase and its adoption as a fully-fledged legal doctrine. The decisions usually cited as prime examples[4] have indeed mentioned 'dignity' in the judicial reasoning, but a declaration such as '[t]he basic concept underlying the Eighth Amendment is nothing less than the dignity of man' found in *Trop* and cited in subsequent decisions, and *Goldberg v Kelly*'s statement that '[f]rom its founding, the Nation's basic commitment has been to foster the dignity and well-being of all persons within its borders',[5] is arguably not the basis of a fully-fledged constitutional doctrine. Even in *Lawrence v Texas*,[6] often presented as heavily influenced by human dignity, the phrase is only used three times, all of them in a discursive fashion, while the term 'liberty' appears no less than 52 times. At best, one can support the argument that the concept of dignity, clearly within the judicial knowledge of US Justices, has been used as an interpretive tool for fleshing out other established rights and doctrines. A recent Supreme Court decision, which upheld a lower court order to substantively improve the conditions offered to California inmates due to prison overcrowding and the severe deprivation of healthcare, refers to 'the concept of human dignity',[7] a possible hint at future recognition of a legal doctrine, but further establishment of a fully-fledged principle is a matter for speculation.

A similar stance can be found in some analyses of Israeli and British jurisprudence that preceded the adoption of texts of constitutional content. It is argued that Israeli courts had

---

4 E.g. *Trop v Dulles*, 356 US 84 (1958); *Planned Parenthood v Casey*, 505 US 833 (1992); *Atkins v Virginia*, 536 US 304 (2002); *Hope v Peltzer*, 536 US 730 (2002); *Roper v Simmons*, 543 US 551 (2005).
5 *Goldberg v Kelly*, 397 US 254, 264–65 (1970).
6 539 US 653 (2003).
7 *Brown v Plata*, No. 09-1233, May 23, 2011, 563 US ___, p. 13, Opinion of the Court (2011).

recognized and protected human dignity before the enactment of the Basic Law: Human Dignity and Liberty in 1992 (Barak 1993), as have pre-HRA British courts (Feldman). Both systems indeed supported values encompassed in the context of human dignity well before their respective constitutional transformations, but the case-law is in our view better interpreted as *pertaining* to dignity, rather than relying on an established doctrine, as in the case of the United States.

15.5.2 Human dignity in the absence of explicit constitutional protection: rhetorical adoption as an 'underlying principle' and application as an interpretative tool

Support for the argument that US courts do no more than use 'dignity' in a discursive fashion, as a term in the English language, can be found by comparing the use of the term in other systems that do not constitutionally recognize human dignity. Such is the case in Canada. Its Charter does not formally protect human dignity. The Canadian Supreme Court has held that human dignity is one of 'the values and principles essential to a free and democratic society', the latter phrase being one element of its limitation clause.[8] An even stronger recognition of the centrality of dignity can be found in *Morgentaler*, in which the court declared that '[t]he idea of human dignity finds expression in almost every right and freedom guaranteed in the Charter', and that the Charter was founded on the respect of human dignity.[9] These *dicta* did not amount to the recognition of a distinct right or doctrine. Dignity has, however, been used extensively to shape the contours of other, formally protected rights, albeit inconsistently and without the formulation of a discernible doctrine (Weinrib; Fyfe).

The jurisprudence of the European Court of Human Rights (ECtHR) has developed in a similar fashion. In the absence of formal recognition, several early decisions sporadically used the phrase 'human dignity'.[10] The elevation of dignity to an underlying principle can be found in the 1990s, in declarations such as 'the very essence of the Convention is respect for human dignity and human freedom'.[11] In a recent decision, the Grand Chamber cited the European Treaty, further emphasizing the EU commitment to the protection of dignity and to human rights at large.[12] However, since dignity as such is not independently protected, it has been considered in conjunction with other rights, most notably Article 3, but has also been extensively linked with other rights.[13] As in Canada, then, usage of the term has not given rise to the introduction of a distinct doctrine, but has had a substantive impact.

The British tone is more muted. The term 'human dignity' is indeed found in decisions, but it is overwhelmingly linked with the application of the European Convention on Human Rights (ECHR) via the Human Rights Act; decisions that grant dignity further attention regularly cite ECtHR decisions.[14] Some cases add references to relevant UN documents (such

---

8 *R v Oakes* [1986] 1 SCR 779. Other named principles ranged from the commitment to social justice to 'faith in social and political institutions'.

9 *R v Morgentaler* [1988] 1 SCR 30.

10 E.g. *East African Asians v UK* (1981) 3 EHRR 76 (1973); *Ireland v United Kingdom* (1979–80) 2 EHRR 25 (1978).

11 E.g. *SW v UK* (1996) 21 EHRR 363 (1995) (no intervention); *Pretty v UK* (2002) 35 EHRR 1 (2002).

12 *MSS v Belgium and France* (2011) 53 EHRR 2, § B.1.

13 The cases cited in notes 10–12 above were concerned with Articles 2, 3, 5, 6, 8, 9, 13, and 14.

14 E.g. *R (Pretty) v DPP* [2002] 1 AC 800; *A v Secretary of State for the Home Department* [2006] 2 AC 221; *R (Purdy) v DPP* [2010] 1 AC 345.

as the Refugee Convention) and to decisions of foreign courts, but the Supreme Court, and its forebear the House of Lords, have not elevated dignity to the status of a domestic principle.[15]

15.5.3 Human dignity in the absence of explicit constitutional protection, judicially recognized as a domestic constitutional principle

The absence of human dignity in the 1789 Declaration of the Rights of Man can be explained once dignity is recognized as a twentieth-century constitutional doctrine, but the lack of recognition in France's two post-war Constitutions requires further attention. Drafts of the 1946 Constitution granted dignity a central place, although not to the degree found in the German Basic Law, but the term was removed, to be replaced by a vague reference in the Preamble. Likewise, the 1958 Fifth Republic Constitution contains no reference to human dignity. In 1993, the Vedel committee proposed the inclusion of a provision explicitly protecting human dignity, but the reform was not introduced.

Not long afterwards, however, both the Conseil Constitutionnel (CC) and Conseil d'État (CE) recognized human dignity as a principle embedded in the system, each of them within its competence. In *Lois Bioéthique* (1994), the CC, deciding upon the constitutionality of two statutes concerned with bioethics and reproduction, opened its decision with a reference to the Preamble of the 1946 Constitution. Referred to in the Preamble of the Constitution of the Fifth Republic as one of the texts through which the French people express their 'attachment to the rights of man and principles of sovereignty'—clearly a declaratory provision, the 1946 Preamble, similarly declaratory, proclaimed that 'each human being, without distinction of race, religion or creed, possesses sacred and inalienable rights'. Citing this part of the Preamble, the CC then established that 'the protection of human dignity against all forms of enslavement or degradation is a principle of constitutional status'.[16] This ruling has been repeated, extending to both civil/political and social rights. It has *inter alia* been the basis for CC recognition of the right for adequate housing.[17]

Further, the duty to consider human dignity is expressly included in a variety of statutes concerning *inter alia* the penal process, bioethics, and public health. Notably, the 1998 framework Act concerned with exclusion of French citizens, which enhanced several social and economic rights, opens with a section that declares its basis on 'the respect of equal dignity of all human beings'.[18]

Yet dignity has not been at the center of a CC unconstitutionality decision. As in *Bioéthique*, arguments on this basis have usually been unsuccessful.[19] In the very few cases in which the CC considered 'dignity' in the context of a successful challenge, other rights were involved and discussed to greater length, and the context was clearly one that was protected by other rights.[20] In addition, for a few decisions concerned with statutes in which the term 'dignity' was one of the considerations to be taken by authorities, the CC repeated the requirement to respect the dignity of the persons concerned.[21]

---

15 E.g. *H.J. (Iran) v Secretary of State* [2011] AC 596.

16 CC 27 juill 1994, *Lois Bioéthique*, 94-343/344 DC, Rec Cons Const 100.

17 CC 19 janv 1995, 94-359 DC, *Diversité de l'habitat*, Rec 176.

18 Loi n° 98-657, 29 juill 1998.

19 See Conseil Constitutionnel, Jurisprudence de Conseil Constitutionnel: Tables d'analyses au 1 août 2011, esp pp 548–51 (http://www.conseil-constitutionnel.fr/conseil-constitutionnel/francais/les-decisions/acces-par-themes-tables-/tables-analytiques.25838.html).

20 E.g. CC 98-403 DC (right to property); CC 21 févr 2008, 2008-562 DC, Rec. 89 (liberty).

21 E.g. 2010-14/22 DC, above; CC 2009-593 DC.

The main contribution of the CE in this respect has been its recognition that the protection of human dignity is part of the administration's duty to keep the peace. In two decisions rendered on the same day, the first being *Commune de Morsang-sur-Orge* (1995), the CE upheld local authorities' interdiction of 'dwarf-tossing' events. Relying on statute-based police authority to keep the public order, security, and health, the CE found that respect for human dignity was an element of the public peace.[22] In the 'pork-soup' case (2007), the CE upheld a police interdiction of an extreme right-wing organization's plan to offer pork soup for homeless people in Paris. The Court ruled that the plan was discriminatory, and that its interdiction was a proper consideration of the potential hurt of the dignity of private persons, which could have endangered the public order.[23] The CE has also addressed dignity in the context of statutes pertaining to the dignity of holders of office and other professionals,[24] and in cases concerned with statute-based social and economic rights, as well as prisoners' rights.[25]

However, on a par with the CC, a similar judicial reticence to accept arguments relying on the breach of human dignity has been noted.[26] As is the case in other systems, successful challenges that have no link to other protected rights have been few and far between.

15.5.4 Human dignity formally recognized, subject to proportionality balancing

Most constitutions that recognize dignity as a distinct right subject the protection of human dignity to limits, typically embodied in a limitation clause. Such is the case in South Africa. In addition to the declaratory Section 1, which lists human dignity as the first of the Republic's values, Section 10 grants 'everyone … inherent dignity and the right to have their dignity respected and protected', encompassing both main concepts of dignity; dignity is also an express element of Section 35, in the context of detention conditions. Section 36 then allows a limitation of rights that is 'reasonable and justifiable in an open and democratic society based on human dignity, equality and freedom, taking into account all relevant factors' (including factors listed in the Section). In Israel, the express general grant of 'life, body and dignity' to which all persons are entitled is then subject to Section 8, in which a violation of the protected rights must be 'by law befitting the values of the State of Israel, enacted for a proper purpose, and to an extent no greater than is required'. Both limitation clauses have been applied *inter alia* through the application of proportionality tests.[27]

Although limitation clauses obviously reject the notion of an absolute right, the protection of human dignity may be extensive. This can derive from wording of the formal recognition,

---

22 CE Ass, 27 Oct 1995, *Commune de Morsang-sur-Orge, Ville d'Aix-en-Provence*, Rec Lebon p 327.

23 CE (ord ref) 5 janv 2007, *Ministre d'État, ministre de l'intérieur et de l'aménagement du territoire*, n° 300311, AJDA 2007, p 601.

24 E.g. CE 21 déc 2007, *M Gabriel A*, req 299993 ; CE 17 mai 2006, *M A*, req 27378. See also Canedo-Paris, at note 43.

25 E.g. CE 8 déc. 2000, *M. Frérot*, Lebon 589 (search of prisoners); CE 8 oct. 2004, *Union Française pour la cohesion nationale*, Lebon p 367 (religious insignia and clothes in schools).

26 Apart from the 'dwarf-tossing' cases, other appeals were unsuccessful. See Canedo-Paris and, as a recent example, CE 12 sept. 2011, n° 352512, *M Ajanthan*.

27 E.g. *National Coalition for Gay and Lesbian Equality v Minister of Justice*, 6 BHRC 127 (CC, 1998), 1998 (12) BCLR 1517 (CC); *Dawood v Minister of Home Affairs*, 2000(8) BCLR 837 (CC); CA 294/91 *Chevra Kadisha Jerusalem v Kastenbaum*, 46(2) PD 464, esp 510–13, 519–24; HCJ 5100/94 *Public Committee Against Torture in Israel v the State of Israel* (1999); HCJ 2605/05 *Academic Center of Law and Business v Finance Minister* (2009). English translations of decisions of the Israel Supreme Court are available at <www.court.gov.il>. When no such translation is available, the Hebrew publication is cited.

especially in systems that accord dignity the status of a principal value in addition to a right; from a dignity-biased application of the limitation clause; and from a general societal agreement regarding the centrality of dignity.

15.5.5 Human dignity as the forebear of other, non-enumerated rights

A unique situation may arise when a constitutional document recognizes human dignity but fails to explicitly protect other human rights. In such cases, the system's express recognition of the centrality of dignity, supplemented by the vagueness of the provision may lead to judicial protection of such non-enumerated rights. Israel's Basic Law: Human Dignity and Liberty, enacted in 1992, formally recognizes the inherent dignity of the person and the duty of the state to protect it, but no such recognition is offered to the classic civil rights—equality, freedom of speech, and freedom of religion—historically the core human rights. The reason for this absence is political. This Basic Law, and its accompanying Basic Law: Freedom of Occupation, were passed following a compromise with ultra-religious political and parliamentary factions that were strongly opposed to the recognition of such rights in a written document, due to the likelihood of a clash between these rights and *halakhic* religious tenets. Human dignity was found acceptable, most likely also due to its religious underpinnings. Still, the Basic Law exempts all pre-1992 legislation from the requirements of the Basic Law. This body of pre-existing statutes, which includes the subjection of all Jews to Rabbinical law in matters of marriage and divorce, is thus safe from judicial review for unconstitutionality, a judicially recognized power deriving from the interpretation of the 1992 basic laws.[28]

In a series of decisions, the High Court of Justice (HCJ) has interpreted some of these non-enumerated rights into human dignity. In *Alice Miller* (1995),[29] a policy of the military that excluded women from service as pilots was invalidated as discriminatory; being degrading, this discrimination also encroached on women's dignity. Further decisions have elaborated upon the guiding principle under which non-enumerated rights were to be protected under the aegis of human dignity. Since then, discrimination arguments are regularly assessed against the Basic Law. The leading test, offered by President Barak, which seems to be 'the autonomy of the private will', covers more than degradation but does not extend to all types of discrimination.[30]

This judicial interpretive exercise, while standing at odds with parliament's original intent, was firmly supported by President Barak in his academic writing as well (Barak 1994, 418–33), and was largely adopted socially and politically, despite some criticism. Freedom of expression and freedom of religion have similarly been declared protected, to a certain extent, by dignity.[31] The court has also recognized the right to minimal living conditions, the right to education, and the right to health as potentially protected when human dignity is found substantially compromised, either through the direct impact on the dignity of the person or through discriminatory provision of these social services.[32] However, the *de facto* protection

28 CA 6821/93, *United Mizrachi Bank v Migdal Cooperative Village* (1995).
29 HCJ 4541/94, *Alice Miller v Minister of Defence* (1995).
30 HCJ 6427/02, *Movement for Quality in Government v The Knesset*, 61(1) P.D. 619 (2006).
31 E.g. HCJ 4804/94, *Station Film v Film Review Board* (1997); HCJ 1514/01 *Gur-Aryeh v Second Television and Radio Authority* (2001).
32 E.g. HCJ 366/03, *Commitment to Peace and Social Justice v Minister of Finance* (2005)); HCJ 1067/08, *Noar KeHalacha v Ministry of Education* (2009).

of social rights has not been broad. Other rights, such as the right to protection of the environment, have not been recognized.[33]

15.5.6 Full formal recognition, extensive judicial application

The model for this alternative is the German system. Germany's post-war Constitution, the Basic Law of 1949, contains a guarantee of human dignity. It starts with this guarantee, thereby showing the value that it attributes to dignity. Art. 1 (1) declares human dignity *unantastbar*. This word is usually translated as 'inviolable' (= *unverletzlich*). *Unverletzlich*, however, appears several times in connection with fundamental rights, whereas *unantastbar* is used only in connection with dignity. A literal translation would be 'untouchable'. In any case, it is considered to be a stronger expression than 'inviolable'.

The text continues in Art. 1 (2): 'To respect and to protect it shall be the duty of all state authority.' This formulation was unique at the time of enactment because it gives dignity not only a negative and 'vertical', but also a positive and 'horizontal' meaning. The word 'respect' is aimed at menaces that emanate from the state. The state has to refrain from action that affects a person's dignity. The word 'protect', to the contrary, is aimed at menaces that emanate from third parties. In such cases, the Basic Law obligates the state to take action in the interest of dignity. Dignity thus becomes a basis for legislative duties. The text continues by saying that 'therefore' (namely due to the recognition of human dignity) the German people acknowledge inviolable and inalienable human rights.

Art. 1 BL plays a prominent role in the jurisprudence of the German Constitutional Court (Enders; Eberle). The guarantee of human dignity is considered a foundational principle, the basis of all that follows, the highest value within the system of constitutionally protected values. The use of the word *unantastbar* in connection with dignity is interpreted as declaring dignity an absolute right, the only one in the Basic Law. 'Absolute' means that it is neither subject to limitation nor to balancing. Any limitation of dignity is *per se* unconstitutional. In case of collision with other rights, dignity always trumps. This is not uncontested in the legal literature, but the Court has repeatedly affirmed its position (see Teifke).

The interpretation of dignity as an absolute right has, however, one obvious consequence: the scope of the right must be narrowly defined. Hence, there are not many cases that were decided solely on the basis of Art. 1 BL.[34] Yet the number of cases decided on grounds of some other fundamental right in connection with Art. 1 is huge. Here, dignity serves as a guideline for the interpretation of other provisions of the Constitution, in a manner similar to other systems, as above. Usually, the combination of another right with Art. 1 enlarges the scope of that right or strengthens its weight when it comes to balancing it against other legally protected goods or interests.

15.6 Conclusion

As this survey shows, human dignity as a legal notion or legal concept is of growing importance. Most recent constitutions contain a guarantee of dignity. The notion has deep and various intellectual roots, and is not bound to a specific theory or creed. This facilitates its

---

33 E.g. HCJ 4128/02, *Adam Teva Ve-Din v The Prime Minister of Israel*, 58 PD 503 (2004).

34 The most important ones are BVerfGE 30, 173; 39, 1; 45, 187; 94, 49; 209, 133; 109, 279; 115, 118; 125, 175.

adoption in different legal cultures and its compatibility with different legal traditions. Its legal status, function, and scope are likewise open to different interpretations and application. However, born out of the atrocities committed by various political regimes in the twentieth century, dignity draws its core meaning largely from the historical experience of totalitarian systems. Against the practice of those systems, the concept of dignity asserts that every human being has an intrinsic value independent of capacity or merit. Certain ways of treating humans, such as slavery, are incompatible with this value. Beyond its core meaning, the doctrine may vary in range and intensity of protection, from rhetorical use to extensive application of a fully recognized right. When legally recognized, dignity is a foundational norm from which other more concrete legal provisions flow or derive their meaning. As a foundational norm, dignity is necessarily abstract, its practical importance depending on the existence of further norms. The more that dignity is translated into concrete legal positions and embedded in an institutional framework, the less it will be relied upon as such in ordinary legal matters. The gap between norms and facts inevitably remains. The absence from a nation's constitution of a guarantee of dignity is no indicator of disregard of human dignity, just as its presence does not indicate compliance with the norm. But the existence of the guarantee offers a platform from which violations of dignity can be rightfully condemned and attempts to justify such violations rejected. To that extent, it matters whether a constitution is based on human dignity or not.

References

Barak, A (1993). *Human Dignity as a Constitutional Right*, 41(3) Hapraklit 271 (Hebrew).
—— (1994). Interpretation in Law (Hebrew).
Brownsword, B (2003). *Bioethics Today, Bioethics Tomorrow: Stem Cell Research and the 'Dignitarian Alliance'*, 17 Notre Dame JL Ethics & Pub Pol'y 15.
Brugger, W (2004). *Communitarianism as the social and legal theory behind the German Constitution*, 2 I-CON 431.
Canedo-Paris, M (2008). *La « dignité humaine » en tant que composante de l'ordre public: l'inattendu retour en droit administratif d'un concept controversé*, RFDA, p 979.
Clapham, A (2006). Human Rights Obligations of Non-State Actors (Oxford, Oxford University Press).
Eberle, EJ (2001). Dignity and Liberty: Constitutional Visions in Germany and the United States.
Enders, C (1997). *Die Menschenwürde in der Verfassungsordnung.*
Englard, I (2000). Human Dignity: From Antiquity to Modern Israel's Constitutional Framework, 21 *Cardozo L Rev* 1903.
Feldman, D (2000). Human Dignity as a Legal Value: Part 2, *Pub Law* 61.
Fyfe, RJ (2007). Dignity as Theory: Competing Conceptions of Human Dignity at the Supreme Court of Canada, 70 *Sask L Rev* 2.
Gewirth, A (1983). Human Dignity as a Normative Concept, 77 *Am J Int'l L* 848.
—— (1992). *Human Dignity as the Basis of Rights*, in Meyer, MJ & Parent, WA (eds), The Constitution of Rights (Cornell University Press: Ithaca, NY), 10.
Goodman, MD (2005). Human Dignity in Supreme Court Constitutional Jurisprudence, 84 *Neb L Rev* 740.
McCrudden, C (2008). Human Dignity and Judicial Interpretation of Human Rights, 19 *Eur J Int'l L* 655.
Paust, JJ (1984). Human Dignity as a Constitutional Right: A Jurisprudentially Based Inquiry into Criteria and Content, 27 *Howard LJ* 145.
Rao, N (2008). On the Use and Abuse of Dignity in Constitutional Law, 14 *Col J Eur L* 201.
—— (2011). Three Concepts of Dignity in Constitutional Law, 86 *Notre Dame L Rev* 183.
Teifke, N (2011). *Das Prinzip Menschenwürde. Zur Abwägungsfähigkeit des Höchstrangigen.*
Weinrib, LE (2004). Human Dignity as a Rights-Protecting Principle, 17 *Nat'l J Const L* 325.
Whitman, JQ (2005). 'Human Dignity' in Europe and the United States: The Social Foundations, in *European and US Constitutionalism* 108 (G Nolte, ed).

The limits of punishment

Martin Scheinin and Denise Meyerson

16.1 Introduction

This chapter[1] provides a comparative assessment of how national constitutions deal with criminal punishment issues. In particular, it explores the extent and rationale of constitutional restrictions on the state's power to punish. While offering a certain modicum of historical context, the discussion is principally limited to modern times. Extensive reference is made to international legal norms because these have significantly influenced the evolution of national constitutions and constitutional law, resulting in a considerable degree of convergence in the way in which national constitutional systems treat issues of punishment. Eastern Europe provides a good contemporary example. While embarking upon transition to democracy from 1989 onwards, Eastern European states have become more engaged with human rights treaties and have altered their constitutions to bring them into line with the international standard (Albrecht, 300).

Typically, the concept of human dignity plays an important role in limiting punishment, either in the form of an express constitutional guarantee of human dignity or as the implicit value underpinning guarantees such as the right not to be subjected to cruel, inhuman or degrading punishment. Other constitutional norms, such as the right to life and the right to bodily integrity, can also play a role. This chapter addresses the various constitutional limits to punishment under five headings. It begins with restrictions on the ultimate punishment, namely the death penalty. Next it turns to judicial corporal punishment, incorporating issues regarding torture. A third section deals with life imprisonment and disproportionate sentencing. This is followed by a treatment of the principles of non–retroactivity, *nulla poena sine lege* and *nullum crimen sine lege*. Finally, the concluding section examines how the national constitution allows or limits punishment within autonomous legal systems operating within its territory.

It is perhaps already evident from what has been said above that fundamental rights considerations play a key role in many of these areas. States are increasingly bound to observe a large

---

1 The authors acknowledge the contribution by Dr Ciaran Burke (EUI) in assisting them in putting together the piece.

number of human rights norms, arising both from regional and global human rights treaties and from customary international law. Often this will also be reflected in the national constitution.

16.2 Capital punishment

Capital punishment has been practised by most societies throughout long historical periods.[2] However, in recent times, a growing number of states have dispensed with the death penalty. According to recent Amnesty International figures, only 58 states actively practise capital punishment, with 96 states having abolished it entirely.[3] Some countries, such as Canada, have abolished it via ordinary legislation,[4] while others proclaim its abolition in the text of their constitutions. Examples are Mexico, Ireland, Gabon, Namibia, Mozambique, Colombia and Uruguay. In South Africa, the Constitutional Court declared the death penalty unconstitutional, finding that it was a violation of the right not to be subjected to cruel, inhuman and degrading punishment, which the Court in turn connected to the rights to life and dignity.[5] During the 1980s, the democratisation of many Latin American countries increased the number of abolitionist states, with the break-up of the Soviet bloc in the 1990s adding further states, such as Romania, Slovakia and Slovenia, to the abolitionist camp.

However, not all Eastern European states have abolished capital punishment at constitutional level. Estonia and Bulgaria, for example, make no reference to the death penalty in their national constitutions, although they are obliged not to practise it by virtue of their memberships of the European Union and the Council of Europe.[6]

Protocol 13 to the European Convention on Human Rights (ECHR) abolishes the death penalty for all crimes. Spain is the most recent state to ratify Protocol 13 (doing so on 16 December 2009). Azerbaijan and Russia have not signed Protocol 13, while Armenia, Latvia and Poland have signed but not yet ratified the Protocol. Russia introduced a moratorium on capital punishment when it joined the Council of Europe. A 2009 decision of the Russian Constitutional Court holds that no capital punishment may be carried out before the ratification of Protocol 13 by the Russian Federation, as to do so would constitute an act of bad faith. The Constitutional Court has been explicit in stating that the effect of this decision is not to extend the moratorium but rather to abolish the death penalty, since the legal practice of capital punishment will no longer be possible.[7]

Article 2 of the Charter of Fundamental Rights of the European Union also prohibits the use of capital punishment. The Charter has been made legally binding by the Treaty of Lisbon and was ratified and rendered fully effective on 1 December 2009. This is highly significant

2 See Laurence, J, *A History of Capital Punishment,* New York, The Citadel Press (1960) for a historical overview in this regard.
3 Amnesty International, 'Abolitionist and retentionist countries' http://www.amnesty.org/en/death-penalty/abolitionist-and-retentionist-countries
4 Bill C-84 was passed in 1976 by a narrow majority, resulting in the abolition of the death penalty, except for certain offences under the National Defence Act. These were removed in 1998.
5 *S v Makwanyane* 1995 (3) SA 391 (CC).
6 The Council of Europe has in practice been prepared to accept a moratorium in lieu of a complete renunciation of the practice, as is the case with regard to the membership of the Council by Russia. Poland and Latvia have also failed to abolish capital punishment during wartime.
7 Lenta.ru: Конституционный суд запретил применять в России смертную казнь http://www.lenta.ru/news/2009/11/19/death/

for EU member states, since many constitutions contain provisions explicitly allowing the *acquis communautaire* to supersede conflicting national laws and national constitutional provisions. Examples are the Constitution of Ireland (Article 29.4), that of the Czech Republic (Article 10, which deals with all international agreements) and the French Constitution (Title XV, which contains a number of reservations concerning, *inter alia*, subsidiarity). In other member state jurisdictions, such a position has been upheld by national courts.[8] This is in accordance with the doctrine of the supremacy of EU law, laid down, *inter alia*, in the case of *Costa v ENEL*.[9] Further, the constitutions of certain EU states contain stipulations stating that any human rights treaties the state becomes party to will also supersede national law in the event of conflict, unless national law contains more favourable provisions. An example is Romania.[10] The Lisbon Treaty also contains a provision for the EU to accede to the European Convention on Human Rights.[11]

Belarus is the only European state that sanctions the use of capital punishment during peacetime. In terms of Article 24 of the Belarusian Constitution, the death penalty is available for 'grave crimes', a term that is elaborated upon by the criminal code, and that comprises 14 offences, including, *inter alia*, conspiracy to seize state power, and murder with aggravating circumstances. The last occasions on which people were executed in Belarus were in March 2010 and March 2012, when on both occasions two men were executed.[12] In 1994, Belarus abolished the death penalty for women, and for those men who committed crimes aged 18 or under, or who are sentenced aged 65 and older.[13]

The UN General Assembly in 2007, 2008 and 2010 adopted resolutions calling for a global moratorium on executions, as a step towards the eventual abolition of the death penalty.[14] This would tend to reflect a prevailing majority against the use of capital punishment amongst the community of states. However, this tells only half the story. Although the majority of states do not currently practise the death penalty, over 60 percent of the world's population reside in states where executions do occur.[15]

Many Asian states retain the death penalty. This trend is also borne out in parts of Africa and the Middle East. Afghanistan, for example, permits executions under national law, *inter alia*, for apostasy and homosexuality[16]; Zimbabwe does so for drug trafficking and

---

8 *49/5/A/2005 WYROK z dnia 11 maja 2005 r. Sygn. akt K 18/04★ W imieniu Rzeczypospolitej Polskiej*,11 May 2005; *R v Secretary of State for Transport, ex parte Factortame Ltd (No 2)* [1991] 1 AC 603.

9 *Costa v ENEL* [1964] ECR 585.

10 Article 20 of the 1991 Constitution, which states that in the event of inconsistency between the Constitution and fundamental rights treaties, the treaties shall prevail, except in cases where the Constitution itself extends a more complete protection concerning a given right.

11 Article 6(2) of the Treaty on European Union, as amended by the Lisbon Treaty and the Protocol Relating to Article 6(2) of the Treaty on European Union on the Accession of the Union to the ECHR. Official Journal, C 306/15.

12 Phillips, Leigh, 'Europe's first ever execution-free year undone by Belarus', EU Observer, 30 March 2010; Michael Schwirtz, 'Belarussian is Executed Over Attack on Subway', New York Times, 17 March 2012.

13 Article 59.2., Belarusian criminal code. The provisions of the code concerning capital punishment are laid out in full at http://www.levonevski.net/pravo/kodeksy/uk/009.html (page in Russian).

14 'General Assembly committee backs global moratorium against death penalty' http://www.un.org/apps/news/story.asp?NewsID=24679&Cr=general&Cr1=assembly; see also UN GA 65/206. Moratorium on the use of the death penalty, 21 Dec. 2010.

15 Notably, India, Indonesia, China and the USA are amongst the remaining retentionist states.

16 Such provision is made under national law. The Afghan Constitution does not mention the death penalty, except to say that sentences of death require the approval of the President to be validated (Article 129).

mutiny[17]; while over 2,000 people were executed in China in 2010 for a variety of offences, though the 1982 Constitution does not mention capital punishment.[18] The United States retains the usage of the death penalty at federal level and within the US military. Although the Eighth Amendment of the US Constitution prohibits the infliction of 'cruel and unusual punishments' (a phrase adopted from the English Bill of Rights of 1689), the US Supreme Court has found that the death penalty is not *per se* cruel and unusual, although it may be so in particular circumstances.[19] Currently, many homicide-related crimes, espionage and treason can be punished with death under federal law. In practice, however, the death penalty is generally reserved for aggravated murder or occasionally for felony murder.[20] In addition, some 34 of 50 US states retain the sanction. The United States executed 46 people in 2010 and it executes more people than any other liberal democracy.[21] The only other countries in the Americas that practise capital punishment are St Kitts and Nevis and Cuba. However, Cuba has not carried out an execution since 2003 and commuted all except three death-row inmates to life sentences in 2008.[22]

While the Second Optional Protocol to the International Covenant on Civil and Political Rights (ICCPR) prohibits capital punishment, there are, to date, only 73 state parties to the Protocol. The role of international law is stronger *vis-à-vis* the question of the execution of juvenile offenders. Article 37(a) of the UN Convention on the Rights of the Child interdicts capital punishment for juveniles, and has been signed and ratified by all UN member states, with the exceptions of the United States and Somalia.[23] The UN Sub-Commission on the Promotion and Protection of Human Rights and the Inter-American Commission on Human Rights have both maintained that the prohibition upon capital punishment for juveniles has become a *ius cogens* norm of customary international law.[24] Article 6.5 ICCPR also prescribes that '[s]entence of death shall not be imposed for crimes committed by persons below eighteen years of age'.

An estimated 365 juveniles have been executed in the United States.[25] However, the US Supreme Court abolished capital punishment for all persons less than 16 years of age in

---

17 Article 15(4) of the 1979 Zimbabwe Constitution (currently the subject of renegotiation between Zanu-PF and the Movement for Democratic Change) prescribes that the death penalty may be used, but that detention and execution must not amount to torture, inhuman or degrading treatment.

18 Amnesty International, 'Death Sentences and Executions 2010', http://www.amnesty.org.au/images/ uploads/adp/Death%20Sentences%20and%20Executions%202010.pdf See also Hands Off Cain News, January 1st, 2011. http://www.handsoffcain.info/news/index.php?iddocumento=15000827

19 *Gregg v Georgia* 428 US 153 (1976). This case represented the beginning of a limiting of circumstances when the death penalty would be acceptable. The later case of *Coker v Georgia* 433 U.S. 584 (1977) prohibited its usage in rape cases, while *Atkins v Virginia* 536 U.S. 304 (2002) and *Roper v Simmons* 543 U.S. 551 (2005) (both discussed below) banned capital punishment of the mentally handicapped and juveniles respectively.

20 Federal Bureau of Justice Statistics: Capital Punishment 2009. http://bjs.ojp.usdoj.gov/index. cfm?ty=pbdetail&iid=2215

21 Amnesty International, 'Death Sentences and Executions 2010', see above, n 18.

22 Cuba's Raul Castro commutes most death sentences, Reuters, 28 April 2008.

23 UNICEF, Convention of the Rights of the Child – FAQ http://www.unicef.org/crc/index_30229. html

24 United Nations Sub-Commission on the Promotion and Protection of Human Rights, Resolution 2000/17 on The Death Penalty in Relation to Juvenile Offenders http://www.unhchr.ch/ Huridocda/Huridoca.nsf/TestFrame/09597876bb508210c125697300448a18?Opendocument; The Michael Domingues Case: Report on the Inter-American Commission on Human Rights, Report No. 62/02, Merits, Case 12.285 (2002).

25 'Execution of juveniles in the US and other countries' http://www.deathpenaltyinfo.org/ execution-juveniles-us-and-other-countries

Thompson v Oklahoma (1988),[26] and for all persons below the age of 18 years in *Roper v Simmons* (2005).[27] Here, the Supreme Court stated that such practices offended the Eighth Amendment's ban on cruel and unusual punishments, with an 'evolving standards of decency' test, based upon the mores of the day, determining where the borderline in such cases would lie. Sociological and empirical research was used to bolster this conclusion. The execution of individuals with intellectual disability was also deemed unconstitutional in *Atkins v Virginia* (2002), as it was also held to violate the Eighth Amendment.[28] A handful of other states continue to execute juveniles, however. Between 2005 and 2008, Pakistan, Iran, Yemen and Saudi Arabia were all reported to have executed children, with Iran being the most persistent in this regard.[29] In Somalia, executions of children have also been common in recent years, including the stoning of a 13-year-old girl in front of 1,000 people at a sports arena in 2008.[30]

16.3 Corporal punishment

Judicial corporal punishment is considered inhumane and unacceptable in the constitutions of many countries. Examples are the constitutions of Poland[31] and Kenya,[32] and the Basic Law of Germany.[33] Often, it is prohibited by way of ordinary law rather than constitutional measures, with restrictions being typically directed toward parental and scholastic corporal punishment rather than state-sponsored judicial corporal punishment. It may sometimes be held to offend against constitutional clauses banning cruel and unusual punishments, torture and inhuman and degrading treatment (see below).

Judicial corporal punishment is entirely abolished in Western Europe. The European Court of Human Rights (ECtHR) has only had cause to deal with this issue once, in the case of *Tyrer v UK*.[34] Here, in the case of the caning of a 15-year-old juvenile inhabitant of the Isle of Man, the Court held that the severity of the punishment did not constitute inhuman punishment, but nevertheless found a violation of Article 3 ECHR due to the degrading nature of the punishment. The Court stated that such punishment constituted a form of institutionalised violence backed by the state, and that it treats a person as an object within the power of the authorities of state. Consequently, judicial corporal punishment violates the essence of Article 3 ECHR, which protects the dignity and physical integrity of individuals. In the United States, no jurisdiction permits judicial corporal punishment.

However, judicial corporal punishment is still regularly used in many other states, especially certain Islamic states. Thirty-three states continue to use judicial corporal punishment for a variety of offences. Most practise punishment via the use of a cane on bare buttocks or through a strap on the guilty party's back. In many countries it is restricted to males only.[35]

---

26 487 US 815 (1988).
27 543 US 551 (2005).
28 536 US 304 (2002).
29 'Execution of juveniles in the US and other countries', see above n 25.
30 'Somalia: Girl stoned was a child of 13.' Amnesty International. 2008-10-31. http://www.amnesty. org/en/for-media/press-releases/somalia-girl-stoned-was-child-13-20081031
31 Article 40 of the 1997 Constitution.
32 Article 29 of the 2010 Constitution.
33 Article 104 of the 1949 *Grundgesetz für die Bundesrepublik Deutschland*, as amended.
34 *Tyrer v UK*, Judgment of 25 April, 2978, Series A, No. 26.
35 'The Fall and Fall of Corporal Punishment', November 1999 Newsletter, EPOCH New Zealand.

In addition, certain states continue to tolerate semi-official judicial corporal punishment by local tribes and authorities.[36]

16.3.1 Torture and inhuman and degrading treatment

Corporal punishment may violate the absolute prohibition on torture and any inhuman, cruel or degrading punishment or treatment. States that have ratified the 1984 United Nations Convention Against Torture have a positive obligation to include provisions prohibiting torture in their municipal laws. In addition, the prohibition on torture constitutes a non-derogable norm of *ius cogens*, and is included in a host of other human rights treaties.[37] As a result, the broad majority of states formally prohibit the use of torture as punishment, many of them in their constitutions.[38]

Torture as punishment was abolished in England in 1640, Scotland 1708, Prussia in 1740, Baden in 1831 and Japan in 1873. The final jurisdictions to prohibit judicial use of torture in Europe were Portugal in 1828 and Glarus (a Swiss canton) in 1851 (Schaff, 80). The 1789 French *Déclaration des droits de l'homme et du citoyen*, still of constitutional value in the Fifth Republic, prohibits submitting suspects to any form of hardship that is not necessary to secure their persons. This position is reinforced by statute law, including the *Code de la Procedure Penale* (Decarpes, 207). In the United States, the customary international law prohibition on torture is recognised, and is actionable under the Alien Tort Claims Act. The status of torturers in the United States was summed up in the *Filartiga v Peña-Irala* decision,[39] which stated that 'the torturer has become, like the pirate and the slave trader before him, *hostis humani generis*, an enemy of all mankind' (at 876).

16.3.2 Non-refoulement

Non-refoulement entails the prohibition, in terms of the 1951 UN Convention Relating to the Status of Refugees, of sending, expelling, returning or otherwise transferring (*refoulement*) of a person (often a refugee) to 'territories where his life or freedom would be threatened on account of his race, religion, nationality, membership of a particular social group or political opinion.'[40] It is widely accepted that the prohibition of forcible return to face persecution

---

36 Examples include Colombia and Bangladesh. See 'End Corporal Punishment – Country Report, Colombia' http://www.endcorporalpunishment.org/pages/progress/reports/colombia. html#Lawfulness and '2005 Country Reports on Human Rights Practices, Bangladesh'. US Department of State, 8 March 2006. http://www.state.gov/g/drl/rls/hrrpt/2005/61705.htm.

37 For example, the International Covenant on Civil and Political Rights, Article 7; the Charter of Fundamental Rights of the European Union, Article 4; the European Convention on Human Rights, Article 3; the American Convention on Human Rights, Article 5; and the African Charter on Human and Peoples' Rights, Article 5.

38 For example, for a list of African constitutions that explicitly prohibit torture in their constitutions, see Viljoen, F & Odinkalu, AC, *The Prohibition of Torture and Ill-treatment in the African Human Rights System*, World Organization Against Torture (OMCT) (2006), p. 94, n 334.

39 *Filartiga v Pena-Irala* 630 F.2d (1980).

40 United Nations Convention Relating to the Status of Refugees, Article 33(1). Non-refoulement is also proscribed by the United Nations Convention against Torture, Article 3; the European Convention on Human Rights, Protocol No. 7, Article 1 (Procedural safeguards relating to expulsion of aliens); the International Covenant on Civil and Political Rights, Article 13; the Charter of Fundamental Rights of the EU, Article 19; and the American Convention on Human Rights, Article 22(8).

constitutes a norm of customary international law. As a consequence, even states that are not party to the Refugee Convention must respect this principle. Outside the context of refugees facing persecution, non-refoulement also applies to protect persons who are under a threat to be returned to a country where they may face torture, inhuman, cruel or degrading treatment, or the death penalty.[41]

This is made explicit in Article 19 of the EU Charter on Fundamental Rights. This effectively entails that (European) states are not only obliged to abstain from torture and inhuman or degrading treatment or punishment, but that they are also obliged not to forcibly transfer any individual to any state where he or she may be subjected to such treatment or punishment. Nevertheless, despite the absolute nature of this prohibition, five EU governments, led by the UK, intervened in the 2006 case of *Ramzy v the Netherlands* before the ECtHR to argue that the right of an individual to be free from torture should be balanced against the national security interests of the state, particularly in terrorism cases.[42] The UK took up the same stance in the case of *Saadi v Italy*. Its arguments were, however, rejected by the ECtHR.[43]

In contrast, the Supreme Court of Canada remarked in the case of *Suresh v Canada*[44] that even if Mr Suresh was protected by the prohibition against non-refoulement, this was a result of the various factors in the 'balance' and the constitutional right to security does not absolutely prohibit deportation to face torture. Although the case has not been overruled, it has been heavily criticised and no one has been deported to face torture under the 'Suresh exception' (Roach, 537).

16.4 Disproportionate sentences and life imprisonment

Grossly disproportionate sentences are constitutionally prohibited in many jurisdictions. Generally, the proportionality test is derived from a prohibition on cruel, unusual, inhuman or degrading punishments (this is the case, for instance, in South Africa) and/or from a prohibition on arbitrariness in criminal procedure (this is the case, for instance, in India). The disproportion may be a function either of the type of sentence or its severity in relation to the seriousness of the offence (Van Zyl Smit & Ashworth, 542–44).

Some jurisdictions are, however, less enthusiastic about the idea that disproportionate punishments are unconstitutional. The United States is an example. Although there are US decisions supporting the idea that the Eighth Amendment includes a proportionality test, it appears from recent US cases that outside the context of the death penalty, which is thought to be 'different', the courts will be very reluctant to find sentences grossly disproportionate. For instance, very harsh sentences imposed for minor offences in terms of 'three strikes' laws have survived scrutiny. The upshot is that proportionality is a virtually toothless concept in non-capital cases in the United States.[45]

In those countries in which the concept of proportionality plays a greater role, it is a matter of controversy whether life sentences without the possibility of release are inherently

---

41 ECtHR, *Ocalan v Turkey*, Judgment of 12 March 2003, para. 213, confirmed by the Grand Chamber in its Judgment of 12 May 2005, para. 169.

42 Observations of the governments of Lithuania, Italy, Portugal, Slovakia and the United Kingdom, intervening in Action No. 25424/05. See 'Non-Refoulement Under Threat, Proceedings of a Seminar Held Jointly By The Redress Trust (REDRESS) And The Immigration Law Practitioners' Association (ILPA)', 16 May, 2006, Matrix Chambers, London.

43 *Saadi v Italy*, Judgment of 28 February 2008.

44 *Suresh v Canada* [2002] 1 SCR 3.

45 *Ewing v California* 538 US 11 (2003); *Lockyer v Andrade* 538 US 63 (2003).

excessive. No single approach to life imprisonment would seem to be predominant, even within Europe. France recently introduced life without parole; whereas Norway and Portugal have abolished life imprisonment altogether. In Portugal, there is a constitutional ban on life imprisonment. The German Federal Constitutional Court found in a landmark case that while life imprisonment is not *per se* unconstitutional, concern for human dignity requires prisoners to retain some hope of regaining their freedom. This led the Court to hold that the legislature was under an obligation to enact legislation setting out a procedure for considering the release of persons sentenced to life imprisonment after a certain period (Van Zyl Smit, 271). Finland restricts use of life imprisonment to murder, but England and Wales make use of the sanction for drugs and sexual offences as well.

The ECtHR has not classified life without parole as inhuman or degrading punishment when used for adults.[46] However, it held in *Weeks v UK*[47] that discretionary life sentences must include a mechanism for the examination of potential release from incarceration once the period of punishment has expired, since the remainder of the sentence may only be justified on security grounds. Such a mechanism must fulfil the requirements of Art 5(4) ECHR, guaranteeing rights to an oral hearing, to present testimony, to cross-examine witnesses and to obtain legal representation.[48] In a subsequent case, the European Commission of Human Rights recognised the distinction between punitive and preventive sentences, while empha-sising the difference between determinate and indeterminate sentences, holding that in the case of determinate (fixed-term) sentences of a number of years (as distinct from life sentences), there was no obligation to provide for the possibility of parole or release after a portion of the sentence had been served.[49]

Many states that impose mandatory life sentences for adults do not do so for juveniles. Some states, such as Finland, do not even allow discretionary life sentences for juveniles, as such punishment is thought to be disproportionate (Kurki, 355–56). Article 37 of the United Nations Convention on the Rights of the Child prohibits life imprisonment for juveniles who were aged under 18 years when they committed the crime unless there is a regular review and the possibility of release. Further, the ECtHR has implied that a mandatory life sentence for a juvenile without parole may amount to inhuman or degrading punishment as prohibited by the ECHR.[50] In the US, over 20 states permit mandatory life imprisonment without parole for juveniles aged 15 or over. In *Harris v Wright*, it was held that these sentences are consistent with 'evolving standards of decency' and are not contrary to the US Constitution.

16.5 Non-retroactivity and related principles

The principles of *nullum crimen sine lege* and *nulla poena sine lege* (no one may be convicted of a crime or subjected to a punishment except in accordance with previously established law) are

---

46 Most recently, see *Vinter and Others v UK*, Judgment of 17 January 2012 (applications nos. 66069/09 and 130/10 and 3896/10), para 93 where the Court concluded that, 'in the absence of … gross disproportionality, an Article 3 issue will arise for a mandatory sentence of life imprisonment without the possibility of parole in the same way as for a discretionary life sentence, that is when it can be shown: (i) that the applicant's continued imprisonment can no longer be justified on any legitimate penological grounds; and (ii) that the sentence is irreducible *de facto* and *de iure*'.

47 *Weeks v UK*, Judgment of 2 March 1987, Series A, No. 114.

48 *Thynne, Wilson and Gunnell v UK*, Judgment of 25 October 1990, Series A, No. 190. See Appleton & Grøver, 608.

49 *Mansell v UK*, Application no. 32072/96, decision of 2 July 1997.

50 *Husain v UK,* Judgment of 21 February 1996.

fundamental principles of justice and they rule out retrospective criminal charges and punishments. They are enshrined in many constitutions[51] and human rights instruments and have also been upheld as general principles of international criminal law (see Raimondo, ch 2). One notable exception is Australia, where there is no express constitutional prohibition on retrospective criminal legislation. In fact, very few rights are expressly protected by the Australian Constitution, which does not contain a bill of rights. Nor is the separation of judicial power of assistance, because the High Court of Australia has held that retrospective criminal legislation does not necessarily offend the separation of powers.[52]

The non-retroactivity of (national) criminal law is not an absolute principle. There are a number of narrow but recurring exceptions. The most prominent modern exception is in respect of international crimes, particularly war crimes and crimes against humanity. For example, while Article 7 ECHR prohibits retroactive penal laws, Article 7(2) allows for 'the trial and punishment of any person for any act or omission which, at the time when it was committed, was criminal according to the general principles of law recognised by civilised nations'.[53] This has, in past cases before the ECtHR, been held to render the punishment of such crimes lawful, even in cases where the domestic law did not provide for such sanctions. In the 2006 case of *Kolk and Kislyiy v Estonia*,[54] which dealt with the actions of two men who had participated in the deportation of civilians to the USSR in 1949, and who had been convicted by Estonian courts of crimes against humanity in 2003 and 2004, it was held that since crimes against humanity were already criminalised in 1949 by 'general principles of law recognised by civilised nations', the Estonian courts had not applied criminal law in a retroactive manner.

Kolk and Kislyiy v Estonia provides an interesting case study, and we shall permit ourselves to dwell on the case a little longer. In 1949, crimes against humanity were punishable by virtue of the affirmation of the 'Nuremberg Principles' by the UN General Assembly in 1949,[55] as well as via Article 6(c) of the Nuremberg Charter. The fact that the General Assembly Resolution had been adopted means that there was consensus amongst the majority of 'civilised' states, and perhaps, indeed, one could argue that a general principle had rapidly emerged after the Second World War, although the more obvious conclusion would be that a customary norm of international law, rather than a general principle, was emerging.

However, the ECtHR failed to mention that in 1949 this 'principle' applied only to crimes against humanity committed in connection with or in execution of war crimes or crimes against peace (Cassese, 413). The applicants' crimes had been committed in a post-war context, and no effort was made by the court to link the post-war Soviet occupation of Estonia to the war itself. This case is therefore indicative of a broader trend, namely that the non-retroactivity of criminal law is not absolute, and that in extreme circumstances, usually connected with war, public emergencies or gross human rights violations, constitutional law may modify this general principle. The London Charter of the International Military Tribunal at Nuremberg is an oft-discussed example of the above, particularly in the case of crimes against humanity, since it is dubious whether many of the crimes tried at Nuremberg were indeed offences under international law at the time they were committed (Clapham).

---

51 According to Gallant 243–44, over four-fifths of the member states of the United Nations recognise *nullum crimen* in their constitutions, while over three-quarters recognise *nulla poena*.
52 *Polyukhovich v Commonwealth* (1991) 172 CLR 501.
53 A similar provision is found in Article 15(1) of the ICCPR.
54 *Kolk and Kislyiy v Estonia*, Applications no 23052/04 and 24018/04 (2006).
55 GA Resolution 95(1) 11 December 1946.

The Nuremberg trials have been discussed in great detail elsewhere.[56] However, there are significant examples from national jurisprudence that also bear out the above position. Two case studies from two different time periods in Irish history serve to bear out this theory, while showing the effect that the human rights *acquis* has had on such considerations. The first is the 1935 case of *State (Ryan) v Lennon*.[57] In the wake of the Irish Civil War, special legislation had been enacted, providing for amendment of the Free State Constitution for a period of eight years by way of ordinary legislation. This was extended, by way of ordinary legislation, to 16 years.[58] Subsequent legislation provided for a standing military tribunal, composed of army officers selected by the executive, which was empowered to try any offence that was referred to it (again, by the executive), from which there might be no right of appeal, and which was empowered to impose any penalty, including death, even if this contradicted ordinary law.[59] The idea of the latter amendment was to quell the unrest prompted by the civil war and to punish those who had fomented said unrest. The fact that the legislation was retroactive was held to be regrettable, but ultimately irrelevant, the potential for rights protection to be effective and immutable being removed by the constitutional caveat allowing for derogations in accordance with law, the content of which may be determined by the legislature. Since the Constitution had been drafted in the aftermath of the Civil War, such a scenario was reasonably foreseeable and no constitutional provision forbade such a course of action by the government.

A modern Irish example serves to demonstrate that while similar considerations play a part, much has changed in this regard, and there is now a high bar that must be surpassed in order to countenance retroactive legislation by virtue of human rights treaties and due process guarantees. In the case of *CC v Ireland and others*,[60] it was held by the Irish Supreme Court that Section 1 of the Criminal Law (Amendment) Act 1935 Act was unconstitutional. This Act covered the area of statutory rape—that is, sexual intercourse between an adult and a juvenile who is incapable of giving his or her consent. The section was struck down as it did not provide for the defence of honest mistake. (In the case in question, a 16-year-old girl had misled an older man about her age and had initiated the intimate contact between them.) The striking down of Section 1 led to a raft of appeals by other offenders who had been convicted under the Act, most of whom were eventually freed. This caused public outcry in Ireland, given that over 200 sex offenders had been released, many of whom were now eligible for state-funded compensation. However, the Irish government, having taken legal advice from several former Supreme Court justices, elected not to pass retroactive legislation to re-imprison the released offenders, instead simply prospectively replacing the 1935 Act with new legislation.[61]

The above cases serve to demonstrate the non-absolute nature of the *nulla poena* principle. Where there are overbearing emergency considerations (*Ryan*) or gross human rights violations at stake (*Kolk and Kislyiy*), courts and state institutions will seek to construe constitutions in order to permit a limited exercise of retroactive punishment. However, *CC* demonstrates that a high threshold must be crossed for such action to be countenanced and

---

56 See, *inter alia*, Davidson.

57 See www.courts.ie/supremecourt/.../State%20(Ryan)%20v%20Lennon_1934.rtf

58 Constitution (Amendment No. 16) Act of 1928.

59 Constitution (Amendment No. 17) Act of 1931.

60 *CC v Ireland, the Attorney General and the Director of Public Prosecutions*, IESC (2006) 33. http://www.courts.ie/judgments.nsf/09859e7a3f34669680256ef3004a27de/877f6b6773b3dcee80257177003c6586?OpenDocument

61 The Criminal Law (Sexual Offences) Act 2006.

for due process guarantees to be cast aside. In reality, the idea utilised in *Kolk and Kislyiy* (perhaps mistakenly) that international crimes have always been repugnant to the legal traditions of 'civilised nations' is likely to be the only circumstance when effective retroactive punishment will be countenanced in states with a developed conception of due process and procedural fairness.

16.6 Criminal punishment and legal pluralism

In the final section of this chapter, we shall examine a rather different kind of limit to punishment, namely, the extent to which national constitutions make room for legal pluralism in the field of criminal law. Latin America, with its large and often geographically isolated indigenous populations, provides some good examples of the constitutional recognition of customary practices of dispute resolution and social control. Such recognition was a response to growing demands for indigenous self-determination (Van Cott, 206–207).

The broad majority of Latin American states have ratified the 1989 Indigenous and Tribal Peoples Convention. This convention, also known as ILO 169, recognises in its preamble 'the aspirations of these peoples to exercise control over their own institutions, ways of life and economic development and to maintain and develop their identities, languages and religions, within the framework of the States in which they live'. In accordance with such considerations, many Latin American states have made arrangements for alternative dispute resolution mechanisms and legal pluralism based upon indigenous law, with a view to enhancing the legitimacy and effectiveness of the legal system. Although indigenous law is generally practised in a way that complements state law, difficult questions arise when, for instance, punishments are not necessarily pre-established; or forms of punishment such as physical punishment, forced labour or loss of community rights are used; or conduct that is not unlawful under positive law, such as witchcraft, is prosecuted. Practices of this kind give rise to the need to decide whether indigenous justice should be limited by human rights standards as contained in constitutional, statutory or international law (Van Cott 215, 222, 230, 233).

In Bolivia, Article 171 of the 1967 Constitution (reformed in 1995 and 2009) states that 'the natural authorities of the indigenous and Campesino communities may exercise functions of administration and application of their own norms as an alternative solution in conflicts, in conformity with their customs and procedures, always providing that they are not contrary to the Constitution and the laws'. The Colombian and Ecuadorian Constitutions contain similar provisions. The Colombian Constitutional Court has found that the indigenous sanctions of corporal punishment and expulsion are not contrary to the constitution because they protect a constitutional right of higher rank (cultural diversity) than the state law that they violate.[62] Article 89 of the 1987 Nicaraguan Constitution gives a very wide discretion indeed to regional authorities, stating that 'the communities of the Atlantic Coast have the right ... to have their own forms of social organization and to administer their internal issues according to their traditions'. Paraguay, Peru and Venezuela also regulate this matter at the constitutional level, though other Latin American states such as Panama, Honduras and Chile prefer to do so via ordinary legislation.[63] In addition, certain states such

---

62 Van Cott, DL, 'Legal Pluralism and Informal Community Justice in Latin America', paper prepared for the conference 'Informal Institutions and Latin American Politics', University of Notre Dame, Indiana, 24–25 April (2003), 10.

63 Ibid 42–44.

as El Salvador and Uruguay are neither parties to ILO 169 nor do they have any specific provision for such indigenous dispute resolution mechanism either in the form of statute law or of constitutional provisions (Chambers, 425–428).

16.7 Conclusion

This chapter has discussed a wide range of constitutional limits to punishment, covering issues related to the death penalty, corporal punishment and torture, life imprisonment and disproportionate sentencing, the principles of non-retroactivity and legality in criminal law and, finally, the way in which national constitutions may allow or limit legal pluralism in the field of criminal law. In order to provide a meaningful comparative study, it was necessary to go beyond the texts of national constitutions that are often silent on many or even all of these issues. Judicial decisions and also ordinary laws were therefore consulted as evidence of what is considered constitutional or unconstitutional in various countries. With respect to many of the issues discussed, international human rights treaties or other international standards were shown to have a significant influence on the understanding of limits to punishment, also for the purposes of constitutionality.

References

Albrecht, HJ (2001). 'Post-Adjudication Dispositions in Comparative Perspective', in Tonry, M & Frase, R (eds), Sentencing and Sanctions in Western Countries, Oxford University Press.

Appleton, C & Grøver, B (2007). 'The Pros and Cons of Life without Parole', 47 *British Journal of Criminology* 597.

Cassese, A (2006). 'Balancing the Prosecution of Crimes against Humanity and Non-Retroactivity of Criminal Law', 4 *Journal of International Criminal Justice* 410.

Chambers, I (1997). 'Untitled Comments', in Gómez, M (ed), Derecho Indígena, Instituto Nacional Indigenista.

Clapham, A (2003). 'Issues of Complexity, Complicity and Complementarity: From the Nuremberg Trials to the Dawn of the New International Criminal Court', in Sands, P (ed), From Nuremberg to the Hague: The Future of International Criminal Justice, Cambridge University Press.

Davidson, E (1997). The Trial of the Germans: An Account of the Twenty-Two Defendants Before the International Military Tribunal at Nuremberg, University of Missouri Press.

Decarpes, P (2010). 'France', in Cape, E, Namoradze, Z, Smith R, & Spronken, T (eds), Effective Criminal Defence in Europe, Intersentia.

Gallant, K (2009). The Principle of Legality in International and Comparative Criminal Law, Cambridge University Press.

Kurki, L (2001). 'International Standards for Sentencing and Punishment', in Tonry, M & Frase, R (eds), Sentencing and Sanctions in Western Countries, Oxford University Press.

Raimondo, F (2008). General Principles of Law in the Decisions of International Criminal Courts and Tribunals, Martinus Nijhoff.

Roach, K (2011). 'Comparative Constitutional Law and the Challenges of Terrorism Law', in Ginsburg, T & Dixon, R (eds), Comparative Constitutional Law, Edward Elgar.

Schaff, P (1882). History of the Christian Church, Volume IV: Mediaeval Christianity. AD 590–1073, Christian Classics Ethereal Library.

Van Cott, DL (2000). 'A Political Analysis of Legal Pluralism in Bolivia and Colombia', 32 *Journal of Latin American Studies* 207.

Van Zyl Smit, D (1992). Is Life Imprisonment Constitutional? The German Experience, *Public Law* 263.

——— & Ashworth, A (2004). 'Disproportionate Sentences as Human Rights Violations', 67 *Modern Law Review* 541.

2. Communication rights

Ancient and modern: access to information and constitutional governance

Thomas Bull and Hugh Corder

17.1 Introduction

The electronic revolution of the past 25 years has facilitated the quest for transparent government. As a result, demands for freedom of information (FOI) have been made with increasing force and frequency, and there has been a corresponding flurry of legislative activity, coinciding especially with the wave of democratisation in Eastern Europe and Asia that resulted from the collapse of the Soviet Union, and elsewhere in the developing world (see Darch and Underwood 2009 for an extensive treatment of this latter area). In 1983, the number of countries with FOI legislation reached double figures for the first time; between 1993 and 2006 a further 70 countries adopted legislation facilitating access to information (Snell 2006). Constitutional protection is increasingly accorded to FOI as a right (Peled & Rabin 2011). There can be no doubt that legislative guarantees of a degree of openness have become a requirement for most benchmarks of good governance in both the private and public sectors since 1990 (Banisar 2006).

Yet in parts of the world, of course, the quest for the cleansing effects of 'sunshine' on governmental practice (this is the kind of phrase used frequently in the United States in relation to FOI measures, the jurisdiction which has in many respects set the pace of change over the past 45 years) has long been in place. This chapter seeks to situate the more recent developments in this field of constitutional law within that historical context, as well as within the reality of the divide between the developed and developing world, by using as sheet anchors the experience of two national systems, those of Sweden (the 'ancient') and South Africa (the 'modern'). Sweden has perhaps the longest-existing formal set of protections for access to information, and is situated firmly within the community of developed nations in Western Europe, as well as the regional power bloc of the European Union. The experience of South Africa, on the other hand, represents much of what is often encountered in the developing nations of the world, as far as the harsh secrecy of history but also the immense potential of political renewal are concerned. Again, the South African experience could provide useful lessons for the potential regulation of the exercise of public power and even the facilitation of the achievement of socio-economic rights (Bentley & Calland 2010) through access to information regimes in generally poor and often highly unequal societies. Indeed, it seems to us that our 'home' systems operate almost as the respective outer limits of a spectrum of legal systems as far as access to information is concerned, in the sense not necessarily of what exists in law, but rather in the extent to which that law has become part of the lived reality of the citizenry in our respective countries.

In what follows, we will be using the experience of our respective legal systems as the basis for high-level comparison of similarities as well as contrasting styles of legal regulation, and as emblematic of the groups of kindred legal systems with which comparison is appropriate (considering not only the civil-law/common-law distinction, but also the differences that exist between established and emerging democracies). In this manner, we hope not only to introduce the reader to the essential elements of legal regulation of freedom of information, but also to provide a sketch of some of the socio-political realities that have to be taken into account when assessing the success or otherwise of such frameworks. As will be seen, the existence of a clear legislative framework can mask an absence of political commitment to the ideals of accountability that lie at the heart of responsive and open government.

17.2 Basic approaches and concepts

South Africa is relatively unusual in the common-law world, in that its approach to FOI underwent revolutionary change in 1994 as a result of the overthrow of apartheid and minority rule and the institution of a constitutional democracy. The legislative framework thus shifted from one of paranoid official secrecy (see, for example, the provisions of the Internal Security Act and the Protection of Information Act, both of 1982) to the inclusion of a right of access to information in the final Constitution (Act 108 of 1996), section 32 of which reads as follows:

> (1) Everyone has the right of access to: (a) any information held by the state; and (b) any information that is held by another person and that is required for the exercise or protection of any rights.
>
> (2) National legislation must be enacted to give effect to this right, and may provide for reasonable measures to alleviate the administrative burden on the state.

This far-reaching entrenchment of access to information must be read together with the rights to administrative justice (in section 33) and to freedom of expression (section 16(1)(b), to receive or impart information or ideas) and the elevation of the 'accountability, responsiveness and openness' of government to the status of a foundational value of the democracy established by the Constitution (see section 1(d)).

These rights are subject to limitation in the normal way (according to the criteria set out in section 36 of the Constitution) but their circumscription has also been specifically authorised by the requirement that legislation must underpin the right. So, we find the Promotion of Access to Information Act (No. 2 of 2000, commonly and hereafter known as PAIA), which attempts in considerable detail to define and regulate the various issues that are typically raised in connection with such legislation, wherever it is enacted. Note, therefore, that the PAIA endorses the active right of accessing information. When there is a constitutional provision complemented by legislation, such as in this instance, questions of law arise from the relationship between the two rules of law: may a litigant, for example, rely directly on the constitutional right, or must they proceed in terms of the legislation? The answers to such questions will depend on the wording used in each law, as well as the judicial policy of the jurisdiction within which they arise; this is not the occasion on which to enter into such a discussion, but the reader should be aware of this complexity.

As the PAIA was drafted by reference to many of the innovative laws enacted in this field in kindred jurisdictions within the common-law sphere, and as it is set at a level at which almost all developing countries have sought to protect and advance access to information, we will use the PAIA as the framework for the discussion that follows, with due regard to other legal systems where appropriate. It is important to note, however, that the PAIA does not seek to protect data, although this is achieved indirectly in some instances.

In most common-law jurisdictions, there is no express right to freedom of information; rather, it is an aspect of or direct implication from the right to freedom of expression, and complemented by specific statutory interventions (see, for example, Canada's Access to Information Act, Australia's FOI Act and New Zealand's Official Information Act, all of 1982). More recently, several developing members of the common-law world have followed suit, such as India's Right to Information Act (2005), Uganda's Access to Information Act (2005) and Liberia's and Nigeria's FOI Acts (of 2010 and 2011 respectively). Several other emerging democracies have draft Bills dealing with access to information, such as Zambia (2002), Kenya (2007) and Ghana (2010). Such legislative interventions are frequently 'balanced' by Privacy Acts. The longstanding and highly developed system of FOI in the USA at federal (FOI Act 1966) and state levels represents in many ways the pioneering advance of the notion of 'government in the sunshine' (Sunshine Act 1976) in the modern era in common-law countries, but is exceptional in its extent and sophistication within that context. It deserves separate and detailed treatment, beyond the scope of this chapter (a perceptive theoretical treatment is to be found in Schauer 2011).

The continental constitutional tradition of Europe is not homogenous, but in several countries there are explicit constitutional provisions on a right to information, as in the German Constitution Article 5 or the Latvian Constitution Article 100. In some countries, such as France, the right to access is a result of interpretation of constitutional norms on control over public power etc., rather than based upon an explicit constitutional provision. In Sweden, the Freedom of the Press Act (FPA), already in its first version of 1766, contained the constitutional rules on FOI. The current FPA devotes the second chapter of the Act to these rules. Section 1 reads:

> Every Swedish citizen shall be entitled to have free access to official documents, in order to encourage the free exchange of opinion and the availability of comprehensive information.

The second section sets out a number of legitimate reasons for restricting the general right to access and stipulates that all such restrictions should be gathered in one single law, the Law on Openness and Secrecy (OSL, recently reformed by law 2009:400). The constitutional system of Sweden includes judicial review of legislation, and ordinary law in conflict with the constitution cannot be applied by courts or public authorities. The provisions of FPA are therefore directly applicable in any legal context where they arise and are given priority over any laws with conflicting content (i.e. Supreme Administrative Court ruling 2006 ref 87). There are three interrelated basic issues that any system of access to information must solve in order to have a functioning system. The first is what kind of information is covered by the right. The second is at what stage in an authority's handling of the information a right to access starts. A third issue concerns which entities are required to disclose information to the public.

(1) *What.* Every system that seeks to advance openness of government requires a definitional device as a 'gatekeeper' in the face of those who seek access to information. In the PAIA, the critical concept is that of a 'record', defined in section 1 as 'any recorded information (a) regardless of form or medium; (b) in the possession or under the control of that public or private body … ; and (c) whether or not it was created by that public or private body'. A 'public' body means a government department at any level or any other 'functionary or institution' exercising public power or performing a public function in terms of legislation, while a private body includes a natural or a juristic person (section 1). The scope of the right to access records is narrower in relation to a private body than a public body, for a requester would have to prove the necessity of having access to such information for the exercise or protection of their rights in the latter case, so the public/private distinction is important. 'Information' is not defined, although 'personal information' enjoys extensive definition. It is important to note that an individual is entitled to their personal information as of right.

Elsewhere in the common-law world, differing approaches are taken to the type of information accessible, and the manner in which it can be obtained. Thus Canada also uses the notion of a (federal government) record, which includes any number of types of documentary material regardless of its form. Australia prefers to impose a duty on Ministers to disclose the structure and functioning of their departments and the processes whereby information can be obtained. Britain's FOI Act of 2000 places an Information Commissioner at the centre of its scheme to promote openness of government (Birkinshaw 2010, chapters 4 and 12).

In Sweden, the approach is that anything that can carry information can also be subject to disclosure through a right to access (FPA Chapter 2 section 3). The form in itself is not the determining factor (Bohlin 2010). Even pastry baked in the form of a message is a form of information and can therefore be a 'public document' in the meaning of the Swedish Constitution. This generous approach is common but not dominant in the European context. More limited approaches can be to connect the right of access to paper products of certain official character, as in Italy (Mezzacapo 2006). The growing use of electronic communication in public administration (e-government) has made issues of what kind of material can be reasonably expected to be accessible from a public authority more problematic. As everything is accessible from everywhere, what counts as a 'public document'? In Sweden, it is clear that any information that has to do with the tasks or functions of a public authority can also be accessible, but it is not yet fully clear how far from such central fields of activity the right to access goes. For example, so-called 'cookies' containing information on what home-pages on the internet publicly employed persons have visited during work hours have been deemed to be accessible by the courts (Supreme Administrative Court 1999 ref 18).

(2) *When.* Swedish law differentiates between information received or sent by the authority on the one hand, and information created at the authority internally but not (yet) spread outside it on the other hand (FPA Chapter 2 section 6 and 7). The typical case of the latter would be drafts, internal memos and other types of communication within the authority. The first kind of information is regarded as accessible at the moment it arrives or leaves the authority. The second kind is accessible only when the matter it relates to is closed, either by an explicit decision or by filing the case material. Persons directly and legally involved in a matter can have a wider right to access, but this follows from administrative law, not from the general right to access in the Constitution.

(3) *Who.* In most modern societies the theoretical boundary between public and private is blurring in many ways. The machinery of government is no exception and all over the world governments are transforming public authorities into private enterprises and/or outsourcing public functions to private actors. This poses a challenge to any system of access of public information, as the information asked for is not necessarily in the hands of the public any more.

The Swedish solution is that, apart from traditional public authorities, some legal subject who performs a function that is akin to using public power is also subject to the requirements of disclosure if they are listed in the OSL. The OSL stipulates that private enterprises owned or controlled by local authorities are subject to the rules on access, but this does not include companies owned by the state. There is no general right to access information held by fully private enterprises. However, if a private company is performing a task on behalf of a public authority, the information held in that capacity is considered to be held on behalf of the authority and therefore still accessible (Supreme Administrative Court 1989 ref 29). In a European context, many countries have some regulation on access to publically owned companies and the method of listing these subjects is not unusual.

17.3 Who can access information and how must it be requested?

The South African PAIA refers to the natural or juristic person seeking information generally as a 'requester', whereas 'personal requesters' (also defined in section 1) may seek information only about themselves. Requests for records must be made to the information officer or head of the body from which the information is sought, and access to the information must be given within 30 days (section 25(1)), provided that the requester has complied procedurally with the Act, has paid any fee levied (section 22) and the information is not protected in terms of Chapter 4 of the Act (section 11(1), and see below). The PAIA also recognises the considerable socio-economic barriers that exist in South Africa in the form of poverty and illiteracy, as well as the secrecy deficit remaining from past practice, and contains many provisions that aim to simplify and enhance access (see generally Chapter 3). This channel for obtaining access to information seems typical of the processes in most common-law countries.

In Sweden, any person has the right to access public information. As seen above, the Constitution refers only to citizens as having the right to access but this has been interpreted as including legal personalities such as companies or associations (i.e. Supreme Administrative Court 2003 ref 83). The FPA includes a specific prohibition on *not* asking for the reasons for wanting access to public information or the identity of the applicant unless it is necessary to have such information in order to decide issues of secrecy (FPA 2 Chapter section 14 (3)). In the most common, uncomplicated cases, it is not necessary to ask any questions of an applicant at all. Many countries in Europe have more detailed demands on anyone seeking access and some will only recognise certain reasons, such as defending a legal interest, as a valid ground for access (Italy and Russia are examples; see Mezzacapo 2006 and Henderson & Sayadyan 2011). The Swedish regulation—as in the rules of some other jurisdictions, such as the United Kingdom and the United States—is based on the idea of transparency as a general means for control of public power and, from that viewpoint, as few obstacles as possible should be raised to anyone seeking access. The other approach is to stress access as a means of individual protection of legal interests, which translates into a much narrower and stricter regulation on access.

17.4 Limits to access and secrecy

Returning to the common-law reference point of South Africa, the PAIA provides that certain categories of information fall entirely outside its scope, and refusal of access is mandatory: those records requested for criminal or civil proceedings (section 7(1)), and of Cabinet, of the judicial functions of courts, and of Members of Parliament (section 12). Such records are effectively declared to be secret, and aspects of such exclusion from the scope of PAIA may be unconstitutional (Klaaren & Penfold, para 62.5). Furthermore, there are several discretionary grounds for refusing access to records, for reasons of: the protection of the privacy of third parties ('unreasonable' disclosure may be refused, see sections 34 and 63, as well as being internationally recognised as a restricting ground, and being a competing right in the Bill of Rights, section 14 of the Constitution); if disclosure could 'reasonably cause prejudice to' the defence, security and international relations interests of the country (section 41(1)); and if broadly defined aspects of the operations of public bodies 'could reasonably be expected' to be frustrated by disclosure (section 44(1)).

The judicial interpretation of statutory language permitting non-disclosure is naturally of cardinal importance, because tolerating their extensive application may work contrary to the constitutional imperative of openness of government. In addition, there exists in the PAIA a 'public-interest override' applicable to both public and private bodies (sections 46 and 70), which mandates disclosure in the public interest in all the above circumstances, except for certain records of the revenue service (section 35(1)). The terms of this override provision should be noted for their similarity to like provisions in other jurisdictions: access to a record will be granted if: '(a) the disclosure … would reveal evidence of (i) a substantial contravention of, or failure to comply with, the law; or (ii) an imminent and serious public safety or environmental risk; and (b) the public interest in the disclosure of the record clearly outweighs the harm contemplated in the provision in question' (section 46). These conditions set the bar high, so that the public-interest override will seldom be invoked, but it nevertheless amounts to an important safety net.

Most common-law jurisdictions seem to adopt the mandatory/discretionary distinction in their approach to limitations on access, and Cabinet documentation is almost always excluded from access, at least for a period of several decades. The South African approach to this issue seems broadly in line with that of other common-law jurisdictions.

The general approach in older democracies to the right of access to information is to recognise such a right limited by a number of interests such as personal integrity and confidentiality. These interests can be overridden if a serious enough public interest is at hand. The common strand is that the regulation demands a test balancing the interests in favour of disclosure with those supporting the withholding of information.

In Sweden, the constitution demands a detailed regulation of every exception to the general rule on access. These rules are all collected in the OSL, containing over 44 chapters and hundreds of sections. The regulation is based on two basic presumptions, one in favour of openness of ordinary information and one in favour of the secrecy of sensitive information. As an example, information on personal income will be kept secret only if it is clear that its disclosure will harm the individual in question, while information on personal health will be secret unless it is clear that it can be disclosed without harm to the individual concerned. The purpose of the detailed regulation is to narrow the room for discretion, which tends to be used to withhold information.

In the European context, the Swedish regulation is somewhat unusual in its detail and most jurisdictions have more open-ended rules. Some countries though, are even stricter than

Sweden and there are examples of regimes where the legislation on access lists subject matters that cannot be held secret at all, notwithstanding conflicting interests (see Henderson & Sayadyan 2011). This must be understood as a reaction to a much too restrictive practice under more flexible regulation.

Another limit to access that exists in some systems is to let the person (or legal body) concerned have a say on the issue of disclosure. This can be a prerequisite for disclosure or it can be an option provided for those 'third parties' that want to stop access. In some countries, such as the USA, Germany and Italy (for example), third parties can stop the disclosure of information in public documents by use of court proceedings if they can show they may be damaged by such a disclosure. Sometimes this possibility is referred to as 'reversed FOI' as it gives third parties a hold on information in the possession of authorities. Such a power is, however, not recognised in other systems such as the British and the Swedish, where the authorities (and ultimately the courts) decide on disclosure without any possibility for 'outsiders' to intervene. This does not mean that the interests of these persons are not considered, just that they do not get a special role in proceedings on disclosure.

17.5 Administrative and judicial regulation

Several issues on the practical matters of access deserve attention, as they are often decisive for how the right works in practice. This includes administrative regulations on such issues as costs and speed of delivery as well as judicial rules on control and appeal.

Both internal administrative appeals and judicial review of the refusal to grant access to a record are contemplated in the PAIA. Essentially, a refusal (or other related decisions) by the information officer of a public body may be appealed against by the requester or even a third party, usually to the political head of the department, and a procedure and the payment of fees are provided for (sections 74–77). After the exhaustion of such internal appeal avenues, an unsuccessful requester may pursue a remedy through an application to court (sections 78–82) in respect of certain decisions of both public and private bodies. Although the level of court and the basis of recourse are not clearly spelled out in the Act, it is highly likely that this is judicial review in a superior court, as commonly understood in most common-law countries (although PAIA also anticipates review by a lower court—before a magistrate, in certain circumstances; section 1 definition of 'court'). Thus the grounds for review are at least that the administrative decision was unlawful, unreasonable or procedurally unfair (the language of section 33 of the Constitution). The reviewing court may grant any order that is 'just and equitable', including interdicts and awards of costs.

Many common-law FOI systems (such as Canada and Australia), while providing for internal review and appeal mechanisms—and ultimate resort to the courts for judicial review of administrative action, as above—also provide for a 'sectoral ombudsman', most frequently styled the Information Commissioner (IC), with the authority to intervene on behalf of dissatisfied applicants for information. While their authority is chiefly non-binding in nature, in certain jurisdictions (such as New Zealand) the IC can make decisions binding on the administration.

The first step in getting access is obtaining information on what kind of documents an authority has access to. This presupposes administrative rules on registers of information and on public archives. The public must be able relatively easily to get a view on what kind of information can be accessed; in Sweden, this is done by computer terminals in the hallways of most authorities where the public can get this information. Another vital aspect is, of course, that public information does not disappear, but is kept in a safe and orderly way.

Well-functioning legislation and practice on archives form an important part of any system of access to information.

When it comes to fees, one approach is to have no fees as such for the access of documentation. If the applicant wants a copy of the information, it can be necessary to pay a fee for the cost of the copies. In Sweden, this is rather strictly regulated and nothing more than the precise cost of copying (somewhat generalized) is permitted. Some Western European countries include fees to cover more than such direct costs, for example time spent gathering the information.

FOI legislation in many countries contains more or less exact time limits within which the information asked for must be provided or a legally sound reason for withholding the information be communicated to the applicant. Usual time limits are between 20 and 30 days. The Swedish approach is less formal and therefore more flexible, yet more demanding. The Swedish Constitution prescribes that public information should be provided immediately or, if that is not possible, as soon as possible (FPA 2 Chapter section 13). The latter has been interpreted in case-law and the opinions of the Parliamentary ombudsman as within a few days in normal cases. In any case, more than two weeks to respond is acceptable only if extraordinary circumstances are at hand. We see here how the mechanisms for judicial control have an impact on the type of administrative regulation necessary to get a system of FOI working.

Another important feature of the Swedish system is the nearly total right to remain anonymous and not to have to give any particular reasons for disclosure. This is not a common starting point for systems of access to public information. Some systems contain requirements for giving reasons for access, such as the protection of a legal interest, and providing information on the identity of the applicant. As the Swedish system generally provides for immediate disclosure, there is normally no need to make contact with the applicant later on and therefore no need for names, addresses etc. In cases where the information sought is (potentially) classified, the authority is permitted to ask for the identity of the applicant and the reason for the application can also be of interest here. For example, a researcher can, under certain conditions, be given access to otherwise secret material for scientific purposes, but this presupposes that the authority gets valid information on the applicant and the use of the information in question. So, a refusal to provide the authority with the information it needs in order to assess the confidentiality of the material will result in access not being granted.

A refusal to grant access in Sweden and most of the rest of Western Europe can be appealed directly to an administrative court of appeal. In Sweden, the court scrutinises the reasons for not disclosing the material and makes an independent assessment of the need for secrecy. If the court finds that the reasons for secrecy are not compelling, it can decide to disclose the material directly or, in more complicated cases, send the case back for a more detailed assessment of exactly what can or cannot be accessed. An illustrative example is a recent case on correspondence between the National Bank of Sweden and its counterparts in the Baltic region during financial crises in the banking system in 2008. The Supreme Administrative Court found that blanket referrals to the secrecy of foreign policy could not prevail and granted access to some of the information sought (2009 ref 59). In most other European countries, the court would limit itself to remanding the case to the authority involved. Court proceedings can also lead to a limited access to certain documents or parts of documents.

As a complementary control, the Parliamentary ombudsman of Sweden makes regular inspections of public authorities and, among other things, controls how the authority handles requests for access to public documents. The ombudsman can also react to individual complaints received. In the ombudsman's decisions, legal and administrative standards are evolved and misconceptions of the FOI system are—at least to a certain extent—corrected. It is usual in many of the European legal systems to have some ombudsman or commissioner with the task of guarding the right to access, but the powers of such institutions vary significantly. In some systems, the commissioner can only make recommendations; in some, they take active part on the side of the applicant; and in others they may take decisions on the issue of disclosure. In Sweden, the ombudsman cannot affect the issue of disclosure as such but will criticise any unconstitutional or illegal decisions and may prosecute civil servants for misuse of public power in flagrant cases (see Court of Appeal in Gothenburg, judgment 2006-02-08).

17.6 Issues for further attention

The review of the current state of legal provision for access to information in the two main legal families of the world indicates a rapidly developing and responsive area of law. Several issues are likely to demand the attention of the courts and those with expertise in the field in the immediate future, such as:

- whether the constitutionalisation of a right of access to information represents an advantage over those regimes which are content to use legislation alone;
- the best means of ensuring that governmental (and, where applicable, private) practice meets the demands of the legal regime applicable within the relevant jurisdiction;
- the effective and fair balancing of the legitimate need for transparent accountability on the one hand with other interests whose advancement is also justified, such as privacy, dignity, equality, the effectiveness and efficiency of public administration and, in limited circumstances, secrecy;
- the potential use of access to information legislation in support of the achievement of other rights granted by law, particularly in the socio-economic sphere;
- the relentless intrusion of the burgeoning capacity of the electronic world, and its relationship with formal legal rules and institutions;
- the usefulness of strict FOI regimes to counter misleading governmental information, and the way that governments try to steer information by granting privileges to some journalists (especially in times of emergency or armed conflict) to the exclusion of others;
- the shifting boundaries within nation states between public and private power, and the enhancement of the latter through the process of economic and financial globalisation; and
- as a consequence of the last point, the need constantly to monitor and reform both the form and substance of civic participation in open government, and the demand for accountability of those who wield power, nationally and supranationally.

One of the greatest challenges likely to undermine the advancement of FOI through the law stems from the seductive nature of secrecy to those wielding public power. While this can rear its head in any country, it is likely to gain greatest purchase in legal systems whose public commitment to transparency is of relatively recent origin, or whose foundations for executive accountability depend more on convention than on statutory regime. So, even in South Africa, notwithstanding the spectacular commitment to openness as a key value of its constitutional democracy, the threats to such commitment are always present. The battle for transparency centres in late 2011 on the proposed enactment of the Protection of State Information Bill, which seeks to grant far-reaching authority to classify information to the Minister of State Security. Such disputes are likely to be replicated in many countries.

In a world that has become more and more protective of what is loosely termed 'personal integrity', the role and rights of third parties are of particular interest from the perspective of access to information. At least from a Swedish perspective, such considerations are foreign to the weighing of interests inherent in an assessment of disclosure, as it will shift the balance in any such exercise. It gives a certain amount of control over the transparency of public administration to private parties and thereby risks undermining the whole project of an open government. As European law in general, and many of the legal systems of Western Europe, are based on such conceptions, there is a real risk that the use of access to public information for control purposes will be diminished.

Freedom of information does not only consist of a right to access information held by public authorities. It also gives a wider right of access to information generally, for example by a positive obligation on the state to provide a basic structure for mass media and mass communication. This is obvious from both national constitutions such as those of Germany (Article 5) or Norway (Article 100), and also follows from the case-law of the European Court of Human Rights on its interpretation of Article 10 on the freedom of expression and information. Traditionally, this right has had few practical legal implications outside the context of prisons and other involuntary restrictions on personal freedom. Nowadays, however, this is changing. In a more multicultural society and with the growing mobility of the population, the demands on access to information in the requester's own language and with a content and form that is accepted will grow and put existing FOI regimes under pressure (see, for example, European Court of Human Rights decision in *Kurshid Mustafa v Sweden*, 2008-12-16).

A last point to make is the almost paradoxical observation that the more ambitious and information-friendly a regulation on FOI is, the more complex and difficult to understand it becomes. In Sweden, this has resulted in a huge legal document that few persons can aspire to be able to grasp completely. The complexity itself can be a hindrance to healthy openness in governance.

References

Banisar, D (2006). 'Freedom of Information around the World: A Global Survey of Access to Information Laws', *Privacy International.*

Bentley, K & Calland, R (forthcoming). 'Access to Information: A Theory of Change in Practice', in Langford, M, Cousins, B, Dugard, J & Madlingozi, T (eds), *Strategies for Socio-Economic Rights in South Africa: Symbols or Substances* (Cambridge, CUP).

Birkinshaw, P (2010). *Freedom of Information: The Law, the Practice and the Ideal* (4th edn) (Cambridge, CUP).

Bohlin, A (2010). Offentlighetsprincipen [The Principle of Openness].

Darch, C & Underwood, PG (2009). *Freedom of Information and the Developing World: The Citizen, the state and models of openness* (Oxford, Chandos Publishing).

Henderson, J & Sayadyan H (2011). 'Freedom of Information in the Russian Federation', *European Public Law.*

Klaaren, J & Penfold, G (2007). 'Access to Information' in Woolman, S et al (eds), *Constitutional Law of South Africa* (Cape Town, Juta), chapter 62.

Mezzacapo, S (2006). 'The Right to Access to Public Bodies Records in Italy and the UK', *European Business Law Review.*

Peled, R & Rabin, Y (2011). 'The Constitutional Right to Information', *Columbia Human Rights Review.*

Schauer, F (2011). 'Transparency in Three Dimensions', *University of Illinois Law Review.*

Snell, R (2006). 'Freedom of Information Practices', *Agenda* 13:291–307.

Additional reading

Allmänna handlingar I elektronisk form – offentlighet och integritet [Public documents in electronic form – openess and integrity] SOU 2010:4 [Public inquiry 2010:4].

Offentlighetsprincipen och den nya tekniken, [The Principle of Openess and new technology] SOU 2001:3 [Public inquiry 2001:3].

Strömberg, H & Lundell, B (2007). Handlingsoffentlighet och sekretess [Access to information and secrecy].

Freedom of expression and association

Iain Currie

18.1 Freedom of expression

18.1.1 Structure and constituent elements of the right

All countries with a Bill of Rights protect freedom of expression.[1] Those that do not have a Bill of Rights will often protect it as a sort of constitutional principle (e.g. the United Kingdom, Australia and Israel; see Stone, 2011). The right is protected by all the international and regional human rights instruments. The ubiquity of the right in the constitutional systems of the world (and, it seems, the ubiquity of its infringement[2]) has spawned a massive and diverse jurisprudence, and an equally massive and daunting body of secondary literature. One might attempt only the most sweeping generalisation about this jurisprudence and literature: though there is general acceptance of the principle of a right to freedom of expression, there is considerable divergence of opinion and practice about its scope and the rationale for having it, and about the extent to which it may justifiably be restricted. Underlying this divergence is, of course, the sheer diversity of history and culture, of context, that underlies the practice of free speech in various jurisdictions. This chapter accordingly can aim to do no more than survey these areas of divergence and draw attention to some common features of both.

For a typical formulation of the right, one can look to article 19 of the International Covenant on Civil and Political Rights (ICCPR), which has influenced a large number of national constitutions:

1. Everyone shall have the right to hold opinions without interference.
2. Everyone shall have the right to freedom of expression; this right shall include freedom to seek, receive and impart information and ideas of all kinds, regardless of frontiers,

---

1 Recent examples: AFGHANISTAN (2004), art 34 ('Freedom of speech is inviolable'); IRAQ (2005), art 13 ('The right of free expression shall be protected'), LIBYA (2011), art 14 ('freedom of communication').

2 See the annual reports and responses to complaints received by the UN Special Rapporteur on the Promotion and Protection of the Right to Freedom of Expression, available at http://www2.ohchr.org/.

either orally, in writing or in print, in the form of art, or through any other media of his choice.

3. The exercise of the rights provided for in paragraph 2 of this article carries with it special duties and responsibilities. It may therefore be subject to certain restrictions, but these shall only be such as are provided by law and are necessary:

    (a) For respect of the rights or reputations of others;

    (b) For the protection of national security or of public order (*ordre public*), or of public health or morals.

The first point to note is the right to 'hold opinions'. Many constitutions include this element and, like the ICCPR, protect it without qualification since there can no plausible justification for interference with freedom of thought (Nowak). As Mill noted, the 'inward domain of consciousness' demands the most comprehensive liberty, 'absolute freedom of opinion and sentiment on all subjects, practical or speculative, scientific, moral, or theological' (Mill).

As soon as an opinion is expressed, made manifest in some way, it becomes of concern to other people and has the capacity to affect them. Mill thought that it was this effect—the potential to cause harm to others—that justified restrictions. But such restrictions could not be on the *holding* of an opinion but only on its *expression*. This fundamental distinction informs the structure of article 19: the right to freedom of expression entails 'special duties and responsibilities' and 'may ... be subject to certain restrictions'. In the jurisdictions that have been influenced by this conception of the right, the possibility of its restriction, by law and in order to protect countervailing interests, is built into its exercise.

A final point can be made about article 19, treated here as paradigmatic of the modern right to freedom of expression. The 'right to freedom of expression' is said to have certain constitutive elements: the freedom to 'seek, receive and impart information' and to do so 'through ... any media'. The older term, freedom of *speech*, tends to suggest only one of these elements—the active imparting of information to others. But freedom of expression encompasses also the right to the passive receipt of information and the right to access information.[3] The latter two concepts are of importance in delineating the purpose and scope of a principle that is sometimes specifically and separately enumerated in national constitutions as a right to freedom of the media.[4] There is no need for specific enumeration, however; with or without enumeration, most jurisdictions have active and developed bodies of jurisprudence relating to the principle of free expression by the media.

A related principle, specifically enumerated in some constitutions, is a prohibition of censorship, usually understood as prior control of publication and sometimes as both pre- and post-publication control. Article 5(1) of the German Constitution is a good example: 'Everyone has the right to freely express and disseminate his opinions in speech, writing, and pictures and to inform himself without hindrance from generally accessible sources. The freedom of the press and the freedom of reporting by means of broadcasts and films are

---

3 On the latter, see Chapter 17 in this volume. Whether a right of access to state information can be derived from the principle of freedom of expression is a question best described as controversial and not yet settled in either international law or national constitutional law.

4 The classic formulation is the First Amendment to the US Constitution (1791): 'Congress shall make no law ... abridging the freedom of speech, or of the press ...' 'Press' is an old-fashioned and potentially restrictive term, particularly in the digital age. Modern texts tend to use 'media'.

guaranteed. There shall be no censorship.' The principle is by no means generally accepted,[5] with most jurisdictions being content to treat publication control as governed by the general right to freedom of expression and by the principles permitting its legitimate restriction.

Just as there is widespread acceptance of the right to freedom of expression, there is little controversy about what could be described as the core guarantees of the right. In most jurisdictions that take the right seriously (I mean those jurisdictions in which the right is independently justiciable at the instance of individual claimants, or at least is susceptible to individual contestation), the freedom of expression would be considered to be infringed by laws imposing political or religious censorship, or ensuring government control of the media and silencing independent or critical voices, or practices such as the intimidation of journalists.[6] Of more interest to the comparative scholar are, accordingly, areas of genuine disagreement. One of these concerns reveals interesting differences in the fundamental understanding of the scope and purpose of the right and these differences will be the focus of this chapter. It is the extent to which free expression can legitimately be restricted in the name of the protection of the rights of vulnerable persons and groups: so-called hate-speech laws and laws forbidding various forms of discriminatory speech.[7]

18.1.2 The scope of the right and its rationale

The US Constitution protects the 'freedom of speech' and does so in textually absolute terms. One way to limit the scope of the right in hard cases is therefore to attempt to delineate what is 'speech' for constitutional purposes and what is not. Restriction of the latter class of conduct is then thought to raise no constitutional difficulty.[8] The classic forms of problem speech that are proscribed in most jurisdictions—incitement ('fighting words'), obscenity, slander, insult, sometimes blasphemy—are then ruled out of constitutional consideration.

But this move has limited utility once it is accepted that 'speech' cannot be taken literally but encompasses other forms of expressive conduct; art, the display of symbols such as swastikas, torch-light parades and similar demonstrations, symbolic conduct such as flag-burning or burnings in effigy are all examples of activities widely held to be constitutionally protected. The term 'expression' used in the more modern formulations seems intended to encompass a wide range of activities that are capable of communicating: it is 'as wide as human thought and imagination', as a New Zealand court put it.[9] Yet, wide though the concept might be, it is not without limit. Terrorism, political assassination, and suicide bombing are undoubtedly political acts intended to convey a message, but most jurisdictions would be reluctant to consider these as constitutionally protected expression (Barendt, 79; Stone).

Another method of dealing with problem speech is to treat it as expression that is constitutionally protected but has relatively little constitutional value. This move is particularly

---

5 Some 27 percent of the constitutions surveyed by the Constitutional Design Group prohibit censorship in absolute terms, 10 percent in qualified terms, while 62 percent have no specific provision: http://constitutionmaking.org/reports.html.

6 Infringements that are depressingly widespread, as the reports of NGOs such as Index on Censorship (www.indexoncensorship.org) and Article 19 (www.article19.org) illustrate.

7 The focus is on laws that restrict speech in the name of dignitarian or anti-discrimination interests rather than those justified by less controversial public-order rationales, for example laws prohibiting incitement to violence.

8 *Chaplinsky v New Hampshire* 315 US 568 (1942).

9 *Moonen v Film and Literature Board of Review* [2000] 2 NZLR 9 (CA).

useful in jurisdictions that accept some or other form of proportionality analysis as the method of resolving the conflict of constitutional principles (on proportionality in rights analysis, see Alexy). Pornography, for example, might comfortably be considered to be a protected form of expression but, at the same time, as expression that is not particularly valuable and therefore relatively easily outweighed by the need to protect countervailing principles—such as the rights of vulnerable groups (e.g. children and women). The same could go for commercial speech, dishonest speech, extreme speech or speech proposing a criminal transaction.[10]

Both moves just mentioned are instances of line-drawing. The difference is that the first is conducted at the stage of determining the scope (the 'coverage') of the right (Schauer 1982). The second is conducted at the stage of balancing the infringement of the right against countervailing principles. Where proportionality analysis is the accepted methodology of rights analysis, much less turns on an initial decision about what is or is not included as protected expression. What matters instead is the relative weight given to a particular form of expression: political speech is usually thought to be more valuable than pornography, artistic expression more valuable than commercial speech.[11] This weight can even vary from case to case, allowing considerable flexibility in decision-making.

But both types of line-drawing exercises can only be conducted with an appropriate metric, a conception of how to measure the value of free speech, or, to put it another way, what the point of the principle of free speech is. There is a massive body of literature on this question,[12] reflecting a considerable divergence of practice in the numerous jurisdictions of the world that have developed a free-speech jurisprudence. Two fundamental and competing traditions have been identified. The first is that of the United States, a jurisdiction with a venerable and voluminous jurisprudence that can be summed up as 'extraordinarily' protective of the freedom of speech and intolerant of almost any limitation on it, particularly those that might involve the state regulating the content of speech (Dworkin). On the other hand, there is a tradition stemming from the international human rights instruments established after the Second World War. This tradition is far more willing to countenance the restriction of free speech, principally when its exercise comes into conflict with the principle of human dignity.

The various justifications for free speech, drawn from political philosophy, can be accommodated, with more or less ease of fit, into the jurisprudential traditions identified above. So, in the general theory of free speech underpinning much of the US jurisprudence, the state should leave the 'marketplace of ideas' to flourish without regulation. Mill thought that the search for truth was the point of free speech, a search that was hindered, not facilitated, by the prohibition of the expression of false opinions: 'If the opinion is right ... [human beings] are deprived of the opportunity of exchanging error for truth: if wrong, they lose, what is almost

---

10 See, for example, the decision of the South African Constitutional Court in *De Reuck v Director of Public Prosecutions* 2004 (1) SA 406 (CC) (child pornography is a constitutionally protected expression, but almost weightless when put in the balance against the principles of dignity and the prevention of harm to others).

11 The weighting approach does not entirely avoid the need for scope-determination, however. For example, it will still be necessary to determine whether a particular instance of expression is pornography (therefore, less valuable) or artistic expression on an erotic subject (more valuable)? Another example: if certain forms of extreme expression (homophobia, religious bigotry) are considered to have little value, does it make any difference if these are uttered in a political context and that their speakers may claim the heightened protection usually accorded to political speech?

12 Schauer 1982 is a fine introduction to this literature.

as great a benefit, the clearer perception and livelier impression of truth, produced by its collision with error' (Mill). As a matter of legal arrangement, it follows that in a free market in ideas, truth will, in the long run, drive out untruth: 'the best test of truth is the power of the thought to get itself accepted in the competition of the market'.[13] Such a theory is suspicious of any form of restriction on speech that appears to entail the state selecting which speech is permissible by its citizens and which is impermissible; hate-speech prohibitions, for example, are unlikely to be considered justifiable. The 'marketplace' theory is best accommodated in a polity with a semi-libertarian ethic and culture.

A second theory of free speech has gained greater traction outside the United States. It emphasises a particular form of speech, public political speech, and singles it out for near absolute constitutional protection. The greatest degree of freedom of expression on political matters is essential to a properly functioning democracy, promoting democratic self-governance—literally, government *by* the people (Meiklejohn). The theory has influenced the development of free-speech doctrines in jurisdictions as diverse as the United Kingdom and Japan (Krotoszynski). Its high-water mark is the famous decision of *New York Times v Sullivan*, which subordinates almost all private interests to the principle of unrestricted political speech: 'debate on public issues should be uninhibited, robust and wide open ... it may well include vehement, caustic, and sometimes unpleasantly sharp attacks on government and public officials'.[14]

An illuminating comparative exercise for tracing the influence of US free-speech jurisprudence on other jurisdictions is to track whether *Sullivan* has been able to gain a foothold. For example, in South Africa, though invited by a new Constitution to craft a law of defamation appropriate for an 'open and democratic society', the courts deliberately did not follow the *Sullivan* route. To have done so would have run the risk of subordinating free speech, even political speech, to the countervailing principle of human dignity.[15] This principle has at least equal weight to the free-expression principle in numerous jurisdictions (particularly those influenced by the European Convention on Human Rights); in some jurisdictions (for example, South Africa, Germany) it is a more weighty principle, even a pre-eminent one (Milo). In the event, as is the position in a number of jurisdictions, the South African law of defamation was developed to recognise a principle of 'reasonable' publication of defamatory material, reasonableness being a flexible standard determined by reference to a set of balancing factors, including the nature of the defamatory speech (political, not political) and the target of the speech (whether a public or private figure), the context of the publication and the right of the target to comment on or reply to the publication. As a consequence, in jurisdictions influenced by a dignity-regarding conception of free speech, political speech is seldom permitted to be quite as robust as it is in the United States; it is tempered by defamation and privacy laws and by laws prohibiting hate speech, religious intolerance or holocaust denial, in addition to milder forms of offence.

But at the same time as it is a limiting principle in speech cases, human dignity can also serve as a value justifying the protection of free speech. The principle, deployed in arguments

---

13 Holmes J in *Abrams v US* 250 US 616.
14 Brennan J in *New York Times* 376 US 254 (1964).
15 *Khumalo v Holomisa* 2002 (5) SA 401 (CC). For other examples of courts disinclined to follow Sullivan, see *R v Keegstra* (1990) 3 CRR (2d) 193 (Canada), *Theophanous v Herald & Weekly Times Ltd and Another* (1994) 124 ALR 1 (Australia) and BVerfGE 198 (1958) (*Lüth*); 30 BVerfGE 173 (1971) (*Mephisto*).

based on speaker or audience autonomy, can be summed as follows: 'We retain our dignity, as individuals, only by insisting that no one—no official and no majority—has the right to withhold an opinion from us on the ground that we are not fit to hear and consider it' (Dworkin, 200). Unlike the argument from democracy, this theory justifies more than the protection of political speech but is a justification for allowing the greatest degree of freedom for all forms of expression by which individuals choose to conduct themselves as responsible moral agents. It serves as a powerful argument against censorship, whether this is motivated by the desire to instil political or ideological orthodoxy or by paternalism. However, the theory is difficult to reconcile with the treatment given in many jurisdictions to speech (even political speech) that harms the dignity of others. How might the moral agency or autonomy of the speaker justify the dissemination by him or her of abusive, defamatory or discriminatory opinions? Might the individual members of a society (moral agents themselves, after all, and therefore entitled to equal respect) not be better off if they were not exposed to such ugliness on a daily basis?[16] The victims of hate speech might indeed be better able to exercise their own rights, including expression, if the climate of fear and marginalisation created by hate speech or discriminatory speech was reduced.

Line-drawing of the type described above is avoided in some jurisdictions by the express exclusion of some types of problem speech from constitutional protection. The model for this is the mandatory prohibition of 'propaganda for war' and 'any advocacy of national, racial or religious hatred that constitutes incitement to discrimination, hostility or violence' required of state parties by article 20 of the ICCPR. Similar obligations are imposed, in relation to racist speech, by article 4 of the International Convention on the Elimination of All Forms of Racial Discrimination. The South African Constitution accordingly specifically provides that 'expression ... does not extend to' the three forms of speech just described. Though a line is still drawn, it is drawn at the stage of formulation of the right and is therefore the product of a democratic pre-commitment on the ambit of the right in future cases.[17]

18.1.3 Justifications for the restriction of the right

As noted above, the near-universal acceptance of a constitutional principle of freedom of expression in the various jurisdictions of the world tells us nothing about the scope of the principle or the conditions in which its restriction is considered permissible. As with its scope, the practice of the limitation of freedom of expression is marked by diversity and shaped by the constitutional history and culture of a particular jurisdiction, by the details of its constitutional text and by the jurisdiction's jurisprudential practices and methodologies.

Most comparative analyses seek to impose some order on this chaos by contrasting the US approach (the oldest body of jurisprudence, after all, and one backed up by a secondary literature of unparalleled depth and richness) with that of other countries, or groups of countries or regions. Contrast, rather than compare, is the appropriate verb, since US jurisprudence is

16 See Waldron, 1621 (hate-speech laws confront the problem of 'public and semi-permanent manifestations of racial and ethnic hatred as visible aspects of the civic environment'). See also Feinberg 1985 (the prevention of offence may justify the restriction of freedom, depending on its scope and intensity and the ease or difficulty with which it may be avoided).

17 See also *Jersild v Denmark* (ECtHR) Series A No 298, para. 35; *Norwood v United Kingdom* (ECtHR) Reports 2004-XI, 343.

usually found to be different, both in the fundamental theory underlying it and in the methodology used to decide cases of conflict between the principle of free speech and other principles and interests, to that of almost everywhere else (Gardbaum).

The underlying theories explaining the valorisation of free speech have been outlined above. As to methodology, one usually begins by noting that the text of the First Amendment to the US Constitution seems to countenance no restrictions of the right at all, a fact that discourages the elaboration of a general theory of limitation; limits are established and imposed on a case-by-case basis. The result is a 'categorisation' approach: speech and speech-restrictions are categorised (e.g. content-based versus content-neutral restrictions, commercial versus non-commercial speech), then rules of restriction applicable to that category are applied (Schauer 2005).[18]

By contrast, though article 19 of the ICCPR appears to state a rule—'Everyone shall have the right to freedom of expression'—this statement is qualified by article 19(3), which specifically envisages that the grant of the right entails 'certain restrictions', when necessary for the protection of the rights of others or other important interests. Article 10 of the European Convention on Human Rights is similarly structured. Such formulations see the grant of the right and the modalities of its exercise as, from the outset, conditioned by the possibility of lawful restriction by the state. Similarly, national jurisdictions either subject the right to a general limitations clause (Canada, South Africa, New Zealand, Russia) or to specific criteria for limitation, along the lines of the ICCPR or the European Convention.

Such a textual structure, as we have seen above, makes the initial exercise of determining the scope of the right less significant than the consideration of its permissible limitation in a concrete case. It is clear that the statement of right is not a categorical prohibition of any restrictions of expression; expression can in fact be restricted in the service of countervailing, constitutionally recognised considerations such as national security, or morals, or to give effect to competing rights such as privacy or dignity. So formulated, constitutional rights have the structure of principles since they state what ought to be realised to the greatest extent relative to what is legally and factually possible (Alexy). Expression must compete with other, countervailing principles: a competition that is resolved by a process of balancing that is conducted either by a legislature when deciding to pass a law that limits expression, or by a court deciding the constitutionality of that limitation.

In those jurisdictions that employ this methodology of rights analysis and adjudication,[19] the emphasis is placed on the relative weight accorded to the principle of free speech versus the weight of the competing principles. There is much diversity of practice and, consequently, of outcome in this weighting exercise. At least two approaches to the exercise are of particular interest and worth noting here. Sometimes a hierarchy of principles is specified in the text or inferred by the courts from the Constitution's overall structure, history or philosophy, and expression is ranked higher or lower in the hierarchy or the value system so established. Human dignity in the German Constitution, for example, outranks, under certain

---

18 Schauer goes on to argue that the exceptional character of the US methodology is overstated. It is in fact no different to the two-stage methodologies (considering, first, the scope of the right and then the legitimacy of restrictions upon it) employed elsewhere. This is because, inescapably, the rationale behind a principle is distinct from the reasons that may exist for overriding it or for refusing to apply it and must be separately considered.

19 Most of them, according to Stone Sweet & Mathews (2008) at 73 (the 'dominant technique of rights adjudication in the world').

conditions, all other principles, including expression.[20] Another approach is to identify a 'core' of the right to freedom of expression, as opposed to non-core or 'peripheral' aspects of the right, and to weigh the former more heavily than the latter in the balancing test. Again, core/periphery analysis requires a metric to be established, either on the basis of clear textual indications or from general theory or from constitutional history. Particular aspects of the freedom of expression, such as press freedom and political speech can, for example, be said to be at the core of a free-speech guarantee, because of their essential importance in a democratic society. Similarly, despite a commitment at the first, definitional stage of analysis to neutrality as to the content of protected expression, the core/periphery distinction invites subsequent ranking of expression based on its content and the contribution of that content to the core project of the constitution and the principle of freedom of expression.[21]

18.2 Freedom of association

Freedom of association is easily as ubiquitous a principle of constitutional law as is freedom of expression. Some 78 percent of the constitutions of the world provide for it in some form or another.[22] Indeed, the two rights are sometimes found in the same provision, reflecting the influence of liberal political philosophy, which regards the rights (along with the freedom of assembly) as fundamental, and interrelated, constituents of individual liberty and foundational to any properly democratic polity.[23] That said, association has nothing like the scope and wealth of jurisprudence and secondary literature that freedom of expression has inspired (Gutman), and there is relatively little comparative treatment of the subject.[24]

The modern conception of the right is usefully exemplified by article 22 of the ICCPR, which protects a right to 'freedom of association with others, including the right to form and to join trade unions for the protection of his interests'. Article 22(2) of the Covenant envisages the possibility of justifiable restrictions of the right 'which are prescribed by law and are necessary in a democratic society in the interests of national security or public safety, public order (*ordre public*), the protection of public health or morals, or the protection of the rights and freedoms of others. This article shall not prevent the imposition of lawful restrictions on members of the armed forces and of the police in the exercise of this right'. Four features of

---

20 BVerfGE 30, 173 (*Mephisto*), [5]: 'If the guarantee of artistic freedom gives rise to any conflict, it must be resolved by construction in terms of the order of values enshrined in the Basic Law and in line with the unitary system of values which underlies it. As part of this system of basic rights, the freedom of art is co-ordinate with the dignity of man as guaranteed by Art. 1 [of the Constitution], the supreme and controlling value of the whole system of basic rights.'

21 See *R v Keegstra* [1990] 3 SCR 697.

22 Data compiled by the Constitutional Design Group: see http://constitutionmaking.org/reports. html. In the absence of an express textual guarantee, the right can be inferred from the constitutional protection of free speech and assembly. The US Constitution does not explicitly mention association, but this has 'proven little barrier to recognition of the right' (Cole, 203).

23 The classic account is Alexis de Tocqueville's admiring account of nineteenth-century America, his observations of the young democracy leading him to conclude that: 'The most natural privilege of man, next to the right of acting for himself, is that of combining his exertions with those of his fellow-creatures, and of acting in common with them. I am therefore led to conclude that the right of association is almost as inalienable as the right of personal liberty. No legislator can attack it without impairing the very foundations of society.' De Tocqueville, chapter 12.

24 That is, of the general association right, as opposed to its specific application to collective labour rights. On this distinction, see immediately below.

this formulation are worth noting. Firstly, the formulation identifies the right as a 'freedom', classically a negative protection of the non-state ('private') sphere against state interference. Though it may be claimed by an association on behalf of its members, it remains, in essence, a constraint on lawful interference (whether by the state or by individuals acting in accordance with the state's laws) on an individual's freedom to form, join and maintain associations. Secondly, although the right is one that, by its nature, can only be enjoyed in association 'with others', it is a right of individuals, not groups.[25] Thirdly, a specifically enumerated component of the right is its application to the formation and joining of trade unions. The specification of trade union rights reflects the historical origins of the ICCPR (and indeed of the European Convention on Human Rights, which contains a similar specification). For the most part, national constitutions do not similarly single out this aspect of the right of assembly for express elaboration.[26]

Even though the freedom of association is the historical predicate of labour rights, such as the right to form and join independent unions and the right to decline to join a union, in most jurisdictions associational rights in the employment context have usually been dealt with and have been developed as a specific and separate area of practice.[27] The associational dilemmas posed by particular collective bargaining arrangements (compulsory membership, agency arrangements, closed shops) are accordingly best treated as specific problem areas of labour law. Fourthly, the right is not absolute but may be limited to protect the rights of others or other important interests, such as the protection of public order or the prevention of crime.

As with the right to freedom of assembly, national formulations of the association right are frequently qualified with reference to the criterion of peacefulness or lawfulness, such as 'associations with lawful purposes' (Venezuela) or 'peaceful associations for a lawful purpose' (Mexico). But even without such qualifications, in most jurisdictions, criminal or violent associations and associations that are opposed to the democratic constitutional order are either excluded from constitutional protection,[28] or their association rights are easily outweighed by countervailing considerations.

25 It must be distinguished, therefore, from the 'individual rights exercised communally' recognised in article 27 of the ICCPR and the various national formulations of minority rights that are based upon it (rights of persons belonging to ethnic, religious or linguistic minorities to enjoy, 'in community with the other members of their group their own culture', to profess and practise their own religion, or to use their own language).

26 But see article 9(3) of the German Constitution: 'The right to form associations to safeguard and improve working and economic conditions is guaranteed to everyone'. Specification may be a good idea: the applicability of the right in the context of collective labour rights seems obvious, but has not always been unproblematically recognised. The Canadian Supreme Court has held, for example, that the constitutional right to freedom of association does not include a right to bargain collectively or a right to strike, and that legislation restricting these activities by public-sector employees does not infringe the freedom of association: Reference re: Public Employee Relations Act [1987] 1 SCR 313.

27 This may reflect the influence of international law, particularly the development of detailed standards by the International Labour Organization (ILO) conventions no. 87 of 1948 (Convention concerning Freedom of Association and Protection of the Right to Organise) and no. 98 of 1949 (Convention concerning the Application of the Principles of the Right to Organise and Collective Bargaining). States parties to these conventions are required to promote the freedom of association in a collective bargaining context.

28 See, for example, article 9(2) of the German Constitution, allowing the dissolution of an association that threatens the democratic constitutional order of the state or articles 68 and 69 of the Turkish Constitution allowing the dissolution of political parties with activities in conflict with 'the principles of the democratic and secular republic'.

Other national formulations of the right are, on the face of it, unqualified, protecting the 'freedom to associate', 'right to association' or 'right to freedom of association'. But, as with the right to freedom of expression, the possibility and parameters of legitimate restriction of the right are a matter of express provision in other parts of the Constitution, or by inference from them, or from theory and practice. Again, as with freedom of expression, the fact of the constitutional recognition of the freedom is of less interest than the modalities of its protection in practice, particularly the reasons for its legitimate restriction.

The space that remains permits only a brief outline of the typical 'problem areas' in association jurisprudence, the areas of genuine disagreement in practice likely to be of interest to comparative analysis. The 'core' guarantee of freedom of association is infringed by preventing someone from joining an association by banning it or imposing penalties on members, compelling someone to join an association, discriminating against someone for joining an association, and interfering with the internal affairs of an association. That said, there is considerable nuance possible in describing the scope and limits of each of these aspects of the right. For example, although an outright prohibition on trade union membership is likely to infringe the right in most jurisdictions, there is considerable divergence on the permissibility of excluding certain classes of workers from membership—for example, military personnel, police, doctors, nurses or teachers.

It is the last of the problem areas mentioned above, state interference in internal affairs, that is perhaps of most interest to comparative analysis. This is particularly so in the case of what could be described as well-intentioned interventions in associational autonomy, interventions aimed at protecting or promoting other constitutional rights and interests, such as non-discrimination.[29] The permissibility of such interventions has engendered an interesting philosophical analysis, as they challenge some of the fundamental premises underlying the simultaneous commitment of liberal democratic states to both the principles of freedom of association and non-discrimination (Kymlicka). These interventions are especially important, and practices vary substantially, in connection with religious institutions—whether the churches themselves or their associated activities such as church-affiliated schools. Often such interventions are addressed not under the heading of the right of association but rather as raising questions of religious freedom.

References

Alexy, R (2001). A Theory of Constitutional Rights (translated by J Rivers) (Oxford University Press).

Barendt, E (2005). Freedom of Speech (2nd edn: Oxford, Oxford University Press).

Cole, D (1999). 'Hanging with the Wrong Crowd: of Gangs, Terrorists, and the Right of Association', *Supreme Court Review* 203.

de Tocqueville, A (1835). Democracy in America (translated by H Reeve).

Dworkin, R (1996). Freedom's Law: The Moral Reading of the American Constitution (Oxford University Press).

Feinberg, J (1985). Offense to Others: The Moral Limits of the Criminal Law: Vol 2 (Oxford University Press).

Gardbaum, S (2008). 'The myth and reality of American constitutional exceptionalism', 107 *Michigan Law Review* 391–466.

Gutman, A (ed) (1998). Freedom of Association (Princeton University Press).

---

29 See, for example, *Roberts v US Jaycees* 468 US 609 (1984) (men-only club could be compelled by anti-discrimination legislation to admit women) and *Boy Scouts of America v Dale* 530 US 640 (2000) (club could not be forced by anti-discrimination legislation to admit a homosexual member).

Krotoszynski, RJ, Jr (2006). The First Amendment in Cross-Cultural Perspective: A Comparative Legal Analysis of the Freedom of Speech (NYU Press).

Kymlicka, W (1995). Multicultural Citizenship: A Liberal Theory of Minority Rights (Clarendon Press, Oxford).

Meiklejohn, A (1960). Political Freedom: The Constitutional Powers of the People (New York: Harper and Brothers).

Mill, JS (1860). On Liberty, Harvard Classics Volume 25 (Collier & Son, copyright 1909).

Milo, D (2008). Defamation and Freedom of Speech (Oxford University Press).

Nowak, M (2005). UN Covenant on Civil and Political Rights: CCPR Commentary 2nd edn (NP Engel, Kehl).

Schauer, F (1982). Free Speech: A Philosophical Enquiry (Cambridge University Press).

—— (2005). 'The Exceptional First Amendment', in Ignatieff, M (ed), American Exceptionalism and Human Rights 29 (Princeton University Press).

Stone, A (2011). 'The Comparative Constitutional Law of Freedom of Expression', in Ginsburg, T & Dixon, R (eds), Comparative Constitutional Law (Edward Elgar Publishing).

Stone Sweet, A & Mathews, J (2008). 'Proportionality Balancing and Global Constitutionalism' 47 Columbia Journal of Transnational Law, 73.

Waldron, J (2010). 'Dignity and Defamation: The Visibility of Hate', 123 Harvard Law Review, 1597–1657.

Additional reading

Hare, I & Weinstein, J (eds) (2009). Extreme Speech and Democracy (Oxford University Press).

Heyman, S (2008). Free Speech and Human Dignity (Yale University Press).

Rosenfeld, R (2003). 'Hate Speech in Constitutional Jurisprudence: A Comparative Analysis', 24 Cardozo Law Review 1523.

Scanlon, T (1972). 'A Theory of Freedom of Expression', 1 Philosophy and Public Affairs, 204–26.

Freedom of religion and religion–state relations

W Cole Durham, Jr and Carolyn Evans

19.1 Introduction

Every constitution on earth deals with religion.[1] Reflecting a drive as deep in human anthropology as the yearning for love, and one that similarly has potential for both good and evil, religion (including its counterparts among secular world views) has been a presence in every society that we know, whether as a dominating force or as an alternative social vision. Because of the significance of religion at the level of society, religion is almost always a formative factor, or at least a source of influence that must be taken into account at the pre-constitutional moment when constituent power is exercised and constitutions are written and adopted. Religion may be viewed as a positive social factor to be advanced and protected, as a negative or reactionary influence from which liberation is needed, as a hypothetical normative factor (perhaps behind a Rawlsian veil of ignorance) or, more typically, as a mixed set of influences that must be taken into account in shaping actual constitutional negotiations.

From this perspective, the religious background is almost always part of the axiological and socio-political context within which constitutions are framed. But religion can figure in constitutional moments in many different ways. It may be viewed by constitutional framers as an atavistic force linked to an older order that is being dismantled and replaced, such as the *ancien regime* at the time of the French Revolution or Shinto in Japan following World War II. It may have been a source of civil discord and even civil war that a new constitutional order seeks to bring to an end with a new foundation of hoped-for peace, security, and, ideally, reconciliation. One role constitutions play is to define the extent to which the rights and structures of pre-existing religious and belief communities will be respected and/or limited within the legal order created by a constitution. Such considerations shape the constitutional framework for religious and belief communities, and the believing individuals that actually live under a constitutional order once it is adopted (whether they were present in the country

---

1 For a tabular breakdown of the world's religion-related constitutional provisions arranged by type of provision, see the Table of Religion-Related Provisions of the World's Constitutions, available at http://www.religlaw.org/index.php?pageId=19&linkId=188&contentId=1622&blurbId=3685 (hereinafter Table of Religion-Related Provisions).

prior to the adoption process or arrived on the scene after the adoption process due to migration, formation of a new religion, schism from an old religion, or conversion). Stated differently, constitutions typically define the nature of the relationship of state institutions to belief communities and individual believers, and to determine whether the state's orientation in this regard is positive, negative, neutral, or, more typically, stratified and mixed in complex ways.

Today, all countries have some measure of religious pluralism. Reflecting this reality, the overwhelming majority of constitutions provide explicit protection for freedom of religion (including freedom to adopt non-religious life stances). As of 2010, all but five countries (Comoros, Maldives, Mauritania, Saudi Arabia, and Yemen) had at least some constitutional provisions calling for religious freedom or equality.[2] The scope of the protection actually provided varies widely, however, from strong and reasonably effective guarantees for all, to mere lip service providing little or no effective protection in practice, particularly for new or unpopular groups.[3] Much depends on the way religious freedom rights are balanced against competing rights and social interests, and on what limitations on religion are ultimately permitted.

19.2 'Religion or belief': scope and definition

Constitutional provisions on religion can be broadly divided into those that single out a particular religion or religions for distinctive treatment (which may be preferential or prejudicial) and those that give equal standing to all religions (and sometimes to all beliefs or convictions as well). The first category includes over 30 countries that have an established or official religion, or affirm that the State itself has a particular confessional orientation (see Table of Religion-Related Provisions).[4] It also includes over 25 more that give special recognition to a particular religion, typically acknowledging the significant role the religion has played in the history of the particular country, while affirming that others are free to practice their religions.

A number of the countries with established religions have reconciled this with strong religious freedom for all (e.g. Denmark and the United Kingdom), but others (such as Iran, Saudi Arabia and a number of other Islamic states) have more restrictive histories. Countries that have populations with a prevailing religion often fall into the first category, but not always. For example, of the 44 countries with majority Muslim populations, 10 declare themselves to be Islamic countries and another 12 specify Islam as the official religion, but 11 (all except Turkey having been either former French colonies or formerly part of the Soviet empire) proclaim the state to be secular. Another 11 have not made any constitutional declaration (Stahnke & Blitt, 954–55). The latter category includes Indonesia, which has a constitutional provision prescribing belief in one God and has recently sustained the constitutionality of blasphemy legislation,[5] but provides constitutional protection for the major world religions.[6]

---

2 Ibid.
3 A credible recent study estimates that 32 percent of the countries on earth (including 70 percent of the world's population) live under high or very high restrictions on religious freedom; Pew Forum, *Global Restrictions*.
4 For analysis of relevant provisions in Muslim countries, *see generally* Stahnke & Blitt.
5 *Decision of the Constitutional Court No. 140/PUU-VII/2009 on the Blasphemy Law* (19 April 2010).
6 Constitution of Indonesia, Sec X, art 28A; Sec XA, arts 28(D)1, 28E(1-3), 28I(1).

In some federal systems, different subunits may be authorized to take different approaches, precisely to take religious differences into account. This has allowed many of the northern states in Nigeria, for example, to implement *shari'ah*.

A few states extend the protection of religious freedom only to particular religions and exclude others from constitutional protection. For example, while Article 36 of the Chinese Constitution theoretically extends protection to all '*normal* religious activities', with normality narrowly conceived, in fact state policy singles out five religions for official protection (state-approved versions of Confucianism, Buddhism, Islam, Protestantism and Catholicism).[7] Moreover, the regime actually privileges atheism, and all members of the Communist Party (which controls most of the key government institutions) must be atheists.

Most liberal democracies do not single out religions for preferential treatment in their constitutional documents or, if they do, it is commonly in acknowledgement of the historically or culturally relevant role of that religion. Older liberal constitutions, such as those of the United States and Australia, tend to extend constitutional protection only to 'religion' (e.g. United States: 'Congress shall make no law respecting an establishment of religion, or prohibiting the free exercise thereof'). Following the pattern established in international instruments, a number of newer constitutions extend protection to 'religion or belief', extending coverage to non-religious life stances.[8]

For those states in which the Constitution refers only to 'religion' or 'religion or belief' rather than more specific religions, one question that arises is how these terms are to be interpreted for constitutional purposes. The question is notoriously difficult, and in some jurisdictions there is a fear that any attempt to define religion might itself be an inappropriate intrusion into religious matters. International law has provided little guidance in resolving the definitional conundrum, other than to say that the concept of religion should be interpreted generously, not be limited to traditional religions and includes 'theistic, non-theistic and atheistic beliefs, as well as the right not to profess any religion or belief.'[9]

This approach makes clear that freedom of religion or belief includes the right to embrace a wide range of traditional and non-traditional religions, and also the right to reject religion. Most liberal democracies take a similarly inclusive approach and extend constitutional protection not only to traditional faiths, but also to new religions as well as to non-religious life stances. Even constitutional provisions that do not explicitly cover 'religion *or belief*' are typically construed to protect atheism and other non-religious world views on the basis that these constitute matters of ultimate concern analogous to religion.

While broad construction eliminates practical problems in most cases, disputes will always arise along the borders, particularly when some within a state believe that a group has adopted the façade of religiosity to evade aspects of legal regulation or to avail itself of benefits such as tax exemption. In such circumstances, it is sometimes necessary for courts to set out the principles that will help to determine whether a group is a religion or not.

A number of approaches have emerged over the past century. The initial forays into this area in many jurisdictions have taken an essentialist tack. That is, they seek to give a verbal formula that defines religion by reference to a discernible essence of religion. To some extent,

---

7 Some academic sources note that these five religions are acknowledged in Party policy (but not in the Constitution); *see*, e.g. Potter, 320.

8 *See*, e.g. Netherlands Const art 6(1); Vietnam Const art 70.

9 UN Human Rights Committee, *General Comment* 22, paragraph 2.

the leading Australian case takes this approach, holding that a religion required first a 'belief in a supernatural Being, Thing or Principle; and second, the acceptance of canons of conduct in order to give effect to that belief.'[10] A second broad approach to the definition problem relies on functional definitions. That is, religion is defined by reference to beliefs or practices that play the same functional role as religious beliefs play in the life of the traditional religious believer. In *United States v Seeger*,[11] for example, the United States Supreme Court invoked Paul Tillich's idea of 'ultimate concern' to hold that a person objecting to the military draft was protected because his ethical beliefs manifested ultimate concern that took the functional place of religion in his life.[12] A third approach involves drawing analogies between a questionable case and phenomena that are clearly religious.[13] This can take the form of multi-factor tests that require fitting some but not necessarily all of a set of factors thought to characterize religion, or it can rely on more open-ended analogical comparisons. Still other approaches involve deference to a group's self-definition (typically subject to some limits to preclude strategic behavior).[14]

No definition of religion or belief is likely to resolve all the complex borderline cases of groups or individuals who claim to be religious. Indeed, even the determination of how to define a religion reflects constitutional values, with states that take a more liberal perspective likely to adopt wider definitions, and those that are more closely tied to a particular religious or political orthodoxy more likely to take a narrower view.

19.3 Comparative perspectives on religion–state relationships

The array of possible religion–state configurations in the constitutions of the world can be thought of in terms of a continuum ranging from regimes where there is a complete and positive identification of religion and the state, as in a theocracy, to a position where there is negative or non-identification, as in militantly anti-religious regimes. In between is a range of types of regimes that exhibit progressively greater distance between religion and state institutions: established religions (i.e. official religions or confessional states), religious status (millet) systems, systems with endorsed religions or preferred sets of (often traditional) religions, systems exhibiting relationships of cooperation, accommodation, or separation (benign, formal, strict, *laïcité*), and regimes that seek to exert substantial secular control over religion.

It is not possible here to provide full elaboration of every possible relationship between religion and states and, indeed, these relationships shift over time in response to changing social, political, and economic factors. For example, debate in Sweden and Norway has led to the disestablishment of their official state churches in the recent past, but discussion continues about the appropriate level and nature of state cooperation. The complexity of the potential relationships has been discussed in more detail elsewhere (Durham, 'Patterns of Religion State Relations'), but for current purposes a few examples will have to suffice of relationships where there is a strong, positive identification between a particular religion and the state;

---

10 *The Church of the New Faith and the Commissioner of Pay-Roll Tax* (1983) 154 CLR 120, 136 (High Court of Australia 1983). See along similar lines from Canada *R v Hunter* [1997] CanLII 1340 (BCSC) at 4.
11 380 US 163 (1965).
12 Similar, although not identical, reasoning is used in *Syndicat Northcrest v Amselem* [2004] SCC 47, at 4.
13 *See*, e.g. Greenawalt (1984), 767–68; *Africa v Commonwealth*, 662 F.2d 1025, 1032, 1035 (3d Cir. 1981) (Adams, J).
14 *See*, e.g. Durham & Sewell; Durham & Scharffs, 52–55.

where the state aims for some degree of neutrality with respect to religion; and where the state is hostile to religion.

(a) The current regime in Iran is probably as close as one gets to a pure theocratic state in the current global context. Established religions have taken many historical forms, ranging from the fairly oppressive state-church regimes of the post-Westphalian period to the reasonably tolerant establishments of modern England and Denmark. Religious-status systems include arrangements such as those found in Israel, India, and a number of countries with significant Muslim populations, where many aspects of personal status, marriage, inheritance, and the like depend on the religious community to which one belongs. Endorsed or preferred religion regimes include countries that do not establish an official religion but give special constitutional recognition to one or a few traditional religions, typically because of their historical importance in the country. Many countries with a Roman Catholic background exhibit this pattern. Greece is a regime closely linked to a dominant religion, but in fact its constitution provides that the Orthodox faith constitutes the prevailing religion,[15] which is somewhat less than making it the official religion of the state, and somewhat more than endorsement without privileged status.

(b) The middle range of the identification continuum includes various forms of cooperation, separation, and *laïcité*. Such constitutional arrangements reflect a commitment to the ideal of state neutrality in its various forms. These represent the dominant positions in modern constitutionalism. Cooperationist regimes maintain a posture of neutrality toward all religions, but openly cooperate with religious institutions in many ways, including providing or facilitating financial subsidies for various religious programs. Most of the countries of Europe, with the notable exception of France, exhibit cooperationist characteristics. (And even secular France allows funding for the support of historical church structures and for secular aspects of parochial education.)

Accommodationist regimes, in contrast, do not allow direct financial subsidization of religion but may allow conferring of indirect financial benefits such as tax exemptions and, more generally, are willing to accommodate conscientious claims by allowing exemption from ordinary laws under appropriate circumstances. Separationist regimes call for even stricter separation of religion and state institutions, and are less inclined to allow any special exemptions for religion. Approximately one-third of the nations on earth have separationist regimes (Temperman, 121–23). French *laïcité* is a particularly strong form of separationism, committed to secularism and a strong insistence that religion be confined to the private sphere. Japan is an interesting amalgam, situated closer to the separationist part of the continuum in many respects, but containing some unique features because of the role of Shinto in Japan's imperial past, and as a relatively weak but nonetheless notable aspect of contemporary culture.

(c) There are also regimes that are hostile to religion, exercising strong regulatory control over them or even trying to eliminate religion outright. China provides a paradigmatic example of a secular control regime—allowing some space for religion, provided it is subject to strong state controls. The most extreme example, historically, of an anti-religious state is arguably Hoxha's Albania, where the effort was made to abolish religion entirely.

---

15 Greece Const, art 3(1).

19.4 The scope of religious freedom protections

The domain protected by freedom of religion or belief is broad but ultimately distinguishable from other major types of human activity and thought such as aesthetics, politics, economics, personal opinion, and (to take dishonest activity into account) fraud.

The core domain of freedom of religion or belief is the realm of inner belief that is central to human dignity. Referred to as the *forum internum*, this domain has long been held in constitutional theory and in human rights law to be absolutely beyond state regulation. This absolute protection reflects in part the notion that lack of access to other minds means that state intervention in this domain is literally impossible, although modern awareness of drug therapies and other types of totalitarian mind control suggest that the internal domain is less immune to attack than may have been thought. The precise outer limits of the *forum internum* are contested, but appear to include the right to have or adopt a religion, as well as the right to change one's religion,[16] and the right (if one so chooses) not to disclose one's religion. For this right to be meaningful, there also needs to be a right to receive information about alternative religions or beliefs, although it is more difficult to say that providing such information is a purely internal forum matter.

Despite the links of conversion rights to the internal forum, a number of jurisdictions continue to maintain anti-conversion legislation. For example, several states in India have adopted such laws, which have been sustained on the basis of a strained interpretation of the right to 'profess, practise and propagate' religion under Article 25 of the Indian Constitution.[17] Similarly, Article 11 of the Malaysian Constitution forbids 'propagation of any religious doctrine or belief among persons professing the religion of Islam.' A Malaysian woman who converted to Christianity and sought to change her name to Lina Joy and her religious designation on her identity card, was prevented from doing so (and blocked from marrying a non-Muslim) by a decision of the Malaysian High Court.[18]

However the outer boundaries of internal forum rights are ultimately delineated, this sphere is quite narrow by comparison to the domain of external religious conduct, or what the international instruments refer to as 'manifestation' of religion. Most constitutional disputes about freedom of religion or belief involve this external domain. Protections of religious freedom in this area are strong, but not unlimited. Here we concentrate on the scope of coverage of the right to freedom of religion or belief. International law protects the 'freedom, either individually or in community with others and in public or private, to manifest [one's] belief in worship, observance, practice, and teaching.'[19] Various constitutions refer to the right to engage in religious conduct in different ways, some echoing the international language of 'manifestation' and some using other formulations such as 'free exercise' or 'free practice.'

---

16 Although international instruments currently describe freedom of religion or belief as a right 'to have or adopt' rather than as a right to 'change' one's religion (as originally provided in Article 18 of the UDHR), this change of locution does not to 'restrict or derogat[e] from any right defined in the Universal Declaration of Human Rights.' See 1981 Declaration, art 8 (implicitly reaffirming the right to change religions); UN Human Rights Committee, General Comment 22, paragraph 5 (noting that the right to 'have or adopt' a religion includes 'the right to replace one's current religion or belief with another or to adopt atheistic views'). For further analysis of the conversion issue, see Interim Report of the UN Special Rapporteur on Freedom of Religion or Belief, A/67/303, transmitted to General Assembly, 13 August 2012; presented at the General Assembly, 25 October 2012; available at http://www.religlaw.org/document.php?DocumentID=5998.

17 *See also* Malaysia Const art 11 (limiting 'propagating').

18 Malaysia, International Religious Freedom Report 2008, released by the US Department of State.

19 ICCPR, art 18 (1).

The precise extent of this freedom depends on both the constitutional language and the way it is interpreted by the courts or other relevant institutions.[20]

Questions that arise in constitutional cases include whether the right to manifest extends only to matters commanded by or required by religion or whether it also extends to other conduct that may be motivated, though not required by, a religion, such as accepting a call to the clergy or assisting religious personnel in carrying out their tasks. While constitutional protections almost always include the right to worship, questions sometimes arise about the right to rent, acquire, own, construct, and use buildings appropriate for worship. For many religious people, however, religious practice goes beyond simply worshipping and extends to a wide variety of activities including: the clothes one wears, the food one eats, the holidays and days of rest one observes, the religious materials one studies, the structuring of family life, and the right to share one's beliefs with others in non-coercive ways. Constitutional courts face complicated questions of determining how far their particular constitutional regimes will recognize behavior as protected free exercise of religion.

In addition, religious freedom is generally exercised within a religious community of some kind. Such communities may be highly structured and formal, and have legal personality, or (at the other end of the spectrum) they may be relatively informal groups of like-minded individuals. The constitutional question that then arises is the extent to which religious freedom protections in constitutions extend to religious communities or groups. Some constitutions extend explicit protection to some or all religious groups, but even those that state the constitutional right as an individual rather than a collective one have tended to recognize that this right must encompass autonomy for religious communities to at least some extent (see generally Robbers 2002). However, the precise scope of this right is contested in many states. For example, while it is clear that religious communities themselves (i.e. churches, synagogues, mosques, and the like) can assert religious autonomy claims, it is not clear how far along the horizontal continuum of religiously affiliated institutions (e.g. theological schools, universities, primary and secondary schools, hospitals, other charitable organizations, religious media institutions, and the like) religious autonomy protections extend.

Similarly, while it is clear that religious communities should have great autonomy in selecting, training, supervising, disciplining, and dismissing their religious leaders and representatives, how deep should religious autonomy reach in its vertical dimension? For example, should it reach down from clergy and official religious representatives, through religious teachers, all the way to teachers of secular subjects in religious schools? What of administrative staff of religious leaders, employees of religiously affiliated hospitals or other charitable organizations? Janitors, gardeners, and others performing tasks that are arguably exclusively secular? Recent major cases in the United States[21] and the European Court of Human Rights[22] have confirmed the right of religious communities to autonomy in appointing clergy and at least some teachers, but it remains unclear how deep, vertically, this autonomy right will extend.

Closely connected to religious autonomy rights is the right to legal recognition and to the acquisition of legal entity status. In contemporary societies, it is difficult to carry out the full range of activities of even a secular non-profit organization without acquiring some form of

---

20 For the leading international catalogue of the types of conduct covered, *see* 1981 Declaration, art 6.
21 *Hosanna-Tabor Evangelical Lutheran Church v EEOC*, 132 S C 694 (2012).
22 *Siebenhaar v Germany*, ECtHR App No 18136/02 (3 February 2011); *Obst v Germany*, ECtHR App No 425/03 (23 September 2010); *Schüth v Germany*, ECtHR App No 1620/03 (10 September 2010); *Fernández Martínez v Spain*, ECtHR App No 56030/07 (15 May 2012).

legal entity status. This is necessary to open bank accounts, rent or acquire property, apply for land use approvals, enter into contracts, hire employees, defend legal rights in court, and so on. There is now an extensive body of jurisprudence in the European Court of Human Rights affirming the right of religious communities to acquire such status.[23]

19.5 Limitations on religious freedom

While protections for freedom of religion or belief are broad and fundamental, they are not unlimited except in the narrow domain of *forum internum*. As a practical matter, it is the determination of the limits that becomes the critical freedom of religion issue in most legal systems. Whether such limitations are expressly stated in constitutional texts,[24] or simply inferred in the process of constitutional interpretation (as in the United States), no system gives people the right to behave in full compliance with their religious beliefs regardless of the harm this may cause. Moreover, even where limitations are expressly spelled out, much still depends on the intellectual constructs that judiciaries develop (e.g. balancing, proportionality, compelling state-interest tests, narrow tailoring, etc.) in applying constitutional limitation provisions in specific cases.

A fundamental issue faced by every constitutional system is what happens when freedom of religion norms collide with the requirements of ordinary legislation. Is the legislative branch the only arbiter of constitutional values in this context, so that only the legislature can approve exceptions to general rules based on conscientious claims? Or can (at least some) judges determine (at least in some contexts) that the constitutional values prevail? If the latter, is the judicial action understood as a judicially crafted exception to legislation, or, on the contrary, as judicial contouring of normal legislation to preclude legislative exceptions to the general and overriding demands of the constitutional order? However this jurisprudential question is resolved, it is clear that one of the central constitutional debates involving religious freedom is whether and under what circumstances judges are authorized to craft exemptions (or contour legislation) to protect manifestations of religious freedom. In the United States, the Supreme Court has said that judges do not have this authority, at least with respect to general and neutral laws.[25] Congress and a majority of the individual states in the United States have held that judges do have that authority (where the law in question is not supported by a compelling state interest or is not narrowly tailored to further such an interest).[26] The result is considerable confusion and ongoing litigation.

The European Court of Human Rights frequently determines that particular legislation or governmental conduct violates provisions of the European Convention on Human Rights (ECHR), such as protection of freedom of religion under Article 9, but must leave correction of the problems to national governments. At the national level, most constitutional courts in Europe do address religious freedom claims, often using essentially the same type of proportionality analysis used by the Strasbourg Court. On the other hand, there are clearly

---

23 *See*, e.g. *Metropolitan Church of Bessarabia v Moldova*, ECtHR App No 45701/99 (13 December 2001); *Moscow Branch of the Salvation Army v Russia*, ECtHR App No 72881/01 (5 October 2006); *Church of Scientology Moscow v Russia*, ECtHR App No 18147/02 (5 April 2007); *Svyato-Mykhaylivska Parafiya v Ukraine*, ECtHR App No 77703/01 (14 September 2007).

24 *See*, e.g. South Africa Const, art 36(1) (1996);

25 *Employment Division v Smith*, 494 US 872 (1990).

26 For a summary of the complex evolution of case-law in this area, *see* Bassett, Durham & Smith, §§ 2.60–2.69.

jurisdictions where constitutional limitations have been construed to allow ordinary legislation to trump religious freedom claims,[27] and there are still other jurisdictions where judicial review to enforce constitutional protections is not available (as in China) or is limited (as in France or Poland).

While specific limitation provisions are diverse, the fact that all but a handful of constitutions have been adopted since the adoption of the Universal Declaration of Human Rights (UDHR) has led to significant convergence in limitation provisions. While some constitutions have a general limitations clause that applies to all human rights provisions (like Article 29 of the UDHR),[28] others have provisions specifically tailored to religious freedom protections (like Article 18(3) of the International Covenant on Civil and Political Rights [ICCPR]).[29] Either way, the basic features of limitation clause analysis are similar.

Typically, before limitations clauses come into play, it is necessary to make a threshold showing that there has been a *prima facie* violation of religious freedom. In the European Court of Human Rights, the question is whether there has been an 'interference' with an Article 9 right. In the United States, the question is whether there is a substantial burden on free exercise of religion. The verbal formula varies slightly, with 'interference' focusing somewhat more on state intermeddling with freedom, and 'burden' focusing more on the weight of the harm imposed. Once this threshold test is met, the state generally has the burden of showing that a particular limitation is permissible. The elements of what must be shown are stated well in Article 18(3) of the ICCPR:

> Freedom to manifest one's religion or beliefs may be subject only to such limitations as are prescribed by law and are necessary to protect public safety, order, health, or morals or the fundamental rights and freedoms of others.

Under this provision, a state must first demonstrate that the particular limitation is 'prescribed by law.' This has come to mean not only that the limitation is formally grounded in law, but also that it is qualitatively consistent with the rule of law in that it is clear and non-retroactive, and does not allow arbitrary or discriminatory application.

Second, the limitation must further one of a limited set of legitimating objectives. Both the UN Human Rights Committee and the European Court of Human Rights have determined that the enumerated objectives specified in the treaties they administer are exclusive. Thus, to the extent that national security concerns are not independently covered by the enumerated grounds, they do not justify limitations on religious freedom.[30] The 'compelling state interest' approach applied by many jurisdictions in the United States allows consideration, at least in theory, of a broader range of justifications for imposing limitations.

Third, even if the first two requirements are met, a limitation cannot be justified unless it is 'necessary' (Article 18 ICCPR) or 'necessary in a democratic society' (Article 9 ECHR). As a practical matter, it is the interpretation of 'necessity' and the proportionality analysis it requires that is typically crucial to determining whether particular limitation are permissible. This requires the state to show that such restrictions are more than merely convenient,

27 *See*, e.g. *Hiang Leng Colin v Public Prosecutor* [1994] 3 SLR(R) [Singapore Law Reports (Reissue)] 209.
28 *See*, e.g. South Africa Const, art 36(1) (1996).
29 *See*, e.g. India Const, art 25; Singapore Const, art 15.
30 General Comment 22, para. 8; *Nolan and K v Russia*, ECtHR App No 2512/04 (12 February 2009).

efficient, or beneficial in some way. It has to demonstrate that the restrictions were necessary. This does not mean that there was no other alternative, but does place a significant burden on the state to make its case.

The precise level of the burden and the type of argument and evidence that will be considered satisfactory to discharge that burden differs from state to state. In some states, courts will take into account—sometimes determinatively—whether there was any 'less restrictive means that could have been taken to achieve the same ends.' Even if those means may have been costlier or less convenient, the state may still be expected to take the more rights-respecting option (although there is usually a limit to the difficulties that a state is expected to surmount before restricting religious freedom can be justified).

In other states, the courts emphasize a proportionality analysis, looking at the degree of restriction on religious freedom and weighing this against the ends that a regulation seeks to achieve. For example, section 2(a) of the Canadian Charter of Rights and Freedoms (Part I of the Constitution Act 1982) on freedom of religion is limited by section 1:

> The rights and freedoms set out in the Canadian Charter are subject only to such reasonable limits prescribed by law as can be demonstrably justified in a free and democratic society.

A two-part test concerning this section was articulated by the Supreme Court of Canada in *R v Oakes*.[31] The first element is that a restriction on this right must be 'an objective related to concerns which are pressing and substantial in a free and democratic society.' The second element, also known as the proportionality test, requires evidence that 'the means chosen are reasonable and demonstrably justified.'[32] This test was later applied in the case of *Multani v Marguerite-Bourgeoys (Commission scolaire)*,[33] where the court considered whether a ban on Sikh students carrying kirpans (ceremonial daggers) for religious purposes in a public school was a permissible limitation on the right to freedom of religion. The majority judgment, delivered by Justice Louise Charron, held that the school could not discharge its burden of proving that prohibiting the daggers was a reasonable limit on the student's constitutional freedom of religion.[34]

The use of a proportionality approach to determine whether a limitation on the right to religious freedom is appropriate has also been employed in South Africa. There, the critical question has been taken to be 'whether the limitation is reasonable and justifiable in an open and democratic society based on human dignity, equality and freedom.'[35]

Still other approaches might require the state to demonstrate a pressing need of some kind in order to restrict religious freedom or to restrict certain elements of religious freedom. For example, the limitation on the right to self-determination of religious communities in Germany depends on the 'law that applies to all,' as set out in article 137 (III) of the Weimar Constitution.[36] Article 137 (III) states that 'Religious societies shall regulate and administer their affairs independently within the limits of the law that applies to all.' This limitation is

---

31 [1986] 1 SCR 103.
32 [1986] 1 SCR 103, at 70.
33 [2006] 1 SCR 256, 2006 SCC 6.
34 [2006] 1 SCR 256, at 49–79.
35 [2002] ZACC 1, 2002 (2) SA 794, at 45.
36 Incorporated into the German Basic Law by art 140.

said to have a 'special meaning'; that is, 'A law that applies to all is only such a law that provides for the *pressing needs* of the society as a whole' (Robbers 2010, 159, emphasis added).

One ground for restricting religious freedom that is common to most constitutional systems is interference with the rights and freedoms of others. Some religious traditional practices may collide with basic human rights. A common conflict of rights is between equality and religious freedom. Many religions traditionally set out at the very least differentiated gender roles for men and women, and often support or reinforce women's subordination and inferiority to men. Inequality remains commonplace today, and it is only in very recent times that any of the mainstream world religions have permitted men and women equal leadership roles (particularly within the clergy or religious leadership). One example of structural change is the General Synod of the Church of England's Priests (Ordination of Women) Measure 1993. The difficult question in this area is whether the state should coerce such ecclesiastical changes, or allow religious communities to determine their approach to these issues internally.

Even more complex problems arise when religious communities operate schools, hospitals, and other welfare organizations. These organizations often wish to discriminate on other grounds in hiring (and sometimes with respect to the groups to which services are provided) in order to give preference to their co-religionists or to exclude people whose behavior is considered wrong or sinful within the religion (for example, gay men and lesbians, or heterosexual couples living in an unmarried relationship). Such employment preferences are seen by at least some religious organizations as an important element of their religious autonomy and freedom, enabling them to live in compliance with their religious teachings. However, with the increase of regulation covering issues such as workplace rights and equal opportunity laws, the capacity of religions to shield themselves from ordinary legal regulation is being challenged. In some states, religious groups are still given considerable protection from the operation of ordinary laws. For example, article 7(2) of the British Employment Equality (Religion or Belief) Regulations No 1660/2003 provides an exemption for employers from the general provisions on religious discrimination if:

(a) being of a particular religion or belief is a genuine and determining occupational requirement;
(b) it is proportionate to apply that requirement in the particular case; and
(c) either:

  (i) the person to whom that requirement is applied does not meet it, or
  (ii) the employer is not satisfied, and in all the circumstances it is reasonable for him not to be satisfied, that that person meets it,

and this paragraph applies whether or not the employer has an ethos based on religion or belief.

Temperman distinguishes between states that allow for exemptions based on 'genuine occupational requirements,' or on the religious ethos of an institution. He cites 22 countries that provide exemptions of the first kind, while giving examples of 19 countries that provide exemptions of the second (Temperman, 267–70).

In other instances, including in the case-law of the European Court of Human Rights, this protection has been limited, and religious groups are at least being obliged to comply with certain procedural requirements to attract a more general immunity. In still others, religious groups are increasingly subject to ordinary laws around issues such as workplace regulation and non-discrimination laws. For example, in the Canadian case of *Re Governing Council of Salvation Army, Canada East et al and Attorney General of Ontario*,[37] the question put to the Ontario Court by the Salvation Army was whether the changes to the provincial pensions legislation were against the autonomy of religious organizations. The court held that right to religious freedom under the Charter of Rights did not require an exemption for religious communities from pension regulations.

One final type of limitation typical in states with various types of separationist constitutions is a constraint on the extent to which religion can be aided by the state and the extent to which religious influence can extend into public affairs. Classic examples of this type of provision are the United States clause forbidding 'establishment' of religion, or Article 14 of the Russian constitutions, which not only forbids any official sponsorship of religion but also requires secularity of the state, separation of religious associations and the state, and equality of religious associations before the law. While constraints of this type have profound practical ramifications in the states that deploy them, they are generally thought of as institutional protections of religious freedom rather than as a narrowing of private manifestation rights.

19.6 Conclusion: areas of current contestation and opportunities for further research and discussion

In liberal democracies, questions about the appropriate role of religion in the public sphere are rising as both secularism and religious diversity increase. For some, the best way to deal with the conflicts between religious and secular world views, or between different religious views, is to keep religion in the private sphere and to maintain public debate as a non-religious realm. For others, such an approach privileges one approach (secular) above religious values and requires religious people to abandon their most deeply held beliefs as a price for entering the public sphere.

As the value and place of religion comes under increasing scrutiny, a number of other questions are being debated. Why should religion have a protected place in constitutions when other preferences do not? As values of equality and secularism rise in many countries and come into conflict with at least some religious traditions, does religious freedom justify permitting religions to make religion-based differentiations in employment and other contexts, or does it constitute impermissible discrimination in violation of human rights? And what branch of government is best suited to balancing out the competing interests when religious rights conflict with other rights or important social values—courts, legislatures, or the executive? These complex issues are not susceptible to easy resolution and the debates over the answers to these questions are likely to continue for many years.

The issues in many less liberal constitutional systems are more stark. Religious organizations and individuals, particularly unpopular minorities, can face hurdles—from administrative burdens to serious violations of their human rights—if they seek to exercise their religious freedom. The constitutions themselves may facilitate this by privileging some religions or condemning others as heretical or dangerous. At other times, ostensible constitutional protections are either not enforced or applied in a discriminatory or haphazard way. In such states, the protection that the constitution appears to provide is a façade that offers little real benefit for those facing restrictions on their rights. The real questions in such systems are not the complex balancing of competing interests within the legal system, but rather political questions about ways in which religious freedom can be enhanced on the ground.

37 (1992) 88 DLR (4th) 238.

References

Bassett, W, Durham, WC & Smith, R (2012). *Religious Organizations and the Law* (New York: Thomson Reuters/West).

Durham, WC (2012). 'Patterns of Religion State Relations', in Witte, J & Green, MC (eds) (2012). *Religion and Human Rights: An Introduction* (Oxford: Oxford University Press), 360–78.

—— & Sewell, E (2006). 'Definition of Religion', in *Religious Organizations in the United States: A Study of Identity, Liberty, and the Law* (Serritella, JA et al (eds), Durham NC: Carolina Academic Press).

—— & Scharffs, B (2010). *Law and Religion: National, International and Comparative Perspectives* (New York: Aspen Publishers, Wolters Kluwer Law & Business).

Greenawalt, K (1984). 'Religion as a Concept in Constitutional Law', *California Law Review* 72: 753–816.

Pew Forum on Religion and Public Life (2009). *Global Restrictions on Religion*, available at http://www.pewforum.org/uploadedFiles/Topics/Issues/Government/restrictions-fullreport.pdf.

Potter, PB (2003). 'Belief in Control: Regulation of Religion in China', *The China Quarterly* 317–37.

Robbers, G (ed) (2002). *Church Autonomy: A Comparative Survey* (Frankfurt: Peter Lang).

—— (2010). *Religion and Law in Germany* (New York: Kluwer Law International).

Stahnke, T & Blitt, R (2005). 'The Religion-State Relationship and the Right to Freedom of Religion or Belief: A Comparative Textual Analysis of the Constitutions of Predominantly Muslim Countries', *Georgetown Journal of International Law* 36:947–1078.

Temperman, J (2010). *State-Religion Relationships and Human Rights Law: Towards a Right to Religiously Neutral Governance* (Leiden: Martinus Nijhoff Publishers).

International documents

Declaration on the Elimination of All Forms of Intolerance and Discrimination Based on Religion or Belief, UN General Assembly Resolution 36/55, November 25, 1981 (1981 Declaration).

International Covenant on Civil and Political Rights, adopted and opened for signature by United Nations General Assembly Resolution 2200A (XXI) on 16 December 1966 (ICCPR).

UN Human Rights Committee, *General Comment 22: The Right to Freedom of Thought, Conscience and Religion (Art 18)*, 48th sess, UN Doc. CCPR/C/21/Rev.1/Add.4 (30 July 1993).

Universal Declaration of Human Rights, UN General Assembly Resolution 217A (III), December 10, 1948 (UDHR).

Additional reading

An-Na'im, A (2008). *Islam and the Secular State: Negotiating the Future of Shari'a* (Cambridge: Harvard University Press).

Choper, J (1982). 'Defining "Religion" in the First Amendment', *University of Illinois Law Review* 1982:579–613.

Evans, C (2001). *Freedom of Religion under the European Convention on Human Rights* (New York: Oxford University Press).

Ferrari, S & Cristofori, R (2011). *Law and Religion in the 21st Century: Relations between States and Religious Communities* (Surrey, England: Ashgate).

Glendon, M & Zacher, H (2012). *Universal Rights in a World of Diversity: The Case of Religious Freedom* (Vatican City: Pontificia Academia Scientiarum Socialium).

Greenawalt, K (2006). *Religion and the Constitution* (2 vols) (Princeton: Princeton University Press).

Grim, B & Finke, R (2011). *The Price of Freedom Denied: Religious Persecution and Conflict in the Twenty-First Century* (Cambridge: Cambridge University Press).

Hill, M, Sandberg, R & Doe, N (2011). *Religion and Law in the United Kingdom* (The Netherlands: Kluwer Law International).

Lindholm, T, Durham, WC & Tahzib-Lie, B (eds) (2004). *Facilitating Freedom of Religion or Belief: A Deskbook* (Leiden: Martinus Nijhoff Publishers).

Martínez-Torrón, J & Durham, WC (eds) (2010). *Religion and the Secular State / La Religion et l'État laïque*, Interim National Reports Issued for the Occasion of the XVIIIth International Congress of Comparative Law (Provo: International Center for Law and Religion Studies), 3–5, available at http://iclrs.org/content/blurb/files/Religion%20and%20the%20Secular%20State%20-%20 Interim%20Reports%202010.07.27.pdf.

Rivers, J (2010). *The Law of Organized Religions: Between Establishment and Secularism* (Oxford: Oxford University Press).

Robbers, G (ed) (2005). *State and Church in the European Union* (2nd edn) (Baden-Baden: Nomos Verlagsgesellschaft).

Sajo, A & Uitz, R (2012). 'Freedom of Religion', in Rosenfeld, M & Sajo, A (eds), *The Oxford Handbook of Comparative Constitutional Law* (Oxford: Oxford University Press), 909–28.

Scolnicov, A (2011). *Right to Religious Freedom in International Law: Between Group Rights and Individual Rights* (New York: Routledge).

Tahzib, B (1996). *Freedom of Religion or Belief: Ensuring Effective International Legal Protection* (The Hague: Martinus Nijhoff Publishers).

Taylor, P (2005). *Freedom of Religion: UN and European Human Rights Law and Practice* (Cambridge: Cambridge University Press).

van der Vyver, J & Witte, J (eds) (1996). *Religious Human Rights in Global Perspective: Legal Perspectives* (Boston: Martinus Nijhoff Publishers).

Vickers, L (2008). *Religious Freedom, Religious Discrimination and the Workplace* (Oxford: Hart Publishing).

3. Due process

Procedural fairness generally

Sophie Boyron and Wendy Lacey

20.1 Introduction

Legal rights and interests are protected in myriad ways and not always in a substantive sense or through entrenched constitutional provisions designed to prescribe or limit power. Procedural safeguards that regulate the exercise of power have historically played an important role in protecting rights to life, liberty and property. As Felix Frankfurter of the United States Supreme Court stated, '[t]he history of liberty has largely been the history of the observance of procedural safeguards'.[1] And, as Jackson J noted in *Shaughnessy v United States*,[2] '[s]evere substantive laws can be endured if they are fairly and impartially applied'.

Still, the treatment of procedural safeguards throughout history has also reflected profound differences between the common law and civil law worlds. While common law jurisdictions attached great importance to the guarantee of liberty through appropriate procedures, civil law jurisdictions gave priority to the detailed identification and declaration of rights as substantive limits on power. Less thought was given in civil law systems to ensuring these rights procedurally. Nowadays, constitutional orders widely recognise the necessity of procedures for preserving the rights and freedoms of citizens and for preventing the abuse of power by governmental institutions. This trend has also been influenced by the increasing recognition, since 1945, of procedural rights in international human rights law.

20.2 The origins of procedural fairness

The concept of procedural fairness—also frequently referred to as natural justice or due process—is historically rooted in the English common law system; specifically, in the context of judicial review of administrative (or executive) action, and, more generally, from the principles of 'natural justice' that apply to the exercise of judicial and quasi-judicial power. 'Due process' is more commonly used in the United States, where a due process clause is contained in the Fifth Amendment to the US Constitution, although the phrase was originally used in

---

1 *McNabb v United States*, 318 US 332 (1943).
2 345 US 206 (1953) (Jackson J).

a 1354 iteration of the Magna Carta. In the twentieth century, procedural protections took root in civil law jurisdictions, where many developed what is commonly called the 'rights of defence'.

The proliferation of international and regional human rights conventions since World War II has witnessed an increased focus on the express protection of individual rights through procedural guarantees. These instruments blend the English approach of protecting the right of an individual to be heard before an impartial authority, with the US and European preference towards the inclusion of express statements of rights in binding instruments. Developments in public international law since 1945 have played a significant instrumental role in the spread of procedural guarantees in domestic constitutional and legal settings throughout the world, but those developments have not resulted in their harmonious adoption and there exist many variations between jurisdictions in the nature and scope to which those principles are both legally and constitutionally protected.

20.2.1 Common law origins

In English common law, the rules of procedural fairness are viewed as manifestations of the rule of law (see Jowell, 12)—a doctrine considered fundamental in the unwritten British constitutional system. The Diceyan conception of the rule of law embodied three elements: first, that individuals should not be subject to the power of officials wielding wide, discretionary powers, or be punished except for breaches of the law established before a court; secondly, that all persons should be subjected equally to one law, and; thirdly, that the constitutional law should be the result of judicial decisions determining the rights of private persons in particular cases.[3] Despite being widely criticised, the Diceyan conception of the rule of law remains influential, as do the values underpinning it; legality, certainty, consistency, accountability, efficiency, due process, and access to justice (see Jowell, 7–13).

Procedural fairness requirements were first reflected in Clause 39 of the Magna Carta, adopted in 1215:

> No free man shall be seized or imprisoned, or stripped of his rights or possessions, or outlawed or exiled, or deprived of his standing in any other way, nor will we proceed with force against him, or send others to do so, except by the lawful judgment of his equals or by the law of the land.

Subsequent versions of the Magna Carta—in particular, a statute of Edward III in 1354 titled 'Liberty of the Subject'—included the phrase 'due process of law'. This terminology, repeated in the Fifth Amendment to the US Constitution, tends to imply a substantive distinction from the mere right to be treated 'according to law'. Under the British Constitution, the protection of procedural fairness is left to the common law, operating primarily through principles of statutory construction and ultimately remaining subject to the doctrine of parliamentary supremacy (and thus to statutory override). The principles of procedural fairness do not act as a direct limit on legislative power but 'as a basis for the evaluation of all laws' (Jowell, 17).

At common law, procedural fairness is frequently used to describe a set of principles that govern the exercise of executive power, whereas natural justice has traditionally been used in

---

3 In reference to Dicey.

reference to procedural requirements attached to the exercise of power by courts and tribunals. Both terms are now used interchangeably. Natural justice contains two basic rules, described by Wade and Forsyth as follows: 'a man may not be a judge in his own cause' (the rule against bias) and 'a man's defence must always be fairly heard' (the fair-hearing rule) (Wade & Forsyth, 440). Both the fair-hearing rule and the rule against bias are designed to ensure that the rights and freedoms of individuals are interfered with only in accordance with the law. In the United Kingdom, the application of procedural fairness requirements to administrative decision-making developed as a component of the *ultra vires* doctrine, based on an implication that, unless Parliament otherwise provides, Parliament does not authorise the exercise of powers in breach of the principles of natural justice.[4] A failure to comply with the principles of natural justice will therefore render a decision void or at least susceptible to being set aside by a court.

In common law systems, procedural rights have historically been protected through judicial review by independent courts equipped with jurisdiction to award various remedies; in civil law systems, review occurs in specialised administrative courts. Many constitutions throughout the world, including Australia's,[5] entrench various prerogative writs and remedies designed to safeguard procedural rights. *Habeas corpus*, for example, is entrenched in the constitutions of Paraguay,[6] Costa Rica[7] and Kenya.[8] Additional prerogative writs have subsequently been adopted in various jurisdictions, including the writ of *amparo* (a remedy available to a person whose life, liberty and security is unlawfully violated or threatened with violation by a public official)[9] and the writ of *habeas data* (a remedy that enables individuals to protect their image, privacy and reputation through the release and correction of information held about them by public officials).[10]

The natural law origins of the principles of natural justice were, at one period, considered to restrain the legislature, enabling the courts to hold laws invalid where they made a man judge in his own cause or were against 'common right or reason'.[11] The doctrine of parliamentary supremacy ultimately prevailed and the rules of natural justice are now approached as common law principles that govern the interpretation and application of valid statutes. In this sense, the principles of natural justice are susceptible to statutory erosion or modification. The likelihood of such statutory override is less pronounced following the incorporation into English law of the European Convention on Human Rights (ECHR), through the passage of the Human Rights Act 1998 (UK); the common law system is now overlaid with the rules and principles contained in the ECHR.

---

4 *Fairmount Investments Ltd v Secretary of State for the Environment*, 1263 (Lord Russell); *Ridge v Baldwin*, 80 (Lord Reid).

5 Australian Constitution, 1900, s 75(v).

6 Constitution of Paraguay, 1992, Article 135.

7 Constitution of Costa Rica, 1949, Article 48.

8 Constitution of Kenya, 2010, Article 25(d).

9 The writ of *amparo* is protected in many constitutions throughout the world, including the Constitution of Mexico, 1917, Articles 103 and 107 and the Philippines Constitution 1987, Article VII, s 5(5), Administrative Matter No. 07-9-12 SC, effective 24 October 2007.

10 The writ of *habeas data* is protected, in various forms, in constitutions including the 1988 Constitution of Brazil, Article 5, LXXII; the 1992 Constitution of Paraguay, Article 135; the Argentinian Constitution (following a 1994 amendment), Article 43; and the Philippines Constitution 1987, Article VII, s 5(5), Administrative Matter No. 08-1-16 SC, effective 2 February 2008.

11 *Dr Bonham's* case (1610) 8 Co Rep 113b at 118a (Lord Coke CJ).

The common law principles of natural justice—now generally referred to as procedural fairness—have been extremely influential in other common law jurisdictions. However, constitutional differences have resulted in important differences in the protection of fundamental process rights. These differences extend to the specific terminology used, the content of fundamental process requirements, the extent to which protection is given to substantive— in addition to procedural—rules, and the degree to which procedural requirements are enforceable by the courts through the process of judicial review.

20.2.2 The US due process clause

By entrenching both judicial review and due process in a written document, the US Constitution protects procedural fairness requirements in a more comprehensive fashion than the English common law. The due process clause in the US Constitution is contained in the Fifth Amendment, which provides that, '[n]o person shall be … deprived of life, liberty, or property, without due process of law'.[12] This amendment applies to federal action; the Fourteenth Amendment extends the due process requirement to the states. The due process clause contained in the US Constitution extends to legislative as well as executive and judicial action. It has also been interpreted by the Supreme Court to protect substantive as well as procedural rights, requiring that governments appropriately justify interferences with an individual's fundamental rights.[13] The rules of procedural fairness identified as constitutional requirements of the Fifth Amendment are not susceptible to complete statutory override, as in the United Kingdom.

Influenced by the interpretation of Lord Coke, the phrases 'law of the land' and 'due process of law' were often used interchangeably, were both reflected in early constitutions of the states within the US and were treated as equivalent terms by the Supreme Court.[14] In early US case law, 'law of the land' and 'due process' clauses in state constitutions were interpreted as not having the effect of restraining the power of the legislature.[15] Consequently, any law could be the 'law of the land' and any process could satisfy the requirement of 'due process of law'. However, that approach did not ultimately prevail, given the absence of a doctrine of parliamentary supremacy under the US Constitution and the acceptance that, in the US, sovereignty resides with the people.[16] This approach was also supported by the availability of judicial review under the US Constitution. As Justice Curtis stated in *Murray v Hoboken*, in reference to the Fifth Amendment,

> [t]he article is a restraint on the legislative as well as on the executive and judicial powers of the government, and cannot be so construed as to leave congress free to make any process 'due process of law', by its mere will.[17]

Arguably, 'due process of law' points to the law's substantive content and implies procedures that are more likely to induce fair or just outcomes. Indeed, the inclusion of a due process

12 Section 1 of the Fourteenth Amendment extends due process of law to the American States.
13 See, for example, *Griswold v Connecticut* 381 US 479 (US); *Roe v Wade* 410 US 113 (US).
14 See Goldberg, 366, citing Justice Curtis in *Murray v Hoboken*.
15 See *Dartmouth v Woodward* 1 NH 111, 65 NH 473 (1817); *State v ----*, 2 NC (1 Hayw.) 50, 52 (1794).
16 See *Taylor v Porter*, 4 Hill at 144.
17 59 US (18 How.) 272, 276 (1855).

clause in the US Constitution, coupled with the power of the Supreme Court to review the constitutional validity of legislation, have combined in the US constitutional context to effect very different methods of protection (when compared with the United Kingdom) for procedural fairness in the exercise of power.

In other common law jurisdictions, such as Australia and Canada, the constitutional protection of procedural fairness or due process requirements reflects elements of both the English and American models. The US Constitution has also been influential in the design of new and amended national constitutions, including its combined features of entrenched judicial review and the due process clause as measures for protecting the individual rights and the rule of law through procedural safeguards. The 1988 Constitution of Brazil, for example, entrenches judicial review and provides that 'no one shall be deprived of freedom or of his assets without the due process of law'.[18] Since 1945, international and regional human rights instruments have provided an additional framework against which nations have modelled new, and amended existing, constitutions. For nations such as the UK, those instruments overlay the existing constitutional system and have the capacity to stimulate change within it (see Wade & Forsyth, 445–8; Lester & Beattie).

20.2.3 The rights of defence in civil law jurisdictions

For many lawyers, the treatment of procedural issues highlights the differences between common and civil law jurisdictions. Yet, this may not constitute an entirely faithful representation of the reality, especially with regard to administrative law. Whilst the *droit administratif* had been roundly criticised by Dicey in the 'Law of the Constitution',[19] French administrative law displayed a healthy interest in procedural matters from an early period. In 1913, the *Conseil d'État* recognised an automatic right to a hearing before any judicial body, in *Tery*.[20] This decision was particularly important as the administration had set up a great many judicial panels for disciplinary matters and the regulation of specific professions (e.g. the medical profession). The landmark case stipulated, unsurprisingly, that applicants before such panels had a right to be heard at first instance and on appeal, even in the absence of any legislative requirement to do so. Soon, other cases indicated that such procedural rights also extended to the administration for certain decisions. In 1944, the *Conseil d'État* asserted in *Trompier-Gravier*[21] the existence of rights of defence (in this case, a right to a hearing) in relation to administrative decisions that imposed a sanction or that affected seriously and detrimentally an individual's position.

Although approached narrowly at first, French courts soon widened this obligation: today, all that is needed is a decision affecting someone adversely, considered on the basis of the individual's behaviour or actions. In fact, this right is even imposed when someone is seeking a licence or a benefit for the first time.[22] Furthermore, the rights of defence have received

---

18 Article 5, LIV.

19 Dicey's criticisms, harsh and ill-informed in the early editions, were more measured in the last (8th, 1915).

20 CE 20 June 1913, rec 736, concl Corneille. A secondary school teacher had been dismissed for disciplinary reasons. He challenged the decision before the appropriate disciplinary panel but lost. He appealed but was unable to attend the appeal hearing for medical reasons. The disciplinary panel confirmed the original judgment despite his justified absence. The *Conseil d'État* declared that the rights of defence had been breached and quashed the appeal.

21 CE Sect 5 May 1944, rec 133.

22 See CE 25 November 1994, Palem, rec 753.

constitutional recognition by the *Conseil constitutionnel*.[23] In a decision of 1987,[24] the *Conseil constitutionnel* specified that the requirements of the rights of defence made it necessary for the decision of the competition council to be reviewed by the administrative courts. It explained that the impact and import of the decisions of the competition council were such that courts involved in reviewing those decisions needed to have powers of interim relief. As the legislation aimed to bestow this review on the private law courts without introducing any interim relief provision, it was held to be unconstitutional.

The protection of the rights of defence and of process rights in general spread to other civil law countries, which commonly recognise and protect a large number of process rights through case law,[25] legislation[26] and constitutional provisions.[27]

20.2.4 Post-war international developments

Since World War II, procedural requirements have increasingly been reflected in international, regional and national human rights instruments and, while the formal declaration of fundamental rights and freedoms is not unique in a historical sense, their development and adoption by nations has had a significant impact on domestic legal systems and the constitutional frameworks that govern them. Perhaps one of the most significant implications of the emergence of international and regional frameworks for human rights protection has been the expansion of the concept of procedural fairness to embody specific *process rights* held by individuals. That shift involves a departure from the common law origins of natural justice and procedural fairness, with its emphasis upon the duties of those exercising power (courts, tribunals, administrative decision-makers) to afford a fair and impartial hearing. It also reflects a departure from the views of Dicey and Bentham on the value of adopting formal statements of the rights and freedoms of individuals.

The development of international legal principles around individual rights, outside international humanitarian law, began with the adoption of the Universal Declaration of Human Rights in 1948. Article 10 of the UDHR provides as follows:

> Everyone is entitled in full equality to a fair and public hearing by an independent and impartial tribunal, in the determination of his rights and obligations and of any criminal charge against him.

The UDHR, though adopted through resolution of the United Nations General Assembly as a non-binding statement of rights,[28] has since acquired a more authoritative status in customary international law and through its use as a model for virtually all subsequent conventions on human rights.[29] Article 6(1) of the European Convention on Human Rights provides that '[i]n the determination of his civil rights and obligations or of any criminal charge against him, everyone is entitled to a fair and public hearing within a reasonable time by an

---

23 The *Conseil constitutionnel* is the equivalent of a constitutional court in the French constitutional order.
24 See C cons n 86-224 DC, competition council.
25 See *il principio del contraddittorio* in Italian public law.
26 See the Dutch General Administrative Law Act of 4 June 1992.
27 See article 105 (c) of the Spanish Constitution: 'The law determines … the procedures to be followed in decision-making; these guarantee the right to a hearing to interested parties when appropriate.'
28 GA Res 217, UN GAOR 3d Sess, UN Doc. A/810 (1948).
29 See generally Hannum.

independent and impartial tribunal established by law'. The International Covenant on Civil and Political Rights (ICCPR) is also replete with procedural guarantees, although articles 9 and 14 are most frequently associated with procedural fairness or due process. Article 2 of the ICCPR, for example, requires member states to ensure that individuals may obtain effective remedies for breaches of their rights before a competent judicial, administrative or legislative authority, and states must also develop the possibility of judicial remedies. The procedural guarantees contained in the major conventions are also seen in human rights instruments dealing with specific subjects, such as children, race, women and disability.[30]

The impact of international instruments on the development of modern constitutions has been significant, and many written constitutions refer expressly to them. The 1993 Constitution of Cambodia, for example, refers directly to the UDHR, the United Nations Charter and other international conventions in Article 31, before setting out a number of procedural guarantees, including the right to file complaints. Other international and regional human rights frameworks providing for the review by supra-national courts or committees have also had considerable impact on domestic legal systems. While some constitutional settings (such as Australia's, where a rigid written document was adopted well before the development of modern international human rights law) have been more resistant to the influences of international human rights law, the general trend worldwide has been to embrace or adapt the provisions of international law in new and revised constitutions.

20.3 The constitutional foundations of procedural fairness

Procedural fairness was not originally conceptualised as a constitutional principle; it was simply a principle of judicial review. Constitutional protection of process rights is strongly influenced by a country's historical origins, legal evolution and political culture, and constitutions vary in their express guarantee of procedural fairness. Most constitutions protect some aspects of procedural fairness, the most common being fairness in criminal procedure.[31]

Judicial adjudication or review is often used as a model when stipulating the hearing rights to be granted prior to an individual determination. Consequently, the principles of judicial independence and impartiality often play a role in the design of the procedure itself. Hearing rights require that the decision-maker explain the arguments that support his/her decision and thereby promote (legal) accountability. Finally, the principle of human dignity plays a significant part in procedural fairness. It is common for process rights to be justified by courts or legislation by reference to a dignitarian rationale; a hearing may not improve the content of the decision (instrumental/utilitarian rationale) but it provides a forum for individuals to present their version of events.[32]

The rule of law is also widely held to justify the requirement of procedural fairness; rules must be clear, accessible to citizens and adopted by transparent processes. The organisation of a hearing ensures that decision-making respects all these requirements. Further, by protecting legal certainty, the rule of law justifies the existence of the principle of procedural legitimate expectations, namely that continual past practices or clear representations by a civil servant create an entitlement to process rights.

---

30 The Convention on the Rights of the Child, for example, requires that a child not be removed from his/her parents unless such decision is authorised by a competent authority subject to judicial review.
31 See articles 33 to 40 of the Japanese Constitution or articles 103 and 104 of the German Basic Law.
32 This dignitarian approach is found in both common law and civil law jurisdictions.

Procedural fairness is also increasingly seen as a way to foster participation in rule-making. The demand of citizens for a larger role in the adoption of primary and secondary legislation has led to a shift; citizens would like to be consulted systematically prior to adoption. Process rights represent a step towards a more participative democracy. The effectiveness of any participation rights relies heavily on the recognition and respect of transparency, another constitutional principle.

Arguably, change or reform of any of these principles affects the content of procedural fairness and the degree to which it is constitutionally protected. Indeed, in some constitutional orders, procedural fairness is in flux because the meaning of these constitutional principles is changing. The case law of the European Court of Human Rights has transformed the principle of judicial independence and impartiality across a number of jurisdictions, for example, effectively requiring that the United Kingdom transform the organisation of its judiciary completely.[33]

20.4 The content of procedural fairness

While other constitutional rights such as freedom of expression have a core meaning that drives their content, procedural fairness is an idea pervading the whole of the decision-making process. A clear determination of the content is complicated by a perceptible transformation of procedural fairness to process rights. Still, it is possible to identify the range of content for procedural fairness across various constitutional orders.

A comparison of the early evolution of the procedural fairness principle in France and in the United Kingdom shows that it arose principally from the need to control the legality (and fairness) of administrative action. Consequently, the content of this principle was strongly influenced by the eventuality of future challenges to the exercise of power in courts. Judicial procedure and adjudication served as a model to determine the exact content of the procedural protection owed to citizens in this context. In both civil and common law jurisdictions, procedural fairness began with the demand for hearing rights when a somewhat detrimental decision was being made by a public body. In France, the *Conseil d'État* declared the existence of a general principle of law[34]—the rights of defence—and annulled the decision of the administration to withdraw a licence for the exploitation of a newspaper's street stand, which had been made without prior hearing of the licence holder.[35] Similarly, in the United Kingdom, the House of Lords decided in *Ridge v Baldwin* that a chief constable should be given notice and heard before his dismissal. In fact, the right of an individual to make oral or written[36] submissions prior to the making of a possibly detrimental determination against them by a public body is widely recognised. Nowadays, many countries have chosen to codify their administrative procedure, defining the circumstances triggering these rights.[37] Some

---

33 See *McGonnell v United Kingdom* (2000) 30 EHRR 289. The Constitutional Reform Act 2005 limited the powers of the Lord Chancellor, created a supreme court and transformed the system of judicial appointments.

34 Although the result of judicial activism, these general principles of law create obligations for public bodies. Their respect is strictly enforced by administrative courts.

35 See CE 5 May 1944 Trompier-Gravier, rec 133. The licence was terminated for fault (an allegation that she had attempted to blackmail her manager).

36 In France, such representations to public bodies can be made in writing. However, citizens can opt for an oral hearing if they wish. Interestingly, few avail themselves of this possibility.

37 See e.g. section 28 of the German Verwaltungsverfahrengesetz of 1976.

constitutions guarantee the right to a hearing when the administration is contemplating a detrimental determination.[38]

To be fully effective, the right to hearing needs to be accompanied by other procedural safeguards. A hearing will be pointless without notice of the decision and of the reasons for it. Information is therefore crucial and procedural fairness generally carries with it a duty to provide reasons for the decision. This is quite important as not all jurisdictions have embedded a general duty to give reasons in their legal system.[39] In the European Union and some other European jurisdictions (e.g. France and Luxembourg) this even extends to a right of access to the file held by the public body.[40] A number of other procedural issues may affect the effectiveness of a hearing, including whether an individual has access to legal representation and sufficient preparation time. The organisation of hearing rights needs the determination of a wide range of procedural issues. If these are not clarified in a detailed administrative code or in the relevant legislation, courts are left to do so, often on a case-by-case basis. While in some circumstances, a notice of the decision with the (factual and legal) reasons and the possibility to submit written representation will be enough, for others, a full oral hearing by an independent panel and access to legal representation will be necessary. In practice, the courts often determine the content of the process rights by reference to the legal and factual context in individual cases: the stronger the right denied and the more detrimental the administrative decision, the wider the process rights are likely to be.[41]

Commentators in common law jurisdictions also ascribe the rule against bias to this search for procedural fairness; the personal or financial interest of the decision-maker is seen to compromise (rightly) the fairness of the procedure. Traditionally, civil jurisdictions did not really conceptualise such cases in this manner; if they involved a judicial body, the independence of the judiciary was said to be breached. However, if this bias came to light in administrative decision-making, a principle of impartiality may be breached.[42] The Italian constitution recognises, in article 97, a principle of impartiality in such circumstances.[43] Interestingly, civil jurisdiction signatories to the European Convention on Human Rights (ECHR) have been affected by the requirement for a fair and impartial tribunal contained in article 6 § 1. While many of the changes imposed on European jurisdictions aimed to strengthen the fairness of the administration of justice, the obligation of a fair and public hearing by an independent and

---

38 See Article 20 of the Greek Constitution: 'The right of a person to a prior hearing also applies in any administrative action or measure adopted at the expense of his rights or interests.'

39 No such duty exists in France or in the United Kingdom. However, the Charter of Fundamental Rights of the European Union has included a duty to give reasons in article 41(2).

40 The file contains all the information that the administrative body has collated prior to the decision being made. In some complex decisions it can be voluminous indeed.

41 For instance, the UK courts are more likely to grant full hearings rights before an impartial tribunal for the renewal of a licence than for an initial application; see *McInnes v Onslow-Fane* [1978] 1 WLR 1520. The French courts will grant hearing rights to any decision that is a sanction (e.g. a dismissal, see CE 26 October 1945 Aramu, rec 213) or the withdrawal/denial of a benefit (e.g. the withdrawal of the state permit to work as a docker, see CE 13 July 1967 Allegretto rec 315). These considerations apply in the European Union as well, see case C-49/88 *Al-jubail Fertilizer v Council* [1991] ECR I-3187 and see article 41 § 2 of the Charter of fundamental rights of the European Union, OJ 2000 C364/1.

42 A regard to personal or financial interests of the decision-maker when making a decision can constitute a misuse of power, a ground that is close to the one of misfeasance in public office in English law.

43 See article 97: Public offices are organised according to the provisions of law, so as to ensure the efficiency and impartiality of the administration.

impartial tribunal is applied more widely to a person's 'determination of civil rights and obligations'. The withdrawal of a licence,[44] the placement of children into care[45] and the sanctions of a regulatory agency[46] must all comply with the requirement of a fair and impartial tribunal. In some cases, this has required that the procedures leading to the adoption of some administrative determinations be transformed to comply with the demands of the European Court of Human Rights.[47] It is also significant that a principle of impartiality was finally recognised by the French *Conseil d'État* in a decision of 1999.[48]

Finally, the content of procedural fairness takes on a completely different complexion when one moves from individual determinations to legislative or general measures. Courts may have felt legitimate in imposing procedural safeguards for the adoption of individual decisions, but they have been much less active with regard to legislative or general measures. When not backed by the constitution or legislation,[49] courts have found it difficult to grant process rights to concerned individuals or interested associations in the context of rule-making. In fact, few constitutional orders grant clear process rights prior to the adoption of legislative or general measures, though they exist in the Spanish Constitution[50] and may soon become a reality in the European Union.[51] However, as the demand for participation in rule-making has risen markedly in recent decades, many countries have organised such participation when administrative procedure was codified in legislation. Even though process rights of the type enshrined in the notice and comment procedure of section 553 of the US Administrative Procedure Act may not be available everywhere, legislation on planning and the environment (to name but two) often include participatory rights in the decision-making process. Also, in common law jurisdictions, a duty to consult 'interested' parties before adopting a general measure may result from legitimate expectations; prior practice[52] or a representation by a public body[53] may constitute a procedural legitimate expectation and bestow some process rights to interested parties.

One must note, however, that the process rights involved in rule-making are rooted largely in different constitutional assumptions than those underlying the right to a hearing or the rule against bias. With general or legislative measures, citizens want to participate in the determination of the content of the measure that holds an interest for them. The judicial process is no longer the model to follow; in rule-making, process rights are strongly

---

44 See *Pudas v Sweden* (1988) 10 EHRR 380.

45 See *Olsson v Sweden* (no. 1) (1988) 11 EHRR 259 PC.

46 See *H v Belgium* (1988) 10 EHRR 339.

47 See the reform in France of the regulation of the financial markets and of the authority for financial markets.

48 See CE Ass 3 December 1999, rec 339.

49 However, many countries have codified administrative procedures and enshrined process rights in rule-making. The US Administrative Procedure Act 1946 describes the various processes of rule-making and stipulates the rights attached to them, such as the notice and comment procedure in section 553.

50 See article 105 (a): 'The law determines: (...) (a) the hearing of citizens, directly, or through the organisations and associations recognised by the law in the process of drawing up the administrative decision which affect them.'

51 However, article 11 of the Lisbon Treaty may well change this. Included in the part on democratic principles, this provision creates an obligation on the institutions of the European Union to consult citizens and representative associations in all areas of decision-making.

52 See *CCSU v Minister for the Civil Service* [1985] AC 374.

53 See *R (on the application of Greenpeace Ltd) v Sec. of State for Trade and Industry* [2007] EWHC Admin. 311.

influenced by an ideal of participative democracy.[54] In addition, these participatory rights can only be effective if concomitant constitutional principles are recognised too. Without a commitment to transparency, the involvement of citizens and their participation in rule-making cannot have much reality: concerned citizens and interested associations need to be fully informed to participate effectively in consultation exercises.[55] Increasingly, constitutional orders recognise a principle of transparency and legislation on freedom of information and access to documents is common. Not only do these foster a more effective and direct involvement of citizens in policy-making, but in turn, they continue to transform the constitutional culture and the expectations of the polity.

20.5 Methods of protecting procedural fairness

The duty to afford procedural fairness, or due process, is enforced by courts and tribunals, but a court's (or tribunal's) role in this respect will depend on the constitutional setting and the extent to which a constitution provides for judicial review. The level of protection given to the rules of procedural fairness will also depend on the extent to which process rights are legally and constitutionally protected, and whether such rights are seen to limit the exercise of legislative power or not. The constitutional framework is therefore determinative of the extent to which procedural fairness, or due process, is both required and protected.

20.5.1 The extent of judicial review

In the United Kingdom, where for a large part the courts lack the power to invalidate Acts of Parliament, the duty to afford procedural fairness is generally required of administrative decision-makers or those exercising public power and is enforced by the courts in the judicial review of administrative action. This common law tradition has now been supplemented by the ECHR, through the operation of the Human Rights Act 1998 (UK). The incorporation of the European Convention has imposed on courts a duty to interpret legislation in line with the Convention and granted them the power to issue a declaration of incompatibility; while this declaration is not legally binding, it highlights the existence of a breach. Furthermore, the Human Rights Act has made the breach of a convention right a new head of judicial review. As article 6 § 1 of the convention imposes the requirement of a fair and impartial tribunal, it is reasonable to argue that procedural fairness is granted quasi-constitutional protection in the United Kingdom.

54　The South African constitutional court encountered these issues in the *Doctors for Life* litigation. The NGO 'Doctors for Life International' argued that key healthcare legislations had been adopted without proper public involvement and that the National Council of Provinces (NCOP) had failed in its duty to facilitate public involvement in the passing of the bills. The court decided that the failure of the NCOP to hold public hearings prior to the adoption of the legislation had breached the duty to facilitate public involvement for two of the legislations. The legislation was invalid as a result, see *Doctors for Life International v the Speaker of the National Assembly and Others* 2006 (12) BCLR 1399 (CC) (S. Afr.). Interestingly, Ngcobo J recognises in the duty to facilitate public involvement an expression of participatory democracy. He rightly insists that such instances of participative democracy do not compete with but complement the South African representative democracy.

55　The notification and consultation of interested parties is the main process right in the context of rule-making.

In Australia, where a written Constitution includes elements of both the English and US Constitutions, judicial review is entrenched, but procedural fairness rights (other than a right to trial by jury for indictable offences[56]) are absent from the constitutional text and must be derived from either the common law or statute. Only the separation of judicial power under Chapter III of the Constitution ensures minimum procedural guarantees for judicial proceedings at both the federal and state levels.[57] However, parliament is free to remove procedural fairness entirely in administrative proceedings. In this respect, while the High Court of Australia has held that the Constitution entrenches judicial review in respect of decisions affected by jurisdictional error,[58] the Court has yet to find that the grounds of review, including procedural fairness, are also entrenched and thus beyond parliament's power to remove as requirements of administrative decision-making.

In Canada, where the Charter of Rights and Freedoms has been constitutionally entrenched since 1982, various procedural rights guaranteed under Articles 7–10 supplement the common law's procedural fairness rules.[59] These legal rights—which extend to the legislature also—include the right to *habeas corpus*, the right to prompt reasons and to retain counsel following arrest or detention. Under Article 24 of the Charter, individuals can apply to a court of competent jurisdiction for remedies where a right or freedom has been denied. However, in accordance with Article 33, the Parliament may declare that an Act of Parliament is to apply, notwithstanding that it conflicts with a right or freedom protected under the Charter. The judicial review capacity of the Canadian Supreme Court has therefore expanded considerably since 1982, as has the constitutional protection afforded procedural safeguards.

In contrast, the US Constitution enables the Supreme Court to invalidate laws at odds with the due process clause, thereby conferring constitutional protection to minimum procedural (and some substantive) requirements. Similarly, many constitutions (especially on the European continent) follow the Kelsenian model of constitutional review by a specialised court. Constitutional courts review the constitutionality of laws and strike them down if they conflict with constitutional provisions or principles. There, what matters is the extent of the protection afforded to procedural fairness by the constitution.

20.5.2 The ambit of the constitutional protection

While most constitutions protect some aspects of procedural fairness, few provide what could be labelled as complete protection. The majority of constitutions are strict on fair trial requirements for criminal litigation but often silent on administrative procedures: for instance, the Japanese Constitution contains many procedural guarantees for criminal trial[60] and, similarly, the German Constitution proclaims a number of judicial rights[61]; neither constitution is concerned with the fairness of administrative procedures. At the other end of the spectrum,

---

56 Conferred under s 80 of the Australian Constitution.
57 See, e.g. *Kable v Director of Public Prosecutions (NSW)* (1996) 189 CLR 51 and *Ebner v Official Trustee in Bankruptcy* (2000) 205 CLR 337.
58 *Plaintiff S157 v Commonwealth* (2003) 211 CLR 476 (in relation to federal decisions); *Kirk v Industrial Court of New South* Wales (2010) 239 CLR 531 (in relation to State decisions).
59 For the common law requirements of procedural fairness, see *Baker v Canada (Ministry of Citizenship and Immigration)* (1999) 2 SCR 817.
60 See articles 33 to 40 of the Japanese Constitution.
61 These are: the right of access to courts (art 19(4)), the right to the lawful judge (art 101), the right to a court hearing (art 103(1)), the principle of clarity of criminal provisions and prohibition of retroactive criminal offence (art 103(2)) and the prohibition of double jeopardy (art 103(3)).

the Spanish Constitution contains detailed guarantees of procedural fairness before the administration: article 105[62] specifies that the right to consultation, the right to a hearing and the right of access to documents must all be implemented by law. Finally, constitutional documents may be (and are often) supplemented by the activism of courts; as explained above, although the French Constitution affords procedural fairness in criminal proceedings only, the French *Conseil constitutionnel* recognised an additional constitutional right of defence. Similarly, the Court of Justice recognised a right of defence in the European Union long before its incorporation in article 41 of the Charter of Fundamental Rights.

20.5.3 Legislative protection

Procedural fairness can be protected efficiently even in the absence of constitutional recognition. Early on, the respect of procedural fairness was often imposed on the administration by courts, but nowadays these early efforts are supplemented increasingly by legislation. For instance, the Netherlands may not have a system of constitutional review but administrative procedure and process rights were codified by legislation in the General Administrative Law Act.[63] In fact, it is perfectly possible to guarantee through legislation that appropriate mechanisms are in place for individuals to make representations before an adverse decision or to ensure that representative associations and interested persons be consulted before the adoption of a legislative or general measure. Indeed, many countries across the world, such as the USA, Germany, the Netherlands, Japan and Spain (to cite but few) have codified their administrative procedure. Although the content of these codifications varies, they all enshrine key process rights: for instance, the Japanese Administrative Procedure Act of 1993 established a duty to give reasons, a right to a hearing, and a comment and notice procedure in rule-making. Even those countries still reluctant to adopt such codification have often needed to enshrine some process rights in legislation to ensure their effectiveness: in France, the right to be heard is now conferred upon citizens by legislation.[64] Still, a full codification has the advantage that other relevant principles such as transparency, access to information and duty to give reasons are addressed at the same time.

Finally, one should not forget that soft law may play an important role in establishing process rights: for instance, although a general right of participation in rule-making is yet to be codified in the European Union, the Commission has chosen to consult the wider public on a number of key reforms since 2002.[65] This has allowed the acclimatisation of these rights ahead of a formal introduction by Treaty amendment.[66]

20.6 Conclusion

Although the origins of procedural fairness lie historically in English common law, its evolution over time has involved an increasing trend towards the express articulation of process

---

62 See Article 105 of the Spanish Constitution.

63 The GALA was adopted in the Netherlands in 1992. This codification was required by article 107 of the Dutch Constitution. Prior to the introduction of the GALA there was a great deal of uncertainty and confusion with regard to administrative procedures and process rights.

64 See the law of 12 April 2000 on the rights of citizens in their relations with their administrations.

65 See the 2002 Communication on Consultation, 'Towards a reinforced culture of consultation and dialogue—General principles and minimum standards for consultation of interested parties by the commission', COM (2002) 704 final.

66 Arguably, this gap has been addressed by article 11 of the Lisbon Treaty.

rights in constitutional documents and in legislation. So much so that for many constitutional orders, procedural fairness is guaranteed by a complex and layered system of protection: constitutional provisions, legislation, case law and even treaty obligations all combine to guarantee process rights. However, a warning may need to be sounded concerning this evolution: in some constitutional orders, this layered approach has led to the various procedural guarantees competing and even clashing. Indeed, many constitutional orders in the European Union may be close to experiencing a process-right overload: there, the growing national guarantees are supplemented by the requirements of the European Convention on Human Rights and in some circumstances those of the Charter of Fundamental Rights. This has engendered some tensions and a degree of legal uncertainty that does not serve the protection of these rights well.

References

Dicey, AV (1885). *The Law of the Constitution*, 10th edn, in Wade ECS (ed) (London: Macmillan, reprinted 1960).

Goldberg, BA (1982). '"Interpretation" of "Due Process of Law"—A Study in Futility', 13 *Pacific Law Journal* 365–405.

Hannum, H (1995–1996). 'The Status of the Universal Declaration of Human Rights in National and International Law', 25 *Georgia Journal of International and Comparative Law* 287–397.

Jowell, J (2007). 'The Rule of Law and its Underlying Values', in Jowell, J and Oliver, D (eds), *The Changing Constitution*, 6th edn.

Lester, A & Beattie, K (2007). 'Human Rights and the British Constitution', in *The Changing Constitution*, 6th edn, 59–83.

Wade, HWR & Forsyth, CF (2004). *Administrative Law*, 9th edn (Oxford: Oxford University Press).

Additional reading

Loveland, I (2006). *Constitutional Law, Administrative Law and Human Rights*, 4th edn.

Rights in the criminal process: a case study of convergence and disclosure rights

Máximo Langer and Kent Roach

21.1 Introduction

The subject of criminal procedure rights can be approached from many angles. Legal systems vary on whether and which rights they give, not only to criminal defendants but also to victims of crime, NGOs, prosecutors, witnesses, citizens, media and the public. Legal systems also vary on the legal status that criminal procedure rights have—as constitutional, international, statutory, common law or regulatory rights; on the nature and structure of these rights; and on how they are enforced. One of the themes of contemporary comparative criminal procedure literature has been that the spread of defendants' rights around the world has accelerated the closure of the gap between common and civil law jurisdictions. According to this claim, the gap is closing because many civil law jurisdictions have moved away from an inquisitorial and toward an adversarial system by adopting more rights (see, e.g., Bradley xxi and xxiv).

This chapter analyzes this convergence claim by concentrating on the defendant's constitutional right to disclosure or to obtain access to elements of proof collected by public officials. This right may not be the most representative or important, but it illustrates some of the complexities and subtleties around the convergence thesis and the debate about rights in comparative criminal procedure. Civil and common law jurisdictions have come to embrace this right as an abstract concept. But their different pre-existing institutional settings and conceptions of the criminal process have led common and civil law jurisdictions to define, debate and regulate this right in varying ways. The spread of rights is not a simple movement of convergence, but rather a more complex process that achieves convergence while simultaneously maintaining existing divergences and creating new ones between common and civil law jurisdictions.

Constitutional rights are seldom absolute. This chapter will also analyze law enforcement and national security considerations as another global converging force that has placed both explicit and implicit limits on constitutional rights to disclosure, especially in organized crime and terrorism cases. But once again, these law enforcement and national security pressures have played out somewhat differently in civil and common law jurisdictions.

Finally, the chapter will move beyond the common/civil law focus of traditional comparative criminal procedure scholarship by briefly comparing American, British and Canadian regulations concerning the right to disclosure. The differences among these regulations cannot be explained in terms of legal traditions, but rather may depend on the contingencies of when these jurisdictions first recognized constitutional rights to disclosure as well as legislative responses to disclosure rights, including legislative assertion of competing rights on behalf of victims or other interests.

Other jurisdictions may be influenced by these and other contingent factors. The recognition of rights within the criminal process emerges as complex. Although some broad patterns of convergence are apparent, they are in turn influenced by legal and institutional traditions and by the concerns of the day.

21.2 The civil and common law dichotomy and rights in the criminal process

The difference between the criminal process in common law and civil law—also sometimes referred to as Anglo-American and Continental jurisdictions or, in a more abstract fashion, as adversarial and inquisitorial systems—has been at the centre of the field of comparative criminal procedure for over 200 years.

One way to conceptualize the differences between the criminal process in common and civil law is by concentrating on two contrasting features. First, in the common law tradition, criminal procedure is conceived as a dispute between two parties—prosecution and defence—before a passive umpire; while in civil law jurisdictions, criminal procedure is conceived as a unitary investigation run by impartial officials (see, e.g., Langer 2004). Second, lay people in a horizontal relationship with each other (e.g., in the form of the jury) have historically been the crucial decision-makers in common law countries, while legal experts who are members of hierarchical public bureaucracies have dominated in civil law countries (Damaška 1986).

These contrasting features are relative rather than absolute. They can be considered ideal types that no jurisdiction actually matches (Packer; Roach 2003). But even as ideal types, they are reflected in actual criminal justice practices and have been, to a certain extent, internalized by institutions and individual actors in common and civil law jurisdictions (Langer 2004).

The concept of rights has played an important role in the academic literature and in policy debate. According to some scholars, the different regulation of defendants' rights was one of the crucial differences between the common law and civil law criminal process from the thirteenth to the nineteenth centuries, because common law jurisdictions conceived criminal defendants as subjects with rights, while civil law jurisdictions conceived criminal defendants as objects of investigation (see, e.g., Maier). This understanding would also be reflected in the different approaches to remedies as exemplified by the iconic status of *habeas corpus* in common law systems, with its focus on the liberty of the subject. Possible reasons for the later development of procedural rights in civil law jurisdictions would include a more authoritarian conception of the state and the administration of criminal justice in continental Europe than in England; the higher importance that codes and legislatures have played vis-à-vis judges in the regulation of procedure in civil law; and the special focus on substantive rather than procedural criminal law in civil law jurisdictions. Whatever its historical accuracy, this characterization no longer describes the two systems, because many members of both types of systems today conceive defendants as subjects with rights, as reflected in domestic constitutions, regional and international human rights instruments, codes and statutes, judicial decisions and actual institutional practices (Bradley; Trechsel).

There has also been a debate in comparative criminal procedure on whether common or civil law countries are more respectful of defendants' rights. One group has claimed that civil law jurisdictions emphasize accuracy over fairness, are less protective of defendants' rights during police investigations, tend to hold defendants in pretrial detention for longer periods or establish weaker trial rights (see, e.g., Damaška 1973; Hodgson; Maffei; Vogler). Other studies have challenged at least some of these characterizations and argued that civil law jurisdictions have other institutional mechanisms that differ from rights to check prosecutors' and judges' power, or have claimed that in actual practice civil law countries may be more respectful of defendants' rights because they do not rely on the widespread use of guilty pleas and plea bargaining and impose milder sentences (Langbein 1979; Langer 2006; Roach 2010b; Ross 2008; Van Kessel) (on punishment and constitutional law more generally, see Chapter 16 in this collection).

A third line of inquiry has sought to explain why certain rights have been defined or debated in a different fashion in common and civil law jurisdictions, given pre-existing differences between them. For instance, it has been argued that there are two different conceptions of the right to privacy in the United States and continental Europe, respectively relying on the ideas of liberty and dignity, and each of these conceptions would have deep historical roots (Whitman 2004).

21.3 The right to know the results of the investigation run by public officials

The right to disclosure has not been explicitly included in constitutions and human rights instruments in either common or in civil law jurisdictions. Rather, courts and legislatures have held that this right is part of the concept of more general rights explicitly established in constitutional and human rights documents such as due process (*Brady v Maryland* in the US); the right to make full answer and defence that would itself be part of the right not to be deprived of liberty except in accordance with the principles of fundamental justice (*R v Stinchcombe* in Canada); the right to have adequate facilities for the preparation of one's defence (see, e.g., *Jasper v United Kingdom* in the European Court of Human Rights); the right to a (fair and public) hearing (*Edwards and Lewis v United Kingdom* in the European Court of Human Rights; Section 103.1 of the German Basic Law); and the rights of defence (see, e.g., Pradel 2004, § 504, regarding France). One of the main rationales for including the right among fundamental rights has been that it is a crucial tool for the defendant to be able to mount a meaningful defence and exercise his other rights. The right to disclosure provides another example of the proliferation of implied rights that are the product of interpretation of basic and general norms. The judicial and legislative creation of disclosure rights underlines the dynamic nature of such rights and the possibility of contraction of rights and the assertion of new and competing rights (Devins & Fisher).

To the extent that both civil and common law jurisdictions have embraced the right to disclosure as a fundamental one, there has been convergence between these two types of jurisdictions at an important level. But the way this abstract concept has been adopted has reproduced pre-existing differences between these jurisdictions and created new ones.

Different expressions have been used to refer to disclosure rights that reflect different conceptions of it. While in civil law jurisdictions it has been defined as the right to access the file (as reflected by expressions such as the *droit de consulter le dossier* in French, *Akteneinsichtsrecht* in German, *derecho a examinar el expediente* in Spanish), in common law jurisdictions the right has been defined as the right to disclosure or discovery of an open-ended list of items, typically possessed by the prosecutor but also at times possessed by the police and other agencies.

The reference to the dossier in the civil law formulation is not coincidental given the central role that the dossier has played in an administration of justice conceived as a Weberian bureaucracy run by impartial legal professionals. In such a conception, investigating officials are supposed to document all their procedural activity—including the gathering of elements of proof. And even if many civil law countries have established public and oral trials, the written dossier still has an important weight in adjudication. First, certain elements of proof collected in the written dossier during the police and pretrial phases—including statements— can be treated as evidence in many civil law jurisdictions (Maffei; Summers). In addition, the written dossier is read by at least one of the members of the trial court before trial—which can create preconceptions about the case—and is used by the court to decide which evidence should actually be presented at trial and in which order, and to interrogate witnesses and expert witnesses at trial.

In contrast, in common law jurisdictions, the right to disclosure does not make a reference to any privileged locus. The historical centrality of the trial by jury as the crucial adjudicatory moment in the criminal process de-emphasized the importance of the pretrial phase and contributed to keeping it relatively informal and flexible. As a consequence, police and prosecution do not need to document all their procedural activity. This means that even a prosecution office with an open-file policy toward the defence may not fully discharge its disclosure duties because there may be information and elements of proof that have been identified in the investigation by public authorities but which have not been included in the prosecutorial file. It also means that the elements the prosecutor has to disclose to the defence include more than notarized documents and real evidence, such as informal notes taken by the police or the name of potential witnesses. It also implies that the prosecutor may have to do more than simply give access to something that is already there and, rather, must actively identify what elements found in the investigation fit the disclosure criteria. The decentralized nature of adversarial disclosure may also reflect the idea of a decentralized state and the idea of a trial as a form of dispute resolution that is similar to that used to resolve civil disputes between private parties in common law. The adversarial system encourages competitive parties to search for the 'smoking gun' that even the government may advertently or inadvertently hide, while the civil law still trusts the dossier and those who compile it (Damaška 1986; Kagan).

Differences between civil and common law jurisdictions may also help explain the history of the right in each of these legal traditions. Given the centrality and weight that the written dossier has had in civil law, it is not surprising that this right has a longer history in these jurisdictions as it would be almost impossible for the defence to meaningfully participate in the criminal process without knowledge of what the dossier contains. For example, even at the height of inquisitorial procedures in continental Europe, according to certain legal authorities the judge was required to disclose incriminating evidence or give the defendant access to the dossier after the collection of incriminating material (Damaška 2011). According to the highly influential Napoleonic *Code d'instruction criminelle* (1808), defence attorneys could make copies of those parts of the dossier that they considered useful for their defence before the trial before the assize court (art 305). And the *loi Constant* (1897) in France established that the defence attorney could access the dossier during the pretrial phase to assist the defendant during his pretrial interrogations (see, e.g., Pradel 2004, ¶ 401). In modern Germany, the original 1877 version of the Criminal Procedure Code already established that the defence attorney was authorized to see the written dossier after the conclusion of the preliminary investigation or after the issuing of the indictment; and in the 1964 reform of the Code, the right to access the dossier was established as a general principle (Lüderssen & Jahn, 995).

In contrast, the United States federal system included such a right at a statutory level only in 1946 with the promulgation of the Federal Rules of Criminal Procedure (see, e.g., Miller *et al*, 753), and the US Supreme Court held that the right had constitutional status that would apply to the states in *Brady v Maryland* in 1963. In Canada, the Supreme Court held that the right had a constitutional status only in 1991 in *Stinchcombe*. In England, disclosure obligations were affirmed in the early 1990s in a number of cases stemming from miscarriages of justice (*R v Ward*) and then were subsequently subject to statutory regulation and restrictions (Corker & Parkison). One can explain this later reception of the right by common law countries as a consequence of a conception of criminal procedure as a dispute resolution process run by self-interested parties rather than as an official process concerned with accuracy and administrative regularity. In adversarial systems, each of the parties in both public and private disputes could plausibly claim that the results of their investigations were theirs and 'the element of surprise was one of the accepted weapons in the arsenal of the adversaries' (*Stinchcombe*). That said, the idea that parties in the adversarial system are self-interested is not absolute and the later assertion of disclosure rights in the United States, England and Canada was also accompanied by assertions about the ethical responsibilities of prosecutors to ensure that justice was done and accurate results achieved at trial.

This brief historical description also reveals that the right to disclosure in common law systems has emerged primarily from case law. Cases such as *Brady* in the United States, *Ward* in England and Wales and *Stinchcombe* in Canada have assumed iconic status in the legal system even when subject to statutory refinement. In contrast, disclosure in many civilian systems is based on explicit obligations in various Codes. Even as the systems converge towards greater disclosure rights, they do so in a manner that follows distinct legal methodologies, reflecting the respective bias of common law and civil law systems towards case-by-case adjudication and legislative regulation.

The elements covered by the right also differ between civil and common law jurisdictions. Since impartial investigators in civil law jurisdictions are supposed to document all their procedural activity, the defendant's access to the dossier means, in theory, access to the whole investigation. Full access may be delayed until some specific point in the proceedings or in certain situations, but there is no question that the defendant will get access to the whole dossier at some point before trial. The question has been thought of differently in common law jurisdictions with a criminal process that has a more informal pretrial phase and that is conceived as a dispute between two competing parties building competing cases. In these jurisdictions, the question has been framed as to whether disclosure should be complete or partial; and, if partial, what it should include. Framing the criterion as to what elements are material or favourable for the defence case has assumed that there is a separate defence case as opposed to one unitary investigation in which the defence participates as in inquisitorial systems. Consequently, the accused's right to disclosure in an adversarial system may depend in part on the specific defence presented by the accused.

Another set of differences involves identifying who has the duty to disclose or give access. In civil law countries, the impartial official in charge of the investigation is the one who has to give access to it to the defence, at least in the first instance. Depending on specific country regulations and the procedural phase the case is at, this official may include not only the prosecutor but also the police and the court. In contrast, in common law jurisdictions, the prosecutor is the official primarily responsible for disclosing elements to the defence. In fact, disclosure is sometimes seen as a matter of prosecutorial ethics as well as legal entitlement.

The role of the court in enforcing these duties in common law jurisdictions is limited to deciding controversial issues that the parties bring, not only because the court is generally not supposed to act on its own motion, but also because the court does not have enough information about the parties' investigations.

The discussion on whether the defence has a duty to disclose the results of its own investigation to the prosecution only makes sense within a criminal process conceived as a competition between the cases of the prosecution and the defence. This helps explain how the right to disclosure has been conceived as a reciprocal right in many common law jurisdictions—at least when it has a statutory status. In this understanding, the prosecution has to honour certain disclosure duties only if the defence is willing to disclose some of its own information or elements of proof in exchange (see, e.g., Federal Rule of Criminal Procedure 16 in the United States). The idea has been foreign to civil law jurisdictions that conceive criminal procedure as a unitary investigation.

When the right is triggered has also been debated and regulated differently in common and civil law jurisdictions. As common law jurisdictions have traditionally conceived the trial as the crucial adjudicatory moment, it is not surprising that some common law jurisdictions have conceived the right to disclosure as a trial right (see, e.g., *US v Ruiz*). Even common law jurisdictions that have challenged this position have instead argued that the prosecution's duty to disclose applies at the latest before the defendant elects a mode of trial or decides to waive his right to trial by jury by pleading guilty (see, e.g., *Stinchombe*). In contrast, in civil law jurisdictions, the right to disclosure generally applies much earlier in the pretrial process because the pretrial phase has historically had more weight. Depending on the jurisdiction and the circumstances of the case, the right may thus kick in before an attorney agrees to serve as counsel for the defendant (CPP Argentina, art 106), before the defendant is interrogated by the investigating judge (CPP France, art 114) or before a decision on pretrial detention (StPO Germany §147.2), to mention some of the choices.

Notice also that this right did not spread from common to civil law jurisdictions. In fact, it was adopted by civil law jurisdictions earlier than common law ones, not necessarily because the former were more due-process oriented than the latter, but probably because the civil law institutional setting with its more formal approach to the pretrial stage made apparent the need to establish and expand this right once the defence was given a (more) prominent role in the adjudication of criminal cases.

Finally, our analysis also suggests that civil law jurisdictions have given a broader scope to this right than common law ones as the former give earlier access to the defence to the whole investigation run by public officials. But once again, this broader scope is not the result of a more due-process orientation in civil law but of the way the issue has been thought of within a pre-existing set of institutional practices and conception of the criminal process. The broader scope of this right in civil law jurisdictions should also not be read as suggesting that civil law jurisdictions are more protective of defendant rights generally. In fact, as the next section will make apparent, some of the very features that have led civil law jurisdictions to give a broader scope to the right to access the dossier may have contributed to these jurisdictions being less protective of other rights of criminal defendants.

21.4 Law enforcement and national security concerns and the right to know the results of the investigation

Besides converging on an abstract agreement on the right to disclosure, civil and common law jurisdictions have been subjected to somewhat similar law enforcement and national security pressure to limit the right's scope. These pressures have relied on the argument that there are elements of proof or information that the defendant should not get access to because it would jeopardize investigations (including those involving transnational co-operation); the safety or well-being of informants, public officials and potential witnesses; or efforts to prevent the commission of crimes. This argument has been raised especially, though not exclusively, in the context of organized crime and terrorism and reveals how pressures to limit rights can be a source of convergence with respect to those rights.

Once again, though, similar pressures to limit disclosure rights have played out differently in civil and common law jurisdictions due to the different institutional contexts already described. Civil law countries have focused on how these rights can be accommodated within a dossier system that generally has had a weaker right to confrontation and cross-examination, operates without a general rule restricting the use of hearsay evidence, and is more accommodating of unsourced or only generally sourced material and anonymous witnesses.

For example, the French Criminal Procedure Code establishes that, for offenses punished with at least three years' imprisonment, a judge may order that the identity of a witness not be revealed if there is danger to the life or physical integrity of that person or members of his family or other people close to him (CPP France, arts 706–57 to 706–63). In undercover operations, only the police officer in charge of the operation has to testify, while the identity of the undercover agents is protected (CPP France, arts 706–81 to 706–87; on similar practice and regulations in Germany, see StPO §110b and Ross 2007). In terrorism cases, police officers who testify do not have to reveal their names or their marital status (CPP France, arts 706–24 to 706–25.2).

France has not been alone in this respect, as reflected by the multiple cases on anonymous witnesses that have reached the European Court of Human Rights (for review of these cases, see, e.g., Maffei; Summers). The European Court of Human Rights has held that 'the use of statements made by anonymous witnesses to found a conviction is not under all circumstances incompatible with the [European] Convention [of Human Rights]' (*Van Mechelen v The Netherlands*, § 54). The Court has also said that even when the anonymous witness does not testify at trial, 'to use as evidence such statements obtained at the pre-trial stage is not in itself inconsistent with Article 6(3)(d) [of the European Convention of Human Rights] provided the rights of the defence have been respected' (*Kostovski v The Netherlands*, ¶ 41). And even if the accused had not had the opportunity to examine the anonymous witness either during the investigation or at trial, a conviction may be valid if it is not based solely or in a decisive manner on the deposition of anonymous witnesses (see, e.g., *Van Mechelen v The Netherlands*).

Besides anonymous witnesses, a number of civil law jurisdictions have used unsourced information as another way to deal with the already described pressures. Jean-Louis Bruguiere, a retired judge who investigated many terrorism cases in France, has stated that the civil law system is more 'flexible' in responding to the threat of terrorism and that the 'common law system is too rigid, it can't adapt because its procedural laws are more important than the criminal law at its base' (Human Rights Watch, 13). Human Rights Watch has criticized the French system for making it difficult for defence lawyers effectively to challenge the very long and unmanageable case files produced in terrorism investigations that often contain unsourced intelligence materials (id, 17–18, 33–37). In Canada, a French investigative file was challenged by a person resisting extradition to France on terrorism charges in part on the basis that it featured unsourced intelligence that could not be challenged and that might have been obtained from foreign agencies on the basis of torture or other forms of mistreatment. The

Canadian government eventually withdrew this information and the accused was ordered extradited on the basis of other evidence (*France v Diab*).

Common law systems have also faced similar pressures with respect to witness protection and the protection of intelligence from disclosure to the accused. But use of anonymous witnesses and intelligence has been more difficult for them, given restrictions on hearsay evidence and a stronger right to confrontation and cross-examination at trial. One common method that common law jurisdictions have used to limit disclosure obligations are public interest immunity proceedings, which allow prosecutors to apply to judges for non-disclosure orders. In England and Wales, the courts have stressed the need for judicial approval of such orders. In a 1993 case that overturned a terrorism conviction in part because the Crown had not made full disclosure, the Court of Appeal criticized the prosecution for acting 'as a judge in their own cause on the issue of public interest immunity' (*R v Ward*, 648). Although British restrictions on disclosure are subject to review by the European Court of Human Rights, the Court has stressed that the entitlement to disclosure of relevant evidence is not an absolute right, and can be outweighed to preserve the fundamental rights of another individual or to safeguard an important public interest (*Edwards and Lewis v the United Kingdom*, ¶ 46).

Public interest immunity proceedings are also used in Australia, Canada, Israel and the United States to limit disclosure rights (Roach 2010a; Kitai-Sangero, 292). In some cases, these proceedings are even conducted at least in part on an *ex parte* basis without full participation from the accused for fear of revealing the secrets. Another available alternative is to allow the accused's interests to be represented by a special advocate, a security-cleared counsel (*R v H and C*).

In the United States, the *Classified Information Procedures Act* PL 96-456 allows prosecutors to obtain non-disclosure orders to protect national security interests. It embraces notions of proportionality by encouraging both the government and judges to provide the accused with disclosure of non-classified substitutes for disclosure of material that might, if disclosed, reveal confidential sources, harm ongoing investigations or breach promises of confidentiality made to other agencies. In some cases, the accused's lawyer may be granted access to the secret material subject to receiving a security clearance and undertaking not to disclose the material to the accused: this procedure has been used in notorious terrorism cases including those of bin Laden and Zacarias Moussaoui (*United States v bin Laden*, 121; *United States v Moussaoui*). Like the British special advocate procedures, these procedures demonstrate how common law systems are willing to qualify the lawyer/client relationship thought to be fundamental to the adversarial system in order to protect other important competing interests such as national security. They also underline how common law systems are prepared to limit the right to disclosure, albeit in a manner that employs nominally adversarial hearings and, as such, differs from the means used in civil systems where investigating judges and prosecutors place less emphasis on confrontation and can use unsourced intelligence in their investigative files. At the same time, real and perceived inflexibility of disclosure requirements in both the US and the UK may have played a role in encouraging both states to use alternatives to the criminal justice system such as military and immigration detention and control orders based, in part, on secret evidence (Roach 2011).

21.5 Comparing American, British and Canadian regulations

This chapter has so far revolved around comparison of disclosure rights in common law and civilian systems. Such comparisons provide a rich source of material for examining how different legal and institutional contexts influence constitutional law. At the same time, however, the common law/civil law axis is not the only axis of comparison and it risks over-estimating the degree of similarities within such systems. In the remainder of this chapter, we will briefly compare American, British and Canadian approaches to disclosure to highlight some important divergences within common law systems. Similar diversity can also be found in civil law systems (see, e.g., Pradel 2002, 467–9).

In the United States, since *Brady v Maryland*, the focus of the constitutional right to discovery has been on favourable evidence to the accused's case, not on any material evidence or evidence that advances a side issue such as a rights violation. In addition, the constitutional right to discovery has been conceived as a trial right (*US v Ruiz*). Case law in the United States continues to provide nuanced divergences in defining what material must be disclosed and when it must be disclosed.

The Canadian Supreme Court in its 1991 *Stinchcombe* decision rejected the *Brady* approach as overly narrow and not responsive enough to the dangers of wrongful convictions. It held that the prosecutor had an obligation to disclose all relevant and non-privileged information in its possession before the accused elected whether to be tried by a jury or not. The different disclosure regimes in the two countries can be explained in part by increased concerns about wrongful convictions when the Canadian right was created by the Supreme Court. (As in the United States, a complex jurisprudence has developed over disclosure, particularly over reme-dies for failure to make disclosure, with the courts drawing fine distinctions between viola-tions of rights that require new trials and those that do not. Even as they embrace broad disclosure rights, common law systems promote nuanced distinctions about the scope and remedies for such rights.)

The British system of disclosure provides a contrast with the American–Canadian system. Broad disclosure rights in the UK were originally the product of common law, not constitu-tional, decisions stemming from wrongful convictions and attempts by prosecutors to with-hold relevant information without judicial approval (*Ward*). Britain has moved away from relying on court decisions to define the prosecutor's disclosure obligations, while legislation has both reduced disclosure obligations and made them more certain. This legislation has also imposed disclosure obligations on the accused with secondary disclosure in response to that disclosure. Disclosure rights today would ultimately be constitutionalized both through the Human Rights Act 1998 and the European Convention on which it is based, but in a more flexible form than in the United States or Canada. Constitutional rights may also reflect on the adequacy of statutory starting points suggesting the need for constitutional lawyers to study the latter as well as the former (Samaha). There is also some evidence that the standards on anonymous witnesses developed in civil law systems have migrated to England, which now provides for a use of anonymous witnesses that would not be accepted in either the United States or Canada (see Criminal Evidence (Witness Anonymity) Act 2008, chapter 15). The migration of constitutional ideas (including reasons for limiting rights) (Choudhry) transcends the civil/common law divide and seems to have been fostered by European human rights institutions.

21.6 Conclusions

This chapter has explored comparative constitutional law in two comparative axes. The first axis was to engage in macro comparisons of countries that have traditionally followed civil and common law systems. We have suggested that while the different legal traditions still have an influence, both systems have embraced broader disclosure rights for those accused of crime. This convergence has occurred despite the absence of explicit provisions for disclosure rights in various constitutions. Although this convergence is important and belies simplistic dichotomies between rights-friendly common law democracies and more statist civilian systems, important differences remain. Although language and other barriers present challenges, we believe that comparative constitutional law should include comparisons across the common law/civil law divide and that modern developments such as supra-national rights protections instruments and international developments such as the International Criminal Court will assist researchers in bridging the common law/civil law divide (see, e.g, Jackson 2008). The divide must be bridged, but attention should still be paid to the enduring significance of these and other different legal traditions. The lessons of such comparisons might also be applied to different legal traditions beyond those of civil and common law, including the influence of religious and indigenous law (Glenn).

The second axis of comparison that we have employed is comparing disclosure rights of similar countries, in this case, Canada, the UK and the US. Such comparisons are a useful antidote to simplification and essentialization that may accompany more macro comparison of countries that have different legal traditions. The more micro comparisons of similar countries should also have a historical dimension as our findings suggest that matters such as the starting points for rights, the timing of rights and the contingency of interests and rights that compete with disclosure rights play an important role. In this sense, comparative constitutional law may follow the path of a history of legal ideas and legal reform (Langer 2007). Another approach would be to focus on events with global repercussions such as the increased emphasis on the prevention of terrorism since 9/11 (Roach 2011). This approach, consistent with our findings on the first axis of comparison, demonstrates both broad convergence in accepting limits on disclosure rights in the name of national security and witness protection, and continued divergence in the precise implementation of these limits on disclosure rights. Again, the glimpse of comparative constitutional law presented in this chapter is one of simultaneous convergence and divergence united by the continued impact of both different legal traditions and global pressures, but also divided by the historical specificity of the law as it is shaped in each country and each era.

References

Bradley, C (2007). 'Overview', in Bradley, C (ed), *Criminal Procedure. A Worldwide Study* 2 d (Durham, Carolina University Press).

Choudhry, S (2006). *The Migration of Constitutional Ideas* (Cambridge: Cambridge University Press).

Corker, D & Parkinson, S (2009). *Disclosure in Criminal Proceedings* (Oxford: Oxford University Press).

Damaška, M (1973). 'Evidentiary Barriers to Conviction and Two Models of Criminal Procedure: A Comparative Study', *University of Pennsylvania Law Review* 121: 506–89.

—— (1986). *The Faces of Justice and State Authority* (New Haven and London, Yale University Press).

—— (2011). *The Quest for Due Process in the Age of Inquisition* (on file with the authors).

Devins, N and Fisher, L (2004). *The Democratic Constitution* (Oxford: Oxford University Press).

Glenn, P (2010). *Legal Traditions of the World* 4th edn (Oxford: Oxford University Press).

Hodgson, J (2005). *French Criminal Justice* (Portland, Hart Publishing).

Human Rights Watch (2008). *Preempting Justice. Counterterrorism Laws and Procedures in France.*

Jackson, J (2008). 'Transnational Faces of Justice: Two Attempts to Build Common Standards Beyond National Boundaries', *Crime, Procedure and Evidence in a Comparative and International Context* (Jackson, J, Langer, M & Tillers, P (eds), Oxford and Portland, Hart Publishing).

Kagan, R (2001). *Adversarial Legalism* (Cambridge, Harvard University Press).

Kitai-Sangero, R (2007). 'Israel', in Bradley, C (ed), *Criminal Procedure: A Worldwide Survey* 2d (Durham: Carolina Academic Press).

Langbein, J (1979). 'Land without Plea Bargaining: How the Germans Do It', *Michigan Law Review* 78: 204–25.

Langer, M (2004). 'From Legal Transplants to Legal Translations: The Globalization of Plea Bargaining and the Americanization Thesis in Criminal Procedure', *Harvard International Law Journal* 45: 1–64.

——, (2006). 'Rethinking Plea Bargaining: The Practice and Reform of Prosecutorial Adjudication in American Criminal Procedure', *American Journal of Criminal Law* 33: 223–99.

—— (2007). 'Revolution in Latin American Criminal Procedure: Diffusion of Legal Ideas from the Periphery', *American Journal of Comparative Law* 55: 617–76.

Lüderssen, K & Jahn, M (2007). '§147', *4 Löwe-Rosenberg Die Strafprozeßordnung und das Gerichtsverfassungsgesetz. Großkommentar* 993 (Volker et al (eds), Berlin, De Gruyter Recht).

Maffei, S (2006). *The European Right to Confrontation in Criminal Proceedings* (Amsterdam, Europa Law Publishing).

Maier, J (2004). *Derecho procesal penal* (2nd edn, Buenos Aires, Editores del Puerto), Vol I.

Miller, F et al (2000). *Criminal Justice Administration* (5th edn, New York, Foundation Press).

Packer, H (1968). *The Limits of the Criminal Sanction* (Stanford University Press).

Pradel, J (2002). *Droit pénal comparé* 2nd edn (Paris, Dalloz).

—— (2004). *Procédure Pénale* 12th edn (Paris, Editions Cujas).

Roach, K (2003). 'The Criminal Process', in Tushnet, M & Cane, P (eds), *Oxford Companion to Legal Scholarship* (Oxford: Oxford University Press).

—— (2010a). *The Unique Challenges of Terrorism Prosecutions* (Ottawa: Government Services).

—— (2010b). 'Wrongful Convictions: Adversarial and Inquisitorial Themes', *North Carolina Journal of International Law and Commercial Regulation* 35: 388–446.

—— (2011). *The 9/11 Effect: Comparative Counter-Terrorism* (New York, Cambridge University Press).

Ross, J (2007). 'The Place of Covert Surveillance in Democratic Societies: A Comparative Study of the United States and Germany', *American Journal of Comparative Law* 55: 493–579.

—— (2008). 'Undercover Policing and the Shifting Terms of Scholarly Debate: The United States and Europe in Counterpoint', *Annual Review of Law and Social Science* 4: 239–61.

Samaha, A (2006). 'Government Secrets, Constitutional Law and Platforms for Judicial Intervention', *UCLA Law Review* 53: 909–76.

Summers, S (2007). *Fair Trials. The European Criminal Procedural Tradition and the European Court of Human Rights* (Oxford and Portland, Hart Publishing).

Trechsel, S (2005). *Human Rights in Criminal Proceedings* (Oxford, Oxford University Press).

Van Kessel, G (1998). 'European Perspectives on the Accused as a Source of Testimonial Evidence', *West Virginia Law Review* 100: 799–845.

Vogler, R (2005). *A World View of Criminal Justice* (Burlington, Ashgate Publishing Company).

Whitman, J (2004). 'The Two Western Cultures of Privacy: Dignity Versus Liberty', *Yale Law Journal* 113: 1151–1221.

4. Non-discrimination

22

General provisions dealing with equality

Brun-Otto Bryde and Michael Ashley Stein

22.1 Equality in political and constitutional theory

In 1776 the American Declaration of Independence stated as an evident truth that 'all men are created equal'. In 1789 the French Revolution proclaimed in the Declaration of the Rights of Man and of the Citizen that '[m]en are born and remain free and equal in rights'. Since then, equality has been a fundamental principle of constitutionalism. Paradoxically, equality is at the same time the most generally accepted principle and a highly controversial one.

There is general agreement that all humans are endowed with the same basic human rights and dignity. Differentiation of rights, and especially political rights, is therefore no longer considered acceptable—yet it took some time to reach this consensus. Women, for example, were excluded from political participation for a long time after the revolutionary declarations of the late eighteenth century. Indeed, Olympe de Gouges went to the guillotine for demanding equal rights for women during the French Revolution. And, although some Western states of the United States, New Zealand, Australia, and Scandinavia initiated female suffrage in the late nineteenth century, it was only in the twentieth century that women were generally enfranchised, with Switzerland as a latecomer among democratic republics in 1971. Similarly, both French and American revolutionaries condoned slavery despite their universal rights rhetoric, and it was only with the demise of the South African apartheid system in 1994 that race disappeared as a means to exclude people from the enjoyment of equal political status.

Today, in constitutionalist democracies, there is general agreement that all citizens enjoy equal political rights, and that all men and women enjoy human rights equally. But beyond that general consensus, controversy starts. The question to what extent the state should further equality is hotly disputed. While egalitarians favour public action to reduce inequalities, libertarians deny the state any right to interfere with an unequal distribution of resources brought about by market forces, and many shades of opinion exist between these positions. There is also political dispute as to whether public action should address only equality of opportunity or also of outcome, and whether it should aim at ensuring adequate basic living conditions for all or include redistribution of resources.[1] These differences are legitimate

---

1 A good discussion of the different positions in this debate is given by Gosepath.

subjects for political debate and constitutional texts that guarantee equality do not solve them. But in many countries, constitutional guarantees help to frame the debate.

22.2 Equality before the law and equal protection under law

In the eighteenth and nineteenth centuries, the demand for equality was a revolutionary one directed against existing laws that treated people differently according to their social status or religion. Once the aim of an equal political status of all *male* citizens was in principle—though not in practice, and with notable exceptions—reached, the constitutional tenet of equality changed focus. Equality became regularly equated with the rule of law and asked administration and courts for the equal application of the law. In principle, it was not directed against the lawmaker. The fact that general laws applied to everybody and were the product of parliaments elected by the empowered body politic was generally considered an adequate protection of equality. In other words, the constitutional equality principle guaranteed equality before the law but not equal protection under the law.

The guarantee of an equal application of the law remains an important aspect of constitutional equality provisions (see below) but increasingly the control of the lawmaker itself has become the main constitutional issue. This shift was of course possible only after judicial review of legislative action spread around the constitutional world. Starting in the United States and increasingly, especially after World War II, in other countries, the lawmaker came under scrutiny as to whether its products met constitutional equality standards. In many constitutional democracies today, an equal protection clause is in practice one of the most important vehicles for judicial review.

22.2.1 Equal protection and discrimination

The concepts of equal protection under law and non-discrimination are closely related. Jurisprudentially, however, they approach equality questions from very different angles. Discrimination is, in principle, forbidden and can be justified only under exceptional circumstances, if at all. The programme for scrutiny of legal provisions runs parallel to that of freedom rights—a law that discriminates with reference to a suspect distinction is *prima facie* forbidden and needs justification.

A general claim for equal treatment meets with much more difficulty. It is by nature vague and open-ended. Every law by necessity treats those cases it covers differently from those it does not. In the words of Ralf Dahrendorf: 'all men are equal *before* the law but they are no longer equal *after* it' (Dahrendorf, 169–70). Therefore, a general constitutional guarantee of equal protection can become a powerful tool for judicial control of the lawmaker in the hands of an activist court. Notably, courts that use it extensively are regularly accused of overstepping into the competence of the democratic lawmaker.[2]

22.2.2 Three basic constitutional models for equality

Despite diverse approaches to apprehending equality and non-discrimination, three basic models dominate the domestic constitutional landscape: (1) constitutions containing only general equality provisions; (2) constitutions with only non-discrimination provisions; and (3) constitutions with general equality provisions and either general discrimination prohibitions or

2 Sherry 89–99 (discussing judicial activism and the Equal Protection Clause).

discrimination prohibitions on the basis of particular characteristics.[3] We note, however, that while these frameworks provide a useful heuristic method for describing constitutional approaches to equality discrimination, the lines drawn are not always as distinct as presented herein.

Equality provisions like those contained in the Italian Constitution ('All citizens have equal social status and are equal before the law, without regard to their sex, race, language, religion, political opinions, and personal or social conditions')[4] and the very similar one in Canada ('Every individual is equal before and under the law and has the right to the equal protection and equal benefit of the law without discrimination … based on race, national or ethnic origin, colour, religion, sex, age, or mental or physical disability')[5] provide a good illustration. Semantically, they can be understood as mere prohibitions of discrimination. This is the case in Canada where the Canadian Supreme Court limits equal protection to 'discrete and insular minorities' who have suffered disadvantage due to a 'personal characteristic'.[6] In Italy, on the other hand, in addition to the discrimination accorded to specific characteristics, the provision has been interpreted as a general equality rule on the basis of which the rationality of laws is scrutinized (Groppi, 11).

Furthermore, these different textual solutions do not necessarily lead to the same consequences. A general equal protection provision might be construed narrowly so that it covers only cases that are treated as non-discrimination, and narrowly worded non-discrimination provisions can be extended by analogy.

22.2.3 General equal protection

One model of constitutional protection is a general equal protection provision, which must then be interpreted and applied by courts. Countries with such provisions include Argentina,[7] Brazil,[8] China,[9] Greece,[10] Luxembourg,[11] Morocco,[12] and Vietnam.[13]

A well-known example arises under the US Constitution, which provides a general equal protection mandate that is in turn juridically differentiated into sub-sections, ranging from rational basis to strict scrutiny. The Fourteenth Amendment to the Constitution, adopted in 1868 to effectuate the abolition of slavery, prohibited American states from abridging 'privileges or immunities' of US citizens, depriving any person of life, liberty, or property without

---

3   We consciously use the term 'general' rather than 'universal' to more accurately capture the fact that some states predicate equality protection on citizenship or residency rather than personhood.

4   Art 3 Costituzione (It.), *translated in Italy—Constitution*, INTERNATIONAL CONSTITUTIONAL LAW COUNTRIES, http://www.servat.unibe.ch/icl/it00000_.html (last visited Mar. 26, 2012). Unless otherwise indicated, all translated quotations from national constitutions cited in this Chapter are taken from this source, which allows readers to locate the identified nation's constitutions.

5   Constitution Act, 1982, *being* Schedule B to the Canada Act, 1982, c. 15 (UK).

6   *Law v Canada (Minister of Employment and Immigration)* [1999] S.C.R. 497 (Can).

7   Argentina Sec 16 ('All its inhabitants are equal before the law').

8   Brazil art 5 ('All persons are equal before the law, without any distinction whatsoever').

9   China art 33 § 2 (2004) ('All citizens of the People's Republic of China are equal before the law').

10   2001 Syntagma [Syn.][Constitution] 2 (Greece), *translated in The Constitution of Greece*, Centre for European Constitutional Law, http://www.cecl.gr/RigasNetwork/databank/Constitutions/Greece.html ('All Greeks are equal before the law').

11   Luxembourg art 11(2) ('Luxembourgers are equal before the law'); *id* art 11(1) ('There is no distinction of orders in the State').

12   Morocco 1996 ('The law is the supreme expression of the will of the nation. All individuals or entities … are equal before it').

13   Vietnam Art 52 (1992) ('All citizens are equal before the law').

due process of law, and from denying 'any person within its jurisdiction the equal protection of the laws'. Traditionally, courts employ a rationality test under equal protection review. That test will uphold governmental action if any differential treatment could rationally be conceived to serve legitimate state interest. However, when the state employs a suspect classification (e.g., race or ethnicity) or creates distinctions in fundamental rights (such as voting or freedom of expression) those actions are subject to strict scrutiny. In that event, courts will uphold only government actions employing classifications that can be demonstrated as necessary for achieving a compelling state interest. An intermediate standard of review applies to gender-based claims where government classifications will only be upheld if they both serve an important state objective and are substantially related to achieving those objectives. This approach has been influential not only in countries that follow this model but also in those that combine a general equal protection clause with specific non-discrimination provisions.

In France, a general equality rule has for a long time been recognized as a general principle of law by the *Conseil d'État* in administrative law. However, it was not until 1971, when the *Conseil Constitutionnel* recognized the Declaration of the Rights of Man and of the Citizen of 1789 as a standard for judicial review, that the equality principle contained in Article 6 of the Declaration gained a constitutional status.[14] Generally, the *Conseil* will accept any rational justification for different treatment.[15]

22.2.4 Countries with no general equality clause but protection against non-discrimination

Some countries do not have a general equality clause but instead feature protection against discrimination or specific cases of unequal treatment.[16] The Constitutions of Denmark and Norway, for example, restrict themselves to outlawing differential treatment that was historically important.[17] This does not force the conclusion that equality is not a constitutional value. Notably, the first case of judicial review in Denmark—the famous *Tvind* case—addressed the denial of legal benefits for private schools to one specifically named school, with the High Court deducing the unconstitutionality of this practice from the separation-of-powers principle.[18]

General prohibitions of discrimination lead to very much the same questions as are seen with general equal protection clauses: they require a differentiated approach to different classes of discrimination cases (see Chapters 23 and 24).

---

14 *Conseil Constitutionnel* [CC][Constitutional Court] decision No 73–51DC, Dec 27, 1973, Rec 25 (Fr).
15 *Conseil Constitutionnel* [CC][Constitutional Court] decision No 83–164DC, Dec 29, 1983, Rec 67 (Fr).
16 For example, Sweden 2:15 ('No Act of law or other statutory instrument may entail the discrimination of any citizen because he belongs to a minority on grounds of race, skin color, or ethnic origin').
17 Danmarks Riges Grundlov [Constitution] June 5, 1953, §§ 4, 6, 66, 67, 68, 70 (Denmark) (pertaining to religion); *id* at §§ 11, 83, 84 (pertaining to aristocratic privileges); *id* at 44, 70–80 (protecting the rights of minorities and liberty generally); Kongeriket Norges Grunnlov [Constitution] May 17, 1814, art 95 (Norway) ('No dispensations, protections from civil arrest, moratoriums or redresses may be granted after the new general code has entered into force'); *id* at art 101 (regarding professional monopolies); *id.* at art 110a ('It is the responsibility of the authorities of the State to create conditions enabling the Sami people to preserve and develop its language, culture and way of life'); *id* at arts 2, 4, 16 (regarding religious equality); *id* at arts 108, 109 (pertaining to aristocratic privileges); *id* at arts 53, 96, 97, 99, 100, 101, 102, 13, 104 (regarding the rights of minorities and liberty generally).
18 Ugeskrift for Retsvaesen [UfR] 1999, p. 841 (Den); Jensen, 492.

22.2.5 General equal protection plus non-discrimination

Since the advent of World War II, a third model has increasingly become prevalent in constitutional protection. This scheme combines a general equal protection mandate with either a general non-discrimination prohibition or a discrimination proscription against enumerated classes of individuals.

Relatively few countries bolster a general equality provision with a general non-discrimination clause. These include Afghanistan,[19] Belarus,[20] Belgium,[21] Costa Rica,[22] Latvia,[23] Lebanon,[24] Paraguay,[25] Poland,[26] and Romania.[27] Much more common are countries that combine a general equality clause with identity-specific non-discrimination protection. These include Albania,[28] Algeria,[29] Bahrain,[30] Bulgaria,[31] Canada,[32] Eritrea,[33] Estonia,[34]

---

19 Afghanistan Jan 26, 2004, art 22 ('The citizens of Afghanistan—whether man or woman—have equal rights and duties before the law'); *id* ('Any kind of discrimination and privilege between the citizens of Afghanistan are prohibited').

20 Belarus, Mar 1, 1994, art 22 ('All shall be equal before the law and entitled, without discrimination, to equal protection of their rights and legitimate interests').

21 Belgium 1994 art 10 ('Belgians are equal before the law'); *id* at art 11 ('Enjoyment of the rights and freedoms recognized for Belgians must be provided without discrimination').

22 Costa Rica, Oct 5, 2005, art 33 ('All persons are equal before the law and there shall be no discrimination against human dignity').

23 Latvia 2003, art 91 ('All human beings in Latvia shall be equal before the law and the courts. Human rights shall be realized without discrimination of any kind').

24 Lebanon, Sept 21, 1990, art 7 ('All Lebanese are equal before the law. They equally enjoy civil and political rights and equally are bound by public obligations and duties without any distinction').

25 Paraguay, June 20, 1992, art 46 ('All residents of the Republic are equal as far as dignity and rights are concerned. No discrimination is permitted').

26 Poland, Apr 2, 1997, art 32(1) ('All persons shall be equal before the law. All persons shall have the right to equal treatment by public authorities'); *id* at art 32(2) ('No one shall be discriminated against in political, social or economic life for any reason whatsoever').

27 Romania, Nov 21, 1991, art 16(1) ('Citizens are equal before the law and public authorities, without any privilege or discrimination').

28 Albania, Aug 4, 1998, art 18(1) ('All are equal before the law'); *id* at 18(2) (enumerating gender, race, religion, ethnicity, language, political, religious or philosophical beliefs, economic condition, education, social status, or ancestry).

29 Algeria, Nov 28, 1996, art 29 ('All citizens are equal before the law. No discrimination shall prevail because of bind, race, sex, opinion or any other personal or social condition or circumstance').

30 Bahrain, Feb 14 2002, art 18 ('People are equal in human dignity, and citizens are equal before the law in public rights and duties. There shall be no discrimination among them on the basis of sex, origin, language, religion or creed').

31 Bulgaria, July 13, 1991, art 6(2) ('All citizens shall be equal before the law. There shall be no privileges or restriction of rights on the grounds of race, national or social origin, ethnic self-identity, sex, origin, religion, education, opinion, political affiliation, personal or social status, or property status').

32 Constitution Act, *supra* note 16 ('Every individual is equal before and under the law and has the right to the equal protection and equal benefit of the law without discrimination and, in particular, without discrimination based on race, national or ethnic origin, colour, religion, sex, age or mental or physical disability').

33 Eritrea, May 23, 1997, art 14(1), *translated in The Constitution for Eritrea*, International Labour Organization, http://www.ilo.org/wcmsp5/groups/.../---ed.../wcms_126648.pdf ('All persons are equal before the law'); *id*. at art. 14(2) (enumerating race, ethnic origin, language, colour, sex, religion, disability, political belief or opinion, or social or economic status or any other improper factors).

34 Estonia, June 28, 1992, art 12(1) ('All persons shall be equal before the law. No one may be discriminated against on the basis of nationality, race, color, sex, language, origin, creed, political or other persuasions, financial or social status, or other reasons').

Germany,[35] Iraq,[36] Kenya,[37] Lithuania,[38] Madagascar,[39] Namibia,[40] Nepal,[41] Netherlands,[42] Oman,[43] Qatar,[44] Serbia,[45] South Korea,[46] Switzerland,[47] Turkey,[48] and Timor Leste.[49]

35 Germany May 23, 1949 BGBI 3(1) (Ger) ('All persons are equal before the law'), *id* at 3(3) ('enumerating sex, parentage, race, language, homeland and origin, faith or religious or political opinions').

36 Article 14, Section 2, Doustour Joumhouriat al-Iraq [The Constitution of the Republic of Iraq] of 2005, *translated in Iraqi Constitution*, United Nations Assistance Mission for Iraq, http://www.uniraq. org/documents/iraqi_constitution.pdf ('Iraqis are equal before the law without discrimination based on gender, race, ethnicity, nationality, origin, color, religion, sect, belief or opinion, or economic or social status').

37 Kenya, art 27(1) (2010) ('Every person is equal before the law and has the right to equal protection and equal benefit of the law'); *id* at art 12(4) (enumerating race, sex, pregnancy, marital status, health status, ethnic or social origin, colour, age, disability, religion, conscience, belief, culture, dress, language or birth).

38 Lithuania, Oct 25, 1992, art 29(1) ('All people shall be equal before the law, the court, and other State institutions and officers'); *id* at art 29(2) (enumerating sex, race, nationality, language, origin, social status, religion, convictions, or opinions).

39 Madagascar, Aug 19, 1992, art 8(1) ('Citizens shall be equal under the law, enjoying the same fundamental liberties protected by law'); *id* at art 8(2) ('enumerating sex, education, wealth, origin, race, religion, or opinion').

40 Namibia Feb 1990, art 10(1) ('All persons shall be equal before the law'); *id* at 10(2) (enumerating sex, race, colour, ethnic origin, religion, creed or social or economic status).

41 Interim Constitution of Nepal, 2007, art 13, *translated in Final Interim Constitution*, World Statesman. org, http://www.worldstatesmen.org/Nepal_Interim_Constitution2007.pdf ('(1) All citizens shall be equal before the law. No person shall be denied the equal protection of the laws. (2) There shall be no discrimination against any citizen in the application of general laws on grounds of religion, race, gender, caste, tribe, origin, language or ideological conviction or any of these. (3) The State shall not discriminate among citizens on grounds of religion, race, caste, tribe, gender, origin, language or ideological conviction or any of these ... (4) No discrimination with regard to remuneration and social security shall be made between men and women for the same work').

42 Netherlands, Feb 17, 1983, art 1 ('All persons in the Netherlands shall be treated equally in equal circumstances. Discrimination on the grounds of religion, belief, political opinion, race, or sex or on any other grounds whatsoever shall not be permitted').

43 Oman, Nov 6, 1996, art 17 ('All citizens are equal before the Law, and they are equal in public rights and duties. There shall be no discrimination between them on the grounds of gender, origin, colour, language, religion, sect, domicile or social status').

44 Qatar , Apr 29, 2003, art 34 ('The Citizens of Qatar shall be equal in public rights and duties'); *id* at art 35 (enumerating sex, race, language, or religion).

45 Serbia, Oct 28/29, 2006, art 21(1 ('All are equal before the Constitution and law'); *id* at art 21(3) (enumerating race, sex, national origin, social origin, birth, religion, political or other opinion, property status, culture, language, age, mental or physical disability).

46 South Korea, art 11 ('All citizens are equal before the law, and there may be no discrimination in political, economic, social, or cultural life on account of sex, religion, or social status').

47 Switzerland, Apr 18, 1999, art 8 para ('All humans are equal before the law'); *id* at art 8, para 2 (enumerating origin, race, sex, age, language, social position, way of life, religious, philosophical, or political convictions, or corporal or mental disability).

48 Turkey, May 10, 2007, art 10 ('(1) All individuals are equal without any discrimination before the law, irrespective of language, race, colour, sex, political opinion, philosophical belief, religion and sect, or any such considerations. (2) Men and women have equal rights. The State shall have the obligation to ensure that this equality exists in practice. (3) No privilege shall be granted to any individual, family, group or class. (4) State organs and administrative authorities shall act in compliance with the principle of equality before the law in all their proceedings').

49 East Timor, May 20, 2002, sec 16(1), *translated in Constitution of the Democratic Republic of East Timor*, The Constitution Society, http://www.constitution.org/cons/east_timor/constitution-eng.htm ('All citizens are equal before the law, shall exercise the same rights and shall be subject to the same duties'); *id* at sec 16(2) (enumerating colour, race, marital status, gender, ethnical origin, language, social or economic status, political or ideological convictions, religion, education and physical or mental condition).

The reasons for the popularity of this model are similar to those informing the development of case law in which courts differentiate between different levels of scrutiny for a general equal protection clause and a general non-discrimination clause; namely, that some forms of unequal treatment have historically been more egregious than others and therefore require closer scrutiny. Within countries that have only a general equal protection clause, the task of differentiating within identity classifications falls to judges while in this model the differentiation is already decreed by the constitution itself.

That this model has become more widespread after World War II has its main reason in increased sensibility regarding discrimination, especially in the fields of race relations and gender. In Germany, which introduced this scheme in advance of most countries, in 1949, the history of prosecution of under Nazi dictatorship was obviously influential.[50] The newly minted Federal Republic acted to replace the general equality provision of the last democratic regime, the Weimar Republic,[51] with a differentiated system in which a general equality provision that proclaims '[a]ll humans are equal before the law'[52] is followed by a extensive list of forbidden discriminations arising from a person's 'sex, parentage, race, language, homeland and origin, his faith, or his religious or political opinions'.[53]

A second reason for the popularity of the general equality plus non-discrimination model, especially in newer constitutions, is international law. Four human rights conventions—the Convention on the Elimination of All Forms of Racial Discrimination,[54] the Convention on the Elimination of All Forms of Discrimination against Women,[55] the International Convention on the Protection of the Rights of All Migrant Workers and Members of their Families,[56] and the Convention on the Rights of Persons with Disabilities[57]—specifically address discrimination against vulnerable persons and groups. General human rights conventions also outlaw discrimination.[58] International human rights law increasingly influences the drafting of constitutions (Bryde, s 191 ff). Therefore it appears natural that when countries draft constitutions they will insert a general equality clause and also highlight those discriminations that are under international opprobrium (*id*). In the constitutional reform of Switzerland, to note one such example, the constitution drafters explicitly give concordance

---

50 Art 3 of the Italian Constitution of 1947 was drafted in a similar spirit; *see* Costituzione [Cost.] (It.), *supra* note 5 ('All citizens have equal social status and are equal before the law, without regard to their sex, race, language, religion, political opinions, and personal or social conditions').

51 The Constitution of the German Empire [Weimar Constitution], Aug 11, 1919, art 109, *translated in Volume 6*. Weimar Germany, 1918/19–1933, German History in Documents and Images, http://germanhistorydocs.ghi-dc.org/pdf/eng/ghi_pol_weimarconstitution_Eng.pdf (last visited Mar 26, 2012) ('All Germans are equal before the law').

52 Grundgesetz für die Bundesrepublik Deutschland [Grundgesetz] [GG] [Basic law], May 23, 1949, BGBl. I at 3(1) (Ger).

53 *Id* at 3(3). Article 6(5) forbids discrimination against children born out of wedlock. *Id* at 6(5). In 1994, the prohibition on the basis of disability was added. Gesetz zur Änderung des Grundgesetzes [Law Amending Basic Law], Oct 27, 1994, BGBl. I at 3146 (Ger). 1249 UNTS 13.

54 Convention on the Elimination of All Forms of Racial Discrimination, Mar 7, 1966, 660 UNTS 195.

55 Convention on All Forms of Discrimination against Women, Dec 18, 1979, 1249 UNTS 13.

56 International Convention on the Protection of the Rights of All Migrant Workers and Members of their Families, Dec 18, 1990, 2220 UNTS 3.

57 Convention on the Rights of Persons with Disabilities, Mar 30, 2007, 993 UNTS 3.

58 International Covenant on Civil and Political Rights arts 4, 26, 16 Dec 1966, 999 UNTS 171; International Covenant on Economic, Social and Cultural Rights art 2(2), 16 Dec 1966, 993 UNTS 3; Universal Declaration of Human Rights, GA Res. 217 (III)A, UN Doc. A/RES/217(III), at art 7 (Dec 10, 1948).

with the international obligations as the main reason for bolstering the general equality rule with non-discrimination provisions.[59] In Europe, the influence of European Union law is also important. With articles 19 TFEU and 21 ChHREU, the European Union has the internationally most comprehensive catalogue of forbidden distinctions.[60]

The relationship between a constitution's general equal protection clause and its specific non-discrimination provisions presents a central question for comparative analysis. Significantly, the Turkish Constitution itself draws a clear distinction between the legal reach of the prohibition of discrimination and the general equality rule contained in Article 10.[61] While the prohibition of discrimination binds all branches of government, the general order to treat people equally applies only to the administrative application of laws and is therefore of special importance for the exercise of administrative discretion.[62] However, most countries that provide both general equality and non-discrimination provisions also bind the legislature, which makes it necessary to clarify the relationship between these two different approaches to equality (see Chapter 30).

In countries that have only a general equal protection provision, case law regularly tends to be developed (as is the case of the United States, above) that creates different standards of scrutiny for different classes of unequal treatment. In countries that combine a general equal protection clause with a prohibition of enumerated discriminations, this task is not left to the courts but in principle undertaken by the constitution itself. One might expect that under such a model the need for a differentiated system of different standards or tests in the framework of the general equality provision does not arise because the constitution has enumerated those classifications that require strict scrutiny and all other equality problems could be treated under a liberal standard allowing for judicial restraint. But this is not necessarily the case. General equal protection clauses are generally vague and cover many different situations such that even where the constitution has regulated some situations specifically, there may still be a need for a differentiated approach.

In Germany, both approaches have been adopted by the Federal Constitutional Court at different times. In the first decades of the Federal Republic, the non-discrimination provisions of Article 3 II and III, especially with relation to gender, and Article 6 V, relating to children born out of wedlock, came to be applied more and more strictly (Currie, 322; Baer, 262). By contrast, under the general equality clause of Article 3 I, lawmakers enjoyed great discretion: only unequal treatment that had no sensible reason at all and was therefore deemed to be arbitrary (*willkürlich*) was forbidden.[63] In a way—and this appears indeed as one possible ('originalist') interpretation of a constitution combining a general equality clause with a heightened protection of specific vulnerable groups—an *argumentum e contrario* was used in which only those interests the constitution itself defined in need of special protection enjoyed such protection.

---

59 Botschaft des Bundesrates über eine neue Bundesverfassung, Nov 20, 1996, BBl 1, S 1, 141f (Switz).

60 These distinctions include sex, racial or ethnic origin, religion or belief, disability, age or sexual orientation. Consolidated Version of the Treaty on the Functioning of the European Union art 19, Mar 30, 2010, 2010 OJ (C 83/01) 47; Charter of Fundamental Rights of the European Union art 21 Mar 30, 2010, 2010 OJ (C 83/02) 389.

61 Türkiye Cumhuriyeti Anayasasi [Constitution of the Republic of Turkey], art 10(1) ('All individuals are equal without any discrimination before the law, irrespective of language, race, colour, sex, political opinion, philosophical belief, religion and sect, or any such considerations').

62 *Id* at art. 10(4) ('State organs and administrative authorities shall act in compliance with the principle of equality before the law in all their proceedings').

63 BVerfGE 1, 14 (52).

Increasingly, the Federal Constitutional Court came to recognize that in the huge field of equality claims not covered by specific non-discrimination prohibitions, there was need for differentiation. In response, it developed a system of different tests for different equality problems within the framework of the general equality rule similar to those used by countries that have only a general equality rule. Today it explicitly holds that the general equality clause is used with different standards, from mere capriciousness to a strict proportionality test similar to the one used for non-discrimination provisions.[64] This is especially true for vulnerable groups in a similar condition to those protected by explicit provisions (e.g., transsexuals, sexual orientation), in which case the Court applies a similar standard of strict scrutiny.[65] Stricter scrutiny is also applied if the distinction employed by the lawmaker affects the enjoyment of other fundamental rights.[66]

In contrast, Canada has taken a single approach toward judicial interpretation of equal protection. When applying the Constitution, and especially Part 1 containing the Canadian Charter of Rights and Freedom, which was designed to protect citizens from illicit government action, the Canadian Supreme Court limits equal protection to 'discrete and insular minorities' who have suffered disadvantage due to a 'personal characteristic'. Thus, gender and race are examined under the same standard. At the same time, there is some evidence that an increasingly strict application of a general equality rule is not uncommon. For example, the jurisprudence of the Indian Supreme Court has applied Article 14 of the Constitution as a judicial tool against all forms of unreasonable policies (Jain, 929).

This new approach, too, can be generalized, as a possible model for countries with a combination of general equality rule and specific non-discrimination rules, where the latter are not used as an *argumentum e contrario* but rather as an inspiration. This may be particularly true in countries where disability is identified as either a protected group in constitutional texts[67] or, *inter alia*, in those countries where ratification of the Convention on the Rights of Persons with Disabilities incorporates the treaty into domestic jurisprudence. (Ecuador is one such example.[68]) People/Persons with disabilities, perhaps more so than other vulnerable population groups, forces a closer examination of the linkage between equality and non-discrimination (Stein), or put another way, the necessity of equality measures to make meaningful prohibitions on discriminatory conduct (Stein & Stein, 1209). This is due to the historic socio-economic exclusion of the group, as noted by the Committee on Economic and Social Rights,[69] as well as the historic inattention to disability in international human rights law and attendant national-level protection, as noted by the Office of the United Nations High Commissioner on Human Rights (Quinn, 23).

By the same token, recent attention to disability as a protected group creates prospects for creative jurisprudence utilizing social rights to leverage non-discrimination mandates (Stein & Lord). This can be seen clearly in the realm of employment, where bans on discrimination

---

64 BVerfGE 126, 400 (416).
65 BVerfGE 88, 87 (96).
66 BVerfGE 121, 317 (370).
67 E.g., Austria, Brazil, Canada, Finland, Fiji, the Gambia, Germany, Ghana, Malawi, New Zealand, South Africa, Switzerland, and Uganda (Degener, 92).
68 Constitución del Ecuador [Constitution of Ecuador] Oct 20, 2008, art 417.
69 Committee on Economic, Social and Cultural Rights, General Comment No 5 Persons with Disabilities, paras 16–17, UN Doc. E/1995/22 (1994) ('[T]o remedy past and present discrimination, and to deter future discrimination, comprehensive anti-discrimination legislation in relation to disability would seem indispensable … Anti-discrimination measures should be based on the principle of equal rights').

against disabled persons yield little results without concurrent equity measures such as vocational training, jobs set-asides, or affirmative action. More challenging issues involve the balancing of equality and redistribution when courts are asked to draw lines between the right of disabled persons not to be involuntarily institutionalized into social-care settings against their right to live in the community,[70] or to delineate the scope of state obligations for facilitating the legal capacity of persons with disabilities to vote, even as those courts overturn state disenfranchisement based on disability status.[71] Recently, the European Court of Human Rights evaded resolving either of those issues[72] presumably in deference to state constitutional or high courts. Hence, an opportunity exists for creative jurisprudence.

Amongst the various countries whose constitutions contain general equality clauses along with non-discrimination prohibitions for specific vulnerable population groups, South Africa's jurisprudence is especially opportune for precipitating integration of equality and equity measures on behalf of persons with disabilities.[73] This is due to the convergence of the self-avowed character of the South African Constitutional Court as progressive in the general field of social rights where it utilizes dignity to lever state obligations, the potential of the UN Conventions on the Rights of Persons with Disabilities, which South Africa has ratified, and the transformative imperative contained in its Constitution.[74] Given the impoverished situation of persons with disabilities in South Africa relative to the non-disabled population, one could well imagine the Constitutional Court not only banning exclusion in terms of access to public accommodations (including court buildings), but likewise requiring the provision of health care, clean water and sanitation, and government-sponsored employment as a means of ensuring social integration.

22.2.6 Equality and social rights

In the political and philosophical discussion about the principle of equality, the distribution of resources and the equality of living conditions take a prominent role.[75] In constitutional law, the question to what extent the state is constitutionally obliged to provide people with basic, comparable, or even equal living conditions is regularly treated not as a subject of general equality provisions but is instead referred to as specific guarantees of social rights or general social justice principles. Nevertheless, equality and social rights are closely related. In constitutional practice, equality provisions have an important role in controlling social security and welfare regulations. Even though the state is generally considered to have great discretion in how generous it is in advancing social benefits, once it has decided to do so it has to respect equality in distributing benefits (see Chapter 29).

This discretionary dynamic is most obvious for the treatment of groups protected by specific non-discrimination provisions. Both the International Convention on the Elimination

---

70　Convention on the Rights of Persons with Disabilities, *supra* note 59, art 19; Quinn & Stein.

71　Convention on the Rights of Persons with Disabilities, *supra* note 59, art 29.

72　*Alajos Kiss v Hungary*, App. No. 38832/06 (Eur Ct of Human Rights, May 20, 2010), para 44; *Stanev v Bulgaria*, App. No. 36760/06 (Eur Ct of Human Rights, Jan 17, 2012), para 159.

73　*See* generally Bhabha.

74　S. Afr. Const., 1996, art 9(3) ('The state may not unfairly discriminate directly or indirectly against anyone on one or more grounds, including race, gender, sex, pregnancy, marital status, ethnic or social origin, colour, sexual orientation, age, disability, religion, conscience, belief, culture, language and birth'). Other statutory provisions bolster this imperative, for example the Employment Equality Act. Employment Equity Act 55 of 198 (S. Afr.).

75　Gosepath, *supra* note 1 ('[H]uman beings should have the same initial expectations of 'basic goods').

of All Forms of Racial Discrimination and the International Covenant on Economic, Social and Cultural Rights protect the enjoyment of social rights from discriminatory policies.[76] But the importance of equality rules goes much beyond this hard case. For those courts that use the general equality provision extensively for a rationality control of the lawmaker (e.g., Austria, Germany, Italy), social security law has been (next to tax law) the foremost area in which to ensure some kind of rationality in rather complex systems.

The linkage between equality and social rights is even stronger where the constitution itself guarantees the equal enjoyment of some rights, especially health and education or access to basic resources like clean water and sanitation. Thus, the Polish Constitution guarantees equal access to health care as well as to education.[77] Similarly, the Constitution of Brazil provides that: 'Health is the right of all persons and the duty of the state and is guaranteed by means of social and economic policies aimed at reducing the risk of illness and other hazards and at universal and equal access to all actions and services for the promotion, protection and recovery of health.'[78] Brazil's Constitution also contains a guarantee of equal access to education, stating that 'Education which is the right of all persons and the duty of the State and of the family, shall be promoted and encouraged with the cooperation of society, aiming at full development of the individual, his or her preparation to exercise citizenship, and his or her qualification for work.'[79] But even without such explicit provisions, courts have ordered equality in the provision of health[80] or access to water.[81]

22.2.7 Relevance of a general constitutional equality provision for courts and administration

For those branches of government entrusted with the enforcement of the law—courts and administrative agencies—a constitutional order to guarantee equality before the law is to a large extent identical with the rule of law (i.e., the obligation to provide equality under law is by definition complied with if the law is applied correctly to everybody).

---

76 International Covenant on Economic, Social and Cultural Rights, *supra* note 60, at art 2(2) ('The State Parties to the present Covenant undertake to guarantee the rights enunciated in the present Covenant will be exercised without discrimination of any kind as to race, colour, sex, language, religion, political or other opinion, national or social origin, property, birth or other status'); International Convention on the Elimination of All Forms of Racial Discrimination, *supra* note 56, at art 5(e) ('State Parties undertake to prohibit and eliminate racial discrimination in all its forms and to guarantee the right of everyone without distinction as to race, colour, or national or ethnic origin, to equality before the law, notable in the enjoyment of the following rights ... (e) Economic, social and cultural rights, in particular ...').

77 Konstytucja Rzeczypospolitej Polskiej [Constitution of the Republic of Poland] Apr 2, 1997, art 68 ('1. Everyone shall have the right to have his health protected. 2. Equal access to health care services, financed from public funds, shall be ensured by public authorities to citizens, irrespective of their material situation'); *id* at art 70(1) ('Everyone shall have the right to education').

78 Constituição Federal [C.F.] [Constitution] art 196 (Braz).

79 *Id* art 205.

80 For example, in *Colombia* T-760/2008 (July 31, 2008), the Columbian Constitutional Court utilized its function of reviewing tutela actions (in this case, some 22 consolidated cases alleging violations of a right to health) to review the state's entire health care system and declare the right to health a fundamental right. The court, in addition, ruled that access to prompt sanitary services was an essential part of that right.

81 *Lindiwe Mazibuko and Others v City of Johannesburg and Others* 2009 [2009] ZACC 28; (3) BCLR 239 (CC) (S Afr).

It is different, however, where an administrative agency enjoys discretion. In this case, constitutional equality provisions become one of the most important principles for controlling the exercise of administrative discretion. The classic US case is *Yick Wo v Hopkins*, wherein a law so 'fair on its face' was administered in an anti-Chinese bias 'with an evil eye and an unequal hand'.[82] The Indian Supreme Court, too, developed extensive case law under Article 14 of the constitution to ensure that the article protects 'not only against arbitrary laws but also against the arbitrary application of laws' (Jain, 970).

By the same token, the fact that equal protection under law is guaranteed by correctly applying the law leads to the question of whether any judgment that is wrong in fact or law is also a violation of the constitution. In theory this question can be answered in the affirmative, but in practice it creates no specific constitutional issue in countries with an integrated court structure. There, the superior courts will quash judgments they think wrong without invoking the constitution.

A different circumstance attends in those countries where constitutional control is vested in a specialized constitutional court apart from the ordinary courts and where, in addition, the violation of constitutional rights by other courts can be challenged in the constitutional courts with a constitutional complaint or similar procedure. In this situation, the definition of any wrong judgment as a violation of the constitutional equality provision could easily defeat the relationship between ordinary courts and constitutional courts envisaged by the constitution, and also allow the constitutional court to acquire generalized supervisory control over other courts.

In Germany, where the combination of a specialized Constitutional Court and a constitutional complaints procedure was introduced in 1951, earlier than in other countries, the proper boundary between the spheres of jurisdictions has been one of the ongoing and (unresolved) debates. The Constitutional Court made clear in 1964 that it was not going to control the correctness of the other courts' judgments[83] and so did not take advantage of the theoretical possibility to define any miscarriage of justice as a violation of the equality provision. But the Federal Constitutional Court made an important exception, against much critique.[84] If decisions of other courts are not just wrong—but so wrong that they are considered arbitrary—the Court will interpret this as a violation of Article 3(1).[85] In a recent judgment, the Court went one step further, holding that a certain line of jurisprudence was so contradictory to the letter of the law and legislative intent that it violated Article 3(1).[86]

22.2.8 Horizontal application

Open and direct racial discrimination by legislation has disappeared with the end of the apartheid system. But indirect social discrimination against minorities (or excluded majorities) unfortunately remains a problem in many parts of the world. Official discrimination in relation to ethnicity or gender has disappeared from the law in most countries, at least in

---

82 *Yick Wo v Hopkins*, 118 US 356, 373 (1886).
83 Structuring procedure, establishing and evaluating facts, interpreting ordinary laws and their application to a concrete case are the exclusive competence of the competent courts and cannot be reviewed by the Federal Constitutional Court. It is only in case of a violation of specific constitutional law that the Federal Constitutional Court can intervene. BVerfGE 18, 85 (92).
84 BVerfGE 42, 64 (78).
85 BVerfGE 42, 64; BVerfGE 57, 39 (41-42); *see also* Currie, 335.
86 BVerfGE 128, 193.

constitutionalist democracies. This does not mean that the fight against social discrimination has become less important. Therefore, the horizontal application of non-discrimination provisions (i.e., their application in the relationship of private parties) is a vital part of any non-discrimination strategy. (See Chapter 14.)

The horizontal application of general equality provisions, on the other hand, would interfere with basic freedoms. Unlike the state, the private citizen is not required to treat all other members of society alike. This does not mean, however, that horizontal application of general equality provisions is completely excluded. On the one hand, we have seen that apart from specific non-discrimination provisions, hard discrimination questions can arise in the framework of a general equality provision. For these, a horizontal application is as relevant as the accepted non-discrimination laws with relation to race or gender.

More generally, in some constitutional systems, powerful social actors who control the lives of other members of society are held to standards comparable to those applied to state actors. Labour law is the classic example. In Germany, the labour courts have developed from the constitutional equality principle a labour-law equality principle that binds employers and the contracting parties of collective bargaining agreements in their treatment of employees.[87] (Similarly, the providers of basic services like water or electricity have been required by courts to provide equal access to their customers.)

References

All constitutional provisions can be found at http://www.servat.unibe.ch/icl, unless otherwise indicated.

Baer, S (1999). 'Equality: The Jurisprudence of the German Constitutional Court', *Columbia Journal of European Law* 5: 249–80.

Bhabha, F (2009). 'Disability Equality Rights in South Africa: Concepts, Interpretation and the Transformation Imperative', *South African Journal of Human Rights* 25: 218–46.

Bryde, B (2003). 'The Internationalization of Constitutional Law', in Groß, T (ed), *Legal Scholarship in International and Comparative Law* (Frankfurt Peter Lang Publishers).

Currie, D (1999). *The Constitution of the Federal Republic of Germany* (Chicago, University of Chicago Press).

Dahrendorf, R (1968). *On the Origin of Inequality Among Men, in* Essays in the Theory of Society 151.

Degener, T (2011). 'Disability Discrimination Law: A Global Comparative Approach', in Lawson, A & Gooding, C (eds), *Disability Rights in Europe: From Theory to Practice* 87–106.

Gosepath, S (2007). *Equality, in* Zalta, EN (ed), Stanford Encyclopedia of Philosophy, *available at* http://plato.stanford.edu/entries/equality.

Groppi, T (2008). 'The Italian Constitutional Court', *Journal of Comparative Law* 3: 100–17.

Jain MP *Indian Constitutional Law* (LexisNexis Butterworths Wadhwa, 2010)

Jensen, JA (1999). 'The 150th Anniversary of the Danish Constitution and a Landmark Decision of the Supreme Court', *European Public Law Journal* 5: 492–99.

Quinn, G et al (2002), Human Rights and Disability: The current use and future potential of United Nations human rights instruments in the context of disability, 23.

—— & Stein, M (2009). 'Challenges in Realising the Right to Live in the Community', in Bulic, I & Parker, C (eds), *Focus on Article 19 of the UN Convention on the Rights of Persons with Disabilities* (European Coalition for Community Living), 28.

Sherry, S (1984). 'Selective Judicial Activism in the Equal Protection Context: Democracy, Distrust, and Deconstruction', *Georgetown Law Journal* 73: 89–126.

Stein, M (2007). 'Disability Human Rights', California Law Review 95: 75–121.

---

87 Weiss & Schmidt, 94.

Stein, M & Lord, J (2011). 'Accessing Socio-Economic Rights: The Rights of Persons with Disabilities', in Langford, M & Reidel, E (eds), *Equality and Socio-Economic Rights: International Law in Theory and Practice*.

—— & Stein, P (2007). 'Beyond Disability Civil Rights', *Hastings Law Journal* 58: 1203–40.

Weiss, M & Schmidt, M (2008). *Labour Law and Industrial Relations in Germany* (The Netherlands, Kluwer Law International).

Additional reading

Baer, S (2012), 'Equality', in Rosenfeld, M & Sajo, A (eds), Oxford Handbook on Comparative Constitutional Law.

Stein, M (2004). 'Same Struggle, Different Difference: ADA Accommodations as Antidiscrimination', *University of Pennsylvania Law Review* 153: 579–673.

Wolfrum, R (ed) (2003). Gleichheit und Nichtdiskriminerung im nationalen und Internationale Menschenrechtsschutz (Berlin/Heidelberg/New York).

Sites of constitutional struggle for women's equality

Ruth Rubio-Marín and Wen-Chen Chang

23.1 Introduction

Constitutionalism and citizenship have been historical paradigms to advance egalitarian, rights-based visions of political justice. Locating the birth of modern constitutionalism with the French and American Revolutions at the end of the eighteenth century, we realize that even in the West, where the liberal revolutions first led to the affirmation of rights-based constitutionalism proclaiming, as the French Declaration of the Rights of Man and of the Citizen did, the 'freedom and equality in rights of men at birth',[1] the word *men* had to be interpreted literally, and not simply as an expression of the generic use of the masculine terminology. Olympe de Gouges's almost contemporaneous affirmation that 'woman is born free and remains equal to man in rights',[2] through which she intended revolutionary constitutionalism to start on a more sex-egalitarian track, was to remain a desideratum for many years.

Political equality for women started to become a reality only at the turn of the twentieth century with access to suffrage. In some cases, this recognition triggered constitutional amendments 'to write women in'.[3] Alternatively, women started to be simply read into the abstract male 'generic' that most constitutions used. But even then, the constitutional grounding of women's political equality was, at the time, understood to be compatible with the persistence of the denial of women's civil equality. In Western liberal democracies, it was not until after 1945 and, as a rule, not before the 1960s and 1970s that marriage and family law, regarded as the paradigmatic realms of tradition, were systematically reformed to ensure women's full equality with men (see Rodríguez-Ruiz & Rubio-Marín 2012), a task undertaken by constitutional litigation and legal reform in Asia only in the late 1980s and 1990s (see, e.g., Chang, in Yap & Lau).

---

1 See Article 1 of the Declaration of the Rights of Man and of the Citizen, adopted 26 August 1789.
2 See Article 1 of the Declaration of the Rights of Woman and the Female Citizen, published in September 1791.
3 This was, for instance, the case of the Nineteenth Amendment to the US Bill of Rights granting women equal suffrage, passed in 1920.

Two consequences follow from the way that constitutionalism and women's access to full citizenship intersected. The first is that, for women, the full emancipatory potential of constitutional rights had to wait until women were recognized as equal citizens. This required more than granting women equal political rights and explains why an important impulse in the process of 'reading women into constitutionalism' came from the recognition of both the principle of non-discrimination on the grounds of sex and the principle of equality in marriage in universal human rights documents of the post-World War II political order. Prior to 1945, prevailing constitutional understandings of human freedom and equality were for the most part regarded as compatible with women's less-than-equal citizenship status. Only in post-WWII constitutionalism did women's full equality in rights make it to the status of a 'defining feature' of liberal democratic constitutionalism itself.

The second important consequence of the late arrival of women's full equality to the constitutional project is that this process of inclusion inherently limited the constitutionally enshrined understanding of human freedom and autonomy. Both post-WWII human rights law and constitutionalism, while including women as human rights holders, ignored for the most part that the rights they enshrined reflected and universalized the male condition. Thus, when women finally arrived at the status of equal fundamental rights holders, by being promised *the same rights as men*, the question was of course begged as to whether women's understandings of autonomy and equality and the set of fundamental rights placed at the service of such values could have been different. And even to this day, short of a massive incorporation of women to the role of norm (including constitutional norm) creation, the promise of full equality for women has yet to be realized.

Against this historical background, this chapter discusses three different ways in which women have come to inhabit constitutionalism around the world. Section 23.2 describes how the promise of the 'same rights as men' has come to life, mostly through the constitutional principles of equality and non-discrimination to assist in the process of ensuring women full civil liberties and marital equality. In section 23.3, we explore the extent to which constitutions have become or failed to become a battlefield to assert women's specific rights claims. For this purpose we choose to focus on the 'female-only person' of the pregnant woman as a legal subject and look at whether her reproductive autonomy, including the right to have an abortion or to carry the pregnancy to term, has been constitutionally fought for and/or recognized. In section 23.4 we discuss constitutional debates around gender political quotas, describing constitutional processes to entrench parity democracy, moving the question of the constitutional incorporation of women beyond the rights debate and into the domain of the defining features of the democratic state and norm creation.

23.2 The right to be treated like men

Constitutional recognition of formal equality enables women's litigation to request courts to affirm equal rights for women. This kind of litigation often began with women's claim to equal rights in the family, where women have traditionally been subordinated to men. Courts asserted equal rights of women in family-related matters by recognizing formal equality. These cases came into the Western courts as early as in the 1960s and 70s, reflecting second-wave feminism's attack on the patriarchal family model, and culminating in international norms such as the Convention on the Elimination of All Forms of Discrimination Against Women (CEDAW), which became effective in 1981. In Asia, women's use of constitutional litigation occurred more recently, as these legal and judicial strategies became available only after the states' progression to social and political reforms in the 1980s and 1990s (Chang, in Yap & Lau). This also explains the later reception of CEDAW in most Asian states.[4]

For instance, the first decision in favour of the equal rights of women in the family by the Constitutional Court of Taiwan was rendered in 1994, holding unconstitutional a provision of the Civil Code that accorded the power of final decision to the father if there was disagreement over the exercise of parental rights in relation to the child.[5] The Court subsequently also invalidated another provision in the Civil Code that required the wife to take the residence of the husband after marriage,[6] and a government regulation that deprived veterans' married daughters—but not married sons—of their equal right to inheritance of government-leased property.[7] Similarly, in South Korea in 2005, the Constitutional Court found unconstitutional the century-long system in which husbands and fathers were always registered as house heads, requiring children to be registered with the household of the father rather than the mother after divorce.[8] Following the same line of reasoning, the Constitutional Court also found unconstitutional the provision in the Civil Code that required adoption of the paternal family name,[9] and the Nationality Act that privileged paternal lineage as the basis of nationality.[10] Given the conservative attitude of Korean society with respect to the role of women in the family sphere, these constitutional decisions were by no means easy.[11] Until the 1990s, Koreans were banned from marrying a spouse of the same surname that followed paternal lineage.[12] Using formal equality to eradicate discrimination against women in the family or other related domains has also occurred in Japan. In the early 1980s, the Supreme Court invalidated a private company regulation that stipulated different mandatory retirement ages for men and women as an irrational discrimination against women.[13] Referring to the constitutional guarantee of sex equality, the Supreme Court extended sex equality to private employment by finding that the different retirement ages contravened 'public policy'. Recently, paralleling the Korean Nationality Act Case, the Supreme Court of Japan interpreted its Nationality Act to allow a child born out of wedlock to a Japanese father and a foreign mother to obtain Japanese nationality.[14]

The cases discussed above shed light on the empowering potential of formal equality. At the same time, this framework has had obvious limitations. To assert the same rights as men have, women must show that they are 'like men' and insist that discriminations based on sex

---

4 See e.g. China (1980), India (1993), Indonesia (1984), Japan (1985), Korea (1984), Malaysia (1995), Singapore (1995), Philippines (1981), and Vietnam (1982). Taiwan voluntarily acceded to CEDAW in 2007, despite not being recognized by the United Nations. See e.g. Thio 1997; Chang 2011.

5 J.Y. Interpretation No. 365 (Sept 23, 1994).

6 J.Y. Interpretation No. 452 (Apr 10, 1998).

7 J.Y. Interpretation No. 457 (Jun 12, 1998).

8 Case on the House Head System, 17-1 KCCR 1, 2001 Hun-Ka 9 *et al*, Feb 3, 2005.

9 Use of Paternal Family Name Case, 17-2 KCCR 544, 2003 Hun-Ka 5 *et al*, Dec 22, 2005.

10 Under the law, children born of a Korean father and a foreign mother automatically acquired Korean nationality whereas children born of a foreign father and a Korean mother remained as foreigners. See Nationality Act Case, 12-2KCCR 167, 97 Hun-Ka 12, Aug 31, 2000.

11 In the Case on the House Head System, a dissenting opinion was issued by two justices with a strong tone to defend the house head system on the basis of culture and tradition.

12 This ban in the Civil Code was held unconstitutional by the Constitutional Court in 1997. See Same Surname Same Origin Marriage Ban Case, 9-2KCCR 1, 95 Hun-Ka 6, etc., Jul 16, 1997.

13 *Nissan Motors, Inc v Nakamoto* (1981). The Nissan Gender Discrimination Case, in Beer & Itoh, 179ff.

14 Case on nationality of a child born out of wedlock to a Japanese father and a Filipino mother, 2006 (Gyo-Tsu) No. 135, 2008.06.04.

or gender must be prohibited. But this leaves out precisely those situations in which women are not equally situated to men, because of their biological or functional differences. In the end, this has meant that relying on different doctrinal constructs (such as proportionality analysis or heightened scrutiny), courts have inevitably had to rely on judgements about when sex-based differentiations were or were not arbitrary, irrational, unreasonable. Differences in treatment in the family domain, as a domain characterized by male power, have been easy targets of correction through formal equality analysis.[15] Other types of differential treatment have found a less unified response, especially given the fact that many constitutions have by now embraced a substantive equality framework, promising to deliver equal opportunities for the enjoyment of rights. The need to accommodate women's distinct biology and statistically significant differential choices regarding the work/family balance, or to compensate for women's past and present disadvantages, have sometimes been seen as justified deviations from formal equality, and sometimes as unjustified deviations with the potential to enshrine the very sex-based stereotypes that equality should abolish.[16] Where even difference and egalitarian strands of feminism disagree, it would have been surprising to find agreement in male-dominated courts.

23.3 The search for women's rights: the constitutionalism of abortion

Women's reproductive autonomy has rarely deserved explicit constitutional protection, and only as recently as the 1990s.[17] Constitutional disputes surrounding abortion have been around only for about four decades. As late as the 1960s, abortion was not generally understood as presenting constitutional questions. Interestingly, constitutional decisions on abortion began in the West in an era when a transnational women's movement was starting to challenge the terms of women's citizenship, precisely coinciding with second-wave feminism's attack against the patriarchal family model (see Siegel).

First in time was *Roe v Wade*, the 1973 US Supreme Court decision in which a pregnant woman and others challenged the constitutionality of a statute making it a crime to 'procure an abortion' except 'by medical advice for the purpose of saving the life of the mother' on the basis that this invaded a right, said to be possessed by the pregnant woman, to choose to

---

15 Examples of case law in Western countries dating back to the 1950s, 1960s and 1970s and relying on formal equality to disestablish women's inferior legal status in the family/marital domain can be found in Baines & Rubio-Marín.

16 For instance, although there is much variation among European countries, there seems to be a contrast between US constitutional anti-discrimination doctrine, which has been mostly concerned with fighting gender stereotypes in general, and those that confine women to the home, perpetuate the breadwinner role and limit women's ability to act as full citizens in particular, and the European sex anti-discrimination model that has thus far prioritized addressing women's real obstacles by accommodating their sex-specificity, both social and biological, at times even at the risk of entrenching gender roles. See Suk.

17 In this regard, Nepal is quite an extraordinary exception. Since the enactment of the eleventh amendment bill, Article 20 of the Interim Constitution of Nepal 2063 (2007) contains an entire provision devoted to Women's Rights (including Article 20.2), which provides that 'every woman shall have the right to reproductive health and rights relating to reproduction'. More generic references, but still fairly recent ones, include the example of the 1994 South African Constitution (Article 12(2)(b)), which refers to the right to control one's body. Another exception is art 55 of the Slovenian Constitution (adopted in 23 December 1991) providing that 'everyone shall be free to decide whether to bear children' and that 'the state shall guarantee the opportunities for exercising this freedom and shall create such conditions as will enable parents to decide to bear children.'

terminate her pregnancy. Although the Court relied on a right to privacy as encompassing a woman's and her practitioner's decision whether or not to terminate her pregnancy, this right was recognized not to be absolute. *Roe* endorsed a framework banning state interference in the first trimester; allowing public powers to regulate abortion to protect the health and life of the pregnant woman after the first trimester; and, finally, to limit or even ban abortion after the point of viability (410 US 113, 152, 164–165 (1973)). Later case law, especially *Planned Parenthood of Southeastern Pennsylvania v Casey*, rejected this scheme and replaced it with a doctrine whereby, so long as the law did not impose an 'undue burden' on the pregnant woman's decision whether to bear a child, the state could assert an interest in protecting unborn life throughout the term of a pregnancy, and not only after the first trimester (505 US 833 (1992)).

In Europe, the constitutionalization of abortion disputes led in the opposite direction, mostly because from the start the process was essentially one of reading the fetus, and not women, into mostly silent constitutions.[18] That process was clearly influenced by the strong counter-mobilization of Catholic groups resisting women's reproductive rights in the name of the sanctity of life. In Europe, constitutions were called to play a role in an attempt to curb, through abstract review, legislative attempts to liberalize access to abortion, either on the indications model (allowing abortion when there were indications that child-birth would cause specified harm to the woman) or on the periodic model (regulating abortions differently depending on when they were sought), when those frustrated with politics have decided to bring their claims to the courts. Also, after a short-lived phase in which courts affirmed these legislative reforms,[19] and until only most recently, the constitutional anchoring of abortion has systematically resulted in constitutional courts more or less aggressively curbing legislative attempts to widen women's autonomy. The most influential and paradigmatic case in Europe was without a doubt the first abortion decision by the German Federal Constitutional Court in 1975, striking down a legislative attempt to decriminalize abortion during the first 12 weeks of pregnancy.[20] For the German Court, as an 'unborn human being', the fetus enjoyed both the protection of the right to life (art 2.2.1 GG) and the protection of human dignity (art 1.1.2 GG), and this ruled out the possibility of signalling different stages in the process of development of the fetus (such as viability) to be deemed relevant for determining different degrees of constitutionally required protection.[21]

---

18 It is exceptional to find the life of the fetus explicitly protected in the Constitution. But there are some examples, including in the Republic of Ireland, where in 1983 the Constitution was amended to provide, 'the State acknowledges the right to life of the unborn and, with due regard to the equal right to life of the mother, guarantees in its laws to respect, and as far as practicable, by its laws to defend and vindicate that right' (Ireland, Eighth Amendment of the Constitution Act, 1983, 1983 Acts of the Oireachtas, 7 October 1983 (amending Ir. Const., art. 40, sec 3.3). Hungary's newly enacted Constitution provides in art. II that 'the life of the foetus shall be protected from the moment of conception'. See Fundamental Law of Hungary, 25 April 2011.

19 In 1974 and 1975 the Australian Constitutional Court and French *Conseil Constitutionnel* both validated liberalizing abortion reform legislation that had been submitted to them. See [1974] Erklaerungen des Verfassungsgerichtshofs 221, decision of 11 October 1974 and *Conseil Constitutionnel* [1975] DSJur 529 [1975] AJDA 134 (of 15 January 1975).

20 Bundesverfassungsgericht 25 Feb 1975, 39 BVerfGE 1.

21 *Ibid* CI1b. The Court found it unnecessary to decide whether a fetus is strictly speaking a constitutional rights bearer because beyond providing subjective defensive rights of protection against the state, fundamental rights also embody an objective order of values that have to be proactively safeguarded by state action. CI3.

This process of reading the fetus into the Constitution as either a rights bearer or embodiment of constitutional values that deserve constitutional protection became the norm in European abortion constitutionalism and was exported to other parts of the world, such as Latin America, where it continues to constrain even the most progressive abortion constitutional decisions.[22] This model has entailed reading pregnant women out or, better, turning them primarily, constitutionally and reproductively speaking into duties (instead of rights) bearers, through a more or less explicitly articulated process of normalizing and naturalizing their motherly obligations. Within this general framework, much constitutional litigation has then turned around the question of where to draw the line separating natural and ordinary duties of motherhood of the pregnant woman from extraordinary circumstances such as those reflected in the indications model. More recently in Europe, a paradigm shift has begun towards the recognition that, even when the protection of unborn human life is constitutionally grounded, the life of the fetus does not have automatic constitutional priority over a woman's reproductive autonomy and that both woman's reproductive autonomy and the life of the unborn deserve some form of constitutional protection, which means that the legislator is necessarily bound to perform an act of balancing and hence to prioritize forms of protection of the unborn that assist rather than punish, threaten or coerce pregnant women.[23]

In contrast with the position in the West, constitutional litigation on abortion has not yet become the main site for Asian women to claim their reproductive rights. Most Asian countries have adopted rather lax abortion policies that allow abortion either on a periodic model or with a system of broad indications ranging from genetic concerns to the mother's physical and mental health, and even to socio-economic grounds or both (Whittaker, 16f). In many countries, such policies have coexisted with provisions criminalizing abortion that have had nearly zero enforcement.[24] This does not, however, reflect the view that abortion is recognized as a right, linked to women's reproductive autonomy, but quite the opposite. Granting

22 The much celebrated Colombian Constitutional Court decision reproduces this architecture when it starts from the necessary protection of unborn life to then argue that the legislative prohibition of abortion in all circumstances is unconstitutional because it extinguishes a woman's fundamental rights, reducing her to the condition of a receptacle of the fetus. See Corte Constitucional, 10 May 2006, Sentencia 355/2006, 26 Gaceta de la Corte Constitucional (Colom). See also the 2008 Mexican Supreme Court decision, upholding a statute of Mexico City decriminalizing abortion during the first 12 weeks (see Suprema Corte de Justica de la Nación. *Acciones de Inconstitucionalidad 146/2008* and *147/2008*, from 28 August 2008).

23 See, for example, the 1998 decision by the Hungarian Constitutional Court striking down an indications model that included as one indication the 'situation of serious crisis' for which a woman's signature was to be sufficient. For the Hungarian Court, a regulation that was only protective of a woman's autonomy was not constitutional. However, the Court acknowledged that decriminalization of abortion coupled with abortion-dissuasive counselling would be a constitutionally valid method of protecting unborn life, which would also be respectful of a woman's right (Alkotmánybíróság (AB) [Constitutional Court], Decision 48/1998 (XI. 23.), Official Gazette (Magyar Közlöny) MK 1998/105 (Hung), 26 *available at* www.mkab.hu/admin/data/file/710_48_1998.pdf.) This new model is allowing European Constitutional Courts to enter the abortion debate to validate the periodic model, as in the 2010 decision by the Portuguese Constitutional Court, upholding legislation allowing women to have an abortion in the first 10 weeks of pregnancy after a counselling process destined to provide women with the information needed to make a free, conscious, and responsible decision and a three-day reflection period, considering this, as well as sexual education and assistance to motherhood owed by the state sufficient constitutional protection of the unborn life. See Acordao N 75/2010, 23.10.2010.

24 Such as in Taiwan, South Korea and Thailand. Whittaker, 11f, 17f.

women access to abortion or not is entirely in the hands of the government and is done to accommodate state interests in genetic health and population control (especially in countries where access to contraceptives and family planning has been extremely limited), as well as in decreasing the mortality rate for women giving birth (*id*, 11ff). There undoubtedly remains a strong need for women to seek formal constitutional recognition of their independent reproductive rights. Why has such litigation not occurred in these Asian countries?

Asian women's reluctance to use constitutional litigation to affirm reproductive rights may be due in part to the fact that most Asian constitutions fail to recognize reproductive rights independently of motherhood. Constitutions extend reproductive protections only to the mother vis-à-vis the child.[25] As we can infer from the European experience, making a claim of reproductive rights may in fact invite the courts to read in the interests of the unborn, not necessarily advancing women's reproductive rights. For example, in a case unrelated to abortion, the Constitutional Court of South Korea stressed that the fetus, as an evolving life, was entitled to constitutional protection while affirming the constitutionality of its Civil Code, which provided tort claims only for the fetus born alive.[26] This evidences the high stakes in using constitutions to advance women's reproductive rights, a much-learned lesson from the West, where religious groups and conservative forces have preferred to deploy constitutional discourse to counter women's reproductive rights demands. In Asia, for the time being, such counterforce has not arisen.

Nonetheless, constitutional affirmation of women's reproductive rights remains paramount not only in recognizing a woman's full citizenship independently of her motherhood but also in providing her publicly funded, safe, and easy access to abortion wherever she finds necessary. A relatively unrestrictive ('lax') policy of abortion still cannot guarantee women reproductive rights to safe and accessible reproductive care. This is a particularly serious concern for poor women and women in less developed countries in Asia.[27] In this regard, Nepal provides an extraordinary example in its recent constitutional recognition of women's reproductive rights. Nepal's abortion law had been one of the strictest and most punitive in the Asian region. Women could be jailed between 3 and 20 years for having an abortion (Whittaker, 22). In 2002, Nepal reformed its abortion law to adopt a less restrictive policy, but this reform continued to face challenges of implementation, especially in ensuring access to abortion for rural women and reducing the mortality rate of women having abortions.[28] The Interim Constitution of 2007 contains an entire provision (Article 20) devoted to women's rights, one clause of which provides that 'every woman shall have the right to reproductive health and rights relating to reproduction'. Taking advantage of this clause, in *Lakshmi Dhikta v Nepal* (2009), the Supreme Court of Nepal interpreted the constitutional recognition of women's reproductive rights as requiring the legislator to remove woman's abortion from the criminal law (as symbolically tainting the exercise of a fundamental right) and demanding that the state ensure that costs are not an impediment for a woman who cannot afford an abortion procedure. The Nepalese experience confirms the constitutional significance in formally recognizing women's independent reproductive rights.

---

25 The protection of motherhood vis-à-vis the child is presented either in the form of a mother's fundamental right such as in Mongolia, the Philippines or Vietnam or in the form of a guiding principle to be operationalized though state policies such as in Taiwan or Cambodia.
26 Claim for Damages of Stillborn Fetuses Case, 2004 Hun-Ba 81, 31 July 2008.
27 Andrea Whittaker (n35), 14f.
28 Whittaker, 22. The current reformed abortion law allows abortion during the first trimester and up to 18 weeks in case of rape or incest.

23.4 Beyond rights: women and democracy

The question of women's disempowerment has come to the forefront in many parts of the world. Among other options, countries have explored gender quotas in electoral lists (see Krook).

In the Asian region, a few constitutions enacted after World War II contemplated quotas to enhance the political representation of disadvantaged groups as well as women, reflecting the commitment to substantive equality to combat the legacy of colonial stratification and subordination, and nation-building interests. The 1947 Republic of China (ROC) Constitution was the first among Asian constitutions to require quotas for women in electoral politics. Article 134 states that in various kinds of elections, the number of women to be elected shall be fixed, and measures prescribed by law. As this constitution was subsequently implemented in Taiwan, since the 1950s women's presence in all legislatures has been greater than 20 percent (Clark & Lu, Table 4). However, this constitution has provided quotas not only for women but also for other ethnic minority groups.[29] Indeed, the making of modern constitutions in Asia was undertaken as an expedited process of state and nation building against foreign threats (Yeh & Chang, 814). Despite being multi-ethnic and multi-linguistic, these Asian states tried to present themselves as a single nation with minorities included, and constitutional quotas became an effective tool to glue these ethnic groups together.[30]

More gender-specific quota came later in Asia in the 1990s, influenced in part by CEDAW and related international movements. In India, the 74th Constitutional Amendment enacted in 1992 added a women's quota into the reserved seats for scheduled castes and tribes in local Panchayats, demanding no less than one-third of those seats allocated for women belonging to the scheduled castes and tribes.[31] Another attempt at adding a women's quota to the national legislature was initiated in 1998, and again in 1999, but it failed in the end as lower-caste men feared that such a quota might increase the number of upper-caste women and undermine their own political representation. After more than a decade's advocacy, in February 2012, India's Upper House again passed a proposal for a women's quota, awaiting further approval from the Lower House and states (Prasad). In Taiwan, despite the quota already stipulated in the ROC Constitution, a constitutional revision in 2005 changed the electoral method of the national legislature once again, demanding that the number of elected female members on each party's list must not be less than one-half of the total number.[32] As a result, in the election of 2012, women for the first time occupied more than 33 percent of the national legislature. A similar strategy was also adopted in the Constitution of Philippines to reserve one-half of the seats allocated to party-list representatives for various minorities including women.[33] In

---

29 Article 64 also stipulates quotas for ethnic minorities, overseas citizens as well as some occupational groups. Article 135 demands the reservations of seats in the national legislature for ethnic minorities.

30 The 1950 Constitution of India also reserved seats for scheduled castes and tribes in the national legislature and the local Panchayats (councils). The equality clause (Article 15) of the Indian Constitution explicitly endorsed these special quota arrangements. In a recent decision by the Indian Supreme Court, these special quotas' constitutionality was affirmed. See *Union of India v Rakesh Kumar & Ors*, 12 January, 2010.

31 Article 243 D (2)–(6) of the Indian Constitution.

32 Section 2, Article 4 of the Additional Articles to the Republic of China Constitution (amended in 2005).

33 Article 4, section 5 (2) of the Constitution. The list of minorities includes the labour, peasant, urban poor, indigenous cultural communities, women, youth, and such other sectors as may be provided by law, except the religious sector.

a recent decision, the Supreme Court of the Philippines added one more group—gays and lesbians—to the list.[34]

In Western countries, gender political quotas entered the constitutional scene later, and often through litigation and constitutional amendment challenging dominant notions of general democratic representation and, for the most part, targeting women's political under-representation as something *sui generis* and conceptually distinct from the underrepresentation of other marginalized groups. In Europe, constitutional battles around gender political quotas had France, the cradle of liberal constitutionalism, as one of its main protagonists. In 1982 the Assembly passed an Act that obliged electoral ballots in municipal elections to have at least 25 percent of candidates of each gender. The Act was successfully challenged before the *Conseil Constitutionnel*, which struck it down calling on the principles of equality before the law, national sovereignty, and the indivisibility of the electoral body.[35] Other European and Latin American courts followed the French example. In 1995 the Italian Constitutional Court,[36] in 1997 and 1998 the Swiss Constitutional Court,[37] and in 2000 the Colombian Constitutional Court[38] all similarly struck down gender quota legislation and initiatives, showing that even when substantive equality mandates are constitutionally enshrined, as they are in Italy, Switzerland, and Colombia,[39] the resistance against subverting the principle of general, free, and equal voting rights through quotas remains; something that can only be explained because of the connection drawn between such principles and the constitutionally enshrined model of representative democracy.[40]

It may be a sign of a growing awareness that the problem is indeed with our conception of democratic representation, and the way it has *de facto* kept women outside politics and power, that a series of constitutional amendments have successfully been passed in several European

34 *Ang Ladlad LGBT Party v Commission on Elections*, GR No 190582 (2010).
35 See CC decision no. 82-146DC, Nov 28, 1982, JO p 3475. For a discussion of the French debate, see Rodríguez-Ruiz & Rubio-Marín 2008, 290–3.
36 See Corte const, n 422/1995, Foro It. For a thorough discussion of the Italian debate see Rodriguez-Ruiz & Rubio-Marín 2008, 294–6.
37 See Bundesgericht [BGer] [Federal Court] Mar. 19, 1997, 123 Entscheidungen des Schweizerischen Bundesgerichts [BGE] I 152 (Switz). For a discussion of the Swiss case, see Rodríguez-Ruiz & Rubio-Marín 2012.
38 Corte const, Mar. 29, 2000, Sentencia C-371/00 (Colom). For analysis of the Colombian decision, see Rodríguez-Ruiz & Rubio-Marín 2008.
39 Art 3.2 in the Italian Constitution provides that: 'It is the duty of the republic to remove all economic and social obstacles that, by limiting the freedom and equality of citizens, prevent full individual development and the participation of all workers in the political, economic, and social organization of the country.' The most interesting case may be that of Colombia, for there the challenged legislation had been passed precisely to implement the requirement of Article 40 of the 1991 Colombian Constitution whereby 'the authorities will guarantee the adequate and effective participation of women at the decision-making levels of Public Administration'. To this end, the legislator had established a 30 percent quota for women in high-level decision-making positions in the public sector. The provisions in the statute were examined and found, for the most part, constitutional as temporary affirmative action measures compatible with the notion of substantive equality, generically sanctioned in Article 13.2 of the Constitution, after surviving a proportionality scrutiny. The Court, however, distinguished between executive appointments and elected positions, and ruled out the possibility of mandatory electoral quotas for the latter, calling on the autonomy of political parties and the principle of popular sovereignty as prevalent in the electoral field.
40 In this respect, the 2008 Spanish Constitutional Court, upholding mandatory electoral gender quotas ensuring that electoral lists include no less than 40 percent of candidates from each gender (see STC, Jan 29, 2008, No. 12/2008) relying mostly on the substantive equality reasoning, constitutes a rare exception. See Rodríguez-Ruiz & Rubio-Marín 2008.

countries to facilitate the introduction of gender quotas. Whereas in some countries, such as Portugal (1997)[41] or Slovenia (2004),[42] constitutional amendments preceded the passing of legislation or came right after it, as a form of constitutional backing, in most other cases the reforms were necessary to overcome a constitutional court's expressed objections, as in France and Italy, where constitutional amendments were required to move from a formal towards a substantive understanding of equality, either in general or specifically in the political domain.[43]

Although much of the new wording introduced into constitutional texts suggests a substantive equality/equal opportunities framing, some of the reforms make explicit reference to democracy,[44] underscoring that what is at stake is not just a question of granting women effective political rights but rather of ensuring women's empowerment as a way of tackling a democratic deficit and of disestablishing the sexual contract based on the gendered division of roles, which modern constitutionalism entrenched (see Rodríguez-Ruiz & Marin 2008). In this respect, probably the most interesting recent evolution is the growing awareness that the empowerment of women must take place in every sphere of male-dominated power, including, if necessary, the adoption of mandatory gender quotas in the corporate world. Not surprisingly, this too has already triggered constitutional contestation[45] and, in some cases, as in France in 2008, constitutional reform.[46] Article 1 of the French Constitution now includes, among the grand principles of the French Republic, a requirement that the French Republic must promote equal access by women and men to elective offices and posts as well as to positions of professional and social responsibility. Interestingly, some of the most recent constitutions including Morocco's 2011 Constitution followed suit in explicitly incorporating the notion of gender parity as framing its entire sex-equality conception.[47]

These are all promising signs. They point to the possibility that constitutional law may be coming to terms with the fact that both the formal and informal institutional arrangements of society tend to maintain existing distributive patterns, even after direct discrimination is eliminated, and that women have been excluded from some domains by the combination of formal institutional rules and informal social norms. Moreover, politics in general and the

---

41 Portugal experienced a constitutional revision in 1997 altering the wording of Articles 109 and Article 9 para h in the Constitution.

42 A new paragraph was added to Article 43 of the Constitution, which recognizes the universal and equal right to vote, whereas at the same time allowing for legal measures to encourage equal opportunities of women and men in standing for election to state and local community authorities.

43 In France, Constitutional Law No 99-569 of 8 July 1999 introduced a fourth paragraph in Article 3 of the French Constitution, whereby 'the law shall favour equality among women and men to have access to electoral mandates and hold elective office'. It also amended Article 4 so as to provide that political parties 'shall contribute to the application of the principle set forth in the last section of Article 3 in accordance with the provisions of the law'. See Law No 99-569 of July 8, 1999, Journal Officiel de la République Française [J.O.] [Official Gazette of France], July 9, 1999, p 10175. For Italy, see Constitutional Law No. 2/2001; Constitutional Law No 3/2001 and Constitutional Law No 1/2003.

44 For instance, Portugal's 1997 constitutional revision altered the wording of Article 109, which now states that 'the direct and active participation of men and women in the political life constitutes a condition and fundamental instrument for the consolidation of the democratic system'.

45 See *Conseil Constitutionnel*, Décision no 2006-533 DC du 16 mars 2006, *Loi relative à l'égalité salariale entre les femmes et les hommes* striking down a law requiring gender corporate quotas.

46 Loi constitutionnelle no 2008/724 du 23 juillet 2008 de modernization des institutions de la Veme Republique, JORF du 24 juillet 2008.

47 Article 19.2 of the new Constitution orders the state to ensure parity between men and women and creates to this effect a 'parity authority' with the task of fighting against all forms of discrimination.

making and administration of the law, including constitutional law specifically, have been largely male-dominated fields of activity and have therefore often failed to prioritize the overcoming of formal and informal obstacles to women's equal enjoyment of rights. Because of this, the massive incorporation of women to the function of norm creation may be the only true way to engender constitutionalism. Nothing else seems adequate in view of the historically shared exclusion of women from the 'founding fathers' clubs' defining rights and shaping democracy as the backbones of constitutionalism.

23.5 Conclusion

Despite its axiomatic foundation on the values of equality and freedom, eighteenth-century constitutionalism left women out simply because constitutions were conceived as instruments to affirm civil and political rights and freedom of some men in the public sphere and as against state interference. In contrast, women were supposed to inhabit the private sphere of the family, where constitutional rights did not apply and inequality was taken to be the natural expression of a hierarchical sex order.

After World War II, constitutions came to recognize the principle of equality with its application to the relationship between the sexes. This has helped women both in the West and in Asia in the fight for civil equality by challenging gender and sexual stereotypes that were typical of the separate spheres tradition. Meanwhile, the constitutional enshrinement of parity democracy should be read as an attempt to overcome the limits of the assimilationist equality model by making sure that women are included not only as rights holders but also as sources of norm creation in occupying the domains of social and political power, which has fared predominantly male; in fact, the very definition of maleness.

References

Baines, B & Rubio-Marín, R (2004). *The Gender of Constitutional Jurisprudence*, Cambridge University Press.

Beer, LW & Itoh, H. The Constitutional Case Law of Japan, 1970 through 1990.

Chang, W-C (2010). 'Public-Interest Litigation in Taiwan: Strategy for Law and Policy Reforms in Course of Democratization', in Yap, PJ & Lau, H (eds), *Public Interest Litigation in Asia*, 136–160.

—— (2011). 'The Convergence of Constitutions and International Human Rights: Taiwan and South Korea in Comparison', 36 (3) *North Carolina Journal of International Law and Commercial Regulations* 593ff.

Clark, C & Lu, PM (2009). 'The Improvement of Women's Status in Taiwan: A Theoretical Model', paper presented at the Annual Meeting of the American Association for Chinese Studies.

Krook, ML (2009). *Quotas for Women in Politics: Gender and Candidate Selection Reform Worldwide*, Oxford University Press.

Prasad, KV. 'Landmark Legislation on Women's Quota in India', available at http://southasia.oneworld.net/women/landmark-legislation-on-womens-quota-in-india

Rodríguez-Ruiz, B & Rubio-Marín, R (2008). 'The Gender of Representation: On Democracy, Equality and Parity', 6 ICON 287.

—— (2012). 'On Parity, Interdependence and Women's Democracy', in Baines, B, Barak Erez, D & Kahana, T (eds), *Feminist Constitutionalism*, Cambridge University Press, 188–203.

—— & Rubio-Marín, R (eds) (2012b). *The Struggle for Female Suffrage in Europe: Voting to Become Citizens*, Brill.

Siegel, S (2012). 'The Constitutionalization of Abortion', in Rosenfeld, M & Sajo, A (eds), *The Oxford Handbook of Comparative Constitutional Law*.

Suk, J (2010). 'Are Gender Stereotypes Bad for Women? Rethinking Antidiscrimination Law and Work-Family Conflict', 110 Columbia. L. Rev. 1, 16.

Thio, L-A (1997). 'The Impact of Internationalization of Domestic Governance: Gender Egalitarianism and the Transformative Potentials of CEDAW', 1 *Singapore Journal of International and Comparative Law*, 278ff.

Whittaker, A (2010). 'Abortion in Asia: An Overview', in Whittaker, A (ed), Abortion in Asia: Local Dilemmas, Global Politics, 16f.

Yeh, J-R & Chang, W-C (2011). 'The Emergence of East Asian Constitutionalism: Features in Comparison', 59 *American Journal of Comparative Law* 805.

Additional reading

Rodríguez-Ruiz, B & Rubio-Marín, R (2009). 'Constitutional Justifications for Parity Democracy', *Alabama Law Review*, Vol. 60, No. 5, 2009, 1167–90.

24

Race and ethnicity discrimination

Patrick Macklem and Adrien K Wing

This chapter will first discuss the concepts of race and ethnicity, and some of the legal roles they play in various political communities. Then, the chapter will highlight the significance of direct or intentional discrimination on the basis of race or ethnicity, a phenomenon that still exists worldwide, but has certainly abated to a large degree in most countries over the last century. Finally, the chapter will discuss the problem of indirect discrimination or disparate impact discrimination, which while diminishing, remains the bulk of the current nature of racial and ethnic discrimination in the twenty-first century. Constitutional orders with written bills of rights appear to be converging in their approaches to racial and ethnic discrimination, with greater convergence occurring with respect to direct discrimination than indirect discrimination. Some constitutional orders require the state to enact positive measures to ameliorate the effects of racial and ethnic discrimination, but there is little evidence to date to suggest convergence on this approach.

24.1 Defining race and ethnicity

Societies have struggled to define 'race' for centuries. The term 'race' is also sometimes used interchangeably with 'ethnicity.' To complicate considerations further, some ethnicities may all be considered to be within one race, and some ethnicities contain several races. In some countries, the concepts intertwine with religious faith as well. However defined, the law has been used historically to classify people on the basis of race or ethnicity. These determinations have resulted in some groups receiving privileged status under the law, directly or informally, and other groups being relegated to an inferior status.

In the nineteenth century, European and American scientists and others attempted to classify human beings into different racial categories. Races were presumed to have distinctive mental, emotional, and moral characteristics as well as physical ones. Using physical characteristics ranging from head shape, nose, eyes, lips, hair, and skin color, they devised a racial hierarchy where Caucasoid, Aryan, or white were terms used to describe the race at the top, and Negroid, Colored, African, or black were terms used to describe the race at the bottom. Additionally, Mongoloid, Oriental, Asian, or yellow were used to describe another racial category. The system presupposed all groups could be fit into one of the racial categories, even though some cultures had characteristics from several races.

Historically, many believed that different races even had different blood. The 'one drop' rule—that even one drop of 'black' blood made a person black—developed. Since minute distinctions were not visible, court cases often involved evaluations of whether the person in question looked black, lived as a white, or Indian (Gross).

Other laws or policies allocating privilege or discrimination on the basis of race, in the United States but also elsewhere, included: laws keeping blacks in slavery for perpetuity rather than a fixed term, as was the case for whites; anti-miscegenation statutes hindering black–white intermarriage[1]; segregated public facilities and accommodations laws delineating 'colored' and white hotels, restaurants, rest rooms, schools, bus seats, and train cars; removal of Indigenous peoples from land desired by settlers; interning Japanese and Japanese Americans, but not other ethnic groups such as Germans or Italians, during World War II[2]; restrictive covenants preventing blacks from buying homes in white areas; and limitations on naturalized US citizenship to whites.

In *St Francis College v Al-Khazraji*, the US Supreme Court recognized how problematic continued efforts at racial characterization are:

> Many modern biologists and anthropologists, however, criticize racial classifications as arbitrary and of little use in understanding the variability of human beings. It is said that genetically homogeneous populations do not exist and traits are not discontinuous between populations; therefore, a population can only be described in terms of relative frequencies of various traits. Clear-cut categories do not exist. The particular traits which have generally been chosen to characterize races have been criticized as having little biological significance. It has been found that differences between individuals of the same race are often greater than the differences between the 'average' individuals of different races. These observations and others have led some, but not all, scientists to conclude that racial classifications are for the most part sociopolitical, rather than biological, in nature.[3]

Despite the lack of any biological foundation to the concept of race[4] and the contemporary rejection of the existence of natural racial hierarchies, discrimination on the basis of race persists throughout the world. What this suggests is that one's racial identity is not biologically constructed, but rather is socially, politically, and legally constructed by assumptions, beliefs, and practices that change over time and vary from nation to nation. As an example, author Wing is regarded as African American in the United States, part of the so-called Colored group in South Africa, and considered white in Brazil.

---

1 These statutes were overturned in *Loving v Virginia*, 388 US 1 (1967).
2 *Korematsu v United States*, 323 US 214 (1944). In 1984, Korematsu's conviction was vacated by a lower federal court, 584 F Supp 1406 (ND Cal 1984), on the grounds of government misconduct in the submission of false information to the Court. In 1988, the US Congress passed a law apologizing for the internment and providing for reparations of $20,000 for each then-living survivor.
3 *St Francis College v Al-Khazraji*, 481 US 604, 610 (1987), confirmed that Arabs as Caucasians could sue for race discrimination under 42 US Code sec 1981.
4 The best current scientific understanding is that the human species originated in Africa. See Zimmer.

As with race, ethnicity has been characterized in many ways. Although some regard ethnicity to be a relatively recent social category, gaining salience in the United States in the 1960s and 1970s (e.g., Glazer & Moynihan at 1; Thompson at 1), the term is derived from the Greek word, *ethnos*, denoting 'others' (Tonkin, McDonald & Chapman at 12–20). An ethnic group generally consists of a set of people who share a sense of identity based on descent, language, religion, tradition, and other common experiences and practices including alphabet, food, music, clothing, and beliefs (Weber at 385–98). As an example, within the US, there is the hyphenated identity notion of ethnicity, a veritable 'salad bowl' of groups, including Irish-Americans, Chinese-Americans, Mexican-Americans and more.

While French thinkers like Jean-Jacques Rousseau developed notions of equality, modern-day France treats equality as inconsistent with recognizing or even officially recording ethnicity. The French maintain the 'melting pot' notion of identity: 'we are all French.' They do not legally recognize the distinctive nature of African, Caribbean, and Arab ethnic groups, who have come mainly from former French colonies. These peoples are often physically distinctive and identifiable by color, language, religion and other characteristics, and are discriminated against in ways that suggest they are not perceived as French by most white French people.

Groups of ethnicities may be referred to as an ethnicity, when it would be more accurate to refer to them in a panethnic fashion. For example, the term 'Asian Americans' can refer to people with connection to China, Japan, Vietnam, Cambodia, Thailand, and elsewhere in Asia. Black American or African American may refer to people who are the descendants of slaves or it may refer to a broader group including people more recently from Africa or the Caribbean. People who arrived more recently in the United States may or may not want to be identified with the Black American group. 'Arab American' may refer to people from countries ranging from Morocco to Lebanon. 'Native American' or 'American Indian' may refer to several hundred different tribes, some recognized officially and some lacking recognition from the federal government. Each one of these tribes has its own standards for determining what percent of Indian 'blood' makes one a member of the tribe.

To complicate our understanding of ethnicity, people from various ethnicities are not always considered within the same racial group. Hispanic as a panethnic identifier does not provide information about the races involved. There are Puerto Ricans who consider themselves white and others who clearly appear to be black. Many people think of Colombians as being of Spanish white stock mixed to various degrees with indigenous people. There are Afro-Columbians as well.

Further confusing the issue, race and ethnicity also get intertwined with religion. One of the best historic examples involves people of the Jewish faith. In the nineteenth century, they were regarded as an inferior 'race' in the United States and Europe; they were not considered white. Nazi Germany valorized the superior Aryan race compared with others, including the inferior Jewish and Roma populations. Today, Jewish Americans may be considered a white ethnic group by many, whether or not an individual Jewish person practices the Jewish religion. In the former Yugoslavia, genocide was committed against Bosnians who were Muslim, a distinct group from Serbian Orthodox or Catholic Croats.

24.2 Racial and ethnic discrimination: direct and indirect

Despite conceptual instabilities surrounding the categories of race and ethnicity, many modern constitutional orders have structural features that take into account the racial and ethnic composition of its citizens. Some have done so in a blatantly discriminatory manner, such as apartheid in South Africa, where the rights of the majority non-white inhabitants of the country were curtailed, and white supremacy and minority rule was maintained.[5] More common today are structural features that protect racial or ethnic minorities from majoritarian politics or seek to minimize the potential for racial or ethnic strife and conflict. Some federal systems, such as Canada and India, vest legislative authority in subunits to confer a measure of autonomy on racial or ethnic minorities. Others, such as Mauritius, create incentives for the creation of cross-cutting allegiances among citizens otherwise divided among racial or ethnic lines. Some constitutional orders, such as Belgium, vest minority rights in racial or ethnic communities to shield them from assimilative tendencies emanating from their broader political community. Others, such as Pakistan and Singapore, provide racial or ethnic communities guaranteed political representation in national political institutions. The structural salience of race and ethnicity in constitutional law is addressed elsewhere in this Handbook. But many constitutions also vest individuals and groups with rights of equality before the law and equal protection of the law. In many of these jurisdictions, race and ethnicity feature prominently as markers of individual and group identity that the exercise of state power must respect in the name of equality. A constitution can thus prohibit direct or intentional forms of racial or ethnic discrimination, but it can also prohibit what is known as indirect or disparate impact discrimination on the basis of race or ethnicity.[6] Some constitutions authorize ameliorative measures aimed at certain racial or ethnic communities. Others go so far as to require the state to enact such measures. The remainder of this chapter addresses in more detail these differing constitutional commitments to racial and ethnic equality.

24.3 Direct or intentional discrimination

Many constitutions prohibit what has been referred to as direct or intentional discrimination on the basis of race or ethnicity. By 'direct discrimination,' we mean laws that distribute benefits and burdens on the basis of racial or ethnic difference. Article 1 of the French Constitution, for example, provides that 'France shall be an indivisible, secular, democratic and social republic. It shall ensure the equality of all citizens before the law, without distinction of origin, race or religion. It shall respect all beliefs.' It is widely understood as requiring the state to treat all French citizens as formal equals and prohibiting legislative or administrative distinctions among them on account of their race or origin, including measures aimed at protecting racial or ethnic minorities. These considerations are often invoked to explain the French refusal to ratify the European framework convention on the protection of national minorities.

---

5 See also *Johnson v M'Intosh*, 21 US (8 Wheat) 543 (1823), where the US Supreme Court ruled that only Indian conveyances of land to the US government were valid.
6 It should be noted that international treaties or conventions also contain equality clauses that include the concept of both intentional discrimination and disparate impact. For example, the International Convention on the Elimination of Race Discrimination states: 'The term racial discrimination shall mean any distinction, exclusion, restriction or preference based on race, colour, descent or national or ethnic origin, which has the purpose or effect of nullifying or impairing the recognition, enjoyment or exercise, on an equal footing, of human rights and fundamental freedoms in the political, economic, social, cultural or any field of public life.' International Convention on the Elimination of Race Discrimination, GA Res. 2106 a (XX), 660 U.N.T.S. 195 (1969). See also European Convention on Human Rights Protocol 12 (general prohibition on discrimination including race), http://www.humanrights.coe.int/Prot12/Protocol%2012%20and%20Exp%20Rep.htm.

The Equal Protection Clause of the Fourteenth Amendment to the United States Constitution provides that 'no state shall … deny to any person within its jurisdiction the equal protection of the laws.' It was adopted after the Civil War in an effort to abolish state discrimination against African Americans. For many years afterwards, however, the Fourteenth Amendment had little impact on racial discrimination. The courts upheld racial segregation, relying on the notorious 'separate but equal' doctrine articulated in the 1896 US Supreme Court case *Plessy v Ferguson*.[7] Under this doctrine, whites and blacks were supposed to be given separate but equal public accommodations and services. In reality, blacks lived a vastly inferior reality.

The US Supreme Court began to revise its views on the legal edifice of racial inequality in the mid-twentieth century after World War II. In its landmark unanimous opinion in *Brown v Board of Education*, the Court declared that 'separate but equal' is 'inherently unequal' and 'has no place' in the field of public education.[8] A follow-up opinion noted that schools should be desegregated 'with all deliberate speed.' Unfortunately, school integration never occurred fully, and some school districts are more segregated now than they may have been at the time of *Brown*.

Modern equal protection jurisprudence in the United States is characterized by a three-tiered approach to the review of legal classifications. Under the first tier, known as strict scrutiny, courts will strike down any legislative classification that is not necessary to achieving a compelling government objective. Strict scrutiny is applied to legislation that classifies on the basis of race or alienage, and legislation that burdens certain fundamental interests. Such laws must be narrowly tailored to meet the compelling governmental objective. If the law is under- or over-inclusive, it will be struck down. The law must use the least restrictive means to achieve its aims. If there are less restrictive means available to achieve permissible goals, it will be struck down. Many have characterized this test as 'strict in theory, fatal in fact.'

In *Parents Involved in Community Schools v Seattle School District No 1*,[9] the Supreme Court prohibited assigning students to public schools solely for the purpose of achieving race integration and failed to recognize racial balancing as a compelling state interest in a case where there was no history of *de jure* segregation. In a 5–4 opinion, the majority held that there was no 'compelling state interest' that would justify the assignment of school seats on the basis of race. Justice Kennedy filed a concurrence indicating that schools can implement 'race-conscious' means to achieve diversity in schools, but that the institutions here did not sufficiently narrow the tailoring of their plans to support their goals.

The second or intermediate tier of scrutiny is applied to classifications on the basis of gender. Legislation will not survive intermediate scrutiny unless the government can demonstrate that the classification is substantially related to an important societal interest. The third tier is known as minimal or rational basis scrutiny. The courts will uphold a law on this approach so long as the classification is reasonably related to a legitimate government interest. Most laws regulating social and economic matters are reviewed and upheld by courts using this minimal level of scrutiny.

Complicating the three levels of scrutiny analysis is the fact that people could be discriminated on the basis of more than one identity simultaneously. Thus, for example, African American women may face discrimination as blacks, as women, and as black women. The law in the US is not set up for proper consideration of an intersectional claim. The

---

7 *Plessy v Ferguson*, 163 US 537 (1896).
8 *Brown v Board of Education*, 347 US 483 (1954).
9 *Parents Involved in Community Schools v Seattle School District No 1*, 551 US 701 (2007).

potential plaintiff would have to choose whether she would prefer to sue as a black and claim strict scrutiny or as a woman and invoke intermediate scrutiny.[10] The problem also exists under Title VII disparate impact analysis, discussed in the next section. Some countries have tried to address the intersectional issue. The South African Constitutional Court has actively accepted the category 'black woman,' rather than make plaintiffs choose between their race or gender.

In the modern era, however, such clauses are now more comprehensive than the US equality clause adopted in the mid-nineteenth century. While Article 14 of the Constitution of India generally provides that '[t]he State shall not deny to any person equality before the law or the equal protection of the laws within the territory of India,' Article 15 specifically prohibits the state from discriminating 'against any citizen on grounds only of religion, race, caste, sex, place of birth or any of them.' Article 3(3) of the German Basic Law provides that 'No person shall be favored or disfavored because of sex, race, language, homeland and origin, or religious or political opinion.' Section 15(1) of the 1982 Canadian Charter of Rights and Freedoms provides: 'Every individual is equal before and under the law and has the right to the equal protection and equal benefit of the law without discrimination and, in particular, without discrimination based on race, national or ethnic origin, colour, religion, sex, age or physical or mental disability.' The 1996 South African Constitution has an extensive list of grounds covered by the equality clause. Art 9(3) says that 'the State may not unfairly discriminate directly or indirectly against anyone on one or more grounds, including race, gender, sex, pregnancy, marital status, ethnic or social origin, colour, sexual orientation, age, disability, religion, conscience, belief, culture, language or birth.'

The Supreme Court of India has held that laws that discriminate on the basis of a ground of discrimination prohibited by art 15 should be subject to 'strict scrutiny,' which it defines as requiring there to be a reasonable relationship of proportionality between the means used and the aim pursued by the law.[11] Laws that do not run afoul of art 15 but that nonetheless deny equality before the law or equal protection of the law contrary to art 14 are subject to more relaxed judicial scrutiny. They must employ a 'permissible classification,' namely, (i) the classification must be founded on an intelligible distinction which distinguishes persons or things that are grouped together from those that are left out of the group; and (ii) the distinction must have a rational relation to the objective sought to be achieved by the statute in question.[12] A final feature of art 14 is that it prohibits 'arbitrary' legislation on the basis that 'equality is antithetic to arbitrariness.'[13] If a classification's objective is illogical, unfair or unjust, then the classification will be held as unreasonable.[14]

Article 13 of the Constitution of Colombia states that 'all persons are born free and are equal before the law, they shall receive the same protection and treatment from authorities and enjoy the same rights, liberties and opportunities with no discrimination on the basis of' several enumerated grounds, including 'race' and 'national origin.' The Constitutional Court of Colombia has deemed these enumerated grounds to be 'suspicious' as they are 'historically associated with behavior' that tends 'to undervalue and place in a disadvantage certain people

---

10 Kimberle Crenshaw and others have written about intersectionality as applied to black women. See Crenshaw; Wing 2003.
11 *Anuj Garg v Hotel Association of India*, (2008) 3 SCC 1.
12 *Budhan Choudhry v State of Bihar*, AIR 1955 SC 191.
13 *Ajay Hasia v Khalid Mujib Sehravardi*, (1981) 1 SCC 722.
14 *Deepak Sibal v Punjab University*, (1989) 2 SCC 145.

or groups' such as women, blacks, homosexuals, and indigenous peoples, among others. According to the Court, race and national origin are 'categories that (i) are based on people's permanent features that they cannot change of their own will without risking their identity; (ii) have been traditionally subjected to patterns of cultural appraisal that tend to belittle them, and (iii) do not comprise, *per se*, criteria enabling a rational and fair distribution of goods, rights or social obligations.' In several cases, it accordingly has ruled unconstitutional measures that directly discriminate on the basis of race or national origin.

Constitutions that prohibit direct discrimination on racial or ethnic grounds commit to a formal principle of equality requiring like cases to be treated alike, and to the proposition that race or ethnic origin should not count as a relevant difference in the exercise of state power. By invalidating legislative or administrative distinctions that rely on race or ethnic difference to distribute benefits or burdens among citizens, constitutional commitments to formal equality possess the potential to secure the same rights and privileges to all, regardless of race or ethnic difference. They thus stand as potentially powerful constitutional instruments to combat laws that withhold legal rights from some citizens on account of their race or ethnicity. Formal equality, however, does not require the state to seek to ameliorate the historical disadvantages that confront some racial and ethnic minorities; such measures would in fact run counter to the proposition that neither race nor ethnic origin should count as a relevant difference in the exercise of state power. Equality provisions that simply prohibit direct discrimination on these grounds therefore do little to remedy the social and economic consequences of past injustices inflicted on racial or ethnic minorities or their ancestors.

24.4 Indirect or disparate impact discrimination

In *Brown v Board*, the US Supreme Court mentioned the need to look beyond direct discrimination, stating 'We must look … to the effect of segregation itself on public education.'[15] Many constitutions therefore complement provisions that require the state to treat individuals and groups equally regardless of their race or ethnicity with provisions that advance substantive equality. One such instrument is the prohibition of what has been referred to as 'indirect discrimination' or disparate impact discrimination on the basis of race or ethnicity. By 'indirect discrimination,' we mean laws or policies that rely on apparently neutral provisions or criteria that have the effect of unjustifiably disadvantaging people on account of their race or ethnicity. While the law does not overtly intend to discriminate, the net effect is that certain racial or ethnic groups end up in a disadvantaged position. Constitutions that prohibit indirect discrimination on racial or ethnic grounds move toward a substantive conception of equality by recognizing that apparently equal treatment can entrench racial or ethnic disadvantage. In the United States, the Civil Rights Act—especially Title VII, which regulates discrimination in the private sector, rather than the equal protection clause—covers this type of discrimination.[16]

Other countries have grappled with how to handle disparate impact cases as well. In Canada, for example, the disparate impact doctrine is called the adverse effects doctrine. There is Canadian case law that expressly stipulates that the adverse effects of legislation can constitute discrimination on the basis of a prohibited ground, such as sex, even though a law

15 347 US at 492.
16 See *Washington v Davis*, 426 US 229 (1976).

might not expressly distinguish between men and women.[17] In *R v Symes*, for example, the Supreme Court of Canada upheld the constitutionality of a provision in the Income Tax Act preventing the deduction of childcare expenses as business expenses from one's income. Although the Court accepted that women disproportionately bear the social burden of childcare in Canada, there was insufficient evidence establishing that women disproportionately bear the actual financial costs of childcare. The Court nonetheless confirmed that facially neutral laws that adversely affect women in their effects can amount to discrimination on the basis of sex.

In South Africa, *City Council of Pretoria v Walker* illustrates how that country is handling the concept.[18] South Africa has emerged from a recent history of *de jure* segregation against a black majority by the white minority. The country now has a Constitutional Court that is interpreting the post-apartheid constitution with a detailed equality clause that covers both intentional *and* unintentional behavior. The *Walker* case implicated issues of race, class, and housing segregation in interesting ways. In that case, white people who lived in Old Pretoria paid more for electricity. They had meters that charged on a consumption basis. The city was in the process of putting meters in two poorer black areas, Atteridgeville and Mamelodi, and was continuing to charge a lower flat tax until all the meters were installed in the area. The city council also had the habit of selectively enforcing collection of arrearages in Old Pretoria, but not in the two poorer areas where there had been a culture of non-payment.

Mr Walker contended that the council's conduct breached s 8 of the interim constitution because there was no rational connection between the discriminatory measures taken and a legitimate governmental purpose. The Court disagreed, finding that the temporary measures were developed to provide service continuity in transitional times, while the city was phasing in equality.

The Court did hold that the council's differential treatment of residents in black areas and residents in white areas constituted indirect discrimination on the grounds of race in violation of s 8(2). The Court suggested it would be artificial to make a comparison between such areas on the grounds of geography alone. The effect of apartheid laws was that race and geography are inextricably linked, and the application of a geographical standard, although seemingly neutral, may in fact be racially discriminatory. Further, proof of intention to discriminate is not required for either direct or indirect discrimination under s 8(2), although the purpose of the conduct or action in question may be relevant in determining whether the discrimination was 'unfair.'

In Brazil, the doctrine has developed as well. In 2005, Brazilian public prosecutors charged five of the country's leading banks with violating the Brazilian Constitution by discriminating against Afro-Brazilian employees and job applicants in hiring, promotion, and compensation. The allegations were based on statistical evidence indicating significant disparities in occupational status and compensation of Afro-Brazilian employees relative to their white colleagues at the banks. The suits also asserted that the banks discriminated in hiring, based on underrepresentation of Afro-Brazilians in the banks' workforce when compared to their share of the local labor market (Hensler).

---

17 See *Symes v Canada* [1993], 110 DLR (4th) 470, 552 (SC) (Can); [1993] 4 SCR 695, 755 (Can); Seiner (observing that the Canadian Supreme Court has recently merged intent and effects tests in employment law).

18 *City Council of Pretoria v Walker* 1998 (3) BCLR 257 (CC), http://www.constitutionalcourt.org.za/uhtbin/cgisirsi/jfn5sP1cBL/MAIN/64690039/9#top.

The indirect discrimination doctrine has developed on a regional basis in Europe. The European Court of Justice (ECJ), which hears cases involving the 27 member states of the European Union, created the doctrine of disparate impact on the basis of Article 119 of the Treaty of the European Community.

Europe has applied the indirect effects notion to a broader array of 'races' than the United States. For example, in *DH and Others v The Czech Republic*, the Grand (Appellate) Chamber of the European Court of Human Rights found the doctrine applied to a case involving the Czech Roma. Nearly 70 percent of these children were placed in special and inferior schools for mentally disabled although they made up only 5 percent of the primary age pupils.[19] The equality clause of the European Convention on Human Rights was violated in a *de facto* school segregation situation even though there was no discriminatory intent.

24.5 Ameliorative measures

Another instrument that advances substantive equality is a constitutional provision permitting the state to distinguish on the basis of racial or ethnic difference to ameliorate historical disadvantages faced by racial or ethnic minorities in society. There are numerous examples of provisions that authorize what, in the United States, is referred to as 'affirmative action.'[20] Numerous articles in the Constitution of India, for example, authorize the state to adopt measures that ameliorate the conditions of disadvantaged individuals and groups. Article 15(3) provides that the state may make 'any special provision for women and children,' and art 15(4) enables the state to make 'any special provision for the advancement of any socially and educationally backward classes of citizens or for specified Castes and the Tribes listed in the Constitution.' Similarly, Article 16, which guarantees to all citizens 'equality of opportunities' in 'matters relating to employment or appointment to any office under the state,' and forbids discrimination against any citizen on various grounds, including race and caste, is qualified by Article 16(4), which enables the state to make any provision for the reservations of appointments or posts in favor of any backward classes of citizens that in the opinion of the state are not adequately represented in the services under the state.

India's Union Parliament has been exceptionally active in seeking to mitigate the effects of caste-based subordination. The constitutionality of such measures is frequently challenged in the courts, and there is a rich line of jurisprudence addressing the extent to which the state can provide preferential treatment, known as 'reservations,' to disadvantaged individuals and groups. The Supreme Court of India made it clear that it would not apply strict scrutiny to reservations or other affirmative action measures contemplated by the Constitution.

Similarly, Article 13(2) of the Constitution of Colombia provides that 'the State will foster the conditions required so that equality may be real and effective and will adopt measures in favor of deprived and unfairly treated groups.' Affirmative action is, therefore, authorized by the Constitution and, consequently, authorities may invoke race or national origin or any other 'suspicious' category 'not to exclude certain people or groups or to perpetuate

---

19 *DH and Others v The Czech Republic*, App. No. 57325/00, Grand Chamber Eur Ct HR 13 Nov 2007.
20 In the US, the equal protection clause has been interpreted by the US Supreme Court to permit affirmative action. See *Regents of the University of California v Bakke*, 438 US 265 (1978) and *Grutter v Bollinger*, 539 US 306 (2003). Quotas are not permitted. See *Gratz v Bollinger*, 539 US 244 (2003).

inequalities, but rather to reduce harmful effects of social behaviors that have placed this same people or groups in unfavorable conditions.'[21]

24.6 Positive obligations

Although there is little evidence to date to suggest that constitutional orders are converging on this approach, some states also impose positive obligations on the state to take measures to ameliorate racial or ethnic discrimination in society. Directive Principles enshrined in the Constitution of India, for example, require the state to adopt affirmative action programs to secure substantive equality for the oppressed and weaker sections of the population. Article 46, for instance, obliges the state to promote with special care the educational and economic interests of the weaker sections of the people, and in particular of the Scheduled Castes and the Scheduled Tribes, and to protect them from social injustice and all forms of exploitation.

The Swedish Constitution also imposes positive obligations to take measures to ameliorate various forms of discrimination, including discrimination on the basis of 'colour' and 'national or ethnic origin.' Specifically, it states that 'public institutions shall combat discrimination of persons on grounds of gender, colour, national or ethnic origin, linguistic or religious affiliation, functional disability, sexual orientation, age or other circumstance affecting the private person.' It states further that '[o]pportunities should be promoted for ethnic, linguistic and religious minorities to preserve and develop a cultural and social life of their own.'[22]

References

Crenshaw, K (1989). Demarginalizing the Intersection of Race and Sex: A Black Feminist Critique of Antidiscrimination Doctrine, Feminist Theory and Antiracist Politics, *University of Chicago Legal Forum* 139-67 (Reprinted in Kairys, D (ed), The Politics of Law: A Progressive Critique 195–217 (2nd edn, Pantheon).

Glazer, N & Moynihan, DP (eds) (1975). Ethnicity: Theory and Experience (Cambridge: Harvard University Press).

Gross, AJ (1998). Litigating Whiteness: Trials of Racial Determination in the Nineteenth-Century South, 108 Yale LJ 109.

Hensler, B (2007). Nao Vale a Pena (Not Worth the Trouble?) Afro-Brazilian Workers and Brazilian Anti-Discrimination Law, 30 Hastings Int'l & Comp L Rev 267.

Seiner, JA (2006). Disentangling Disparate Impact and Disparate Treatment: Adapting the Canadian Approach, 25 Yale L & Pol'y Rev 95.

Thompson, RH (1989). Theories of Ethnicity: A Critical Appraisal (NY: Greenwood).

Tonkin, E, McDonald, M & Chapman, M (1989). History and Ethnicity (London: Routledge).

Weber, M (1968). Economy and Society, vol. 1 (New York: Bedminster).

Wing, AK (ed) (2003). Critical Race Feminism (New York: NYU Press 2nd edn).

Zimmer, C (2005). The Smithsonian Intimate Guide to Human Origins (New York, HarperCollins Publishers).

Additional reading

Bell, D (2008). Race, Racism and American Law (Aspen 6th edn).

Cheadle, M et al (2002). South African Constitutional Law: The Bill of Rights.

21 Law on Shares Case, Constitutional Court of Colombia, Decision C-371 (2000).
22 Chapter 1, Article 3 of the Instrument of Government of Sweden.

Currie, I & de Waal, J (2005). The Bill of Rights Handbook 260–264 (Juta Press 5th edn).

Delgado, R (2001). Critical Race Theory (New York: NYU Press).

Dorsen, N, Rosenfeld, M, Sajo, A & Baer, S (2010). Comparative Constitutionalism: Cases and Materials (West Press 2nd edn).

Gotanda, N (1991). A Critique of our Constitution is Colorblind, 44 Stan L. Rev 1.

Jackson, VC & Tushnet, M (2006). Comparative Constitutional Law (Foundation Press 2nd edn).

Kentridge, J (1999). Equality, in Chaskelson, M et al (eds), Constitutional Law of South Africa 14-55 to 14-66.

Lawrence, C, III (1987). The Id, the Ego, and Equal Protection: Reckoning with Unconscious Racism, 39 Stan L Rev 317.

Loenen, T & Rodriques, P (ed) (1999). Nondiscrimination Law: Comparative Perspectives (Hague: Kluwer).

Motala, Z & Ramaphosa, C (2002). Constitutional Law 252–302 (London, Oxford University Press).

Perea, P, Delgado, R *et al* (2007). Race and Races: Cases and Resources for a Diverse America (Thomson/West 2nd edn).

Pildes, R (2008). Ethnic Identity and Democratic Institutions: A Dynamic Perspective, in Choudhry, S (ed), Divided Societies: Integration or Accommodation? 173 (London, Oxford University Press).

Prewitt, P (2005). Racial Classification in America: Where Do We Go from Here?, 134 Daedalus 5 (Winter 2005).

Williams, G (1996). Life on the Color Line: The True Story of a White Boy Who Discovered He Was Black (NY: Dutton).

Wing, AK (ed) (2000). Global Critical Race Feminism (New York: NYU Press).

Wing, AK (2009). Review of Laws Having Racially Disparate Impacts, in Tushnet, M & Amar, V (eds), Global Perspectives on Constitutional Law 88 (London, Oxford University Press).

25

Affirmative action

Robert J Cottrol and Megan Davis

25.1 Introduction

Affirmative action refers to a range of governmental policies designed to foster greater opportunities for racial and ethnic groups that have traditionally been victims of discrimination. These policies are also frequently extended to women and to individuals who have suffered from socio-economic disadvantage. Affirmative action has generally been less controversial when based on class or gender instead of race. Affirmative action policies have taken the form of quotas for members of previously disadvantaged groups, preferential weighting of applicants for employment and university admissions and governmental pressure to increase recruitment of members of groups that have long suffered from discrimination. In some nations—the United States and the Republic of South Africa are examples—affirmative action takes place against a background of previous histories of formal, legally mandated discrimination against non-white groups. In other nations—Brazil is an example—affirmative action occurs in the absence of a history of formal legal discrimination. In such nations there are often nonetheless very real histories of racial discrimination and stigmatization of and often very strong patterns of racially linked class disadvantage (Cottrol). Affirmative action policies are found in a diverse set of nations in the modern world including such nations as Brazil, Colombia, India, Israel, Malaysia, Nigeria, South Africa and the United States (Sowell, 2–22).

Affirmative action frequently creates constitutional and judicial dilemmas in the nations that have or contemplate such policies. By the end of the twentieth century, and especially after the fall of South Africa's apartheid regime in 1993, the principle of the equality of all citizens before the law had become a virtually universal constitutional norm. But how would affirmative action policies that did confer preferences and benefits on traditionally disfavored groups be reconciled with the equality principle? A strict reading of the equality principle that is found in most modern constitutions would argue that applications for employment or university admissions be judged without regard to race, ethnicity, gender, or a nation's previous history of discrimination. Yet such a strict adherence to the equality principle would allow entrenched patterns of social, economic and, in some cases, political inequalities to continue, not taking into account either historic disadvantage, or the very real persistence of discrimination against traditionally disfavored groups. Various international conventions proscribing discrimination, in particular the UN Convention on the Elimination of All Forms of Discrimination, and treaty bodies have weighed in on this issue, indicating that measures designed to benefit historically excluded groups do not violate the equality principle because substantive equality acknowledges that there are situations where concrete circumstances may necessitate unequal treatment for unequal matters.[1] It is accepted in international law that the principle of equality

> [do]es not require absolute equality or identity of treatment but recognizes relative equality ie, different treatment proportionate to concrete individual circumstances. In order to be legitimate, different treatment must be reasonable and not arbitrary and the onus of showing that particular distinctions are justifiable is on those who make them (McKean).

As Judge Tanaka famously held in the South West Africa Case (Second Phase):

> The principle of equality before the law does not mean absolute equality, namely the equal treatment of men without regard to individual, concrete circumstances, but it means the relative equality, namely the principle to treat equally what are equal and unequally what are unequal ... To treat unequal matters differently according to their inequality is not only permitted but required.[2]

The extent to which this viewpoint has become accepted law in different nations has, of course, depended on the actions of national courts and legislatures, the reception of international human rights law and the era in which constitutional drafting occurred.

This Chapter examines the treatment of affirmative action in the constitutional law of four nations, selected to highlight differences and similarities in connection with the common law or civil law background, and differences and similarities in connection with the historical origins of the conditions that have led policy-makers to develop affirmative action policies.

25.2 United States

Affirmative action in the United States developed out of the civil rights movement and the struggle of black Americans against systematic patterns of segregation and discrimination, frequently mandated by law. In 1865, more than two centuries of slavery on the North American continent would come to an end: the results of Northern victory in the American Civil War. In the wake of that conflict, the US Constitution was amended with three new provisions, specifically designed to provide equal rights for the newly emancipated black population. These provisions included the Thirteenth Amendment, which prohibited slavery, and the Fifteenth Amendment, which eliminated racial restrictions on voting. The new provision that would become the subject of much constitutional litigation was the Fourteenth

---

1 *International Convention on the Elimination on All Forms of Racial Discrimination*, opened for signature 7 March 1966, 660 UNTS 195 (entered into force 4 January 1969). See also Human Rights Committee, General Comment No 18: Non-Discrimination (10 November 1989); See also, Judge Tanaka in South West Africa Case, (second phase) ICJ Report 18 July 1966.
2 Judge Tanaka in South West Africa Case, (second phase) ICJ Report 18 July 1966.

Amendment, which contained an equal protection clause designed to bring the principle of equal treatment of people of different races into the American constitutional order.

If the period after the American Civil War would see the enactment of constitutional measures designed to equalize the status and treatment of Americans of different races, by the beginning of the twentieth century, the principle of equal treatment under the law was being largely ignored in many parts of the nation. By the beginning of the twentieth century, a system of racial segregation, popularly known as 'Jim Crow,' was developing in the southern states of the America, home to a majority of the nation's black population. The Jim Crow system, which at its height would mandate separate railroad coaches, separate seating on buses, separate park benches and water fountains, separate schools and segregation in almost every visible facet of public life, was approved by the US Supreme Court in the 1896 case *Plessy v Ferguson*.[3] In that case, the Court declared that the equal protection principle was not violated by separate facilities for people of different races as long as the facilities were equal. In the Southern states, and a good part of the rest of the nation, separate facilities were common but equal facilities rare.

The fight against the Jim Crow system would gain increasing momentum after World War II. One important early victory was *Brown v Board of Education*, the case that declared school segregation unconstitutional and implicitly reversed the separate but equal doctrine of *Plessy*.[4] The efforts of the Civil Rights movement would ultimately lead to comprehensive national legislation, the Civil Rights Act of 1964 which outlawed many of the then existing patterns of racial discrimination in public accommodations. It also prohibited discrimination on the basis of race and sex in employment.

By the late 1960s, many proponents of civil rights had come to believe that the simple elimination of previously existing restrictions would not be sufficient to overcome the disadvantages that had been suffered by blacks and other minorities during generations of discrimination. Civil rights activists urged the adoption of affirmative action measures in employment and university admissions designed to compensate for previous, and indeed still existing, patterns of racial exclusion. A number of these programs would be brought before the Supreme Court with constitutional challenges claiming that reverse discrimination and thus violations of the Fourteenth Amendment's equal protection clause.

The Court would make its first examination of affirmative action in the field of higher education in the 1978 case of *Regents of the University of California v Bakke*.[5] *Bakke* examined an admissions program at the University of California at Davis School of Medicine in which a certain number of spaces were reserved for minority students. In what would become the operating rationale of the case, Justice Lewis Powell wrote an opinion stating that quotas, such as the one administered by the University of California, were unconstitutional and violations of the Fourteenth Amendment's equal protection clause. Powell's opinion went on to state that public universities could consider race in admissions in order to add to the diversity of the student body. The Supreme Court would re-affirm the operating principle in *Bakke* that some degree of considering race in university admissions was constitutionally permissible, but that rigid numerical formulae using race were constitutionally forbidden in its 2003 examination of two affirmative action programs at the University of Michigan.[6]

---

3 165 US 537 (1896).
4 347 US 483 (1954).
5 438 US 265 (1978).
6 *Gratz v Bollinger*, 539 US 244 (2003); *Grutter v Bollinger* 539 US 306 (2003).

The Supreme Court has been willing to give a limited constitutional sanction to affirmative action in American public universities, in part on the rationale offered by Justice Powell, that racial diversity contributes to a university's educational mission by fostering contact between students of different backgrounds. The Court has generally taken a somewhat stricter view of affirmative action in public employment. Although the Court ruled that an affirmative action program by a private employer did not violate Title VII of the 1964 Civil Rights Act in the 1979 case *United Steel Workers of America v Weber*,[7] it has taken a more narrow view of what is permissible for public agencies. The Court's view of the equal protection principle has been that affirmative action involving preferences for minority job candidates or contractors requires 'strict scrutiny' of the highest level in American constitutional jurisprudence. In effect, this means that governmental entities intending to adopt affirmative action measures have to demonstrate that these measures are remedial measures designed to remedy a specific history of discrimination in the agency proposing the affirmative action measure. The Court has rejected the view that affirmative action can be justified as a broad measure to remedy societal discrimination in general.[8]

25.3 Brazil

Affirmative action developed in the United States as an outgrowth of the African American struggle against formal legal barriers to racial equality. The push for affirmative action in Brazil would take place against a somewhat different historical background. Brazil has a long history of often profound racial inequality, but this inequality existed in the absence of formal, legally mandated racial discrimination. Although slavery in Brazil lasted for a generation longer than it did in the United States, ending in 1888, the South American nation did not have, after emancipation, the system of legally mandated segregation that existed in the United States. Indeed, throughout much of the twentieth century, the South American nation was hailed as a 'racial democracy' lacking the kind of rigid, legally mandated racial segregation or apartheid found in much of the United States and later in the Republic of South Africa. This image, frequently promoted by the Brazilian government, served to mask the very real and persisting racial inequalities in Brazilian society, including widespread discrimination in employment and significant differences in educational levels between Afro-Brazilians and whites. Although Brazil adopted seemingly far-reaching national civil rights legislation in 1951, prohibiting racial discrimination in all facets of public life, discrimination in employment, public accommodations, and the provision of public services would be a continued fact of life for many Afro-Brazilians throughout the twentieth century and indeed into the twenty-first century (Cottrol). Throughout the post-war period, social science investigators, including some sponsored by the UN Educational, Scientific and Cultural Organization (UNESCO), documented the pervasive nature of discrimination and inequality in Brazilian life (Chor Maio, 153; Fernandes, 134–44).

In the 1970s and 1980s, Afro-Brazilian activists were becoming increasingly assertive in their criticism of racial barriers in Brazilian life. Their efforts were encouraged by the anti-apartheid and anti-colonial struggles in Africa and the success of the civil rights movement in the United States, including the relative success that African Americans had in

---

7 443 US 103 (197).
8 See e.g. *City of Richmond v JA Croson*, 488 US 469 (1986).

breaking down traditional racial barriers. The increasingly visible presence of blacks in the US media, the professions, the senior ranks of the armed forces, and the diplomatic corps— and the absence of Afro-Brazilians in similar positions—made the traditional assertions that Brazil was a racial democracy seem increasingly hollow. The Afro-Brazilian push for greater racial inclusion and the elimination of racial barriers was inhibited in the 1970s and 1980s by the nation's military government, which was suspicious of all independent political movements. With the return of democratic rule in 1985, the movement for greater racial equality gained increased momentum. The adoption of a new democratic constitution in 1988, which Afro-Brazilian political activists had played a significant role in drafting, further spurred efforts to place the problem of racial inequality on the national agenda.

The new constitution had strong provisions prohibiting racial discrimination. Title I of the 1988 Constitution, the document's statement of 'Fundamental Principles,' declares the nation's obligation to promote 'the well-being of all people, without prejudice on the basis of origin, race, sex, color, age or any other form of discrimination.' Title II proclaims the equality of all persons under the law and declares racism to be a crime.[9] The 1988 Constitution also had provisions recognizing the cultural contributions of Afro-Brazilians and the nation's indigenous population. It is silent on the question of race-based affirmative action. Measures were adopted in the 1990s guaranteeing a minimum level of political representation for women, with relatively little controversy. Throughout the 1990s, opponents and proponents of race-based affirmative action would debate the desirability and constitutionality of possible affirmative action measures. Proponents would point to the strong disparities in income and education between Afro-Brazilians and Brazilians of European descent. Opponents of affirmative action would respond that such measures would violate the new constitution's strong equality principle and that race-based affirmative action was inappropriate in a nation that lacked a history of legally mandated racial discrimination. Many opponents of affirmative action argued that the disparities between whites and Afro-Brazilians were the results of class inequality and not racial discrimination, and that affirmative action measures based on race would be inappropriate. Other opponents of affirmative action also argued that in a society like Brazil, with its large degree of racial mixture and lack of agreed-upon definitions as to who was white and who was Afro-Brazilian, it would be difficult—if not impossible— to make the kind of racial determinations that affirmative action required.

Affirmative action programs would begin with the nation's public universities. The South American nation had long had a system of first-class public universities available to students free of charge. Entrance to these universities was controlled by a rigorous exam known as the vestibular. Overwhelmingly, the students who did well on these exams were those who had had strong secondary school preparations, usually in private schools. Disproportionately, students from wealthy families were the ones who scored high on the exams and were able to attend the good public universities, which were frequently the key to professional success in Brazil. In 2001 the state of Rio de Janeiro became the first state to announce a program of affirmative action for its public universities, requiring them to set quotas for Afro-Brazilians and the graduates of public secondary schools. In the years that followed, other state and federal universities also adopted affirmative action programs with quotas for Afro-Brazilians, indigenous people, and in many cases, graduates of public schools regardless of race.

The new policies, which were also accompanied by new affirmative action programs for Afro-Brazilians in a number of governmental ministries, were met with an extensive body of

9 Constitution Title I, Art 4 § VIII, Title II, Art 5§ 1, No. XLII (Brazil, 1988).

academic and polemical commentary pros and cons throughout the Lusophonic nation. To date, the programs have not been the subject of any decisions on the part of O Supremo Tribunal Federal, the South American nation's Supreme Court. In March 2010, the high court agreed to hear a case involving an affirmative action program at the Federal University of Rio Grande do Sul. The Court invited a wide segment of interested parties—those supporting, opposing, or merely commenting on affirmative action—to testify before the Court. More than 40 presentations were heard.

Two of the presentations presented the views of the administration of President Luiz Inácio da Silva ('Lula'), supporting the constitutionality of affirmative action. Deborah Duprat, then Vice Procuradora of the Republic, argued that the 1988 Constitution should be viewed as a break with the nation's past, a past in which the legal and constitutional order worked to protect the privileged while excluding the underprivileged. She argued that the 1988 Constitution should be viewed as an effort to bring about the inclusion of those who had traditionally been excluded and that, hence, the affirmative action measures were consistent with the equality principle in the new constitution.[10] Duprat's colleague Edson Santos de Souza, Minister of the Special Secretariat for Public Policy for the Promotion of Racial Equality, documented the strong patterns of racial discrimination and inequality in Brazilian life, and argued that these justified the new affirmative action measures.[11]

On 26 April 2012, Brazil's Supremo Tribunal Federal declared university affirmative action programs constitutional in a case involving another university, the University of Brasilia, a federal university. In a unanimous 10–0 vote, the Brazilian High Court supported a decision authored by STF Minister Ricardo Lewandowski. The Lewandowski opinion held that the university's affirmative policies were justified on three grounds: first, that the university had an interest in having a diverse student body and in combating racial inequality; second, that the university's program used proportional means to achieve its goals; and third, that the university's program was temporary and required periodic review. The Court concluded that the university's affirmative action program was within the principles of equality and human dignity set forth in the 1988 Constitution.[12] On August 29th 2012 Brazilian President Dilma Rouseff signed legislation requiring public universities to reserve half their admissions slots for graduates of public secondary schools. This action is expected to siginificantly increase the number of Afro-Brazilians attending public universities.[13]

25.4 India

Affirmative action in India is aimed at addressing the historical inequality of the caste system and the continuing impact that this deeply embedded discrimination and social subordination continues to have upon those at the bottom of the caste system. It has been described as a 'feudal system of hierarchical inequality embodied in the caste system that had been nurtured by an intermeshing of religion, culture and socio-legal practice' (Jackson, 223). It was envisaged that the post-independence Constitution would be transformative for those at the

---

10 *Audiência Publica: Arguição de Descumprimento de Precieto Fundamental 186, Recurso Extraordinário 597.285*, 'Palestra de Senhora Deborah Duprat (Vice-Procuradora Geral da República)' (Brasilia, 2010) (website Supremo Tribunal Federal).

11 *Ibid*, 'Palestra de Edson Santos de Sousa.'

12 'STF julga constitucional política de cotas na UnB,' *Noticias STF* (Quinta-feira, 26 de abril de 2012) http://www.stf.jus.br/portal/geral/verlmpressao.asp

13 'Brazil Enacts Affirmative Action Law for Universities' *New York Times*, August 30, 2012 (online addition).

bottom rung of the system and they are identified in the Constitution as Scheduled Castes, Scheduled Tribes, and social and educationally backward classes of citizen. The Indian Constitution was intended to provide the legal architecture to address the entrenched inequality that is a feature of the caste system through affirmative action. Yet, identifying who within those groups—in particular, other backward classes—should benefit has proved complicated and controversial since the Mandal Commission's attempt at designation.

Indeed, the Preamble to the Indian Constitution emphasizes equality of status and of opportunity, which reflects this commitment and imbues the text of the Constitution with this aim. Even so, the courts have struggled with the tension between equality before the law as a principle and the need to address the contemporary manifestations of caste and rigid social hierarchy. There exists a duality to this struggle in the Supreme Court whereby one approach is to view affirmative action as an exception to equality and the other approach is to read affirmative action as a composite feature of equality. The tension between equality and non-discrimination is particularly magnified in the context of access to employment in the public sector, and access to educational institutions, which has attracted significant domestic controversy.

Articles 14 and 15 of the Constitution enshrine equality before the law and non-discrimination, and are aimed at addressing the inequality of the caste system:

14. Equality before law.

The State shall not deny to any person equality before the law or the equal protection of the laws within the territory of India.

15. Prohibition of discrimination on grounds of religion, race, caste, sex or place of birth.

(1) The State shall not discriminate against any citizen on grounds only of religion, race, caste, sex, place of birth or any of them.
(2) No citizen shall, on grounds only of religion, race, caste, sex, place of birth or any of them, be subject to any disability, liability, restriction or condition with regard to—

(a) access to shops, public restaurants, hotels and places of public entertainment; or
(b) the use of wells, tanks, bathing ghats, roads and places of public resort maintained wholly or partly out of State funds or dedicated to the use of the general public.

(3) Nothing in this article shall prevent the State from making any special provision for women and children.
(4) [(4) Nothing in this article or in clause (2) of article 29 shall prevent the State from making any special provision for the advancement of any socially and educationally backward classes of citizens or for the Scheduled Castes and the Scheduled Tribes.]
(5) [(5) Nothing in this article or in sub-clause (g) of clause (1) of article 19 shall prevent the State from making any special provision, by law, for the advancement of any socially and educationally backward classes of citizens or for the Scheduled Castes or the Scheduled Tribes.]

In general, the courts have held that under article 15, equality before the law means the right to equal treatment in similar circumstances and, to date, the judiciary's approach to interpreting article 14 has been to recognize the limitations on the implementation of such a right. Bakshi locates the origins of article 14 in 'the American and Irish Constitutions' and connects the constitutional commitment to equality of status and opportunity with the freedom movement in India (Bakshi, 17). According to Bakshi, the relationship between arts 14 and 15 is, in a general sense, that article 15 lays down the detail of article 14; 'discrimination,' on the other hand, has been found to mean 'making an adverse distinction with regard to' or 'distinguishing unfavorably from others,'[14] and 'only' in article 15(1) has been interpreted as meaning that if the discrimination is based on a ground not connected to religion, race, caste, sex, or place of birth, then the discrimination would be valid (Bakshi, 27).

An area where the tension between equality and affirmative action has been amplified is reservations or quotas in educational institutions. In a decision on 12 August 2005, the Indian Supreme Court delivered a judgment that found that the state cannot impose its reservation policy on minority and non-minority unaided private colleges and professional colleges.[15] Moving swiftly, the state adopted an amendment to the Constitution to article 15 that any special provision for the advancement of 'any socially and educationally backward classes of citizens or for the Scheduled Castes or the Scheduled Tribes includes private educational institutions, whether aided or unaided by the State' (Article 15(5)).[16] This proposal was a commitment to, and aimed at, achieving the goal of equality by providing the lower castes have access to educational opportunities and facilities.

The constitutionality of this amendment was challenged in the Supreme Court decision *Thakur v India* in 2006. The grounds included that the amendment violated the basic structure of the Constitution because it transgressed the principle of secularism by favoring one minority group over another; that the determination of who is classified as 'other backward classes' is inconsistent with the principle of equality in the Constitution and, in particular, the 'creamy layers' should be excluded from the benefit of these reservations and stricter scrutiny should be given to the classification of other backward classes.

Here, it is important to note that the challenge to the central government's proposal was twofold: that it discriminated against meritorious students who did not have a disadvantaged background; and that such reservations are monopolized by the elite or so-called 'creamy layer' of the other backward classes.[17] The 'creamy layer' is a term given to the wealthier and more affluent members of the other backward classes. The concern is that members of the 'creamy layer' have the benefit of these reservations solely by virtue of their membership of a caste without regard to other rational factors that may differentiate them from other members of the caste, including their income, assets, and level of education. Indeed, in *Jagdish Negi v State of Uttar Pradesh*, a case pertaining to public-sector employment, the Supreme Court held that backwardness is not static; that no one is entitled to remain a member of the other backward classes in perpetuity; and that there should be some review of how citizens are classified. Once members of the other backward classes advance and achieve success economically and socially, that 'creamy layer' should not be entitled to the reservation because the aim of preferential treatment is to advance the situation of those in the caste who are: that is to say, these measures should be temporary, not permanent, and cease to provide a benefit once the aim is achieved. Although related to s 16 (4) and dealing with public-sector employment, the Supreme Court in *Indra Sawhney v Union of India* found that if the connecting link is social backwardness and some of the members become too socially and economically advanced, then the connecting thread between them and the class snaps.

---

14 *Kathi Raning Rawat v State of Saurashtra* (1952) SCR 435, 442.
15 *PA Inamdar & Ords v State of Maharashtra & Ors.*
16 Constitution (Ninety-Third Amendment) Act 2005.
17 Note: Justice Krishna Iyer, in *State of Kerela v NM Thomas*: 'benefits of the reservation shall be snatched away by the top creamy layer of the backward class, thus leaving the weakest among the weak and leaving the fortunate layers to consume the whole cake.'

In *Thakur*, the Supreme Court found that the Constitution (Ninety-Third Amendment) Act 2005 was not unconstitutional because it did not violate the basic structure of the Constitution.[18] While they left open-ended the question of whether the amendment was valid in relation to private education institutions, they did find that such reservations should exclude the 'creamy layer' of the other backward classes. The Court found implied in the Act that the failure to exclude the 'creamy layer' from monopolizing the benefits of reservation would render the reservation for other backward classes under the Act unconstitutional.

The debate in India is ongoing over the role of affirmative action in achieving a classless society and whether it is contrary to the principle of equality. Constitutionally valid affirmative action measures that mandate preferential treatment of some groups over others, particularly in the context of education and public-service jobs, continue to fuel ongoing tensions and debate about whether these measures entrench class divisions and perpetuate caste rather than foster a more egalitarian society.

25.5 South Africa

Like India, the South African Constitution is intended to be a transformative instrument aimed at addressing the historical exclusion of black South Africans during the apartheid regime. The language of the Preamble to the Constitution lays bare this intent: *'Recognise the injustices of our past'*; *'Honour those who suffered for justice and freedom in our land'*; *'Heal the divisions of the past and establish a society based on democratic values, social justice and fundamental human rights'*; *'Lay the foundations for a democratic and open society in which government is based on the will of the people and every citizen is equally protected by law'*. The challenge South Africa has faced in regard to affirmative action has been that the historically oppressed group is now the majority.

Equality is protected in ss 7 to 39 of the Constitution in the South African Bill of Rights. The commitment to equality is enshrined in s 1 (a) of the Constitution and can only be amended by a 75 percent majority of the National Assembly supported by six of the nine provinces. Section 9 of the South African Constitution provides:

Section 9 Equality

(1) Everyone is equal before the law and has the right to equal protection and benefit of the law.
(2) Equality includes the full and equal enjoyment of all rights and freedoms. To promote the achievement of equality, legislative and other measures designed to protect or advance persons, or categories of persons, disadvantaged by unfair discrimination may be taken.
(3) The state may not unfairly discriminate directly or indirectly against anyone on one or more grounds, including race, gender, sex, pregnancy, marital status, ethnic or social origin, color, sexual orientation, age, disability, religion, conscience, belief, culture, language and birth.
(4) No person may unfairly discriminate directly or indirectly against anyone on one or more grounds in terms of subsection (3). National legislation must be enacted to prevent or prohibit unfair discrimination.

18 Writ Petition (civil) 265 of 2006; see also Writ Petition (civil) No. 265 of 2006 decided on 10 April 2008.

(5) Discrimination on one or more of the grounds listed in subsection (3) is unfair unless it is established that the discrimination is fair.

Section 9 includes equality before the law, non-discrimination, and affirmative action, and is comprehensive including race, gender, sex, pregnancy, marital status, ethnic or social origin, color, sexual orientation, age, disability, religion, conscience, belief, culture, language and birth. The limitations to equality are expressed in s 36 (1). The equality jurisprudence in the Constitutional Court is mostly based on s 8 of the interim Constitution, which came into force on 27 April 1994. Although it was not the product of a democratically elected assembly, the 1996 Constitution was drafted and adopted by a democratically elected assembly. Section 9 is the successor of s 8 in the interim constitution and, according to Currie and De Waal, s 8 of the interim constitution applies to the 1996 Constitution (Currie & De Waal, 234).

In regard to Affirmative Action, s 9 (2) is the relevant provision. According to Currie and De Waal, the constitutional drafters were adamant that South Africa would avoid the controversies of affirmative action that has beleaguered the United States, and instead emphasized that affirmative action is an integral aspect of equality and s 9 (2) must be read only in the context of South Africa's unique history (Currie & De Waal, 264). There has also been a readiness on the part of the Court to provide group redress for discrimination (ibid).

In a 1995 decision, the Court had to grapple with the legacy of the apartheid regime classification system. In post-apartheid South Africa, 'black South Africans' were classified by the African National Congress as including black Africans, coloreds, and Indians, displaying a unity among those who were discriminated against during apartheid. In *Motala v University of Natal* an Indian student argued that he was unfairly discriminated against when he was refused admission to the University of Natal medical school despite the fact that he had obtained five distinctions in senior.[19] In this case, the medical school had limited its intake of Indian students to 40, the rationale being that, given the history of limited or no access to quality education for African students, a merit-based entrance system would unfairly discriminate against them. The Court held that the admission policy had a reasonable justification because it was a special measure designed to achieve the advancement of a group that was more disadvantaged under apartheid than South Africans of Indian descent. According to Currie and De Waal, this decision was 'clearly correct' because the measures were in proportion to the degree of disadvantage suffered; however, 'when the effect of a programme is to disadvantage, on the basis of race, people who had also been victims of discrimination in the past, the court ought to focus on the second requirement of the affirmative action clause and satisfy itself that the programme is rational and carefully constructed so as to achieve equality' (Currie & De Waal, 267).

In 2004, the Constitutional Court set down a substantive approach to s 9 (2) affirmative action in *Minister of Finance v Van Heerden*.[20] This case involved an appeal against the High Court declaration that Rule 4.2.1 of the Political Office-Bearers Pension Fund was constitutionally invalid because it was discriminatory. Van Heerden was a former parliamentarian who served with the National Party from 1997 to 2004, and served until 1999 as a member of the National Assembly. This meant he was covered by both the Pension Fund and the Closed Pension Fund. Van Heerden challenged the Pension Fund because Rule 4.2.1 prescribed categories of members and, as such, employer contributions differentiated between members and discriminated against him. Prior to the leave to appeal to the Constitutional

---

19 *Motala v University of Natal* 1995 (3) BCLR 374 (D).
20 *Van Heerden v Minister of Finance* 2004 (6) SA 121 (CC).

Court, the High Court had found that the Pension Fund and the Minister had violated the constitutional right of equality because they had not discharged their onus to establish that the affirmative action measures promoted the achievement of equality.

The Constitutional Court found that such remedial measures do not violate the principle of equality. The Court held that measures are 'not a derogation from, but a substantive and composite part of, the equality protection envisaged by the provisions of section 9 and of the Constitution as a whole. Their primary object is to promote the achievement of equality' (para 32). Moseneke J laid down three grounds on which s 9 (2) can be achieved: the majority of the group targeted by the measures must be designated as disadvantaged by unfair discrimination; the measure must be designed to protect or advance the disadvantaged group; and the measure must promote the achievement of equality (para 37). On each of these grounds the majority found that Rule 4.2.1 of the Pension Fund did satisfy these grounds because the means to achieving equality were targeted at the achievement of equality in a restitutionary sense.

Debates are ongoing in South Africa about the effectiveness of affirmative action policies and division caused by a rigid adherence to affirmative action measures. Again, as in other jurisdictions, the community must grapple with the balance between whether affirmative action measures are having an impact in terms of addressing historical disadvantage or whether such measures serve to entrench and perpetuate divisions along racial lines.

25.6 Conclusion

The affirmative action debate occurs worldwide and represents an ongoing struggle to strike a balance between the equality principle found in contemporary constitutions and the very real problem of entrenched structural inequality in modern societies. Different nations have found the balance between the competing considerations difficult to achieve. Some nations, such as France and the other nations of the European Union, have largely rejected the idea of ethnically or racial-based affirmative action because of their underlying conceptions of citizenship and the state, although there are significant European advocates for such programs. In other nations, affirmative action policy is a matter of constant debate and revision. The Ecuadoran Constitution of 2008 had adopted provisions permitting affirmative action for the South American nation's indigenous and Afro-Ecuadoran populations.[21] On 21 February 2012, the United States agreed to hear a challenge to an affirmative action program at the University of Texas, potentially calling into question race-based affirmative action programs in American public universities.[22] The battle over affirmative action, both as a matter of policy and as a matter of constitutional law, will remain an ongoing area of controversy in the twenty-first century.

References

Bakshi, PM (2000). *The Constitution of India with Comments and Subject Index* (Universal Law Publishing).

Chor Maio, M (1999). 'O projeto UNESCO e a agenda das Ciências Sociais no Brasil dos Anos 40 e 50,' *Revista Brasileira de Ciências Sociais* 14, no. 41 (Outubro): 141–58.

Cottrol, RJ (2004). '*Brown* and the Contemporary Brazilian Struggle Against Racial Inequality: Some Preliminary Comparative Thoughts, 66 *U Pitts L R* (Fall): 113–29.

21 Republica del Ecuador, Constituciones de 2008, Art II, Sec II.
22 *Fisher v University of Texas at Austin* 2012 WL 538328 (cert granted).

Currie, I & De Waal, J (2005). *The Bill of Rights Handbook* (Juta, 5th edn).

Fernandes, F (1971). *The Negro in Brazilian Society* (New York: Atheneum Books for Young Readers).

Jackson, VC (2010). *Constitutional Engagement in a Transnational Era* (Oxford University Press).

McKean, W (1983). *Equality and Discrimination under International Law* (University of Michigan, Clarendon Press).

Sowell, T (2009). *Affirmative Action Around the World* (New Haven, Yale University Press).

26

Minorities and group rights

Michael M Karayanni and Roberto Gargarella

26.1 Liberalism, neutrality and the constitution

For many decades, it was assumed that liberal constitutions had to be neutral in relation to different ways of life and conceptions of the good, so as to be equally respectful of them all. Philosophers referred to this idea of neutrality as 'the priority of the right over the good' (Rawls 1971, 1988). John Rawls, for example, maintained this view of neutrality, which he extended to the constitution. For him, the constitution had to limit itself to the establishment of a fair procedure through which rival parties would seek approval from the people. It had to set up 'a form of fair rivalry for political office and authority' (Rawls 1971, 227). So organized, the constitution was seen as an expression of *imperfect procedural justice*.[1]

Constitutional neutrality was the way in which liberalism responded to a world characterized by 'the fact of pluralism' (Rawls 1991).[2] The US Constitution represents a good illustration of what this response could imply, namely, a system of checks and balances (aimed at ensuring that the exercise of power remained under control), and a bill of rights (which came to set limits to the state, and thus to protect individual rights). The US Constitution's endorsement of the principle of neutrality appears particularly clear in its First Amendment, and the idea that 'Congress shall make no law respecting an establishment of religion, or prohibiting the free exercise thereof; or abridging the freedom of speech, or of the press …' The Amendment was a moral compromise reached at a time of extreme religious confrontations,

---

1 We have *perfect procedural justice* when we have both an independent criterion for deciding what is a fair outcome and a procedure that guarantees that we get that outcome. In the case of the constitution, we do have an independent criterion for defining what is fair, but lack a procedure that could guarantee us such a result.

2 As the moral philosopher Michael Sandel has put it, liberals assumed that '[since] people disagree about the best way to live, government should not affirm in law any particular vision of the good life. Instead, it should provide a framework of rights that respects individuals as free and independent beings, capable of choosing their own values and ends' (Sandel 1996, 4; Taylor 1989, 172, 178). By so doing, liberals asserted 'the priority of fair procedures over particular ends' (ibid).

when colonists obliged members of their communities to take part in religious activities, and dissidents suffered from ruthless physical punishment, imprisonment, and exile.[3]

By the end of the eighteenth century, with the enactment for the first modern constitutions in the United States and France, the model of the neutral constitution became the established rule. Sometimes, as in the United States, it gained unquestioned stability, and at other times, as in most Latin American countries, it did not. Yet, for a long period, constitutional neutrality became the focal point—the obvious point of departure in all constitutional debates. Neutrality seemed to be the proper answer in the face of social diversity, moral perfectionism, and political factionalism.

Another basic tenet of liberal thought was that the rights-bearing entity is the individual and not the group. Central to this conception is the great emphasis that liberalism places on individual autonomy. From the point of view of liberalism, all individuals are to be treated equally by state institutions. Individuals have, of course, the right to associate themselves in corporations and associations, but have no right to ask for preferential treatment based on their group membership (Barry 2001).

By the end of the twentieth century, things began to change as a consequence of a plurality of factors. Kymlicka and Norman have listed some of these: 'the collapse of communism in 1989 sent waves of ethnic nationalism ripping through Eastern Europe ... the nativist backlash against immigrants and refugees in many Western countries (especially France, Britain, Germany, and the United States); the resurgence and political mobilization of indigenous peoples, resulting in the Declaration of the Rights of Indigenous Peoples at the United Nations (although many countries of concern, including the US, Canada and Australia voted against it); and the ongoing, even growing, threat of secession within some of the most flourishing Western democracies, from Quebec to Scotland, Flanders, and Catalonia' (Kymlicka & Norman 2000, 2–3). Indigenous groups around the world began to claim a place within constitutional orders that seemed to ignore their needs and more urgent demands. In the face of these renewed claims, the old solution of constitutional neutrality seemed insufficient, if not directly wrong.

26.2 Group rights in the new constitutional order

In effect, by the end the century, it became clear that the model of the neutral constitution was having serious difficulties in fulfilling its promise of equal respect for all. The problems surfaced everywhere. Thus, the constitutional system invoked the ideal of equal treatment, but allowed the state to communicate only through the language that the majority spoke; it claimed neutrality among different religions, but organized the national holidays and celebrations according to the values of the dominant groups; it alleged respect for all, but chose a system of economic organization that was hostile to communal forms of organizing property; it made proud references to its impartial character, but left no room for alternative understandings of justice. Given the fact that members of the majority group are the ones that govern in most branches of government, it is inevitable that government bodies will be more

---

3 As M Konvitz put it, 'the Virginia colony banished Puritan clergymen, Quakers, and Catholic priests. The Puritans at Plymouth gave the suffrage only to orthodox believers and legislated against Quakers. At Massachusetts Bay the voting privilege was given only to church members (there was only one church); the church and clergymen were supported by taxes, and church attendance was compulsory. The Puritans at New Haven conformed to this theocratic pattern' (Konvitz 1957, 18).

attuned to majority interests than to those of the minority. For members of minority groups, it seemed obvious that the constitutional system in place was not giving due consideration to some of their most fundamental interests: it proved unable to grant them a proper voice in the defense of their own affairs; considered their own systems of justice to be simply unfair; dismissed the value of their traditions and religious ceremonies; directly rejected their claims for autonomous rule; and ensured no protection for their cultural heritage.

Neutrality did not seem to be the proper answer in a world of unjustified inequalities, and particularly so when these inequalities were created and maintained through the use of the state's coercive apparatus. In such a context, equal respect seemed to require differential treatment, rather than state blindness towards existing differences. The principle of neutrality went through a process of substantial reinterpretation. Something similar happened with the liberal principle of not treating people differently based on circumstances beyond their control. The principle was easily invoked and usually applied in the face of racial or gender differences. For example, it seemed clear that men and women, black and white, deserved the same treatment by the state, in spite of the—morally irrelevant—differences that existed between them. However, the principle was never invoked in other substantially similar cases, which included, for example, cultural differences between groups. Thus, it was normally the case that the state failed to make relevant distinctions between members of majority and minority groups, applied the same rules to all of them, and thus mistreated members of cultural or ethnic minorities for reasons beyond their control. This is what happened, for example, when the state spoke only through the official—majority—language, or failed to recognize the special needs of members of religious minorities.

One fundamental question emerged as a consequence of this gradual change of perspectives. The question was 'whether the familiar system of common citizenship rights within liberal democracies—the standard set of civil, political, and social rights which define citizenship in most democratic countries—(was) sufficient to accommodate the legitimate interests which people have in virtue of their ethnic identity' (Shapiro & Kymlicka 2000, 4). The answer seemed to be clearly 'no.'

The emergence of these new concerns for the rights of minorities explains the wave of profound constitutional and legal change that took place at the end of the twentieth century, in large sections of the world. By that time, many countries began to modify their basic legal rules in order to accommodate some of the, until then, unattended claims of minority groups. In the Philippines, an Indigenous Peoples Rights Act was enacted in 1997, trying to help remove serious forms of discrimination against minority groups; in Norway, a special legislative body was created to allow the Sami people to gain control over their own affairs; in Canada in 1982, the Constitution Act gave explicit protection to the practices and traditions of aboriginals; in Kenya, the 2010 Constitution recognized individual and collective rights of indigenous peoples.

Also, in recent years, most Latin American countries changed their constitutions, trying to address the problem of centuries of discrimination against indigenous communities. The new constitutions included numerous and original responses to those largely ignored problems. Thus, and for example, we find reserved seats in the Parliament for indigenous groups, in Colombia, Panama, and Venezuela; reserved seats at the municipal level in Mexico; recognition to specific forms of indigenous justice in Bolivia, Ecuador, Mexico, Peru, and Venezuela; greater degrees of political autonomy for indigenous communities in Bolivia, Colombia, Ecuador, Guatemala, Paraguay, Peru, and Venezuela; protection to their cultural heritage in Bolivia, Colombia, Ecuador, Guatemala, Honduras, and Venezuela; special protection for their communal lands in the vast majority of the existing constitutions; new rights for the exploitation and use of their own resources in Argentina, Bolivia, Brazil, Colombia, Ecuador, Mexico, Nicaragua, Paraguay, Peru, and Venezuela; protections to their language rights in Argentina, Brazil, Bolivia, Colombia, Costa Rica, Ecuador, Guatemala, Nicaragua, Paraguay, Peru, and Venezuela (Aguilar *et al* 2010). We can also find a similar evolution in the European context. For example, in the Copenhagen criteria (1993), European countries established that respect for minority rights was a pre-condition for entering into the European structure. The European Charter for regional or minority languages (1992) aims at protecting and promoting regional and minority languages. Also in 1995, European countries passed the Framework Convention for the Protection of National Minorities (see, for example, Kymlicka 2006).

26.3 On the justifications for group rights

One important rationale for group rights is past discrimination (Sowell 2004). In a number of countries it was resolved that, to repair past injustices, members of groups that were discriminated against in the past must be given preferential treatment today (Anderson 2004). Through such measures, a previously discriminatory society would be able to compensate for the past injustice and provide members of the disadvantaged group with the prospect of an opportunity for equality in the future. Measures of affirmative action that have often been employed in these cases usually include favorable admission policies to institutions of higher education and preferential treatment in government jobs or in handing out government contracts. Although racial or religious minority groups are usually considered for affirmative action policies, other groups might qualify at times as well. Some argued that affirmative action measures were justified for women, and in some cases for the majority group as in the case of South Africa, given the fact that such groups have also suffered from discriminatory treatment. Affirmative action policies envision a future in which the preferential treatment accorded the designated groups will end. The Convention on the Elimination of All Forms of Racial Discrimination provides explicitly in Article 2.2 that the separate rights accorded to the different racial groups shall not be maintained 'after the objectives for which they were taken have been achieved.'

Yet group rights can be justified on the basis of values concerned with the present well-being of individual members of minority cultures, irrespective of whether these groups have suffered from discrimination in the past. Some authors—many of whom were once labeled communitarians—have argued that the ties individuals have to their society, history, and culture are significant aspects of identity and part of one's being. People are to be understood as 'constituted by relations with others without which they will cease to be who they are' (Sandel 1982). In his important work on the 'ideal of authenticity,' Taylor has argued that the recognition of identity is a 'vital human need' (Taylor 1994, 26). Identity, for him, is discovered by each person within herself, but also shaped and constructed through our relationship with others. According to Taylor, that process of discovery is fundamentally dialogical, and realized against a background—which defines our 'horizon of meaning'—that is set by the community within which we live. This is why the protection of identity requires 'the affirmation of group members in their particular and authentic identities' (ibid, 37). Similarly, Kymlicka has argued in defense of group rights, assuming that groups are crucial for our capacity for deliberative judgment: our community defines the range of options between which we choose how to live, and provides us with the tools necessary for assessing those options (Kymlicka 1989).

Taking such assumptions as their starting points, many have argued that it is then inevitable for a liberal political structure that values individual autonomy to grant groups certain accommodations. Without such special accommodations, an individual's own autonomy will be undermined, especially if the individual belongs to a minority group (Kymlicka 1989, 1995; Raz 1994; Taylor 1994). Unlike the majority, minority groups are under the continuous threat of assimilation, marginalization, exclusion, and other forces that work to diminish their capacity to maintain themselves as a group. According to this strand of thought, a strand that became known as liberal multiculturalism, concepts of tolerance, and state neutrality—which are the standard liberal concepts for managing a diverse and pluralistic society—are not sufficient for safeguarding individuals. To attend to the needs of individuals, the state must not only tolerate the group that that individual belongs to or be neutral to its various group identities, but must actively accommodate the group. If 'individual freedom and prosperity depends on full and unimpeded membership in a respected and flourishing community, then liberalism makes it necessary to devise accommodations that work to secure the existence and flourishing of cultural minorities' (Raz 1986; Deveaux 2000).

This rationale for group rights can have a broad application. Its focus is those cultures that are threatened to be eliminated by the majority culture, either because this majority culture seeks to assimilate minority members or because the majority seeks to weaken, or even eradicate, other cultures without offering to assimilate them. However, the rationale is limited to those groups that qualify as culture groups (i.e. groups that envision a specific way of life and a certain value system identifiable as special and different) (Margalit & Halbertal 1994). Consequently, certain groups that might be discriminated against but do not necessarily form a cultural group, such as women, may not be entitled to accommodations under this rationale, but might be entitled to accommodations under the first one.

A third rationale for group rights focuses on the democratic process. Its objective is to make that process more inclusive. Without special group accommodations for minority groups, their voice will be excluded and the democratic process undermined. Societies composed of a majority group and minorities cannot be neutral among all of their members, even if they adopt the most democratic form of government. To make a democracy more inclusive, minority groups must be guaranteed representation in government bodies (Young 1989). Without such protection the minority group could be assimilated, thereby endangering its very nomos (Shachar 2001).

Another basic issue that has drawn attention in the discussion on group rights is whether there should be a distinction between indigenous minority groups and immigrant minority groups. Immigrant groups, some suggest, can be expected to adjust to the reality and culture of their new country whereas indigenous groups cannot fairly be placed under the same expectation. To the contrary, it is the state that came on to them, and therefore the state should adjust to their reality and culture. Although one cannot easily disregard this distinction, it is important to also acknowledge the fact that people at times emigrate from their home countries in light of harsh conditions there and not totally by choice.

26.4 The type of group rights

Group rights can take different forms. This is a list of the most common forms of group rights (Levy 1997).

1. Exempting minority members from the need to abide by certain norms, especially those that deem certain acts as criminal (helmet laws and the Sikhs; Jews and Muslims and humane slaughter laws);
2. Granting minorities special assistance and funding, affirmative action, support of minority cultural activities; special representation quotas;

3. Self-government powers; the power to have courts and devise norms; exclusive power over persons of territories;
4. Recognition: recognizing the official status of minority language; recognizing minority holidays.

26.5 The problems with group rights

Two major problems are associated with group rights. The first is of a vertical nature and focuses on intragroup norms that are illiberal in nature; norms that now have the backing of special accommodations. The second is horizontal in nature, attuned to possible tensions among groups; tensions that can become worse given the cultivation and promotion of group identity.

26.5.1 Problem I: Illiberal intra-group norms

There is much discussion in the literature dealing with group rights and multiculturalism on what became known as the 'minority within a minority' problem (Green 1995; Eisenberg & Spinner-Halev 2005). The major question posed in this respect is how can a liberal democracy work to justify the accommodation of a minority group when that group will work to apply illiberal norms to its members? Two intra-minority groups have been identified as especially vulnerable to intra-group illiberal norms: women and children. Let us assume that the group seeking accommodation is a group that still adheres to patriarchal norms by which women are considered as less equal members of society and is even prepared to openly accord women lesser rights than those accorded to men (Okin 1999). Should such a group be accommodated? But how could it be when accommodations are anchored *within* liberalism! The same applies to children. The case of *Wisconsin v Yoder* (405 US 205, 1971) exemplifies this quandary. Following an Amish tradition, four Amish parents had their children leave school at the age of 14. However, according to the relevant state law, children are to remain in an accredited school until the age of 16. The parents were eventually prosecuted and convicted for violating state law. The US Supreme Court held that these parents were absolved from criminal liability because of their constitutionally guaranteed freedom of conscience. This resolution surely accords the Amish a special protection that promotes their values and teachings among their children. Yet this outcome is problematic from a liberal point of view, given that children are denied the opportunity to complete a course of education that adequately equips them with the tools and skills that enable them to decide for themselves and become citizens capable of weighing the various contending views in society (Shapiro & Arneson 1996). So can the accommodations for the Amish infringe on the rights of Amish children?

A number of suggestions have been put forward to address this liberal predicament. The first proposes a distinction between accommodations that work to protect the minority group from the majority (external protections) and accommodations that permit the minority group to make internal regulations that govern their members' conduct (internal restrictions) (Kymlicka 1995). According to this view, only the first kind of accommodations (i.e. external protections) should be permitted. If so, then the group will not be permitted to apply its own illiberal norms to its members and thus the predicament can be contained. Another suggestion argues that internal restrictions are an inevitable consequence of accommodating minorities, given the fact that internal restrictions are at times intertwined with the group culture itself. Moreover, external protection can have the same effect as internal restriction and thus will not really do the job of eliminating the internal illiberal norms. For example, designating a specific neighborhood for the exclusive residence of minority members might be taken as an external protection, but at the same time it will work to foster the minority culture, including minority illiberal norms. In light of this reality, it has been suggested that illiberal groups can and should be accommodated as long as their individual members will have the option of exiting the group, and by doing so relieving themselves from the internal illiberal practice (Kukathas 1992). Moreover, once exit from the group is possible, the voice of individuals within the group calling for reform and even-handedness will become more effective given the essential drive of the group to prevent its members from leaving (Karayanni 2007). An enhanced right of exit will thus enhance the voice of internal minorities.

However, strong arguments can be offered against the justification of accommodating illiberal groups based on the existence of a right to exit. One can doubt whether certain individuals can actually exercise the right of exit in light of their circumstances. For example, one can reasonably argue that children cannot really exercise a right to exit their group. Second, the right to exit is at times unfair, offering a binary option under which one is brought to choose between his or her culture and the culture and norms of the majority.

26.5.2 Problem II: Inter-group tensions

The claims raised by different groups for special accommodations are often raised in the context of inter-group conflicts. Thus there is the basic fear that if group identities are cultivated and strengthened by the fact of group rights, existing tensions between groups will become worse. So, while group rights will offer some remedies for past injustice, attend to one's individual needs, and make democracy more inclusive, such rights might also make inter-group relations much worse than they are at present.

This is an empirical argument that depends on the reality that exists in an individual nation. Indeed, some have argued that diversity and pluralism can lead to a healthier state of being for those who belong to different cultures. It is assumed that those living in a society of different groups will be engaged in a constant process of self-reflection, given the fact that their daily lives bring them to always confront the values practices of other cultures (Deveaux 2000). Cultural diversity is also beneficial to politics. As one scholar has argued: 'the presence of citizens of diverse social and cultural backgrounds brings different moral perspectives into political life and may enhance debate and decision-making in the context of deliberative, democratic arrangements' (Deveaux 2000).[4]

Even if inter-group tensions may rise as a result of group rights, measures can be taken to contain and perhaps even eliminate these tensions. One important measure in this respect is the promotion of what Joseph Raz has termed a 'common culture' (Raz 1994). This common culture will cultivate such ideas as mutual toleration and respect as well as promote educational programs designed to encourage studying the history and culture of other groups. Additionally, the interaction within one economic and political system will also work to promote some common ideals that all groups will work to respect. In this vein, one could also imagine favorable government funding for joint inter-group activities and projects that will not only serve the quest to create some common spheres of values but also indicate, by their very existence, the high value of co-existence and joint activities.

---

4 In its decision T-422-96, the Colombian Constitutional Court made reference to the importance of protecting minority groups in order to 'ensure social equity and consolidate internal peace in the country' See http://www.corteconstitucional.gov.co/relatoria/1996/T-422-96.htm

26.6 Group rights in non-Western democracies

Most of the discussions of group rights have so far taken place in the context of Western democracies, and in that context assumes the existence of some basic guiding constitutional principles even if questions remain about whether such principles are applicable to all groups and, if so, whether they are equitably enforced. One such guiding principle is the drive to maintain the state as neutral as possible; another is the centrality of liberalism with its strong hold in the autonomous individual in constructing rights and freedoms. However, these basic tenets of Western democracies do not necessarily apply everywhere. In some countries the state itself is officially identified with one group, and in others political arrangements are explicitly determined based on group affiliation. For example, Israel is generally defined as a Jewish nation state in which special privileges are accorded to Jews and Jewish collective ideals, especially in the laws pertaining to Israel's immigration policy, state institutions, and state symbols (Jacobsohn 1993, 2010). On the other hand, Israel has also committed itself to certain democratic norms and has recognized some special rights for its Palestinian–Arab citizens. However, so far, Israel lacks a common institution of citizenship for Jews and Arabs alike, something that makes it almost impossible to build a common culture (Karayanni 2007). Additionally, some of the group rights that are recognized accord religious institutions with the right to establish courts, and apply their own religious law in matters of family law, namely matters of marriage and divorce—laws that explicitly discriminate against women. Similarly, Lebanon's existing political and constitutional structure maintains consensual arrangements under which basic governmental positions are distributed among the different groups (Zuhur 2002). As in Israel, Lebanon, and many other Middle Eastern countries, the law of the relevant religious community governs a number of family law matters (Mallat 2007). These different underlying constitutional characteristics can have major implications for the justification and content of group rights in such Middle Eastern countries as well as elsewhere in Asia and Africa. Because of the states' formal identity, they can severely restrict the group rights of certain minorities, especially if such rights will challenge the hegemony of the dominant group, while at the same time generously backing the inner handlings of the non-dominant minority groups so as to compensate for the official bias.

References

Aguilar, G, LaFosse, S Rojas, H & Steward, R (2010) 'Análisis Comparado del Reconocimiento Constitucional de los Pueblos Indígenas en América Latina', SSRC: Conflict Prevention and Peace Forum.

Anderson, TA (2004). *The Pursuit of Fairness: A History of Affirmative Action* (Oxford, Oxford University Press).

Barry, B (2001), *Culture and Equality: An Egalitarian Critique of Multiculturalism* (Cambridge, Harvard University Press).

Deveaux, M (2000), *Cultural Pluralism and Dilemmas of Justice* (Ithaca, Cornell University Press).

Eisenberg, A & Spinner-Halev, J (eds) (2005). *Minorities within Minorities: Equality, Rights and Diversity* (Cambridge, Cambridge University Press).

Green, L (1995). 'Internal Minorities and Their Rights', in Kymlicka, W (ed), *The Rights of Minority Cultures* (Oxford, Oxford University Press), 256–74.

Jacobsohn, GF (1993). *Apple of Gold: Constitutionalism in Israel and the United States* (Princeton, Princeton University Press).

—— (2010). *Constitutional Identity* (Cambridge, Harvard University Press).

Karayanni, MM (2007). 'Multiculture Me No More! On Multicultural Qualifications and the Palestinian-Arab Minority of Israel', *Diogenes* 54: 39–58.

Konvitz, M (1957). *Fundamental Liberties of a Free People: Religion Speech, Press, Assembly* (Westport, Conn., Greenwood Press Publishers).

Kukathas, C (1992). 'Are There Any Cultural Rights?', *Political Theory* 20: 105–39.

Kymlicka, W (1989). *Liberalism, Community, and Culture* (Oxford, Oxford University Press).

—— (1995). *Multicultural Citizenship: A Liberal Theory of Minority Rights* (Oxford, Oxford University Press).

—— (2006). 'The Evolving Basis of European Norms of Minority Rights: Rights to Culture, Participation and Autonomy', in McGarry, J & Keating, M (eds), *European Integration and the Nationalities Question* (Routledge, London, 2006), 35–63.

—— & Norman, W (2000). 'Citizenship in Culturally Diverse Societies: Issues, Contexts, Concepts', in Kymlicka, W & Norman, W (eds), *Citizenship in Diverse Societies* (Oxford, Oxford University Press), 1–41.

Levy, JT (1997). 'Classifying Cultural Rights', in Shapiro, I & Kymlicka, W (eds), *Ethnicity and Group Rights: NOMOS XXXIX* (New York, New York University Press), 22–66.

Mallat, C (2007). *Introduction to Middle Eastern Law* (Oxford, Oxford University Press).

Margalit, A & Halbertal, M (1994). 'Liberalism and the Right to Culture', *Social Research* 61: 491–510.

Okin, SM (1999). *Is Multiculturalism Bad for Women?* (Princeton, Princeton University Press).

Rawls, J (1971). *A Theory of Justice* (Cambridge, Harvard University Press).

——(1988). 'The Priority of Right and Ideas of the Good', *Philosophy and Public Affairs* 17: 251–76.

—— (1991). *Political Liberalism* (New York, Columbia University Press).

Raz, J (1986). *The Morality of Freedom* (Oxford, Clarendon Press).

—— (1994). 'Multiculturalism: A Liberal Perspective', *Dissent* 41: 67–79.

Sandel, MJ (1982). *Liberalism and the Limits of Justice* (Cambridge, Cambridge University Press).

—— (1996). *Democracy's Discontent: America in Search of a Public Philosophy* (Cambridge, Harvard University Press).

Shachar, A (2001). *Multicultural Jurisdictions: Cultural Differences and Women's Rights* (Cambridge, Cambridge University Press).

Shapiro, I & Arneson, R (1996). 'Democracy and Religious Freedom: A critique of *Wisconsin v Yoder*', in Shapiro, I & Hardin, R (eds), *Political Order: NOMOS XXXVIII* (New York, New York University Press) 365–411.

—— & Kymlicka, W (eds) (2000). *Ethnicity and Group Rights: Nomos XXXIX* (New York, New York University Press).

Sowell, T (2004). *Affirmative Action around the World: An Empirical Study* (New Haven, Yale University Press).

Taylor, C (1989). Sources of the Self: The Making of Modern Identity (Harvard University Press).

—— (1994). 'The Politics of Recognition', in Gutmann, A (ed). *Multiculturalism: Examining the Politics of Recognition* (Princeton University Press), 25–74.

Young, IM (1989). 'Polity and Group Difference: A Critique of the Ideal of Universal Citizenship', *Ethics* 99: 250–74.

Zuhur, S (2002). 'Empowering Women or Dislodging Sectarianism?: Civil Marriage in Lebanon', *Yale Journal of Law & Feminism* 14: 177–208.

5. Rights and society

27

Rights of non-citizens

Atsushi Kondo and Dragoljub Popović

27.1 Types of constitution and interpretation

The historical development of constitutional rights of non-citizens can be divided into three periods. In the late eighteenth century, constitutional rights were not limited to a state's citizens because of the influence of the natural rights doctrine. The Declaration of the Rights of Man and of the Citizen in France is one example, even where the rights of the citizen were defined as being limited to citizens. The Bill of Rights in the United States is another. Thereafter, in the nineteenth and early twentieth centuries, constitutional rights came to be limited to citizens (or subjects) because of the nationalistic spirit of this time.[1] Finally, after 1945, constitutional rights have again extended beyond citizens because of the human rights renaissance and the influence of international human rights treaties. Although, shortly after World War II, non-citizens' rights were not clearly stipulated in constitutions such as those of Japan and Italy, they have come to be more clearly defined in relatively new constitutional laws. The 1974 Swedish Constitution proved most detailed, in which fundamental rights were accorded to 'citizens', but non-citizens were equated to citizens in respect of certain rights.[2] However, the 2010 Amendment of the Swedish Constitution generally accords fundamental rights to 'everyone', while special limitation for non-citizens may be introduced with respect to certain rights.[3]

---

1 For example, the French Constitutional Charter of 1814 (or Japanese Constitution of 1889).
2 Non-citizens were equated to citizens in respect of protection against discrimination, expropriation, coercion to manifest an opinion, or to belong to an association; protection of personal integrity in connection with automatic data processing; protection against capital punishment, corporal punishment and torture; the right to a fair trial, industrial action or an education (see Chapter 2 Art 20 of the 1974 Instrument of Government). The Swedish Constitution consists of four fundamental laws, of which the most important is the Instrument of Government.
3 Special limitation for non-citizens may be introduced in freedom of expression, information, assembly, demonstration, association and worship; protection against coercion to divulge an opinion, body searches, house searches and other such invasions of privacy, deprivation of liberty and violations on grounds of an opinion; public court proceedings; intellectual property rights; the right to trade, practise a profession and freedom of research (see Chapter 2, Art 25 of the 2010 Amended Instrument of Government).

Currently, constitutional interpretation of the rights of non-citizens can be divided into two types: 1) 'word-oriented', and 2) 'nature-oriented'. This classification is attributable to the way of thinking at the time of constitution-drafting. In 'word-oriented' countries such as Germany, linguistic interpretation according to the founders' will comprises the starting point, and then evolutive interpretation adjusts to social developments. For example, the German Constitution designated the right to freely choose one's occupation under Art 12.1 as being exclusively for the protection of 'all Germans', but the protection has since been expanded in given respects for certain non-citizens under Art 2.1, which guarantees 'every person' the right to free development of his or her personality.[4]

In 'nature-oriented' countries such as Japan and South Korea, linguistic interpretation of the 'national' rights clause is not the starting point, and comparative constitutions or international human rights law are more important for understanding the nature of rights that can be applicable to non-citizens. Although Art 22.1 of the Constitution stipulates: *Every person shall have the freedom to choose and change his residence*, the Japanese Supreme Court decided that 'according to customary international law a nation is under no duty to admit non-citizens to its territory . . . consequently, in constitutional law . . . non-citizens are not guaranteed the rights claimed of staying in Japan', and 'the guarantees of fundamental human rights contained in Chapter 3 of the Constitution, except for those deemed to be guaranteed only to citizens from the nature of the right, shall apply equally to all non-citizens residing in Japan.'[5] Under Art. 6.2 of the South Korean Constitution, 'the status of non-citizens is guaranteed as prescribed by international law and treaties'.

It is often stated that civil and political rights are first-generation rights, while economic, social and cultural rights are second-generation rights. Indeed, citizens in constitutional states were first given civil, then political and finally social rights. However, non-citizens have obtained access to the same rights in another order and not to the same degree (Hammar, 54). Non-citizens were first given most civil rights under the principle of the legal state (*Rechtsstaat*); then social rights were guaranteed to permanent or regular residents based on the principle of the welfare state; but some political rights are limited to citizens (nationals) in accordance with the principle of democratic state or national sovereignty (*souveraineté nationale*) (Eriksen & Weigård, 15; Kondo 2003, 10, 20 f). Furthermore, some economic rights such as the right to choose an occupation are not guaranteed to certain non-permanent residents, while cultural rights such as the right to enjoy one's own culture are significant for non-citizens. In addition to the general constitutional law framework for the rights of non-citizens, the specific guarantees of family reunification and asylum law are important (Hofmann & Tietje, 216 ff).

We begin by classifying the main types of non-citizens with reference to their rights protection. Then we consider what kinds of civil rights are limited to what kinds of non-citizens. Then we examine economic, social and cultural rights and conclude with a discussion of political rights and citizenship.

---

4 See BVerfGE 78, 179 (1988); 104, 337 (2002).
5 32 *Minshuu* [Supreme Court Reports about Civil Cases] 1223 (1978). See Beer & Itoh, 477.

27.2 Three types of non-citizens and their rights

If we omit some special factors and generalize the classification according to the Three Gates Model as described by Hammar (16), the state of non-citizens' rights in most countries[6] can be categorized into three groups: permanent residents, other regular residents and irregular residents. Non-citizens pass through the immigration control gate for entry permission first, and receive most civil rights and partial social rights as regular residents. Second, after staying for a designated period, regular residents pass through the gate for permanent residency, and receive more stable rights in the fields of residential, employment and social rights. Third, permanent residents may choose to naturalize and obtain full rights including political rights as citizens.

Before the oil shock of 1972, the problem of irregular residents was not so serious because they could be regularized after they found jobs with ease. However, in the current economic and political climate, regularization is more difficult. In some European countries, irregular migrants tend to be asylum seekers but in other places they work clandestinely without seeking asylum. In the US Supreme Court, the distinction between resident aliens and undocumented aliens is important (Bosniak 2006, 49 f). As to social rights, minimum rights such as emergency medical care are available to irregular residents in most countries. However, in practice, most social rights are limited. The French Constitutional Council has noted that 'foreigners shall enjoy the rights to social security, when they reside stably and regularly in the French territory'.[7] The Japanese Supreme Court upheld the constitutionality of excluding irregular residents from the recipients of public assistance.[8] Economic rights such as the right to unionize are guaranteed to irregular workers in many countries. Yet, the US Supreme Court held that an undocumented worker fired in relation to his support of union organizing was ineligible for back pay.[9] Therefore, such rights are limited, in practice. However, cultural rights such as the right to education at public schools are guaranteed to undocumented children.[10] With respect to political rights, irregular residents may have liberty of political expression, but clandestine migrants know that their public appearance may lead to deportation. Irregular residents do not have voting rights, even in countries where local voting rights for permanent (or long-term) or privileged (such as EU citizens) foreign residents are granted.

27.3 Civil rights

Scholars describe three generations of human or fundamental rights, as they are also called; the first being civil and political, the second economic and social, and the third environmental (Cohendet, 136 f).[11] Political rights, being eminently the rights of political participation, can however be distinguished from civil rights. Political rights are usually limited to citizens.[12] Some constitutional texts have introduced a clear distinction between various

---

6 In traditional immigration states such as the US, 'immigrants' are permitted permanent residence at the time of arrival, therefore the two-gates model is applied to them. However, there are also many non-immigrants and the Three Gates Model is also applicable to them.

7 93-325 DC (1993).

8 1768 *Hanrei Jiho* [Law Cases Report] 48 (2001).

9 *Hoffman Plastic Compounds, Inc v National Labor Relations Board*, 583 US 137 (2002).

10 See *Plyler v Doe*, 457 US 202 (1982).

11 For the definitions and concepts of civil, fundamental and human rights, cf. Häberle 1997, 291.

12 However, there is a trend of expanding these rights (Secker).

fundamental rights. The Italian Constitution provides an example in this respect. In its first part it provides for the rights and duties of citizens, devoting a separate chapter to each type of right: civil, social, economic and political.

Civil rights are fully granted to non-citizens insofar as they are not closely connected either with political rights on the one hand, or economic and social rights on the other. Examples of such rights are the right to life, the right to liberty and security, and the right to a fair trial. Within the framework of the United Nations these civil rights are guaranteed by the International Covenant on Civil and Political Rights of 1966.[13]

The wording of constitutional provisions in which these rights are based displays the difference between two types of rights. Compare Art. 2.2 of the German Constitution, which provides in the first sentence: *Every person shall have the right to life and physical integrity*, with Art. 9.1 of the same Constitution: *All Germans shall have the right to form corporations and other associations*.

Similarly, the wording of the Fifth and Seventh Amendments of the US Constitution differs from that of its Fifteenth Amendment. The former provisions guaranteeing the due process of law and a trial by jury do not refer to citizen status, while the Fifteenth Amendment—forbidding discrimination in electoral rights—clearly mentions the citizens of the United States.

The Spanish Constitution provides in Art. 29.1 that the right of petition belongs to all Spaniards, while under Art. 15 of the same Constitution, '*everyone has a right to moral and physical integrity*'. By so doing, this constitutional text construes the right of petition as linked to political rights. These provisions show that a certain right, reserved to citizens, is perceived as having a participatory connotation, although it may not necessarily be the case by its nature. Voting in elections or forming associations may be components of political participation, but that is much less evident with respect to the right to address authorities by a petition.

Other constitutions grant the right of petition to both citizens and non-citizens, regardless of their status. Such is the case of Art. 33 of the Swiss Constitution, for instance, as well as Art. 17 of the German Constitution. The right of petition in Switzerland and Germany is therefore considered to be a civil right. In contrast, Art. 50 of the Italian Constitution, providing that all citizens have a right of petition, finds its place in the chapter on political rights.

Among civil rights, some specifically apply to non-citizens. The most important among these are the rights to enter a country, as well as the right to establish residency. Non-citizens' right of entry to the territory of a sovereign state is usually restricted. Constitutional texts construe this right in the same way as the right to circulate freely over the state territory, granting it exclusively to citizens. Examples of this kind are to be found in Art. 19 of the Spanish Constitution.

States usually impose restrictions on the freedom of entry for foreigners. A non-citizen is required to present a valid passport and a visa to be allowed to enter the state territory.[14] If a non-citizen wishes to remain within the country, he/she is to follow a procedure provided for by the domestic law of the host country to receive a residence permit. These permits vary

---

13 Cf Part III of the Covenant, Articles 6–27. Political rights are granted by Art. 25 (right to vote, to stand in elections and have access to public service), whereas Art. 27 guarantees minority rights.

14 There are agreements on visa exemption for a limited period staying in certain states. For the European Union member states and their practices, see Carlier, 251 f.

in character. They can be permanent or time limited, automatically renewable or not, and so on. Some countries require that a person applying for a residence permit be in possession of sufficient assets to sustain him/herself, or otherwise be financially independent.

Countries with large migration influxes have programmes aimed at full integration for permanent immigrants. It should also be noted that the European Union developed a whole set of rules concerning immigration, which led to the emergence of the EU immigration law (Labayle, 427–29).

Residential rights are considered to be 'the most fundamental' civil rights. Those rights are guaranteed to non-citizens, once they enter the country, but only if the entry was legal. However, non-citizens who have illegally entered a country are not automatically subject to expulsion. The European system of protection of human rights absolutely prohibits collective expulsion of aliens.[15] In many cases certain persons enjoy protection of international law regardless of how they entered a country. Such is the case of asylum seekers and refugees.

There is no definition of asylum seeker in international law. An asylum seeker is a person 'who has left a country of origin in order to seek international protection' (Weissbrodt, 110). The international protection is echoed at national level, because constitutions of many countries deal with the right of asylum. That is the case of Germany, whose Constitution reads in Art. 16a.1: 'Persons persecuted on political grounds shall have the right of asylum.' Nation-states have developed integration procedures to be followed by asylum seekers and domestic authorities in order to establish whether a certain individual fulfils the requirements to be accorded protection (Weissbrodt, 115–19; see also Laacher, 369–75).

Refugees are also a special class of non-citizens who enjoy protection under international law. The Convention Relating to the Status of Refugees of 1951, concluded within the framework of the United Nations, provides requirements to be met if a person is to be granted refugee status. The core element is a well-founded fear of persecution in the country of permanent residence of a person seeking protection, or that person's country of departure (Weissbrodt, 153). Granting refugee status to an individual also implies procedures at the domestic level of the country of refuge.

Once given rights of residence in the host country, a non-citizen is basically entitled to enjoy other civil rights, although some of those may be subject to restrictions. A distinction can be introduced, as far as rights of residence are considered, between permanent and non-permanent residents. The former are usually entitled to enjoy a wider scope of rights than the latter. Permanent residents are in a more favourable position than non-permanent and they are less vulnerable in practice. That is why the international bodies tend to distinguish certain categories of non-citizens, such as immigrants and resident migrants.[16] However, even the freedom of movement over the national territory and the freedom to choose an occupation can be restricted in the case of non-citizens, although the restrictions occur mostly in the fields of economic, social and cultural rights.

Countries of emigration for their part tend to include in their constitutions provisions for maintaining links with the emigrants. Such is the case of Serbia, whose constitution provides in Art. 13.2: 'The Republic of Serbia shall develop and enhance relations of Serbs living abroad with their home country.'

---

15 Art. 4 of the Fourth Additional Protocol to the Convention for the Protection of Human Rights and Fundamental Freedoms; the protocol was opened for signature in 1963. See also the ruling of the European Court of Human Rights in *Conka v Belgium*, ECHR 2002-I.

16 That is the case of the Council of Europe; cf Salama, 16–18.

27.4 Economic, social, and cultural rights

The rights of non-citizens to some economic, social and cultural rights are often restricted. The background idea of such restrictions cannot be properly defined in terms of an overwhelming formula. If citizen status is decisive for restricting participatory rights of non-citizens, there is no common denominator to justify restrictions of economic, social and cultural rights. That is why these rights should be considered separately.

27.4.1 Economic rights

Restrictions of economic rights of non-citizens occur in various ways. Owning of property in certain areas of the country and sometimes throughout the territory can be limited. The same applies to self-employment of non-permanent residents and other designated categories of non-citizens. In some countries citizenship may be required to appoint certain companies' management (Kondo 2001, 236 f). The restrictions vary from one country to another. In Germany, for instance, immigrants must wait a certain period to become eligible to establish business (id, 237).

The forms of discrimination of non-citizens are diverse and not necessarily reflected at the legal level. It is not only as regards self-employment that non-citizens face less favourable treatment than citizens. Recent research shows the existence of discrimination of non-citizens in terms of employment in general. Immigrants and non-citizens have a lower employment rate than native-born citizens; they are paid less than others and are more vulnerable in case of unemployment (Salama, 34–43).

In many countries there is a restriction for non-citizens to be employed as civil servants. In European countries, however, a distinction is drawn between posts of civil servants with public status and those of employees with private contract conditions of employment. The restrictions apply only to the former. The European Union has lessened restrictions in this respect and made public-sector employment accessible to non-citizens who are members of an EU member state (Kondo, 2001, 237).

27.4.2 Social rights

The international protection of social rights is construed as universal and non-discriminatory, as evidenced by the wording of Art. 9 of the International Covenant on Economic, Social and Cultural Rights 1966. However, the protection of social rights emerged at national levels as the outcome of welfare states' social policies, tending to steer social integration beyond frontiers performed by market mechanisms favoured in liberal philosophy (cf Evers, 470).

As the enjoyment of social rights demands positive state action, it encompasses financial schemes and budgetary expenses. That is why a distinction is to be made between contributory and non-contributory benefits that states nowadays usually provide to the population.

In general, non-citizens are not excluded from enjoying contributory benefits, provided they had contributed to the respective scheme. In Europe, the international protection of human rights was decisive. The European Court of Human Rights ruled in a landmark judgment in favour of equal treatment of citizens and non-citizens in respect of contributory benefits.[17]

---

17 *Gaygusuz v Austria*, ECHR Reports, 1996-IV; for comments on the case see Popović, 141 f.

In contrast, non-contributory benefits are not provided generally, but only in areas where the assistance is most needed, which led nation-states to supply it both to citizens and non-citizens on an equal basis. An example of the kind is medical emergency assistance, which is normally accorded to everyone, although there are countries that make it accessible only to regular residents. The type of a person's residence within a country is the crucial point in this respect, although citizen status can also play a role.

Constitutional provisions on social rights differ. Some do not distinguish between citizens and non-citizens, at least in certain aspects. An example is to be found in the Swiss Constitution, which deals with social goals in Art. 41, assuring positive action of the Confederation and the cantons in favour of everyone. In contrast, the Spanish Constitution guarantees in its Art. 41 the social security to all citizens and in Art. 50 a pension to the citizens having attained advanced age.

Equality of treatment of citizens and non-citizens was on many occasions introduced by international treaties, such as in case of accident compensation (basically a non-contributory benefit), as early as 1925, or for social security (a contributory benefit) in 1962 (Kulke, 446–50).[18] The right to social security has the most developed set of provisions in the vast field of social rights. Founded on a contributory basis, it spread over national borders owing to international cooperation, to become almost universally accepted (Hirose, Nikač & Tamagno, 19–102).

27.4.3 Cultural rights

Cultural rights are closely linked to social rights and, in constitutional texts, they usually find their place under the same heading. A striking example is the Swiss Constitution, which provides for both in one long article, devoted to social goals. There is a difference between citizens and non-citizens in respect of cultural rights, but it is also important whether a person is a regular or irregular resident of a country. This issue has particular salience for the cultural rights of indigenous groups, where they are not treated as citizens. (See Chapter 30 in this volume.)

The most important among cultural rights is the right to education. Many constitutions deal with this right without limiting it to citizens, like Art. 7 of the German Constitution. Many countries have developed programmes for integration of migrants' children within the scope of national education systems (Marin & Dasen, 285–320; see also Salama, 45–53). A special problem arises in this field, consisting of providing education in mother-tongue for immigrants' children. It had originally been introduced in view of remigration to the countries of origin, but it expanded beyond that particular intention (Kondo 2001, 236). It is nowadays considered to be a means of integration in the host country. Public authorities either financially support the activities, tending to offer education in mother-tongue at least as complementary to the regular education, or tolerate actions of the governments of the countries of origin to provide such classes for migrants' children.[19]

18 On the Migrant Workers Convention, which entered into force in 2003, cf Weissbrodt, 182–93.

19 The former is the case of German Länder in respect of various ethnic groups and the latter is the practice of Swiss cantons for immigrants from, e.g., Italy, Spain, Greece or Serbia. It should be noted that some of the Swiss cantons apply the German pattern and contribute themselves to the mother-tongue education.

The continuous character of the migration processes, bringing a huge number of people to countries other than those of their origin on one hand, and the hosting countries' policies tending to cope with problems arising from migration on the other, have brought new topics to the agenda. It is not only questions of education or language adaptation that create problems of integration and setting the migrants in a favourable environment in the host country. The cultural situation of migrants is perceived in a broader perspective, founded on the fact that migrants are a minority and that they should be accorded protection as such (Eide 2007, 372–86). (See Chapter 26 in this volume.)

27.5 Political rights

National electoral rights are limited to citizens in most states, but local electoral rights are permitted to non-citizens in some. It is reported that 65 of the world's 192 states permit some form of non-citizen voting, and in 36 of these, voting is available to 'denizens' (Andrès, 80). 'Denizens' are currently referred to as persons who are 'foreign citizens with a legal and permanent resident status' (Hammar, 15). There are three types of non-citizens' vote: 1) denizen type; 2) reciprocity type; and 3) traditional type. Long-term or permanent-resident citizenship, which includes an array of rights and duties, is currently called 'denizenship'. In some states such as Sweden, denizens are granted local electoral rights regardless of their nationality. European citizenship has a character of reciprocity. Member states of the EU confer electoral rights on EU citizens in local and European elections. Commonwealth citizenship has a relation with the colonial legacy and falls within the category of tradition-based voting rights. The United Kingdom grants electoral rights to British Commonwealth citizens and Irish citizens in national and local elections, but while some Commonwealth countries maintain this type based on tradition, some have already withdrawn electoral rights from former British subjects, and others have adopted denizen type.

Some constitutional decisions reject the extension of voting rights to non-citizens due to the national sovereignty clause. Even if the constitutional term of the sovereignty holder is '*peuple*' in France[20] and '*Volk*' in Germany,[21] the nationalistic sentiment is decisive for their interpretation. The French Constitutional Council initially rejected the constitutionality of EU citizens' local electoral rights, but after amending the Constitution, the Council upheld the constitutionality because EU citizens are excluded from participating in the exercise of national sovereignty in the final stage of the election of the Senate, although the designation of municipal councillors has an impact on the election of senators.[22] This means that Article 3 of the French Constitution on national sovereignty has posed no decisive obstacle for non-citizens' local voting rights only.

In contrast, the term 'people' in Ireland has been rather sympathetic to transnational citizenship, although the Irish Supreme Court interpreted it as comprising the 'Irish people', and not as referring to the 'general public'.[23] Since 1985, British citizens have had the right to vote and stand for election in the national Parliament, and it should be noted that EU citizens have the right to vote and stand for local election and may also be granted suffrage in Ireland's Parliament under the condition of reciprocity (O'Leary 1996, 220–3). Additionally, the

20 92–308 DC (1992).
21 BverfGE 83, 37 (1990); BverfGE 83, 60 (1990).
22 92–312 DC (1992).
23 [1984] IR 268. See Kelly, 38.

majority opinion of the Swedish Voting Commission in 1984 remarked that the definition of the 'people (*folk*)' was difficult and it was not 'Swedish citizens', which the minority opinion understood.[24] Although the Spanish Constitutional Court recommended a constitutional amendment before ratifying the EU treaty, the reason was not the popular sovereignty clause (Art. 1.2) but the previous, only local, suffrage extension clause (Art. 13.2).[25] The Government had argued that the Constitution did not define 'Spanish' and, therefore, did not impede EU citizens from being treated as 'Spanish' for the purposes of EU treaty and local elections (O'Leary, 226). The Japanese Supreme Court denied that the Japanese Constitution secured the local suffrage of non-citizens because of a 'national sovereignty' clause, but noted that from the viewpoint of the constitutional principle of local autonomy, it does not prohibit the Diet from granting local suffrage to non-citizens who have a particularly close relationship with a local public entity, such as permanent residents.[26] The 'national sovereignty' clause of the South Korean Constitution has not prevented local suffrage for permanent residents since 2005.

Who is the sovereign and what is sovereignty are not clear in the recent extension of local electoral rights to non-citizens. The principle of national sovereignty has two elements: democracy and nationalism. If we focus on democracy, which refers to the 'identification between the ruling and the ruled', 'the ruled' includes denizens. Since those who are affected for a long time by the execution of the state power must be able to take part in political decisions, there is an argument that sovereign people are not those who have citizenship but those who have sufficient ability for political decision-making. On one hand, if we focus on nationalism, the traditional popular sovereignty (i.e., national sovereignty) principle could be based on the idea of national democracy, which prohibits non-citizens' vote. On the other hand, if we focus on the principle of local autonomy contrary to state sovereignty, autonomy by the residents of local public governments allows local voting rights for denizens. In some countries, national sovereignty is only a matter of national legislative power or of constitutional amending power. For this reason, there is an argument that the local election is not a matter of sovereignty.

The right to be employed as a civil servant in national government has been limited to citizens in most states. Some constitutions, such as Portugal, have formulated a general criterion of 'mainly technical position', which has been interpreted as intending to deny non-citizens access to public functions with public authority, and others such as Sweden have a negative list of high civil servants (see Beenen, 139–51). However, employment as local civil servants is more open to non-citizens. For example, there are no citizenship requirements for posts at the local government level in Sweden.[27]

Let us cite some constitutional cases to illustrate this point. The US Supreme Court voided the total exclusion of non-citizens from a state's competitive civil service,[28] while non-citizens have been disqualified in some states from serving as probation officers, teachers or police officers.[29] This right has been categorized as a political right, but the right to be employed in

---

24 Rösträttskommittén, SOU 1984: 11, 164.
25 BOE-T-1992-17448 (1992).
26 49 *Minshû* [Supreme Court Reports about Civil Cases] 639 (1995).
27 SOU 1999: 34, 120.
28 *Sugarman v Dougall*, 413 US 634 (1973).
29 *Foley v Connelie*, 435 US 291 (1978); *Ambach v Norwich*, 441 US 68 (1979); *Cabell v Chavez-Salido*, 445 US 432 (1982).

most administrative positions should be categorized as an economic right, because such activity should not be regarded as encompassing a political function. In contrast to electoral rights, the national sovereignty clause has a relatively weak influence on non-citizens' rights to be eligible as non-elective civil servants. In public administration, it is not a matter of the formation of the will of the nation, but a matter of its enforcement; therefore, it is often said that national sovereignty is not related to eligibility for administrative positions in Germany (Isensee, 1546). The French Constitutional Council grants legislators broad discretion over which public functions can be separated from the exercise of sovereignty.[30] The Japanese Supreme Court has ruled that non-citizens are not assumed to take on public official positions with public authority under the national sovereignty clause in the Constitution.[31] However, they are not forbidden from doing so, and the issue is left to the local governments' discretion.

Traditionally, rights to expression and to form association are not guaranteed for non-citizens because of public order. Currently, however, non-citizens can establish political parties, enjoy the freedom of electoral campaigning, and express their opinions. Yet, in some countries they are under pressure to limit their political activities, in case protesting against the government results in deportation.

27.6 Denizenship and/or multiple citizenship

Denizenship and European citizenship are categories of membership for certain privileged non-citizens.[32] As discussed in the previous section, residential and universal citizenship such as 'denizenship', or regional and reciprocal citizenship such as 'European citizenship', are challenging the transformation of the traditional principles of popular sovereignty. The Nordic states such as Norway, Denmark, Finland and Iceland had previously applied the 'reciprocity type', but they have gradually turned to the 'denizen type' because reciprocity resulted in discrimination based on national origin.

Even if denizens acquire some local electoral rights, their rights are far less secure than those of citizens; denizens, for example, are still in danger of being expelled in the case of serious crime. In most states, the introduction of multiple citizenship does not pose any constitutional obstacles[33] and there is a tendency to allow for multiple citizenship. However, denizens originating from countries that prohibit dual citizenship still confront problems, even where the host country permits multiple citizenship.

References

Andrès, H (2007). 'Le droit de vote des étrangers: Une utopia déjà réalisée sur cinq continents', *Migrations Société* 19:114: 65–81.

30 91–293 DC (1991).
31 59 *Minshû* [Supreme Court Reports about Civil Cases] 128 (2005).
32 Gronendijk (1996) adds one more type as 'quasi-citizenship', whose status is similar, but not completely identical to citizenship. For example, because of complicated historical reasons, Moluccan immigrants in the Netherlands are to be treated as Dutch citizens, with the exception of the right to participate in national elections.
33 As an exception, the Australian High Court in 1992 rejected the eligibility for the House of Representatives of two candidates who held or had dual citizenship (see *Sykes v Cleary* (1992) 176 CLR 77). However, in 1997, the Parliament deleted Section 44 (i) of the Constitution, which provided for the disqualification of a 'citizen of a foreign power' from being chosen as the member of the Parliament.

Beenen, N (2001). *Citizenship, Nationality and Access to Public Service Employment* (Groningen: European Law Publishing).

Beer, LW & Itoh, H (1996). *The constitutional case law of Japan, 1970 through 1990* (London: University of Washington Press).

Bosniak, L (2006). *The Citizen and the Alien: Dilemmas of Contemporary Citizenship* (Princeton, Princeton University Press).

Carlier, J-Y (2007). 'L'Europe et les étrangers', in Chetail, V (ed), *Globalization, migration and human rights: international law under review, Vol. II* (Bruxelles, Bruylant), 239–80.

Cohendet, M-A (2006). *Droit constitutionnel* (Paris, Montchrestien).

Eide, A (2007). 'Minority rights of non-citizens', in Jorgensen, RF & Slavensky, K (eds), *Implementing Human Rights—Essays in honour of Morten Kjaerum* (Copenhagen, Danish Institute for Human Rights).

Eriksen, E & Weigård, J (2003). 'The End of Citizenship?', in McKinnon, C & Hampsher-Monk, I (eds), The Demands of Citizenship (London, Continuum), 13–24.

Evers, A (2001). 'Sozialpolitik', in Nohlen, D (ed), *Kleines Lexikon der Politik* (München, CH Beck).

Gronendijk, K (1996). *The Legal Status of Long-Term Migrants in Europe*, Council of Europe document CDMG (96) 27 (Strasbourg: Council of Europe).

Häberle, P (1997). *Europäische Rechtskultur* (Baden-Baden, Suhrkamp).

Hammar, T (1990). *Democracy and the Nation State: Aliens, Denizens and Citizens in a World of International Migration* (Aldershot: Avebury).

Hirose, M, Nikač, M & Tamagno, E (2011). *Social Security for Migrant Workers—A rights-based approach* (Budapest, ILO).

Hofmann, R & Tietje, C (1999). 'Constitutional Rights of Non-Citizens in Germany', in Starck, C (ed), *Constitutionalism, Universalism and Democracy—a comparative analysis* (Baden-Baden, Nomos), 199–226.

Isensee, J (1994). 'Öffentliche Dienst', in Benda, E *et al* (eds), *Handbuch des Verfassungsrechts der Bundesrepublik Deutschland* 2nd edn (Berlin, W de Gruyter), 1527–77.

Kelly, JM (1994). *The Irish Constitution*, 3rd edn (London: Butterworths).

Kondo, A (2001). 'Comparative Citizenship and Aliens' Rights', in Kondo, A (ed), *Citizenship in a Global World: Comparing Citizenship Rights for Aliens* (New York, Palgrave Macmillan).

—— (2003). 'Transnational Citizenship and Constitutional Principles', in Kondo, A & Westin, C (eds), *New Concepts of Citizenship: Residential/Regional Citizenship and Dual Nationality/Identity* (Stockholm: CEIFO at Stockholm University).

Kulke, U (2007). 'Filling the gap of social security for migrant workers: ILO's strategy', in Chetail, V (ed), *Globalization, migration and human rights: international law under review, Vol. II* (Bruxelles, Bruylant, 2007), 435–74.

Laacher, S (2007). 'Immigration, asile et sécurité d'état', in Caloz-Tschopp, M-C & Dasen, P (eds), *Globalization, migration and human rights: international law under review, Vol. I* (Bruxelles, Bruylant), 369–76.

Labayle, H (2006). 'L'étranger dans l'Union européenne', *Le droit à la mesure de l'homme—Mélanges en l'honneur de Philippe Leger* (Paris, Éditions A Pedone).

Marin, J & Dasen, PR (2007). 'L'éducation face à la mondialisation, aux migrations et aux droits de l'homme', in Caloz-Tschopp, M-C & Dasen, P, *Globalisation, migration and human rights: a new paradigm for research and citizenship* (Bruxelles, Bruylant).

O'Leary, S (1996). *The Evolving Concept of Community Citizenship* (The Hague: Kluwer).

Popović, D (2009). *Protecting Property in European Human Rights Law* (Utrecht, Eleven International Publishing).

Rösträttskommittén (Voting Rights Committee), SOU 1984: 11 Rösträtt och medborgarskap (Voting Rights and Citizenship).

Salama, P (2011). *Migrants and fighting discrimination in Europe* (Strasbourg: Council of Europe Publishing).

Secker, E (2009). 'Expending the concept of participatory rights', *International Journal of Human Rights*, Vol. 13, No. 5 December 2009.

SOU 1999: 34. *Svenskt medborgarskap* (Stockholm: fakta info direct, 1999).

Weissbrodt, D (2008). *The Human Rights of Non-Citizens* (Oxford, Oxford University Press).

Additional reading

Aleinikoff, TA & Klusmeyer, D (eds) (2000). *From Migrants to Citizens: Membership in a Changing World* (Washington, DC: Carnegie Endowment for International Peace).

Frowein, JA & Stein, T (eds) (1987). *Die Rechtsstellung von Ausländern nach Staatlichem Recht und Völkerrecht / The Legal Position of Aliens in National and International Law/ Le régime juridique des étrangers en droit national et international* (Berlin: Springer).

Huddleston, T *et al* (eds) (2011). *Migrant Integration Policy Index III.* Brussels: British Council and Migration Policy Group. Available at: http://www.mipex.eu/.

28

Proprietary constitutionalism

Jeremy Webber and Kirsty Gover*

28.1 Introduction

Most textbooks treat constitutional provisions with respect to property as though they conformed to a simple story: property rights arise outside the constitution; the state may seek to infringe those rights; constitutional protections limit the extent to which the state can do so.

That story is, however, too simple. To begin with, it assumes that all constitutional provisions with respect to property are designed to protect privately owned assets. A review of constitutions worldwide makes clear this is not the case.[1] The protection of private property is certainly a principal aim of constitutions in the liberal tradition—although, as we will see, there are variations even in those constitutions: liberal constitutions frequently protect public as well as private property; and they sometimes state that private property is subject to limitations and conditions in the public interest, suggesting that the 'private' sphere might not be as separate from the 'public' as is often assumed. And beyond these variations on the liberal model, there are constitutions that reflect very different visions of property: communist constitutions, in which the great bulk of productive assets are kept within the public domain; and constitutional provisions that recognise indigenous and other forms of communal title.

But more generally, the simple story neglects the way in which constitutions work together with property law to define the fundamental political and economic order of societies. Relations between government and people, even the very structure of government, are in substantial measure a function of the property rights in that society, so that property rights are not merely protected by the constitution but seamlessly interwoven with it. It is not simply that property law is tied to the distribution of resources within society, so that political power is to some extent a product of who holds property (although that is true). Rather, there is an intimate and

* Our thanks to Ardith Bailey, Rafael Plaza, Emma Poole, Jared Wehrle and the Melbourne Law School Research Service for able research assistance, and to Ardith Bailey, Thomas Fleiner, Nguyen Van Cuong, Qu Xiangfei, Ren Danli, Cheryl Saunders, Mark Tushnet, Lael Weis and Zhang Qianfan for their comments on previous versions of this chapter.
1 This chapter is based on an examination of 130 constitutions worldwide, which we cite only by country.

integral relationship between property and constitutionalism, where principal features of the political constitution are determined by what are, at first sight, proprietary mechanisms.

This was certainly true historically in the parts of Europe subject to feudalism. There, political and economic responsibilities (obligations to one's lord including military service; the right to administer justice; compulsory labour for public works; entitlement to natural resources; the right to hold a market; the right to maintain a mill) were incidents of rights in land.

But it is also true in post-feudal countries, in which the structure of property-holding shapes the relationship between individuals and their governments, determining the degree of individuals' independence both from each other and from the state; the control exercised by private actors over such productive assets as land, water and mineral resources; the terms applicable to the expropriation of private property; the very extent to which a public sphere is separate from a private sphere; and so on. Think, for example, of the ways in which gated communities, where property is held in condominium, restructure the relationship between their residents and municipal governments, replacing the latter's responsibility for policing, service provision and even (through arbitration) the resolution of disputes. It also is no accident that the structure, distribution and incidents of property were crucial to the transition from communism in central and eastern Europe, or to South Africa's rejection of apartheid, where many feared that apartheid might be recreated in the 'private' sphere. One is reminded of Morris Cohen's claim (in 1927) that property rights should be conceived as devolved sovereignty, allocating spheres of autonomous power to property-holders.

We use the term 'proprietary constitutionalism' to capture the way in which constitutions and property law together determine the foundational structure of the political order. We conceive of proprietary constitutionalism as a compound of three elements, each evident in written constitutions: the nature and distribution of control over productive assets, the governance arrangements that interlock with that structure, and the ideational conceptions that bind everything together, providing rationales for the different components and suggesting how they interrelate.

We set out three models of proprietary constitutionalism extant in contemporary constitutions: 1) the *liberal model*; 2) the *communist model*; and 3) *traditional models of communal property*. In describing these models, we provide an overview of the constitutional structures that address property rights worldwide. We spend most time on the liberal model because it is hegemonic and because three principal variants are evident within it, suggesting that it may be in the process of transformation. In any case, the models are often combined, either as a society transitions between liberal and communist forms of proprietary constitutionalism, or where social and political changes result in the recognition of different proprietary orders within a single state.

We focus specifically on the role of written constitutions in affirming and supporting these models of proprietary constitutionalism. Although we cannot explore the role of property law in depth, it is important to keep the broader nature of proprietary constitutionalism in mind, for the written constitutions are never self-sufficient. They presuppose the existence of proprietary orders extending well beyond the terms of the constitution. Indeed, the respective roles assigned to the constitution and to property law often differ: usually, but not always, constitutions are vehicles for expressing general principles and property law provides the framework within which competing claims are managed, but different constitutions draw these lines in different places.

We will then describe three modalities in the constitutional treatment of property: 1) the question of what counts as property; 2) the extent to which conceptions of property are engrained in other constitutional provisions, so that, in effect, the latter protect property rights; and 3) the constitutional regulation of major changes in the proprietary order.

28.2 Models of proprietary constitutionalism

28.2.1 The liberal model

The vast majority of constitutions today are premised on an essentially liberal model of proprietary constitutionalism. They are based on a relatively clear distinction between a public sphere of government-determined action and a private sphere in which private actors' decisions are the principal motive force. They anticipate that the private sphere will be extensive, with many productive assets held and deployed by private parties. They presume that the predominant role of law is not to determine every action in society but rather to establish general rules within which private parties should be free to pursue their own ends.

This division between public and private spheres is generally presumed rather than defined in constitutions, although some do define the spheres' outer limits, declaring that the state owns those assets that are not held by private actors,[2] or stipulating that natural resources, culturally significant assets, air space, water, watercourses, marine zones, ocean frontage or a wide variety of other objects are retained within state control or vested in the populace as communal property,[3] and sometimes regulating the disposal of publicly owned property[4] or forbidding government actors from corrupt dealing in public property.[5] For the most part, however, the definition of the boundary between the spheres is left to other areas of law, especially the law of property.[6]

---

2 Mongolia, art 6(2).
3 Afghanistan, art 9; Algeria, art 17; Angola, art 12(1); Azerbaijan, art 14; Bahrain, art 11; Bolivia, arts 339(II), 349, 359(I), 369(I), 372(I), 374; Chad, art 57; Chile, art 19(24); Hong Kong, art 7; Taiwan, arts 108(1)3 and 12, 109(1)2, 110(1)5, 143(1), 143(2); Colombia, arts 63, 102, 334; Costa Rica, art 121-14; Cambodia, arts 58, 69; Croatia, art 2(1); Cyprus, art 1; East Timor, section 139(1); Ecuador, arts 1, 261(7) and (11), 379, 400, 408; El Salvador, art 103; Equatorial Guinea, art 28; Greece, art 24(6); Guatemala, art 121, 122; Guinea-Bissau, art 9; Hungary, art P, art 38(1); India, art 297; Indonesia, art 33(3); Iran, art 45; Iraq, art 111; Ireland, art 10(1) and (4); Japan, art 88 ('all property of the Imperial Household'); Kazakhstan, art 6(3); Kuwait, art 21; Kyrgyzstan, art 12(5); Liberia, art 22(b); Lithuania, art 47(1), (2), and (4); Macedonia, art 56(1); Mexico, art 27; Mongolia, arts 5(5) ('livestock of the country'), 6(1); Nicaragua, art 102; Paraguay, art 112(1); Peru, arts 21, 66; Philippines, arts XII(2), XIV(16); Portugal, arts 80(d), 84(1); Romania, art 135(4); Serbia, art 87(1); Slovakia, art 4; Spain, art 132(2); Syria, art 14(1); Tonga, arts 104, 109; Turkey, arts 168, 169; Ukraine, art 13; Uruguay, art 34; Vanuatu, art 80; Venezuela, arts 11, 12; Yemen, art 8. Botswana, art 8(3), regularizes the taking of possession of minerals 'if that law makes provision for the payment at reasonable intervals of adequate royalties.'
4 Bolivia, art 349(I); British Virgin Islands, section 41; Cayman Islands, section 38; Taiwan, arts 102(1)6, 110(1)2; Colombia, art 150; Costa Rica, arts 121–14, 174; Croatia, art 52; El Salvador, art 104; Hungary, art 38(3) and (4); India, art 298; Iran, art 83; Ireland, art 10(3) and (4); Kuwait, art 121, 138; Lithuania, art 128(2); Mexico, art 27; Philippines, art XIII(1); USA, art IV(3).
5 Albania, art 70(3); Bahrain, arts 81, 86(b); Benin, art 37; Iraq, art 127; Japan, art 8; Korea (South), art 46(3); Kuwait, arts 121, 131; Peru, art 41; Norway, art 75(e); Philippines, arts XI(15), XVIII(21); Yemen, arts 118, 136.
6 This is explicit in Czech Republic, art 11(1); Slovakia, art 20(2); Turkmenistan, art 9; Ukraine, art 92(7).

The predominant focus of provisions on property in liberal constitutions is the affirmation and protection of the sphere of private rights. Sometimes the right to own property, either generally or with its attributes listed, is protected.[7] Some of the more extensive lists of attributes appear in post-communist constitutions, and may be designed to shift the proprietary norm from one of social ownership to private ownership.[8] Sometimes, state actors are obligated to protect property.[9] Some constitutions name property as a prohibited ground of discrimination[10] or prohibit discrimination in the enjoyment of property, with non-discrimination occasionally extended to non-citizens.[11] But most extensively and characteristically, liberal constitutions regulate state intrusions on property, either generally or by regulating expropriation and search and seizure.[12]

7 Albania, art 41; Algeria, art 52; Argentina, section 14; Armenia, arts 8, 28; Azerbaijan, art 29; Bahrain, art 9(c); Belarus, art 44; Bolivia, art 56(I), (II) and (III); Brazil, art 5(XXII and XXX); Bulgaria, art 17(1); Cambodia, art 44; Chile, arts 23, 24; Cook Islands, section 64(1)(c); Croatia, art 48(1); Cyprus, art 23(1); Czech Republic, Charter art 11(1); Dominican Republic, art 8(13); East Timor, section 54(1); Ecuador, arts 66(26), 69(2), 321; Egypt (2011) art 5; El Salvador, arts 2, 22, 23, 103; Equatorial Guinea, art 29; Estonia, art 32; Finland, section 15; Georgia, art 21(1); Germany, art 14(1); Guatemala, art 39; Hungary, art XIII(1); Indonesia, art 28G(1); Iraq, art 23; Ireland, art 43; Japan, art 29; Kazakhstan, arts 6, 26; Korea (South), art 23(1); Kyrgyzstan, art 42; Latvia, art 105; Liberia, arts 11, 22(a); Liechtenstein, art 28(1); Macedonia, arts 8, 30; Mongolia, arts 5(2), 16(3); Nicaragua, art 44; Peru, art 2(16); Poland, arts 21(1), 64; Portugal, art 62(1); Romania, arts 41(1), 42; Russia, art 35; Rwanda, art 29; Serbia, arts 58, 59; Slovakia, art 20(1); Slovenia, art 33; Spain, section 33(1); Sudan, art 43(1); Switzerland, art 26(1); Taiwan, art 15; Thailand, section 41; Turkey, art 35; Turkmenistan, art 9; Ukraine, art 41; Uruguay, art 7; Venezuela, art 115. Eritrea, art 23(1), Ethiopia, art 40(1), Hong Kong, art 7, and Tonga, arts 1, 104 protect private ownership, but with the important exclusion of land.
   There are specific provisions for the enjoyment of intellectual property in Argentina, section 17; Azerbaijan, art 30; Bolivia, arts 100(II), 101, 102; Chile, art 25; Czech Republic, Charter, art 34(1); Dominican Republic, art 14; East Timor, section 60; Ecuador, arts 22, 322; El Salvador, art 103; Georgia, art 23(1); Guatemala, art 42; Guinea-Bissau, art 42; Kyrgyzstan, art 49(3); Mongolia, art 7(2); Paraguay, art 110; Philippines, art III(13); Russia, art 44(1); Slovakia, art 43(1); Slovenia, art 60; Sweden, ch 2, art 16; Syria, art 24(2); Thailand, section 86(2); Turkmenistan, art 9; Ukraine, arts 41, 54; Uruguay, art 33; Venezuela, art 98.
8 See, e.g., Albania, art 41(2); Armenia, arts 8, 28; Azerbaijan, art 29; Belarus, art 44; Georgia, art 21; Kazakhstan, arts 26; Kyrgyzstan, art 42; Lithuania, art 46; Macedonia, art 55; Nicaragua, art 44; Poland, arts 21(1), 64; Russia, arts 34–36; Turkmenistan, art 9.
9 See, e.g., Colombia, art 2; Greece, art 17(1); Hong Kong, art 6; Ireland, art 40(3); Kazakhstan, art 6(1); Kyrgyzstan, art 12(4); Macedonia, art 8(1); Peru, art 166; Romania, arts 41(2), 135(1); Russia, art 8(2); Rwanda, art 171; South Africa, art 205(3); Taiwan, art 143(1); Ukraine, art 13; Venezuela, art 55; Turkmenistan, art 9; Zambia, art 104(a).
10 British Virgin Islands, sections 9, 26(1)(a); Bulgaria, art 6(2); Cayman Islands, section 16(2); Croatia, art 14(1); Czech Republic, Charter of Fundamental Rights and Freedoms, art 3(1); Estonia, art 12(1); Georgia, art 14; Iceland, art 65; Kazakhstan, art 14(2); Macedonia, arts 9(1), 54(3); Mongolia, art 14(2); Poland, art 233(2); Romania, art 4(2); Serbia, art 21(3); Slovakia, art 12(2); Turkmenistan, art 17; Ukraine, art 24.
11 See, e.g., Chad, art 15; Djibouti, art 18; Peru, art 71. Some constitutions require the property rights be enjoyed equally between men and women: Bolivia, art 402(2); Ecuador, arts 69(2) and (3), 324; Ethiopia, art 35(6); Japan, art 24; Liberia, art 23; Zimbabwe, art 23(3a).
12 Afghanistan, art 40; Andorra, art 27(1); Angola, art 12(4); Antigua and Barbuda, art 3(a); Armenia, art 28; Azerbaijan, arts 29(IV), 31(II); Bahrain, art 9(c)–(d); Barbados, art 11(b); Belarus, art 44(3); Belize, art 3(d); Benin, art 22; Bermuda, section 1(c); Bosnia and Herzegovina, art 2(1)(k); Botswana, art 3(c); Brazil, art 5(XXII); Bulgaria, art 17(5); Cambodia, art 44; Chad, art 4(1); Chile, art 24; Colombia, arts 58, 59; Cook Islands, section 40; Croatia, arts 34, 50; Cyprus, art 23; Czech Republic, Charter art 11(4); Denmark, sections 72, 73; Djibouti, art 12; Dominica, section 6;

The expropriation provisions in particular can be very detailed.[13] They often require that dispossession occur only by process of law, such as by the judgment of a court under statutory authority. They sometimes require that there be a right of appeal to the courts. They often stipulate permissible grounds for expropriation, usually some variation of 'public interest' or 'public purpose', thereby excluding, ostensibly, the use of the state's expropriation power to transfer property between private parties. Some constitutions contain a codified list of public purposes or other exemptions from the general prohibition, allowing expropriations for the satisfaction of a debt, to protect public health and safety, and, importantly, to conserve natural resources or protect the environment.[14] Cyprus, Greece and Ireland specifically protect property belonging to religious institutions.[15] Confiscation of property for crimes is sometimes eliminated.[16] They also typically require compensation, generally stipulating that it should be 'just' or 'fair' (or 'equivalent' or 'full'—apparently more demanding formulations), or constitute market value. Some require that compensation be fixed by statute. Many require that compensation be paid in advance, immediately or within a reasonable period.

By contrast, protections against intrusion, search and seizure tend to state the right generally or simply require that search and seizure should occur by process of law.[17] There is, however, a family of Caribbean and African constitutions (and a few other constitutions) that contain detailed conditions for search and seizure.[18] Some provisions specifically protect the sanctity of the home, often within the framework of rights of privacy.[19]

Dominican Republic, art 8(13); East Timor, section 54(3); Ecuador, art 323; Egypt (2011), art 5; El Salvador, arts 20, 106; Equatorial Guinea, art 29; Estonia, arts 32, 33; Eritrea, art 23(1); Estonia, art 32; Ethiopia, art 40(8); Georgia, art 21; Germany, arts 13, 14(3); Greece, art 17; Guatemala, art 40; Hungary, art XIII(2); Iceland, arts 71, 72; India, art 31A; Iraq, art 23; Italy, art 42; Japan, art 29; Kazakhstan, art 26(3); Korea (South), art 23(3); Kuwait, art 18; Kyrgyzstan, arts 12(2), 12(3), 30; Latvia, art 105; Lebanon, art 15; Liberia, arts 20, 21, 24(a); Liechtenstein, arts 34, 35; Lithuania, art 23; Macedonia, art 30; Mexico, arts 16, 27; Mongolia, art 16(3); Netherlands, art 14; Nicaragua, art 44; Norway, arts 104, 105; Paraguay, art 109; Peru, art 70; Philippines, art III(1), (2) and (9); Poland, art 21(2); Portugal, art 62(2); Romania, arts 41(3)-(5); Russia, art 35(3); Rwanda, art 29; Serbia, art 58; Slovakia, art 20(4); Slovenia, art 69; South Africa, art 25(1)-(4); Spain, section 33(3); Sudan, art 43(2); Sweden, art 15; Switzerland, art 26(2); Thailand, section 42; Tonga, art 18; Turkey, art 46; Ukraine, art 41; US, Fifth Amendment; Uruguay, art 32; Venezuela, art 115; Yemen, art 7(c); Zambia, art 16; Zimbabwe, section 16.

13 See *ibid.*

14 See, e.g., Bermuda, section 13(1)(a); Bolivia, art 57; Botswana, art 8(1); British Virgin Islands, section 25(3); Cayman Islands, section 15(2); Chile, art 24; Cook Islands, section 40(2); Cyprus, art 23; Dominica, s 6; Ecuador, art 323; India, art 31A(1)(e); Liberia, art 24(a); Thailand, section 42; Tonga, art 18; Zambia, art 16(2); Zimbabwe, art 16(1).

15 Cyprus, art 23(10); Greece, arts 18(8), 105(2); Ireland, art 44(2)(6°).

16 See, e.g., Argentina, section 17; Belgium, art 17; Columbia, art 34; Cyprus, art 12; El Salvador, art 106; Guatemala, art 41; Greece, art 7(3); Paraguay, art 20(2); Uruguay, art 14.

17 See, e.g., Afghanistan, art 40; Belgium, art 15; Cambodia, art 40; Chad, art 42; Czech Republic, art 12; Djibouti, art 12; Eritrea, art 18(2); Estonia, art 33; Fiji, section 26(2); Iceland, art 71; Kazakhstan, art 25(1); Rwanda, art 22; Syria, art 31.

18 Antigua and Barbuda, art 10; Barbados, arts 17.1, 17.2; Belize, art 9; Bermuda, section 7; Botswana, art 9; British Virgin Islands, section 19; Cayman Islands section 9; Dominica, section 7; Zambia, art 17; Zimbabwe, section 17. See also Croatia, art 34; Germany, art 13; Mexico, art 16; Romania, art 27; Serbia, art 40(2) and (3).

19 Antigua and Barbuda, art 3(c); Azerbaijan, art 31(II); Barbados, art 11(b); Belarus, art 29; Belgium, art 15; Belize, art 3(c); Bermuda, sections 1(c), 7; Botswana, arts 3(c), 9; British Virgin Islands section '19(1); Cayman Islands, section 9(1); Chad, art 42; Costa Rica, art 23; Croatia, art 34; Cambodia, art 40; Czech Republic, art 12; Denmark, section 72; Djibouti, art 12; Dominica,

The rights stated thus far could protect a right conceived purely in terms of an individual's entitlement, allowing an essentially unlimited accumulation of property. Indeed, many liberal constitutions do appear to protect property rights regardless of the extent of accumulation (although accumulation might be dampened by, for example, redistributive taxation or generous welfare provision). This model might be called *Liberal Model 1*. However, many constitutions expressly qualify individual property rights by some notion of the common good, social function or social responsibility.[20] The German Basic Law states, for example: 'Property entails obligations. Its use shall also serve the public good.'[21] Indeed, there appear to be two variants on the liberal model.

One, *Liberal Model 2a*, still favours private ownership as the dominant form of property, but prefers modestly sized holdings over large holdings. It is committed to some form of material equality, not simply to protecting private property. This approach may be heir to a notion of republican politics, now long eclipsed, in which the best guarantee of political liberty and democratic equality lies in a society of roughly equal land-holders (Pocock 2003, 386–91, 532–9). Indications of *Liberal Model 2a* are diverse—so diverse that they may be responses to discomfort with unlimited accumulation rather than a genuinely alternative model. Nevertheless, the examples are striking.

First, several constitutions contemplate land redistribution as a remedy for inequality in land ownership or past dispossessions, clearly preferring some measure of equality to security of accumulated wealth.[22] Some directly limit the size of agricultural holdings or empower governments to limit them.[23]

Second, some extend special consideration to small-holders.[24] This is true of the Brazilian Constitution, which states 'the small rural property . . . provided that it is exploited by the family, shall not be subject to attachment for the payment of debts incurred by reason of its

section 1; El Salvador, art 20; Eritrea, art 18(2); Estonia, art 33; Ethiopia, art 26(1); Germany, art 13(1); Guinea-Bissau, art 48; Iceland, art 71; Italy, art 14; Kazakhstan, art 25(1); Korea (South), art 16; Kyrgyzstan, art 30(1); Lebanon, art 14; Lithuania, art 24(1); Mexico, art 16; Netherlands, art 12(1); Norway, art 102; Paraguay, art 34; Peru, art 2(9); Poland, art 50; Portugal, art 34(1); Romania, art 27(1); Rwanda, art 22; Serbia, art 40(1); Slovakia, art 21(1); Slovenia, art 36; South Africa, art 14; Spain, section 18(2); Sudan, art 37; Turkey, art 21; Turkmenistan, art 24; Ukraine, art 30; Uruguay, art 11; Vanuatu, art 5(j); Zambia, arts 11(d), 17(1).

20 Azerbaijan, art 13(3); Bolivia, arts 393, 397; Brazil, art 5(XXIII); Colombia, art 58; Croatia, art 48(2); East Timor, section 54(2); Ecuador, art 66(26); El Salvador, art 103; Estonia, art 32(2); Germany, art 14(2); Greece, art 17(1); Hungary, art XIII(1); India, art 39(b); Ireland, art 43(2); Italy, art 42; Japan, art 29; Kazakhstan, art 6(2); Korea (South), art 23(2); Kuwait, art 16; Latvia, art 105; Liberia, art 7; Macedonia, art 30(2); Mongolia, art 6(4); Nicaragua, art 5; Philippines, art XII(6); Romania, art 41(6); Slovakia, arts 20(3), 67; Spain, sections 33(2), 128; Turkey, art 35; Yemen, art 8.

21 Germany, art 14(2).

22 Colombia, arts 60, 64; Cyprus, art 23(6); Dominican Republic, art 8(13)(a); Ecuador, arts 281(4), 282; El Salvador, arts 104, 105; Ethiopia, art 44(2); Italy, art 44; Mexico, art 27(XVII); Nicaragua, arts 106ff; Paraguay, arts 114ff; Philippines, art XIII(4); Portugal, arts 81(h), 94–96; South Africa, art 25(4)–(8); Taiwan, art 142; Thailand, section 85(2); Turkey, art 44; Zimbabwe, arts 16A, 16B. See the general commitment to equitable distribution in India, art 39; Iran, art 31 (for housing); Ireland, art 45(2). But see Greece, art 18(4) and Portugal, art 95, which contemplate the combining of small parcels.

23 See, e.g., Angola, art 90(j); Bolivia, art 398; Ecuador, art 282; El Salvador, art 105; Italy, art 44; Mexico, art 27(XVII); Syria, art 16.

24 Bolivia, art 394(1I); Ethiopia, art 40(4); Italy, art 44; Mexico, art 27(XV).

productive activities, and the law shall establish the means to finance its development'.[25] Angola stipulates: 'The State ... shall give special support to small and medium-scale economic activity, in accordance with the law.'[26]

Third, there may be a distinctively Islamic version of the model, in which an essential commitment to private ownership is framed by religious and moral obligation. The Bahrain Constitution has special provisions to protect small farmers and states: 'Property, capital and work, in accordance with the principles of Islamic justice, shall be fundamental constituents of the social structure of the State and the national wealth. They are all individual rights with a social function regulated by the law.'[27] Iran states that 'ownership ... is protected by the laws of the Islamic Republic, in so far as this ownership ... does not go beyond the bounds of Islamic law, contributes to the economic growth and progress of the country and does not harm society'.[28]

Fourth, some countries limit accumulation by prohibiting or limiting land ownership by either non-nationals or non-residents,[29] or by excluding non-citizens from protections against expropriation.[30] These constraints may simply be ways to favour the economic interests of nationals and resist overseas investment in the limited resource of real property, but they may also represent a desire to resist the full commercialisation of land and to reserve land rights for those with a long-term commitment to the society. Many of these restrictions have come under heavy pressure in trade and investment negotiations. As a result, some countries have expressly included protections for foreign ownership in their constitutions.[31]

The limited conception of property rights in *Liberal Model 2a* brings those rights into closer accord with the spirit underlying social and economic rights. No longer do social rights function as partial remedies for the inequitable distribution of property. A sense of social value, of social purpose, is written into the very protection of property.

Indeed, it has been argued that private property is now so limited by regulation, public access, duties and control, and is so routinely subject to exceptions and reservations (such as the exclusion of mineral rights from the private ownership of land, limitations on the sale of cultural or archaeological objects, or the imposition of environmental conditions on owners), that it is best to conceive of property rights, especially over immovables, as composite bundles of rights organised around two principles: 1) the private actor's right to use and control access to the resource; and 2) the government's (or public's) interest in land use and control, which

---

25 Brazil, art 5(XXIII) and (XXVI).

26 Angola, arts 11(3).

27 Bahrain, art 9(a) and 9(g).

28 Iran, art 44(5). See also Yemen, art 7.

29 Afghanistan, art 41; Armenia, art 28; Bolivia, art 396(II); Cambodia, art 44; East Timor, section 54(4); Iceland, art 72; Iraq, art 23(3)(a); Liberia, art 22(a); Mexico, art 27(I); Mongolia, art 6(3); Romania, art 41(2). These constitutions expressly contemplate or impose limitations on foreign ownership. Other constitutions permit such limitations without expressly mentioning foreign ownership. See the West Indian constitutions that stipulate restrictions on land acquisition should not be held to violate mobility rights (e.g., Barbados, section 22.3(d)). In addition, some constitutions prohibit foreign ownership close to the country's borders for security reasons (Bolivia, arts 262; Guatemala, art 123; Mexico, art 27(I); Peru, art 71) or generally permit restrictions on foreign ownership (Estonia, art 32; Slovakia, art 20(2)).

30 Belize, art 17(4)(b).

31 Angola, art 11(4); Argentina, section 20; Brazil, art 5; Bulgaria, art 22; Hong Kong, art 105(3); Macedonia, art 31; Serbia, art 85; Slovenia, art 70. See also Botswana, art 8(2) (re foreign remittance of compensation for expropriation).

may themselves approximate property rights (Gray 2010). The composite conception of property might be considered yet another variant on the liberal model: *Liberal Model 2b*. Under this variant, the concept of property itself is redefined, so that private property is seen to be a complex product of public power and not (as in *Liberal Model 1*) an independent and original right, amounting in principle to full dominion over the thing. Instead, the bundles can include a spectrum of entitlements, marking gradations in the degree of exclusive control they afford and blurring the line between 'public' and 'private'. Constitutional provisions stating that property rights are intrinsically limited by a public interest, or by obligations of ownership, might express such a notion.[32] Certainly there is no bright line between the concept of a public interest in land and the state's sovereign authority to make laws governing the use of 'things'. This lack of a bright line has bedevilled constitutional provisions on expropriation, as we will discuss below. Some scholars argue that *Liberal Model 2b* is more appropriate to our interdependent world, where global environmental concerns are critical, as well as a more accurate description of contemporary systems of land-use regulation and the complex regimes governing new objects of property (such as electromagnetic spectra) (Gray 2010).

Will either of these alternative liberal models become dominant? It is unclear. Doubtless, there is considerable strength left in the ideological underpinnings of *Liberal Model 1*. But the ostensibly absolute concept of private property, often asserted under *Liberal Model 1*, appears to have been significantly eroded, an erosion evident in constitutional provisions with respect to property. The question now is whether the ideational element too will shift, so that *Liberal Models 2a* or *2b* come to reflect the dominant understanding of the nature of property, and constitutional provisions be interpreted accordingly.

Finally, we should not give the impression that all liberal orders have imposed constitutional protections of private property rights. Until recently, the British tradition clearly favoured parliamentary sovereignty over the constitutional protection of rights, including property rights. Indeed, in the aftermath of World War II in the United Kingdom, the newly elected Labour government consciously sought to break up landed wealth in order to dismantle the remnants of the country's aristocratic system. However, the UK Human Rights Act 1998, Schedule 1, Part II, art 1 now protects some property rights, based on the European Convention on Human Rights. For its part, the Australian Constitution requires that expropriations occur on 'just terms', but this limitation applies to the federal and territorial governments, not to the states.[33] And when the Canadian Charter of Rights and Freedoms was framed during the early 1980s, the protection of property rights was rejected because it was feared that a guarantee of property rights might be used to strike down social legislation (as in the United States during the *Lochner* era) (Alvaro 1991, 317–26; Tribe 2000, 1332–57).[34] There is a substantial commitment to an essentially liberal proprietary order in these countries, but this has generally been combined with a commitment to preserving the capacity of the government to act in ways that might limit property rights.

---

32 *Supra*, note 20.
33 Australia, section 51 (xxxi).
34 There is, however, an interpretive presumption that compensation must be provided when property is expropriated unless the relevant statute clearly states otherwise (*A-G v DeKeyser's Royal Hotel* [1920] AC 508, 542 (HL)), and it is often suggested that some property rights have been protected under other provisions of the Charter, notably mobility rights.

28.2.2 The communist model

As the notes to the previous section reveal, the liberal model of proprietary constitutionalism is hegemonic in the world today. With the collapse of the Soviet Union, it has been embraced by many former communist countries and even, to some extent, by countries that are still nominally communist, such as China and Vietnam. The liberal model has not completely occupied the field, however. There remain at least one clear example of the communist model in the world today; countries like China, whose constitutions combine elements of the liberal and communist models; and countries that expressly rejected the communist model but nevertheless have framed their constitutions to manage the transition.

The communist model treats all or substantially all productive assets as the common property of the society. It rejects the idea that productive resources should be vested in private parties. Rather, it insists that assets be held by the government or by state-supervised cooperatives and administered ostensibly in the interests of society as a whole.[35] The communist model tends to structure the entire relationship between state and society very differently from the liberal model: much of social activity is managed directly by the state as part of its exercise of property rights—by its managerial authority rather than by its enactment of general rules. Indeed, the very concept and role of law has long been contested in communist societies. Contemporary communist states retain or have reinstituted at least some notion of law, but in a manner that often combines state control, managerial direction and legal determination.

Perhaps the regime with the purest communist constitutional order is North Korea. It has an expansive definition of state property—stipulating, for example, that 'there is no limit to the property that the State can own'—and it declares that state property belongs to all the people. It stipulates that the state 'plays the leading role in the economic development of the country' and that state property should be developed on a preferential basis. Natural resources and the principal industrial facilities are vested exclusively in the state, although smaller facilities, land, farm machinery and ships can be vested in cooperatives. Nevertheless, the state '[leads] the cooperative property so as to combine the two forms of property in an organic way, and consolidates and develops the socialist cooperative economic system by improving the guidance and management of the cooperative economy and gradually transforms the property of cooperative organizations into the property of the people as a whole based on the voluntary will of all their members'. Provisions protect the inviolability of state and cooperative property.[36] Private property is not entirely absent—indeed, the state is said to 'protect' it—but it is limited to consumption goods: assets 'derived from socialist distribution according to work done and from supplementary benefits granted by the State and society' and 'the products of individual sideline activities including those from kitchen gardens . . .' Nominally, 'Citizens are guaranteed inviolability of the person and the home . . .'[37]

Countries such as China and Vietnam have moved away from a purely communist model but, as yet, without embracing a thoroughly liberal one. They tend to recognise both public and private property, stating that the latter is inviolable, but allowing substantial latitude to legislation to determine precisely what can be owned privately. Ostensibly, there

---

35 Cuba, arts 15, 19, 20, 24, however, permits small farmers to own, sell and inherit land and extends special protections to them, also encouraging them to form cooperatives.

36 North Korea, arts 21–23, 35, 84, 125(10), 147, 156, 162.

37 North Korea, arts 24, 79. See also Cuba, arts 56–57.

are protections against expropriation of private assets, although in practice there has been deep dissatisfaction with confiscations for development.[38] In China, the constitution states that urban land is owned by the state and rural land by collectives, and in Vietnam land is owned by the state, although in both, substantial private rights are permitted by leasehold. This means that the communist character of these and other constitutional orders is now a matter of degree, determined by the extent to which property is retained, empirically, within the state sphere, and state enterprises and state planning play a directive role in the economy.[39] Certainly in China and Vietnam, the activity of private and parastatal enterprises has been actively encouraged, foreign investment particularly so. The Vietnamese Constitution formally exempts foreign investments from nationalisation.[40] Indeed, some once- or still-Communist countries declare their commitment to mixed economies.[41]

The communist model has, since 1989, suffered a precipitous decline, both through outright rejection (as in the post-Communist states of central Europe) and through incremental abandonment (as in China). That decline has occurred through a dramatic shift in the proportion of productive assets held publicly. This in turn has reduced the extent to which those countries rely on managerial authority to organise social life. Several of them remain less than democratic, constitutions continue to recognise the leading role of the Communist Party, and the constitutions are generally not independently enforced, but nonetheless these countries rely increasingly on law as an instrument of social organisation.

28.2.3 Traditional models of communal property

A third type of proprietary constitutionalism is evident in some constitutions, which recognise forms of property that either predate the infrastructure of the state (for example, indigenous tenures) or are otherwise adapted to communal forms of life. Generally, the relationship between property and social ordering in these traditional forms differs materially from that in the state as a whole (although communal tenures are dominant in some Pacific Island states[42]). This communal property is not strictly public or private. Indeed, the 'property' interest often serves as a means of recognising a domain in which landholding is governed by indigenous law, so that, within that domain, the community determines the specific rights that are to be held by individual members or kinship groups.

Sometimes, constitutional provisions of this kind are directly analogous to federal structures or local government, acknowledging the existence of tribal or ethnic jurisdictions within the state and allocating to those communities the authority to manage communal

---

38 China, art 13 (as amended in 2004); Vietnam, art 23. See also Cuba, arts 19, 25; Syria, art 15. Compensation tends not to be specified as clearly or as generously as in liberal constitutions (Zhang 2012).

39 China, art 10; Vietnam, arts 17–18. See also Zhang (2012); Sidel (2009: 90–92). Many Communist or post-Communist constitutions contain a substantial list of assets held within state control or confer an open-ended power on legislatures to determine property to be reserved to the state: Algeria, art 17; Angola, art 11(1); Belarus, art 13; Cuba, art 15. Some retain land in state ownership: Eritrea, art 23; Ethiopia, art 40(3). Iran, art 44, also specifies an extensive state sector.

40 Vietnam, art 25.

41 Equatorial Guinea, art 27 and 29; Guinea-Bissau, art 11 and 12; Kyrgystan, art 12; Mongolia, art 5; Nicaragua, art 103; Peru, art 60; Portugal, arts 80(b), 82; Syria, art 14; Vietnam, art 15.

42 See especially Tonga, art 104; Vanuatu, arts 73–79.

property regimes.[43] In other cases, the provisions are expressed in purely proprietary terms, without any formal allocation of jurisdiction.[44] It is clear, however, that communal property must, of necessity, carry some elements of governance with it. The community must have rules to regulate the rights of individuals and groups *inter se* (including rules governing land use, stewardship, succession and transfer) and decide how the general interest of the community should be advanced through the shared use of resources. Communal or traditional forms of property therefore have significance extending far beyond the accommodation of minority interests in land and resources. They reveal the continued vitality of forms of social organisation that do not depend on the delineations typical of the liberal model of proprietary constitutionalism.

Communal property regimes are multiple and variegated even within a particular state. Some are continuations of precolonial orders while others are communal forms of land tenure granted by the state as in-kind reparation for past injustices (the dispossession of indigenous peoples, or the historic enslavement of persons now forming distinct ethnic communities). Grants of this kind may reflect traditional usages, but continuity with those forms is less obvious than in the recognition of ancient property rights.[45] Constitutional mechanisms recognising communal titles may serve both reparative and distributive functions; some constitutions expressly enable the distribution of public lands to communities in order to further the economic development of certain minority groups.[46] Significantly, provisions recognising communal title do not determine the content of indigenous property rights; rather, they serve as markers of the continuing importance of traditional systems of proprietary constitutionalism, usually affirming a general recognition of indigenous property or territory, sometimes alongside protections for indigenous culture and traditions.[47]

Some constitutions specify that indigenous rights are inalienable, a move that excludes indigenous peoples from the market and prevents them from selling, leasing or mortgaging their land.[48] It also places indigenous property in a category of its own and cements the identity boundary between indigenous and non-indigenous communities: the property rights of individuals are defined by the laws of that group, and cannot be alienated outside of it. Inalienability has the effect of protecting indigenous lands from exploitation, but it also insists on equating 'traditional' with 'non-commercial' uses of land. It may also assert, indirectly, the importance of those lands to the populace as a whole, treating them in effect as the patrimony of the people, and so subject to state oversight and protection. Sometimes traditional property regimes, especially if expressly inalienable, can coincide with (or function as a proxy for) environmental protection.[49] In all these ways, public lands, and the protection of indigenous interests on those lands, have become hallmarks of settler-state identity and legitimacy.

---

43 Bolivia, art 403, Colombia, art 329, 330; Ecuador, art 57, Guatemala, arts 67, 68; Nicaragua, arts 5, 89, 107, 180ff; Peru, art 89; Vanuatu, sections 73-79; Venezuela, arts 119-24. See also the abrogated constitution of Fiji, arts 6, 186.

44 Brazil, art 231; Canada, Charter of Rights and Freedoms, section 35; Cook Islands, section 64(1) (c); Mexico, art 27(VII–XIV); Paraguay, art 64; Philippines, art XII, section 5; Tonga, art 104.

45 See, e.g., Bolivia, art 32; Brazil, art 68; Colombia, provisional art 55; Guatemala, art 68.

46 See, e.g., Argentina, art 68; Paraguay, art 115(4); Guatemala, art 68.

47 This is clearest in Bolivia, arts 2, 30.

48 Bolivia, art 394; Brazil, art 231; Colombia, art 329; Ecuador, art 57(4); Paraguay, art 64; Tonga, art 104; Venezuela, art 119.

49 See, e.g., Colombia, arts 310, 330.

Other ethnic minorities and peasant communities sometimes receive constitutional recognition of their property rights and jurisdiction.[50] The separate regulation of the property of churches and religious institutions, in some constitutions, may similarly amount to the recognition of a non-commercial sphere within the general proprietary order.[51] One might be tempted to think that the ownership of land by rural communes in China approximates this model, but the role of the party/state in establishing, directing and removing that tenure makes clear that they are thoroughly incorporated within the state's regime.

28.3 Modalities of the constitutional regulation of property

Within the principal models of proprietary constitutionalism, especially the liberal model, certain themes recur.

28.3.1 What counts as property

To this point, we have treated the objects of property rights—the assets, the resources—as though they were unambiguously defined. But this is not the case. Objects are also created and defined by law, with great variety of approaches among countries. Consider, for example, the complex structures of condominium or the licensing schemes governing ownership of electromagnetic spectra.

The bulk of that definition occurs within property law, but some definitional elements find their way into constitutions. Many exclude certain natural resources or natural features (e.g. watercourses, foreshores) from the domain of private property. Communist constitutions commonly exclude land. Some things are excluded from the scope of property altogether, often for supervening moral reasons. The clearest example would be prohibitions on slavery,[52] but restrictions on the ownership of cultural heritage, monuments and artefacts may also be premised on moral, as opposed to commercial, conceptions of value.

More recently, a growing number of states, especially in Latin America, have either eliminated or restricted private property in water.[53] These reflect the importance of water as a cultural and economic resource, but also the risks that attend the commodification of water. This is a concrete, not abstract, concern. Many developing countries that created a market in water (sometimes under international pressure) have suffered from attendant scarcity and over-pricing, the resulting civil unrest in some cases, notably Bolivia, creating conditions of crisis that promoted wholesale constitutional reform. Constitutional protections of scarce public resources are sometimes a response to the overreach and failures of neoliberal markets.

Indeed, one can observe a spectrum in the classification of different types of property across constitutions: a) things subject to private ownership; b) things that can be owned but that are subject to significant restrictions, lifting them beyond a purely private realm (church

50 Bolivia, arts 32; 394 (III), 395 (intercultural communities, Afro-Bolivians, peasant communities); Brazil, art 68 (ancient runaway slave communities); Colombia, provisional art 55 (Black communities); Ecuador, art 60 (Afro-Ecuadorians, coastal back-country (Montubios) peoples); Nicaragua, arts 89, 180, 181 (ethnic communities of the Atlantic Coast).

51 Cyprus, art 23-9, 23-10, 110; Germany, art 138(2); Greece, art 105(2); Guatemala, art 37; Liechtenstein, art 38; Norway, art 106; Uruguay, art 5.

52 These are very common. See, e.g., Liberia, art 12; USA, Amendment XIII.

53 Bolivia, arts 373–74; Ecuador, arts 12, 318; Guatemala, art 127; Venezuela, art 304.

property; indigenous lands; in some cases water); c) things subject only to public ownership; d) things that cannot be owned.

There is also a question of the range of property interests that are covered by constitutional protections. Do they apply to rights *in rem* alone, or are all rights with economic value included (including contractual rights and rights to sue)? Most constitutions focus on rights *in rem* (generally land), but the 'contracts clause' of the US Constitution is a famous example of the latter.[54] Even with respect to rights *in rem*, is all value protected, or does protection only apply to a stripped-down right of ownership? This has been the great question in expropriation, namely whether regulations that limit what one can do with one's property, especially the right to 'rents and profits', amount to a partial expropriation, giving rise to compensation. Constitutional courts have generally distinguished between regulation and expropriation, but the line has been difficult to draw (see Tribe 1988, 590–604).[55] Indeed, the very fact that regulation does not give rise to compensation suggests that something like *Liberal Model 2b* may be operative, with the courts implicitly recognising a continuing public interest in the use made of private property.

28.3.2 Implied protection of property rights

In addition to constitutional provisions that specifically address property, there are also implied or disguised protections of property, accomplished through the interpretation of other provisions.

These implied protections may be extensive. It is often argued that, in liberal constitutions, rights are founded on a proprietary model (Ingram 1994, 25–89). All rights protect a sphere of private autonomy that is presumed to include not just the holder's person but also their property. When a person benefits from freedom of religion, they can deploy not just their bodies but also their property to religious ends. The same might be said of virtually any other human right.

This proprietary dimension can sometimes predominate, perhaps displacing other values distinctive to the right. A classic example would be the US Supreme Court's decision in *Citizens United v Federal Election Commission*, 558 US 50 (2010), ostensibly based on freedom of speech. The right to use one's wealth to purchase election advertising trumped any sense that expenditures might be constrained in order to foster rough equality in political discourse.

Other provisions too might be given a proprietary gloss. The Australian provision that 'trade . . . among the States shall be absolutely free' was used to strike down laws that had the effect of reducing interstate commerce, including the nationalization of banks—until, in 1988, the High Court ruled that the provision was meant simply to prohibit custom duties between the states.[56]

These proprietary protections are often subtle and tacit, built into judges' presumptions about the meaning of liberty and the importance of a private domain. They are the expression of proprietary constitutionalism in judicial interpretation.

---

54 USA, art 1, section 10.
55 Some constitutions attempt to guide the consideration; see, e.g., Poland, art 64(3); Serbia, art 58(3); Sweden, art 15 (prescribing compensation for substantial impairment by regulation).
56 Australia, section 92; *Cole v Whitfield* (1988) 165 CLR 360.

28.3.3 Transitions in proprietary constitutionalism

Finally, some constitutions attempt to manage large-scale social and economic reform, transforming the nature of property in the state.

We have already mentioned the changes wrought in communist and post-communist constitutions. Sometimes, those constitutions address the cost of transformation. Bosnia-Herzegovina provides for the restoration of property, or compensation for losses, resulting from the hostilities following the break-up of Yugoslavia.[57] The constitutions of Colombia, Portugal and Serbia regulate privatisation, something that most countries leave to ordinary legislation.[58]

In recent years, several constitutions have responded to the dispossession of indigenous peoples or other marginalised groups, recognising their title, requiring the state to restore property and/or requiring the distribution of public land to impoverished communities. Bolivia's 2009 Constitution is the most far-reaching. It accomplished a revolutionary indigenisation of Bolivian political life, shifting public power and property to the country's indigenous majority. The proprietary provisions confirm the rights of 'nations and native peasants' to exercise self-determination and organise themselves in accordance with their 'political, economic and legal systems' as well as protecting their 'collective title to lands and territories'.[59]

Finally, South Africa's 1996 Constitution contains complex provisions designed to reverse the effects of apartheid, affirming property rights, providing for restitution of property taken during apartheid and authorising redistribution.[60]

28.4 Conclusion

It is sometimes said that the true constitution of France is the *Code civil des français*. The dictum points to a more general truth. A state's fundamental political and economic order is a function not simply of its formal constitution but of the way in which the constitution interacts with the country's proprietary order to form a consolidated whole. That is proprietary constitutionalism. Its recognition is essential to understanding the variety and the interplay of constitutional provisions with respect to property.

References

Alvaro, A (1991). 'Why Property Rights Were Excluded from the Canadian Charter of Rights and Freedoms' Canadian Journal of Political Science 24: 309.

Cohen, M (1927). 'Property and Sovereignty' Cornell Law Quarterly 13:8.

Gray, K (2010). 'Regulatory Property and the Jurisprudence of Quasi-Public Trust' Sydney Law Review 32:221.

Ingram, A (1994). *A Political Theory of Rights* (Oxford: Clarendon Press).

Pocock, JGA (2003). *The Machiavellian Moment: Florentine Political Thought and the Atlantic Republican Tradition* (Princeton: Princeton University Press).

Sidel, M (2009). *The Constitution of Vietnam: A Contextual Analysis* (Oxford: Hart Publishing).

Tribe, L (1988). *American Constitutional Law*, 2nd edn (Mineola, NY: Foundation Press).

—— (2000). *American Constitutional Law*, 3rd edn, vol 1 (Mineola, NY: Foundation Press).

Zhang, Q (2012). *The Constitution of China: A Contextual Analysis* (Oxford: Hart Publishing).

57 Bosnia and Herzegovina, art 4.
58 Colombia, art 60; Portugal, art 293; Serbia, art 86. Compare Ukraine, art 85.
59 Bolivia, art 32.
60 South Africa, arts 25(6) and (7).

Fundamental social rights

George Katrougalos* and Paul O'Connell†

29.1 Introduction

Fundamental social rights are constitutionally protected entitlements that impose substantive, legally binding obligations on the state to provide for the basic material needs (e.g. housing, health and education) of people. They should be distinguished from mere legislative welfare entitlements, which are basically discretionary in nature. In contrast, the essential fulfillment of fundamental social rights, as of every other constitutional right, is beyond the discretion of changing governmental policies.[1] While in international law the term generally used is 'social and economic rights' (or economic, social and cultural rights), the term 'fundamental social rights' is preferred here, to underline their constitutional character (Iliopoulos-Strangas). This term also distinguishes the rights discussed here from the right to property—the basic economic right in the continental European tradition—which, as the archetypical civil right of liberalism, has a qualitatively different character from the class of rights considered here.

Fundamental social rights, in this sense, are enshrined in many constitutional charters worldwide and in major international instruments.[2] The most important among them are the rights to basic subsistence, to housing, to healthcare, to education, to social security and social assistance, to work and to decent working conditions. In some legal systems, social rights are also considered to be rights related to the organisation of the labour class, such as the rights to form and join a trade union, and the rights to bargain collectively and to strike. In most European continental legal orders, the latter are considered civil rights and liberties. The

---

* Professor of Law, Demokritos University of Thrace.

† Reader in Law, University of Leicester.

1 In this regard, it is instructive that Alon Harel argues that 'To say that one has a right is different from saying that it would be good, nice, or noble that one is provided with the good in question or with what one desires to have. More particularly, stating that one has a right implies an imperative, nondiscretionary requirement.' Harel, 191.

2 Such as the Universal Declaration of Human Rights, the UN Covenant on Economic, Social and Cultural Rights as well as other UN Treaties, the European Social Charter and the EU Charter of Fundamental Rights.

aim of social rights is not to guarantee a luxurious life but to ensure the protection of essential human needs, in conformity with the principle of human dignity. This core obligation is not necessarily minimal in covering only the barest necessities of life. The extent of the state's obligations is defined by the historical evolution of each right, its concretisation in case law, and the economic and material conditions in each country. It could therefore be said that the minimum protection social rights offer is the historically and economically maximum possible for all. While such rights are guaranteed to every member of society equally, they are of particular relevance to poor people and disadvantaged groups within society (Michelman).

This chapter begins by sketching the historical development of the concept of social rights, and by highlighting the continuing divergence between legal systems grouped broadly into the European Social State model, and the Anglo-American Liberal model when it comes to the recognition, or acceptance, of fundamental social rights *qua* rights. The chapter's second half highlights a number of ongoing debates about the nature of social rights, and the continuing objections to them voiced in many legal systems, showing that for each of these objections, coherent alternative accounts have emerged, both in theory and practice. Finally, the chapter reflects on the challenges facing social rights in the future.

29.2 Historical formation and national variations

There is a clear dividing line between European and American (or Anglo-American) legal cultures regarding the conceptualisation of fundamental social rights and the corresponding obligations of the state. European 'social states' have a distinct constitutional ethos, which determines their entire legal systems, albeit with important variations in the conceptualisation of traditional rights and freedoms. The roots of the divergence extend to the eighteenth century, and the intrinsic difference between the American and French Revolutions. The former aimed at political independence as an end in itself, whereas the latter aimed primarily at the creation of a different social and legal order, and only when this proved unfeasible under the *ancien régime* was the monarchy overthrown (see Grimm, 139). It is illustrative that, already in 1793, Robespierre had proposed to the Convention a Bill of Rights that recognised as legally enforceable the rights to work and to social assistance and which treated the right of property not as a natural or absolute right, but as one limited by the law and the needs of other people.

Still, it was the nineteenth century that shaped definitively the European legal concept of social rights, as a response to the great 'social question' of that century: how could the market and the representative, democratic system be made compatible with the extension of political and social rights, without a socialist revolution? This question was not posed in the USA, or at least not in the same terms. Throughout the nineteenth century, the social tensions there had not acquired the same explosive character as in Europe, because, among other things, the vastness of the country's resources and its 'new, open frontiers' provided land and opportunities on a scale unknown in the Old Continent. As de Tocqueville put it, the reason the social question was not as prominent in America was because there 'are no proletarians in America. Everyone, having some possession to defend, recognizes the right to property in principle'.[3]

---

3 A de Tocqueville (trans. G Lawrence), *Democracy in America* (New York, Harper 1988), 238. Cf FD Roosevelt who said, quoting Jefferson, that America had no paupers, as 'most of the labor class possessed property'. FD Roosevelt, 'New conditions impose new requirements upon Government and those who conduct government, Campaign Address, 1932', in *The Public Papers of Franklin Roosevelt* (1938), San Francisco. Naturally, even the American nineteenth century was not entirely

In Europe, two opposite historical currents—a revolutionary and a counter-revolutionary one—tried to give an answer to the 'social question'. The recognition of enforceable social rights was one of the main demands of the pan-European social revolutions of 1848, especially with regard to the rights to work and education. The conservative counter current, archetypically represented by the Bismarckian paradigm, tried to solve the 'social question' with the introduction of social insurance, in tandem with repressive measures, such as the laws against the trade unions and the socialist organisations. This reformist alternative was ideologically reinforced by the 'Christian Social Teaching' of the Catholic Church (*die Katholische Soziallehre*) and its first important encyclical on social rights, *De Rerum Novarum*, in 1891.

The subsequent introduction of social legislation in continental Europe did not, therefore, signify constitutional recognition of social rights on an equal footing with civil and political rights. Quite the opposite: social rights were established on the basis of socialisation of risk, through the expansion of the insurance technique, and not as fundamental rights of the same nature as traditional liberties. The constitutionalisation of the social obligations of the state through fundamental social rights is, predominantly, a twentieth-century phenomenon. Their incorporation became widespread in Europe only in the aftermath of World War I. This was mainly the outcome of a political compromise between liberal and social democratic political forces (reflected also in the early legislative work of the International Labour Organization, founded in 1919), which aimed at the insulation of western European societies from the influence of the Russian October Revolution. Even before the emblematic Constitution of Weimar Republic (1919), social rights were included in the Constitution of Finland and subsequently a number of other constitutions followed suit.[4]

Still, the introduction of social rights, albeit incomplete and not yet constitutional, represented a breach in the liberal tradition. The insurance principle is not alien to the logic of the market, as it implies an exchange of equivalents, a *quid pro quo* (social contributions versus insurance premiums). However, the compulsory element of social insurance and the non-contributory character of social assistance schemes represented a radical break with the postulates of nineteenth-century liberalism. Until then, in classical liberal thought, human rights had been conceived as inherent in human nature and inalienable, possessed at birth, not granted by either society or state. The role of government was not to establish these rights, since they preceded it, but simply to respect them and guarantee their free exercise. Social rights, as individual or collective claims towards the state, could never be conceived as prior to society, because their role was precisely to compensate societal risks and alleviate extreme inequalities produced by the functioning of the market.

Nonetheless, social rights are not 'socialist rights'. They simply provide the legal basis for a political intervention in the economic sphere, in order to alleviate major inequalities, without infringing the primacy of the market. They constitute a public interface between the market, the state and the individual, formalising a kind of institutional solidarity that does not threaten the primacy of market relationships. Hence, they do not constitute a breach of the

idyllic and 'pauper-free'. This is shown by many dramatic incidents of class warfare, such as the violent strike against the Pennsylvania Railroad in 1877 or the industrial war at Andrew Carnegie's Homestead steel plant in 1890. See among others, Beatty.

4 For example: Estonia (1920), Poland (1921), Italy (1927), Greece (1927), Portugal (1933), Spain (1931, 1938) and Ireland (1937).

capitalist system, but rather a breach *within it*. They have created a different kind of market from the supposedly self-regulated liberal one,[5] defined later by the conservative Ordoliberalists in Germany as the 'social market economy' and a different kind of state, the 'social state'.

29.3 The 'Social State' principle

Usually the terms 'Welfare State' (*Wohlfahrtstaat/Etat-Providence*) and 'Social State' (*Sozialstaat/Etat social*) are used interchangeably. However, there is a qualitative distinction between the two: the first term (welfare state) describes the universal type of state that evolved in all industrialised countries during the twentieth century. The emergence of the welfare state responds to a functional necessity of the modern capitalist economy, related to the reproduction of a well-educated working class, as 'a problem of industry' (Beveridge). On the other hand, the social state is a normative, prescriptive principle, which defines a specific polity where the state has the constitutional obligation to assume interventionist functions in the economic and social spheres and to guarantee fundamental social rights to all citizens. In this sense, the USA or Australia are 'welfare' but not 'social' states, as social policy therein has no constitutional foundation.

In contrast, countries such as India or South Africa, although lacking the basic infrastructure of a mature welfare state, can be considered as social states due to their constitutional arrangements regarding the protection of social rights. Even though these two countries have quite distinctive historical and institutional starting points, they both nonetheless have found ways to effectuate the social state principle. In India, the fact that the Constitution does not include explicit guarantees of social rights has not precluded the Supreme Court from reading the Constitution as a whole, and in particular the right to life in Article 21, as including the right to livelihood with human dignity and several other social rights.[6] In contrast, the South African Constitutional Court is able to draw on an extensive catalogue of explicitly recognised social rights in the South African Constitution, and adjudicates on the reasonableness of state policy in advancing such rights, taking into account available resources.[7]

While the concept of the social state finds its origins in German legal thought, it is now widely accepted throughout Europe—and further afield[8]—as a fundamental normative and general organisational principle of the Constitution, on a par with the Rule of Law. Nearly all countries in Europe—with the most notable exception being the United Kingdom—are

---

5 Even proponents of the 'spontaneous order of the market', like Hayek, are not against the regulation of the market according to criteria of economic efficiency, not social justice, such as the removal of discriminations. See Hayek, 141.

6 See *Olga Tellis v Bombay Municipal Corporation* (1985) 3 SCC 545, *Francis Coralie Mullin v Union Territory of Delhi* AIR 1981 SC 746 at 753, and Kothari.

7 See *Government of the Republic of South Africa and Others v Grootboom and Others* (CCT11/00) [2000], and Liebenberg.

8 Indeed, the Mexican Constitution of 1917—still in force—was the first Constitutional Charter in the world to set out social rights. Social rights are included nowadays in most South American Constitutions and in the majority of Asian and African Constitutions. Still, in some cases the constitutional provisions are interpreted as mere programmatic principles of state policy, not as subjective rights. In other cases, as in East Asia, the influence of the traditional values of Confucianism results to a situation in which roles, rights and duties are intermingled.

social states, either comprising an explicit 'Social State' clause in their Constitutions,[9] or an analytical enumeration of social rights,[10] or both. It is broadly accepted that the principle can be deduced from the overall corpus of constitutional legislation, even without explicit reference to it. Therefore, the explicit inclusion of social rights in the Constitution is not a prerequisite for a polity to be a social state.

The archetypical social states of Germany and Austria, for example, do not have such rights in their constitutional charters, and the Nordic Constitutions—with the exception of Finland—contain only minimal provisions. The constitutional recognition of social rights implied a change of the functions of the state: instead of regulating the market only on the basis of norms that derive from the private law of contract, property and tort (Hayek, 141), the European state uses, in addition, 'political power to supersede, supplement or modify operations of the economic system in order to achieve results, which the economic system would not achieve on its own . . . guided by other values than those determined by open market forces' (Marshall, 15).[11] This 'market-correcting' function impregnates the legal culture (Deakin & Browne, 28), in the sense that, in the words of Raymond Aron, 'the concept of State and law is not any more merely negative, but also positive, so that the law is considered to be not only the juridical foundation but also the source of the material conditions for its fulfilment' (Aron, 242).

In contrast, the functions of the Anglo-American state have remained essentially negative, consisting mainly in the removal of arbitrary legal impediments (e.g., anti-trust legislation) and not in the provision of positive means for the exercise of rights. In this type of polity, not only are there no constitutional social rights but there can be no positive constitutional obligation of the state, not even as a guarantee of traditional liberties.[12] Therefore, the fundamental division of European 'social' and Anglo-American 'liberal' states cannot be reduced only to the legal differences between the common law and continental legal traditions. Rather, it reflects much more profound political, moral and societal choices, regarding the redistributive functions of the state,[13] and its intrusive role in the market. In Europe, in the words of Abbé Sieyès, the citizens feel they have a right to demand from the state everything it can do for them.[14] Consequently, in the words of Duguit, 'if the state fails to ensure to anyone (. . .) the necessary means of subsistence, it fails a compelling obligation (*Il manqué à un devoir stricte*)'.[15] In the USA, the traditional mistrust towards the state has resulted in a much

---

9 As in art 20 para 1 of the German Fundamental Law; art 1 of the Constitution of France; art 1 para 1 of the Constitution of Spain; art 2 of the Constitution of Portugal; the Preamble of the Constitution of Bulgaria; and Art 1 para 1 of the Constitutions of Croatia and FYR of Macedonia; Art 2 of Slovenia; Art 6 para 1 of Russia.

10 See, e.g., the Constitutions of Belgium (art 23), Italy (art 2-4, 31, 32, 35-38, 41, 45, 46), Luxembourg (11, 23, 94), Netherlands (19, 20, 22) Greece (21, 22), Spain (39-52, 129, 148, 149), Portugal (56, 59, 63-72, 108, 109, 167, 216).

11 Marshall was referring to social policy in general, but his description defines very precisely also the basic functions of the social state principle.

12 See the now (in)famous cases of *Harris v MacRae*, 448 US 297 (1980), and *Deshaney v Winnebago County Department of Social Services*, 489 US 189 (1989).

13 Many empirical studies reaffirm this deep clash of values between Europe and America. See, for instance, Alesina & Angletos.

14 'Il suffit de dire que les citoyens en commun ont droit à tout ce que l'Etat peut faire en leur faveur.' Abbe Sieyès, *'Des droits de l'homme et du citoyen', lu les 20 et 21 juillet 1789 au comité de la Constitution* (Hermann Paris 1939), 70.

15 Duguit, 291; Spanou, 123.

more individualistic, Lockean *Weltanschauung* and, especially, a fundamentally different conceptualisation of equality and rights.

Therefore, the social state does not entail only the constitutional protection of social rights, but a whole series of new functions for public power that are specific to it and alien to the liberal state. (a) The Social State principle functions as a fundamental interpretative 'meta-rule', constituting both a means of consistent interpretation of other constitutional rules and of control of the generation of infra-constitutional ones. (b) It contributes to the formulation of an objective system of values, which constitutes a different constitutional 'ethos' from that of a liberal state. Hence, concepts such as human dignity, social justice or substantive equality acquire not only a programmatic but also a normative, binding content. (c) It guarantees a constitutional 'floor', a 'standstill' effect for social legislation, i.e., a minimum of protection that the legislator is not allowed to withdraw (referred to as '*effet cliquet*' in France and as '*Bestandsgarantie*', '*Bestandschutz*' or '*Rückschrittsverbot*' in Germany). Thus, a minimum core of welfare protection is beyond the scope of the powers of both the legislature and the administration, no longer 'something that might be changed or abolished whenever the administration changes its political hue', but a constitutive element of social citizenship. And, (d) the social state offers constitutional justification for the limitation of economic freedom and the right to property, allowing state regulation of the economy both on the demand and the supply side.

29.4 Objections to social rights

From the foregoing it can be seen that differing views and approaches to social rights have their roots in specific historical divergences and fundamental, normative, political positions. However, along with these debates there is also a hodgepodge of arguments against the protection of social rights, which seek to differentiate them from civil and political rights, and thereby exclude them from constitutional protection and judicial enforcement. These arguments assert a number of supposedly inherent dichotomies between the two sets of rights, all of which masquerade under the rather nebulous, umbrella concept of non-justiciability. These arguments include, but are not limited to[16]: the assertion that social rights, unlike civil and political rights, are by their nature resource intensive, and consequently unrealisable in practice (Neier; Weede); the claim that courts cannot adjudicate on social rights because of the positive obligations they impose, whereas civil and political rights are said to impose only negative obligations (Macklem, 115–30); the claim that the courts, because of their procedural set-up and the skill set available to the average judge, are institutionally ill-suited to adjudicate on matters with potentially significant economic and social policy implications[17]; and the rather nebulous claim, which is both an argument in its own right and an umbrella term for all of the arguments against social rights, that they are non-justiciable (Dennis & Stewart).

The first response to the argument about resources is that it is a common cause that certain civil and political rights, such as the right to legal representation or the right to participate in elections, will involve considerable costs, whereas the social rights to join trade unions, or to the peaceful enjoyment of one's home, are cost-free. It is inaccurate to say that civil and

---

16 This non-exhaustive list is drawn from the useful summary provided by Koch, 5.
17 Captured famously in the concept of polycentric disputes (Fuller).

political rights are free and social rights are resource intensive (Hunt, 55-7), as noted by the South African Constitutional Court in its *First Certification Judgment*.[18] Even more to the point, empirical research demonstrates that 'there is no evidence that enforceable [social rights] means that the government must spend itself into the poorhouse' (Makinen, 43). And while there are certainly other studies that appear to demonstrate the 'resource draining' potential of social rights and the potential of judicial enforcement of such rights to skewer and undermine complex social programs (Ferraz), such examples are by no means the norm.

The argument that the courts are institutionally ill-suited or ill-equipped to deal with the sort of issues implicated in cases involving the assertion of social rights builds on Lon Fuller's concept of polycentric disputes (King). Fuller defined polycentric disputes in a general sense as being cases that 'involve many affected parties and a somewhat fluid state of affairs' (Fuller, 397); as an archetypal example, Fuller noted any case that would concern the distribution or otherwise of public funds, and concluded that such cases 'present too strong a polycentric aspect to be suitable for adjudication' (id, 400). Yet, if the argument justifies excluding the courts from addressing social rights cases on the basis of their resource implications, then surely it should also exclude courts from adjudicating on, for example, tax appeals, which patently have substantial resource implications, but are nonetheless routinely dealt with by the courts (King).

Alternatively, one could adopt Paul Hunt's approach of saying that if the institutional and procedural *status quo* is a barrier to adjudicating on social rights, and a given society wishes to adjudicate on such rights, then the structures should be changed (Hunt, 26). This latter approach was the one adopted by the Indian Supreme Court when it launched its now much lauded Public Interest Litigation (PIL) initiative in the late 1970s.[19] The Supreme Court held that it was necessary to 'democratise' the judicial process and make it more accessible to the marginalised.[20] Following from this, the Indian courts fundamentally re-cast their rules on standing, fact-finding and remedies, so as to give meaningful protection to social rights (see Desai & Muralidhar). So, whatever other criticisms there may be of the Indian social rights jurisprudence,[21] the experience at least demonstrates that the claim of polycentricity and institutional incompetence is overstated.

The positive–negative dichotomy posits an inherent difference between positive social rights and negative civil and political rights, with the latter being appropriate for judicial enforcement, and the former being wholly unsuited.[22] This argument has been undermined by the widespread acceptance of a tripartite typology initially developed by Henry Shue, which acknowledges that all human rights impose three levels of obligation on states: the obligation to respect, protect and fulfil (Eide, 23). This taxonomy makes it clear that all human rights, whether social or civil and political, impose a bundle of both positive and

---

18 See *Ex parte Chairperson of the Constitutional Assembly: In re Certification of the Constitution of the Republic of South Africa 1996* 1996 (10) BCLR 1253 (CC) at paras 77–78.

19 For discussion of the Indian experience with social rights, see Muralidhar.

20 See *SP Gupta v Union of India* (1981) Supp SCC 83.

21 Among the more prominent criticisms of the Indian Supreme Courts PIL/social rights jurisprudence are the arguments that the courts' activism undermines the separation of powers, and the more recently articulated argument that the Supreme Court has, in recent years, abandoned the interests of the poor and marginalised, and rubber-stamped state-sponsored, neo-liberal development projects. On these criticisms see Cassels; Rajagopal.

22 See Dennis & Stewart, and the majority judgments of the Irish Supreme Court in *Sinnott v Minister for Education* [2001] 2 IR 241, and *TD v Minister for Education* [2001] 4 IR 545.

negative obligations on states. As expressed by Sandra Fredman, 'rights cannot coherently be distinguished by the kind of duty to which they give rise' (Fredman, 67). Indeed, it was accepted by the Joint Human Rights Committee of the UK Parliament that '[no] clear line of demarcation can be drawn between the substance of rights classified as civil and political and those classified as economic, social and cultural' on the basis of the obligation they purportedly give rise to.[23] The articulation of the tripartite typology of state obligations with respect to all human rights therefore goes a long way towards negating the positive–negative dichotomy posited by opponents of social rights.

The final argument to consider here is the purported non-justiciability of social rights. The first point to note in this context is that the terms justiciable/non-justiciable are used fairly haphazardly by both opponents and advocates of entrenched social rights (Dennis & Stewart, 473). For this reason, the justiciability argument is often presumed to embrace all of the other arguments against social rights discussed here. The first problem in this context is that the concept of justiciability is a multifaceted one, precluding the courts from entertaining cases on the basis, *inter alia*, that the plaintiff lacks standing, that the point being argued is moot, that the issue concerned is a 'political question' for determination by the elected branches of government, or any number of other, jurisdiction-specific prohibitions, all of which come under the umbrella of the justiciability doctrine (Siegel, 76–7) (see Chapter 9). To fruitfully engage with this concern, it is essential to be precise about what is meant by justiciability. Martin Scheinin argues that at the level of domestic constitutional law, justiciability is concerned with 'the search [for] a proper procedure that is capable of providing an adequate remedy' in response to the violation of social rights (Scheinin, 20). In similar terms, Fons Coomans notes that justiciability refers to 'the extent to which an alleged violation of an economic or social subjective right invoked in a particular case is suitable for judicial or quasi-judicial review' (Coomans, 4).

It can be said, then, that insofar as justiciability is concerned with identifying and securing a judicial role in the enforcement and vindication of social rights, the argument of non-justiciability is ultimately an assertion that the courts cannot play a role in adjudicating such rights. However, if we take into account Jonathan Siegel's observation that justiciability quite often operates as a 'discretionary judicial avoidance mechanism',[24] we might question the apparently neutral assertion that the courts cannot adjudicate on such rights and surmise that underlying this assertion are certain assumptions about the judicial role in the vindication of social rights. If, for example, those who genuinely apprehend that judicial enforcement of social rights would require the courts to make extensive mandatory orders that sap the public finances and inhibit the functioning of government; or alternatively, that the enforcement of social rights will put the courts in a position where they have to make extensive and expansive orders that are simply ignored by the elected branches of government, it might be thought better to simply avoid these undesirable vistas by denying social rights claims a hearing in the first instance.

Viewed in this light, 'justiciability' ceases to be an abstract account of what the courts *can* do, and is shown to be a normative view of what courts *should* do. The claim of non-justiciability is thus absorbed into a broader account, which sees judicial enforcement of social

---

23 House of Lords/House of Commons Joint Committee on Human Rights, *The International Covenant on Economic, Social and Cultural Rights* (Twenty-First Report of Session 2003-04, HL Paper 183, HC 1188, Published 2 November 2004) at p. 11.
24 Siegel, 109; and see Fallon.

rights as inherently inimical to the maintenance of the separation of powers. As Craven notes, the 'main argument [against judicial enforcement of social rights] . . . is not that courts are unable to deal with particular subject-matters, but that they should not involve themselves in distributive decision-making: that function is one assigned to governments or legislatures' (Craven). But if courts are to shy away from social rights, and deem them non-justiciable because of a fear that such rights fundamentally undermine the separation of powers, then surely they should be expected to be equally cautious when it comes to the enforcement of the obligations arising from civil and political rights. However, this is quite often not the case. The Canadian Supreme Court's unwillingness to enforce the social rights of welfare claimants on the basis, *inter alia*, of concerns regarding separation of powers (that it should be for the elected branches of government to decide how much, if any, social welfare an individual or group should receive)[25] contrasts strikingly with the same court's willingness to vindicate the rights of private healthcare consumers (and providers) irrespective of equally, if not more, pressing concerns about separation of powers (that the choice of healthcare system—a real 'hot button' issue in Canada—should be one for the elected, and accountable, representatives of the people and not the courts),[26] then the argument rings a little hollow.

Furthermore, in the recent *Hartz IV Judgment*,[27] the German Constitutional Court has shown that judicial involvement in the implementation of social rights is possible, without the usurpation of legislative discretion. In this case, the Court declared unconstitutional a law reducing benefits for social assistance, primarily on the basis that the legislator had failed to respect the fundamental right to guarantee a subsistence minimum, which is derived from the principles of human dignity and the social state. According to the Court, its substantive review was restricted to ascertaining whether the benefits are evidently insufficient according to the actual need, in line with reality, by examining: a) whether the legislator has chosen a reasonable and scientific method for assessing the subsistence minimum levels; and b) whether it has used plausible and suitable figures with consistency. This is just one of the many examples of cases in which the separation of powers concerns, which animate the charge of non-justiciability against social rights, were shown to be overstated. The German Constitutional Court in this case has demonstrated that, where the will exists, national superior courts can play a role in enforcing social rights, without running roughshod over the imperatives of parliament and the other democratically accountable branches of government.

29.5 Concluding remarks

The most important conclusion is that the oft-posited arguments against the recognition and enforcement of fundamental social rights are by no means dispositive. Instead, the different ways in which different legal systems treat social rights and their associated interests reflect fundamental, normative political judgments. It is not a case of a divide between common law and civil law approaches, or even of embedded versus crumbling welfare systems. Instead, the decision of a country, such as South Africa in the recent past, to adopt and protect social rights reflects a political commitment to the equal worth of all citizens and, by implication, the further position that such equal worth will not be protected by the market, but requires explicit and conscious collective action. In contrast, a nation's decision not to recognise and

---

25 See *Gosselin v Quebec (Attorney General)* [2002] 4 SCR 429.
26 See *Chaoulli v Quebec (Attorney General)* [2005] 1 SCR 791.
27 *Hartz IV* BVerfGE 125, 175 of 9 February 2010.

protect social rights reflects a view that, left to their own devices, atomistic, utility-maximising market actors will, in the end, be best able to protect their own rights and interests (Woods). Designating such divergences as fundamentally ideological is, by no means, to denigrate them. Rather, it simply highlights the fact that whatever future may lie in store for social rights, it will be decided as much, in fact more, in the political arena as it will in the judgments of superior courts.

References

Alesina, A & Angeletos, M (1983). 'Fairness and Redistribution: US versus Europe', *Harvard Institute of Economic Research Working Papers* (Harvard—Institute of Economic Research 2002).

Aron, R (1972). *Etudes Politiques* (Paris, Gallimard).

Beatty, J (2007). *Age of Betrayal, The Triumph of Money in America, 1865–1900* (New York, A. Knopf).

Beveridge, W (1909). *Unemployment: A Problem of Industry* (London, Longmans).

Cassels, J (1989). 'Judicial Activism and Public Interest Litigation in India: Attempting the Impossible?' 37 *American Journal of Comparative Law* 495.

Coomans, F (2006). 'Some Introductory Remarks on the Justiciability of Economic and Social Rights in a Comparative Constitutional Context', in Coomans, F (ed), *Justiciability of Economic and Social Rights* (Intersentia, Antwerp), 1.

Craven, M (2005). 'Assessment of Progress on Adjudication of Economic, Social and Cultural Rights', in Squires, J, Langford, M & Thiele, B (eds), *The Road to a Remedy: Current Issues in the Litigation of Economic, Social and Cultural Rights* (Sydney: University of New South Wales Press), 27.

Deakin, S & Browne, J (2003) in Hervey, T & Kenner, J, *Economic and Social Rights Under the EU Charter of Fundamental Rights—A Legal Perspective* (Oxford-Portland Oregon, Hart Publishing) 27.

Dennis, M & Stewart, D (2004). 'Justiciability of Economic, Social and Cultural Rights: Should There Be an International Complaints Mechanism to Adjudicate the Rights to Food, Water, Housing and Health?' 98 *American Journal of International Law* 462.

Desai, A & Muralidhar, S (2004). 'Public Interest Litigation: Potential and Problems', in Kirpal, Desai, Subramanium, Dhavan & Ramachandran (eds), *Supreme But Not Infallible: Essays in Honour of the Supreme Court of India* (Oxford University Press, New Delhi), 159.

Duguit, L (1901). *L'Etat, le droit objectif et la loi positive* (Paris, Albert Fontemoing).

Eide, A (2001). 'Economic, Social and Cultural Rights as Human Rights', in Eide, A, Krause, K & Rosas, A (eds), *Economic, Social and Cultural Rights: A Textbook* (2nd edn Martinus Nijhoff, The Hague), 9.

Fallon, R (2006). 'The Linkage Between Justiciability and Remedies—and Their Connection to Substantive Rights', 92 *Virginia Law Review* 633.

Ferraz, O (2011). 'Harming the Poor Through Social Rights Litigation: Lessons From Brazil', 89 *Texas Law Review* 1643.

Fredman, S (2008). *Human Rights Transformed: Positive Rights and Positive Duties* (Oxford University Press, Oxford).

Fuller, L (1978). 'The Forms and Limits of Adjudication', 92 *Harvard Law Review* 353.

Grimm, D (2005). 'The Protective Function of the State', in Nolte, G (ed), *European and US Constitutionalism* (Cambridge, New York, Cambridge University Press), 137.

Harel, A (2005). 'Theories of Rights', in Golding, M & Edmundson, W (eds), *The Blackwell Guide to the Philosophy of Law and Legal Theory* (Blackwell Publishing Ltd., Oxford) 191.

Hayek, FA (1980). *Law, Legislation and Liberty: a new statement of the liberal principles of Justice and Political Economy* (London, Routledge).

Hunt, P (1996). *Reclaiming Social Rights: International and Comparative Perspectives* (Dartmouth Publishing Company, Aldershot).

Iliopoulos-Strangas, J (ed) (2000). *La protection des droits sociaux fondamentaux dans les Etats Membres de l'Union Européenne* (Athènes, Bruxelles, Baden-Baden, Bruylant, Nomos Verlag, Ant. N. Sakkoulas).

King, J (2008). 'The Persuasiveness of Polycentricity', *Public Law* 101.

Koch, IE (2003). 'The Justiciability of Indivisible Human Rights', 2 *Nordic Journal of International Law* 3.

Kothari, J (2007). 'Social Rights Litigation in India: Developments of the Last Decade', in Barak-Erez, D & Gross, A (eds), *Exploring Social Rights* (Oxford, Hart Publishing) 171.

Liebenberg, S (2010). *Socio-Economic Rights: Adjudication Under a Transformative Constitution* (Juta Academic Press).

Macklem, T (2006). 'Entrenching Bills of Rights', 26 *Oxford Journal of Legal Studies* 107.

Makinen, A (2001). 'Rights, Review and Spending: Policy Outcomes With Judicially Enforceable Rights', 39 *European Journal of Political Research* 23.

Marshall, TH (1975). *Social Policy* (London, Routledge).

Michelman, F (2003). 'The Constitution, Social Rights and Liberal Political Justification', 1 *International Journal of Constitutional Law* 13.

Muralidhar, S (2008). 'India: The Expectations and Challenges of Judicial Enforcement of Social Rights', in Langford, M (ed), *Social Rights Jurisprudence: Emerging Trends in International and Comparative Law* (Cambridge University Press, Cambridge), 102.

Neier, A (2006). 'Social and Economic Rights: A Critique', 13(2) *Human Rights Brief* 1.

Rajagopal, B (2007). 'Pro-Human Rights But Anti-Poor? A Critical Evaluation of the Indian Supreme Court From a Social Movement Perspective', 8 *Human Rights Review* 157.

Scheinin, M (2005). 'Justiciability and the Indivisibility of Human Rights', in Squires, J, Langford, M & Thiele, B (eds), *The Road to a Remedy: Current Issues in the Litigation of Economic, Social and Cultural Rights* (University of New South Wales Press, Sydney), 17.

Siegel, J (2007). 'A Theory of Justiciability', 86 *Texas Law Review* 73.

Spanou, K (2005). *The Reality of Rights* (Athens, Savvalas).

Weede, E (2008). 'Human Rights, Limited Government and Capitalism', 28 *Cato Journal* 35.

Woods, JM (2003). 'Justiciable Social Rights as a Critique of the Liberal Paradigm', 38 *Texas International Law Journal* 763.

Additional reading

Arango, A (2001). *Der Begriff der sozialen Grundrechte* (Nomos Verlagsgesellschaft, Baden-Baden).

Barak-Erez, D & Gross, A (eds) (2007). *Exploring Social Rights* (Oxford, Hart Publishing).

Coomans, F (ed) (2006). *Justiciability of Economic and Social Rights* (Intersentia, Antwerp).

Eide, A, Crause, K & Rosas, A (eds) (2001). *Economic, Social and Cultural Rights: A Textbook* (Leiden, Kluwer Law International).

Gay, L (2007). *Les «droits-créances» constitutionnels* (Bruylant, Bruxelles).

Hepple, B (ed) (2002). *Social and Labour Rights in a Global Context* (Cambridge, Cambridge University Press).

Iliopoulos-Strangas, J (ed) (2000). *La protection des droits sociaux fondamentaux dans les Etats Membres de l'Union Européenne* (Athènes, Bruxelles, Baden-Baden, Bruylant, Nomos Verlag, Ant. N. Sakkoulas).

Katrougalos, G (2008). 'European "Social States" and the USA: An Ocean Apart ?', 4 *European Constitutional Law Review* 225.

O'Connell, P (2012). *Vindicating Socio-Economic Rights: International Standards and Comparative Experiences* (Routledge, Oxford).

Squires, J, Langford, M & Thiele, B (eds) (2005). *The Road to a Remedy: Current Issues in the Litigation of Economic, Social and Cultural Rights* (University of New South Wales Press, Sydney).

30

Linguistic and cultural rights

Bipin Adhikari and Carlos Viver Pi-Sunyer

Although language rights have cultural content, there are differences between language and cultural rights, which justify separate analysis. From a comparative perspective, language rights have distinctive characteristics: weak international and constitutional protection and the influence of different domestic language policies on their content and their protected scope. Cultural rights necessarily differ because of problems associated with the definition of culture. We start with a provisional approach, then describe the relevant content of international and domestic legal instruments, and finally deduce from these texts the main characteristics of these rights. The latter are usually established through general clauses of vague and sometimes evanescent content that, in turn, weaken their position among fundamental rights. However, they have intrinsic importance and are directly connected with human dignity and peaceful coexistence among peoples and communities.

30.1 Language rights

30.1.1 Main characteristics of language rights

Language rights can be broadly understood as rights, the object of which is the use of a given language and, more strictly, the use one's own language or one's chosen or preferred language.

In the first instance, they are rights of freedom that seek to avoid interference by public authorities in the use of languages, in the strictly private sphere, in *inter privatos* relations that have public significance (e.g., in socio-economic relationships), and in relations with public authorities. A few such rights extend the objective of protection to include some characteristics of the participation rights. Many have positive dimensions, imposing obligations on individuals and especially on governments.

Language rights have specific characteristics that, collectively, distinguish them from other rights. Firstly, they vary considerably between countries and sometimes also within each state, depending on the territory and the languages protected. Secondly, it is often difficult to determine their content, their limits and their binding strength; sometimes their very existence as proper rights. Thirdly, they are poorly protected under international law and even under constitutional law: domestic legislation plays a major role in the area of language rights. Fourthly, in many cases language rights interact as a zero-sum game.

In comparative terms, the diversity of state regulation is noticeable. The international community has not established relevant common standards. The diverse situations of languages spoken in different states and the disparate language policies in each country are the cause and effect of precarious international standards, and the transfer of much regulation to diverse and plural domestic legislators.

Few linguistic rights are explicitly recognized under international or domestic constitutional law. Most language rights have been deduced by courts and academic doctrine: first, from the implicit linguistic content of other constitutional rights such as freedom of expression, the right to privacy and family life, the right to education and the right of association; second, from principles such as non-discrimination on grounds of language, from legal statements that attribute official status to a particular language or from simple institutional uses that *de facto* grant official character to one or more of the languages. The implicit nature of these rights leads to disputes about their identification and content. These controversies contribute to a weakening of their legal effectiveness or 'enforceability'. Moreover, the few rights expressly recognized as such under international or constitutional law tend to have ambiguous content, which also weakens their legal effectiveness and promotes diversity of the laws that implement such generic provisions. Controversy also accompanies questions about the enforceability of legislative implementation of international and constitutional rights that are set forth in such general terms.

Special mention should also be made of rights deduced from obligations to promote and protect certain languages or language groups, imposed by international instruments or programmatic constitutional provisions. Problems often arise in determining whether these measures are to protect and promote real rights or not, and, if so, what kind of rights are concerned since, in the sphere of language rights, both collective and individual rights are important. Collective rights, however, have some controversial features. On some approaches, collective rights are no more than individual rights necessarily exercised within language groups, which governments alone have the duty to protect through positive action. In others, language groups are the holders of true collective rights.

Within countries, language rights are likely to be diverse, in terms of scope and status. More than one language is spoken in most countries, so a plurality of language groups live side by side. Yet, in no country are languages and language groups afforded a position of legal equality.

In all countries, there are one or more languages that, *de jure* or *de facto*, have special status as the official language of the state, offering speakers the full range of language rights in the private, public and official spheres, with few limits imposed on their exercise. Alongside these official languages, there may be others corresponding to language groups that the government decides to protect for some reason, which are also given a special status of official language in part of the territory of the state. Alternatively, they may have the status of 'regional' or 'minority' language, conferring language rights on their speakers that may be less than the rights afforded to speakers of official languages throughout the state. Finally, there are language groups, including some immigrant groups, without specific language rights.

Together with differences attributable to the spoken language, there is disparity between the status of languages and, consequently, language rights that depends on where different languages are intended to be used. Some official and minority languages have this status only in a part of the state's territory, but outside this area—such as in the relations with the central government—they have no special protection. In Switzerland, for example, the Constitution recognizes principally four official languages, while the cantons decide on the official languages recognized in their territory. By contrast, in Spain there is only one official language of the central institutions; other official languages are confined to the territory of a region.

The diversity of legal status attributed to the different languages spoken in a country, together with the diversity of language rights, is a consequence of two factors. One is the objective situation of these languages in each country (the number of languages, their territorial distribution, the number of speakers, the evolution and degree of standardization of the languages, the political, economic and social relevance of the language groups, the capacity of the state to effectively manage linguistic diversity, or the role of the language as a basic element of the various national or cultural communities within plurinational countries).

Diversity in legal status results from the varying language policies adopted by individual governments. These policy options respond to disparate objectives and are based on a wide range of justifications. In comparative law, we find examples such as policies that tend to recognize only one language and to suppress any manifestation of the others, even in private, by trying to justify this option on economic, religious or political grounds—such as to preserve internal cohesion or encourage nation-building—and by reference to the values of inclusion and the promotion of equality. Thus, Turkey and Spain developed language assimilation policies that included language repression. Articles 26 and 28 of the Turkish Constitution 1982 limited and prohibited the use of regional, migrant and indigenous languages in the press, printed documents, videotapes and publications. Since 2001, Article 10 of the Turkish Constitution has required non-discrimination on the basis of language and the official attitude is more flexible, but the Kurdish minority still does not have positive linguistic rights, with their indigenous language banned by Article 42. Another example of prohibition of language rights was the case of the Catalan and Basque languages during the Franco dictatorship in Spain. Using these languages was forbidden in street, commercial and road signs, private documents, books and schools.[1] Elsewhere, however, policies seek to achieve maximum equality among a large number of the languages spoken and among diverse national communities in plurinational or multicultural countries. These choices are justified by the need to protect the country's linguistic diversity and cultural heritage, to make up for historical discrimination or even to encourage nation-building through procedures and with final aims opposed to those of the previous model.

Between these two extremes, there is a wide range of alternatives under which, although one language has privileged status, speakers of other languages not only have the right to use their language in private, but also certain rights in the public and official spheres. As examples of proportioned restrictions, in Catalonia language laws establish language quotas for films and media and require that civil servants know Catalan. In Belgium, language laws establish quotas for civil servants. A Belgian law requiring the labelling of foodstuffs for sale exclusively in the language of the region, without allowing for the possibility of using another language easily understood by purchasers or of ensuring that the purchaser is informed by other measures, exemplifies disproportionate or spurious regulations.[2]

---

1 See *Kurdish Language Rights in Turkey*, Yildiz & Düzgören, 2002, and Toksabay, Burcu, *Conflict over language rights: the case of Kurds and Circassians in Turkey,* doctoral thesis, unpublished, 2005. See also Solé i Sabaté & Villaroya.

2 The European Court of Justice held that regulation inconsistent with Article 30 of the EEC Treaty and Article 14 of Council Directive 79/112/EEC of 18 December 1978 (Judgment of the Court 18.06.1991, Case 369/1989).

Normally, language models based on the principle of territoriality tend to give priority to linguistic homogeneity, the protection of a language and the reduction of tensions between language rights, while the principle of personality tends to give priority to linguistic diversity and individual language rights. Here too there are intermediate models where the principle of territoriality is combined with the principle of personality to balance the protection of languages with the granting of language rights.

Importantly, all speakers of any of the languages found in a specific area typically have a few language rights in common. Common rights are essentially those that affect the freedom to use the preferred language in purely private relations, rights relating to the public sphere derived from the linguistic content of other human and constitutional rights, and certain rights of defendants in criminal proceedings, such as the right to an interpreter.

Finally, in many cases the recognized rights of speakers of a given language—and, more generally, some of the measures protecting a language—may limit the exercise of these rights by speakers of other languages in contact: sometimes the relationship between language rights is a zero-sum game.[3] The tension between the language rights of persons belonging to different language groups and the—very often—legitimate measures to protect certain languages is a constant almost everywhere. Limits to the exercise of language rights relate to different objectives, from the protection of a minority language group within a territory to the promotion of linguistic homogeneity at the expense of minority groups. These limits usually involve the use of language in dealings with public authorities; however, in some cases they also affect the use of a language in *inter privatos* relations that are of public relevance (e.g., in trade relations) and even, in exceptional cases, strictly private uses. The legitimacy of these restrictions[4] depends on the legitimacy of their objectives and the necessity, reasonableness and proportionality of their application case by case. Some regulations are reasonable and proportionate, others spurious.

30.1.2 Language rights in international law

There has been a significant increase in recent years in the number of international instruments that refer to languages, which impose obligations on states to protect certain groups that claim language rights.[5] This increased presence of language rights at the international level has led to better domestic regulation of those rights. Nevertheless, international standards are still quite scarce and weak.

---

3 In specific circumstances, business people may consider that their freedom to use their preferred language is limited by the right of their customers to be dealt with in their own language, while the protection measures for other languages may limit their linguistic freedom in relation to outdoor commercial advertising. In Quebec, language laws restrict the use of languages in public signage and within private business exceeding a certain size. The Supreme Court of Canada ruled as unconstitutional the requirement that only French be used on outdoor commercial signs but allowed the Quebec government to require that French have 'greater visibility' or 'marked predominance' on them (*Ford v Québec* (PG), 1988, 2 RCS 172).

4 As well as restrictions that language rights may impose on the exercise of other rights such as the freedom of enterprise or the equality of access to certain public positions.

5 An extensive list of the international instruments related to language rights can be found at http://www.unesco.org/most/In2.htm

30.1.2.1 Universal international law

The Universal Declaration of Human Rights (UDHR) does not recognize proper language rights. It declares only (in Article 2.1) the principle of non-discrimination on the grounds of language, but only in connection with the other rights and freedoms contained in the Declaration. This principle, reflected as well in the International Covenant on Civil and Political Rights (ICCPR) and the International Covenant on Economic, Social and Cultural Rights (ICESR), imposes an obligation on states to take affirmative action to prevent discrimination with respect to protected rights that does indeed occur as a result of the language spoken by certain people or language groups.

The ICESR enshrines two rights: one for language minorities to use their own language (Article 27) and one for defendants in criminal proceedings so that they can be informed—in a language that they understand (not necessarily their preferred language)—of the reason why they have been charged and also to have an interpreter present in cases where they do not understand the language used in the court (Article 14).

The vagueness of Article 27 is a good example of the difficulty involved in deducing the specific content of the right that it is intended to lay down. The United Nations Human Rights Committee has tried to clarify case-by-case certain points of this precept. The Declaration on the Rights of Persons Belonging to National or Ethnic, Religious and Linguistic Minorities, approved by the UN General Assembly in 1992, expands the need for states to carry out affirmative action to ensure the freedom to use the minority language. However, the content of this right is not specified and although it makes clear that the freedom of use refers to both the private and public spheres, it excludes from the latter individuals' relationships with governments.

The UN has promoted other instruments with linguistic content—related to childhood, education and indigenous peoples—although those rights are no less precarious than the previous ones. The UN Educational, Scientific and Cultural Organization (UNESCO) has also promoted several conventions in defence of language diversity and against discrimination in the area of education; nevertheless, they have the same problems of indeterminacy and lack of guarantees just discussed.

In the universal international field, the majority doctrine and some courts still point out that certain fundamental rights contained in the main international instruments implicitly incorporate language content, which would consequently also have a fundamental and universal character. Thus, freedom of expression and opinion would incorporate the right to express oneself in one's own language; freedom of assembly and association would involve at least the right not to be banned from meetings or associations because of the language used in them; the right to privacy and family life would entail the freedom to use the language in the private sphere and to have an official name in each person's language; the rights of detainees and criminal defendants would include the rights to be informed in an intelligible language and, where applicable, an interpreter; and lastly the right to education would incorporate the right of children to receive teaching in an understandable language. Today, there is almost unanimous acceptance of the existence of language rights implicit in fundamental rights.

Nevertheless, there is also a very general acceptance of the difficulty in specifying the scope of those rights and specifying the consequent obligations for states. The diversity in the way that these rights have been developed at the domestic level is a good example of these difficulties.

In recent years there have been increasing efforts to delineate some universal language rights or some language content of fundamental international rights, but the results are still limited (Milian).

30.1.2.2 International regional law

In all regions there are international instruments under which obligations on states are imposed in respect of certain languages and language groups, and the rights of these groups and citizens are recognized.

Europe is perhaps the region where this regulation is most complete. The main instruments come from the Council of Europe. Among these instruments, notable for its detail and the advanced nature of its content is the European Charter for Regional or Minority Languages.[6] However, it is not a charter of rights but rather of obligations on states to protect languages. The explanatory report makes clear that 'the charter sets out to protect and promote regional or minority languages, not language minorities . . . The charter does not establish any individual or collective rights for the speakers of regional or minority languages' (Arzoz, 16).

The instruments of international law in the American region are limited to incorporating the right to non-discrimination on the grounds of language and the right to an interpreter during criminal proceedings. Since February 1997, work has been done on drafting a Declaration of Rights for Indigenous Peoples, containing important references to language rights. However, so far, no definitive agreements have been reached.

Influenced by global international law, the regional system for the protection of human rights established under the Organization of African Unity has similarly addressed linguistic rights issues in two treaties. The African Charter on Human and Peoples' Rights, which entered into force in 1986, provided for the entitlement of every individual to enjoy the rights and freedoms recognized and guaranteed in the Charter without distinction of any kind including language (Art 2). Under the African Charter on the Rights and Welfare of the Child, every child has a similar right (Art 3).

Unlike Europe, Africa and the Americas, Asia does not have an intergovernmental convention on human rights.

30.1.2.3 Inter-state rights

Another relevant type of international instrument are the numerous international and cross-border treaties and accords signed between neighbouring states that recognize language rights for members of minorities or language groups established territorially on both sides of the state borders.

30.1.3 Language rights in domestic law

30.1.3.1 Constitutional law

Although most constitutions have articles devoted to the use of languages, few expressly establish rights related to linguistic content. Usually, they are limited to declaring the official or national nature of one or more languages and, in some cases, imposing certain obligations on governments aimed at preserving linguistic diversity and protecting part of the minority languages (Italy, Hungary and Slovenia). The courts and doctrine have, not without controversy, deduced language rights at constitutional level from these official statements as well as

---

6 Also, the Framework Convention for Protection of National Minorities (1995). On the European Charter see Woehrling.

from the programmatic provisions referred to (especially those that protect regional language minorities) and from other constitutional rights.

Notable among the few constitutions that expressly proclaim authentic language rights are Canada (in the 1982 Bill of Rights), Finland, South Africa, Peru and the countries of Eastern Europe. Some constitutions, such as in Belgium, Switzerland and Bolivia, proclaim language freedom.

In Africa, constitutions such as those of Senegal, Ghana, Nigeria, Rwanda, Kenya, Ethiopia and Mauritius have dealt with language rights in varying degrees. The 1996 Constitution of South Africa not only recognizes 11 languages as the official language of the country, but intends to enhance 'the historically diminished use and status of the [se] indigenous languages'. By requiring that the national government and each provincial government must use at least two official languages, the Constitution also obliges municipalities to take into account the language usage and preferences of their residents. All official languages must enjoy parity of esteem and must be treated equitably. Apart from this, a language board has also been envisaged by the Constitution itself. The 1994 Constitution of Ethiopia ensures all Ethiopian languages 'equal state recognition'. Although it establishes only one language as the working language of the federal government, members of the federation may by law determine their respective working languages.

The Asian countries also have diversity in their constitutional formulations. India, Indonesia, Singapore and East Timor are multilingual and this status is reflected in their constitutions. Some of these countries, to avoid conflicts between languages, use as an official language—alone or among others—a 'neutral' language such as English (as in India and Pakistan) to avoid linguistic conflicts. Pakistan also adopted Urdu, spoken by a small minority, as a 'neutral' language. The 2002 Constitution of East Timor provides for two languages (Tetum and Portuguese) as official languages and Indonesian and English as working languages of the civil service. The 1949 Constitution of India includes the right to conserve one's distinct language (Art 29). In Nepal, the preliminary draft of the new constitution contains a complete regulation of the status of all the languages spoken in the country and of some of the language rights of the citizens.[7]

Finally it must be noted that within federal states the constitutions of the subnational units in some cases also regulate language rights, often in greater detail than in the federal constitutions (see Chapter 12).

30.1.3.2 Domestic legislation and regulations

Most language rights are enshrined in laws and regulations. Their content differs across different states.[8] There is a surprising heterogeneity even among legal systems of countries that share the same legal culture and which, in terms of other rights, share very broad common minimum standards. In any case, the number and profile of language rights is increasing in all countries because of the need to regulate the growing multilingualism that is now common in almost all countries, and the increase in the public services provided by governments.

---

7 A list of constitutional provisions relating to language rights can be found in Fiangold.
8 A catalogue of the language rights contained in domestic legislation can be found in the website of the International Research Centre on Language Planning at http://www.ciral.ulaval.ca/alx/amlx-monde/accmonde.htm

The heterogeneity of language rights—in terms of content and of the interests that they seek to protect—makes it difficult to draw up meaningful categories. Similarly, the limits on those rights, which have a very important practical significance, differ greatly from one system to another.

30.2 Cultural rights

30.2.1 Delineation of the object

Delineation of cultural rights has always posed problems. It has always been difficult to determine a useful concept of culture,[9] and yet most fundamental rights traditionally contained in international and domestic law have, among their objects, human activities that can be considered cultural activities. Post-1945 legal instruments that proclaim human or fundamental rights do include rights aimed at culture in general—a culture as a whole differentiated from the cultural content of other rights—as well as rights associated with quite specific cultural activities such as literary production, which have an autonomous treatment differentiated from the cultural content that the other fundamental rights with a broad content might have.

This section focuses on the 'general' rights to the culture as a whole and the 'residual' or 'autonomous' specific cultural rights currently regulated in international and domestic law.

30.2.2 Regulatory sources of the right to culture

The right to culture is proclaimed and regulated in both the domestic laws of an important part of the states and in many different instruments of international law, of universal or regional scope. With regard to cultural rights, unlike language rights, international law has played and still plays an important role in comparison with domestic law; although we must recognize from the start that in both international and domestic law, cultural rights have a marginal position and little practical significance.

30.2.2.1 International and supranational law

The first regulation with theoretical and practical significance is UDHR Art 27, which proclaims a person's right freely to participate in the cultural life of the community, to enjoy the arts, and to share in scientific advancement and its benefits, as well as the protection of the moral and material interests resulting from any scientific, literary or artistic production of which he is the author.

This right was incorporated in ICESCR Art 15. This provision adds a series of measures that signatory states must take to ensure the exercise of these rights: measures for the conservation, development and diffusion of science and culture, respect for the freedom for research and creative activity, and for the promotion of international relations and cooperation in

---

9 However, it should be noted that nowadays there is a widespread consensus on the essential elements of the concept of culture and cultural rights built on the ground of the definitions such as those of the Universal Declaration on Cultural Diversity (UNESCO), one of the General Comments num. 21 of the Committee of Economic, Social and Cultural Rights of 2009 – paragraph 13, or of the Fribourg Group www.1umn.edu/humanrts/instree/Fribourg%20Declaration.pdf.

scientific and cultural fields. This article has been interpreted broadly, especially as regards the right to participate in cultural life, and has had a significant impact on international law and domestic law of states.

Article 27 of the ICCPR refers to a particular aspect of the right to cultural life—the right of ethnic minorities to their own cultural life—that has recently acquired special importance.

UNESCO, as a UN organization specialized in the field of culture, has promoted several international instruments that proclaim cultural rights. Prominent among them is the Universal Declaration on Cultural Diversity 2001, and the subsequent Convention on the Protection and Promotion of the Diversity of Cultural Expressions, 20 October 2005. Cultural diversity presupposes but also complements the existence of cultural rights.

In the American region, the American Declaration of the Rights and Duties of Man (Bogotá 1948) reproduces Art 27 of the UDHR. The Charter of the Organization of American States of April 1948 and the American Convention on Human Rights contain only generic commitments regarding the promotion of culture, cultural exchanges and the enjoyment of culture by the whole population. The Additional Protocol to the American Convention on Human Rights on economic, social and cultural rights (San Salvador Protocol) incorporates Art 15 of ICESCR.

The European Convention on Human Rights does not include any cultural rights, but within the Council of Europe other international instruments contain rights of national and language minorities. The fundamental treaties of the European Union state, among their objectives, respect for cultural and linguistic national and regional diversity, and the need for cooperation between Member States to promote awareness and dissemination of culture, cultural heritage protection, cultural exchanges, and artistic and literary creation. In 2010 the Charter of Fundamental Rights of the European Union was incorporated into the Treaties. The Charter proclaims freedom of arts and sciences (Art 13) and a generic mandate to respect cultural, religious and linguistic diversity (Art 22).

The African Charter on Human and Peoples' Rights protects the right to education in Article 17, and also every individual's right to freely take part in the cultural life of his community. The state has been given the responsibility to promote and protect morals and traditional values recognized by the community. The right to self-determination allows people to pursue their social development, and struggle against cultural domination (Art 20). There is also the right to their cultural development with due regard to their freedom and identity, and in the equal enjoyment of the common heritage of mankind. There is a resolve that '. . . it is henceforth essential to pay particular attention to the right to development and that civil and political rights cannot be dissociated from economic, social and cultural rights in their conception as well as universality and that the satisfaction of economic, social and cultural rights is a guarantee for the enjoyment of civil and political rights'.

No regional arrangement for cultural rights operating exists in the Australasian region.

30.2.2.2 Domestic law

In European countries the recognition and regulation of cultural rights takes place more at the legislative than at the constitutional level. Many constitutions make no express reference to culture or are limited to legislative mandates aimed at the promotion of culture or protection of cultural heritage (e.g., Italy). In a few constitutions a mandate related to some specific right to culture is included, as for example the right of access to culture (e.g., Spain). Only three constitutions identify authentic, though quite specific, cultural rights (e.g., copyright protection in Sweden, free development of arts in Bulgaria). In contrast, eight constitutions proclaim cultural rights of national and ethnic minorities; in addition to the cases of Finland and Norway, with longstanding guarantees, six constitutions in Eastern Europe have incorporated such rights.[10] The exception to the rule is the Portuguese Constitution of 2005, which incorporates many of the rights and freedoms to culture and many mandates directed to public authorities.

In European countries organized on a federal or politically decentralized basis, subnational entities often have significant powers in matters of culture and the constitutions of these entities often regulate some cultural rights.

The constitutional references to cultural rights in Anglo-American constitutions are limited. The Constitution of Canada refers to the preservation and enhancement of the multicultural heritage of Canadians, the rights of the aboriginal peoples and the equality of status of English and the French linguistic communities in some provinces. In federal and provincial legislation (culture is a competence of the provinces) there is abundant regulation concerning cultural rights of migrants, national minorities and aboriginal peoples. The US Constitution has no provision concerning the question of cultural rights. There are treaties with aboriginal peoples or tribes in establishing groups with cultural rights, and some state constitutions also recognize cultural, economic and social rights of indigenous peoples.

Elsewhere in the Americas the constitutional regulation of cultural rights is uneven, although one should highlight the complete and detailed regulation contained in some constitutions, especially regarding minority rights. This wide range of regulations begins with the Constitution of Chile, which regulates only creative freedom and copyright; the Constitution of Venezuela follows, which, besides declaring the multiculturalism of Venezuelan culture, adds to the two rights mentioned above the mandate of promoting culture; and the Constitution of Mexico, which also makes reference to rights to natural resources of the 'Indians' and foresees that the law will protect the development of languages, customs, traditions, resources and forms of social organization of indigenous peoples. At the other extreme lie the Constitutions of Ecuador, Brazil and Guatemala, which give greater scope to the rights of citizens to culture both as individuals and as indigenous minorities: they recognize the rights of access to culture and to cultural identity, the freedom to decide membership in one or more cultures, the right to know their own and other cultures, and more. In between these two models are the Constitutions of Argentina and Peru, which recognize the right to cultural identity, individually and collectively; the right to the cultural plurality; and the main rights to culture of indigenous communities, though without as much detail as the previous three.

30.3.1 Content and limitations of cultural rights

30.3.3.1 Content

Cultural rights, as defined in legal texts,[11] by the courts and in scientific doctrine, are complex. They attach to individuals or groups or, in another formulation, to individuals acting alone or in association with others or within in a group or community.

---

10 They are Poland, the Czech Republic, Hungary, Bulgaria, Romania and Slovakia.
11 See especially the General Comment num. 21 to Art 15.1 of the International Covenant on Economic, Social and Cultural Rights made by the Committee on 15 December 2009. Note also the Fribourg Declaration on Cultural Rights in May 2007.

The collective dimension of this right, especially when it relates to ethnic, religious, linguistic or national minorities existing in almost every state, has today special characteristics. The cultural rights of these minorities are mutually conditioned by the recognition of political,[12] economic[13] and social[14] rights of such minorities. This Chapter discusses only the right to culture generally (see Chapter 26).

Cultural rights typically encompass:

- The right to choose their own cultural identity, without impositions or assimilation by another culture. That is, the right to have, create, express and disseminate freely their own values, beliefs, customs, traditions, ways of life and languages, oral and written literature and artistic expression, through which individuals and communities express their 'humanity' and the meaning they give to their existence.
- The right to know their own culture and that of others.
- The right to access and participate in cultural life or in the cultural lives in which each person chooses to join and also the right not to participate: freely contributing to its creation, enjoying the protection of moral and material interests resulting from this contribution to cultural activities, enjoying the existing cultural activities, goods and services, and taking part in the definition and implementation of cultural policies and decisions that impact on cultural rights.

Legal texts frequently mention groups of people for whom these rights must be especially assured: children, women, youth, the elderly, prisoners and, above all, migrants, national and ethnic minorities and indigenous peoples.

Rights to culture impose obligations on public authorities. Some are negative obligations of non-interference in cultural freedoms, non-discrimination for cultural identities and respect for cultural diversity, or the abstention from imposing philosophical, aesthetic or political guidelines to its education and culture programmes.

Other obligations require positive action from the public authorities, and are specified in mandates to perform certain actions to ensure the effective exercise of those rights by their holders. These obligations include:

- The establishment of cultural policies ensuring access to all cultural expression and to media and broadcasting.
- The protection and enrichment of cultural heritage and cultural expressions, including the promotion of cultural goods, services and industries.
- The promotion of exchanges, cooperation and solidarity in the cultural field.
- The establishment of an educational system that, in addition to respect for the diverse cultural identities and freedoms of parents, contributes to the development of cultural identity.
- The promotion of the participation in the definition and implementation of cultural policies.

---

12 As, for example, the right to some kind of self-government of minorities, especially national minorities, or to some kind of mechanisms for participation in specific organs or national decision-making processes.

13 In this sense should be emphasized the inseparable connection of the cultural rights of indigenous peoples with rights to lands and territories and resources traditionally held.

14 For example, the right to maintain some specific forms of social organization.

- The protection of cultural rights against threats from non-state actors such as markets and the media.

30.3.3.2 Limits

Like most rights, cultural rights are subject to limits that in practice define their content. The determination of limits raises numerous conflicts. In most international instruments, these limitations are derived from the existence of other internationally recognized human rights. Cultural rights do not shelter practices, customs, traditions and the like, which infringe on other human rights. There is no cultural relativism in this area; nor does the fact of belonging to a minority culture remove its members from the application of the rules governing human rights. However, according to these international instruments, both determining and applying the limitations must respect the principles of minimum intervention and proportionality.

At the national level there is an important disparity in establishing the limitations of cultural rights. The greater or lesser restriction depends on the type of rights that can be used as a limitation (rights of consumers, rights of employers and the like), the possibility of using as limits other constitutional values or goods (such as the mandate to promote a common cultural identity, foreseen in some constitutions), the application of criteria of political organization (such as the need to ensure minimal cultural homogeneity shared by the human groups that form the state citizenship, or the need to avoid social 'ghettoization' of certain groups), or simply the criteria derived from economic limitations of the states in order to promote the rights to culture. The long controversy between the *communitarian, intercultural* and *multicultural* approaches illustrates the tension between rights to culture, particularly—but not exclusively—in its collective dimension and its multiple juridical and political limitations. This is a permanent and general tension, although in some states and in some historical moments, due to political and economic reasons, it acquires a remarkable intensity as shown, for example, in the recurrent revolts in some European countries, and more extreme cases such the civil war in Sri Lanka or the destruction of indigenous communities in Amazonia.

30.4.1 The rights to culture in practice

Despite the intrinsic importance of cultural rights, directly connected with human dignity and in many cases a necessary condition for peaceful and fruitful coexistence between people and communities, in practice these types of rights still occupy a very marginal position among human rights and have a very limited practical significance.

The causes of these phenomena are diverse:

(a) The right to culture raises problems of identification of its contents. The rights are incorporated into national and international legal instruments through general clauses of vague or programmatic or aspirational content that can include almost anything or nothing, and often it is not clear whether they are simple mandates to governments or authentic rights. Neither the ad hoc committees created to implement international agreements, nor doctrine, nor the sparse jurisprudence of the courts have made this content more precise. In fact, the unspecific nature of cultural rights could explain the relatively limited access of these rights to judicial remedies. And when they are brought to tribunals, generally the request is related to education or language rights, rather than to the right to culture as such. This is similar with regard to the rights of indigenous peoples, whose claims usually refer more to the right to land, natural resources, or political rights, than to cultural rights.

(b) Constitutional systems often lack effective tools to repair the frequent violations of cultural freedoms and especially to accomplish the realization of positive action that require the greater part of the cultural rights.

(c) Legal and factual limitations determine the effective realization of these rights. Limitations derive, for example, from certain obligations of 'integration', not always negligible, imposed by the dominant culture or from the need for public spending that governments do not usually consider a priority.

References

Arzoz, X (2007). 'The Nature of Language Rights', *Journal on Ethnopolitics and Minority Issues in Europe* 6. 2: 1–35, 16.

Fiangold, E (2004). 'Language Rights and Language Justice in the Constitutions of the World', 28 *Language Problems & Language Planning*, 11.

Milian, A (2010). Drets Linguistics per a Tothom (Palma, Lleonard Luntaner).

Solé i Sabaté, JM & Villaroya, J (1994). *Cronologia de la repressió de la llengua i la cultura catalanes*, 1936–1975.

Toksabay, B (2005). 'Conflict over language rights: the case of Kurds and Circassians in Turkey' (MA Thesis, Sabanci University, Spring 2005).

Woehrling, JM (2005). *The European Charter for Regional or Minority Languages: A Critical Commentary* (Council of Europe Publishing, Strasbourg).

Yildiz, K & Düzgören, K (eds) (2002). Türkiye'de Kürtçe (Beyoğlu, İstanbul: Senfoni).

Additional reading

Francioni, F & Scheinin, M (eds) (2008). *Cultural Human Rights* (Leiden/The Netherlands; Martinus Nijhoff Publishers).

Kymlicka, W (2011). 'Liberal multiculturalism and human rights', in Requejo, F & Caminal, M (eds), *Political Liberalism and Plurinational Democracies* (Usa and Canada: Routledge) 73–92.

Stamatopoulou, E (2007). *Cultural Rights in International Law* (Leiden/Boston: Martinus Nijhoff Publishers).

Symonides (1998). 'Cultural Rights: A Neglected Category of Human Rights', 158 *International Journal Social Science* 158: 595.

Environmental rights and future generations

Hong Sik Cho and Ole W Pedersen

31.1 Introduction

Constitutionally enshrined environmental rights have gained an increasingly prominent role in the last 25 to 30 years, for many reasons. The mounting regulatory attention afforded to environmental problems domestically and internationally is testament to the fact that the environment is generally considered a common good in need of preservation. This increase in environmental concern has occurred just as a general trend of protecting societal values through the vocabulary and use of rights developed. Thus, the constitutionalization of environmental rights serves to support the observation that environmental elements such as air, water and soil are finite resources worth protecting, while also highlighting the value that modern societies attach to the environment (Nedelsky).

The result has been widespread support for declaring a constitutional right to the environment. Often these rights aim to secure a minimum level of environmental protection, thereby protecting humans from incidents of pollution threatening human survival. Environmental rights have also been used to secure access to basic environmental amenities such as clean water. Sometimes they have been successfully used to stop developments threatening nature conservation areas and other protected areas. More than 70 countries have some kind of constitutional environmental provisions, and at least 30 among them take the form of environmental rights (Hayward 1998, 152–6, 178; May). Environmental rights appear in constitutions across the world—in developed as well as developing countries. Most commonly, environmental rights are found in recently adopted or amended constitutions. For example, many post-communist countries adopted environmental rights when rewriting their constitutions following the breakdown of the Soviet Union. Likewise, constitutions that have undergone significant changes (such as the Constitution of Iraq) or constitutions that are regularly amended include environmental rights in some form.

Constitutionalizing the environment raises many questions, including: (i) Should the state constitutionalize the environment, and, more importantly, in what form? (ii) What do the constitutional provisions protect and, more importantly, to what degree? (iii) How can courts implement and enforce the constitutional provisions?

These questions involve difficult jurisprudential or policy issues. As to policy, for example, how far society should protect the environment is a highly contentious political question on which there is no clear societal consensus. Implementation and enforcement might be easy once a regulatory regime is created. Yet, even where such a regime exists, one can seek judicial protection against currently unregulated activities. Courts also may worry about how to ensure that the administrative agency implements and enforces the legislative mandate even in the face of factual uncertainty, budgetary restraints and political hostility.

31.2 Humans and the environment

At the international level, one can find noteworthy steps in the direction of adopting the environmental rights vocabulary.[1] Environmental protection has been recognized as so essential to human rights protection that it would not be inappropriate to add an environmental right to the existing portfolio of rights. Perhaps the most cited form of environmental right in this direction is the one proposed in the Legal Principles put forward in the Brundtland Report by the World Commission on Environment and Development: '[a]ll human beings have the fundamental right to an environment adequate for their health and well-being'.[2] By looking only to the adequacy for *human* health and well-being as the criterion of environmental protection, this formulation arguably fails to capture all aspects of environmental concern, which may extend beyond anthropocentrism.

One important criticism of this human-centric formulation challenges the instrumental base that the protection affords the environment; environmental protection need not be contingent on human interests. For present purposes we focus not on the right *of* nature, but rather the right *to* nature. Having said that, while most constitutions maintain an anthropocentric focus on environmental rights, some constitutions provide for a right *for* nature. Ecuador's Constitution now famously includes a right for nature to be restored independent of human proprietary interests. Insofar as one explores the desirability of *constitutionalizing* the environment, one must take into account the political, economic and legal constraints imposed upon humans. This is true even when one focuses on the good of non-humans. The issue here is not about *wholesale* transformation of our society (cf. Eckersley), and the constitutional environmental right is not offered as a cure-all for all aspects of the environmental problem. Furthermore, something less than wholesale transformation is better than nothing: once a fundamental right, anthropocentric though it may be, is institutionalized, social norms may evolve to support more progressive aims (Hayward 2000, 559–60).

31.3 Forms of constitutional environmental provisions and their practicality

Constitutional environmental provisions can take various forms. At the weak end of the continuum, the constitution simply gives the legislature authority to enact environmental legislation. While these general provisions are important, they take the form of policy aims

---

1 To name a few international documents in this direction: Principle 1 of the Stockholm Declaration on the Human Environment of 1972; the Brundtland Report of 1987; the Draft Declaration of Principles on Human Rights and the Environment; and the 1989 UN Convention on the Rights of the Child.
2 World Commission on Environment and Development 1987, 348.

and objectives, and serve to delegate a particular mandate to a legislative or executive body rather than facilitating a specific right (Brandl & Bungert, 17). A slight step beyond occurs when the constitution sets out a constitutional policy to protect the environment. This type of provision may not be self-executing, which means that state or private entities are not required to take any particular actions. A step further is taken where the constitution requires the legislature to address particular environmental issues, awards environmental rights to citizens, or both. These more substantive constitutional provisions may vary in, for example, the specificity by which the constitution sets out environmental goals, the extent to which they recognize competing values, and the degree to which they allow standing to citizens to seek judicial enforcement of environmental provisions, and more (Thompson, 162).

Environmental rights thus seek to promote a specific right to a particular environmental good (substantive as well as procedural), vested in an individual or a group, which creates a corresponding obligation on public authorities, individuals or private enterprises. These rights consequently include substantive rights to a 'healthy', 'safe' or 'balanced' environment, and procedurally focused rights to environmental information or to administrative or judicial redress of decisions relating to the environment (Pedersen).

One common example of environmental rights is found where a constitution provides a substantive right to the environment on a stand-alone basis, as in the environmental charter added to the French Constitution in 2005. This states that all French citizens have the right to live in a 'balanced environment, favorable to human health' (see also Marrani). An example of a procedural environmental right is found in the Constitution of Ukraine, which prohibits secrecy in relation to environmental information, and in the Norwegian Constitution, which provides for a right for people to be 'informed of the state of the natural environment and of the effects of any encroachments on nature that are planned or commenced'.[3] In some constitutions, environmental rights provisions like these are placed alongside traditional civil and political rights, while in others the rights are placed alongside socio-economic rights (see generally May & Daly). The environmental right in the Portuguese Constitution to 'a healthy ecologically balanced human environment' is, for example, placed in the part of the constitution providing for 'Social Rights and Duties'.[4]

In addition to these explicit provisions, environmental rights are at times also derived from other rights. Most commonly, this type of environmental right is derived from the 'right to life'. Examples of this include Indian case law, based on interpreting a constitution that does not refer to any environmental rights. Nevertheless, the Indian Supreme Court has ruled that under Indian law every individual has a fundamental right to the 'enjoyment of pollution-free water and air'.[5] Elsewhere, environmental rights have been derived from other rights, including the right to privacy. Examples of this are most prominently found in the case law from the European Court of Human Rights where the right to respect for private and family life in Article 8 has been interpreted, in line with the Court's practice of interpreting the Convention in light of 'present day' conditions, to include severe environmental pollution and environmental risks (see generally Pedersen).

---

3 Constitution of the Kingdom of Norway, Art 110b and Constitution of Ukraine, ch. II, Article 50: '[e]veryone is guaranteed the right of free access to information about the environmental situation, the quality of food and consumer goods, and also the right to disseminate such information. No one shall make such information secret'.
4 Constitution of Portugal, Article 66.
5 See *Subhash Kumar v State of Bihar* (1991) 1 SCR 5 (Supreme Court of India). Cf. Dam & Tewary.

In many respects the increase in environmental rights provisions in domestic constitutions exemplifies an ongoing convergence or harmonization of constitutions whereby domestic constitutional principles increasingly reflect each other across state borders. Consider the recently enacted Constitution of Iraq, which provides every individual with 'the right to live in a safe environment',[6] and the South African Constitution of 1996, stating that 'everyone has the right to an environment that is not harmful to their health or well-being'.[7]

In the United States, a number of states have adopted environmental rights provisions in their constitutions. These include, *inter alia*, the Constitution of Massachusetts stating that '[t]he people shall have the right to clean air, water, freedom from excessive and unnecessary noise, and the natural, scenic, historic, and aesthetic qualities of their environment'[8] and the Constitution of Illinois granting '[e]ach person . . . the right to a healthful environment'.[9] However, even where state constitutions provide substantive environmental provisions, courts have used a number of different arguments to avoid 'constitutionalizing' environmental considerations. Courts may hold that the provision is not self-executing, that there is no cause of action, and that plaintiffs may lack standing or present an unripe claim (Fernandez). Likewise, courts may narrowly interpret the scope of environmental provisions, allow strong deference for administrative actions and apply reasonableness standards (see Chapter 9).

Notwithstanding hesitant judicial attitudes, constitutionalization of environmental protection as a fundamental right remains attractive. People generally assume that rights, especially those enshrined in the constitution, embody values that cannot easily be compromised. The environmental cause might benefit were people to regard environmental protection as the substance of a constitutional right.

Yet, this potential advantage can be hard to realize in practice. Inclusion of a new right, especially at the highest political level, may be difficult because the new right aims to articulate its inherent *new* substance in 'an institutionalized discourse with some established mechanisms of enforcement' (Hayward 2000, 560). This new substance likely has some aspects where it is in conflict with other existing structures of government, which may impose unnecessary burdens on the legal system (Ruhl 1996).

In the absence of any relevant jurisprudence or societal consensus, critics assert that it would be unwise to constitutionalize an environmental right with no ensuing legislative efforts to clarify its content. Where a constitutional environmental right provision is in place, it is not always the case that the right can be implemented and enforced. Much is left to clarify about the nature, content and scope of the right. Is it positive or negative? Does it give rise to duties of the state or other non-state actors? Are there legal rules available for establishing causation and standard of liability (which often become a decisive factor in environmental cases). Constitutional entrenchment of an individual environmental right with no subsequent attempts to clarify its content might open floodgates to the courts (Ruhl 1997), give the judiciary a *carte blanche* about how to decide cases, and ultimately lead to an environmental version of a Hobbesian war of all against all; that is, a 'war of all environmental rights against all environmental rights'. This is more so if one takes seriously the proposition that environmental rights, just like other rights, mark the 'trumping' status of environmental concerns.

6 Constitution of Iraq, Article 33.
7 Constitution the Republic of South Africa, Article 24.
8 Constitution of the Commonwealth of Massachusetts, Article XCVII.
9 Constitution of Illinois, Article XI section 2.

Furthermore, the issue of indeterminacy is not only conceptual but scientific as well. Causation in environmental problems is often difficult to establish accurately enough to impose on individuals those legal obligations corresponding to the constitutional right to an adequate environment. This is the case even where the right is enforceable against the state. Even if environmental quality has fallen below a threshold that a constitutional provision is interpreted to guarantee, courts cannot be expected to impose on the responsible authority a duty to take appropriate actions. Such decisions often involve difficult trade-offs between environmental protection and other competing values such as economic interest.

Constitutional entrenchment of a new environmental right, whether substantive or procedural, may be superfluous if either existing substantive rights or other constitutional provisions (in the form, for instance, of policy principles) suffice to achieve the desired goals. Environment-friendly interpretation of existing substantive rights such as a right to life, a right to health and a right to physical integrity may have sufficient potential to achieve similar results (Churchill). Other legal or policy principles specified in a wide variety of environmental protection legislation may also work. Some have asserted that such well-known principles as the 'precautionary principle' have constitutional force (see, e.g., Miller).

Even where environmental protection provided for by the existing legal instruments is not sufficient, there is not necessarily a compelling need to constitutionalize an environmental *right*. It might suffice to create general statutory obligations. As John Austin observes, there can be 'some obligations as absolute duties, which exist independently of any correlative right' (Austin, 413–15). By enacting statutes that obligate the general public to protect the environment, harmful activities to the environment can be controlled. In other words, one can effectively protect the environment by enacting objective legal rules that command and control individuals' behaviours, not by enacting subjective legal rules that define individuals' rights.[10] In the US, for instance, the passage of environmental legislation has reduced the potential importance of the constitutional environmental right in most contexts. The state constitutional provisions have rarely been invoked in litigation, and when they have been, the constitutional arguments have often been secondary to the statutory claims (Thompson 158; Fernandez).

31.4 Environmental problems as a political problem

The drive to constitutionalize environmental rights in the early 1970s is to some extent a result of a 'combination of political idealism and scientific naivety' (Thompson, 187). Environmental issues are often discussed in absolute, moral terms: environmental degradation is morally wrong, which justifies outlawing it just as discrimination is outlawed. For example, the Brundtland definition of environmental rights presupposes that current societies can readily achieve certain basic, absolute levels of environmental protection. Only with such presuppositions can one conceive a constitutional provision *guaranteeing* an environment adequate to human health and well-being.

---

10 A statute to remedy 'natural resources damage' such as the Comprehensive Environmental Response, Compensation and Liability Act (CERCLA) in the US would be a good example of such objective legal rules. Sections 107(a)(4)(C) and (f)(1) of the CERCLA authorize the federal and state governments to recover damages for injury to 'natural resources' statutorily defined. Damage recovered must be used to restore the equivalent of the injured resource. On the other hand, CERCLA does not authorize a damage remedy for private owners of natural resources.

Scientific uncertainty and difficult trade-offs are pervasive. The core question of environmental law and policy is mostly how much society should sacrifice economic prosperity in the face of scientific uncertainty in order to achieve environmental health; often this leads to another value-laden question of how to assign liability and responsibility for environmental protection.

No policy-maker can now claim environmental absolutes without considering the regulatory costs needed to achieve them. What a society regards as 'clean' or 'healthy' may depend on existing environmental conditions and the technological and economic limitations facing the society. Therefore, environmental law must grapple with the question of how much environmental protection is worth, which logically leads to the question of how much remediation is affordable. In this light, how well-equipped are courts at resolving these trade-offs in a *constitutional* setting? There may not be public consensus or settled societal norms to guide a resolution. Legislatures have often taken a full range of approaches to environmental trade-offs, from the precautionary principle, technological feasibility and economic feasibility to a broad cost–benefit comparison. In the absence of a prevailing societal norm or public consensus, courts often feel at a loss as to how to strike a proper balance between jobs and the environment. Furthermore, comparing costs and benefits in environmental disputes is not straightforward. A single metric is necessary to measure the costs and benefits of particular actions. Because there is often no market for environmental goods and services, costs and benefits in environmental conflicts are often incommensurate (Sunstein).

To most courts, a key question in deciding whether an environmental provision is self-executing is whether the provision sets out a sufficient rule by which to decide cases without any legislative guidance. From an analytic viewpoint, environmental problems can be boiled down to the question: how adequate is adequate enough? In fact, much discussion over environmental problems is a process of negotiation between different standards applied by different people to different questions. The fact that people have different answers to these questions reflects the diversity of values. Some value creating jobs over protecting natural habitats, while some willingly give up their material abundance to protect endangered species in a remote corner of the planet. The essence of environmental problems is the conflict of competing values.

In contemporary political philosophy, it is widely accepted that values are not only plural but also incommensurable and incomparable. Plurality of values means that the values cannot be encompassed by a value from a higher stratum, and incommensurability or incomparability means that there is no common standard or measure to determine which one prevails over the other. As a matter of fact, there are abundant examples of incommensurable values in everyday life. Joseph Raz describes one such situation by comparing a walk in the park and reading a book with a glass of whisky on a Friday evening (Raz, ch. 13). Given this, it is natural for most courts to feel uncomfortable determining the appropriate methodology and standards for evaluating environmental issues such as the permissible level of pollution or appropriate land uses.

All these considerations may make courts characterize environmental trade-offs as political questions, which implies that the political process, not the judicial process, is appropriate to resolve them. This is still so even where a constitution places a clean and healthy environment at the top of its list of fundamental rights; courts cannot evade the economic trade-offs common in the environmental field. Even in cases of traditional fundamental rights, realities of law are likely to push courts toward a more flexible approach that takes into account trade-offs. For example, while no one can negate that right to life is a paramount right among constitutional rights, no civilized country bans automobiles even though allowing cars will inevitably result in violation of the right to life by increasing the number of fatalities by car accidents (Calabresi). When courts decide on issues related to a constitutional provision, balancing is almost always required against other constitutional provisions. The list of fundamental rights in constitutions does not stop with environmental rights, but goes on to include rights such as liberty of freedom and property. Virtually all environmental–economic trade-offs involve economic rights. In this way, substantive constitutional environmental rights, even where provided in absolute terms such as 'clean' or 'safe', should be read to inherently incorporate a balance.

Under these circumstances, substantive constitutional environmental rights cases may threaten to turn the courts into the ultimate societal arbiter of environmental trade-offs. Policy analysts historically have assumed that legislatures have a comparative advantage both in fact-finding needed to formulate environmental law and in its implementation (see generally Chayes; Rebell & Hughes). Compared with courts, legislatures and executives have advantage in terms of budgets and expert staffs. This is more problematic with substantive environmental rights because these are positive rights requiring the state to actively provide certain substantive goods or services. As compared to legislative and regulatory branches, courts cannot create government programmes on their own, do not systematically overview governmental policy and lack bureaucratic arms. If a right is not enforceable in practice, then constitutionalizing it would arguably do more harm than good by degrading the normative force of other enforceable rights (Alston; cf. Hayward 1998, 65–66).

Procedural inflexibility may also cause problems when it comes to adjudication. When faced with a specific claim, a court may not have anyone before it who can adequately represent the broader public environmental interests. Without relevant legislation, courts may have to evaluate unfamiliar information and use it to formulate new policies reflecting existing laws in the face of complexities of new environmental challenges.

31.5 Distrust or passive virtue?

A powerful argument for constitutionalizing the environment is distrust of democracy. By constitutionalizing environmental rights, one can put them above capricious everyday politics. When one evaluates this argument, however, one must also consider it in relation to another point: entrenchment of a right implies a transfer of as much power from an elected legislature to the judiciary. To apply certain provisions, courts have to interpret them. This brings with it the prospect of courts becoming the final arbiter concerning central societal values by revising and adapting basic rights. If environmental problems are caused by distorted representation of the interests concerned in decision-making processes, courts may have a legitimate reason to intervene. In the ideal world, legislatures are the most representative and responsive to the public. Insofar as judicial intervention moves legislatures toward that ideal, the public is better served. In this regard, citizen's access to courts is certainly an important feature of constitutional democracy.

As Joseph Sax points out, the problem in the context of environmental conflicts is that a diffuse majority is often made subject to the will of a concerted minority (Sax). If environmental problems can be recognized as the disproportionate representation in the decision-making process, all that must be done is to even out the political and administrative postures of the parties concerned. If representative equalization can be done judicially, one can properly leave the ultimate decision to the democratic process. Thus, it is only to provide the most appropriate climate for democratic policy-making that courts can intervene.

Finally, one argument that supports the promulgation of constitutional environmental rights, and thereby the delegation of decision-making power to the courts, is the fact that such rights aim at facilitating a bare minimum of environmental quality, in turn contributing to human survival. That is to say, where government agencies (and private entities) fail in their responsibilities to provide protection of basic living conditions, enforceable constitutional environmental provisions can be relied on to offer judicial remedies securing the containment of pollution threatening basic living conditions.

31.6 Rights of future generations

By their very nature, environmental rights are strongly linked to the question of how to strike a balance between the needs of current generations and the interests of future generations. A strong argument in support of including rights of future generations in constitutional documents is that, like the environment itself, future generations cannot present themselves to today's law-makers, and so cannot make representations aimed at guaranteeing that their needs are taken into account. While rights for future generations inevitably create certain problems (see below), the inclusion of these rights in a constitution aims to protect the needs of an otherwise vulnerable group. Inevitably, political and legal decisions affecting the environment will have an effect on future generations and their ability (or inability) to experience comparable environmental conditions. Having said that, it is not merely environmental decisions that will be of relevance to future generations. Economic, fiscal and monetary decisions, as well as decisions relating to pension contributions and healthcare, all potentially affect future generations. In legal debates, however, the relationship between current and future generations has played a prominent role in environmental law settings. The urge to ensure that the needs of future generations are taken into account has found support in calls for 'intergenerational justice', 'intergenerational responsibility' and 'intergenerational rights' (to mention a few).

From a constitutional law point of view, intergenerational considerations manifest themselves in a number of ways. First and foremost, a number of constitutions make explicit reference to future generations. Some constitutions make a general reference in the preamble of the constitution to the responsibility toward future generations. The Constitution of Switzerland states that the Swiss people and the Cantons (regions) are 'conscious of their common achievements and their responsibility towards future generations'.[11] The Ukrainian Constitution likewise observes in the Preamble that the Ukrainian Parliament is 'aware of our responsibility before God, our own conscience, past, present and future generations',[12] and the Constitution of Poland refers in the Preamble to the obligation to 'bequeath to future generations all that is valuable from our [. . .] heritage'.[13] While the references to future (and past) generations in the preamble of a constitution serve as a backdrop for the rest of the constitution and often provide an interpretive background, the preambular provisions are necessarily contingent on the rest of the constitution. In other words, the preambular provisions are often not self-executing and do not create any rights of action on their own.

Elsewhere, the substantive part of the constitution refers to intergenerational responsibilities. Often this is done in the context of an environmental provision or a provision relating to financial rules and responsibilities. Examples of constitutional environmental provisions with reference to future generations are found across the globe in Latin and South America, Europe

---

11 Constitution of Switzerland, Preamble.
12 Constitution of Ukraine, Preamble.
13 Constitution of Poland, Preamble.

and Africa. The Constitution of Argentina refers to the need to meet 'present needs without endangering those of future generations' in the provision providing for a right to healthy environment.[14] The Constitution of Germany notes that 'mindful also of its responsibility toward future generations, the State shall protect the natural bases of life',[15] and the Constitution of South Africa refers to the right 'to have the environment protected, for the benefits of future and present generations'.[16]

As discussed above, the application of the constitutional environmental rights provisions are often hampered by reference to issues of self-execution and judicial restraint. One significant exemption to this, however, is found in the celebrated decision delivered by the Supreme Court of the Philippines in *Minors Oposa*.[17] There the Court found in favour of the plaintiffs who sought the cancellation of timber operations in the area in which they lived, by relying on a constitutional provision affording the people a right to a healthy environment. While the plaintiffs in the case were all minors (duly represented by their parents), they based their claim on the argument that they 'represent their generation as well as generations yet unborn'. The Court noted *obiter dictum* that the ability to 'sue [o]n behalf of the succeeding generations can only be based on the concept of intergenerational responsibility' and that 'every generation has a responsibility to the next to preserve the . . . full enjoyment of a balanced and healthful ecology'.[18] As a result, the *Oposa* decision has been heralded as a watershed in the attempt to secure intergenerational responsibilities in domestic constitutions. Nevertheless, as argued by Gatmaytan, the significance of the decision has often been overstated; the case was never pursued in the lower courts after being remanded by the Supreme Court, no timber licence was cancelled as a result of the decision and the groundbreaking statements of the Court were merely *obiter dictum* (Gatmaytan).

A third category of intergenerational provisions not linked to environmental issues are found where constitutional provisions seek to secure a certain level of financial stability. Such provisions are fewer than the intergenerational environmental rights provisions and often do not explicitly refer to intergenerational responsibilities. Examples include the German Constitution, which provides for a nominal cap on federal borrowing of 0.35 percent of GDP,[19] and the Constitution of Poland, which contains a provision seeking to limit national public debt to three-fifths of GDP.[20]

An altogether different approach to the question of intergenerational responsibility is found in the Israeli Constitution (which notably is not codified into one single text like the constitution of most other countries). In Israel, the parliament (Knesset) opted for establishing a Commission for Future Generations tasked with assessing the effects that bills passing through Parliament would have on future generations. This novel institution was established as a result of the tendency among elected politicians to focus on current problems and needs at the expense of future generations (see generally Shoham & Lamay).

---

14 Constitution of Argentina, ch 1 s 41(1).
15 Constitution of Germany, art 20A.
16 Constitution of South Africa, art 24.
17 *Minors Oposa v Secretary of the Department of Environment and Natural Resources (DENR)* (1993) 224 SCRA 792; (1994) 33 ILM 173 (Supreme Court of the Philippines).
18 *Minors Oposa v Secretary of the Department of Environment and Natural Resources (DENR)* (1994) 33 ILM 173, 177, 185 (Supreme Court of the Philippines).
19 Constitution of Germany, art 115(2).
20 Constitution of Poland, art 215(5).

The Commission, which was established as an internal advisory part of the Knesset, had the power to request information from government entities and could delay the legislative process in order to prepare reports describing the implications that a bill would have on future generations. The Commission came to rely on the concept of sustainable development, which famously asks us to balance competing intergenerational considerations.[21] Notwithstanding the innovative approach taken by the Knesset (but perhaps symptomatic of the problems associated with trying to take into account the needs of future generations), the Commission stopped functioning only a few years after its adoption.

The concept of sustainable development has found its way into a number of constitutions. The French Environmental Charter provides that 'in order to secure sustainable development, the choices made to meet the needs of the present should not jeopardize the ability of future generations and other peoples to meet their own needs',[22] and the Constitution of Sweden states that the 'public institutions shall promote sustainable development leading to a good environment for present and future generations'.[23]

As highlighted by the short tenure of the Commission for Future Generations, constitutional reference to future generations is not problem-free. Where such references are made in the language of rights, classic understandings of rights instruct us that we must identify a rights holder. The problem this raises in relation to future generations becomes immediately clear when we consider that future generations are, for obvious reasons, not currently able to assert such rights. Critics of intergenerational rights often point out that future generations cannot have anything, let alone rights (Beckerman & Pasek). To this, proponents of intergenerational rights argue that future generations will surely *come* to hold rights once they are born (Tremmel). Other problems relate to how we identify future generations. Are we referring to future individuals or groups of individuals?

The relationship between present and future generations is addressed in numerous constitutions. These provisions are often vague and their exact implications are not clear. Most provisions simply refer to the need to take into account future generations without necessarily providing for any administrative framework for how to do so or any checks and balances to secure that adequate consideration has been afforded future generations.

31.7 Conclusion

As the public consensus concerning environmental controls develops, the argument for substantive constitutional environmental rights is likely to grow. Although constitutional environmental rights have the potential to add impetus to the need for environmental protection, these developments are far from problem-free. The main problems with constitutionalizing environmental rights, as discussed here, relate to the vagueness of such provisions and lack of statutory guidance. As a result, constitutional environmental rights provisions often remain subject to the will of judiciaries and so the extent to which the right is actually protected may be illusory.

---

21 Shoham & Lamay observe that the focus on sustainable development, to some extent, has driven the agenda away from strict environmental issues (which are often considered controversial) into less divisive topics such as economic and social problems: at p. 254.
22 Constitutional Amendment on the French Environment Charter, art 2.
23 Constitution of Sweden, art 2.

References

Alston, P (1984). 'Conjuring Up New Human Rights: A Proposal for Quality Control', *American Journal of International Law* 78:607.

Austin, J (1873). Lectures on Jurisprudence (4th edn, revised and edited by Robert Campbell). (Oxford University, J Murray).

Beckerman, W & Pasek, J (2001). *Justice, Posterity and the Environment* (Oxford, Oxford University Press).

Brandl, E & Bungert, H (1992). 'Constitutional Entrenchment of Environmental Protection: A Comparative Analysis of Experience Abroad', *Harvard Environmental Law Review* 16:1.

Calabresi, G (1985). *Ideals, Beliefs, Attitudes, and the Law: Private Law Perspective on a Public Law Problem* (Syracuse, Syracuse University Press).

Chayes, A (1976). 'The Role of the Judge in Public Law Litigation', *Harvard Law Review* 89:1281.

Churchill, R (1996). 'Environmental Rights in Existing Human Rights Treatise', in Boyle, A & Anderson, M (eds), *Human Rights Approaches to Environmental Protection* (Oxford, Clarendon).

Dam, S & Tewary, V (2005). 'Polluting Environment, Polluting Constitution: Is a "Polluted" Constitution Worse than a Polluted Environment?', *Journal of Environmental Law* 17:383.

Eckersley, R (2004). *The Green State: Rethinking Democracy and Sovereignty* (Cambridge, MIT Press).

Fernandez, JL (1993). 'State Constitutions, Environmental Rights Provisions, and the Doctrine of Self-Execution: A Political Question?', *Harvard Environmental Law Review* 17:333.

Gatmaytan, DB (2010). 'Judicial Restraint and the Enforcement of Environmental Rights in the Philippines', *Oregon Review of International Law* 12(1):1.

Hayward, T (1998). *Political Theory and Ecological Values* (New York, St Martin Press).

—— (2000). 'Constitutional Environmental Rights: A Case for Political Analysis', *Political Studies* 48:558.

Marrani, D (2008). 'The Second Anniversary of the Constitutionalisation of the French Charter for the Environment: Constitutional and Environmental Implications', *Environmental Law Review* 10:9.

May, JR (2005–2006). 'Constituting Fundamental Environmental Rights Worldwide', *Pace Environmental Law Review* 23:113.

— & Daly, E (2010). 'Vindicating Fundamental Environmental Rights Worldwide', *Oregon Review of International Law* 11: 365.

Miller, C (1995). 'Environmental Rights, European Fact or English Fiction', *Journal of Law and Society* 22:374.

Nedelsky, J (2008). Reconceiving Rights and Constitutionalism, *Journal of Human Rights* 7: 139–173.

Pedersen, OW (2008). 'European Environmental Human Rights and Environmental Rights: A Long Time Coming?', *Georgetown International Environmental Law Review* 21:73.

Raz, J (1986). *The Morality of Freedom* (Oxford, Oxford University Press).

Rebell, MA & Hughes, RL (1997). 'Efficacy and Engagement: The Remedies Problem Posed by *Sheff v O'Neill* and a Proposed Solution', *Connecticut Law Review* 29:1115.

Ruhl, JB (1996). 'Complexity Theory as a Paradigm for the Dynamical Law-and-Society System', *Duke Law Journal* 45:849.

—— (1997). 'An Environmental Rights Amendment: Good Message, Bad Idea', *Natural Resources and Environment* 11:46.

Sax, J (1970). 'The Public Trust Doctrine in Natural Resources: Effective Judicial Intervention', *Michigan Law Review* 68:471.

Shoham, S & Lamay, N (2006). 'Commission for Future Generations in the Knesset: Lessons Learnt', in Tremmel, JC (ed), *Handbook of Intergenerational Justice* (Cheltenham, Edward Elgar).

Sunstein, CR (1999). *Free Market and Social Justice* (New York, Oxford University Press).

Thompson, BH (2003). 'Constitutionalizing the Environment: The History and Future of Montana's Environmental Provisions', *Montana Law Review* 64:157.

Tremmel, JC (2006). 'Establishing Intergenerational Justice in National Constitutions', in Tremmel, JC (ed), *Handbook of Intergenerational Justice* (Cheltenham, Edward Elgar).

World Commission on Environment and Development (1987). *Our Common Future* (Oxford, Oxford University Press).

Additional reading

Anton, DK & Shelton, D (2011). *Environmental Protection and Human Rights* (New York, Cambridge University Press).

Dworkin, R (1995). 'Constitutionalism and Democracy', European Journal of Philosophy 3:2.

Hayward, T (2005). *Constitutional Environmental Rights* (Oxford, Oxford University Press).

Hiskes, R (2009). *The Human Right to a Green Future: Environmental Rights and Intergenerational Justice* (New York, Cambridge University Press).

Nickel, J (1993). 'The Human Right to a Safe Environment: Philosophical Perspectives on Its Scope and Justification', *Yale Journal of International Law* 18:281.

Key words

Environmental rights, constitution, environmental protection, future generations

Part IV

New challenges

32

Asylum and refugees

Michelle Foster* and Jonathan Klaaren†

32.1 Introduction

The need for individuals to seek asylum outside their country of nationality or habitual residence is not a new phenomenon; rather, refugees have been recognised as such at least since
the Treaty of Westphalia established the modern state system in 1648.[1] However, it was not
until the early part of the twentieth century, which witnessed a series of significant population displacements following World War I (Hathaway 1990, 136), that the international
community, and specifically European states, apprehended the need to develop normative
standards for the recognition of those seeking asylum (Hathaway 1991, 1–6), a development
that ultimately culminated in the formulation of the 1951 Refugee Convention, the 'cornerstone of the international refugee protection regime' today.[2] While the Convention was
generally respected and implemented in the early decades following its inception, and indeed
its scope expanded by an amending Protocol in 1967,[3] a range of factors—including changed
geo-political dynamics, the increased ease of travel and concomitant erection of barriers by
many (mainly Northern) destination states—has meant that vindication of the right to seek
asylum has indeed become a new challenge.

* I am grateful to Louise Brown, LLB, Melbourne Law School, as well as the Library Research
Service at Melbourne Law School, for excellent research assistance for this chapter. This author
acknowledges the support of the Australian Research Council (DP1096791).

† I am grateful to Elizabeth Power, LLM, Wits Law School, for excellent research assistance for this
chapter. This author acknowledges the support of the National Research Foundation.

1 Barnett, 239, discussing the Huguenots who fled France in 1685. See also Hathaway 1990, 134–5.

2 UNHCR Executive Committee, *Conclusion on the Provision of International Protection including through
Complementary Forms of Protection*, No 103 (LVI)- 2005 at [1]. The *Convention relating to the Status of
Refugees*, 189 UNTS 137, was adopted on 28 July 1951, and entered into force on 22 April 1954.

3 *The Protocol Relating to the Status Refugees*, 606 UNTS 267, adopted 31 January 1967 and entered into
force on 4 October 1967, removed the temporal and geographical restrictions on the scope of the
1951 Convention, meaning that henceforth it was able to be applied to all refugees regardless of
when and where their need for protection arose.

While a significant number of domestic constitutions contain a right of asylum, or associated right or power, international and regional legal regimes are increasingly significant for a state determining refugee status and hence for individuals seeking to realise this right. However, constitutional rights more broadly have remained an important source for both asylum seekers (those who claim protection but have not yet been determined as refugees) and refugees in seeking protection from the excesses of executive action, including in the areas of access to judicial review, detention and rights related to dignity such as the right to work. The salience of constitutional rights has become particularly apparent as the challenge of refugee protection has intensified in recent years.

32.2 Constitutional recognition of refugees and asylum

France, which recognised a constitutional right to asylum following the 1789 Revolution,[4] appears to have one of the few constitutions that recognised such a right prior to World War II.[5] The massive population movements during and after the War, which had underlined the need for a new and enduring international instrument for the protection of refugees, were also clearly in the minds of those drafting new national constitutions during this time. Hence, while one study estimates that approximately 32 percent of modern constitutions grant a right to asylum or contain provisions for the protection of stateless individuals, it notes that the number of constitutions containing a right to asylum 'increased dramatically after the end of World War II'.[6]

Although described broadly as a 'right to asylum', an analysis of the specific relevant provisions in modern constitutions reveals distinct methods by which asylum is recognised or mentioned in domestic constitutions. Such provisions vary significantly and range from the conferral of rights of considerable weight and direct applicability, to those that merely confer a power to grant asylum rather than endowing any specific rights on individuals.

Four aspects are particularly noteworthy. First, some constitutions recognise a positive right to asylum in a way that appears to confer a subjective right on an individual: for example, the Basic Law for the Federal Republic of Germany provides that, '[a]nybody persecuted on political grounds shall enjoy the right of asylum'.[7] Second, some constitutions recognise the right to asylum as a subjective right but appear to condition it by reference to 'the order of the

---

4 Article 120 of the Constitution of 1793: see Lambert, Messineo & Tiedemann, 17.
5 The study by ConstitutionMaking.org, states that '[i]n 2000 about 40% of constitutions in force granted the right to asylum as opposed to almost none in the 1940s': at [3].
6 Report on 'Right to Asylum', 20 May 2008 by ConstitutionMaking.org Option Reports at [3].
7 Article 16(II)(2), Basic Law 1949; now Article 16a(1) following a 1993 amendment: see Hailbronner, 160–1. See also *Constitution of the Republic of Haiti*, 1987, Article 57; *Constitution of the Republic of Indonesia*, 1945, Article 28G (2); *Constitution of the Republic of Macedonia* 1991, Article 29; *Constitution of the Republic of Paraguay*, 1992, Article 43; *Constitution of the Republic of Portugal* 1976, Article 33.8; and *Constitution of the Republic of Serbia*, 2006, Article 57; *Constitution of the Bolivarian Republic of Venezuela*, 1999, Article 69. In other constitutions the relevant provision is phrased more as an obligation on the state, but presumably would have a similar effect: see *Constitution of the Republic of Costa Rica*, 1949, Article 31; *Constitution of the Republic of Cuba*, 1976, Article 13; *Charter of Fundamental Rights and Basic Freedoms*, Czech Republic, Article 43; *Constitution of the Arab Republic of Egypt*, 1971, Article 53; *Socialist Constitution of the Democratic People's Republic of Korea*, 1972, Article 80; *Constitution of the Russian Federation*, 1993, Article 63; *Constitution of the Republic of Bulgaria*, 1991, Article 98.10.

laws and regulations in force',[8] or similar phrase,[9] which may be interpreted as providing discretion to the law-making branch of the relevant state to condition the content of the right.[10] Third, some constitutions embody only a negative right; that is, the right of political refugees *not* to be extradited or deported,[11] which leaves open the question of whether the status of refugee or asylum has any positive content. Finally, some constitutions define the right as belonging to the state (in some cases specifically the president),[12] which for example, 'may grant the right of asylum to persons persecuted in other states for political or religious beliefs or their ethnic affiliation'.[13] Such provisions do not appear materially different from those constitutions that do not explicitly mention asylum or refugees, but confer plenary power in the (often federal) parliament with respect to 'aliens', 'immigration' or a similarly generic concept.[14]

As this survey indicates, constitutional reference to, or recognition of, the concept of asylum is often highly conditional and thus, in practice, provides little protection to asylum seekers in many states. Yet, even in those states whose constitutions provide the most robust protection, international and regional instruments have become much more significant both

8 *Constitution of Burkina Faso*, 1991, Article 9.

9 See for example, *Constitution of the Republic of Albania*, 1998, Article 40; *Political Constitution of Columbia*, 1991, Article 36; *Constitution of the Italian Republic*, 1947, Article 10; *Constitution of the Republic of Poland*, 2006, Article 56; *Constitution of the Republic of Rwanda*, 2003, Article 25; *Constitution of the Republic of Slovenia*, 1991, Article 48; *Constitution of the Democratic Republic of East Timor*, 2001, Section 10; *Constitution of the Republic of Hungary*, 1949, Article 65; *Constitution of the Republic of Moldova*, 1994, Article 19(3); *Constitution of the Slovak Republic*, 1992, Article 53; *Permanent Constitution of the State of Qatar*, 2004, Article 58; *Constitution of the Republic of El Salvador,* Article 28; *Constitution of the Islamic Republic of Afghanistan*, 2004, Article 4.

10 This is the case for example in Italy, where the relevant constitutional provision has no effect until legislation implementing it is enacted, which has not to date occurred: Messineo in Goodwin-Gill & Lambert, 89–90.

11 For example, the *Constitution of the Democratic and People's Algerian Republic*, 1989, Article 69; *Constitution of the Republic of Yemen*, 1991, Article 46; *Constitution of the Kingdom of Bahrain*, 1973, Article 21; *Constitution of the Hashemite Kingdom of Jordan,* 1952, Article 22; *Constitution of the State of Kuwait*, 1962, Article 46; *Basic Statute of the State of Oman*, 1996, Article 36; *Constitution of the Tunisia Republic*, 1959, Article 17; *Constitution of the United Arab Emirates*, 1971, Article 38.

12 See for example, *Constitution of the Republic of Armenia*, 1995, Article 55; *Constitution of the Republic of Kazakhstan,* 1995, Article 43.14; *Constitution of the Republic of Uzbekistan*, 1992, Article 93.22.

13 *Constitution of the Republic of Belarus*, 1994, Article 12; *Constitution of the People's Republic of China*, 1982, Article 32; *Constitution of the Islamic Republic of Iran*, 1979, Article 155; *Constitution of Mongolia*, 1992, Article 18.4; *Spanish Constitution* 1978, Article 13.4. See also *Basic Law* of Saudi Arabia, 1992, Article 42, clearly reposing discretion in the state; *Constitution of the Republic of Croatia*, 1990, Article 33; *Angolan Law of Constitutional Revision*, 1992, Article 26, and *Constitution of the Republic of Montenegro* 2007, Article 44.

14 See for example, the *Australian Constitution*, s 51 (xix) and (xxvii); Canadian *Constitution Act*, 1867, s 91(25). In the US, while there is no specific Constitutional provision concerning immigration, the long-established 'plenary power' doctrine provides that 'Congress and the executive branch have broad and often exclusive authority over immigration decisions' (Motomura, 547). For an excellent overview of current US asylum law, see Legomsky in Kneebone (ed). For a more specific reference to refugees or asylum in the context of the allocation of power in a federal system, see *A Proclamation of the Constitution of the Federal Democratic Republic of Ethiopia*, 1995, Article 51.18; Iraqi Constitution, 2005, Article 110-Fifth; *Constitution of the Republic of Uganda*, 1995, Article 189.

for states and for individuals wishing to assert a right to remain in a state by virtue of their need for international protection.[15]

This phenomenon can be explained by at least three factors. First, the Refugee Convention enjoys a large number of state ratifications, with 147 states being party to either the Convention or Protocol, or both.[16] Although not automatically operative in most domestic legal systems, because most are dualist, many states have decided to implement the key terms of the Convention into their domestic law by way of legislation. The 1951 Convention sets out a universal definition of qualification for refugee status,[17] as well as a range of rights to which refugees are entitled—that is, it provides the content of such status.[18] The Convention defines a refugee as a person who has a well-founded fear of being persecuted for reasons of race, religion, nationality, membership of a particular social group or political opinion. This is often significantly broader than the concept as embodied in domestic constitutions,[19] where states have often combined the different sources into a more comprehensive status largely based on the Refugee Convention definition.[20]

To a certain extent, this dilution of the significance of constitutional-based refugee status has reflected and coincided with the recognition that idiosyncratic domestic constitutional approaches to defining qualification for asylum or refugee status cannot legitimately be relied upon to colour the 'true autonomous and international meaning' of an international treaty.[21] Hence, for example, the earlier approach of German courts, which restricted Convention status to those who feared persecution by *state* agents—and thus conversely excluded those fleeing from *non-state* agents—was criticised because of its origin in domestic constitutional principles.[22]

A second significant influence has been the important parallel developments in three regions of the world. Nations in Africa, Latin America and Europe have relied both on the notion that 'international co-operation' is required to find 'a satisfactory solution' to the 'social and humanitarian' challenge of refugee protection,[23] as well as the drafters' explicit hope that contracting parties would expand international protection beyond the definition of 'refugee' as provided in the Convention,[24] to conclude regional treaties and agreements that largely expand the application of Convention rights to others in need of international protection.

---

15 See for example, Lambert *et al*, who conclude that in relation to France, Germany and Italy, 'international obligations and recent European Commitments have absorbed [constitutional asylum's] distinctiveness, making it a redundant, almost obsolete, concept': at 16.
16 As of 1 April 2011: see http://www.unhcr.org/3b73b0d63.html; 142 states are party to both (last checked 14 February 2012).
17 Article 1A(2). It should also be noted that the Convention does not distinguish between asylum seekers and refugees; rather, a person is a refugee as soon as they factually meet the definition.
18 See Articles 2–34.
19 For example, in Germany the Basic Law refers only to the 'politically persecuted' (Article 16a(1)); in France to 'any foreigner who is persecuted for his action in pursuit of freedom' (Article 53.1); and in Portugal to those whose political activities put them at risk (Article 33.8).
20 See Lambert *et al*, 18–21 (France), at 25 (Italy) and 31–32 (Germany).
21 *R (ex parte Adan) v Secretary of State for the Home Department* [2001] 2 A.C. 477 per Lord Steyn.
22 See, for example, Marx. This has since been altered by the Qualification Directive. But we note that Germany retains an idiosyncratic approach to defining religious persecution that is also based on its constitution and has been heavily criticised: see Geldbach.
23 Preamble to the Refugee Convention.
24 See para E of the Final Act of the United Nations Conference of Plenipotentiaries on the Status of Refugees and Stateless Persons.

The Organization of African Unity (now African Union) formulated the first such agreement in 1969.[25] It is designed to expand refugee status to include 'every person who, owing to external aggression, occupation, foreign domination or events seriously disturbing public order in either part or the whole of his country of origin or nationality, is compelled to leave . . . in order to seek refuge in another place . . .'[26] It is the dominant legal instrument governing refugee protection in Africa, having now been ratified by 45 of the 53 member states of the African Union[27] and implemented in much of the relevant domestic legislation for the protection of refugees in individual African states,[28] as well as guiding and shaping UNHCR's considerable work in Africa.[29]

The second regional arrangement is embodied in the *Cartagena Declaration*, adopted by 10 Latin American states in 1984,[30] which similarly extends refugee protection to ' . . . persons who have fled their country because their lives, safety, or freedom have been threatened by generalized violence, foreign aggression, internal conflicts, massive violations of human rights or other circumstances which have seriously disturbed public order'.[31] Although not formally binding on participating states, it has nonetheless come to be very significant in expanding refugee protection in Latin America, with 15 states having incorporated the more expansive criteria for qualification for protection, in addition to the Convention definition, into domestic legislation.[32]

Third, the 27 Member States of the European Union (EU) have in recent decades developed a 'Common European Asylum System' whereby all Member States (already party to the 1951 Refugee Convention) are now also governed by the Charter of Fundamental Rights of the European Union, which guarantees the right to asylum.[33] A key method of realising the objective of a common asylum system has been the formulation of a series of Council Directives concerning both procedural standards and those designed to ensure uniform interpretation of international standards.[34] Since all such Directives are required to be transposed into the domestic law of Member States, they will have a significant impact on the scope of protection available in individual Member States.[35] The final element of the common system

25 1969 Organization of African Unity Convention Governing the Specific Aspects of Refugee Problems in Africa, 1001 UNTS 45, adopted 10 September 1969, entered into force 20 June 1974.

26 *Id*, Art I(2).

27 As at 02/08/2011; http://www.au.int/en/sites/default/files/Refugee_Problems_in_Africa.pdf (last checked 20 February 2012).

28 Okoth-Obbo, 97–98. For a very precise and current description of relevant legislation, see Van Garderen & Ebenstein in Zimmermann, 196–201.

29 See statement by *UNHCR spokesperson Andrej Mahecic, on 8 September 2009, 40th anniversary of the OAU Convention;* see also Rankin, 419. Of course, *implementation* of refugee law is a significant problem in Africa: see Crisp, [22]–[33].

30 See Annual Report of the Inter-American Commission on Human Rights 1984-85, OEA/Ser.L/ II.66, doc. 10, rev. 1, at 190–3.

31 *Id*, Conclusion 3.

32 Piovesan & Jubilut in Zimmermann, 219–20.

33 Article 18; see Gil-Bazo.

34 Council Directive 2004/83/EC of 29 April 2004, OJ 2004 L 304, and corrigendum, OJ 2005 L 204, Preamble para 6. We note that a revised version of this Directive was approved in December 2011: see 20.12.2011; L 337/9.

35 Although there is concern that in some respects the Qualification Directive adopts an approach that is narrower than that required by the Refugee Convention. In general, see Klug, 'Regional Developments: Europe' in Zimmermann (ed), 117–144 and Battjes.

is embodied in the Dublin Regulation, which allocates responsibility for refugee status determination to the state through which an applicant first entered the EU.[36] In at least one Member State, France, a constitutional amendment has been effected in order to authorise the conclusion of such agreements with 'European States that are bound by commitments identical with its own in the matter of asylum and the protection of human rights and fundamental freedoms'.[37]

A unique aspect of the EU governance structure is that, by contrast to other regions, a court (the Court of Justice of the European Union) is responsible for enforcing and implementing EU law, and it is evident that the Court's jurisprudence has and will continue to exercise significant influence over the formulation of asylum and refugee law and policy in Member States.[38] Further, the European Court of Human Rights—which enforces the European Convention on Human Rights to which the 47 Member States of the Council of Europe are party—has long issued binding decisions establishing the scope of entitlement to, and the content of, the protection required to be extended to asylum seekers and refugees pursuant to the European Convention,[39] which has in turn had a significant impact on state policy in this area (see for example Mole). So, in Europe, regional refugee law, as interpreted and enforced by regional courts, has had the most significant impact upon state sovereignty in relation to asylum.

A final important reason why many of the constitutional provisions vis-a-vis asylum and/ or refugees may have limited practical significance in determining qualification for refugee status is that many of the states with such provisions, particularly those in the developing world, either tend to predominantly produce rather than receive refugees themselves (as in North Korea) or, more commonly, simply have not established adequate procedures for determining status; hence leaving the right effectively redundant. In many such states, the UN refugee agency (UNHCR) undertakes refugee status determination, which is carried out by reference to international rather than domestic standards.[40]

32.3 Constitutional rights and refugees

Thus far this chapter has considered the relevance of explicit constitutional guarantees relating to asylum and the impact of international and regional refugee law on the ongoing relevance of such provisions. We now turn to consider an important second source of constitutional protection for securing the rights of refugees, namely general human rights

---

36 Council Regulation (EC) No 343/2003 of 18 February 2003, OJ 2003 L 50.
37 French Constitution, Article 53.1. See Guendelsberger, 142–52. See also discussion of reform in Germany by Hailbronner, 160–4 and Marx & Lumpp.
38 See for example the judgment of the Grand Chamber in *N.S. (C-411/10) v Secretary of State for the Home Department and ors*, 21 December 2011, Joined Cases C-411/10 and C-493/10 in relation to the Dublin Regulation.
39 For a recent very important decision, see the decision of the Grand Chamber in *Case of MSS v Belgium and Greece*, Application no. 30696/09, 21 January 2011.
40 A good example is Indonesia, where the UNHCR notes, ' . . . due to the absence of national refugee legislation and procedures, UNHCR continues to be the primary provider of protection and assistance to refugees and asylum-seekers, undertaking responsibility for registration, RSD and the search for durable solutions': 2012 Regional operations profile - South East Asia, available at: http://www.unhcr.org/cgi-bin/texis/vtx/page?page=49e488116 (last checked 15 February 2012). Another is Egypt: see US Committee for Refugees,World Refugee Survey 2009, http://www.refugees.org/resources/refugee-warehousing/archived-world-refugee-surveys/2009-wrs-country-updates/egypt.html.

and fundamental rights protection. Paradoxically, general constitutional provisions regarding due process or fundamental rights, interpreted so as to apply to non-citizens including refugees and asylum seekers, have proven more effective in vindicating the right to asylum.

The ability of domestic courts to impose limits on executive action by reference to constitutional rights has proven particularly important in limiting the populist and utility-driven concerns that underpin the treatment of asylum seekers and refugees in many states.

32.3.1 Due process

Refugee policy in many states is marked by an inherent tension between the desire of the executive to exercise ultimate control over the composition of the population—including any intake of non-citizens—and legal limitations in constraining such discretion. One persistent site of struggle is access to judicial review of executive action. Here, constitutional guarantees concerning access to the courts have proved crucial for asylum seekers in resisting discretionary and often arbitrary treatment by the executive.

In Australia, this fundamental tension between the executive and judicial branches has manifested in an attempt by successive governments over several decades to restrict the ability of the judicial branch—including the High Court of Australia—to review executive determinations of refugee status as well as decisions in other immigration matters. Although Australia has no constitutional Bill of Rights, instrumental in resisting such efforts has been the ability of applicants to rely on s 75(v) of the Australian Constitution, which confers original jurisdiction on the High Court in which a remedy is sought 'against an officer of the Commonwealth'. Applicants for refugee status have pushed and tested the boundaries of the High Court's constitutionally conferred jurisdiction (see Gageler), leading to the High Court's declaration that s 75(v) represents an 'entrenched minimum provision of judicial review',[41] impervious to legislative interference.[42] This constitutional guarantee was central to the High Court's rejection, in a recent landmark case, of the notion that the Commonwealth had legitimately established a so-called 'non-statutory' process of refugee status determination on Christmas Island, which is physically part of the territory of Australia but deemed an 'excised offshore place' by the Migration Act.[43] The Court rejected the notion that this scheme was non-statutory and hence capable of operating outside the limits of Australian substantive and procedural law, holding instead that the process was amenable to supervision by the federal courts and governed by the ordinary rules of legality and procedural fairness.[44] The decision had enormous practical importance to the significant numbers of asylum seekers whose negative determinations have subsequently been quashed in the federal courts for jurisdictional error.[45]

41 *Plaintiff S157/2002 v Commonwealth* (2003) 211 CLR 476 at 513 [103].
42 For a similar argument concerning the influence of litigation regarding Chinese exclusion and the development of American due process law, see Salyer.
43 *Plaintiff M61/2010E v Commonwealth of Australia; Plaintiff M69 of 2010 v Commonwealth of Australia* (2010) 272 ALR 14 [2010] HCA 41 (11 November 2010).
44 For further details, see Foster & Pobjoy.
45 The Austrian Constitution also provides for a comprehensive system of judicial review, which has similarly been relied upon in the asylum context: see Kotschy, 692–3.

Reliance on ordinary principles of judicial review has also sometimes been important in securing protection for asylum seekers in states that are not party to the Refugee Convention and have no established legal system for refugee protection. For instance, in Hong Kong, the Court of Final Appeal in 2005 held that since Hong Kong had adopted a policy of complying with Article 3 of the Convention Against Torture (the obligation not to remove a person at risk of torture), any decision pertaining to the application of the policy to an individual must be made according to 'high standards of fairness',[46] and would be subjected to 'rigorous examination and anxious scrutiny to ensure that the required high standards of fairness have been met'.[47] This decision has since led to the creation of a 'torture-screening' mechanism administered by the Hong Kong Immigration Department (Loper, 407).

In a number of other states, asylum seekers have relied on explicit constitutional human rights protections such as those pertaining to the right to life and liberty, and the right not to be subjected to torture, in asserting a right not to be expelled without recourse to a fair procedure.[48] In Canada, for example, a landmark decision of the Supreme Court in 1985 recognised that section 7 of the *Canadian Charter of Rights and Freedoms*, which provides that '[e]veryone has the right to life, liberty and security of the person and the right not to be deprived thereof except in accordance with the principles of fundamental justice', applies to 'every human being who is physically present in Canada'.[49] Since the appellants' section 7 rights were found to be at issue in the determination of their applications for refugee status in Canada, the Supreme Court held that the administrative decision-making process adopted by the government to determine eligibility for asylum was required to accord 'fundamental justice', which at a minimum includes 'the notion of procedural fairness'. Although the government had argued that a compromised system of determination was necessary to avoid the administrative and financial burden of according procedural fairness, the Supreme Court rejected this on the basis that 'the guarantees of the Charter would be illusory if they could be ignored because it was administratively convenient to do so'.[50] This constitutional right has been instrumental in shaping the high-quality refugee status determination procedure that exists in Canada today, which makes an oral hearing 'an indispensable feature' of the process (Macklin, 88–9).[51]

32.3.2 Substantive refugee rights

Constitutional rights have proven significant in vindicating substantive rights in the asylum context in several important respects; here we consider two of the most controversial. First, a particularly vexed issue is the administrative detention of asylum seekers pending determination of status. One of the most extreme forms of such detention is exemplified in Australia's immigration laws establishing mandatory indefinite detention of all asylum seekers, including

46 *Secretary for Security v Sakthevel Prabakar* [2005] 1 HKLRD 289 at [44].

47 *Id* at [45].

48 See for example, the decision of the Indian Supreme Court in *National Human Rights Commission v State of Arunachal Pradesh and Anor,* 1996 Supreme Court Cases (1) 742, 9 January 1996, at [20].

49 *Singh et al v Minister for Employment and Immigration* [1985] 1 S.C.R. 177.

50 *Singh* [1985] 1 SCR 177 at [70]; see Audrey Macklin, 'Asylum and the Rule of Law in Canada: Hearing the Other (side)' in Kneebone, 88–9.

51 See also the more recent decision in *Suresh v Canada (Minister of Citizenship and Immigration)* [2002] 1 S.C.R. 3. In South Africa, see *Kiliko and Others v Minister of Home Affairs and Others* 2006 (4) SA 114 (C), and *Kiliko and ors v Minister of Home Affairs and Ors* [2009] ZAWCHC 79 (9 March 2009).

children. Largely due to a lack of a constitutional Bill of Rights, the Australian High Court has rejected attempts to strike down the legal regime of mandatory detention.[52] However, in many other jurisdictions, constitutional rights to freedom of movement have been important in securing the rights of asylum seekers in this regard.[53]

A particularly good example of this phenomenon is South Africa, where the Constitutional Court has held that the rights contained in sections 12 (right to freedom and security of the person) and 35(2) (rights of detainees) of the Constitution are integral to the values of human dignity, equality and freedom that are fundamental to the constitutional order, and that the denial of these rights to human beings who are physically inside the country at sea and airports merely because they have not entered South Africa in a technical sense would constitute 'a negation of the values underlying our Constitution'.[54]

In another case, the High Court of South Africa held that a detention facility operated by the South African police service and not appropriately designated for detention by the Director-General of the Department of Home Affairs was unlawful, and that the conditions of detention, including in relation to children, were unlawful and unconstitutional.[55] Similarly, in yet another case, the High Court of South Africa held, in relation to the treatment of unaccompanied foreign children who were detained at a repatriation centre with adults and were destined for deportation that section 28 of the Constitution (children's rights) is not subject to a limitations clause and therefore imposes a direct duty on the state to ensure that unaccompanied children are provided with the basic necessities of life.[56] Further, the Court held that their detention was unlawful, invalid and shameful.[57]

A second particularly contested area relates to the provision of socio-economic rights to both asylum seekers and refugees, particularly the right to work and to receive social welfare assistance. States have often sought to argue for greater discretion in deciding the extent to which such rights are to be accorded to non-citizens, including those seeking international protection. But, the highly politicised nature of policy determination in relation to asylum seekers has highlighted the importance of constitutional rights and the availability of judicial enforcement mechanisms for the vindication of such rights.

In some contexts, courts have refused even to consider policy concerns, particularly where the fundamental right at issue is one that admits no limitation, as was the case in *Limbuela*—a decision in which the House of Lords considered the legitimacy of the government's policy to prohibit asylum seekers from the right to work and to refuse support where a claim had not been made 'as soon as reasonably practicable'.[58] In finding that this policy violated the United Kingdom's obligations under the non-derogable Article 3 of the European Convention on Human Rights—namely, not to subject a person to inhuman or degrading treatment—the House of Lords emphasised that engagement in the political debate surrounding asylum seekers was irrelevant to the court's decision, since it 'forms no part of the judicial function'.[59]

---

52 *Al Kateb v Godwin* (2004) 219 CLR 562.

53 See Field & Edwards for a useful discussion of domestic constitutional protections regarding detention. For discussion of the position in Austria, see Kotschy, 694–5.

54 *Lawyers for Human Rights v Minister of Home Affairs* [2009] ZACC 12 at [26].

55 *Lawyers for Human Rights v Minister of Safety and Security* [2009] ZAGPPHC 57 at [8].

56 *Centre for Child Law and Another v Minister of Home Affairs and Others* 2005 (6) SA 50 (T).

57 *Id* at [23].

58 *R (Limbuela) v Secretary of State for the Home Department* [2006] 1 A.C. 396.

59 *Id* at [14] per Lord Hope of Craighead.

Indeed, even where a court is more willing to consider the aims and objectives as well as particular policy choices of the government in the context of undertaking an assessment of the availability of a constitutional limitations clause, populist and unsustainable justifications for violations of the fundamental rights of non-citizens have been rejected. For example, in holding unconstitutional the policy of the South African government to prohibit asylum seekers from engaging in employment and study, the Supreme Court of Appeal of South Africa considered the impact that the denial of the freedom to engage in productive work would have on the first respondent's human dignity—a right secured by Section 10 of the Constitution—which was said to have 'no nationality', it being 'inherent in all people, citizens and non-citizens alike, simply because they are human'.[60] While it agreed that states have the right to determine the conditions under which asylum seekers are accommodated within host countries, and that the right to human dignity in South Africa is not absolute and may be limited,[61] the Court found that, in the absence of state support for asylum seekers, 'the deprivation of the freedom to work assumes a different dimension where it threatens positively to degrade rather than merely to inhibit the realisation of the potential for self-fulfilment'.[62] Further, the Court was not convinced that the state's purported justifications—namely, to prevent abuse by fraudulent asylum-seekers and to protect the jobs of citizens—could justify the application of such a general prohibition on the right to work for asylum seekers.[63]

Similarly, the Israeli Supreme Court (sitting as the High Court of Justice) found in 2006 that the policy of imposing a restrictive employment arrangement on foreign workers violated their human dignity and liberty,[64] and that the government had failed to establish that its policy was not 'the least harmful measure',[65] its figures tending to suggest that the policy undermines, rather than furthers, the purpose for which it was intended.[66]

32.4 Conclusion

This chapter has explored the notion that constitutional guarantees relating to the right to asylum, existent in a wide range of state constitutions, have become less relevant in practice as the development of international and regional refugee law has become increasingly significant in the governance of domestic refugee law. However, in light of the ongoing challenges for both asylum seekers and refugees in gaining access to international protection, constitutional guarantees relating to fundamental human rights remain of enormous significance in protecting against the arbitrary, politicised and restrictive refugee policies adopted by many states today.

---

60 *Minister of Home Affairs and Others v Watchenuka and Others* [2004] 1 All SA 21 (SCA) at [25]. For a South African Constitutional Court case on the right to receive social assistance, see *Khosa and Others v Minister of Social Development and Others, Mahlaule and Another v Minister of Social Development* 2004 (6) SA 505 (CC).
61 *Watchenuka* at [28].
62 *Id* at [32].
63 *Id* at [33].
64 *Kav LaOved Worker's Hotline and ors v Government of Israel and ors* [2006] (1) IsrLR 260 at 286 [29]–[30], as found in s 1 of the Basic Law.
65 306 [52].
66 306 [51].

References

Barnett, L (2002). 'Global Governance and the Evolution of the International Refugee Regime', 14 *International Journal of Refugee Law* 238.

Battjes, H (2006). *European Asylum Law and International Law* (Martinus Nijhoff).

Crisp, J (2000). *Africa's Refugees: Patterns, Problems and Policy Challenges*, UNHCR Working Paper No 28.

Field, O & Edwards, A (2006). *Alternatives to Detention of Asylum-Seekers and Refugees*, UNHCR Legal and Protection Policy Research Series, POLAS/2006/03, April.

Foster, M & Pobjoy, J (2011). 'A Failed Case of Legal Exceptionalism? Refugee Status Determination in Australia's "Excised" Territory', 23(4) *International Journal of Refugee Law* 583–631.

Gageler, S (2010). 'Impact of Migration law on the Development of Australian Administrative Law', 17 *Australian Journal of Administrative Law* 92–105.

Geldbach, E (2009). 'Is there a Minimum of Religious Existence?' in Kilp and Saumets, *Religion and Politics in Multicultural Europe: Perspectives and Challenges* (Tartu University Press, Estonia).

Gil-Bazo, M (2008). 'The Charter of Fundamental Rights of the European Union and the Right to be Granted Asylum in the Union's Law', 27(3) *Refugee Survey Quarterly* 33–52.

Goodwin-Gill GS & Lambert, H (eds) (2010). *The Limits of Transnational Law* (Cambridge University Press).

Guendelsberger, J (1994). 'New Limits on Asylum in France: Expediency versus Principle', *Am. U. J. Int'l L. & Pol'y* 129.

Hailbronner, K (1994). 'Asylum Law Reform in the German Constitution', *American University Journal of International Law and Policy* 159.

Hathaway, J (1990). 'A Reconsideration of the Underlying Premise of Refugee Law', 31 (1) *Harvard International Law Journal* 129.

—— (1991). *Law of Refugee Status* (Butterworths).

Kneebone, S (ed) (2009). *Refugees, Asylum Seekers and the Rule of Law* (Cambridge University Press).

Kotschy, B (2006). 'Austria: Asylum law in conflict with the Constitution', 4 (4) *International Journal of Constitutional Law* 691.

Lambert, H, Messineo, F & Tiedemann, P (2008). 'Comparative Perspectives of Constitutional Asylum in France, Italy, and Germany: Requiescat in Pace?', 27 (3) *Refugee Survey Quarterly* 16.

Loper, K (2010). Human Rights, *Non-refoulement* and the Protection of Refugees in Hong Kong', 22 (3) *International Journal of Refugee Law* 404 at 407.

Marx, M & Lumpp, K (1996). 'The German Constitutional Court's Decision of 14 May 1996 on the Concept of "Safe Third Countries"– A Basis for Burden-Sharing in Europe?' 8(3) *International Journal of Refugee Law* 419.

Marx, R (2000–2001). 'The Notion of Persecution by Non-State Agents in German Jurisprudence' 15 *Georgetown Immigration Law Journal* 447.

Mole, N (2007). *Asylum and the European Convention on Human Rights* (Council of Europe, 4th edition).

Motomura, H (1990). 'Immigration Law after a Century of Plenary Power: Phantom Constitutional Norms and Statutory Interpretation', 100(3) *The Yale Law Journal* 545.

Okoth-Obbo, G (2001). 'Thirty Years On: A legal review of the 1969 OAU Refugee Convention Governing the Specific Aspects of Refugee problems in Africa', 20(1) *Refugee Survey Quarterly* 79 at 97–98.

Rankin, M (2005). 'Extending the Limits or Narrowing the Scope? Deconstructing the OAU Refugee Definition Thirty Years On', 21 *South African Journal on Human Rights* 406.

Salyer, L (1995). *Laws Harsh as Tigers: Chinese Immigrants and the Shaping of Modern Immigration Law* (University of North Carolina Press).

Zimmermann, A (ed) (2011). *The 1951 Convention Relating to the Status of Refugees and its 1967 Protocol: A Commentary* (Oxford University Press).

Additional reading

Goodwin-Gill, GS & McAdam, J (2007). *The Refugee in International Law* (Oxford University Press).

Hathaway, J (2005). *The Rights of Refugees under International Law* (Cambridge University Press).

The competing effect of national uniqueness and comparative influences on constitutional practice

*Zaid Al-Ali and Arun K Thiruvengadam**

33.1 Introduction

This chapter focuses on theoretical, historical and contemporary trends in constitutional drafting with a particular focus on how local context and characteristics that are unique to particular countries interact with comparative influences. The latter have played a major role in shaping significant domestic constitutional decisions. This historical fact continues to be manifested in contemporary constitutional cultures. We examine the effect of forces of globalization and other phenomena that have led scholars to suggest that we are in an era of convergence of constitutionalism. Our analysis shows that even as there is a movement towards similar constitutional institutions and principles, significant differences lead us to doubt that the moment of convergence is imminent. Our chapter analyzes these questions by focusing in particular on the experiences of postcolonial constitutions and recent events in the Arab region.

33.2 Theoretical and historical background

The question of the portability of basic legal institutions and ideas across legal systems and cultures has been called 'one of the grand old topics of comparative law' (Langbein, 48) and continues to be a contested issue in our times. Dating back to the eighteenth century, philosophers such as Savigny and Montesquieu argued that there is an inherent relationship between the laws of a state and its society. Montesquieu, for instance, declared that:

> [the political and civil laws of each nation] . . . should be so closely tailored to the people for whom they are made, that it would be pure chance [un grand hazard] if the laws of one nation could meet the needs of another . . . (Montesquieu, book I, ch. 3).

Scholars of comparative law have been influenced by such thinking, and have traditionally undervalued the importance, and viability, of law's ability to travel across boundaries. One

---

* We thank the editors for inviting us to join this significant collaborative project, and for their close review and constructive suggestions on earlier drafts.

example is the work of Otto Kahn-Freund on comparative legislation, which, while conceding that laws move across jurisdictions in some contexts, contends that in most contexts, law is so deeply embedded in a nation's life that transplantation is rendered impossible (Kahn-Freund). By contrast, other scholars who have focused on the historical evolution of legal systems have noted that each of the four major exporters of Western law in the modern era—France, Germany, the United Kingdom and the United States of America—had, in its primary stage, drawn from existing foreign models. They argue that this makes the reception of law an integral element of the evolution of all national legal systems of the Western tradition (Glenn).

The scholar who has arguably produced the largest body of scholarship on law's ability to travel is the Scottish legal historian, Alan Watson. Watson's historical writings are focused on Roman law, and he documents, in minute detail, the spread of Roman law by a process of legal transplantation throughout continental Europe. He demonstrates that the very same rules of contract can operate in the very different eras of Julius Caesar and the medieval Popes, of Louis XIV, of Bismarck and of the twentieth-century welfare state (see generally Watson, 1974; Watson, 1977, 79).[1] Based on these findings, Watson's argument is that history has shown that because of the nature of the legal profession, legal change in European private law has taken place largely by transplantation of legal rules. Therefore, law is, at least sometimes, insulated from social and economic change. Watson's ideas have been contested by several scholars including, most famously, Pierre Legrand, and this has given rise to a rich and sophisticated body of literature analyzing the basic terms of this debate, much of which is beyond the scope of our focus.[2] For our purposes, it is relevant, as Ewald has noted, that Watson's theories are based principally on his investigations of Roman law, and specifically of Roman *private* law. Ewald therefore contends that Watson cannot claim that his theory holds good either for non-Western cultures, or even for European *public* law. In fact, Watson himself has been careful to note that his conclusions are properly applicable to the development of private law (Watson 1977, preface).

The question that then arises is: can and does public law exhibit tendencies similar to those asserted for private law in its capacity to travel across jurisdictions? In this respect, the following statement of Christopher Osakwe, one of the co-authors of a leading text on comparative law, would seem particularly apposite:

> The problems of the comparability of laws are particularly acute in the area of public law. Public law, more than private law, is infused with indigenous political, social and economic realities. Much more than private law, public law is closely linked to national tradition. Whereas nations are more inclined to borrow building blocks from the outside in the process of erecting their private law, they prefer to re-invent the wheels on which their public law is constructed. Public law reflects an inner relationship—a sort of spiritual and psychical relationship—with the people over whom it operates. This historical contact between public law and national identity is not readily transplantable from one country to another (Osakwe, 876).

Osakwe's statement suggests that one would expect to find public law regimes developing very differently around the world, responding to a potentially varied range of internal stimuli.

---

1 For a bibliographic listing of Watson's scholarly output and a comprehensive overview of his approach to legal transplants, see Ewald; for an insightful analysis contrasting the views of Kahn-Freund and Watson, see Stein.
2 For a good overview of this debate, see Nelken. For an overview of the Watson–Legrand debate from the perspective of constitutional law, see Frankenburg.

However, a survey of constitutional developments across the twentieth century suggests that this has not been the case. Indeed, comparing constitutional regimes across the 192 nations that are members of the UN in the contemporary world reveals a remarkable degree of similarity in terms of constitutional institutions and ideals. In the survey that follows, we examine how two of these have become particularly widespread: written bills of rights and the institution of judicial review.

At the dawn of the twentieth century, very few nations had adopted written constitutions. The dominant model of constitutionalism was not the American model characterized by a strong court with wide powers of judicial review, but instead, the model of legislative supremacy exemplified by the British (parliamentary sovereignty) and French (legislative supremacy) models (Gardbaum). Prior to World War II, few courts had the power to review the constitutionality of national legislation for violation of fundamental rights.[3] This, however, changed after the War. Countries that adopted the new model, with its emphasis on bills of rights and judicial review, included: Germany (1949), Italy (1948), Japan (1947), Spain (1978), Portugal (1982), Greece (1975), Cyprus (1960), Turkey (1961) and Belgium (1984).

The end of World War II also signalled the end of colonialism, and led to the creation of new states in Asia and Africa, many of which adopted bills of rights and judicial review as integral parts of their model of constitutionalism. For instance, the Constitution of India (1950) created a strong Supreme Court with wide powers of judicial review.[4] While some nations in Africa also adopted this model (including Nigeria, Uganda, Kenya, Botswana and Zambia), many other countries (including Ghana, Liberia, Ethiopia, Malawi and Tanzania) decided to continue with the British model of legislative supremacy. However, starting from the mid-1980s, many African countries began a series of measures of constitutional reform with the result that more than 20 new constitutions were adopted across Africa, most of which now contain bills of rights and courts with powers of judicial review (Alston, Ihonvbere). Similarly, recent years have witnessed several countries in Asia (including Taiwan, South Korea and Mongolia) undergoing constitutional reforms designed to confer wider powers of judicial review on courts (see generally Ginsburg).

Likewise, many countries in Latin America—a region with a long history of constitutions and constitutionalism—have contemporary constitutions that contain bills of rights and provide for judicial review. It is worth noting that most of these countries retain several aspects of the civil law tradition in their legal systems, thereby raising doubts about the supposed impossibility of transfers between different legal traditions. Since the collapse of the Soviet Union in 1989, a 'burst of constitutionalization' (Gardbaum) has occurred in Central and Eastern Europe. Many of these nations have also opted for judicial review and bills of rights.[5] Our analysis finds empirical support in recent scholarly findings showing that of the 106 national constitutions that have been adopted since 1985, every one contained a written bill of rights, and all but five established a mode by which rights can be reviewed (Stone Sweet; Law & Versteeg).

---

3 Gardbaum records the following instances: Ireland (judicial review was established under its 1937 Constitution); the constitutional courts in Austria (1920–33) and Czechoslovakia (1920–38); Spain (1933–36); and Weimar Germany (more in theory than in actual practice).
4 For an analysis of the impact of foreign constitutional models on the drafting of the Constitution of India, see generally Austin.
5 For details of the constitution-making processes employed in these and other countries in the region, see generally Elster; Arato.

At the beginning of the second decade of the twenty-first century, as one surveys the legal and constitutional landscape of the world, one is struck by its relative homogeneity, both in terms of existing legal traditions and extant constitutional structures. With the disappearance of the 'socialist' legal family, the homogeneity of existing legal traditions has increased. Taken together, civil and common law cultures cover 70 percent of the population of the world, in over 62 percent of the legal jurisdictions of the world (Koch, 2). From a constitutional point of view, as the survey indicates, courts wielding powers of judicial review can be found in virtually every corner of the globe. Ran Hirschl has insightfully described how courts in jurisdictions as diverse as Canada, Russia, Hungary, Israel, South Africa, New Zealand, Peru, Turkey, Chile, Trinidad and Tobago, Madagascar, Zimbabwe, the Philippines, Thailand, Pakistan and Fiji are becoming 'crucial political decision-makers', harkening a 'global transition to juristocracy' (Hirschl 2002, 217–218; Hirschl 2004).

In highlighting the rapid spread of bills of rights and judicial review, we do not take a normative position on this trend. This phenomenon has found strident critics and supporters amongst a diverse range of scholars from across the world. Scholars have also argued against understanding these trends in simplistic terms, as pointing to the triumph of liberal democracy and other universalistic ideals. As Morton Horwitz has shown, the move towards judicial review around the world can be viewed as a distrust of the very institutions that constitute democracy, and a move towards institutions that are independent of democratic politics (Horwitz).

Our focus, instead, is on other constitutional actors, such as those involved in drafting constitutions, to see how much they are influenced by foreign and comparative models. Given that constitution-making is bound to be focused on questions of national identity and indigenous issues, one expects that local factors will predominate, but our survey suggests that the forces of harmonization also have a role to play in such processes. The rapidity with which nations around the world have adopted bills of rights suggests that constitution-makers have indeed looked beyond their borders for inspiration and for content.

We also focus on the potentially harmonizing role that judges exercising strong judicial review in nations across the world can play when they look to each other's practices, and seek to emulate them in their home jurisdictions. Courts will particularly be susceptible to the tendency of looking to each other as it is a part of most legal traditions to look to past practices for evolving solutions to problems that confront them. On the other hand, pressures to decide important issues of national importance by looking inward into their local legal tradition will act as a countervailing force against the impulse of engaging in cross-judicial dialogue, or being a recipient of cross-judicial transplants.

Our analysis also engages with an emerging body of scholarship that has debated the correct terminology for discussing constitutional transplants (the consensus is in favour of the metaphor of 'migration' over that of 'borrowing') and whether the effect of these trends points to a convergence in constitutional ideals (see Choudhry 2006; Perju).

Convergence of and foreign influence on constitutional ideas has today become a fact of life. Certain concepts, including fundamental rights and the separation of powers, have become the cornerstone of constitutional thought across many countries. Despite this seeming universality, a survey of a number of constitutional systems and the manner in which they evolved over time shows that convergence has proceeded differently depending on the political system in place. The cornerstones have somewhat different shapes in different nations. A tension can be discerned between an outward (i.e. essentially theoretical) and an inward (i.e. as reflected in the details of the applicable laws, regulations and practices, which are not always in conformity with the constitutional text) perspective on constitutional rights. Indeed, an outward commitment to universal principles sometimes masks an inward legal framework that conflicts violently with those same principles. With increased democratization, the outward/inward tension essentially disappeared within most constitutional systems; outward commitments to fundamental rights were more adequately reflected within national legal systems. However, that tension was replaced by a new phenomenon: with increased democratization has come a commitment by some national constitutional systems to principles that do not necessarily conform with universal principles, thus establishing a firm limit to convergence. These issues are discussed in greater detail below.

33.3 Constitutional migration and national uniqueness in practice

33.3.1 External and internal convergence

33.3.1.1 Introduction

Each of the world's countries has a unique history that has impacted its value system. Language, religion, geography, economic and political circumstance influence those principles that are common to the inhabitants of individual countries and to the members of individual nations. Nevertheless, as the concept of the nation state spread and established itself in all parts of the world during the nineteenth and twentieth centuries, a large number of the constitutional texts that were designed to govern those territories were similar in the wording, concepts and format that they adopted. Many emerging constitutional orders were merely following the precedents that had been established in the United States, Great Britain and France. In other parts of the world, colonialism, and the fact that many of those texts were either directly written or inspired by European officials and scholars, played their part. The individuality of many post-colonial countries (although not all, see below) was either ignored or repressed in the process.

In the post-colonial period, that practice was continued, albeit not always for the same reason. Many new constitutions established a narrative based on freedom, human development and generous (often merely aspirational in nature) social rights. A distinction must be drawn, however, between countries such as India, where elites had acquired an extraordinary degree of autonomy during the constitution-drafting process and were motivated by a desire to democratize their country, and regimes that were mainly motivated by a desire to monopolize power for extended periods of time. Despite their non-democratic tendencies, the latter were nevertheless mindful of the need to maintain some form of international and internal legitimacy. As a result, they formally maintained many of the same concepts and norms (sometimes even strengthening the wording in their respective texts) while putting in place mechanisms and institutions that they hoped would concretize their hold on power. In other words, world constitutions converged with Western liberal principles, but to varying extents, depending essentially on the political system in place. Others engaged in external convergence (e.g. on fundamental rights) but avoided internal convergence (on the separation of powers).

33.3.1.2 Fundamental rights under post-colonial constitutions

Many of the constitutional frameworks that emerged in the twentieth century made sure to pay lip service to the notion of human rights in their fundamental texts, while at the same time enacting legislation that would allow for the spirit of those same rights to be routinely violated. In many (although not necessarily all) cases, this type of framework was enacted in a deliberate attempt to maintain the capacity to violate rights that had been developed by colonial frameworks. In Iraq, all of the constitutions that were drafted since nominal independence was granted in the 1920s included provisions that guaranteed the protection of a certain number of rights, while at the same time subjecting those same rights to future legislation and therefore (given the constitutional framework) to the will of an unelected government.[6]

By way of example, Iraq's post-colonial constitutional texts were all permeated with extensive social and economic rights including the right to work, free health care and education.[7] Freedom of expression, religion and association as well as the right to human dignity were also, in theory, guaranteed by all of Iraq's fundamental texts. They were, however, usually followed by the prescription that these should be exercised 'within the limits of the law', without any clear indication as to what types of limits could be established by legislation. Even where there was no constitutional authority to do so, Iraq's governing authorities still legislated a large number of measures that curbed the enjoyment of specific rights.[8] A similar trend can be identified in many other post-colonial constitutional frameworks. The Kingdom of Morocco has revised its constitutional framework on a large number of occasions since independence, but on each occasion it has maintained wording guaranteeing freedom of expression[9] and complete equality between all citizens,[10] rights that were routinely violated.

---

6 Iraq was a constitutional monarchy (and proceeded under the 1925 Constitution drafted under the British Mandate) from 1925 until 1958. From 1958 to 1970, a series of non-democratic military and political transfers of power took place, many of which resulted in short-lived interim constitutions (including the 1958, 1964 and 1968 Constitutions). The 1970 Interim Constitution remained in force until the war in 2003, which resulted in the 2004 Transitional Administrative Law (yet another interim constitution). A new permanent constitution was drafted in 2005 and entered into force in 2006.

7 Iraq's 1964 Constitution provides for due process rights (Article 20 to 25), the right to free education (Article 33) and free health care (Article 36).

8 For example, although Article 22(a) of the 1970 Interim Constitution provided, without the possibility for future legislative limitations, that '[t]he dignity of man is safeguarded. It is inadmissible to cause any physical or psychological harm', Decree 59 (1994) provided that the punishment for theft was hand amputation, while Decree 115 (1994) provided that abandoning military service was punishable by ear amputation (Article 1).

9 See for example, Article 9(b) of the 1996 Constitution of the Kingdom of Morocco, which provides that all citizens shall enjoy 'freedom of opinion, of expression in all its forms, and of public gathering'. That same right was readopted virtually unchanged in Article 25 of the 2011 Constitution. The Moroccan authorities have nevertheless curbed the free expression of ideas throughout the post-colonial period.

10 Article 5 of the 1996 Moroccan Constitution provides that Moroccans are all 'equal before the law' and does not allow for any restriction. Article 19 of the 2011 Constitution is more explicit, providing that: 'Men and women enjoy, in equality, the right and freedoms of civil, political, economic, social, cultural and environmental character, set out in this Title and elsewhere in this Constitution.' Nevertheless, Article 475 of the Moroccan penal code provides that 'where a minor is kidnapped or raped and marries her abductor or rapist, the latter cannot be criminally prosecuted [. . .]'. Article 475 was applied in the case of one 16-year-old girl in March 2012 who was raped and forced to marry her rapist, who then escaped prosecution. The girl later committed suicide.

The Hashemite Kingdom of Jordan offers similar guarantees and has applied limitations to the application of those guarantees.[11]

33.3.1.3 The separation of powers and judicial independence

A similar trend was established in relation to those same countries' governance structures, which often paid lip service to democracy and to the separation of powers but were typically designed to maintain one-party, or even one-man rule. Pursuant to a 1952 military *coup d'état* that was principally motivated by a desire to end foreign interference, corruption and social inequality, a 'Constitutional Declaration' was issued in Egypt that established a 'Revolutionary Command Council', an unelected and unaccountable body that was dominated by the military and controlled the country over the coming period. That model was replicated in a large number of countries, including in Iraq. That country's 1970 Interim Constitution (which contained a far more detailed and generous section on fundamental rights than all of Iraq's previous constitutional frameworks) provided that the country is a 'sovereign people's democratic republic' (Article 1), but also provided for the existence of a 'Revolutionary Command Council'. The Council was accountable only to itself (Article 40) and was defined as the 'supreme institution in the State' (Article 37), which enjoyed both full legislative and executive authority (Article 42). The first parliamentary elections that were organized pursuant to the 1970 Constitution took place in 1980. Other post-colonial constitutions established similarly anti-democratic institutions, while at the same time promising to liberate their local populations from inequality.[12]

Likewise, many post-colonial regimes understood the need to preach judicial independence while at the same time ensuring that the courts remained firmly under the control of the executive. Iraq's 1970 Interim Constitution contained a single provision on the judiciary, which granted and withdrew independence in practically the same breath. Article 60(a) provided unambiguously that 'the judiciary is independent' but added that the judiciary 'is subject to no other authority save that of the law'. Given that the 1970 Interim Constitution provided that the (unelected and unrepresentative) Revolutionary Command Council enjoyed both executive and legislative power (Article 42), the judiciary was effectively under the control of a small group of individuals who had granted themselves unlimited power over

---

11 Article 15 of the 1952 Jordanian Constitution provides that: 'The State shall guarantee freedom of opinion. Every Jordanian shall be free to express his opinion by speech, in writing, or by means of photographic representation and other forms of expression, provided that such does not violate the law.' One such law that criminalizes the act of insulting the king has been applied regularly against pro-democracy activists, including in March 2012 when more than 30 protesters were detained.

12 Morocco has maintained, throughout its modern constitutional history, a strongly monarchical system of government, in which the king has executive, legislative and judicial authority. The 2011 Constitution maintains much of this same system, with some commentators arguing that it merely codifies much of what was previously customary, effectively preventing any significant reduction in the monarch's powers in the future. See Maghraoui. Syria's 1973 Constitution maintained that all citizens were equal before the law (article 25(3)) and also provided that the Socialist Arab Ba'ath Party was the 'leading party in society and in the state' (article 8). Thus, the right to equality was violated by the fact that only Ba'ath Party members enjoyed access to high public office.

the state.[13] A number of other post-colonial constitutions have also subjected judges to the will of the executive while at the same time professing adherence to the principle of judicial independence.[14]

33.3.2 Increased democracy as an instrument of convergence

33.3.2.1 Introduction

The wave of democratization that came prior to, during and after the fall of the Soviet Union brought with it a strong convergence of constitutional ideas in many countries that had hitherto only adopted some of the external features of liberal constitutionalism. Democracy, or the free expression of popular will within the confines of a particular political system, has led to a convergence of constitutional cultures, and has also pushed many apart. When allowed to make their own democratic choices, nations are more likely than not to opt in favour of a separation of powers that guarantees a genuinely independent judiciary, and of a system of government that protects the rights of the individual.

At the same time, several factors have been working against convergence during this same period. First, although democratization has progressed apace in many of the world's regions, vested interests within each individual country often work against full democratization as a way to maintain access to power. That dynamic has led to many outdated practices being maintained in several countries (see below). Secondly, when allowed to freely express their will, nations often favour the application of illiberal principles or choose to adopt a system of government that does not entirely conform with mainstream liberal principles (e.g. religiously inspired sexual discrimination; see below). That trend has become particularly acute as an increasing amount of former colonies have transitioned to more democratic systems of government. As they become free to express their independent will, they often choose to confine themselves within a set of rules that are deeply rooted in local culture, and which sometimes sanction discrimination on the basis of sex, race or social class.

---

13 The 1970 Interim Constitution was in conformity with Iraqi tradition on this point: although judges were nominally independent under the 1925 Constitution (Article 71), the entire functioning of the courts was to be determined by law (Article 70) and judges themselves were to be appointed by the king (Article 68); under the 1958 Interim Constitution, judges were also nominally granted independence but the judicial sector was to be organized by law (Article 23), under a system in which the unelected government was granted legislative power (Article 21).

14 The 1973 Syrian Constitution provided that 'The judicial authority is independent. The President of the Republic guarantees this independence with the assistance of the Higher Council of the Judiciary' (Article 131) and provides that 'The President of the Republic presides over the Higher Council of the Judiciary. The law defines the method of its formulation, its powers, as well as its internal operating procedures' (Article 132). The 2011 Moroccan Constitution provides that judges are independent of the legislative power and of the executive (Article 107) and even provides significant detail as to what constitutes interference in judicial affairs and what should be done in case of such interference (Article 109). At the same time, the 2011 Constitution establishes a High Judicial Council that oversees the judicial sector and ensures that judicial independence is respected (Article 115), and notes that the Council is 'presided by the King' who amongst other things nominates five of its members.

33.3.2.2 A greater adherence to checks and balances, including judicial independence

As noted above, Western nations generally converged towards similar constitutional norms as a result of a number of factors, not least that they share many of the same cultural and political values and are generally free to express them. Since the end of the post-colonial period, they have been joined by a number of non-Western nations that have used constitutional learning as a means to remedy the democratic deficit and other flaws in their own constitutional designs. Politicians, jurists and various stakeholders have looked to other countries as sources of inspiration while trying to construct their own national pacts. Most famously perhaps, South Africa's constitutional negotiators turned to experts from several countries, including Germany, for lessons that could be useful in constructing various sections of their own charter, though the drafters also asserted that they kept those advisers at arm's length so that the new constitution could be described as autochthonous. Former Soviet bloc countries, motivated by the prospect of European Union membership, naturally looked towards Western liberal traditions for inspiration in redesigning their own constitutional frameworks. In the post-colonial world, countries such as India took an early lead in developing democratic traditions and institutions; those that underwent a period of totalitarian rule also eventually adopted many of the features of democratic rule in their own national charters. This applies to a number of African, Latin American and (more recently, and at the time of writing still somewhat tenuously) Arab countries.

As comparative constitutional culture has become more democratic, a number of points of convergence have emerged. In particular, outside Western liberal circles that had already adopted many of these principles in the past, world constitutions moved to prevent the predominance of unrepresentative and unelected executives by institutionalizing political competition, regular elections and a genuine system of checks and balances (including an independent judiciary), as well as a commitment to respecting fundamental rights. Iraq is a case in point: following an extended period of dictatorial rule, the 2006 Constitution provides for regular multi-party parliamentary elections (Article 56), the indirect election of a president (Article 70) and the nomination by the president of a prime minister from the largest parliamentary bloc (Article 76). Iraq's 2006 Constitution also firmly separates powers and establishes a number of checks on the exercise of executive power. The concept of parliamentary oversight was established and the mechanism through which oversight is to be exercised was also codified in the Constitution. Thus, the Board of Supreme Audit (Iraq's supreme audit institution) is for the first time protected by the 2006 Constitution, which guaranteed it 'financial and administrative independence' (Article 103(1)) (See Al-Ali). Insofar as the protection of fundamental rights is concerned, the incidence of external influence between nations that have sought to turn a page after a period of abuse is particularly acute. For example, a direct line can be drawn between the limitation clauses that are included in Germany's Basic Law, the Canadian Charter of Rights and Freedoms, South Africa's 1996 Constitution and Kenya's 2011 Constitution (Sarkin).

On the notion of judicial independence, approximately 60 percent of the world's constitutions have now established judicial councils in some form or another, as a means to insulate courts from the political process and interference. Judicial councils are typically responsible for appointments, budgetary issues and training, including continued legal education. Many of the countries that have opted for the establishment of judicial councils drew heavily from developments in OECD (Organisation for Economic Co-operation and Development) countries.[15] Kenya's 2011 Constitution is a recent example: it provides for the establishment of a Judicial Service Commission, which is responsible for 'promot[ing] and facilitat[ing] the independence and accountability of the judiciary and the efficient, effective and transparent administration of justice' (Article 171). The difficulty for each country has been to establish rules and procedures within the context of existing traditions and working methods in a way that is likely to increase independence from political interference. By way of example, after a century-long tradition of abandoning the judiciary to the mercy of unelected executives, Iraq's 2006 Constitution establishes a Higher Judicial Council, which is solely responsible for managing judicial affairs (Article 91).

Despite this development, major flaws have undermined the progress that has been made. First, a significant number of constitutions still grant significant control over judicial affairs to unelected and unrepresentative executives, including in relation to appointments (a crucial issue).[16] Secondly, even where a council is established and granted nominal independence, a lack of detail often opens the door to political interference. For example, Iraq's 2006 Constitution leaves the Higher Judicial Council's composition and its rules of operation to future legislation (Article 90).[17] The constitutional drafters could not come to an agreement on this issue, and left the matter to the ordinary political process in the hope that the parliament's complicated composition would prevent the passage of a law that will allow for the Council to be politicized.[18] This absence of a clear body of rules has contributed to a monopolization of decision-making power within the judiciary. A single judge is the head of the Higher Judicial Council (which does not have a clear decision-making process) and the Federal Supreme Court, which has opened the door to political influence.[19]

33.3.2.3 The increased codification of processes and establishment of independent agencies

In addition to all of the above, comparative constitutional culture has in fact moved in a new direction of late. Setting aside a, by now outdated, belief that constitutions should be devoid of detail to ensure flexibility and longevity (Elkins, Ginsburg & Melton), an increasing number of constitutions include significant detail on issues including the legislative process, financial decentralization and the electoral process. Research on how nations organize their budgetary processes has found remarkable similarities between a significant number of

---

15 See Judicial Appointments and Judicial Independence, United States Institute of Peace (January 2009), available at www.usip.org/files/Judicial-Appointments-EN.pdf (accessed 23 May 2012).

16 See for example Article 98 of Jordan's 1952 Constitution (updated in 2011) according to which: 'Judges of the Civil and Sharia Courts shall be appointed and dismissed by a Royal Decree in accordance with the provisions of the law.'

17 Jordan's 1952 Constitution is even sparser on this issue. Its Article 98(2) merely provides that: 'A Judicial Council responsible for matters related to civil judges shall be established by a Law'. Morocco's 2011 Constitution also provides for the establishment of a High Judicial Council (Article 113), which is presided over by the King (Article 115). The 2011 Constitution does not include any detail in relation to how the Council should take its decisions and what role and power the King will dispose of in that context.

18 At the time of writing, the Iraqi parliament had not passed any legislation relating to the Council, which is therefore still governed by Coalition Provisional Order 35 (2003).

19 Failing oversight: Iraq's unchecked government, International Crisis Group, Middle East Report Number 113 (26 September 2011).

countries.[20] Although that convergence has mostly been among members of the OECD, the systems that are in place in those countries have started spreading to post-colonial countries as well.[21]

Another important example is the increasing popularity of independent commissions to manage elections, particularly in countries that have or are transitioning from a period of autocratic rule. Reforms in the Arab region since popular uprisings began in December 2010 are particularly relevant: Tunisia, Egypt, Libya and Jordan have all now established their own independent commissions. Also, Iraq has had its own electoral commission since 2004.[22]

Once again, although these reforms were motivated by a desire to bridge the gap between democratic theory and practice, significant progress remains to be made. Political realities on the ground have meant that the progress that has been made remains tenuous for now. At the time of writing, Tunisia, Egypt and Libya have not adopted their own permanent constitutions, so it remains to be seen to what extent their respective electoral commissions' independence will be protected. Iraq provides an important lesson learned in that regard: although the 2006 Constitution nominally protects its independence and provides that it is 'subject to monitoring' by the legislature, poor drafting by the constitutional drafting committee in 2005 created a number of loopholes for the executive to exploit, ultimately resulting in a 2010 Supreme Court decision, which held that although the commission is to be monitored by the legislature, it should be 'attached' to the council of ministries (which has come under the control of a particular political alliance).[23] The concept of independent commissions was thereby undermined, and the credibility of future elections has been put at risk.

33.3.2.4 The re-emergence of local values and norms in constitutional texts as inspired by each country's starting point

Although increased democracy has meant a greater adherence to some of the universal principles set out above and to a consolidation of a number of mechanisms, it has also contributed to a re-emergence of local values that have by now taken root in constitutional culture, and in a way that does not always conform with these same universal principles, or even with Western liberal values. Even where the principle of irrevocable individual rights is nominally accepted, it can sometimes nevertheless be subject to interpretation or qualification according to local values, which are sometimes considered to be of a higher order than constitutional law. In particular, religious values that have been elevated to the level of constitutional principles have in some countries (but not all) translated into official and enduring sexual discrimination. At other times, divided societies have struggled to define their parameters of coexistence and in the process have established governance mechanisms that place group rights over individual rights.

During the post-colonial period, popular forces in the Arab region struggled for greater representation in government against unrepresentative elites. Those same popular forces called for the institution of a more democratic form of government in which local values (in

---

20 The Legal Framework for Budget Systems, An international comparison, OECD Journal on Budgeting, Volume 4, No. 3 (2004).

21 Since it was amended in 2011, the Jordanian Constitution includes similar detail in relation to how its annual state budget law should be passed (Article 112).

22 By virtue of Coalition Provisional Authority Order 92 (2004).

23 Federal Supreme Court, Decision 88 (2010).

particular, religious values) would play a significant role under the constitution. Although the previous ruling elites made some concessions in that regard over time (in particular, in Egypt), large segments of the population were not satisfied. Since the beginning of the Arab uprisings in December 2010, the inclusion or reinforcement of Sharia in the region's constitutions has since become a *cause célèbre* for some of those some forces, and an important debate is ongoing as to what the implications might be, in particular on the principle of non-discrimination against women. As democracy has increased, so have the calls for constitutional reform in favour of a model that places less emphasis on universally accepted principles and more on religion. In 1999, religious values also inspired El Salvador to amend its constitution so as to recognize that rights extend to 'every human being since the moment of conception'.

Also, as increasing numbers of post-colonial countries emerge from periods of autocratic or of minority rule, redistributive politics tend to find their way into constitutional texts, typically through generous social and economic rights and sometimes through the institution of financial transfers between provinces. Iraq provides a dramatic example of how (quasi) democracy plays a role in the evolution of constitutional rights. Iraq's 2004 interim constitution, which was mainly drafted behind closed doors by a small number of American and Iraqi–American jurists and political scientists who were appointed by the US and UK occupation authorities, did not include the types of social and economic rights that Iraqis had been accustomed to seeing in their constitutions (although it did provide for an explicit right to bear arms, a principle that was alien to Iraqi constitutional culture; Article 17) (Diamond, 141–5). Iraq's 2006 permanent Constitution, which was the product of a deeply flawed but partially democratic drafting process, included perhaps the most generous economic and social rights that Iraq has seen to date (including the rights to health care, to a safe environment, to free education, to work and to practise sports). The same phenomenon has been noted in Latin America, where recent constitutional drafting processes involving representatives of disenfranchised masses produced texts that were for the first time heavily slanted towards social and economic rights (Brinks & Forbath).

33.3.3 Courts as agents of constitutional migration

Courts have been making references to, and relying upon, judicial decisions from foreign jurisdictions dating back to the beginning of the modern era. Though there is evidence of trans-judicial influence among countries in Continental Europe dating back to the eighteenth century (Glenn, 275), the practice appears to have gained widespread currency during the period of British colonialism and in territories that were subjected to the common law (Lester). Perhaps colonial habits of referring to judicial decisions from other countries seeped into the legal cultures of former colonies and lingered beyond the age of empire, with the result that judges in a number of former colonies continue to make extensive use of foreign law in their contemporary decision-making (Saunders).[24]

In respect of former colonies, the pressure to cast off the imperialist past and establish strong foundations of indigenous constitutionalism has acted as a counter to the historical reasons favouring trans-judicial influence. Nevertheless, two factors have ensured that the

---

24 See generally Drobnig & Erp (detailing how judiciaries in several former colonies have continued to apply or defer to judicial authorities from the former colonial power several years after the grant of formal independence).

many nations that became independent from colonial rule in the mid-twentieth century have remained connected with 'global dialogues' about constitutionalism. First, a predominant majority of the countries that obtained freedom from colonial rule adopted the constitutional models and structures of their former colonial masters (often at the behest of the colonial powers who, of course, believed that their own forms of government were the best).[25] Second, many of these former colonies adopted language from the emerging corpus of international human rights law in the aftermath of World War II directly into their independence constitutions, thereby creating more opportunities for dialogue among judges from different countries.

Our survey in the first section of this chapter noted how widespread written bills of rights and judicial review have become since the middle of the twentieth century. Many of the newly instituted constitutional and supreme courts sought to draw upon the jurisprudence of their more established counterparts, often with a view to emulating important facets of their constitutional jurisprudence. Lorraine Weinrib has argued that these and other factors in the aftermath of World War II resulted in a 'post-war paradigm' of domestic constitutional law that relies extensively on comparative engagement. Weinrib identifies Germany and Canada as countries that fall within this category but asserts that it includes courts in other liberal democracies that have embraced the emerging jurisprudence of human rights (Weinrib).

In recent years, a number of additional factors have contributed to an increase in trans-judicial influence. A selective list of these contributory factors would include: i) the greater quantity of comparative constitutional jurisprudence as a number of constitutional and supreme courts have built up their corpus of domestic constitutional law over several decades; ii) the similarity in issues that such courts are asked to decide upon, which makes trans-judicial influence more natural and logical (these issues include construing the ambit of freedoms of speech, religion, reproduction, privacy; language rights of minorities; equality issues; constitutional limits on punishment; rights of accused; and the ambit of war and emergency powers of the executive); iii) the greater access to foreign judicial decisions due to the internet and the willingness of courts to translate their decisions into English; iv) the increasingly global nature of legal education, which causes law students (who are future lawyers and judges) to be exposed to the constitutional jurisprudence of other nations in their domestic contexts, and to more sustained levels of interaction when they study in other jurisdictions in exchange and post-graduate programmes; and v) the increasing interaction among judges of different nations at specially organized conferences and through inter-court exchanges that are held at regular intervals in several jurisdictions (see generally Rahdert).

It is therefore not surprising that the practice of trans-judicial influence in the specific area of constitutional adjudication is now widespread. Judges in several countries in Asia, Australia, Africa, Europe, North America and South America engage with foreign and comparative law decisions from other countries in considering questions of domestic constitutional law (McCrudden; Markesinis & Fedtke). A number of scholars have identified the creative and

---

25 Although this appears to have proved viable in a few countries (India is one such example), in the majority of postcolonial states, such efforts proved disastrous, and the independence constitutions had to be subsequently revised to account for local political, social and economic conditions and structures. Go (2003) notes that 'at least 91 countries' became free from Western colonial rule in the twentieth century, all of which went on to adopt constitutions of their own, usually based on that of their former colonial masters—as many as 65 percent of these countries had to substantially rewrite and revise their constitutions in later years.

multiple ways in which foreign decisions are actually used in constitutional adjudication by judges across nations (Markesinis & Fedkte; Tushnet 1999).

In recent years, the use of foreign and comparative decisions has attracted controversy and considerable scholarly commentary in several jurisdictions, most notably in the United States. Judges of the US Supreme Court and an army of scholars have cast doubt on the use of comparative law by raising a number of objections: that the practice is undemocratic as it vests great discretion in judges with respect to the foreign decisions they can cite in support of their results; that such use is unprincipled, haphazard and lacking in method (Perju; Halmai). Critics of the use of foreign law echo the sentiments expressed by Montesquieu and Osakwe on the uniqueness of domestic constitutional law regimes. Similar skepticism has been expressed by judges in Australia and Singapore, albeit for different reasons (Thiruvengadam). Analysis of the debate over the use of foreign law reveals that the disagreement is often over far more fundamental differences in approaches to constitutional interpretation, and the way protagonists conceive of the proper role of judges as actors within a constitutional system in relation to the relative powers of other constitutional actors such as legislators and members of the executive. There is a clear correlation between judges whose self-perception of the legitimate role of judges is relatively narrow and a reluctance to refer to or use foreign law in domestic constitutional interpretation.

In the rest of the world, however, the use of foreign decisions as persuasive authority has been relatively uncontroversial. Detailed studies show that judges in Canada, India and South Africa have made extensive use of foreign decisions. What is more, this is typically done in ways that do not undermine the important local issues that arise. Scholars have demonstrated that engagement with foreign decisions has been used to enhance particular aspects of their domestic constitutional culture (Choudhry; Roy).

33.4 Conclusion

In recent years, several scholars have drawn attention to the forces of globalization that have an increasingly discernible impact on what were once considered domestic constitutional ideals and principles (Law; Tushnet 2009). The question that then arises is whether we are living in or heading towards an era of convergence. Scholars have warned us about the dangers of viewing this question in simplistic terms, and being sanguine about its implications (Goldsworthy; Scheppele).

Our analysis provides support for the argument that constitutional ideas today are more similar at a macro level than they were at the beginning of the twentieth century. Yet, despite this overall similarity in constitutional institutions and principles, our analysis equally shows that there is great divergence and difference in the details of the constitutional systems of different countries, lending support to the proposition that 'globalization does not entail uniformity' (Tushnet 2009, 987).[26] As globalization continues to interact with increased democratization, particularly at a local level, constitutional processes and judicial borrowing are likely to continue to converge but within the framework of a more determined articulation of local values.

---

26 This is also the conclusion of scholars who have closely studied significant recent constitutional developments, such as the drafting of Bills of Rights that occurred in Canada, South Africa and Northern Ireland. See Smith.

References

Al-Ali, Z (2011), 'Constitutional Legitimacy in Iraq: What Role Local Context?, in Rainer Grote and Tilmann J. Röder (eds.), *Constitutionalism in Islamic Countries: Between Upheaval and Continuity* (Oxford University Press).

Alston, P (1999). *A Framework for the Comparative Analysis of Bills of Rights*, in Alston, P (ed), Promoting Human Rights Through Bills of Rights: Comparative Perspectives 1–2.

Arato, A (2000). Civil Society, Constitution, and Legitimacy (University of Michigan, Rowman & Littlefield Publishers).

Austin, G (1966). The Indian Constitution: Cornerstone of a Nation (Oxford: Clarendon Press).

Brinks, DM & Forbath, W (2011). *Commentary: Social and Economic Rights in Latin America: Constitutional Courts and the Prospects for Pro-poor Interventions*, 89 Tex L Rev 1943.

Choudhry, S (ed) (1999). 'Globalisation in Search of Justification: Towards a Theory of Comparative Constitutional Interpretation', 74 Indiana Law Journal 819.

—— (2006). The Migration of Constitutional Ideas (Cambridge, Cambridge University Press).

Diamond, L (2005). Squandered Victory (Times Books; First Edition edn), 141–5.

Drobnig, U & Erp, SV (eds) (1999). The Use of Comparative Law by Courts (Kluwer Law International: London).

Elkins Z, Ginsburg, T & Melton, J (2009). The Endurance of National Constitutions (Cambridge University Press).

Elster, E (1995). *Forces and Mechanisms in the Constitution-making Process*, 45 Duke L J 364.

Ewald, W (1995). *Comparative Jurisprudence (II): The Logic of Legal Transplants*, 43 Am J Comp L 489.

Frankenburg, G (2010). Constitutional Transfer: The IKEA Theory Revisited, 8 International Journal of Constitutional Law, 563–79.

Gardbaum, G (2002). *The New Commonwealth Model of Constitutionalism*, 49 Am J Comp L 707.

Ginsburg, T (2003). Judicial Review in New Democracies (Cambridge University Press).

Glenn, HP (1987). Persuasive Authority, 32 McGill Law Journal 261.

Go, J (2003). *A Globalising Constitutionalism? Views from the Postcolony, 1945–2000*, 18 International Sociology 71.

Goldsworthy, J (2006). 'Questioning the migration of constitutional ideas: rights, constitutionalism and the limits of convergence', in Choudhry, S (ed), The Migration of Constitutional Ideas.

Halmai, G (2012). 'The Use of Foreign Law in Constitutional Interpretation', in Rosenfeld, M & Sajo, A (eds), The Oxford Handbook of Comparative Constitutional Law (Oxford, Oxford University Press), pp 1328–48.

Hirschl, R (2002). *Resituating the Judicialization of Politics: Bush v Gore as a Global Trend*, 25 Canadian J L & Juris 191.

—— (2004). Towards Juristocracy: The Origins and Consequences of the New Constitutionalism (Harvard).

Horwitz, MJ (2009). Constitutional Transplants, 10 Theoretical Inquiries in Law, 535–60.

Ihonvbere, J (2000). *Towards Participatory Mechanisms and Principles of Constitution Making in Africa, in* The Path to People's Constitution (Committee for the Defence of Human Rights, Lagos).

Kahn-Freund, O (1972). *On Uses and Misuses of Comparative Law*, 37 Mod L Rev 1.

Koch Jr, CH (2003). *Envisioning a Global Legal Culture*, 25 *Michigan Journal of International Law* (Fall 2003) 1–76.

Langbein, JH (1997). *Cultural Chauvinism in Comparative Law*, 5 Cardozo J Intl & Comp L 41.

Law, D & Versteeg, M (2001). *The Evolution and Ideology of Global Constitutionalism*, 99 California Law Review 1163–1257.

Law, DS (2008). 'Globalization and the Future of Constitutional Rights', 102 Northwestern University Law Review 1277.

Lester, A (1988). *The Overseas Trade in the American Bill of Rights*, 88 Colum L Rev 537.

Maghraoui, D (forthcoming 2012), *A critical analysis of the 2011 Moroccan Constitution* (International IDEA).

Markesinis, B & Fedtke, J (2009). Engaging with Foreign Law (Hart).

McCrudden, C (2000). 'A Common Law of Human Rights? Transnational Judicial Conversations on Constitutional Rights', 20 Oxford Journal of Legal Studies 499–511.

Montesquieu, C (1748). De L'Espirit Des Lois, book I, ch 3.

Nelken, D (2003). Comparatists and Transferability, in Legrand, P (ed), Comparative Legal Studies:

Tradition and Transitions (Cambridge) pp 437–66.

Osakwe, C (1984). *Introduction: The Problems of the Comparability of Notions in Constitutional Law*, 59 Tul L Rev 875.

Perju, V (2012). 'Constitutional Transplants, Borrowings and Migrations', in Rosenfeld, M & Sajo, A (eds), The Oxford Handbook of Comparative Constitutional Law (Oxford University Press), pp 1304–27.

Rahdert, M (2006). *Comparative Constitutional Advocacy*, 56 Am U L Rev 2007 13.

Roy, B (2004). 'An Empirical Survey of Foreign Jurisprudence and International Instruments in Charter Litigation', 62 University of Toronto Faculty Law Review 99.

Sarkin, J (1998). *The Effect Of Constitutional Borrowings On The Drafting Of South Africa's Bill Of Rights And Interpretation Of Human Rights Provisions*, 1 U Pa J Const L 176.

Saunders, C (2006). *The Use and Misuse of Comparative Constitutional Law*, 13 Ind J Glob Leg Stud 1.

Scheppele, KL (2006). 'The migration of anti-constitutional ideas: the post 9/11 globalization of public law and the international state of emergency', in Choudhry, S (ed), The Migration of Constitutional Ideas (Cambridge University Press).

Smith, A (2011). *Internationalization and constitutional borrowing in Bills of Rights*, 60 ICLQ 867–93.

Stein, E (1977). *Uses, Misuses – and Nonuses of Comparative Law*, 72 Nw U L Rev 198.

Stone Sweet A (2012). 'Constitutional Courts', in Rosenfeld, M & Sajo, A (eds), The Oxford Handbook of Comparative Constitutional Law (Oxford University Press), 816–30.

Thiruvengadam, AK (2009). Comparative Law and Insights from Constitutional Theory, in Tan, K & Thio, L (eds), Evolution of a Revolution: Forty Years of the Singapore Constitution (Routledge-Cavendish).

Tushnet, M (1999). 'The Possibilities of Comparative Constitutional Law', 108 Yale Law Journal 1225.

—— (2009). 'The Inevitable Globalization of Constitutional Law', 49 Virginia Journal of International Law 985.

Watson, A (1974). Legal Transplants: An Approach to Comparative Law (Edinburgh, Scottish Academic Press).

—— (1977). Society and Legal Change (Edinburgh, Scottish Academic Press).

Weinrib, L (2006). The Post-War Paradigm and American Exceptionalism, in Choudhry, S (ed), The Migration of Constitutional Ideas, pp 84–111.

Multicultural societies
and migration

Pierre Bosset, Anna Gamper and Theo Öhlinger

34.1 Introduction

Multiculturalism has been truly called the 'challenge of our time' (Fleiner & Basta-Fleiner, 511). Although multicultural societies have been an outcome of migration processes[1] perhaps for as long as we speak of states, the extent to which *worldwide* migration has changed social life almost everywhere has previously been unknown. This new global dimension of multiculturalism dramatically challenges both states and their constitutions.

Constitutions, however, respond differently to this challenge. Some of them expressly use the terms 'multicultural', 'pluricultural', 'plurinational', 'multiethnic', 'pluralist' or 'cultural diversity' as (partly synonymic) legal concepts. Others do not explicitly refer to multicultural societies, but nevertheless deal with the subject in equal measure. At the theoretical level, multiculturalism may assume different meanings. In a narrow sense, the term is restricted to a culturally diverse society, while a wider meaning—which is adopted in this chapter—also encompasses diversity caused by different ethnic or national origin, apart from diversity as to religion or language (see McCrudden, 202, with additional references).

This chapter explores the impact of multicultural societies and migration on constitutional systems worldwide as well as the different ways in which constitutions can treat these phenomena. The chapter shows that a wide range of constitutional themes are relevant in this context, including nearly all principles that are considered to be essential in the view of modern constitutionalism.

34.2 Constitutionalism and culture(s)

Constitutions not only express a certain legal culture, they also need to be understood against the general cultural background in which they are embedded (Häberle; Sajó; Dorsen,

---

1 Even indigenous peoples may have a migration background if their history is traced back to pre-historic times. Apart from that, indigenous issues are only an indirect outcome of migration (through colonization, if colonization is conceived as a migration process). Indigenous issues will be treated here as part and parcel of multicultural societies.

Rosenfeld, Sajó & Baer). Cultural constitutional law, being the effigy of that relation, builds constitutional identity (Tushnet). Often bearing an integrative character, it includes preambles that narrate the history of a nation, refer to a national culture or religion, or design the subject of constitutional identity as 'we the people'.[2] Integrative preambles, however, differ as to whether they authorize a certain culture to dominate with a view to assimilating those from another cultural background and to disestablish the need for cultural diversity, or whether they address a homogeneous *legal* subject to which the *pouvoir constituant* and *constitué* are ascribed—'the' people of a state, without prejudice to possible *cultural* diversity of that people. The South African Constitution, for example, addresses a single body as 'we, the people' in its preamble, whilst at the same time stressing that 'South Africa belongs to all who live in it, united in [. . . their] diversity'; seemingly an oxymoron, but actually attesting that multiculturalism and national identity are compatible through constitutional integration. The preamble of the Constitution of France, an ex-colonial power that is otherwise a unitary if decentralized state, includes a constitutional 'offer to the overseas territories that adhered to France'.[3] Some preambles do not merely refer to a multicultural national, but also a multinational identity. The preamble of the Ethiopian Constitution mentions the 'proud cultural legacies' of 'the Nations, Nationalities and Peoples of Ethiopia', while the preambles to the Russian and Chinese Constitutions refer to a 'multinational people' and the 'people of all nationalities' respectively, united in a joint endeavour for nation-building. 'The preamble to the controversial new Constitution of Hungary claims that nationalities form part of the Hungarian political community, while the "freedom and cultures of other people" are respected.'

Mostly, though, when preambles allude to different cultures, these cultures have an indigenous or at least ancient tradition that is accommodated in the concept of nation, without considering non-citizens or even immigrant citizens of the present. Other preambles do not seek to integrate or accommodate different cultures with due respect for their diversity, but bear a clearly monocultural character. In the latter case they stress a specific ethnicity, history or religion, such as Islam or Christianity (see, e.g., the Preamble to the Irish Constitution), though there are preambles that evidently present a more liberal notion of spirituality, such as the preambles to the Polish or Fijian Constitution. To avoid conveying a discriminatory message about non-Christians and non-believers, the idea of mentioning God or the Christian heritage of Europe, as discussed during the preparatory phase of the draft Treaty establishing a Constitution for Europe, was abandoned (von Bogdandy, 300–305).

Apart from preambles, which may or may not have a legally binding character under a specific nation's laws, state symbols and state objectives are constitutional elements particularly qualified for the entrenchment of cultural constitutional law, either by protecting a certain tradition, religion or cultural heritage due to a monocultural concept or by the express recognition of distinct cultures. Art 9 para 2 of the Bolivian Constitution, for example,

---

2 Another question is who belongs to 'the people': the preamble of the German Basic Law, e.g., originally presupposed 'the German people' in the *Länder* of West Germany (which was extended to 'the Germans' in the *Länder* after reunification), while the phrase in the US Constitution was used to avoid the enumeration of states instead of 'the people' as the source of sovereignty rather than applied to native Americans at that time; see Perry, 99–151; Orgad, 718–721.

3 This invitation should not obscure the fact that, under the Constitution, the 'French people' is 'indivisible'. Thus, a proposal for the constitutional recognition of the Corsican people was rejected as unconstitutional: *Conseil constitutionnel*, Decision No. 91–290, 9 May 1991.

stipulates as a state objective mutual respect as well as an intracultural, intercultural and plurilingual dialogue among persons, nations, peoples and communities, thus distinguishing even among different kinds of multiculturalism. Multicultural constitutional law is also richly embedded in both fundamental rights and institutional law as the two prime structures of modern constitutionalism (Jackson & Tushnet, 212–243). Multicultural institutional law is not limited just to federalism or citizenship issues, but also includes rules on linguistic or ethnic representation in state bodies (Belgium, or Bosnia and Herzegovina[4]) as well as on the role of traditional leaders in some African and Oceanian constitutions. Indigenous peoples are increasingly recognized by Meso and South American constitutions, including their right of self-organization (Stavenhagen 2002, 24–44; Sieder, 184–207). At a meta-level, finally, multicultural constitutional law is entrenched in provisions like Sec 27 of the Canadian Charter of Rights and Freedoms, which requires an interpretation of the Charter 'in a manner consistent with the preservation and enhancement of the multicultural heritage of Canadians' (see 34.5 below, 'Rights'), or the admittance of traditional customary law of aboriginal and indigenous peoples in many South American, African, South and East Asian and Oceanian constitutions, as well as the Canadian Constitution. Such provisions are particularly far-reaching, as they relativize the supremacy and monopoly of the 'established' law in favour of other sources of law derived from a certain non-majoritarian culture.

Although it would thus seem that multiculturalism is a key value of modern constitutionalism, this thesis faces two great challenges. First, multicultural constitutional law is most frequently confined to cases where there is a long-standing tradition of multiculturalism. Constitutions respond to multiculturalism most easily if there is a 'homogeneously heterogeneous' people with broadly the same culturally mixed background. An example is the preamble to the Fijian Constitution, which accurately narrates the history of settlement by the ancestors of the indigenous people and the arrival of settlers from several parts of the world that has 'made [. . . them] what [. . . they] are',[5] while the preamble to the Constitution of the Marshall Islands conversely attests resistance to 'impact of other cultures'. Where ancient migration processes are finalized before the enactment of the constitution, it appears easier for constitutions to accommodate multiculturalism even along more divided cultural lines, as in multinational states, federal states or states with strong minorities or indigenous peoples, endowing all individuals belonging to that multicultural society with citizenship. Within the closed circle set by nationhood and citizenship, multiculturalism is thus not only tolerated, but even established as a constitutional value. A good example is Sec 51A, para e of the Indian Constitution according to which it is the duty of every citizen of India to promote harmony and the spirit of common brotherhood amongst all the people of India transcending religious, linguistic and regional or sectional diversities, and to value and preserve the rich heritage of 'their' composite culture. Its limits, though, are obvious: neither the duty nor the protection guarantee goes beyond Indian citizens.

4 Note that Bosnia and Herzegovina's institutional arrangements regarding representation in state bodies have been ruled contrary to the anti-discrimination provisions of the European Convention for the Protection of Human Rights and Fundamental Freedoms and its Protocol No. 12 *Sejdic and Finci v Bosnia and Herzegovina*, [GC], nos. 27996/06 and 34836/06, 22 December 2009 [access to House of Peoples and Presidency limited to members of 'constituent peoples'].

5 The preamble stands in sharp contrast to the tensions between the indigenous Fijians and Indo-Fijians, which led to several constitutional coups; see Ghai & Cottrell, 287–315.

If a society becomes multicultural due to immigration after the enactment of the constitution, the question arises whether the identity of the constitutional subject changes over time and whether this requires another kind of constitutional accommodation. This is even more difficult for old and rigid constitutions, but it is also an eminently political question if, and how, a constitution wants to recognize '(im)migrant multiculturalism' as a distinctive constitutional feature. It often seems that constitutions are reluctant to do so, not only in case of (im)migrant non-citizens, but also if they acquired citizenship, although the reverse may be true for some states, such as Canada. The treatment of 'new' immigrants is thus less a matter of constitutional principles than a question of immigration and perhaps linguistic policy, even though this is seen in the light of universal human rights. A much more radical response, therefore, would be the enactment of restrictions on immigration, not just in ordinary legislation, but in the constitution itself.

Second, multiculturalism as a constitutional principle has to be put in context with other, sometimes antithetic, constitutional principles. For example, the ban on civil servants wearing religious garb in France is based on the laicism of the state (*laïcité*), while it also challenges the cultural rights of religious civil servants. The prohibition on building minarets in Art 72 para 3 of the Swiss Constitution was inserted after a referendum that was held in line with the high constitutional standing of direct democracy in Switzerland. If constitutions abstain from clear answers, it is ultimately for the courts to balance such clashes of principles. They arrive at highly different solutions, as the example of the diverse treatment of anti-multicultural hate speech in various jurisdictions shows (see 34.5 below, 'Rights').[6]

34.3 Citizenship

Although citizenship does not necessarily imply constitutional recognition of cultural differences between citizens, it is still a crucial factor for the treatment of cultural diversity. Generally, citizens enjoy better constitutional protection than persons who are not citizens of the state in which they live. The importance of citizenship is deeply rooted in the theory of the social contract, as the *pactum unionis* is concluded between those who are to be the citizens of the state that is being founded. As Rousseau put it: 'Si donc lors du pacte social il s'y trouve des opposants, leur opposition n'invalide pas le contrat, elle empêche seulement qu'ils n'y soient compris; ce sont des étrangers parmi les citoyens.'[7] The presumption is that persons born and living in a state tacitly agree to accept the authority of that state, whilst the cosmopolitan idea that a state has to take care of the diverse cultural backgrounds of non-citizens, however short their residence in that state may be, is much younger: at its onset stands the concept of universalism of human dignity and human rights, which is not only at the core of international human rights protection, but also enshrined in many constitutions. One theoretical possibility for constitutions to recognize multiculturalism, as a result of increasing migration, is therefore to extend citizenship to immigrants and to adopt a multicultural concept based on a pluralist understanding of demos. A more common constitutional response to migration is to draw a distinction between (immigrant) citizens, resident non-citizens and refugees. Among these, citizenship is the most privileged status, but also the status most difficult to acquire, although states differ considerably as to the requirements to be complied with,

6 Rosenfeld, 181–97; Jackson & Tushnet, 1484–1587.
7 Rousseau, book IV, chapter II.

ranging from mere requirements of residence to the observance of the laws of the host state, or to 'active' accomplishments, such as basic training in the national language and culture.

One of the most interesting examples where 'responsive' constitutions differently address resident non-citizens is the right to vote. Traditionally, this has not been a human right, but a citizen right. Due to the right's political nature, international law refrains from requiring states to extend it to foreign residents. Nevertheless, Art 6 para 1 of the Council of Europe's Convention on the Participation of Foreigners in Public Life at Local Level requires that every foreign resident be entitled to vote and stand for election in local authority elections, provided that he fulfil the same legal requirements that apply to nationals and, furthermore, has been a lawful and habitual resident for the five years preceding the elections. While it is thus not unusual for states to let non-citizen residents participate at local level, their admission to national or regional elections is still exceptional. In New Zealand, foreigners are entitled to vote at national level, if they are permanent residents (Rodriguez). The UK and many other Commonwealth countries grant similar privileges to citizens of other Commonwealth countries, mostly at statutory level, though. Within EU member states, the right to vote is generally not granted to foreigners (not even foreign EU citizens), although there are rare exceptions (e.g., UK citizens who may vote in Ireland). However, EU law entitles the citizens of member states to vote in European Parliament and local elections when residing in another member state, under the same conditions as nationals (Lansbergen & Shaw). This is the most striking effect of the concept of 'citizenship of the European Union'. According to Art 9 TEU, every national of a member state is a citizen of the Union, but citizenship of the Union shall be additional to and not replace national citizenship. Citizenship of the Union is thus a rather flamboyant term for a legal status that derives from national citizenship and presently neither constitutes an independent form of citizenship nor alters the (still, if atypically) confederal character of the European Union. In particular, it does not resemble federal citizenship, at least not that of fully-fledged federal systems (Kadelbach, 443–478; Schönberger).

Nevertheless, multi-tiered citizenship poses the question how a hybrid organization like the EU manages multiculturalism and migration. According to the preamble of the EU Charter of Fundamental Rights, the Union respects the diversity of the cultures and traditions of the peoples of Europe as well as the national identities of the member states, which corresponds with several constitutions that explicitly claim their state's contribution to cultural diversity in Europe. Apart from this general recognition of the different cultures of *states*, the rights of *persons* and the principle of pluralism are also enshrined in EU primary law. These concepts are not always compatible, as the recognition of diversity between member states is clearly limited by the rights and freedoms enjoyed by the citizens of these member states—in particular, the non-discrimination principle and the guarantee of free movement of persons allow EU citizens to migrate from one member state to another as well as to work and reside there permanently and unrestrictedly. While internal border controls were thus abolished within the so-called Schengen area, both the EU and member states, in their endeavours for a joint immigration policy, seek to fortify external borders to control excessive immigration, while some states even want to re-establish border controls at their internal frontiers.

A last issue to be mentioned in the context of citizenship is the relationship between nation and minorities. Here again, citizenship proves to be a powerful tool for an efficient protection of minorities either as collective entities or as individuals belonging to them. Although, in recent years, the Council of Europe's Parliamentary Assembly found it difficult, if not impossible, to arrive at a common definition of the concept of nation—either as a civic or as an ethno-cultural community—it identified a general trend from the ethnic state into a civic state and further into a 'multicultural state where specific rights are recognized with regard not only to physical persons but also to cultural or national communities'.[8] The question, however, is not just whether such rights are individual or collective rights, but whether citizenship is a crucial factor for the enjoyment of those rights. The Council of Europe's Framework Convention for the Protection of National Minorities, which applies to 'national minorities' without defining the term, leaves it to member states to determine whether national minorities consist only of citizens or not. However, the Convention's preamble stresses that cultural diversity enriches, not divides, a society, while Art 6 demands effective measures to promote mutual respect, understanding and cooperation 'among all persons living on their [the Parties'] territory', irrespective of those persons' ethnic, cultural, linguistic or religious identity, which means that citizenship is not obligatory. The Council of Europe's Venice Commission has encouraged states to extend their guarantees of protection to minorities that consist of non-citizens, since fundamental rights, except political rights, were universal human rights.[9] Clearly, though, minorities worldwide do not enjoy homogeneous protective standards (if at all) and citizens, for democratic reasons, still have better claims to active and fully-fledged protection from the state than immigrant (or, such as Roma, migrant) non- or 'second-class' citizens (Ringelheim, 108).

34.4 Federalism

Federalism is often described as a constitutional tool to accommodate the diverging principles of unity and diversity (Fleiner & Basta-Fleiner, 528). According to the traditional concept of federalism, diversity means that a number of states constitute a federal state, which does not necessarily mean that the constituent states differ ethnically or culturally from each other or that the federal state has a multicultural character solely because of the federal concept. Nevertheless, federalism may very well function towards accommodating multiculturalism if territorial diversity goes along with ethnic or cultural diversity (Jackson & Tushnet, 1040–138). Such management of diversity cannot only be performed by federal constitutions that provide a dual system of government, but to a smaller extent also by the constitutions of otherwise decentralized or regionalized states. Certain insular autonomies, such as Greenland, Åland, the Faroe Islands and the Azores, were asymmetrically accommodated even in otherwise highly unitary states. While secession would be the ultimate though precarious solution for a territorially divided multicultural society, federalism seeks to reconcile diversity and unity by granting the constituent units the right of internal self-determination. A federal solution compatible with the unity of the state has thus been proposed in order to resolve the bi- or multicultural conflicts in Sri Lanka, Iraq or Cyprus, while China, despite its constitutional commitment to multinationalism, still refuses an asymmetric form of regional self-government for Tibet. Best practice examples where constitutions successfully manage cultural diversity can be found particularly in 'Western' federal or highly regionalized states: these are the well-known cases of Quebec, Catalonia and South Tyrol, where a strong national minority constitutes the majority of a certain regional population. Multiculturalism in Belgium and Switzerland has a different aspect in so far as the federal 'people' is not split into

---

8 *Recommendation 1735 (2006)*, Council of Europe Parliamentary Assembly.
9 European Commission for Democracy through Law (Venice Commission), *Report on Non-Citizens and Minority Rights*, December 2006, CDL-AD (2007) 001, 36.

one large majority and one or more smaller minorities, but two or three larger and one or two smaller groups. The case of the linguistic communities in Belgium is, moreover, unique since in that case a personal entity instead of a territorial entity is endowed with constituent institutions and rights—a concept particularly developed by the Austrian Karl Renner, though not implemented, to resolve the conflict of nationalities in the Austrian and Austro-Hungarian Empire (Renner, 15–47). Multicultural overlaps of the personal and territorial dimension, however, may cause tensions between the accommodation of territorial groups through federalism and non-territorial groups or between majority and minority in the constituent territory (Fleiner & Basta-Fleiner, 511–521). While respect for cultural diversity was a fundamental condition for the foundation of 'coming together' federations (cf., strikingly, the preamble to the Micronesian Constitution), recent processes of migration, due to globalization, war or economic crisis, have not as yet correlated with a shift towards territorial decentralization.

34.5 Rights

The universalistic ideal of human rights has always co-existed uneasily with the reality of citizenship and its privileges, especially in matters of voting and other political rights. It is in fact not uncommon for constitutions to limit the enjoyment of fundamental human rights by non-citizens, especially migrants, whether in regular or irregular situation (Cholewinski). The Constitution of the People's Republic of China, for example, guarantees fundamental rights only to citizens (with the sole exception of the right to rest, which extends to all 'working people'). The Constitution of Sweden has an impressive list of rights for which 'special limitations' may be imposed on foreign nationals; the list includes freedom of expression, freedom of association, freedom of worship and protection against deprivation of liberty. To ensure conformity with international law, the Swedish Constitution also provides that no law may be adopted that contravenes Sweden's undertakings under the European Convention for the Protection of Human Rights and Fundamental Freedoms, thereby illustrating the now frequent interplay between constitutional law and international legal standards in the field of human rights. South Africa took a different approach to non-citizens in its post-apartheid constitution: it couched rights in universalistic terms ('everyone has the right to . . .', 'no one may be subjected to . . .') while subjecting limitations on the rights of non-citizens—like any other limitation on rights—to the normal requirements of purpose, relevance and proportionality. This latter approach seems to be in keeping with current trends in international law. Thus, the International Convention on the Protection of the Rights of All Migrant Workers and Members of their Families, adopted in 1990, seeks explicitly to discourage recourse to irregular migrant workers, by promoting recognition for the fundamental rights of all migrant workers. This was designed to compensate for the fact that the rights of migrant workers (cf. preamble of the Convention) 'have not been sufficiently recognized everywhere and therefore require appropriate international protection'. The Convention's approach has found support in an advisory opinion by the Inter-American Court of Human Rights to the effect that, under international law, undocumented migrant workers enjoy the same labour human rights as other workers.[10] This does not easily find favour with the states concerned: as of September 2012, the list of signatories to the Convention

---

10 *Juridical Condition and Rights of Undocumented Migrants* (2003), Advisory Opinion OC-18/03, Inter-Am Ct. H.R. (Ser. A), no. 18 (paras. 128–160).

still failed to include a single major 'receiving' state.[11] The enduring differential treatment of migrants at the national level is to be contrasted with recent pronouncements by expert UN organs emphasizing that human rights are, in principle, to be enjoyed by 'everyone including non-nationals, such as refugees, asylum-seekers, stateless persons, migrant workers and victims of international trafficking, regardless of legal status and documentation'.[12]

Whether it is the outcome of recent or ancient migrations or stems from a long-standing history of diversity (e.g., indigenous peoples), multiculturalism often raises sensitive issues in both legal and human rights terms. These include the scope of equality (whether limited to equality of rights, or extending to equality of opportunities, or even results); whether the recognition of cultural differences would conflict with other human rights (e.g., gender equality); the extent of free speech in relation to race or religion; or the proper relationship of the state vis-à-vis religions. In the quest for legal answers to such issues, courts—acting as 'philosopher kings' (Christie)—will adopt a wide range of national approaches to certain issues. Approaches to equality under the law, for example, will often range from somewhat formalistic ones, at one end of the spectrum, focussing on equality before the law, to substantive ones at the other end, possibly encompassing affirmative action and reasonable accommodation of cultural differences.[13] To some extent, discrepancies in national approaches may result from specific requirements of constitutions, such as *laïcité* in France (or Turkey); but they may also reflect how courts choose to frame an issue. Thus, it is remarkable how differently various courts in Europe and North America have addressed the controversial question of whether crosses should be allowed in public buildings. On the one hand, some courts held that the cross denoted Christianity and thus infringed on the freedom of religion of non-Christians or non-believers (Germany; Switzerland; Canadian province of Quebec); whilst others considered the cross a cultural symbol with no impact on other denominations (Austria; Italy; Grand Chamber of the European Court of Human Rights with respect to Italy). In other cases, the borrowing of foreign legal concepts may turn out to be only a rhetorical device with little regard to the original meaning of the concept; this is what happened, for example, to the North American concept of reasonable accommodation of cultural differences, which a French official report on *laïcité* chose to re-interpret as meaning that individuals should refrain from expressing their cultural identities for the sake of social cohesion.[14] Finally, constitutions themselves, or judicial decisions, may define the extent of and limitations on human rights, suggesting an implicit hierarchy of rights. A clear illustration is the legal treatment of hate speech. Under international law, there is a strong current in favour of limitations on anti-multicultural hate speech, as in the explicit provisions of a number of UN human rights treaties. In practice, national approaches range from constitutional classifications of racism as a crime (Brazil), or outright exclusions of hate speech from any

---

11 See: http://treaties.un.org/Pages/ViewDetails.aspx?src=TREATY&mtdsg_no=IV-13&chapter=4& lang=en.

12 UN Committee on Economic, Social and Cultural Rights, *General Comment No. 20: Non-Discrimination in Economic, Social and Cultural Rights*, para. 30; UN Committee on the Elimination of Racial Discrimination, *General Recommendation No. 30: Discrimination against Non-Citizens*, para. 3.

13 For a comparative study of the United States, Canada and Europe, see Bribosia, Ringelheim & Rorive. On the backlash against policies of accommodation, especially of religious differences, and the emergence of a so-called 'post-multiculturalism', see McCrudden, 201–205.

14 France, Commission de réflexion sur l'application du principe de laïcité dans la République, *Rapport remis au Président de la République*, Paris, La Documentation française, 2003, 16–17.

constitutional protection (e.g., South Africa) at one extreme, to a value-neutral conception of free speech that will tolerate hate speech, as long as it does not amount to defamation or incitement at the other extreme (US).

Given the wide range of approaches to human rights interpretation in plural societies, it may be queried whether greater consistency might be achieved by resorting to an overarching constitutional value or principle, such as recognition or even promotion of multiculturalism.[15] As indicated above, an attempt to specifically link human rights interpretation with multiculturalism features in the Canadian Charter of Rights and Freedoms, which provides that human rights shall be interpreted consistently with the preservation and enhancement of the multicultural heritage of Canadians. Multiculturalist interpretation has had some notable influence on the outcome of a number of significant Canadian cases. Thus, courts have ruled that an absolute prohibition on wearing a Sikh kirpan in public schools would contradict the promotion of multiculturalism, thereby violating the proportionality requirement: the child involved in that case was allowed to wear a kirpan, provided that basic safeguards were observed.[16] Similarly, the enhancement of the social participation has been invoked in Canada to justify limitations on freedom of expression in a multicultural society. In stark contrast with the US approach to free speech, Canadian hate speech cases emphasize the commitment to multiculturalism which, according to them, bears notice 'in emphasizing the acute importance of the objective of eradicating hate propaganda from society'.[17]

Even accepting that significant constitutional developments (e.g., in equality law) may occur without any overarching principle of multiculturalist interpretation, an explicit or judicial rule of multicultural interpretation clearly provides a framework for interpreting human rights in plural societies. A number of constitutions adopted or modified over the last two decades, especially in South and Central America (Bolivia, Colombia, Ecuador, Mexico, Nicaragua, Paraguay and Peru), explicitly recognize the multicultural nature of societies. Yet, the constitutional recognition of multiculturalism, and judicial interpretations thereof, have been criticized for not challenging the liberal paradigm of individual self-fulfilment and insufficiently taking 'radical' diversity (i.e., traditional communities that reject liberal values) into account.[18] Indeed, it is interesting to note that, in the Canadian cases cited above, an underlying element was the consideration given to the symbiotic relationship between an individual and the cultural group he belongs to. Thus, the Chief Justice of Canada explicitly linked group belonging and cultural rights to individual self-fulfilment when he wrote that the Canadian Charter emphasized the need 'to prevent attacks on the individual's connection with his or her culture, and hence upon the process of self-development'.[19] The liberal paradigm of self-fulfilment is also implicitly present in substantive concepts of equality such as reasonable accommodation, which emphasize the right of individuals, but not groups as such, to take part on an equal footing in the broader society.

15 On 'values' and 'principles', see Venter, 55–58.

16 *Multani v Commission scolaire Marguerite-Bourgeoys*, [2006] 1 SCR 256.

17 *R v Keegstra* [1990] 3 SCR 697 at p. 757.

18 Thus, with respect to Colombian multiculturalism: Bonilla Maldonado, *La Constitución multicultural* (Bogotá, Universidad de Los Andes, 2006) at pp. 158 ff.

19 *Keegstra, loc. cit.*

The category of cultural rights, as part of the so-called 'third generation' of rights,[20] is useful when approaching the inherent tension between group rights and individual self-fulfilment (see Chapters 30 and 31). It is a crossroads for a vast array of rights—civil, political, social and cultural proper—that have culture as their object. Freedom to create, access to and participation in culture, and respect for cultural identity, are fundamental elements of cultural rights. Respect for cultural identity—taken here in the anthropological sense (Stavenhagen 1995, 66 ff)—entails a positive obligation to take group specificities into account when public policy is being developed. Thus, the UN Committee on Economic, Social and Cultural Rights has developed the concept of cultural adequacy, which refers to the idea that every human right (e.g., the right to housing or the right to health) has a *cultural component* that public policies should respect. Yet, in a recent general comment, the Committee has emphasized that the right to take part in cultural life should above all 'be characterized as a freedom', thereby implying a right for individuals not to claim belonging in a specific group, to claim belonging in more than one cultural group, or to change such choice over time, which brings us back within the fold of the liberal paradigm.[21]

Even where multiculturalism is constitutionally recognized or promoted, the view of culture that is put forward remains an essentialist one that ignores the impact of cross-influencing and cross-fertilization in the development of culture (Stamatopoulou). Perhaps the notion of interculturalism (see the Constitution of Bolivia), which encourages cross-cultural interaction and the development of a shared culture based on the initial cultural identities, but eventually transcending them, should be given more attention in the future. Based on the premise that culture is a process, not a prison, both cultural rights and interculturalism have the potential to harmoniously integrate the individual, the social and the identitarian dimensions of human rights, while ontologically respecting the fluid nature of culture. Within the liberal paradigm outlined above, they should therefore be considered as useful conceptual tools in giving meaning to human rights in multicultural societies.

34.6 Conclusion

Has the globalization of migration issues and multiculturalism led to a homogenization of constitutional approaches? The question is closely related to current discussions about constitutional convergence and the globalization of law, a broader phenomenon.[22]

Generally speaking, legal globalization is seen as regulating and, above all, facilitating the mobility of goods, capital and labour. However, legal globalization is inspired also by competing ethical concerns, such as respect for the environment, the sanction of crimes against humanity or the protection of human rights. Thus, it could legitimately be hypothesized that the globalization of human rights, based on concepts of dignity, freedom and equality, would have a uniformizing effect on constitutions in terms of citizenship, fundamental rights and possibly even institutional multinationalism. This hypothesis rests on the assumption that human rights are univocal, an assumption that disregards the fact that rights

---

20 For the classic presentation of rights in terms of generations, see: Vasak, 'Le droit international des droits de l'homme', 140 *Recueil des cours*, Hague Academy of International Law (1974).

21 UN Committee on Economic, Social and Cultural Rights, *General Comment No 21: The Right of Everyone to Take Part in Cultural Life*, E/C.12/GC/21 (2009).

22 Legal globalization is understood here as the process through which the transnational and international character of human activity (including law itself) influences the creation of law. For an overview of current debates on legal globalization, see Mockle.

are objects of interpretation. Perhaps this would be less problematic were constitutional interpretation to be based on principles such as multiculturalism (or interculturalism) and on fluid notions of culture, as put forward here. However, this is not borne out by facts, as constitutions continue to react to multiculturalism and migrations in widely different, sometimes antithetic, ways.

Legal globalization, as regards migration and multiculturalism, is therefore much less one-sided, univocal and linear than any superficial outlook would suggest. Clearly, further empirical research is needed on the nature, extent and impact of interactions between legal orders (national and international) on the constitutional treatment of migration and multiculturalism. Nevertheless, it seems safe to assume that cultural constitutional law, as described above, continues to influence the reception and interpretation of legal concepts and that, where resorting to foreign or international 'models' occurs, its function—as exemplified by the re-interpretation of the concept of reasonable accommodation—may be rhetoric as well as normative. In short, legal globalization is not 'a slow and peaceful river' (Allard & Garapon, 9); it is a process, sometimes even a battlefield. Therefore, analyzing how constitutions react to migrations and multiculturalism should focus not just on the 'black-letter' law (in constitutions or in case law), but also on how legal discourse is invoked, perhaps even instrumentalized, by constitutional actors. This is an exercise in the sociology of law as well as in constitutional law.

References

Allard, J & Garapon, A (2005). *Les juges dans la mondialisation: La nouvelle révolution du droit* (Paris, Seuil).

Bonilla Maldonado, D (2006). *La Constitución multicultural* (Bogotá, Universidad de Los Andes).

Bribosia, E, Ringelheim, J & Rorive, I (2009). 'Aménager la diversité: le droit de l'égalité face à la pluralité religieuse', *Revue trimestrielle des droits de l'homme* 78: 319–373.

Cholewinski, Ryszard (1997). *Migrant Workers in International Human Rights Law: Their Protection in Countries of Employment* (Oxford, Oxford University Press).

Christie, GC (2011). *Philosopher Kings? The Adjudication of Conflicting Human Rights and Social Values* (Oxford, Oxford University Press).

Dorsen, N, Rosenfeld, M, Sajó, A & Baer, S (2010). *Comparative Constitutionalism* (2nd edn, St Paul, West Law School).

Fleiner, T & Basta-Fleiner, LR (2009). *Constitutional Democracy in a Multicultural and Globalised World* (Berlin/Heidelberg, Springer).

Ghai, Y & Cottrell, J (2008). 'A tale of three constitutions: Ethnicity and politics in Fiji', in Choudhry, S (ed), *Constitutional Design for Divided Societies: Integration or Accommodation?* (New York/Oxford, Oxford University Press) 287–312.

Häberle, P (2011). *Europäische Verfassungslehre* (7th edn, Baden-Baden, Nomos).

Jackson, V & Tushnet, M (2006). *Comparative Constitutional Law* (2nd edition, New York, Foundation Press)

Kadelbach, S (2011). 'Union Citizenship', in Bogdandy, A & Bast, J (Eds), *Principles of European Constitutional Law* (2nd edition, Munich/Oxford, Beck/Hart).

Lansbergen, A & Shaw, J (2010). 'National membership models in a multilevel Europe', *International Journal of Constitutional Law* 8: 50–71.

McCrudden, C (2011). 'Multiculturalism, freedom of religion, equality, and the British constitution: The JFS case considered', *International Journal of Constitutional Law* 9: 200–229.

Mockle, D (ed) (2002). *Mondialisation et État de droit* (Brussels, Bruylant).

Orgad, L (2010). 'The preamble in constitutional interpretation', *International Journal of Constitutional Law* 8: 714–738.

Perry, MJ (1998). 'What Is "the Constitution"? (and Other Fundamental Questions)', in Alexander, L (ed), *Constitutionalism: Philosophical Foundations* (Cambridge, Cambridge University Press) 99–151.

Renner, K (2005). 'State and Nation', in Nimni, E (ed), *National Cultural Autonomy and its Contemporary critics* (London, Routledge) 15–47.

Ringelheim, J (2010). 'Minority Rights in a Time of Multiculturalism – The Evolving Scope of the Framework Convention on the Protection of National Minorities', *Human Rights Law Review* 10: 99–128.

Rodriguez, CM (2010). 'Noncitizen voting and the extraconstitutional construction of the polity', *International Journal of Constitutional Law* 8: 30–49.

Rosenfeld, M (2009). 'Regulation of Hate Speech', in Amar, VK & Tushnet, MV (Eds), *Global Perspectives on Constitutional Law* (New York/Oxford, Oxford University Press) 181–197.

Rousseau, JJ (1762). *Du contrat social, ou Principes du droit politique*.

Sajó, A (2010). 'Emotions in constitutional design', *International Journal of Constitutional Law* 8: 354–384.

Schönberger, C (2007). 'European Citizenship as Federal Citizenship', *European Review of Public Law* 19: 61–82.

Sieder, R (2002). 'Recognising Indigenous Law and the Politics of State Formation in Mesoamerica', in Sieder, R (ed), *Multiculturalism in Latin America* (Houndmills/Basingstoke/Hampshire/New York, Palgrave Macmillan) 184–207.

Stamatopoulou, E (2007). *Cultural Rights in International Law* (Leiden/Boston, Nijhoff).

Stavenhagen, R (2001). 'Cultural Rights and Universal Rights', in Eide, A, Krause, C & Rosas, A (eds), *Economic, Social and Cultural Rights: A Textbook* (Dordrecht, Nijhoff).

—— (2002). 'Indigenous Peoples and the State in Latin America: An Ongoing Debate', in Sieder, R (ed), *Multiculturalism in Latin America* (Houndmills/Basingstoke/Hampshire/New York, Palgrave Macmillan) 24–44.

Tushnet, M (2010). 'How do constitutions constitute constitutional identity?', *International Journal of Constitutional Law* 8: 671–676.

Vasak, K (1974). 'Le droit international des droits de l'homme', 140 *Recueil des cours,* Hague Academy of International Law 333–416.

Venter, F (2010). *Global Features of Constitutional Law* (Nijmegen, Wolf Legal Publishers).

von Bogdandy, A (2005). 'The European constitution and European identity: Text and subtext of the Treaty establishing a Constitution for Europe', *International Journal of Constitutional Law* 3: 295–315.

Additional reading

Asmal, K (2007). 'The South African Constitution and the Transition from Apartheid: Legislating the reconciliation of rights in a multi-cultural Society', *Amicus Curiae* 69: 26–32.

Bosset, P (2011). 'Complex Equality, Ambiguous Freedoms: Lessons from Canada (and Québec) on Human Rights in Plural Societies', *Nordic Journal of Human Rights* 29(1): 4–37.

Charters, C (2011). 'Comparative constitutional law and Indigenous peoples: Canada, New Zealand and the USA', in Ginsburg, T & Dixon, R (eds), *Comparative Constitutional Law* (Cheltenham/Northampton, Edward Elgar) 170–188.

Choudhry, S (ed) (2008). *Constitutional Design for Divided Societies: Integration or Accommodation?* (Oxford, Oxford University Press).

Preuss, UK & Requejo, F (eds) (1998). *European Citizenship, Multiculturalism, and the State* (Baden-Baden, Nomos).

Rubenstein, K & Lenagh-Maguire, N (2011). 'Citizenship and the boundaries of the constitution', in Ginsburg, T & Dixon, R (eds), *Comparative Constitutional Law* (Cheltenham/Northampton, Edward Elgar) 143–169.

Saxena, R (ed) (2011). *Varieties of Federal Governance. Major Contemporary Models* (New Delhi, Cambridge University Press India).

Sieder, R (ed) (2002). *Multiculturalism in Latin America. Indigenous Rights, Diversity and Democracy* (Houndmills/Basingstoke/Hampshire/New York, Palgrave Macmillan).

Tierney, S (ed) (2007). *Multiculturalism and the Canadian Constitution* (Vancouver/Toronto, UBC Press).

Constitutions, populations and demographic change*

Brian Opeskin and Enyinna Nwauche

35.1 Introduction

In late 2011 the world marked the arrival of its seven-billionth human inhabitant. It had taken just 12 years for the last billion people to be added to world population; the next billion is expected to be added within 14 years, by 2025. The United Nations projects that 2.4 billion people will be added to the world's 2010 population by 2050. Some 97 percent of this growth will be in less developed regions—mostly in Africa and Asia—and nearly all in urban centres. Europe, by contrast, is projected to decline in absolute population, despite significant immigration.

Changes of this scale generate significant long-term social transformations within countries, as populations change in size, composition and spatial distribution. It might be expected that constitutions would anticipate or reflect such changes because constitutions are intended to establish an enduring legal architecture for the governance of social and political communities. While many constitutions reveal an awareness of population dynamics, for others the impact can be subtle or fragmented.

The link between constitutions and populations attracted attention in the 1970s and 1980s, after Paul Erlich's book, *The Population Bomb*, generated widespread international concern about the Malthusian calamity that might arise from unchecked population growth in a world of finite resources (Ehrlich). In that context, several scholars examined how the US Constitution might regulate demographic processes, but the issue has now largely slipped from view.

This Chapter seeks to address this gap. It surveys the nature of population change, globally and in selected case studies, and then examines how population dynamics are relevant to four constitutional domains. The *political domain* addresses structural issues about government and representation. The *socio-economic domain* considers how constitutions affect populations through their effects on individuals as economic and social beings, and their decision-making

* The authors wish to thank Bronwyn Lo for research assistance, and Denise Meyerson, Nick Parr and the editors for insightful comments on a draft.

about fertility, mortality and migration. The *ethno-cultural domain* examines how constitutions address issues of demographic composition, especially ethnic diversity. Finally, the *scientific domain* explores the ways in which governments acquire knowledge about populations through national censuses and other means, thus informing action within the other domains.

The Chapter focusses on the experience of six countries—Australia, Brazil, India, Indonesia, Nigeria and the United States—a choice informed by the desirability of including some of the most populous countries (they accounted for more than 30 percent of global population in 2010), as well as representatives of federal and unitary states, old and new constitutions, developed and developing states, and states from different legal traditions. Other constitutions are referred to where relevant.

35.2 The nature of population change

Four attributes of a country's population affect constitutional design or operation: the size of the population and how it changes over time; the spatial distribution of the population; the structure or composition of the population; and the relative contribution of three population processes (fertility, mortality and migration), which drive all population change. Demographic change is a highly complex phenomenon and what follows is no more than a sketch of its main features. Key data are presented in Table 35.1.

35.2.1 Population size

For some 200,000 years, the presence of humans on earth was scarcely noticeable because high death rates kept the population at relatively low and stable levels (Weeks, 34). World population gradually reached one billion shortly after 1800, but the Industrial Revolution brought social changes that came to be reflected in greatly accelerated population growth. The change from patterns of high fertility and mortality to patterns of low fertility and mortality has been explained by the theory of the 'demographic transition'. Better nutrition, sanitation and medicine reduced high rates of mortality, thus removing the pressure to have large families; but the decline in fertility often lagged decades behind the decline in mortality, leading to exponential population growth in the interim. Globally, the rate of population growth peaked in 1970 at 2.07 percent per annum. Despite the slower rate of annual growth today (1.16 percent), substantial numbers are added to world population each year—95 million in 2011 alone.

The demographic transition has been experienced at different times and rates in different societies, and the case studies reflect this varied experience. India and Nigeria are currently growing much faster than the global average, underpinning their projected population growth from 1.23 to 1.69 billion and from 158 to 390 million, respectively, by 2050. By that year, India is projected to be the most populous country in the world (overtaking China), and Nigeria the fourth most populous. All the case-study countries will experience significant population growth between 2010 and 2050, but the population of some other countries (e.g., Russia and the Baltic states) is projected to decline. Population size has constitutional salience in the political domain because of its impact on the size of legislatures and on state formation.

35.2.2 Population distribution

The spatial distribution of a population responds to many factors, including differential rates of growth in different localities and the capacity to migrate internally and internationally.

Table 35.1 Demographic data, selected countries

	Year	Unit	Australia	Brazil	India	Indonesia	Nigeria	USA	World	Source
Adoption of current constitution	–	year	1901	1988	1950	1945	1999	1787	–	(d)
Human development world rank	2011	range: 0 to 187	2	84	134	124	156	4	–	(a)
States (internal territories)	2011		6(2)	26(1)	28(7)	–	36(1)	50(1)	–	(a)
Population	2010	millions	22.3	194.9	1224.6	239.9	158.4	310.4	6895.9	(a)
Population world rank	2010	range: 0 to 187	51	5	2	4	7	3	–	(a)
Rate of population change	2005–10	% per year	1.75	0.94	1.43	1.08	2.5	0.89	1.16	(a)
Projected population	2050	millions	31.4	222.8	1692.0	293.5	389.6	403.1	9306.1	(a)
Projected population world rank	2050	range: 0 to 187	61	7	1	5	4	3	–	(a)
Population density	2010	persons/km^2	3	23	373	126	171	32	51	(a)
Urbanisation	2009	%	89	87	30	44	50	82	50	(b)
Projected urbanisation	2050	%	94	94	54	66	75	90	69	(b)
Median age	2010	years	36.9	29.1	25.1	27.8	18.5	36.9	29.2	(a)
Population aged 60+	2010	%	19	10.3	7.6	8.2	5.3	18.4	11	(a)
Total fertility rate	2005–10	children per woman	1.93	1.90	2.73	2.19	5.61	2.07	2.52	(a)
Life expectancy at birth (males)	2005–10	years	79.1	68.7	62.8	66.3	49.5	75.4	65.7	(a)
Life expectancy at birth (females)	2005–10	years	83.8	75.9	65.7	69.4	51.0	80.5	70.1	(a)
Infant mortality rate	2005–10	deaths per 1000 births	5	23	53	29	96	7	46	(a)
Stock of immigrants	2005	% of population	21.3	0.4	0.5	0.1	0.7	13.0	3.0	(c)
Annual net migration	2005–10	thousands per year	225	–100	–600	–259	–60	991	0	(a)

(a) United Nations Department of Economic and Social Affairs, Population Division, World Population Prospects: The 2010 Revision
(b) United Nations Department of Economic and Social Affairs, Population Division, Urbanization Prospects: The 2009 Revision
(c) United Nations Development Programme, 'Human Development Report 2009: Overcoming Barriers – Human Mobility and Development' (UNDP, 2009)
(d) United Nations Development Programme, 'Human Development Report 2011: Sustainability and Equity: A Better Future for All' (UNDP, 2011)

Globally, population density averaged 51 persons/km² in 2010, but this masks large disparities between countries—from just 3 persons/km² in Australia to 373 persons/km² in India—and even larger disparities within countries.

One of the most significant demographic trends of our age is the steady urbanisation of the population, as people leave rural areas in search of employment in towns and cities. In 1800, less than 1 percent of world population lived in cities of more than 100,000 people (Weeks, 46). Today, more than one-third of the world's population live in cities of that size, 50 percent live in towns and cities of any size, and this is projected to rise to 69 percent by 2050. The effects of increasing urbanisation will be most pronounced in developing countries. This can be seen in the case studies, where urbanisation is projected to increase from 30 percent to 54 percent in India, and from 44 percent to 66 percent in Indonesia, over the period 2009–2050. Population distribution has constitutional salience in the political domain because of its impact on electoral representation and funding for states and other sub-national units.

35.2.3 Population structure

Populations vary in the proportion of males and females at different ages (the age–sex structure) and across other attributes such as education, social status and ethnicity. With respect to age, countries in the earlier stages of the demographic transition tend to have young populations due to high fertility and low life expectancy. Nigeria and India exemplify this with their low median ages (18.5 and 25.1 years) and small aged populations. Countries that have completed the demographic transition have older populations due to low fertility and high life expectancy. Australia and the United States exemplify this with their high median ages (both 36.9 years) and a high proportion of their populations in older age groups (18–19 percent are aged 60+). Population structure has constitutional salience in the socio-economic domain if there are mandated social protections (e.g., retirement pensions) for the elderly, or universal free education for the young. In the political domain, changing population structures also affect the size and composition of the voting-age population.

35.2.4 Population processes

All population change is driven by just three processes—fertility (births), mortality (deaths) and migration. The balance between these components varies from one country to another and over time. Births and deaths are biological processes, and the balance between them reflects different stages of the demographic transition. Historically, some societies experienced fertility rates as high as 10 children per woman if no attempt was made to limit childbirth, but fertility has fallen globally since the 1970s and today averages just 2.52 children per woman. Nigeria and India exceed this average, while fertility in the other case studies is below the 'replacement level' of about 2.1 children per woman. Many constitutions make provision for the interrelated issues of fertility, marriage, family planning and abortion.

Mortality has undergone an 'epidemiological transition', from an age of pestilence and famine when lives typically spanned 20–30 years, to an age of degenerative and man-made diseases marked by dramatically increased life span (Omran). Global life expectancy at birth is now 65.7 years for males and 70.1 years for females. In Nigeria, life expectancy falls well below this average; conversely, life expectancies in Australia and the United States are among the highest in the world.

Migration is the third demographic process but its patterning is complex because it responds to fluctuating economic conditions and government policy. The cumulative impact of net international migration means that about 3 percent of the world's population live outside the country of their birth. For settler societies the figure is much higher—24 percent of the population in Australia, and 13 percent in the United States, are migrants. Conversely, Brazil, India, Indonesia and Nigeria experienced sizeable net emigration over the period 2005–2010. The regulation of cross-border movement is central to defining social membership, and constitutions thus routinely empower legislatures to make laws on that subject. Migration raises important constitutional questions, especially in Europe, which are dealt with in more detail elsewhere in this volume (see Chapter 34).

35.3 Population and the political domain

35.3.1 Size of the legislature

It is a common experience that the size of legislatures in representative democracies expands over time as the population increases. This is partly a principled response to the desire to maintain a close connection between electors and their representatives, and partly a pragmatic response to the challenges faced by legislators in managing complex modern economies. However, the growth in legislatures is typically less than proportional to the growth in population because, as the size of the chamber increases, parliament is less capable of functioning as an assembly (Dahl & Tufte, 80). At some point, there are practical limits to further growth.

The pressure for expansion is felt most acutely in the lower chamber of bicameral systems because these are, in name or function, people's houses. Yet, upper chambers are not necessarily immune from population pressures, especially where there is a formal nexus between the sizes of the two houses. This is the case in Australia, where the House of Representatives must be twice the size of the Senate (s 24), and thus any measure to increase the size of the former has consequences for the latter.

Constitutions play diverse roles in the process of legislative expansion, some being permissive and others prescriptive. Some constitutions, such as Indonesia's, do not indicate the number of members in the lower chamber but leave the matter entirely to the legislature (currently 560 members) (arts 2, 19, 22C). Other constitutions, such as Nigeria's, specify the exact size of the lower chamber (360 members), with no express mechanism for growth other than through the regular processes of constitutional amendment (s 49). Other constitutions stipulate an initial size and leave it to the legislature to alter the number of representatives as it thinks fit. In 1787, the US Constitution specified 66 members of the House of Representatives (art I s 2), but federal law gradually expanded the lower house to its present 435 members, the last expansion occurring in 1911. The only constitutional constraints are that each state has at least one member and that there be *no more* than one member for every 30,000 people—long since made irrelevant by the country's rapid population growth. Still other constitutions include a constitutional formula for determining the total number of members, with or without a cap. The Brazilian Constitution (art 45) stipulates that the total number of Deputies in the lower chamber shall be 'in proportion to the population' but determined by law, which since 1993 has capped that number at 513. In India, the lower chamber is capped at 530 members from the states and 20 from the territories (art 81).

35.3.2 Electoral representation

Demographic change also affects the spatial dimensions of electoral representation. Although imperfectly realised, the guiding democratic principle is 'one vote, one value'. The

459

mechanism for achieving this, in systems with single-member electorates, is that electoral boundaries should be drawn to ensure that, as nearly as is practicable, each electorate contains the same number of voters.

This conception of political equality is generally absent from representation in upper chambers. In federations, upper chambers usually follow a federal principle by which each state elects an equal number of members regardless of the state's population—in the United States it is 2; in Brazil and Nigeria, 3; in Australia, 12; while India is atypical in that its Council of States comprises unequal numbers of representatives from each state, ranging from 1 to 31.[1] Non-federal states may contain similar features: in Indonesia, up to one-quarter of the People's Consultative Assembly ('MPR') is drawn from a regional council ('DPD') whose members are drawn in equal numbers from the 30 provinces (arts 2, 22C).

In lower chambers, population proportionality is the dominant organising principle. In Nigeria, for example, the boundaries of each federal constituency shall be such that 'the number of inhabitants thereof is as nearly equal to the population quota as is reasonably practicable' (s 72). In some federations, the organising principle operates twice over—seats are allocated to the states in proportion to each state's population and, within each state, single-member electorates are required to contain equal numbers of voters.[2]

The application of population proportionality to lower chambers is not perfect, and the imperfections come from many sources. First, inequalities arise because of indivisibilities that result from allocating people to a small and finite number of electorates. Second, voter equality achieved at one point in time can deliquesce in the face of dynamic populations, necessitating periodic adjustments. Third, floors and ceilings to state representation in the national legislature can introduce anomalies—the former resulting in over-representation of the least populous states and the latter resulting in under-representation of the most populous. In the United States, each state is entitled to a minimum of one seat in the House of Representatives; in Australia it is 5; in Brazil there is a minimum of 8 and a maximum of 70; and in India the proportionality rule does not apply to small states (those under six million people).[3] Fourth, the way in which population is defined can have a distorting effect. In 1976 the Indian Constitution was amended to fix the population of the states as at the 1971 census for the purpose of allocating seats in the national parliament to the states (art 81). The data will not be revised until at least 2026, by which time the population figures will be 55 years out of date. The reason for the freeze was ostensibly to prevent the rapidly growing northern states from being rewarded—by extra seats—for poor performance in lowering birth rates, in contradiction of the government's policy of reducing population growth (Haub & Sharma, 14).

35.3.3 State formation in federations

For those countries with a federal constitution, population change may also drive the formation of states within the union. Historically, this can be seen in the way in which the 13 original states of the United States expanded to 50, growing westward to fill the entire continental land mass. While the US Constitution provides that new states may be admitted

---

1 Australia s 7; Brazil art 46; India art 80, sch 4; Nigeria s 48; United States art I s 3.
2 Australia s 24; United States art 1, s 2; India art 81. The second requirement (equally sized electorates within a state) derives from legislation in Australia and case law in the United States: see *Wesberry v Sanders* 376 US 1 (1964) and its progeny. See also Brazil art 45.
3 Australia s 24; United States art I s 2; Brazil art 45; India art 81.

into the Union, it left Congress to fashion the conditions of entry. The Northwest Ordinance (1787) addressed this issue by stipulating that a territory could petition for admission as a new state only once its population reached 60,000. This established a precedent by which the United States expanded through the addition of new states.

All federal constitutions provide for the admission of new states, but where existing states already occupy all available land territory, new states can only be added by new territorial acquisitions or, more commonly, by carving out new states from old. The procedures for doing so vary, requiring federal legislation, consent of the affected state legislatures, a referendum of the affected population, or a combination of these.[4] Of the case studies, the Nigerian Constitution is the most onerous, requiring: (a) support from two-thirds of the representatives of the National Assembly, the state legislature and the local government council from the affected area; (b) a popular referendum; (c) a simple majority of all states of the federation; and (d) a two-thirds majority of each chamber of the National Assembly. With such a high threshold, Nigeria is unlikely to see any short-term alteration to the boundaries of its existing 36 states. By contrast, India's more liberal provisions have facilitated the merging and splitting of states on many occasions since 1950. This has been a response to pressures of changing population size and composition, including the desire of less prosperous regions for greater political influence. In 2011, territory splitting was also attempted unsuccessfully in Brazil's Para state.

35.4 Population and the socio-economic domain

The socio-economic domain covers an expansive set of constitutional provisions that have both direct and indirect bearing on the demographic processes of fertility, mortality and migration.

35.4.1 Fertility

Prescriptions, or lack thereof, about marriage, divorce, family planning, sterilisation and abortion are key examples of the ways in which constitutions can affect reproductive decision-making by individuals and hence the population's fertility. Marital status is one of the most important determinants of fertility, even in countries with liberal attitudes to ex-nuptial births. The regulation of marriage formation and dissolution therefore has repercussions at a population level. Globally, the marriageable age for females ranges from around 13 years to 20 years. While none of the constitutions under review prescribes a marriageable age, several expressly authorise the legislature to make such laws.[5] In federations, this power may lie with federal or state legislatures, and may be exclusive or concurrent. In Nigeria, the National Assembly's exclusive power does not extend to marriages under Islamic or customary law, which generally permit marriage at younger ages. In Indonesia, the tension between Islamic law and the secular principles that underpin the constitution has been accommodated in the context of family law through the grant of wide-ranging regional autonomy.

Access to family planning has been a major concern of the international community for many years. At a UN conference held in Cairo in 1994, countries affirmed 'the basic right of all couples and individuals to decide freely and responsibly the number, spacing and timing

---

4 Australia ss 123–124; Brazil art 18; India arts 2–3; Nigeria s 8; United States art IV s 3.
5 Australia s 51(xxi); India art 246, sch 7, List III-5; Nigeria sch 2, Part I-61.

of their children and . . . to make decisions concerning reproduction free of discrimination, coercion and violence'.[6] While this commitment was directed to promoting individual freedom of choice in reproductive matters, the state also has an interest in fertility because of its long-term demographic consequences. Individual interests and state interests do not always coincide, and they may be pro- or anti-natalist. This ambivalence can be seen in the diverse constitutional provisions.

In Indonesia, the human rights chapter introduced into the Constitution in 2000 includes the right of every person 'to establish a family and to procreate based upon lawful marriage' (art 28B). In India, a constitutional amendment made in 1976 during the emergency period introduced a new head of concurrent legislative power with respect to 'population control and family planning'—thus enabling greater state regulation (art 246, sch 7, List III-20A). Brazil's 1988 Constitution sets out rights and responsibilities, stating that 'couples are free to decide on family planning' and that the state must provide 'educational and scientific resources for the exercise of this right, prohibiting any coercion on the part of official or private institutions' (art 226(7)). All these provisions have been adopted within the past generation, but concern for family planning is also evident in judicial interpretation of older constitutions, such as the notion of reproductive freedom enjoyed under the US Constitution as a hallmark of personal liberty.

Two aspects of fertility control deserve special mention—sterilisation and abortion. Both procedures have been integral to population control in China under the 'one-child policy', which was introduced in 1978 and given a formal legislative (but not constitutional) basis in 2001. Among the case studies, voluntary sterilisation is a common means of family planning in countries such as Brazil. Coerced mass sterilisation as a means of population control has generated great controversy, and India's experience of it in the 1960s and 1970s 'has become emblematic of everything that can go wrong in a program premised on "population control" rather than on reproductive rights and health' (Connelly, 629). Millions of male sterilisations were performed during this period, often coerced by 'negative incentives' such as withdrawal of healthcare, education, housing and employment from families with more than three children. While legislative proposals for compulsory sterilisation were never adopted, the declaration of a state of emergency in 1975—prompted in part by the 'population crisis'—had the effect of suspending constitutional rights that may otherwise have prevented such coercive action (art 359).

The control of fertility through induced abortion is also a controversial issue, as evidenced by the 'one-child policy' in China, where 6.3 to 14.4 million abortions have been reported annually since the late 1970s. This has been elevated to a constitutional level in some countries, although others have resisted the pressure to do so. For example, in deliberations leading to the adoption of Brazil's Constitution, church groups sought to include the 'right to life from conception' but this was successfully resisted by women's groups (Guedes, 71). Where abortion is constitutionalised, approaches vary widely. At one end of the spectrum lie countries such as Ireland and Kenya, whose constitutions expressly ban abortion.[7] In Ireland, there was no constitutional regulation of abortion until 1983, when an amendment acknowledged 'the right to life of the unborn'. A subsequent referendum to liberalise abortion laws was narrowly defeated in 2002. The Kenyan Constitution also states that abortion is not permitted but, unlike the Irish provision, makes exceptions where there is a need for emergency

6 International Conference on Population and Development, *Programme of Action*, s 7.3.
7 *Constitution of Ireland* (1937) art 40.3.3; *Constitution of Kenya* (2010) art 26(4).

treatment, the life or health of the mother is in danger, or abortion is permitted by another law. The last qualification has the potential to neutralise legislatively the pro-natalist stance of Kenya's constitutional ban on abortion.

Contrasting with the restrictive approaches in Ireland and Kenya is the well-known decision of the United States Supreme Court in *Roe v Wade*.[8] There the Court held that a constitutional right to privacy in reproductive decision-making arose from the concept of personal liberty protected by the Fourteenth Amendment. This right limited a state's capacity to criminalise abortion, depending on the gestational stage of the foetus. In the wake of the decision, the rate of legal abortions in the United States nearly doubled, although the approach in recent jurisprudence has been less liberal.

35.4.2 Mortality

The role of constitutions in influencing mortality is perhaps the least obvious of the three components of population change. In individual cases, constitutions may have something to say about end-of-life decisions such as euthanasia, the liberty to refuse unwanted medical treatment or the availability of the death penalty in criminal cases. However, these are unusual situations and the first two, in particular, are of interest primarily to developed countries with advanced medical systems. More significant at a population level is the capacity of governments to promote public health, provide appropriate health services and support the well-being of individuals as they age. It is notable that the most significant improvements in life expectancy in modern times have come from reductions in child and maternal mortality, which form part of the United Nations' Millennium Development Goals. Improvements directed to that end may come through constitutional articulation of rights and duties, empowerment of legislatures to make laws on those subjects, and authority to spend on health programmes and services.

Some constitutions impose general duties on the state to take health-related action, such as the injunction in the Netherlands Constitution (1983) that 'the authorities shall take steps to promote the health of the population' (art 22). Constitutions that include social and economic rights as part of their fabric may include more specific rights. The Brazilian Constitution includes health and nutrition as social rights, while urban and rural workers have the additional right to a retirement pension, which is an important factor in promoting access to aged healthcare (arts 6, 7(xxiv), 196). The Constitution describes health as the right of all and the duty of the national government, which is to be guaranteed by policies aimed at 'reducing the risk of illness and other maladies' through universal and equal access to services. Similarly, the Indian Constitution includes the improvement of public health as a primary duty of the state, but only as a non-enforceable 'directive principle' (art 47). Constitutional courts have recognised that realisation of the right to health or medical treatment is often tempered by resource constraints and that governments may ration available resources through policies that attend to the larger needs of society rather than the specific needs of individuals.[9] In some countries, such as Australia, by far the most significant role of government in relation to mortality stems not from legislative powers over health but from financial control exercised by making tied grants to constituent states and appropriating funds for direct government programmes (ss 81, 96).

---

8 *Roe v Wade* 410 US 113 (1973).

9 *Soobramoney v Minister of Health (KwaZulu-Natal)* [1997] ZACC 17 (Constitutional Court of South Africa, 27 November 1997).

35.4.3 Migration

Many constitutions guarantee the right of individuals to move freely within the country.[10] This freedom of movement enables the spatial redistribution of the population, such as the rural–urban drift noted above, although some constitutions expressly seek to slow the rate of urbanisation by reducing disparities in the standard of living between rural and urban areas.[11] By contrast, international movement of persons touches a key attribute of sovereignty and is tightly regulated by granting the national legislature exclusive, or sometimes concurrent, power to make laws with respect to immigration and emigration.[12]

Many constitutions also make indirect provision for international migration by defining membership of their societies through the concept of nationality or citizenship. Because nationals have a right to enter their own country under international law (which some constitutions also reflect),[13] broader or narrower conceptions of nationality can impact on the size and composition of a population. Some constitutions (e.g., United States) follow the principle of *jus soli*, providing that nationality at birth is acquired merely by being born in the territory of the state; others (e.g., Nigeria) follow the principle of *jus sanguinis*, providing that nationality at birth is acquired by any person who is descended from nationals; while still others (e.g., Brazil, India) recognise both bases.[14]

35.5 Population and the ethno-cultural domain

In the modern world no country has a homogeneous population—even Iceland (the most homogeneous) has experienced increasing diversity in recent times due to international migration. This diversity is often seen across language, culture, religion, ethnicity and race. To what extent do constitutions recognise these compositional attributes of a population? At one end of the continuum lie countries like Indonesia, whose 240 million people span an archipelago of substantial ethnic and linguistic diversity but whose original 1945 Constitution established a unitary republic that gave no formal recognition to this diversity. This constitutional silence was seen as a means of establishing a strongly centralised and integrated state, in the face of pluralism, after a long period of Dutch colonial rule (Bertrand, 206). Only more recently have secessionist conflicts in the provinces of Aceh and Irian Jaya led to constitutional amendments that recognise, in somewhat abstract terms, the 'diversity of each region' and the 'special and distinct' features of regional units (arts 18A, 18B). However, the Indonesian Constitution does not itself accommodate diversity, relegating this to the national legislature, where special autonomy laws have since been passed for these fractious provinces.

The Indian Constitution provides a stark contrast to Indonesia in addressing the issue of diverse sub-populations—it protects diversity through a framework of rights, including positive measures to protect the least advantaged. The Constitution provides that citizens

---

10 Australia s 92; Brazil art 5(xv); Nigeria ss 15(3), 41. In the United States this derives from judicial interpretation of the privileges and immunities clause: art IV s 2. Contrast India, where the federal legislature has exclusive power to *regulate* interstate migration (sch 7, List I-81).

11 *Bangladesh Constitution* (1972), s 16.

12 Australia s 51(xxvii); Brazil art 22(xv); India art 246, sch 7, List I-19; Nigeria s 4, sch 2, List I-30. In the United States this derives from judicial interpretation of the naturalisation power: art I s 8.

13 *International Covenant on Civil and Political Rights*, opened for signature 16 December 1966, 999 UNTS 171 (entered into force 23 March 1976) art 12(4). See, e.g., Nigeria s 41.

14 Brazil art 12(i); India art 5; Indonesia art 26; Nigeria s 25; United States amend XIV s 1.

have a right to conserve their 'distinct language, script or culture', and that minorities have the right to 'establish and administer educational institutions of their choice' (arts 29–30). In an environment where language differences have been a frequent social irritant, states within the Union are authorised to adopt official languages in addition to Hindi, and the President may direct a state to recognise a language if so desired by a 'substantial proportion' of the state's population (arts 345–347). Indeed, the re-drawing of state boundaries in India, noted above, has been driven to a large degree by the desire to form more linguistically homogeneous territorial units, especially in the south (Mawdsley, 39–40).

More remarkable are the constitutional provisions for affirmative action (positive discrimination) in relation to certain castes, tribes and 'other backward classes'.[15] The constitution establishes a process of one-off executive notification for defining the beneficiaries of the affirmative action provisions, which may be amended only by legislation (arts 341–342). The affirmative measures include the reservation of seats in the lower chambers of the Union and the states in proportion to the population of the affected groups in each state; 'consideration . . . in the making of appointments to services and posts' in the public sector; and the establishment of national commissions to monitor the constitutional safeguards (Part XVI). Originally set to expire in 20 years, the provisions have been extended time and again (Sourell).

In Nigeria, the object of achieving national unity in a country characterised by more than 250 ethnic groups, 500 indigenous languages and diverse religions (50 percent Muslim, 40 percent Christian, 10 percent indigenous) has been approached openly. The constitutional response has been partly structural (the 1999 Constitution is federal in character) and partly proscriptive—Nigeria's multi-religious make-up is accommodated by prohibiting the adoption of a state religion (s 10). The Constitution also contains directive principles that require, at the federal level, that 'there shall be no predominance of persons . . . from a few ethnic or other sectional groups'; and, at the state and local levels, that the conduct of government affairs shall 'recognise the diversity of the people within its area of authority' (s 14). The Federal Character Commission is given power under the Constitution to give effect to s 14 by working out an equitable formula for the distribution of all cadres of posts in the public service, armed forces, police force and government-owned companies. The Commission also has power to promote, monitor and enforce compliance with the principles of proportional sharing of all bureaucratic, economic, media and political posts at all levels of government (sch 3, s 8). This goes well beyond minority rights; it provides an institutional framework for programmatic action. The constitution demands not merely that 'regard' be had to the diversity of each region (as in Indonesia) or that the claims of disadvantaged groups to jobs 'be taken into consideration' (as in India), but that the distribution of public goods accords with the robust principle of proportionality, backed up by measures for legal enforcement.

35.6 Population and the scientific domain

How do constitutions promote the availability of relevant, timely and accurate scientific knowledge about populations, so as to inform the political, socio-economic and ethno-cultural domains identified above? Population data come from many sources. The best known

---

15 The practice of 'untouchability' was abolished by art 17 but discrimination against Dalit communities persists in practice.

is the population census, which is a complete enumeration of a population at a specific point in time. Other important data sources are registers of vital events (births, deaths, marriages, divorces); administrative collections maintained by governments for other purposes (immigration control, healthcare claims, school enrolments); population registers, which keep complete and continuous records of all vital events experienced by residents in the small number of countries that keep such registers; and sample surveys. Constitutions may promote the collection, analysis and dissemination of population data from any of these sources through provisions they make about processes, institutions or substantive counting rules.

35.6.1 Processes for collecting population data

The process for collecting population statistics most frequently identified in constitutions is the population census. The US Constitution provided an early model in mandating that a census of the American people be conducted within three years of the first meeting of Congress, and every 10 years thereafter (art I, s 2). The purpose of that census falls squarely within the political domain, namely, to adjust the number of congressional representatives elected from each state and to augment the total number of representatives as the population grows (Hamilton, Jay & Madison). Many other countries have shied away from a constitutional mandate for a periodic census but instead authorise the legislature to make such laws on that topic as it thinks fit. Thus, the federal legislature has exclusive power over 'census' in India and over 'national systems of statistics' in Brazil, while in Australia it has concurrent power over 'census and statistics'.[16] The international norm is to hold censuses every 10 years, but countries such as Australia conduct them every five years. In some countries, constitutional rights to privacy limit the nature of information that can be collected during a census or disclosed subsequently. The Indian Constitution also recognises methods of data collection beyond the census: the power to make laws with respect to 'vital statistics including registration of births and deaths' is shared concurrently by federal and state legislatures, whereas the Nigerian Constitution makes vital registration an exclusive federal power.[17]

35.6.2 Institutions for analysing population data

Most countries now have well-established institutions for conducting periodic censuses and reporting on population issues. The work of these national statistical institutes often informs issues of electoral representation but also extends well beyond this domain in informing social and economic policy. Nigeria is unusual, however, in giving such an institution constitutional status.[18] The Nigerian Constitution establishes the National Population Commission as an independent authority with wide-ranging functions. These include enumeration of the population through censuses and surveys, maintaining the machinery for registering births and deaths, advising the President on population matters, and publishing population data for the purpose of economic and development planning. The Commission's census reports are given special prominence by reason of the fact that they must be delivered to the President and, if accepted, tabled in the national legislature. The delicate accommodation of diverse

---

16 India sch VII, List I-69; Brazil art 22 (xviii); Australia s 51(xi).
17 India sch VII, List III-30; Nigeria sch 2, Part I-8.
18 Nigeria ss 153, 158, 213, sch 3 ss 23–24.

ethnic and religious interests probably accounts for the profile given to the work of this constitutional body.

35.6.3 Rules for using population data

Constitutions may also set out substantive rules about the use of population data. A simple example is the requirement in Australia and Nigeria that electoral representation be determined using the 'latest' statistics or census data, which contrasts with the requirement in India that outdated statistics be used, as discussed above.[19] Less benign is the provision in the US Constitution (art 1, s 2) that excluded some Native Americans and two-fifths of slaves from the population count for the purpose of apportioning congressional representatives to the states; or the provision in the Australian Constitution (s 127) that completely excluded indigenous Australians from being counted in estimates of the Australian population. Consistent with this, every Australian census held from federation in 1901 until the provision was repealed by referendum in 1967 included a question on race for the purpose of excluding 'Aboriginal natives' from official population counts.

The illustrations reflect the experience of many countries that the way in which people are counted can be highly politically charged, especially when race, religion or privacy are involved. This can make the census difficult to execute, since successful enumeration depends on the trust of those enumerated. In the United States, for example, there has been ongoing legal controversy about whether the 'actual enumeration' mandated by the Constitution permits the Census Bureau to adjust raw population data for net undercount (i.e., the difference between the number of people who were not counted but should have been, and the number who were counted but should not have been), which disproportionately affects African Americans and Hispanics (Siegel, 559–65).

35.7 Conclusion

The relationship between constitutions and populations deserves more attention than it has received. Populations are far from immutable, but the forces that drive change reflect deep social processes that evolve unhurriedly, but nonetheless insistently, over time. Demographic change and constitutional change operate in a similar multi-generational timeframe, which ought to encourage a reflexive relationship between them.

This Chapter has examined the ways in which constitutions reflect and respond to population change. The relationship is a complex one, reflecting contrasts in population histories, economic development, constitutional styles and judicial attitudes. Modernising social processes have resulted in profound transformations in all populations over the past century. If constitutions are to provide sound architectures for the governance of people far into the future, they need to have population dynamics firmly in mind in their design and subsequent evolution.

19 Australia ss 24, 105; India art 81; Nigeria s 75.

References

Bertrand, J (2008). 'Indonesia's Quasi-Federalist Approach: Accommodation amid Strong Integrationist Tendencies', in Choudhry, S (ed), *Constitutional Design for Divided Societies: Integration or Accommodation?* (Oxford University Press), 205.

Connelly, M (2006). 'Population Control in India: Prologue to the Emergency Period', 32(4) *Population and Development Review* 629.

Dahl, R & Tufte, E (1973). *Size and Democracy* (Stanford University Press).

Ehrlich, P (1968). *The Population Bomb* (Ballantine Books).

Guedes, A (2000). 'Abortion in Brazil: Legislation, Reality and Options', 8(16) *Reproductive Health Matters* 66.

Hamilton, A, Jay, J & Madison, J (1788). *The Federalist No 58*.

Haub, C & Sharma, O (2006). 'India's Population Reality: Reconciling Change and Tradition', 61(3) *Population Bulletin* 1.

Mawdsley, E (2002). 'Redrawing the Body Politic: Federalism, Regionalism and the Creation of New States in India', 40(3) *Commonwealth and Comparative Politics* 34.

Omran, A (1971). 'The Epidemiological Transition: A Theory of the Epidemiology of Population Change', 49 *Milbank Memorial Fund Quarterly* 509.

Siegel, J (2002). *Applied Demography: Applications to Business, Government, Law, and Public Policy* (Academic Press).

Sowell, T (2004). *Affirmative Action Around the World: An Empirical Study* (Yale University Press) 23.

Weeks, J (2005). *Population: An Introduction to Concepts and Issues* (9th edn; Wadsworth Publishing Company).

Additional reading

Barnett, L & Reed, E (1985). *Law, Society, and Population: Issues in a New Field* (Cap and Gown Press).

Choudhry, S (ed) (2008). *Constitutional Design for Divided Societies: Integration or Accommodation?* (Oxford University Press).

Juriansz, J & Opeskin, B (2012). 'Electoral Redistribution in Australia: Accommodating 150 Years of Demographic Change', 58 *Australian Journal of Politics and History*.

Lee, R (2003). 'The Demographic Transition: Three Centuries of Fundamental Change', 17(4) *Journal of Economic Perspectives* 167–190.

Opeskin, B (2010). 'Constitutions and Populations: How Well has the Australian Constitution Accommodated a Century of Demographic Change?', 21 *Public Law Review* 109–140.

Skerry, P (2000). *Counting on the Census? Race, Group Identity, and the Evasion of Politics* (Brookings Institution Press).

United Nations Department of Economic and Social Affairs (2010). *World Population Policies 2009* (United Nations).

United Nations Department of Economic and Social Affairs (2011). *World Population Prospects: The 2010 Revision* (United Nations).

Supranational organizations and their impact on national constitutions

Markus Böckenförde and Daniel Sabsay

36.1 Introduction

National constitutions increasingly interact with institutions at a regional or international level. Globalization and regionalization are not only catchwords, but real twentieth-century trends that are likely to accelerate in the next decades. National constitutions are affected by international and supranational organizations at different stages and in different forms. At the stage of constitution-making they may serve as advisors or caretakers to support or guide constitutional processes. Later they might be involved in implementation and capacity-building. Globalization also involves the emergence of complex and influential bodies of supranational law and regulations that increasingly shape national legislation, by establishing criteria for membership or partnership that frame the constitutional design of states eager to join. Sometimes constitutional design in member states is directly affected by regional integration.

This chapter reviews the impact of international and supranational organizations on national constitutions. The first part briefly addresses the role of the United Nations (UN) in constitution-building processes as part of transitional arrangements, using the cases of Namibia and East Timor to illustrate different forms of involvement. The second part examines regional organizations that foster integration between neighbouring countries, using Europe and South America as examples.[1]

36.2 The role of the UN in post-conflict constitution-building processes

36.2.1 Introduction

Since its founding, the UN has been involved in peace-keeping operations and state-building activities, with varying effects. The development of UN peace-keeping operations is often

---

1 Written by scholars of the respective regions, this part expresses to a certain extent the authors' different views about how supranational organizations support, influence and affect domestic constitutions.

described in terms of generations. In the first generation, during the cold war, peace-keeping was an instrument to manage traditional inter-state conflicts. In the second generation, after the fall of the Berlin wall, the focus turned to intra-state conflicts where the UN acted in times of transition from a war-torn society to a peaceful state. Scholars have identified four types of involvement: the UN acted as a supervisory authority with nearly comprehensive governing powers; as an executive authority; as an administrative authority; or through facilitation and monitoring (Doyle & Sambanis, 332). The UN's role in constitution-building initiatives differed according to the type of involvement. Our examples are Namibia and East Timor, both late cases of decolonialization. The UN Transition Assistance Group (UNTAG) in Namibia operated as a caretaker during Namibia's struggle to independence and the drafting of the first post-independence constitution. It marked the transition from 'traditional' to 'complex' peace-keeping operations (Malone & Wermester). In East Timor the UN's mandate was broader in scope and ambition than anything that went before. The UN Transitional Administration of East Timor (UNTAET) was empowered to exercise sovereign authority within a fledgling nation and served as a 'surrogate mother' to a new state (Griffin & Jones; Chopra).

36.2.2 Namibia (UNTAG)

Constitution-building was at the heart of Namibia's peace-building and national reconciliation initiatives for almost two decades, and is probably the finest example of a 'transition through constitutionalism' (Wichers). UNTAG was formally established in 1978 (SCR 435) with the mandate to conduct free and fair elections for a Constituent Assembly under a transitional authority composed jointly by the South African Administrator General and the UN Special Representative. Although UNTAG remained dormant until 1989 because of South Africa's resistance,[2] in 1981, the Western Contact Group led by the United States managed to reach an agreement with all interested parties (i.e., Frontline States, SWAPO, South Africa) to draw up constitutional principles to guide both the process for creating, and the final content of, a new constitution. Although not officially adopted by the Security Council, the 1982 'Principles concerning the Constituent Assembly and the Constitution for an Independent Namibia' were submitted to the UN Secretary General and somehow considered part of SCR 435. After free and fair elections took place in 1989, the Constituent Assembly at its first meeting adopted the constitutional principles as a 'framework to draw up a constitution for South West Africa/Namibia'.[3] The eight principles called for a unitary, sovereign and democratic state with an independent judiciary, respect for and enforceability of human rights consistent with the Universal Declaration of Human Rights, and free and fair elections. In February 1990, the Constituent Assembly unanimously approved Namibia's Constitution. After the Secretary General reported to the Security Council that the Constitution complied with the principles, Namibia became independent, the Constitution entered into force, and the newly elected president was sworn in by the UN Secretary General. The UN's role in the constitution-building process was significant, although not dominant. This might also be due to the fact that the process fell short in terms of public participation, which was confined to the election of members to the Constituent Assembly. Once the elections occurred, this was an elite-driven process.

2 For a detailed analysis see Melber & Saunders.
3 Constituent Assembly Resolution of 21 November 1989.

36.2.3 East Timor (UNTAET)

East Timor's constitutional passage to independence was quite different. In Namibia, the UN provided political oversight and capacity-building to a somewhat functional, pre-existing set of administrative institutions. In East Timor, the UN stepped into a political and administrative vacuum. SCR 1272 established the UN Transitional Administration in East Timor (UNTAET) after massive violence followed a successful vote for independence. UNTAET was given overall responsibility for the administration of East Timor and empowered to exercise all legislative and executive authority, including the administration of justice. SCR 1272 did not specify how the shift from a transitional administration to an independent East Timor would take place, nor was there any statement specifying that a constitution would be a component of the state-building effort (Aucoin & Brandt, 250). Both were developed later on. Subsequent Security Council resolutions extended the mandate and urged 'further measures to delegate authority to East Timorese people'.

The UN's impact in the constitution-building process was immense. The design of the process was determined by key UN officials and a few political elites. Whether the country benefited from this dominant role is even doubted by former UN-staff in East Timor: '[T]he process in East Timor was rushed, did not create the conditions necessary to include the public in the process, and emphasized an electoral process that in the East Timorese context led to single-party domination of the Constitutional Assembly and a resulting constitution that largely reflected the desires of one party rather than the aspirations of the country as a whole or even of other key elite power bases.'[4] The Constitutional Assembly convened in September 2001. Due to the limited time, neither a constitutional agenda nor common constitutional principles to guide the process could be prepared. The dominant party's draft was left essentially unchanged and was adopted in March 2002 after only a couple of weeks of public consultations.

Today, both cases are considered success stories of UN intervention. In Namibia, the UN's role was one of a midwife, attending and supporting the birth of a new nation. In East Timor, the UN was sitting in the driver's seat, influencing the constitution-building process considerably. This role of a 'surrogate mother' resulted in part from the specific context in East Timor, but in part also from UNTAET's flawed commitment to support an inclusive Timorese-owned process instead of maintaining a 'UN's Kingdom of East Timor' for too long.

36.3 Regional organizations and their effect on domestic constitutions

Supranational organizations at a regional level—whose primary aim is to foster the integration among member states by exercising rights transferred to them by member states—support and influence domestic constitutions in a number of ways and to different degrees. Domestic constitutions are directly affected by supranational organizations through their legal acts, decisions or (if courts are involved) judgements. Other effects are less direct. The organization might set up criteria and constitutional standards for membership that frame the constitutional design of states eager to join the organization or partner with it. Or the legal agreements drafted under the auspices of such an organization might serve as a prototype for others to follow or borrow from.

---

4 Aucoin & Brandt, 246; see also id, 254 for further examples of unfortunate UNTAET Regulations.

From a legal perspective, the impact of supranational institutions on domestic law depends on two factors: (1) The legal authority vested in the supranational organization and that its institutions are vested with, and (2) the way in which domestic constitutions define their relationship to international law and to the organization. Countries have chosen different approaches to ranking international agreements within their national legal order, even apart from their use of monism or dualism with respect to international law generally.

36.3.1 Europe

36.3.1.1 The Council of Europe

a) Introduction

The Council of Europe (COE) was the first European political organization founded with a view to achieving closer unity among its members. Emerging from the ideas of the 'Hague Congress' in 1948, it was established by the 10 founding states a year later and now comprises 47 members—including all European nations other than Belarus. Despite the formation of the European Communities and the European Union later on, the COE has remained an important forum due to a wider membership and a potentially almost unlimited remit. It has addressed practical pan-European cooperation in various fields such as human rights, legal cooperation, culture, education, public health, social cohesion and youth. Based on the principles of democracy and respect for human rights and the rule of law, the COE gained a new political dimension with the fall of the Berlin wall in 1989. The two main outputs of the COE's inter-governmental work are 'conventions and agreements', as well as 'recommendations to the governments of members' (Art. 15 COE Statute) (Polakiewicz). More than 200 international treaties have been adopted by the COE, and many of them have prepared the ground for codification at the global level as well as regional levels elsewhere.

Two instruments of the COE are of special interest: the European Convention on Human Rights (ECHR) and its court, which has contributed to the creation of a pan-European standard of human rights; and the European Commission for Democracy through Law, which offers constitutional advice to countries in transformation.

b) The European Convention on Human Rights and the European Court of Human Rights

The European Convention for the Protection of Human Rights and Fundamental Freedoms (ECHR) was signed in Rome on 4 November 1950 and entered into force almost three years later. The European Court of Human Rights (ECtHR) was established in 1959. Over the decades, substantial new guarantees have been added and new procedures developed. Probably the most successful feature of the Convention has been the fact that individuals have the right to individual application before the court (since 1998, directly) (Frowein).

(1) The status of the ECHR in the legal hierarchy of its members

From a formal legal perspective, the impact of the ECHR and the rulings of the ECtHR depend on two factors: whether the Convention is applied as internal national law and, if so, what legal status is accorded to it. The Convention is now internally applicable in all member states, but the status of the ECHR in the legal hierarchy of the members differs considerably. In the Netherlands and Moldova, the ECHR is ranked above all national laws, including constitutional law.[5] The status in the United Kingdom is similar, but was achieved in a more complex legal terrain. Pursuant to the principle of parliamentary sovereignty, Acts of Parliament already are the highest norm, binding the judges. The Human Rights Act 1998 (HRA) empowered the courts to review legislation for compliance with many of the rights enshrined in the ECHR. And although it does not allow courts to disapply the law, the HRA requires them either to interpret legislation in compliant ways or declare it incompatible (providing parliament with the opportunity to adjust the law accordingly).[6] Parliamentary sovereignty may survive in form, but not as a matter of political reality: the ECHR (including the ECtHR's decisions) has become a quasi-constitutional bill of rights, serving as a yardstick for national legislation. In Austria, the ECHR has constitutional status and all its rights can be asserted before the Constitutional Court like genuine domestic fundamental rights.[7] Many Eastern European States sandwiched international agreements like the ECHR between the constitution and national law. Apparently, countries that previously suffered from authoritarian rule attempted to entrench certain political choices through the incorporation of treaties as higher law, be it in fear or anticipation that a future illiberal regime will roll back liberal gains.[8] Again in other countries, like in Italy, Germany and the Scandinavian countries, the ECHR ranks as a national law.

However, the formal legal rank alone does not yet conclude the role of ECHR in a legal system. In some countries, the lower legal rank was compensated through an upgrade by means of interpretation. In Germany, the ECHR has been accorded with a 'leading interpretative role' by the Constitutional Court, putting it on the same footing as constitutional provisions:

> The Federal Constitutional Court contributes to achieving a far-reaching harmonisation by consulting the text of the Convention and the case-law of the European Court of Human Rights, which it has raised to the level of constitutional law, as 'interpretation aids' for the determination of the content and scope of the fundamental rights and rule of law guarantees of the Basic Law. In this manner, the fundamental decisions of the European Court of Human Rights have the effect of legal precedents and a function of normative guidance and orientation (Voßkuhle).[9]

(2) The constitutional impact of the ECHR on member states

Over the last 60 years, the ECtHR has had to navigate carefully between the aim of the Convention and the need to respect national traditions and sensitivities. Due to the general acceptance and faithful implementation of its decisions in most countries, a European bill of rights with quasi-constitutional effects has been created. In interpreting the Convention as 'dynamical' or 'evolutive', the Court managed to keep the European human rights

---

5 Art 4 and Art 8 of the Constitution of Moldova 1994 as amended to 2003; Art 91 (3) and 93 of the Constitution of the Kingdom of Netherlands. See also Alkema; Blanke & Mangiameli.

6 Art 3 and 4 HRA. See also Bellamy, 87; Bamforth, 80, 83.

7 Art 2 No 7 of the Resolution of the National Council in 6 April 1964, amending the Federal Constitutional Law. Available at: http://www.ris.bka.gv.at/Dokumente/BgblPdf/1964_59_0/1964_59_0.pdf.

8 Bulgaria 1991 as amended to 2003 (Art 5); Albania 1998 (Art 122); Czech 1992 as amended to 2002 (Art 10).

9 In 2012, Voßkuhle was the President of the Federal Constitutional Court.

standard abreast of present-day conditions, thereby setting new standards for national courts to follow. Consequently, the ECtHR has not shied away from effectively over-ruling decisions of national constitutional courts, whose traditional way of interpreting human rights norms was no longer accepted by the court. Two recent cases may illustrate those dynamics: in *Oršuš and Others v Croatia*, the ECtHR decided that Roma-only classes in some schools of Croatia, held legal by the Constitutional Court of Croatia, are discriminatory and therefore in violation of the Convention.[10] In *Obst v Germany* and *Schüth v Germany*, the ECtHR balanced the right of churches to impose religious-based moral standards (as manifested in the employment contract) to their employees and the employees' right to respect for their private life.[11] Whereas the German courts (including the Constitutional Court) generally confirmed the dismissal of church employees for adultery, the ECtHR now required considering the specific nature of the position concerned.

(3) Relevance of the ECHR to constitutions of non-member states

The constitutional relevance of the ECHR is not limited to member states because the Convention has served as a model for constitutional drafters elsewhere. Probably the most immediate incentive was to prepare the ground for future membership to the COE. Respect for democracy and the rule of law and human rights and fundamental freedoms are prerequisites for membership. Compliance with these principles is the subject of strict scrutiny within COE institutions before a final decision on accession is taken. And although COE members are not obliged to sign or ratify the ECHR, it has become common practice that ratification of a number of core conventions, mainly in the fields of human rights and legal cooperation, has become a condition for membership (Polakiewicz, 2–3). The Copenhagen Criteria of 1993,[12] which must be met as a precondition for joining the EU, require both accession to and implementation of the ECHR.[13] Consequently, some constitutional drafters in Central and Eastern European countries have followed almost exactly the same language as contained in the Convention in order to qualify more easily for future membership.[14]

The impact of the ECHR was not limited to Europe. It played an important role in the independence constitutions of the former British colonies in Africa. Driven by concerns that emerged out of the socio-political context at the time, some Nigerian leaders were cautious of possible oppression by the other regional ethnic groups upon the withdrawal of the British[15] and thus of the need for constitutional guarantees. The Nigerian Constitution of 1960 included provisions for fundamental rights to which the Convention served as a model. Either through direct influence or indirectly through the Nigerian Constitution serving as a precedent, many other African countries adopted the Convention as a model, such as Sierra Leone, Uganda, Kenya, Malawi, Gambia, Botswana, Lesotho, Mauritius, Swaziland, the Seychelles and Zimbabwe.[16]

---

10 Grand Chamber, Application no 15766/03, 16 March 2010.

11 Application no 425/03 and 1620/03, 23 September 2010.

12 See Presidency Conclusions at the Copenhagen European Council, 7.A available at http://www.europarl.europa.eu/enlargement/ec/cop_en.htm.

13 Council of Europe, Parliamentary Assembly, Doc 11533, 18 March 2008; Marktler, 345.

14 See, for instance, the Constitution of the Republic of Kosovo (2008) as the latest example.

15 Nigeria had been fundamentally divided into three regions, each with different ethnic groups, and each of the three major political parties represented one of the three regions. See Go, 578.

16 Id; Moderne, 326.

c) The European Commission for Democracy through Law

The European Commission for Democracy through Law, commonly known as the Venice Commission, was established in 1990 and now includes all 47 member states.[17] It is the Council's advisory body on constitutional matters. Members are experts in constitutional law, senior academics and practitioners alike, acting on the Commission in their individual capacity. They are appointed for four years by the participating countries.

The Commission has supported the constitution-making processes in Central and Eastern Europe through various means of constitutional assistance. In addition to preparing comparative studies and analysis on constitutional issues, its primary task has been to assess legal questions that have been raised in the process of revising an old or drafting a new constitution. In providing opinions on new or revised constitutions, the Venice Commission primarily checks whether their provisions are in compliance with the ECHR and in line with the democracy and rule-of-law standards and fundamental values commonly shared by the member states of the Council of Europe.[18] But the Venice Commission occasionally also acts upon the request of the Parliamentary Assembly of the COE, as it did recently with the revision of the Constitution in Hungary.[19]

36.3.1.2 The European Union

The idea of European integration is not new; some visions of an integrated Europe date to the late Middle Ages (Streinz, 3–4). Shortly after 1945, forums were established to pursue that idea. In 1951, a Constitutional Commission comprising 72 members of the COE prepared a preliminary draft of a European Federal Constitution. After this initiative failed, European integration was pursued by continuously strengthening the three European Communities.[20] The Communities originated with the idea of safeguarding peace within Europe by fostering economic integration and pooling war-essential industries under a common administration.[21] They were then transformed into the European Union through six consecutive treaties. In parallel, successive treaties of accession let the Community grow from six to 27 member states. This continuous process of integration has come along with a considerable shift of national powers towards powers of the European Community / European Union. It has

---

17 Partial agreements allow a limited number of member states to carry out a certain activity within the institutional framework of the COE in spite of the abstention of other member states. Due to their flexibility and capacity to mobilize additional resources, partial agreements have become an important feature within the COE's institutional framework. In 2002, the Commission became an enlarged agreement, allowing non-European states to become a member. Polakiewicz, 6.

18 The working method adopted by the Commission when providing opinions is to appoint a working group of rapporteurs to advise national authorities. After discussions with the national authorities and stakeholders in the country, the working group prepares a draft opinion on whether the legislative text meets the democratic standards in its field and on how to improve it on the basis of common experience. The draft opinion is discussed and adopted by the Venice Commission during a plenary session, usually in the presence of representatives from that country. After adoption, the opinion becomes public and is forwarded to the requesting body. See the website of the Venice Commission at: http://www.venice.coe.int/site/main/Constitutional_Assistance_E.asp.

19 Opinion no 618 / 2011, 20 June 2011, CDL-AD(2011)016.

20 European Coal and Steel Community (1951), European Atomic Energy Community, and European Economic Community (both signed in 1957).

21 See Schuman Declaration of 9 May 1950, available at http://www.eppgroup.eu/Activities/docs/divers/schuman-en.pdf.

developed into a legal system of a new kind and quality, thereby creating a sort of multi-level constitutionalism. Community law in part directly affects and entitles citizens in the national states as European citizens. This setting—already surpassing the status of a mere confederation, but not having yet achieved the configuration of *one* federal state—is what many European lawyers have in mind while using the term 'supranational' narrowly.

a) Integration clauses

Although the European Union is obviously an international organization, the present legal system of the EU cannot be considered merely as a system of treaty-based international law, which usually aims at coordinating rather than integrating different states' interests. This perception is also reflected in many constitutions of member states. Progress in EU integration meant that ordinary provisions for the incorporation of public international law into domestic legal systems were increasingly considered insufficient. The majority of member states have now adopted specific constitutional 'integration clauses' to better reflect the substantial share of sovereign powers between the two levels.[22] Most of them introduce additional requirements for the accession to the European Union or the ratification of major amendments to the EU treaty, ranging from parliamentary approval with special majorities (similar or equal to those required for constitutional amendment), referendum requirements or prior constitutional amendment (Woelk, 7).

b) The rank of EU law in the national legal hierarchy

The successful process of continuous integration relies on the precedence of the integrating norms and thus requires that EU law prevail over national law.[23] From the national perspective domestic constitutions remain the apex of the legal hierarchy. In the overwhelming majority of member states, the supremacy of EU law over *domestic statutes* is well established. This is particularly obvious where the respective 'integration clauses' refer specifically to the EU, ranking its law explicitly or implicitly above statutory law. As the discussion of the COE showed, in member states that resort to constitutional clauses relating to the ratification of international treaties, conflicts are usually resolved in favour of international (EU) law.

The situation is less clear with respect to the precedence of EU law over domestic constitutional law. Some countries explicitly accord supremacy to international treaties over national law (Netherlands). A number of other countries followed this path with

---

22 Scholars have described various categories of integration clauses, clustering them as 'limitation of sovereignty clauses', 'transfer of power clauses' or 'common exercise of power clauses'. See Hoffmeister, 375.

23 This longstanding interpretation of the European Court of Justice (ECJ) since *Costa v ENEL Case* ('the law stemming from the Treaty, an independent source of law, could not, because of its special and original nature, be overridden by domestic legal provisions, however framed, without being deprived of its character as Community law [. . .]' (at 594)) was explicitly included in Art. I-6 of the failed Treaty Establishing a Constitution for Europe (2004): 'Constitution and law adopted by the institutions of the Union in exercising competence conferred on it shall have primacy over the law of the Member States.' Although, due to the sensitivity of the matter, it hadn't been included in the Lisbon Treaty, Member States manifested in the 'Declaration concerning Primacy' at the Lisbon conference: 'in accordance with well settled case law of the Court of Justice of the European Union, the Treaties and the law adopted by the Union on the basis of the Treaties have primacy over the law of Member States, under the conditions laid down by the said case law'. See Gaja.

respect to EU law alone (Ireland, Estonia).[24] Again some countries generally accepted the supremacy of EU law subject to some limitations. Those limitations often relate to constitutional essentials that are not open to change even for the constitutional legislator (immutable clauses). In such a scenario, the same essentials are also safeguarded against a (theoretically) deficient piece of EU law (Hoffmeister, 96). But the majority of member states have preserved the possibility that constitutional law takes precedence over EU law. In those countries, incompatibilities between EU law and national constitutional law require the respective states to amend their constitution prior to ratification of a new treaty (for instance on issues such as voting rights at municipal level or extradition of nationals). In France, Spain and Poland, the highest courts have identified areas where constitutional law had to be 'Europeanized' to conform to EU law (Claes). In other member states, the highest courts constituted themselves as final guardians on whether fundamental rights as guaranteed in their respective constitutions are generally maintained by EU law and ECJ's jurisprudence; in Denmark, the highest court reserves a final say on *ultra vires* actions of EU institutions.

c) The European Court of Justice (ECJ) and the Preliminary Reference Procedure

The fundamental role of the ECJ is to ensure that EU institutions and member states comply with their obligations.[25] As pointed out by Tridimas, '[T]his role is *par excellence* a constitutional one. The ECJ carries out, in effect, review of constitutionality of EU and Member State action' (Tridimas, 738). Like almost all other international/regional tribunals, the ECJ does not have the power to declare national measures void, but the ECJ has an instrument to strengthen a uniform interpretation of EU law in member states. The *preliminary reference procedure* provides that domestic courts in EU member states can, and in some cases must, refer to the ECJ questions about the interpretation of the treaties or the validity or interpretation of acts of EU institutions (Art. 267 TFEU). The procedure provides not only an avenue for direct inter-court communication, but also offers the ECJ the opportunity to direct the 'Europeanized' interpretation of the constitutional law of member states. In exercising its interpretive function, the ECJ enjoys significant discretion. Scholars have identified three different degrees of specificity in ECJ rulings, providing ready-made solutions to the dispute, offering guidelines as to how to resolve the case, or answering the questions in such vague terms that it amounts to a deferral to the national judiciary on the point in issue (id, 739).

d) Constitutions of non-member states affected by the EU

Three different categories of effects of the EU on the domestic constitutions of nonmembers should be distinguished.

1) Candidates for EU membership. EU membership has a number of constitutional implications. Art. 49 TEU refers to the principles of the rule of law, democracy, liberty and respect for human rights as criteria for accession. Candidate countries need to take into account a growing body of 'constitutional acquis' as the basis for future membership. Candidates amended their constitutions significantly in order to conform to those requirements (Czuczai, 421).

---

24 See Art 4 para 10 of the Irish Constitution. The Estonian Act Supplementing the Constitution has been interpreted by the Estonian Supreme Court to grant unconditional supremacy to EU law as well.

25 Art 19 (1) of the Treaty of the European Union (TEU).

2) Nations with partnerships with the EU. The EU has been linked since 1975 to a set of African, Caribbean and Pacific (ACP) countries in a partnership focused mainly on development cooperation. An array of cooperation facilities and instruments has gradually been developed to that end. The Cotonou Agreement that legally frames this partnership sets out various aims and objectives that also have a considerable impact on the constitutions of partner countries. In recognition that impunity contributes to cycles of violence and insecurity, the preamble and article 11.6 of the revised Cotonou Agreement include a clear commitment of ACP and EU states to combat impunity and promote justice through the International Criminal Court.[26] Implementing the Rome Statute of the International Criminal Court (ICC) requires various regulations that potentially affect national constitutions (for instance the extradition of nationals under specific circumstances).

3) The EU has also served as a prototype for other systems of regional integration.

36.3.2 South America

Although the impulse toward integration in South America dates to the nineteenth century, little effective action was taken until the late twentieth century. We use Mercosur and the inter-American system of human rights to exemplify the role of regional institutions in contemporary constitutionalism in South America.

36.3.2.1 The Mercosur

Argentina, Brazil, Paraguay and Uruguay decided to establish a common market called the 'Common Market of the South' (Mercosur) to ensure the free movement of goods, services and factors of production; to establish a common external tariff and a common commercial policy; to coordinate macroeconomic and sectoral policies between States Parties; and to harmonize their legislation in relevant areas to strengthen the integration process. The initial legal regime of Mercosur was formed by a treaty and five annexes. These six international instruments should be interpreted harmoniously. The Asunción Treaty of 1991 fixed as its main objective the expansion of domestic markets through integration.

The regulatory framework for the integration is completed with the signing of protocols. The Ouro Preto protocol established Mercosur's legal structure and gave it international legal status. The Brasilia protocol established a system for resolving disputes to contribute to strengthening relations between the parties, based on justice and equity. Disputes arising between States Parties concerning the interpretation, application or violation of the provisions contained in the Treaty of Asunción and the agreements concluded in the framework, and the decisions of the Common Market Council and the Common Market group resolutions, will be submitted to the specified settlement procedures.

Finally, the 'democratic clause' states that any country that has abandoned the democratic system of government is immediately excluded from Mercosur. The Montevideo Agreement creates fundamentally intergovernmental institutions, not a 'Community' with separate institutions. The constitution of the common market referred to in art. 1 of the Treaty of

---

26 See Second Revision of the Cotonou Agreemment – Agreed Consolidated Text, 11 March 2010 available at http://ec.europa.eu/development/icenter/repository/second_revision_cotonou_agreement_20100311.pdf.

Asunción is only a goal. An initial deadline of 1994 has been missed completely, and after two decades it is impossible to know when it is going to happen. It is an imperfect customs union and an incomplete free-trade area.

The intergovernmental structure of Mercosur means that none of its clauses produces a transfer of attributes of state sovereignty in favour of a structure located above the governments of the States Parties.

36.3.2.2 The Mercosur and the EU

The EU has an organizational structure where decisions are in part taken by majority rather than consensus or unanimity as in the case of Mercosur. This structure reflects the principle of separation of powers that should prevail in any constitutional democracy. As such, it is worth noting the existence of a court or tribunal of the European Union whose powers allow it precedence over the judicial hierarchy of each member state, as well as the achievement of a jurisprudence that is building a common understanding of the rules that give life to the Union.

In contrast, Mercosur is not provided with supranational bodies. It acts through representatives of States Parties and its actions are functionally dependent of state entities. The will and the national interest of each State Party are expressed in rules emanating from the various 'intergovernmental' bodies.

36.3.2.3 The American system of the protection of human rights

The countries of Central and South America have built their own system of protection of human rights within the Organization of American States to implement the Inter-American Convention on Human Rights.

a) Inter-American Commission on Human Rights

The Human Rights Commission is an autonomous organ of the Organization of American States (OAS) responsible for the promotion and protection of human rights in the Americas. Consisting of seven independent members who act in a personal capacity with headquarters in Washington, it can receive and consider complaints of human rights violations by the states members. The members are elected by the OAS General Assembly for a period of four years and must meet the requirements of high moral and professional skills in human rights.

People who have suffered human rights violations can get help by filing a petition before the Commission. The Commission investigates the situation and may make recommendations to the state responsible for restoration of the enjoyment of the rights to the extent possible, so that similar incidents do not recur in the future and that the events are investigated and repaired.

Any person, group of persons or non-governmental entity legally recognized may file complaints, grievances or individual petitions to the Commission for violation of the rights, freedoms and guarantees recognized in the Convention. The Regulations of the Commission have been reformed in recent years to advance the strengthening of the American system through the participation of victims, to give greater guarantees to procedural fairness, and to ensure publicity and transparency.

In fulfilling its mandate, the Commission receives, analyzes and investigates individual petitions that allege human rights violations, both in terms of OAS member states that have ratified the American Convention, as well as those states that have not ratified it. A State Party can request the Commission's attention to claims that another State Party has committed human rights violations. The Commission also examines the overall situation of human rights in member states and publishes special reports on the situation. In doing so, it visits countries to carry out a detailed analysis of the overall situation and/or investigate specific situations. In addition, it stimulates public awareness of human rights in America. To this end, the Commission conducts and publishes reports on specific topics such as: measures to be taken to ensure greater access to justice; the effects of internal armed conflicts on certain groups; human rights for children, women, migrant workers and their families, persons deprived of liberty, human rights defenders, indigenous peoples, and persons of African descent; freedom of expression; and public safety and terrorism and its relation to human rights.

The Commission also recommends that the OAS member states adopt measures that contribute to the protection of human rights in the Southern Hemisphere of the Americas, and can call on member states to adopt 'precautionary measures'. The Commission presents cases and can request advisory opinions from the Inter-American Court, and appears before the Court during the processing and consideration of them.

The word 'recommendations' should not be interpreted literally as they are not mere suggestions, but are strictly binding. The courts of the member states determine their effects within domestic law. The Argentine Supreme Court has said that the jurisprudence of international courts for the interpretation and application of the Inter-American Convention on Human Rights should guide the interpretation of the conventions to the extent that the Argentine state recognized the jurisdiction of the Inter-American Court to hear all cases concerning the interpretation and application of the Convention.[27] Similarly, in a ruling in 1996, the Court stated the opinion of the Inter-American Commission on Human Rights that determining a 'reasonable period of detention without trial' was 'of significant importance' in deciding whether a national law on pretrial detention was consistent with the American Convention on Human Rights.[28] The reports and views of the Commission are considered 'valuable legal criteria of interpretation and valuation of organization of the clauses of the American Convention on Human Rights, which must be taken into account for decisions in the domestic law harmonized with the former'.[29] The Court also explained that the Inter-American Commission directives constitute an indispensable guideline for interpretation of the duties and obligations under the American Convention on Human Rights.[30]

b) Inter-American Court of Human Rights

In 1969, the American Convention on Human Rights (Pact of San José de Costa Rica) created the Inter-American Court of Human Rights. The Court was established in 1978 when the treaty entered into force. Headquartered in San José (Costa Rica), it is composed of seven judges, elected for their personal capacity from among jurists of moral prestige and professionals in human rights, for a term of six years, renewable only once.

Article 1 of the Court's Statute states that it is an autonomous judicial institution whose purpose is to apply and interpret the American Convention on Human Rights. It has two

---

27 'Giroldi, Horacio David y otro s/ recurso de casación – causa n° 32/93'. Fallos 318:514.
28 'Bramajo, Hernán Javier s/ incidente de excarcelación – causa n° 44.891'. Fallos 319:1840.
29 Fallos 326:3268, opinión of Justice Juan Carlos Maqueda.
30 Fallos 328:2056.

functions: judicial and consultative. Only the Commission and the States Parties to the American Convention that have recognized the jurisdiction of the Court are authorized to submit a case before the Court. A State's declaration recognizing the Court's jurisdiction may be made unconditionally to all cases or, on condition of reciprocity, for a time or to a specific case.

The American Convention provides that any member state of the Organization of American States may consult the Court regarding the interpretation of the American Convention or other treaties concerning the protection of human rights in the American States. The Court may also, at the request of any member state of the organization, issue an opinion on the compatibility of any of its domestic laws and treaties concerning the protection of human rights in the American States.

The advisory jurisdiction has in view to contribute to the fulfilment of international obligations of States. Through these opinions, the interpretation of the Convention can be achieved as well as other treaties dealing with human rights. While compliance is not compulsory, practice shows that the advisory jurisdiction is always respected by the countries. Its strength lies in the Court's moral and scientific authority.

36.3.2.4 How supranational institutions affect domestic constitutions in South America

The link between domestic and international law is one of the key issues in a country's constitutional law. In Latin America there has been a tendency towards the adoption of rules close to monism, giving precedence to international law over national law. This has happened in the area of human rights as a result of the conclusion of treaties since the end of World War II, a phenomenon that has led many countries to draw up their common legal framework. Latin American countries have acceded to the international human rights system to which is added the regional ones centred in the American Convention on Human Rights.

How this situation has been reflected in relation to the Mercosur and then with the regional human rights system deserves note. Constitutional regimes of the member countries of Mercosur have a mismatch. Argentina (1994) and Paraguay (1992) have constitutional provisions describing the supremacy of treaties over national laws, with special provisions aimed at facilitating regional integration processes in accordance with a very similar system. By contrast, the constitutions of Brazil and Uruguay have not changed their pre-existing dualist system. That this 'constitutional floor' is not shared is one of the most important challenges for advancing the integration process because of the distrust and general legal uncertainty that it provokes.

The 1994 constitutional reform in Argentina changed the international treaty regime, establishing that 'treaties take precedence over laws'. It also ordered that 11 international declarations and treaties that provide international and regional systems of human rights have constitutional status. According to Article 75, paragraph 22 of the Constitution, these treaties 'can only be vetoed, if any, by the Executive, following approval of two-thirds of the total membership of each house'. The Constitution establishes the possibility that other human rights treaties will acquire the same constitutional status. To do this, after being approved by Congress the treaty would take on special status after a new vote by two-thirds of all members of each House. Paragraph 24 of the same article provides for the delegation of powers to supranational organizations through integration agreements, subject to compliance with the democratic system and human rights regime. The rules issued by these organizations will be superior to national laws.

Brazil amended its Constitution in 1988 without considering specific rules that facilitate integration processes, either by changing the priority of its internal rules, giving the possibility to internal organs to delegate powers to a regional order, or establishing a procedure to ease the incorporation of the rules arising from decisions taken by a regional organ. The Constitution is contradictory; on the one hand, art. 4 provides that 'The Federal Republic of Brazil seeks the economic, political, social and cultural integration of the peoples of Latin America, approving the formation of a Latin American Community of Nations'. However, despite this principle, other provisions limit the opening of a common market as a consequence of the national monopoly on mining, transportation and other activities listed in arts 177 and 178 of the constitution.

Thus today, Brazilian participation in the process of integration is limited to an intergovernmental structure and not to a community-type system. The Federal High Court has maintained a consistent case law of dualism, stating that national law prevails internally over that of Mercosur, in cases of contradiction between them.

The Paraguayan Constitution of 1992 sets out principles similar to Argentina's, including the primacy of treaties over laws. In regard to the integration processes, Article 145 states: 'the Republic of Paraguay, on an equal basis with other states, allows a supranational legal order that guarantees respect for human rights, peace, justice, cooperation and development, political, economic, social and cultural development. Such decisions may be taken by an absolute majority of each House of Congress'. The 1966 Uruguayan Constitution provides a classic dualist system in regard to the relationship between laws and treaties. It endorses integration in the social and economic areas but states that Uruguay's participation is limited to associative processes and cooperation. It is contemplated that the nation cannot accept the binding nature of legislative measures emanating from supranational bodies.

36.4 Conclusion

The effects of supranational organizations on domestic constitutions differ substantially, both in kind and quality. At the international level, the impact of the UN on national constitutions becomes most relevant where states are going through a transition, predominately in post-conflict settings. UN missions have supported constitution-building processes to varying degrees, always with the intention of building peace, democracy and the rule of law, and to a lesser extent political or economic integration. In contrast, regional supranational organizations pursue integration, in different designs and with different pace, ranging from intergovernmental settings to multi-level constitutionalism.

References

Alkema, EA (2010). 'International Law in Domestic Legal Systems', Electronic Journal of Comparative Law 14.3 (December 2010), 3, available at: http://www.ejcl.org/143/art143-1.pdf

Aucoin, L & Brandt, M (2010). 'East Timor's Constitutional Passage to Independence', in Miller, LE (ed), Framing the State in Times of Transition – Case Studies in Constitution Making (Washington), 245.

Bamforth, N (2011). 'Current issues in United Kingdom constitutionalism: An introduction', I•CON 9: 1, 79.

Bellamy, R (2011). 'Political constitutionalism and the Human Rights Act', I•CON 9: 1, 86.

Blanke, HJ & Mangiameli, S (2006). 'Introduction', in Blanke, HJ & Mangiameli, S (eds), Governing Europe under a Constitution (Heidelberg), xxiv.

Chopra, J (2000). 'The UN's Kingdom of East Timor', Survival, 42: 3, 27.

Claes, M (2007). 'The Europeanisation of National Constitutions in the Constitutionalisation of Europe: Some Observations Against the Background of the Constitutional Experience of the EU-15', Croatian Yearbook of European Law and Policy 3: 3, 1.

Czuczai, J (2001). 'Practical Implementation by the Acceding Countries of the Constitutional Acquis of the EU – Problems and Challenges', in Kellermann, A, De Zwaan, J & Czuczai, J (eds), EU Enlargement: The Constitutional Impact at EU and National Level (The Hague), 411.

Doyle, MW & Sambanis, N (2006). United Nations Peace Operations – Making War & Building Peace (Princeton).

Frowein, JA (1950). 'European Convention for the Protection of Human Rights and Fundamental Freedoms', in Max Planck Encyclopedia for Public International Law.

Gaja, G (2011). 'European Community and Union Law and Domestic (Municipal) Law', in Wolfrum, R (ed), Max Planck Encyclopedia of Public International Law (MEPIL) (Oxford, Oxford University Press), 1–6.

Go, J (2009). 'Modeling the State: Postcolonial Constitutions in Asia and Africa', Southeast Asian Studies 39, 558.

Griffin, M & Jones, B (2000). 'Building Peace through Transitional Authority: New Directions, Major Challenges', International Peacekeeping 7: 4, 75.

Hoffmeister, F (2007). 'Constitutional Implications of EU Membership: A View from the Commission', Croatian Yearbook of European Law and Policy 359.

Malone, DM & Wermester, K (2000). 'Boom and Bust? The Changing Nature of UN Peacekeeping', International Peacekeeping 7: 4, 37.

Marktler, T (2006). 'The Power of the Copenhagen Criteria', Croatian Yearbook for European Law and Policy 2, 343.

Melber, H & Saunders, C (2007). 'Conflict Mediation in Decolonisation: Namibia's Transition to Independence', Africa Spectrum 42: 1, 73–94.

Moderne, F (1990). 'Human Rights and Postcolonial Constitutions in Sub-Saharan Africa', in Henkin, L & Rosenthal, AJ (eds), Constitutionalism and Rights: The Influence of the United States Constitution Abroad, 315.

Polakiewicz, J (2011). 'Council of Europe (COE)', in Wolfrum, R (ed), Max Planck Encyclopedia of Public International Law (MEPIL) (Oxford, Oxford University Press) 1–16.

Streinz, R (2006). 'European Integration under Constitutional Law', in Blanke, HJ & Mangiameli, S (eds), Governing Europe under a Constitution, Heidelberg, 1.

Tridimas, T (2011). 'Constitutional review of member state action: The virtues and vices of an incomplete jurisdiction', I•CON, Vol. 9, 737.

Voßkuhle, A (2010). 'Multilevel Cooperation of the European Constitutional Courts: Der Europäische Verfassungsgerichtsverbund', Eur. Const. L. R. 6: 175.

Wichers, M (2010). 'Namibia's Long Walk to Freedom – The Role of Constitution Making in the Creation of an Independent Namibia', in Miller, LE (ed), Framing the State in Times of Transition – Case Studies in Constitution Making (Washington), 81.

Woelk, J (2011). Constitutional Challenges of EU Accession for South East European Applicant Countries: A Comparative Approach. Unpublished conference paper, on file with Markus Broeckenforde.

New technologies and constitutional law

Thomas Fetzer* and Christopher S. Yoo†

37.1 Introduction

One of the most controversial issues among legal academics is the extent to which constitutional interpretation should adjust to reflect contemporary values. On the one hand, constitutions are often lauded for their relative insulation from contemporary politics and for their ability to embody fundamental commitments that do not change with the public opinion of the moment. On the other hand, proponents of a living constitution emphasize how much society's moral commitments have changed over time and point out the difficulties that can arise if constitutional principles are not permitted to evolve in response.

What has received less attention is the extent to which changes in constitutional interpretation are driven not by shifts in political mores, but rather by new developments in technology. Technological innovation can affect constitutional interpretation in many ways. It can alter the factual context surrounding an existing technology in ways that raise new questions about the manner in which the constitution applies to that technology. It constantly creates new technologies that require courts to determine how existing constitutional principles apply to them. It can also present opportunities for individual self-fulfillment and personal liberty that are comparable to those given explicit constitutional protections, but that fall outside the strict letter of the constitution. In the process, technological change can cause previously latent theoretical conflicts to surface. These forces are likely to become increasingly important as the pace of technological change continues to accelerate.

This Chapter illustrates each of these dynamics by focusing on specific examples in which such a transformation has occurred. The examples are drawn from US and German constitutional law, not simply because those are the systems with which the authors are most familiar, but also because constitutional law in those nations provides crisp illustrations of dynamics we

* Professor of Law, Chair of Public Law and Taxation, University of Mannheim Law School, and Lecturer in Law, University of Pennsylvania Law School.

† John H. Chestnut Professor of Law, Communication, and Computer & Information Science and Founding Director of the Center for Technology, Innovation and Competition, University of Pennsylvania.

believe occur wherever constitutional law must deal with new technologies. Other examples could of course be given from fields such as genetic engineering and reproductive technologies, but the dynamics we describe either have appeared, or are quite likely to appear, when constitutional law deals with those technologies as well. A better understanding of the potential impact of new technologies should provide a deeper appreciation of the manner in which constitutional law evolves over time.

37.2 Reapplying existing constitutional principles to existing technologies

New technologies can cause courts to rethink the way that constitutional law applies to existing technologies. One classic example is broadcast regulation. The United States has traditionally embraced a liberty-oriented vision of free speech that defines free speech in terms of freedom from government coercion (see, e.g., Berlin 1969). This vision does not permit the restriction of speech that some people find objectionable. Indeed, "the fact that society may find speech offensive is not a sufficient reason for suppressing it. Indeed, if it is the speaker's opinion that gives offense, that consequence is a reason for according it constitutional protection" (*FCC v Pacifica Foundation*, 438 US 726, 745 (1978)). The traditional solution to low-value or dangerous speech is more speech, not government regulation (see, e.g., *Whitney v California*, 274 US 357, 377 (1927) (Brandeis, J, concurring)). Although this means that people will sometimes encounter material they find offensive, this approach also presumes that people are sufficiently robust to tolerate such exposure. Rather than restrict the speech, US law typically expects those who are exposed to such speech unwillingly to "avoid further bombardment of their sensibilities simply by averting their eyes" (*Cohen v California*, 403 US 15, 21 (1971)).

Notwithstanding this hostility toward governmental restrictions on private editorial choices, the Supreme Court has upheld the imposition of negative content restrictions and affirmative content obligations on broadcasters. The primary justification became known as the "scarcity doctrine," which held that electromagnetic spectrum placed an absolute limit on the number of people who could speak. The seminal case announcing the doctrine states, "Unlike other modes of expression, radio inherently is not available to all. That is its unique characteristic, and that is why, unlike other modes of expression, it is subject to governmental regulation" (*NBC v United States*, 319 US 190, 226 (1943)).

Characterizing broadcast channels as scarce "turn[s] speech into a zero-sum game" in which enabling any one person to speak inevitably crowds out another's ability to do so. By suggesting that the total amount of speech is strictly limited, this characterization attempts to foreclose the classic argument that the solution to low-value speech is more speech, not government regulation (Yoo 2011). The supposed need to ensure that this limited resource is placed in its highest and best use was invoked by the US Supreme Court to uphold the imposition of affirmative content obligations on broadcasters (*Red Lion Broadcasting Co v FCC*, 395 US 367 (1967)).

The Supreme Court later recognized a second justification for restricting broadcast programming, holding that broadcasting represented a "uniquely pervasive presence in the lives of all Americans" and is "uniquely accessible to children." The absence of effective filtering mechanisms justified placing limits on broadcast programs deemed to be indecent (*FCC v Pacifica Foundation*, 438 US 726, 748, 749 (1978)).

Both of these rationales have been subjected to extensive academic criticisms challenging their analytical coherence (see Yoo 2003, 2010, reviewing the literature). At the same time, technological developments have begun to undercut both of these rationales. The shift to digital transmission has caused a dramatic increase in the number of television stations. The advent of cable television eliminated the inherent limitations on the number of speakers imposed by the electromagnetic spectrum (*Turner Broadcasting System, Inc. v FCC*, 512 US 622, 637, 639, 656 (1994)). Video programming is also available from direct broadcast satellite (DBS) systems such as DirecTV and BSkyB, as well as from services offered by telephone companies such as FiOS and U-verse (Yoo 2005, 2011). The shift to Internet-based distribution of video will undermine this rationale still further, as there are no natural limitations to the number of people who can speak via the Internet (*Reno v ACLU*, 521 US 844, 868, 870 (1997)). Indeed, the Supreme Court has recognized, "the market for high-speed Internet service is now quite competitive," with "DSL providers fac[ing] stiff competition from cable companies and wireless and satellite providers" (*Pacific Bell Telephone Co v linkLine Communications, Inc.*, 555 US 438, 448 n2 (2009)).

The US Supreme Court has also exhibited considerable reluctance to extend the rationales it articulated in *Pacifica* to other communications media. For example, the Court refused to extend *Pacifica* to dial-a-porn, cable television, and the Internet, in part because the would-be recipient must take affirmative steps before receiving the communication and because effective filtering technologies were available (*Sable Communications of Cal, Inc v FCC*, 492 US 115, 127–31 (1989); *Reno v ACLU*, 521 US 844, 869-70, 877, 879 (1997); *United States v Playboy Entertainment Group, Inc.*, 529 US 803, 814-26 (2000)). Indeed, significant doubts exist as to whether *Pacifica* remains good law even with respect to broadcasting (Yoo 2003). As Justice Thomas noted in his concurrence in the first *Fox Television* decision, modern broadcasting is no more pervasive than other media, and the existence of the V-chip now gives parents who wish to screen out indecent content the ability to do so (*FCC v Fox Television Stations, Inc.*, 556 US 502 (2009) (Thomas, J, concurring)). On remand, the Second Circuit echoed both of these concerns, even going so far as to opine that the existence of effective filtering technologies rendered restrictions on broadcast indecency unconstitutional (*Fox Television Stations, Inc. v FCC*, 613 F3d 317, 326–27 (2d Cir 2010)). In addition, *Pacifica* provides little purchase in a world increasingly dominated by video on demand, in which receiving content requires the type of affirmative steps sufficient to render indecency restrictions unconstitutional (Yoo 2003).

The mandatory deployment of the V-Chip has brought to the surface a fundamental theoretical conflict that the previous technology allowed to remain latent. Restrictions of the type upheld in *Pacifica* always enjoy the support of those who paternalistically regard indecency as low-value speech unworthy of full First Amendment protection. When effective filtering remained impossible, civil libertarians could also support the decision based on viewers' inability to filter out content they did not wish to see or hear. The emergence of filters that can permit individuals to choose for themselves what content they wish to see has introduced a wedge between those who supported the constitutionality of indecency regulations out of a desire to enhance individual autonomy, and the more conservative voices who wish to restrict speech in the name of promoting a particular conception of the public good (Yoo 2011).

On June 21, 2012, the US Supreme Court issued its second decision in the *Fox Television* litigation, overturning the sanctions because the US Federal Communications Commission failed to give broadcasters fair notice of its decision to begin enforcing the indecency prohibition against isolated or occasional uses of expletives instead of limiting punishment to deliberate and repetitive uses occurrences. Because the Court disposed of the case on procedural grounds, it explicitly reserved judgment on *Pacifica*'s continuing constitutionality

(*FCC v Fox Television Stations, Inc*, 132 SCt 2307 (2012)). Justice Ginsburg issued a concurrence in the judgment arguing that *Pacifica* was wrongly when it was initially decided and that "[t]ime, technological advances, and the Commission's untenable rulings in the cases now before the Court show why *Pacifica* bears reconsideration," citing Justice Thomas's concurrence in the first *Fox Television* decision. Although *Fox Television* did not properly present the issue of whether *Pacifica* should be overruled, the skepticism expressed both by the Second Circuit and by two US Supreme Court Justices, and the lack of support for *Pacifica* in the academic commentary, suggest that the Court may well overrule that decision if presented with an appropriate case.

Quite comparable to the US case law, the German Federal Constitutional Court (Bundesverfassungsgericht) has held in a series of cases that the constitutional provision of the freedom of broadcasting in Article 5, paragraph 1 of the German Basic Law (Grundgesetz) not only protects private television and radio stations from governmental regulation, but also allows some kind of governmental content regulation.[1] The Court interpreted the constitutional provision also to comprise an "objective concept of diversity of opinions" (Ladeur, 122). According to the Court's case law, the Freedom of Broadcast provision requires that the government establish a "positive legal order" that ensures the constitutionally mandated diversity of opinions (Bundesverfassungsgericht [BVerfG] Feb 28, 1961, 12 Entscheidungen des BVerfGE 205 (262) (FRG)). The court decided that the constitutionally protected freedom of broadcast is closely linked to the freedom of speech of Article 5, paragraph 1 of the Basic Law. The Constitutional Court argued that both freedoms are of utmost importance for a democracy, which can only work if the sovereign—the people—has access to a wide variety of opinions. Moreover, the Court argued that economic competition alone would not be able to secure a broadcasting market, which provides for a diverse program that reflects all relevant groups of society.

Two main factors drove the Court's determination: first, the number of possible television and radio channels has long been limited due to physical constraints—the scarcity of spectrum. The Court argued that it is necessary on the one hand to prevent the government from gaining control over the limited number of channels, to prevent a repetition of the experience of the Third Reich. One important factor for the Nazis' successful way to obtain the power was the use of mass media, especially film and radio, as propaganda tools. On the other hand, the Court stated that the unregulated control of television stations by private parties, motivated simply by economic considerations, might lead to a survival of those television stations with the most sensational and scandalous programming (Bundesverfassungsgericht [BVerfG] Jan 24, 2001, 103 Entscheidungen des BVerfGE 44 (67) (FRG)). High-quality programs that contribute to the constitutionally mandated diversity of opinions would not be able to succeed economically and therefore would not be able to occupy one of the limited channels. This—according to the Federal Constitutional Court—requires government

---

1 See the following decisions of the Federal Constitutional Court (short-form citations given after the first): Bundesverfassungsgericht [BVerfG] [Federal Constitutional Court] Feb 28, 1961, 12 Entscheidungen des Bundesverfassungsgericht [BVerfGE] 205 (FRG); BVerfG July 27, 1971, 31 Entscheidungen des BVerfGE 314; BverfG June 16, 1981, 57 Entscheidungen des BVerfGE 295; BVerfG Nov 4, 1986, 73 Entscheidungen des BVerfGE 118; BVerfG Mar 24, 1987, 74 Entscheidungen des BVerfGE 297; BVerfG Feb 5, 1991, 83 Entscheidungen des BVerfGE 238; BVerfG Oct 6, 1992, 87 Entscheidungen des BVerfGE 181; BVerfG Feb 22, 1994, 90 Entscheidungen des BVerfGE 60; BVerfG Feb 17, 1998, 97 Entscheidungen des BVerfGE 228; BverfG Sept 11, 2007, 119 Entscheidungen des BVerfGE 181.

regulation of broadcasting. Hence, the Court argued, it is necessary to protect the diversity of opinions by imposing certain content regulations on private broadcasters and by establishing an independent public television system that is not motivated by profit and thereby can represent content that has no commercial value but is important for political debate.

The second factor that justifies the special regulation of broadcasting is—according to the Federal Constitutional Court—that television is so intrusive and persuasive that the government must prevent anti-democratic elements from gaining control over the few possible television stations. Otherwise those elements would have a powerful tool in their hands to fight the democratic state. Whereas the first argument pretty much resembles the case law of the US Supreme Court, the latter argument is a clear reaction to the specific historical experience in Germany with the totalitarian Nazi regime.

As a consequence the Court established the so-called "Dual Broadcasting Order." One pillar of this dual order is the public broadcast system, which consists of regional and national television and radio stations that are funded by a mandatory monthly fee that every household must pay. These stations are insulated from governmental influence by a specific organizational structure. They also need to provide for basic broadcast services that reflect all "relevant groups of society" (Bundesverfassungsgericht [BVerfG] June 16, 1981, 57 Entscheidungen des BVerfGE 295 (325) (FRG)). The second pillar of the dual order consists of private broadcasters. However, to operate a television or radio station, private companies need governmental permission and need to fulfill certain content-related requirements concerning the diversity of their programs. Moreover, strict rules regulate the broadcasting of indecent and youth-endangering content, which can only be broadcast during the evening hours in order to protect children.

As with US law, one would expect that the special interpretation of the Freedom of Broadcast provision in the German Basic Law by the Federal Constitutional Court would change once the scarcity problem is solved by alternative transmission technologies like cable, IPTV, satellite television, and more efficient use of the existing spectrum: if the limitation of possible fora for the presentation of different opinions is no longer an issue, content regulation of the existing forum should be lifted. Quite the opposite is true: rather than restricting the scope of government regulation and lifting it from broadcasters, the Federal Constitutional Court has demonstrated a tendency to expand traditional broadcast regulation to the new technologies. The Court started to reinterpret the Basic Law in 2006 when it stated that the scarcity argument is not the only justification for the special broadcast regulation (Bundesverfassungsgericht [BVerfG] June 16, 1981, 57 Entscheidungen des BVerfGE 295 (322) (FRG)). Instead, the Court argued that the intrusive and persuasive character of television requires special content regulations of television stations even if the number of possible stations is no longer limited. According to the Federal Constitutional Court, the intrusive and persuasive character of television distinguishes broadcasting from all other kinds of media, including the Internet. The Court argued that this fact requires governmental oversight of private television stations and the maintenance of public television stations that prevent the television landscape from being dominated by yellow-press style programs that do not contribute to the diversity of opinions (Bundesverfassungsgericht [BVerfG] Sept 11, 2007, 119 Entscheidungen des BVerfGE 181 (FRG)).

In an apodictic way, the Court even acknowledges that scarcity of programs might no longer be a problem, but that this has no consequence for the justification of broadcast regulation (Bundesverfassungsgericht [BVerfG] Sept 11, 2007, 119 Entscheidungen des BVerfGE 181). Hence, the advent of new technologies has not triggered a change in the interpretation of the constitution by the Court as far as the outcome is concerned, but only as far as the rationale for the special content regulation is concerned.

It remains to be seen how the Federal Constitutional Court will deal with the diversity of opinions that exist on the Internet. If scarcity and intrusiveness are the justifications for the special content regulation of television, there should be no reason to apply the traditional broadcast regulatory regime to the Internet. The Internet is not a scarce medium, nor is it any more intrusive than the print media or movie theaters since it is—unlike television, which is a "push" medium, meaning the audience will get a fixed program—a "pull" medium in which the user decides what she wants to see and when. Users—and parents as far as children are concerned—can exercise a much higher level of control over the content to which they want to expose themselves. However, some have argued that public television stations have a constitutional duty to protect the diversity of opinions in the Internet also. One argument is that the Internet provides an overabundance of content that makes it hard for users to identify valuable content. This argument flips the traditional rationale for special media regulation through 180 degrees: traditionally, scarcity was the problem and content regulation was the cure; now overabundance would be the problem, but the cure would remain the same.

In short, technological change has undercut the doctrines traditionally used to justify regulating broadcasters' speech. They also have no purchase on new technologies, such as the Internet. This has not prevented courts from expanding traditional doctrines to new technologies. Some constitutional courts have exhibited a reluctance to rescind government regulation merely because the technological basis has changed. At least in Germany, the answer to new technologies seems to be to keep the old doctrines for the old technologies and expand them to the new ones as well.

37.3 Applying existing constitutional principles to new technologies

In addition to forcing courts to re-evaluate the application of constitutional principles to old technologies, the process of innovation also requires courts to determine how constitutions apply to emerging technologies. Technologies that did not exist when a constitution was drafted can raise particular challenges in this regard.

A classic example is the application of constitutional protection against unreasonable searches and seizures to new means for conducting surveillance. For example, the Fourth Amendment of the US Constitution states, "The right of the people to be secure in their persons, houses, papers, and effects, against unreasonable searches and seizures, shall not be violated." By its nature, this protection must change as the frontier of sciences continues to shift. As the US Supreme Court observed, "It would be foolish to contend that the degree of privacy secured to citizens by the Fourth Amendment has been entirely unaffected by the advance of technology" (*Kyllo v United States*, 533 US 27, 33–34 (2001)).

The initial touchstone of what constituted a search that implicated the Fourth Amendment was the physical occupation of private property. Indeed, *Olmstead v United States*, 277 US 438, 464 (1928) initially suggested that physical invasions of property represented the *sine qua non* of a Fourth Amendment violation when it held that attaching wiretaps to telephone wires on public streets did not constitute a search because "[t]here was no entry of the houses or offices of the defendants."

The Court later overruled *Olmstead* and expanded the scope of the Fourth Amendment beyond the bounds of property law in its landmark decision in *Katz v United States*, 389 US 347 (1967), which held that the placement of an eavesdropping device in a telephone booth violated the Fourth Amendment. Subsequent Supreme Court decisions embraced the test articulated in Justice Harlan's concurrence, which suggested that the scope of people's Fourth Amendment rights be determined by their "reasonable expectation of privacy."

The aftermath of *Katz* left a latent ambiguity. Some commentators have drawn on the language stating that "the Fourth Amendment protects people, not places" to argue that *Katz* completely displaced the property-oriented approach associated with *Olmstead* and that the scope of the Fourth Amendment was determined exclusively by reference to the reasonable-expectation-of-privacy test (see, e.g., Israel and LaFave 1993). Others suggested that the property-oriented approach remained intact and that the reasonable-expectation-of-privacy test represented an additional basis for Fourth Amendment protection that augmented the traditional rule (see, e.g., Kerr 2004).

The US Supreme Court clarified this ambiguity in *United States v Jones*, 132 SCt 942 (2012), which held that attaching a Global Positioning System (GPS) tracking device to the underside of a vehicle without a warrant violated the Fourth Amendment. After reviewing the history of its Fourth Amendment jurisprudence, the Court concluded that it did not need to address the government's argument that no search occurred because the defendant had no reasonable expectation of privacy with respect to the bottom of his vehicle. The fact that the attachment of the GPS tracking device to the vehicle constituted a trespass to Jones's private property was sufficient by itself to implicate the Fourth Amendment. In the process, the Court clarified that *Katz* expanded the scope of the Fourth Amendment by adding reasonable expectations to the property-oriented approach rather than displacing the property-oriented approach altogether when it noted that "the *Katz* reasonable-expectation-of-privacy test has been *added to*, not *substituted for*, the common-law trespassory test" (*id* at 952).

Unlike the US Supreme Court, the German Constitutional Court declared the surveillance of a car with a GPS device not to violate constitutional rights (Bundesverfassungsgericht [BVerfG] Apr 12, 2005, 112 Entscheidungen des BVerfGE 304 (FRG)). The Court held that the attachment of a GPS device to a car does affect the constitutionally protected right to informational self-determination of Article 2, paragraph 1 of the German Basic Law. This right gives every individual the power to decide who knows what about the individual. Hence, the government must not collect personal data of individuals without their consent or a statutory provision (Bundesverfassungsgericht [BVerfG] Dec 15, 1983, 65 Entscheidungen des BVerfGE 1 (FRG)).

This right is not absolute, meaning that the government can collect personal information if there is a justifying reason. However, the right to informational self-determination gains the character of an absolutely protected right with respect to the core of a private sphere into which the government must not intrude. Examples that fall within this core are religious beliefs and sexual orientation. The Federal Constitutional Court argued that the GPS surveillance does not touch the core sphere of privacy and therefore is permissible as long as there is a statutory basis for the GPS surveillance. Since the GPS surveillance device only affects a person when it is leaving her private sphere and enters the public sphere, the Court did not see a violation of constitutional rights in this case. The Court argued that on the other hand, GPS surveillance is a very important tool for the police and criminal prosecutors.

The Federal Constitutional Court's GPS decision is in line with its decisions on other, more traditional surveillance technologies, in which the Court has asked to what extent a surveillance technology affects the core of the private sphere of an individual and how useful the technology is for the police and criminal prosecutors. In a decision concerning the permissibility of wiretapping operations in private houses, the Court argued that every individual is entitled to a core sphere of privacy without fear of government intrusions (Bundesverfassungsgericht [BVerfG] Mar 3, 2004, 109 Entscheidungen des BVerfGE 279 (FRG)). Hence, the core sphere of privacy is constitutionally protected against all kinds of intrusions no matter what technology is used by the government. On the other hand, the government can investigate private spheres outside this core as long as there is a statutory basis for such an investigation, no matter what technology is used.

The GPS decisions thus represent a particularly cogent example of how the courts apply established constitutional principles to new technologies. The new context provided by the innovation can offer the opportunity to shed new light on those principles' proper scope.

37.4 Recognizing new constitutional rights

New technologies can also prompt the recognition of new constitutional rights. Consider, for example, remote searches of personal computers. Under US law, the result is fairly straightforward. Because the Fourth Amendment protects people's "persons, houses, papers, and effects," it encompasses personal as well as real property. Moreover, courts have concluded that people have a legitimate, objectively reasonable expectation of privacy in their personal computers such that any remote search of that computer by a state actor implicates the Fourth Amendment (*United States v Heckenkamp*, 482 F3d 1142 (9th Cir 2007)).

This situation is quite different in Germany. In 2008, the German Constitutional Court had to address the constitutionality of so-called online searches based on a state law of the State of North Rhine–Westphalia (Bundesverfassungsgericht [BVerfG] Feb 27, 2008, 120 Entscheidungen des BVerfGE 274 (FRG)). The statute authorized state police to conduct remote (online) searches of computers of people who were believed to be planning a crime, such as a terrorist attack. The police were allowed to search hard disks of a computer and to follow online activities that were executed on the computer in order to collect evidence.

The Court argued that the use of new technologies like the Internet has gained an unprecedented importance for personal self-determination. People no longer only meet other people in their homes, but also in their "virtual homes" like online communities. People now write diaries on computers instead of in physical books. People no longer communicate by mail or phone, but by email, instant messaging, and social networks. All those traditional activities, however, are protected by the Constitution to allow the individual to develop her own personality based on the interaction with others and that can be intruded by the government only under very limited conditions. The Court held that the traditional interpretation of the privacy rights of the German Constitution does not provide for an adequate level of protection against violations of the "cyber-privacy sphere" of individuals.

The Court acknowledged the utmost importance of the use of information technology systems for the development of personality of many citizens. If people are using new technologies for legal purposes, chances are that they will also use them for illegal activities. Preserving the pre-existing balance between the interests of criminal defendants and state authorities requires that those new technologies and virtual meeting points cannot remain immune from government inspection. Yet, the Court saw that surveillance of the use of such systems and the evaluation of the data stored on the storage media can be highly illuminating as to the personality of the user, and may even make it possible to form a profile of that user. Hence, the Court saw a high temptation for the government to collect this kind of information on the basis of a precautionary principle.

The Court held that the guarantees contained in Article 10 of the German Basic Law (secrecy of telecommunication) and Article 13 of the Basic Law (inviolability of the home), as well as the general right of personality previously developed in the case law of the Constitutional

Court, do not adequately take account of the need for protection arising as a consequence of the development of information technology. Therefore, the Court decided that the traditional interpretation of the right to personal self-determination in Article 2, paragraph 1 of the Basic Law needs to be supplemented by a new fundamental right to the guarantee of the confidentiality and integrity of information technology systems. Hence, the Court basically created a new right by interpreting an existing constitutional provision to fill a constitutional gap that was caused by the advent of new technologies that were not foreseen by the founders of the Constitution. The Court decided the online-search statute to violate this "new" constitutional right was based on the disproportionality of the statute authorizing online searches.

37.5 Conclusion

The examples discussed in this Chapter provide only the barest overview of the ways in which technological innovation can alter the scope of constitutional principles. Not only can new technologies cause constitutional rights to expand or contract; applying constitutional principles to new contexts can also shed new light on the rationales underlying those principles. Most importantly, the challenges posed by new technologies can lead courts to recognize new constitutional rights.

Interestingly, constitutional courts often seem reluctant to regard the emergence of new technologies as an opportunity to reduce the level of governmental regulation of existing technologies. Rather, there seems to be a tendency to expand the existing doctrines to the new technologies. One reason might be that one of the distinctive characteristics of constitutional law is—or at least should be—its consistency and stability. Constitutional courts focus on the consistency and stability of their case law and are therefore reluctant to react to new technologies too quickly. Notably, this suggests that, though constitutional courts everywhere will respond to technological change in structurally similar ways, the content of their responses will be influenced by their national constitutional traditions and so may vary quite substantially from one nation to another.

To the extent that government regulation that limits constitutionally protected rights is justified by arguments rooted in technology, a change in that technology should force the government to limit the scope of traditional regulations in order to foster the individual's liberty. Leaving these questions up to the courts would open the door to arbitrary decisions on the question of which new technologies receive which kind of regulatory burden; decisions that might be in line with the court's case law, but do not reflect the current status of technology. These decisions might more properly belong to the legislature rather than to the judiciary.

On the other side, the Federal Constitutional Court of Germany has demonstrated that new technologies might provide not only a reason to rethink existing regulation, but also a need for new protections against government actions. If new technologies take over functions that are constitutionally protected, there can be a constitutional gap that needs to be filled—either by the legislator or by reinterpreting the existing Constitution. It seems that European Courts have been more willing to create new rights out of existing provisions (Schwartz 2011). The German Federal Constitutional Court has demonstrated its willingness to interpret the Constitution in such an extensive manner at least two times: in 1983 the Court developed the right to informational self-determination out of the right to personality, which is protected by Article 2, paragraph 1 of the Basic Law (Bundesverfassungsgericht BVerfG Dec 15, 1983, 65 Entscheidungen des BVerfGE 1 (FRG)). This was a response to the emergence of data-processing technologies, which made it possible for the government to process personal data on a large scale and thereby create personality profiles of individuals. In 2008, the Court developed the right to confidentiality and integrity of information technology systems that is also rooted in Article 2, paragraph 1 of the Basic Law. At least under German constitutional law, this kind of decision lies at the center of the Federal Constitutional Law Court's authority: the protection of fundamental rights belongs to the judiciary rather than to the legislature. New technologies therefore not only pose new challenges to the substantive constitutional law; they also raise the classic question of which branch has sufficient democratic legitimacy to develop constitutional law.

References

Berlin, I (1969). "Two Concepts of Liberty", in *Four Essays on Liberty* (New York: Oxford University Press).

Israel, J & LaFave, W (1993). *Criminal Procedure in a Nutshell*, 5th edn (St Paul, Minnesota: West Publishing Co).

Kerr, O (2004). "The Fourth Amendment and New Technologies: Constitutional Myths and the Case for Caution", *Michigan Law Review* 102: 801–88.

Ladeur, K-H (2012). "Medienverfassungs- und Europarecht", in Paschke, M, Berlit, W and Meyer, C (eds), *Hamburger Kommentar Gesamtes Medienrecht*.

Schwartz, P (2011). "Regulating Governmental Data Mining in the United States and Germany: Constitutional Courts, the State, and New Technology", *William and Mary Law Review* 53: 351–87.

Yoo, C (2003). "The Rise and Demise of the Technology-Specific Approach to the First Amendment", *Georgetown Law Journal* 91: 245–356.

—— (2005). "Architectural Censorship and the FCC", *Southern California Law Review* 78: 669–731.

—— (2010). "Free Speech and the Myth of the Internet as an Unintermediated Experience", *George Washington Law Review* 78: 697–773.

—— (2011). "Technologies of Control and the Future of the First Amendment", *William & Mary Law Review* 53: 747–75.

Index

Made in the USA
Middletown, DE
31 December 2016